CIMA

Paper E1

Enterprise Operations

Study Text

PUBLISHING

WORKING TOGETHER FOR YOU

PUBLISHING

CIMA Publishing is an imprint of Elsevier
The Boulevard, Langford Lane, Kidlington, Oxford, OX5 1GB, UK
225 Wyman Street, Waltham, MA 02451, USA
Kaplan Publishing UK, Unit 2 The Business Centre, Molly Millars Lane, Wokingham, Berkshire
RG41 2QZ

Notice
No responsibility is assumed by the publisher for any injury and/or damage to persons or property as
a matter of products liability, negligence or otherwise, or from any use or operation of any methods,
products, instructions or ideas contained in the material herein.

British Library Cataloguing in Publication Data
A catalogue record for this book is available from the British Library

ISBN: 978-0-85732-568-6

Printed and bound in Great Britain

12 13 14 10 9 8 7 6 5 4 3 2 1

Contents

Paper Introduction

How to Use the Materials

These Official CIMA learning materials brought to you by Elsevier/CIMA Publishing and Kaplan Publishing have been carefully designed to make your learning experience as easy as possible and to give you the best chances of success in your *'Enterprise Operations'* exam.

The product range contains a number of features to help you in the study process. They include:

- a detailed explanation of all syllabus areas;

- extensive 'practical' materials;

- generous question practice, together with full solutions;

This Study Text has been designed with the needs of home-study and distance-learning candidates in mind. Such students require very full coverage of the syllabus topics, and also the facility to undertake extensive question practice. However, the Study Text is also ideal for fully taught courses.

This main body of the text is divided into a number of chapters, each of which is organised on the following pattern:

- *Detailed learning outcomes* expected after your studies of the chapter are complete. You should assimilate these before beginning detailed work on the chapter, so that you can appreciate where your studies are leading.

- *Step-by-step topic coverage*. This is the heart of each chapter, containing detailed explanatory text supported where appropriate by worked examples and exercises. You should work carefully through this section, ensuring that you understand the material being explained and can tackle the examples and exercises successfully. Remember that in many cases knowledge is cumulative: if you fail to digest earlier material thoroughly, you may struggle to understand later chapters.

- *Activities*. Some chapters are illustrated by more practical elements, such as comments and questions designed to stimulate discussion.

- *Question practice*. The test of how well you have learned the material is your ability to tackle exam-standard questions. Make a serious attempt at producing your own answers, but at this stage do not be too concerned about attempting the questions in exam conditions. In particular, it is more important to absorb the material thoroughly by completing a full solution than to observe the time limits that would apply in the actual exam.

- *Solutions*. Avoid the temptation merely to 'audit' the solutions provided. It is an illusion to think that this provides the same benefits as you would gain from a serious attempt of your own. However, if you are struggling to get started on a question you should read the introductory guidance provided at the beginning of the solution, where provided, and then make your own attempt before referring back to the full solution.

You should plan to attempt the mock tests just before the date of the real exam. By this stage your revision should be complete and you should be able to attempt the mock exam within the time constraints of the real exam.

If you work conscientiously through the official CIMA Study Text according to the guidelines above you will be giving yourself an excellent chance of success in your exam. Good luck with your studies!

Icon Explanations

Definition – these sections explain important areas of knowledge which must be understood and reproduced in an exam environment.

Key Point – identifies topics which are key to success and are often examined.

Supplementary reading – indentifies a more detailed explanation of key terms, these sections will help to provide a deeper understanding of core areas. Reference to this text is vital when self studying.

Test Your Understanding – following key points and definitions are exercises which give the opportunity to assess the understanding of these core areas.

Illustration – to help develop an understanding of particular topics. The illustrative exercises are useful in preparing for the Test your understanding exercises.

Exclamation Mark – this symbol signifies a topic which can be more difficult to understand, when reviewing these areas care should be taken.

Study technique

Passing exams is partly a matter of intellectual ability, but however accomplished you are in that respect you can improve your chances significantly by the use of appropriate study and revision techniques. In this section we briefly outline some tips for effective study during the earlier stages of your approach to the exam. Later in the text we mention some techniques that you will find useful at the revision stage.

Planning

To begin with, formal planning is essential to get the best return from the time you spend studying. Estimate how much time in total you are going to need for each subject you are studying for the Managerial Level. Remember that you need to allow time for revision as well as for initial study of the material. You may find it helpful to read "Pass First Time!" second edition by David R. Harris ISBN 978-1-85617-798-6. This book will provide you with proven study techniques. Chapter by chapter it covers the building blocks of successful learning and examination techniques. This is the ultimate guide to passing your CIMA exams, written by a past CIMA examiner and shows you how to earn all the marks you deserve, and explains how to avoid the most common pitfalls. You may also find "The E Word: Kaplan's Guide to Passing Exams" by Stuart Pedley-Smith ISBN: 978-0-85732-205-0 helpful. Stuart Pedley-Smith is a senior lecturer at Kaplan Financial and a qualified accountant specialising in financial management. His natural curiosity and wider interests have led him to look beyond the technical content of financial management to the processes and journey that we call education. He has become fascinated by the whole process of learning and the exam skills and techniques that contribute towards success in the classroom. This book is for anyone who has to sit an exam and wants to give themselves a better chance of passing. It is easy to read, written in a common sense style and full of anecdotes, facts, and practical tips. It also contains synopses of interviews with people involved in the learning and examining process.

With your study material before you, decide which chapters you are going to study in each week, and which weeks you will devote to revision and final question practice.

Prepare a written schedule summarising the above and stick to it!

It is essential to know your syllabus. As your studies progress you will become more familiar with how long it takes to cover topics in sufficient depth. Your timetable may need to be adapted to allocate enough time for the whole syllabus.

Students are advised to refer to the notice of examinable legislation published regularly in CIMA's magazine (Financial Management), the students e-newsletter (Velocity) and on the CIMA website, to ensure they are up-to-date.

The amount of space allocated to a topic in the Study Text is not a very good guide as to how long it will take you. For example, the material relating to Section B 'Information Systems' and Section D 'Marketing' each account for 20% of the syllabus, but the latter has more pages because there are more models and illustrations, which take up more space. The syllabus weighting is the better guide as to how long you should spend on a syllabus topic.

Tips for effective studying

(1) Aim to find a quiet and undisturbed location for your study, and plan as far as possible to use the same period of time each day. Getting into a routine helps to avoid wasting time. Make sure that you have all the materials you need before you begin so as to minimise interruptions.

(2) Store all your materials in one place, so that you do not waste time searching for items around your accommodation. If you have to pack everything away after each study period, keep them in a box, or even a suitcase, which will not be disturbed until the next time.

(3) Limit distractions. To make the most effective use of your study periods you should be able to apply total concentration, so turn off all entertainment equipment, set your phones to message mode, and put up your 'do not disturb' sign.

(4) Your timetable will tell you which topic to study. However, before diving in and becoming engrossed in the finer points, make sure you have an overall picture of all the areas that need to be covered by the end of that session. After an hour, allow yourself a short break and move away from your Study Text. With experience, you will learn to assess the pace you need to work at.

(5) Work carefully through a chapter, making notes as you go. When you have covered a suitable amount of material, vary the pattern by attempting a practice question. When you have finished your attempt, make notes of any mistakes you made, or any areas that you failed to cover or covered more briefly.

(6) Make notes as you study, and discover the techniques that work best for you. Your notes may be in the form of lists, bullet points, diagrams, summaries, 'mind maps', or the written word, but remember that you will need to refer back to them at a later date, so they must be intelligible. If you are on a taught course, make sure you highlight any issues you would like to follow up with your lecturer.

(7) Organise your notes. Make sure that all your notes, calculations etc can be effectively filed and easily retrieved later.

Structure of subjects and learning outcomes

Each subject within the syllabus is divided into a number of broad syllabus topics. The topics contain one or more lead learning outcomes, related component learning outcomes and indicative knowledge content.

A learning outcome has two main purposes:

(a) To define the skill or ability that a well prepared candidate should be able to exhibit in the examination

(b) To demonstrate the approach likely to be taken in examination questions

The learning outcomes are part of a hierarchy of learning objectives. The verbs used at the beginning of each learning outcome relate to a specific learning objective e.g.

Explain process design.

The verb **'explain'** indicates a level two learning objective.

These verbs are outlined in the first chapters of the text.

These verbs are outlined in the first chapter of the text.

PAPER E1
ENTERPRISE OPERATIONS

Syllabus overview

This paper addresses several functional areas of business, as well as introducing candidates to the economic, social and political context of international business. For each of the sections dealing with information systems, operations, marketing and managing human capital, the learning requirements alert students to major developments in the field as well as tools and techniques important to each functional area.

Syllabus structure

The syllabus comprises the following topics and study weightings:

A	The Global Business Environment	20%
B	Information Systems	20%
C	Operations Management	20%
D	Marketing	20%
E	Managing Human Capital	20%

Assessment strategy

There will be a written examination paper of three hours, plus 20 minutes of pre-examination question paper reading time. The examination paper will have the following sections:

Section A – 20 marks
A variety of compulsory objective test questions, each worth between two and four marks. Mini scenarios may be given, to which a group of questions relate.

Section B – 30 marks
Six compulsory short answer questions, each worth five marks. A short scenario may be given, to which some or all questions relate.

Section C – 50 marks
One or two compulsory questions. Short scenarios may be given, to which questions relate.

E1 – A. THE GLOBAL BUSINESS ENVIRONMENT (20%)

Learning outcomes
On completion of their studies students should be able to:

Lead	Component	Indicative syllabus content
1. explain the social, political and economic context of business. [2]	(a) explain the emergence of major economies in Asia and Latin America; [2] (b) explain the emergence and importance of outsourcing and offshoring; [2] (c) explain the impact of international macroeconomic developments (e.g. long-term shifts in trade balances), on the organisation's competitive environment. [2]	• Cross-cultural management and different forms of business organisation. [2] • Emerging market multinationals. [2] • Liberalisation and economic nationalism. [2] • Outsourcing and offshoring. [2] • Major economic systems including US, European and transition economies. [2] • National account balances (especially from international trade), monetary policy and their impact on markets. [2]
2. analyse the relationship between the internal governance of the firm and external sources of governance and regulation. [2], [3]	(a) explain the principles and purpose of corporate social responsibility and the principles of good corporate governance in an international context; [3] (b) analyse relationships among business, society and government in national and regional contexts; [3] (c) apply tools of country and political risk analysis; [2] (d) discuss the nature of regulation and its impact on the firm. [3]	• Corporate governance, including stakeholders and the role of government. [3] • Principles of corporate social responsibility and the scope for international variation, e.g. between developed and developing economies. [3] • Business-government relations in developed and developing economies. [3] • Regulation in the national and international context and its impact on the firm. [3] • Role of institutions and governance in economic growth. [3] • Corporate political activity in developed and developing markets. [3] • Country and political risk. [2]

E1 – B. INFORMATION SYSTEMS (20%)

Learning outcomes
On completion of their studies students should be able to:

Lead	Component	Indicative syllabus content
1. discuss the wider business context within which information systems operate. [4]	(a) identify the value of information and information systems organisations; [4] (b) discuss the reasons for organisations' increased dependence on information systems; [4] (c) discuss the transformation of organisations through technology. [4]	• The role of information systems in organisations. [4] • Emerging information system trends in organisations (e.g. Enterprise-wide systems; knowledge management systems; customer relationship management systems, e.g. E-business, Web 2.0 tools). [4] • Information technology enabled transformation; the emergence of new forms of organisation. [4] • Geographically dispersed (virtual) teams; role of information systems in virtual teams and challenges for virtual collaboration. [4]
2. analyse how information systems can be implemented in support of the organisation's strategy. [5]	(a) discuss ways for overcoming problems in information system implementation; [5] (b) discuss ways of organising and managing information system activities in the context of the wider organisation. [5]	• Assessing the costs and benefits of information systems; criteria for evaluating information systems. [5] • Privacy and security. [5] • System changeover methods (i.e. direct, parallel, pilot and phased). [5] • Information system implementation as a change management process; avoiding problems of non-usage and resistance. [5] • Information system outsourcing (different types of sourcing strategies; client-vendor relationships). [5] • Aligning information systems with business strategy (e.g. strategic importance of information systems; information systems for competitive advantage; information systems for competitive necessity). [5]

E1 – C. OPERATIONS MANAGEMENT (20%)

Learning outcomes
On completion of their studies students should be able to:

Lead	Component	Indicative syllabus content
1. explain the relationship of operations management to other aspects of the organisation's operations. [6], [7]	(a) explain the shift from price-based to relational procurement and operations; [6], [7] (b) explain the relationship of operations and supply management to the competitiveness of the firm; [7] (c) explain the particular issues surrounding operations management in services; [6] (d) explain the importance of sustainability in operations management. [6]	• Supply chain management as a strategic process. [7] • An overview of operations strategy and its importance to the firm. [6] • Supply chains in competition with each other; role of supply networks; demand networks as an evolution of supply chains. [6], [7] • Design of products/services and processes and how this relates to operations and supply. [6], [7] • The concept of sustainability in operations management. [6]
2. apply tools and techniques of operations management. [6], [7], [8]	(a) apply contemporary thinking in quality management; [8] (b) explain process design; [7] (c) apply tools and concepts of lean management; [8] (d) illustrate a plan for the implementation of a quality programme; [8] (e) describe ways to manage relationships with suppliers. [6], [7]	• Different methods of quality measurement (e.g. Servqual). [8] • Approaches to quality management, including Total Quality Management (TQM), various British and European Union systems as well as statistical control processes. [8] • External quality standards. [8] • Systems used in operations management: Manufacturing Resource Planning II (MRPII); Optimized Production Techniques (OPT) and Enterprise Resource Planning (ERP). [6] • Use of process maps to present the flow of information and product across supply chains and networks. [7] • Methods for managing inventory, including continuous inventory systems (e.g. Economic Order Quantity, EOQ), periodic inventory systems and the ABC system (Note: ABC is not an acronym; A refers to high value, B to medium and C to low value inventory). [7] • Methods of managing operational capacity in product and service delivery (e.g. use of queuing theory, forecasting, flexible manufacturing systems). [6] • Application of lean techniques to services. [8] • Practices of continuous improvement (e.g. Quality circles, Kaizen, 5S, 6 Sigma). [8] • The characteristics of lean production. [8] • Criticisms and limitations of lean production. [8] • Developing relationships with suppliers, including the use of supply portfolios. [7]

E1 – D. MARKETING (20%)

Learning outcomes On completion of their studies students should be able to: Lead	Component	Indicative syllabus content
1. explain developments in marketing. [9], [11]	(a) explain the marketing concept, and the alternatives to it; [9] (b) describe the marketing environment of a range of organisations; [9] (c) explain marketing in a not-for-profit context; [11] (d) explain the social context of marketing behaviour; [11] (e) describe theories of consumer behaviour. [9]	• The marketing concept as a business philosophy. [9] • The marketing environment, including societal, economic, technological, political and legal factors affecting marketing. [9] • Marketing in not-for-profit organisations (i.e. charities, non-governmental organisations; the public sector). [11] • Theories of consumer behaviour (e.g. social interaction theory), as well as factors affecting buying decisions, types of buying behaviour and stages in the buying process. [9] • Social marketing and corporate social responsibility. [11]
2. apply tools and techniques used in support of the organisation's marketing. [10], [11]	(a) explain the relationships between market research, market segmentation, targeting and positioning; [10] (b) apply tools within each area of the marketing mix; [10] (c) describe the business contexts within which marketing principles can be applied; [11] (d) describe the market planning process; [10] (e) explain the role of branding and brand equity. [10]	• Market research, including data gathering techniques and methods of analysis. [10] • Segmentation and targeting of markets, and positioning of products within markets. [10] • How business to business (B2B) marketing differs from business to consumer (B2C) marketing in its different forms (i.e. consumer marketing, services marketing, direct marketing, interactive marketing, e-marketing, internal marketing). [10], [11] • Promotional tools and the promotion mix. [10] • The 'service extension' to the marketing mix. [10] • Devising and implementing a pricing strategy. [10] • Experiential marketing. [10] • Marketing communications, including viral, guerrilla and other indirect forms of marketing. [10] • Distribution channels and methods for marketing campaigns. [10] • The role of marketing in the business plan of the organisation. [10] • Brand image and brand value. [10] • Product development and product/service life-cycles. [10] • Internal marketing as the process of training and motivating employees so as to support the organisation's external marketing activities. [11] • The differences and similarities in the marketing of products, services and experiences. [10] • Product portfolios and the product mix. [10]

E1 – E. MANAGING HUMAN CAPITAL (20%)

Learning outcomes
On completion of their studies students should be able to:

Lead	Component	Indicative syllabus content
1. explain the relationship of Human Resources (HR) to the organisation's operations. [12], [13]	(a) explain how HR theories and activities can contribute to the success of the organisation; [12] (b) explain the importance of ethical behaviour in business generally and for the line manager and their activities. [13]	• Theories of Human Resource Management relating to ability, motivation and opportunity. [12] • The psychological contract and its importance to retention. [12] • The relationship of the employee to other elements of the business. [12] • Personal business ethics and the fundamental principles (Part A) of the CIMA Code of Ethics for Professional Accountants. [13]
2. discuss the activities associated with the management of human capital. [12], [13]	(a) explain the HR activities associated with developing the ability of employees; [13] (b) discuss the HR activities associated with the motivation of employees; [12] (c) describe the HR activities associated with improving the opportunities for employees to contribute to the firm; [12] (d) discuss the importance of the line manager in the implementation of HR practices; [13] (e) prepare an HR plan appropriate to a team. [13]	• Practices associated with recruiting and developing appropriate abilities including recruitment and selection of staff using different recruitment channels (i.e. interviews, assessment centres, intelligence tests, aptitude tests, psychometric tests). [13] • Issues relating to fair and legal employment practices (e.g. recruitment, dismissal, redundancy, and ways of managing these). [13] • The distinction between development and training and the tools available to develop and train staff. [13] • The design and implementation of induction programmes. [13] • Practices related to motivation including Issues in the design of reward systems (e.g. the role of incentives, the utility of performance-related pay, arrangements for knowledge workers, flexible work arrangements). [12] • The importance of appraisals, their conduct and their relationship to the reward system. [13] • Practices related to the creation of opportunities for employees to contribute to the organisation including job design, communications, involvement procedures and appropriate elements of negotiating and bargaining. [12] • Problems in implementing an HR plan appropriate to a team and ways to manage this. [13] • HR in different organisational forms (e.g. project based, virtual or networked firms) and different organisational contexts. [13] • Preparation of an HR plan (e.g. Forecasting personnel requirements; retention, absence and leave, wastage). [13]

Understanding the CIMA Verb Hierarchy for E1

Chapter learning objectives

CIMA VERB HIERARCHY

CIMA place great importance on the choice of verbs in exam question requirements. It is thus critical that you answer the question according to the definition of the verb used.

The E1 syllabus contains 38 learning outcomes using the following verbs that you need to understand:

Level 2 verbs

- "Explain" – occurs 17 times
- "Describe" – occurs 6 times
- "Illustrate" – occurs once
- "Identify" – occurs once

Level 3 verbs

- "Apply" – occurs 4 times
- "Prepare" – occurs once

Level 4 verbs

- "Discuss" – occurs 7 times
- "Analyse" – occurs once

The verbs given in the syllabus limit the scope of the question requirements that the examiners can ask.

For example, syllabus learning outcome C2(b) is "**explain** process design". "Explain" is a level 2 verb, so the examiner would not be allowed to ask you a level 3 or 4 verb here, such as to "**discuss**" a firm's process design approach.

This chapter looks at the verbs and the differences between them.

1 Operational Level Verbs

It is vital that you identify which verb is used in an exam question requirement and answer accordingly. The examiner has repeatedly said that students in the real exam are generally good at the knowledge aspects of questions but poor when discussion and/or application to a scenario is required.

Level 1: KNOWLEDGE

What you are expected to know

VERBS USED	DEFINITION
List	Make a list of
State	Express, fully or clearly, the details of / facts of
Define	Give the exact meaning of

Level 2: COMPREHENSION

What you are expected to understand

VERBS USED	DEFINITION
Describe	Communicate the key features of.
Distinguish	Highlight the differences between.
Explain	Make clear or intelligible/state the meaning or purpose of.
Identify	Recognise, establish or select after consideration.
Illustrate	Use an example to describe or explain something.

Level 3: APPLICATION

How you are expected to apply your knowledge

VERBS USED	DEFINITION
Apply	Put to practical use.
Calculate	Ascertain or reckon mathematically.
Demonstrate	Prove with certainty or exhibit by practical means.
Prepare	Make or get ready for use.
Reconcile	Make or prove consistent/compatible.
Solve	Find an answer to.
Tabulate	Arrange in a table.

Level 4: ANALYSIS

How you are expected to analyse the detail of what you have learned.

VERBS USED	DEFINITION
Analyse	Examine in detail the structure of.
Categorise	Place into a defined class or division.
Compare/contrast	Show the similarities and/or differences between.
Construct	Build up or compile.
Discuss	Examine in detail by argument.
Interpret	Translate into intelligible or familiar terms.
Prioritise	Place in order of priority or sequence for action.
Produce	Create or bring into existence.

2 Further guidance on operational level verbs that cause confusion

Verbs that cause students confusion at this level are as follows:

Level 2 verbs

- **The difference between "describe" and "explain".**

  An explanation is a set of statements constructed to describe a set of facts which clarifies the **causes**, **context**, and **consequences** of those facts.

  For example, if asked to **describe** the features of a marketing orientation you could talk, among other things, about understanding the customer's needs and adopting a strategy producing products with the benefits and features to fulfil these needs. This tells us what the marketing orientation looks like.

  However if asked to **explain** the marketing orientation, then you would have to talk about why firms may be dissatisfied with alternative approaches to selling their products and may consider switching to the marketing orientation, and the implications for firms (consequences) in terms of the benefits of adopting a marketing orientation.

  More simply, to describe something is to answer "what" type questions whereas to explain looks at "what" and "why" aspects.

- **The verb "to illustrate"**

  The key thing about illustrating something is that you may have to decide on a relevant example to use. This could involve drawing a diagram, performing supporting calculations or highlighting a feature or person in the scenario given. Most of the time the question will be structured so calculations performed in part (a) can be used to illustrate a concept in part (b).

  For example, you could be asked to explain and illustrate what is meant by an "quality programme".

Level 3 verbs

- **The verb "to apply"**

  Given that all level 3 verbs involve application, the verb "apply" is rare in the real exam. Instead one of the other more specific verbs is used instead.

- **The verb "to reconcile"**

  This is a numerical requirement and usually involves starting with one of the figures, adjusting it and ending up with the other.

  For example, in a bank reconciliation you start with the recorded cash at bank figure, adjust it for unpresented cheques, etc., and (hopefully!) end up with the stated balance in the cash "T account".

  This verb will rarely be used in paper E1.

- **The verb "to demonstrate"**

  The verb "to demonstrate" can be used in two main ways.

  Firstly it could mean to prove that a given statement is true or consistent with circumstances given. For example, the Finance Director may have stated in the question that the company will not exceed its overdraft limit in the next six months. The requirement then asks you to demonstrate that the Director is wrong. You could do this by preparing a cash flow forecast for the next six months.

  Secondly you could be asked to demonstrate **how** a stated model, framework, technique or theory could be used in the particular scenario. Ensure you do not merely describe the model but use it to generate some results.

Level 4 verbs

- **The verb "to analyse"**

  To analyse something is to examine it in detail in order to discover its meaning or essential features. This will usually involve breaking the scenario down and looking at the fine detail, possibly with additional calculations, and then stepping back to see the bigger picture to identify any themes to support conclusions.

  For example, if asked to analyse a set of financial statements, then the end result will be a set of statements about the performance of the business with supporting evidence. This could involve the following:

  (1) You could break down your analysis into areas of profitability, liquidity, gearing and so on.

  (2) Under each heading look at key figures in the financial statements, identifying trends (e.g. sales growth) and calculating supporting ratios (e.g. margins).

  (3) Try to explain what the figures mean and why they have occurred (e.g. why has the operating margin fallen?)

(4) Start considering the bigger picture – are the ratios presenting a consistent message or do they contradict each other? Can you identify common causes?

(5) Finally you would then seek to pull all this information together and interpret it to make some higher level comments about overall performance.

The main error students make is that they fail to draw out any themes and conclusions and simply present the marker with a collection of uninterpreted, unexplained facts and figures.

- **The verb "to discuss"**

To discuss something is very similar to analysing it, except that discussion usually involves two or more different viewpoints or arguments as the context, rather than a set of figures, say. To discuss viewpoints will involve looking at their underlying arguments, examining them critically, trying to assess whether one argument is more persuasive than the other and then seeking to reach a conclusion.

For example, if asked to discuss whether a particular technique could be used by a company, you would examine the arguments for and against, making reference to the specific circumstances in the question, and seek to conclude.

- **The verb "to prioritise"**

To prioritise is to place objects in an order. The key issue here is to decide upon the criteria to use to perform the ordering. For example, prioritising the external threats facing a firm could be done by considering the scale of financial consequences, immediacy, implications for the underlying business model and so on.

The main mistake students make is that they fail to justify their prioritisation – why is this the most important issue?

2

Introduction to the Global Business Environment

Chapter learning objectives

Lead	Component
A1. Explain the social, political and economic context of business.	(a) Explain the emergence of major economies in Asia and Latin America.
	(b) Explain the emergence and importance of outsourcing and offshoring.
	(c) Explain the impact of international macroeconomic developments (e.g. long-term shifts in trade balances), on the organisation's competitive environment.
A2. Analyse the relationship between the internal governance of a firm and external sources of governance and regulation.	(c) Apply tools of country and political risk analysis

1 Introduction

Today's global business environment is changing at a fast pace. This presents a number of challenges for global managers who must be able to deal with a wide range of labour, environmental, social, cultural, ethical and governmental issues.

Some of these will give rise to opportunities for the firm, for example:

- New markets in developing nations
- The possibility of reducing production costs by outsourcing and off-shoring
- The achievement of economies of scale through becoming a multi-national enterprise (MNE)

However, there may be problems and threats to deal with as well, such as:

- Domestic markets may become open to competition from foreign firms
- Some countries may be difficult to penetrate due to them joining a regional trade bloc
- World Trade Organisation (WTO) intervention may change the balance of power in some markets

Today's global managers are expected to possess entrepreneurial qualities beyond those of judgement, perseverance and knowledge of business. Above all, global managers must have an understanding of the complexities of the modern world and how to deal with people from a wide range of backgrounds and cultures.

The huge issue facing many of today's global leaders is what to say about corporate governance when the rules and expectations of society are changing so quickly. What do you teach managers about the global competitive landscape, when countries like China and India are fundamentally changing the rules of the game?

Chapters 2 and 3 explore some of these issues in more detail and also review the role of government in the global business environment.

2 Different Economic Systems

2.1 Introduction

There are three main types of economic system:

Planned   Mixed   Free market

2.2 Planned economic systems

In a **planned economy** the government owns all the resources and makes decisions about their use on behalf of the population. The government fixes or controls the prices of goods and services.

Test your understanding 1
Identify examples of planned economies.

2.3 Free market economic systems

In a **free market (capitalist)** system, individuals decide how resources will be used, acting as producers and consumers of goods and services. It is not considered immoral to use these resources for the attainment of private profit.

There is no real life example of a free market economy.

Illustration 1 – Free market economies
The USA and the UK come relatively close to the definition of a free market economy as there is a limited degree of government intervention in the provision of healthcare, education and welfare services. In the USA, the government plays a much smaller role in the provision of healthcare facilities than in the UK.

2.4 Mixed economic systems

In a **mixed economic system**, resource allocation is undertaken partly by the government and partly by the private sector. The government will also intervene to influence the behaviour of the private sector.

2.5 Transition economies

 A **transition economy** is an economy which is changing from a planned economy to a mixed (or even free market) economy.

The former Soviet Union and China would be classed as transition economies.

Growth in these economies has been triggered by a number of factors. For example:

- **Offshoring** (this is discussed later in this chapter).

- **Foreign direct investment (FDI)** – overseas companies (multinational enterprises) want to share in the growth of these countries and may invest by acquiring a local company or by creating new facilities in the host country to take advantage of local conditions. The two main types of FDI are:

  - **Acquisitions** – the multinational enterprise (MNE) acquires a local company and so gains control of its assets and markets. The acquired company becomes a division of the parent company. Future profits will be exported back to the parent company and therefore the local economy may only benefit if the firm was subject to imminent collapse.

  - **Greenfield investment** – the MNE will create new facilities in the host country, taking advantage of local conditions. Although future profits will still be exported to the parent company the host country will benefit from new jobs, knowledge transfer, increased productive capacity and access to global economies.

How transition economies change

As countries seek to become more competitive, they will attract investment from overseas firms, eager to share in the growth of the country. The investment that those companies make is known as foreign direct investment (FDI).

The firms that make these investments are known as multinational enterprises (MNEs), and retain control of the entity in which they have invested. This is often met with mixed feelings by the population, who are grateful for the creation of wealth and jobs but resentful of the country being "bought by foreigners". Similarly there can be resentment in countries whose firms invest abroad, particularly when there is domestic unemployment.

The current trend to offshore call centres and computing services has been a hotly debated issue since it began, but it is a phenomenon that has been occurring for many years. Originally the preserve of OECD countries (i.e. countries involved with the Organisation for Co-operation and Development) it is now a truly global feature of the world economy.

Many countries are seeing their economy boosted by the arrival of foreign firms, as is the case of Russia, where growth in the domestic economy is being fuelled by the arrival of multinational retailers who have established bases in the country. In 2005 Russia attracted $16.7 billion of FDI, with Coca Cola acquiring a fruit juice maker, Heineken acquiring local brewers and both Toyota and Volkswagen establishing automobile factories. Other companies establishing factories include Carlsberg, Nestle and Whirlpool (the domestic appliance manufacturer) in partnership with the Turkish company, Vestel Group.

FDI is often the "trigger" to an economy, and can lead to rapid growth in wealth and skills. Countries that are beginning to benefit from FDI are known as "transition" economies, and they sometimes develop significant domestic economic infrastructure as a result. Other transition economies are triggered into growth by offshoring, and the economic gain can lead to the development of a local pool of highly skilled labour. Some local organisations grow, until they too are ready to enter the world stage.

3 Free Trade and Protectionism

3.1 International trade

The global economy is not a new concept and international or global companies have existed for many years. The British East India Company, founded in 1600, is popularly cited as the world's first international and global company. Today, however, it is no longer the case that international business means western multinational companies selling or operating in world markets.

3.2 Liberalisation – free trade

Free trade means that there are no barriers to the free flow of goods and services between countries.

Benefits of free trade include:

- **Specialisation** – free trade allows nations to specialise in the production of goods or provision of services for which they have a natural advantage, e.g. Saudi Arabia extracts oil, Argentina rears beef and Britain provides financial services. Specialisation normally enables an industry to benefit from large scale production. This should improve the economies of scale obtained and result in lower prices and better products.

- **Competition** – greater competition should be fostered by free trade resulting in lower prices and greater choice for consumers.

- **Surpluses and deficits removed** – a country with a surplus, e.g. of oil, can export its resource and a country with a deficit can improve the resource. This should improve economic prosperity and the standard of living.

- **Closer political links** – the development of trading links, e.g. the European Union, should result in closer political relationships between countries.

Free trade agreements

In many parts of the world, governments have created trade agreements and common markets to encourage free trade. However, the World Trade Organisation (WTO) is opposed to these trading blocs and customs unions (e.g. the European Union) because they encourage trade between members but often have high trade barriers for non-members.

From a business perspective such agreements give major opportunities to firms within the area specified but create barriers to entry for those outside. This is the reason why Japanese car manufacturers have built factories within the EU, so they can avoid quotas.

The different types of agreement are as follows:

Bi-lateral and multi-lateral trade agreements

These are agreements between two or more countries to eliminate quotas and tariffs on the trade of most (if not all) goods between them. Examples include:

- The Closer Economic Relations (CER) agreement between Australia and New Zealand.

Free trade areas

If the members of a multi-lateral free trade agreement are all in the same geographical area then it is sometimes described as a free trade area (FTA). Examples include

- The North American Free Trade Agreement (NAFTA) between Canada, the United States, and Mexico.
- The ASEAN Free Trade Area (AFTA) is an agreement by the Association of Southeast Asian Nations (Brunei, Indonesia, Malaysia, Philippines, Singapore, Thailand, Vietnam, Laos, Myanmar and Cambodia).
- South Korea is currently negotiating a free trade agreement with the EU. Trade between South Korea and the EU totalled $92.2 billion in 2010.

Customs unions

A customs union is a free trade area with a common external tariff. The participant countries set up common external trade policy, but in some cases they use different import quotas. Examples include:

- Mercosur is a customs union between Brazil, Argentina, Uruguay, Paraguay and Venezuela in South America.

Countries may chose to move from a FTA to a customs union to eliminate some of the trade distortions of FTAs where different member countries have different export rules to the same target country. To avoid local regulations producers may sell to a partner in another member country with less stringent regulations who then sells to the target customer. This results in the need for rules to determine the origin of goods.

Single markets (economic communities)

A single market is a customs union with common policies on product regulation, and freedom of movement of all the four factors of production (land, labour, capital and entrepreneurship). Advocates argue that this gives a more "level playing field" for producers in different countries as they all have to meet the same standards.

Examples include:

- The Economic Community of West African States (ECOWAS).

Economic unions

An economic and monetary union is a single market with a common currency.

The largest economic and monetary union at present is the Eurozone. The Eurozone consists of the European Union member states that have adopted the Euro.

Arguments abound regarding the effects of regional trading blocs.

- Their supporters say that they encourage *trade creation by harmonizing economic policies* and standards within member countries and reducing prices as trade restrictions are removed.

- Opponents state that they lead to *trade diversion*. Member countries buy within the regional trading bloc when cheaper sources are available outside.

- Common external tariffs can encourage a regional fortress mentality which can lead to conflicts between different regional trading blocs. For example, NAFTA has complained over the EU's agricultural imports while the EU has complained over NAFTA's restrictions on steel imports.

- The fear is that regional trading blocs could lead to the development of protectionism worldwide at a time when the WTO is seeking to create free trade.

3.3 Economic nationalism – protectionism

In theory, free trade between nations is desirable, but often in practice various forms of protection are used.

Protectionism is where one country, or group of countries, attempts to restrict trade with another country, to protect their producers from competition.

Test your understanding 2

Explain the arguments for restricting free trade.

There are a number of ways in which markets can be protected:

- **Tariffs** – the imposition of taxation on imported goods, pushes up their price and discourages their purchase.

Illustration 2 – Tariffs

In 2002 the US steel industry was making heavy losses. As a result, George W. Bush (the US President at the time) announced that the industry was to receive protection from imported steel. Tariffs of between 8% (on steel wire) and 30% (on steel plates) were imposed. The decision was met with dismay from around the world. The Americans were accused of putting domestic politics ahead of the country's international legal agreements.

- **Quotas** – restrictions on the amount of certain goods that can be imported.
- **Embargoes** – ban on certain imports and exports.

Illustration 3 – Embargoes

In 2006, a European Commission ban on British beef exports officially ended, 10 years after it was imposed to prevent the spread of BSE or "mad cow disease" throughout Europe.

- **Subsidies** – on domestic products to give them a price advantage over imports. For example, the Common Agricultural Policy protects small farmers in European countries through the payment of subsidies.
- **Administrative regulations** – designed to deter imports.

Illustration 4 – Administrative regulations

Some countries insist on stringent standards of quality, health and safety, packaging or size to restrict what may be imported. At one point, as part of its environmental legislation, Germany insisted that large firms importing goods into Germany were responsible for collecting and removing packaging from the country. Costs increased to such a high level that imports were deterred.

- **Buy national campaigns** – sometimes a country will encourage or force its citizens to buy locally produced goods.

One way in which a firm can try to get round such barriers is to consider some sort of **alliance** or **joint venture** with a domestic firm in that market.

Most developed nations have agreed to abolish protectionism, and policies that favour free trade are encouraged through organisations such as the World Trade Organisation (**WTO**).

Institutions influencing free trade

Most companies will face markets where free trade dominates and others where there is more protectionsim. However, these situations are rarely set in stone so here we consider some of the major institutions that influence free trade.

The World Trade Organisation (WTO) and the General Agreements on Tariffs and Trade (GATT)

As trade began to recover after the Second World War attempts were made to reduce barriers to free trade around the world. The General Agreements on Tariffs and Trade (GATT) came into being in 1948. Regular rounds of talks were held to agree trading patterns around the world and to negotiate removal of trade barriers.

These negotiations have become more prolonged and complex as time has gone on.

In 1995 the World Trade Organisation based in Geneva replaced GATT. It has a number of roles:

- to ensure compliance of member countries with previous GATT agreements
- to negotiate future trade liberalisation agreements
- to resolve trading disputes between nations.

The WTO has much greater authority than GATT as it has the power to police and 'enforce' trade agreements. It faces an increasingly difficult role as the facilitator for global free trade talks.

The WTO is opposed to the development of trading blocs and customs unions such as the EU and NAFTA. Although they promote free trade between members of the union, there are normally high trade barriers for non-members, e.g. the difficulties faced by non-EU food producers when they attempt to export to the EU.

Example

There is growing tension between the developed and the developing world. The developing world regards heavy subsidy of EU and American farmers as a huge barrier to trade for their domestic farmers. At the same time, the developed world complains about export of low cost manufactured goods from the developing world that are not subject to the same health, safety and environmental regulations that they face.

The European Union (EU)

The EU is an example of a single market and, within the Eurozone, an economic union (see above). It has its origins in the Treaty of Rome (1957).

The aims of the treaty were as follows:

- the elimination of customs duties and quotas on imports and exports between member states

- the establishment of a common customs tariff and a common commercial policy towards non-member states

- the abolition of obstacles to the free movement of persons, services and capital between member states

- the establishment of common policies on transport and agriculture

- the prohibition of business practices that restrict or distort competition

- the association of overseas countries in order to increase trade and development.

The Group of Eight (G8)

The Group of Eight (G8) consists of Canada, France, Germany, Italy, Japan, Russia, the United Kingdom, and the United States. Together, these countries represent about 65% of the world economy.

The agenda of G8 meetings is usually about controversial global issues such as global warming, poverty in Africa, fair trade policies and AIDS but has implications for global trade.

The 31st G8 summit in 2005 resulted in a stated commitment to reduce subsidies and tariffs that inhibit trade.

The G8 summit has consistently dealt with:

- Macroeconomic management

- International trade

- Energy issues and climate change

- Development issues and relationships with developing countries

- Issues of international concern such as terrorism and organised crime.

The G8 does not have any formal resources or powers as is the case with other international organisations such as the WTO. However, it provides a forum for the most powerful nations to discuss complex international issues and to develop the personal relations that help them respond in effective collective fashion to sudden crises or shocks. The summit also gives direction to the international community by setting priorities, defining new issues and providing guidance to established international organisations.

3.4 Balanced trade

This is another alternative to free trade policies.

 With **balanced trade**, two countries attempt to maintain a fairly even relationship between their respective imports and exports so that neither country runs a large trade deficit.

4 Emerging Market Multinationals

4.1 Globalisation

 Globalisation is the economic and social process whereby local markets and cultures are increasingly dominated by global markets and cultures.

Most of the emphasis of globalisation relates to the ability of larger and larger **multinational** organisations to operate globally, taking advantage of local specialism. They may do this, for instance, through outsourcing their IT operations to India where the expertise is as high and the costs are significantly lower than, in say, the United States.

Multinational companies

A **multinational** business owns or controls foreign subsidiaries in more than one country, i.e. it has production or service facilities in more than one country.

Size – most of the world's largest firms, e.g. Wal Mart and Shell, are multinationals but there are also thousands of very small multinationals

Owernership – Overseas subsidiairies may be wholly owned or joint ventures may be established

Nature of Business – cover all areas from manufacturing to service provision and finance

Diversity among multinationals

Productive locations – may be located in a small or large number of countries

Overseas business relative to total business –only one fifth of Wal Mart's sales come from overseas subsidiaries compared to four fifths of BP's sales

The **benefits** of going multinational include:

Ownership advantages

- Ownership of superior technology – this will enhance productivity and result in superior-quality products.

- Research and development (R&D) capacity – multinationals can invest heavily in R&D since they can spread the cost over a large output.

- Managerial skills – managers of multinationals are often more experienced and may be more innovative in the way that they do things.

Locational advantages

Multinationals will take advantage of the most appropriate location to make their products or services. They can locate:

- where the required resources can be found.
- where labour is relatively cheap.
- where the quality of the resources is better.
- in a foreign country to avoid transport costs and tariffs.
- in a foreign country to take advantage of government incentives.

Internalisation

The cost of setting up an overseas subsidiary is often less than the cost of arranging a contract with an external party, e.g. an overseas importer.

Illustration 5 – Globalisation

Most people are affected by globalisation in a number of ways and are aware of global brands either through personal experience or via the media. Thinking about what you are doing at the moment, it is quite possible that:

- You are reading a book written in the UK
- Using software developed in North America
- Which was typeset in India
- Printed locally wherever you live
- Bought using a credit card issued by an international bank
- You are drinking a coffee made from Columbian beans
- Wearing trainers made in Vietnam
- Clothes made in China
- Or possibly from Egyptian cotton
- You may be listening to music recorded locally
- But playing on equipment made in Japan
- You may even be studying in a foreign country where you have gone to work

Illustration 6 – Globalisation and supermarkets

The expansion of European and American grocer retailers into global markets has been underway for a number of years. Limited growth opportunities at home resulted in the major players expanding their overseas operations with mixed success. Tesco entered the Thai market in 1998 and now has over 500 stores. The advantage for these international retailers was expertise in systems, distribution and the range of products. However, the businesses have had to learn to adapt to local conditions, e.g. Walmart sells whole roasted pigs and live frogs in its Chinese stores.

Test your understanding 3

Identify the main drivers of globalisation.

The impact of globalisation on firms

Firms are affected by globalisation in many ways, including:

Industrial relocation

Many firms have relocated their manufacturing base to countries with lower labour costs – offshoring (this is discussed in more detail later in the chapter).

However, this can give the impression that the only form of expansion is from "First World" to "Third World". This is not always the case as illustrated by Nissan (a Japanese company) building a car factory in Sunderland in the United Kingdom to avoid EU import quotas and tariffs.

Some non-Western countries are developing regional areas of excellence. For example, Bangalore in India is recognised globally for its expertise in telecommunications.

Managing (often complex) global supply chains has only been made possible by the advances in information technology.

Emergence of growth markets

As mentioned above, many previously closed markets, such as China, are opening up to Western firms.

In addition, if tastes are becoming more homogeneous, then this presents new opportunities for firms to sell their products in countries previously discounted.

Access to markets and enhanced competition

The combination of firms' global expansion plans and the relaxation of trade barriers have resulted in increased competition in many markets. This can be seen in:

- greater pressure on firms' cost bases with factories being relocated to even cheaper areas
- greater calls for protectionism.

Developments in information technology have also facilitated greater access to markets, for example by selling via the Internet.

Cross-national business alliances and mergers

To exploit the opportunities global markets offer many firms have sought to obtain expertise and greater economies of scale through cross-national mergers and acquisitions. For example:

- In 2004 American brewer Anheuser-Busch Limited purchased the Chinese company Harbin Brewery Company Ltd.
- The merger of Hoechst (a German company) and Rhone Poulenc (French) to create Aventis in 1999 created the second largest drugs manufacturer in the world at the time.

Widening economic divisions between countries

Many opponents of globalisation argue that it is creating new gaps between the rich and the poor. For example:

Rich countries have much greater access to the Internet and communications services. In the current information age wealth is created by the development of information goods and services, ranging from media, to education and software. Not all poor countries are taking part in this information revolution and are falling further behind the "digital divide".

The relentless drive to liberalise trade, i.e. to remove trade barriers, promote privatisation, and reduce regulation (including legal protection for workers), has had a negative impact on the lives of millions of people around the world.

Many poor countries have been pressured to orientate their economies towards exporting and to reduce already inadequate spending on public services such as health and education so that they can repay their foreign debt. This has forced even more people into a life of poverty and uncertainty.

4.2 Emerging market multinationals – the BRIC economies

A recent trend has been a rise in multinational companies from the emerging "BRIC" economies.

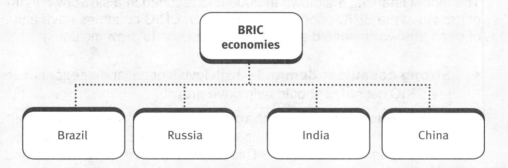

BRIC are the world's largest emerging economies.

Two key factors have resulted in the growth of these economies:

- **globalisation** (see 'test your understanding 3' on the drivers of globalisation)
- **internal developments** – these include:
    - large and rapid growth rates
    - a move towards a free market economy
    - relative political stability
    - availability of labour
    - low wage rates
    - improvements in education
    - availability of natural resources.

By 2050, the combined BRIC economies are expected to outstrip the G6 economies (Germany, France, Italy, Japan, UK and the USA).

China is predicted to become the world's largest economy, as early as 2027.

In 2012, Brazil replaced Britain as the 6th Largest world economy.

In June 2009, the first summit of heads of state of the BRIC countries was held. The forming of an alliance will help to increase their economic and political power.

Organisations in BRIC economies are moving from being recipients of foreign direct investment to actually investing in and even becoming owners of major Western businesses. For example, there is a strong move in China to export capital and to make foreign acquisitions.

The future of the BRIC economies

The global financial meltdown in 2008 has resulted in a slowdown in the rate of growth of the BRIC economies. However, BRIC countries have a number of strengths which should allow them to continue to grow including:

- **Strong consumer demand** – high levels of consumer expenditure in the BRIC countries should help drive growth.
- **High levels of foreign exchange reserves** – these reserves will allow the government to boost public spending in the economy, e.g. on transport and infrastructure. This will enhance the environment and lead to further economic growth.

The BRIC economies seem to have withstood the shakings of the world's economic foundations, and emerged more robust than ever.

Threats for BRIC economies

The global slowdown of 2008 has resulted in a number of threats for the BRIC economies. For example:

- Foreign investment in BRIC economies from developed countries has slowed.
- Consumer demand in the developed world has slowed. This will impact the BRIC economies, e.g. two thirds of China's exports are to the developed world, with exports accounting for over one third of their wealth.
- India's economy depends on developed countries outsourcing services to them. A recession in the developed world will reduce the level of outsourcing.

A second tier of emerging economies, which demonstrates some similar characteristics to those of the BRIC nations, is Indonesia, Vietnam, Colombia and Ukraine. Economic growth in these countries is beginning to drive consumer spending on domestic goods. The size of their populations means there is unlikely to be any reversal of this trend.

Major institutions and international development

The principal institutions encouraging world trade have been discussed earlier in this chapter. Here we consider institutions more involved with international development and financing.

The World Bank

The International Bank for Reconstruction and Development (IBRD), also known as the World Bank, was created at the Bretton Woods meeting in 1944. The original purpose of the IBRD was to help finance the reconstruction of economies damaged by the war. However, it soon shifted the focus of its lending to countries of the developing world.

The bank now comprises three principal constituent elements:

(1) The IBRD proper whose function is to lend long-term funds for capital projects in developing economies at a commercial rate of interest. The main source of these funds is borrowing by the IBRD itself.

(2) The International Development Association (IDA) which was established in 1960 to provide 'soft' loans to the poorest of the developing countries. The IDA:

(a) is mainly financed by 20 donor countries providing funds every 3 years. Funding therefore depends on the generosity or otherwise of these countries.

(b) provides loans on concessionary terms, normally interest free loans repayable over 50 years.

(3) The International Finance Corporation, which promotes the private sector in developing countries by lending or by taking equity.

The World Bank is clearly an important source of capital funds for the developing countries. However, it has been criticised in recent years over the nature of its lending conditions.

The International Monetary Fund (IMF)

The IMF was also founded in 1944 at Bretton Woods in the USA but did not really begin to fully function until the 1950s. The so called Bretton Woods System, that the IMF was to supervise, was to have two main characteristics: stable exchange rates and a multilateral system of international payments and credit.

In particular the IMF became responsible for:

- promoting international financial co-operation and establishing a system of stable exchange rates and freely convertible currencies
- providing a source of credit for members with balance of payments deficits while corrective policies were adopted
- managing the growth of international liquidity.

European Bank for Reconstruction and Development

The European Bank for Reconstruction and Development was established in 1991 when communism was crumbling in Central and Eastern Europe and ex-soviet countries needed support to nurture a new private sector in a democratic environment.

Today the EBRD uses the tools of investment to help build market economies and democracies in 27 countries from central Europe to central Asia.

5 Country and Political Risk

5.1 Introduction

Globalisation can be a huge opportunity for a company to engage in business with many countries around the world. However, investing abroad may be accompanied by risk. This section will review two such risks:

- Political risk
- Country risk

5.2 Political risk

Political risk is the possibility of an unexpected politically motivated event in a country affecting the outcome of an investment.

- Political risk is greater in countries with developing economies.

- A change in government can sometimes result in dramatic changes for a business.

- Political risk could have a **direct** effect on a business. For example:
    - The risk of nationalisation of foreign owned assets.

    - The risk of a government decision to raise taxation.

    - The risk of a government decision to restrict payments to foreign shareholders.

    - The risk that politically motivated terrorists cause damage to property and/or employees.

    - The risk of changes in the law, such as employment law.

    - The risk that contracts are cancelled or revised.

    - The risk that lobby groups within a country put pressure on the government to support home based business rather than foreign business.

- Political risk can also be **indirect**, because of the effect of government policies on the economy, e.g. changes in interest rates and exchange rates.

Illustration 7

In 2001, British Prime Minister Tony Blair had to personally intervene to protect the investment in the Ukraine by the British oil company JKX Oil and Gas plc. The Ukraine's State Property Fund had attempted to expropriate JKX's investment but after intervention by the British Prime Minister the Ukrainian court ruled that the action was illegal.

Groups that can generate political risk

- Current government

- Opposition groups

- Organised interest groups such as students and teachers

- Terrorist or anarchist groups

- International organisations such as the UN

- Foreign governments that have entered into international alliances with the country or are supporting the opposition within the country.

Managing political risk

Three main methods of managing political risk

Understand political risk before investing	Review risks regularly during the period of investment	Take action after the risk has materialised
• Is the risk less than the potential economic return?	• New risks may emerge or existing risks may become more material	

Test your understanding 4

Explain what steps may be taken to manage political risk:

(a) before the investment takes place.

(b) during the period of investment.

(c) after the risk has been realised.

5.3 Country risk

Country risk is the risk arising from operating or investing in a particular country, with risks relating to matters such as:

- political interference, e.g. currency controls
- political stability
- the social and economic infrastructure
- the culture of the country
- and its attitude to foreign business.

Country risk is a much more general term than political risk and relates to all of the risks of operating or investing in a particular country.

Illustration 8

Oil company BP has explained on its website how it approaches the task of identifying and assessing country risk.

BP carries out a country risk assessment whenever it faces a strategic decision about whether to invest in a new country. Country risk assessments are also made when the political or social environment changes, or if a significant change in the size of investment is under consideration.

This process culminates in an intensive discussion with active participation from outside experts and BP personnel with experience of the region and relevant BP operations. Over two days many strands of thinking and research are brought together to form a view of the country in question, which then informs all major decisions, including investment decisions, relating to BP's involvement in the country. The results of these assessments remain, by their nature, confidential to the business.

Country risk analysis

Country risk can be analysed in three ways

Political analysis
Considers:
- stability of govern-ment
- corruption by officials
- different religious beliefs
- ethnic tensions

Financial analysis
- Can country meet its debt obligations?
- Consider factors such as exchange rate stability, past loan defaults

Economic analysis
- Growth in GDP (gross domestic product)
- Per capita GDP
- Inflation rates

When all of these risks are taken together, an overall assessment of country risk can be made.

Risk mapping

When an initial review is carried out to identify and assess risks, the assessment of both probabilities and impact might be based on judgement and experience rather than on a detailed statistical and numerical analysis.

- In an initial analysis, it might be sufficient to categorise the probability of an adverse outcome as 'high', 'medium' or 'low', or even more simply as 'high' or 'low'.

- Similarly, it might be sufficient for the purpose of an initial analysis to assess the consequences or impact of an adverse outcome as 'severe' or 'not severe'.

Each risk can then be plotted on a risk map. A risk map is simply a 2 × 2 table or chart, showing the probabilities for each risk and their potential impact.

		Impact/ consequences	
		Low	**High**
Probability/	**High**		
likelihood	**Low**		

6 Outsourcing and Offshoring

6.1 Outsourcing

Outsourcing means contracting-out aspects of the work of the organisation, previously done in-house, to specialist providers.

Before making a decision to outsource a company must consider what competencies exist within their business. There are two types of competencies:

Threshold competencies – actions or processes that you must be good at just to be considered as a potential supplier to a customer. They are the same as competitors' competencies and easy to imitate.

For example, in clothes retail it may be the case that most firms have outsourced to Chinese manufacturers in order to gain low costs. Outsourcing may be essential just to be a feasible player in the market.

Core competencies – something that you are able to do that drives competitive advantage and is very difficult for your competitors to emulate. You must possess these if you want to compete effectively in the market concerned.

For our clothing retailer the core competences may relate to design and brand management.

It may be unwise to outsource aspects of the work in which you have a core competence as this could erode your competitive advantage.

Quinn and Hilmer

According to Quinn and Hilmer (1994), a major strategic factor in sourcing decisions is core competence. There are three basic tests that can be employed to identify the core competences of an organisation.

- First, a core competence should provide potential access to a wide variety of markets.

- Secondly, a core competence should also make a significant contribution to the perceived benefits as experienced by the customer of the product.

- Finally, a core competence should be difficult to imitate by competitors.

Based on these ideas, Quinn and Hilmer developed a decision matrix incorporating three factors:

(1) The potential for competitive edge derived from the activity,

(2) Any strategic vulnerability introduced by outsourcing and the need for flexibility, and

(3) The transaction costs incurred due to outsourcing.

The output from the decision matrix identifies the level of control the organisation needs to exercise on the particular activity. For example:

- If the potential for competitive edge derived from a given activity and the degree of strategic vulnerability are both "high," then a "high" level of control is in order. Coupled with a "low" need for flexibility required (due to demand variability, say), this suggests full ownership of the activity in question by the organisation.

- On the other hand, when the flexibility requirement is "high," then the authors propose outsourcing of the activity based on a short-term contract.

Naturally, there are other possible actions between these two extremes, such as partial ownership and long-term contracts, depending on the level of control and flexibility needs.

Outsourcing has become increasingly common in organisations. The advantages and disadvantages include:

Advantages

The main reason for outsourcing is that it is cheaper. **Cost advantages** can come from a number of sources:

- A large supplier may benefit from economies of scale in production.
- The firm concerned will benefit from reduced capital expenditure on machinery to make the items now outsourced.
- Reduced headcount in terms of workers no longer needed to make the items.
- Research and development expenditure on the components, say, concerned will also be saved.

There can also be **quality advantages**:

- The supplier may have skills and expertise that allow them to make better products
- Outsourcing may solve the problem of the company having a skills shortage in certain areas.

Other advantages include the following:

- The supplier may have greater production expertise and efficiencies, leading to faster and more flexible supply of components.

- The management of the customer are no longer distracted by fringe areas and so can focus on core business activities.

- The organisation can exercise buyer power over suppliers ensuring favourable terms and conditions.

- The organisation has greater flexibility to switch suppliers based on changing cost/quality considerations.

Disadvantages

- Cost issues – the supplier will want to make a profit margin, suggesting it may be cheaper to do the work in house. In addition, if dealing with a major supplier we may be vulnerable to future price rises.

- Loss of core competence – the service may represent (or contribute to) a core competence for the organisation and therefore outsourcing may lead to a loss of competitive advantage.

- Transaction costs – arise from the effort put into specifying what is required, co-ordinating delivery and monitoring quality. (Note: transaction costs are discussed in more detail later on in the chapter).

- Finality of decision – once a service has been contracted out it may be difficult to take back in-house at a later date, e.g. due to a loss of in-house expertise.

- Risk of loss of confidential information.

- Risk of continuity of supply if the supplier has problems.

- Difficulty agreeing/enforcing contract terms.

- Damage to employee morale if redundancies occur or if organisational culture is eroded.

Service level agreements

At least some of the potential disadvantages can be controlled though the use of effective service level agreements.

 A **service level agreement** (SLA) is a negotiated agreement between the supplier and the customer and is a legal agreement regarding the level of service to be provided.

Service level agreements

Service level agreements should include the following factors:

- A detailed explanation of exactly what service the supplier is offering to provide.
- The targets / benchmarks to be used and the consequences of failing to meet them.
- Expected response time to technical queries.
- The expected time to recover the operations in the event of a disaster such as a systems crash, terrorist attack, etc.
- The procedure for dealing with complaints.
- The information and reporting procedures to be adopted.
- The procedures for cancelling the contract.

Test your understanding 5

Could accountancy services be outsourced? Are there problems in so doing?

6.2 Transaction cost theory

Transaction costs are the indirect costs (i.e. non-production costs) incurred in performing a particular activity, for example the expenses incurred through outsourcing.

When outsourcing, transaction costs arise from the effort that must be put into specifying what is required and subsequently co-ordinating delivery and monitoring quality.

A number of kinds of transaction cost have come to be known by particular names:

- **Search and information costs** – for example, the cost of determining which supplier is cheapest.
- **Bargaining costs** – the cost of agreeing on an acceptable SLA.

- **Policing and enforcement costs** – are the costs of making sure the other party sticks to the terms of the contract, and taking appropriate action (often through the legal system) if this turns out not to be the case.

High transaction costs for outsourcing may suggest an in-house solution whereas low transaction costs for outsourcing would support the argument to outsource.

Transaction cost theory

Transaction cost theory (Wiliamson)

Organisations choose between two methods of obtaining control over resources:

- the ownership of assets (hierarchy solutions – decisions over production, supply, and the purchases of inputs are made by managers and imposed through hierarchies) and

- buying-in the use of assets (the market solution – individuals and firms make independent decisions that are guided and co-ordinated by market prices).

The decision is based on a comparison of the transaction costs of the two approaches.

Transactions have three dimensions that determine the costs associated with them:

- uncertainty – the more uncertain the environment the harder it is to write effective long-term contracts and the more likely the acquisition of a supplier is;

- the frequency with which the transactions recur; and

- asset specificity – the extent to which the transacting firms invest in assets whose value depends on the business relationships remaining intact. The greater the specificity of the assets involved, the greater the likelihood that a transaction will take place within the firm.

These factors translate into 'make-or-buy' decisions: whether it is better to provide a service from within the organisation, with hierarchical co-ordination, or from outside the organisation, with market co-ordination.

Williamson argues that it is the third dimension, the degree of asset specificity, which is the most important determinant of transaction. The more specific the assets are to a transaction then, all other things being equal, the greater will be the associated transaction costs and the more likely that the transaction will be internalised into a hierarchy. Conversely, when the productive assets are non-specific the process of market contracting is the more efficient because transaction costs will be low.

Asset specificity

An asset is said to be transaction-specific if its value to a given transaction is greater than its value in its best alternative use. The greater the gap between these two values, the greater the degree of specificity of the asset. Williamson has suggested six main types of asset specificity:

- Site specificity – suggests that once sited the assets may be very immobile.

  For example, a car components manufacturer locating a components factory near to a large customer's manufacturing plant.

- Physical asset specificity – when parties make investments in machinery or equipment that are specific to a certain task these will have lower values in alternative uses.

  For example, a supplier of wet cement to building sites may invest in wet cement delivery trucks (a 'hierarchy' solution) since these trucks are so specific to this task that they cannot be sourced via a network.

- Human asset specificity – occurs when workers may have to acquire relationship-specific skills, know-how and information that is more valuable inside a particular transaction than outside it.

  For example, a consultant may have to acquire detailed knowledge of a client's in-house developed systems but this knowledge may not be useful on other clients.

- Brand name capital specificity refers to becoming affiliated with a well-known 'brand name' and thus becoming less free to pursue other opportunities.

  For example, an actor may become 'typecast' in a particular role or show.

- Dedicated asset specificity entails investments in general-purpose plant that are made at the behest of a particular customer.

  For example, the car components manufacturer above invests in dedicated machinery to make bespoke components for just one manufacturer. Should the contract be lost, these components may have to be adapted for sale elsewhere.

- Temporal specificity – arises when the timing of performance is critical, such as with perishable agricultural commodities where a farmer may struggle to find alternative processors at short notice.

6.3 Offshoring

Offshoring is the relocating of corporate activities to a foreign country.

The bulk of offshored activities include call centres, IT enabled services (e.g. software development) and business process operations (e.g. human resource management and payroll processing).

Illustration 9

Reuters, the world's biggest news agency, employs dozens of journalists in Bangalore, India. They work overnight so that they can report US financial news live as it happens on the New York Stock Exchange.

These Indian financial journalists can be employed by Reuters for a fraction of the cost of employing a journalist in the New York office.

This system became feasible as a result of IT developments:

- **Obtaining information** – most US companies now put out their press releases on the internet, just as the stock market opens. Therefore, the journalists in Bangalore can access the same basic information as their colleagues in the US.

- **Sending information** – the reduced cost of telecommunications links means that the news written in Bangalore can be sent around the world as quickly as the news written in New York.

Benefits of offshoring for the home country

Over the last decade, India has emerged as an attractive destination for offshoring. Explain why many UK companies have taken the decision to offshore their services to India.

Disadvantages of offshoring for the home country

The disadvantages for the home country, for example the UK, include:

- **Differences** – cultural, language and time differences between the home country and the recipient country may make offshoring difficult.

Illustration 10

A team of retired teachers from the UK have set up a company in India where they conduct general knowledge classes for the Indian call centre workers to teach them how to handle calls from UK customers. The call centre agents not only learn about regional accents around the UK, but also the cultural variations and political make-up of the UK.

- **Stability of the offshore countries** – economic and political instability exists in many of the countries providing the services.
- **Cost savings** – the promises of cost savings and improved productivity are not always realised.
- **Job losses** – it is argued that when jobs are lost people are freed up to do higher skilled and higher paid work. But in reality, whilst the economy as a whole may evolve in time to a higher level, the individuals who lose their jobs are not necessarily the ones gaining the new jobs.
- **Safety of information** – there is an increased risk that confidential information, e.g. customer's details, may be lost.
- **Exchange rate effects** – make offshoring risky

Impact of offshoring on the recipient countries

The benefits of offshoring for the recipient countries, such as India, include:

- The creation of much needed jobs
- Improvement in skills
- Advances in infrastructure and technology

In addition to the disadvantages for the home country, concerns to do with decent working conditions, e.g. wages, working hours, and other aspects of good practice (such as technology transfer), exist in the recipient country.

Illustration 11

Employees in Indian call centres are exposed to a host of health problems because of the time difference between India and the US. Working from late evening until early dawn can result in digestive problems, hair loss, back pain and stress.

These factors contribute to the high turnover in Indian call centres; approximately 30–40% of employees resign each year.

7 Cross-cultural Management

7.1 Introduction

Managers are increasingly exposed to working with, or within, many different business cultures. This involves working in other countries, working in organisations that have operations in other cultural environments, or working with colleagues from a wide range of cultures.

Culture is the 'sum total of the beliefs, knowledge, attitudes, norms and customs that prevail in an organisation or country'.

Managers need to display cross-cultural competence and reconcile cultural differences.

Cross cultural management

David Foster argues that cross-cultural management is a shorthand term that summarises a number of different elements:

- First, it describes the range of organisational behaviour which exists within both countries and cultures.

- Second, it compares and contrasts organisational behaviour across countries and cultures.

- Third, it seeks to understand and improve the interaction of co-workers, clients, suppliers and partners from different countries and cultures."

Cross-cultural education and training are thus needed to achieve the following purposes:

- To encourage people to study and evaluate the components of their own culture so that they become more aware of their own hidden cultural assumptions which interfere with effective intercultural action.

- To expand people's repertoire of culturally appropriate behaviours so that they can operate more effectively in cross-cultural encounters in the workplace.

- To evaluate the impact of cultural factors on job performance. It can be argued that cultural traits and differences are so ingrained that it is hard for individuals even to understand they are there or that they have an influence on behaviour. These traits influence individual action, how relationships are formed and maintained, how products are perceived and located in markets and the success of communication.

Illustration 12

HSBC brands itself as 'the World's local bank'. The company understands that there are cultural differences between the countries in which they operate and celebrate that people have different points of view. They believe that these points of view are supported by their business values and promote these values in their advertising. This understanding of cultural differences has helped this 'local bank' to become one of the world's largest and most successful banks.

7.2 The Hofstede model

During his work with IBM Hofstede found that national culture can be a greater influence on behaviour and performance than corporate culture. This means that even firms with a very strong corporate culture need to understand the different national cultures in which they operate. The challenge for managers is thus knowing where and how national cultures vary.

Hofstede has identified five dimensions in which national culture seems to vary:

Power distance – how much society accepts the unequal distribution of power, for instance the extent to which supervisors see themselves as being above their subordinates. In some cultures, particularly South American ones, disparities of power were tolerated more than in North European cultures.

Individualism versus collectivism – how much people prefer a tight-knit social framework based on 'loyalty' to an involvement based on individual cost and benefit. Some cultures are more cohesive than others, with Anglo Saxon cultures more individualistic than the collectivist cultures of South America.

Masculinity versus femininity – used as shorthand to indicate the degree to which 'masculine' values predominate: e.g. assertive, domineering, material wealth and competitive, as opposed to 'feminine' values such as sensitivity and concern for others. A masculine culture is one where gender roles are distinct, with the male focus on work, power and success. Such cultures include Japan, and Italy. Feminine cultures, such as Finland, have smaller differences in gender roles and success is likely to be regarded as a social, rather than personal activity.

Uncertainty avoidance – how much society dislikes ambiguity and risk, and the extent to which people feel threatened by unusual situations, paralleled by how far persons and ideas deviate from the accepted norm. Some cultures, such as France and Japan, dislike uncertainty and use planning and bureaucracy to reduce it. Other cultures, such as Jamaica and Denmark, tend to be less uncomfortable with uncertainty and ambiguity. High uncertainty avoidance traits means risk taking is discouraged.

Long term orientation – first called 'Confucian dynamism' it describes societies' time horizon. Long term oriented societies (e.g. China) attach more importance to the future. They foster pragmatic values oriented towards rewards, including persistence, saving and capacity for adaptation. In short term oriented societies (e.g. Germany), values promoted are related to the past and the present, including steadiness, respect for tradition, preservation of one's face, reciprocation and fulfilling social obligations.

It is important to see that Hofstede was attempting to model aspects of culture that might influence business behaviour, rather than produce national stereotypes.

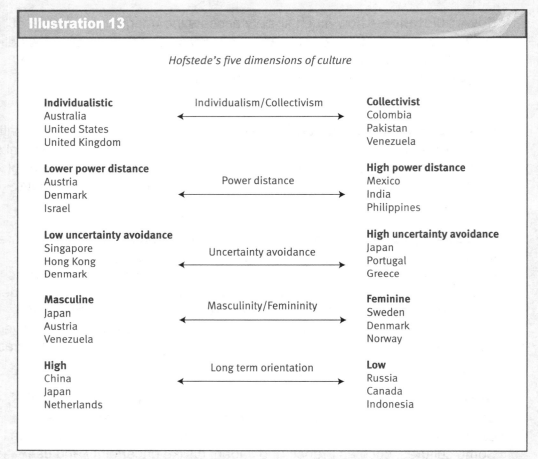

Illustration 13

Hofstede's five dimensions of culture

Individualistic	Individualism/Collectivism	**Collectivist**
Australia		Colombia
United States		Pakistan
United Kingdom		Venezuela

Lower power distance	Power distance	**High power distance**
Austria		Mexico
Denmark		India
Israel		Philippines

Low uncertainty avoidance	Uncertainty avoidance	**High uncertainty avoidance**
Singapore		Japan
Hong Kong		Portugal
Denmark		Greece

Masculine	Masculinity/Femininity	**Feminine**
Japan		Sweden
Austria		Denmark
Venezuela		Norway

High	Long term orientation	**Low**
China		Russia
Japan		Canada
Netherlands		Indonesia

Culture in the BRIC economies

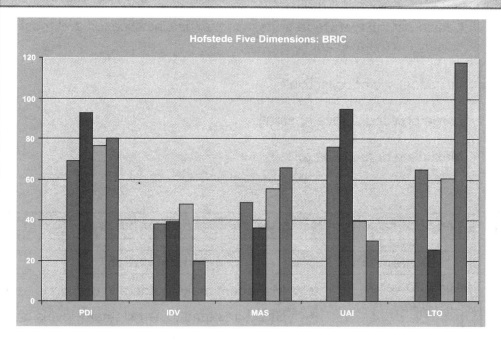

Key:

PDI = power distance
IDV = individualism
MAS = masculinity
UAI = uncertainty avoidance
LTO = long term orientation

For each dimension the chart shows the results in the order of Brazil, Russia, India, China.

Test your understanding 7

In the Hofstede model, a national culture which supports single status pay arrangements, informal styles of address in the workplace and self-managed team working would be classified as:

A   individualist

B   masculine

C   low power distance

D   high uncertainty avoidance

Test your understanding 8

Looking at the **Hofstede** traits, choose the classification that most closely fits Great Britain.

Individualistic or collective?

Large power distance or small?

Masculine or feminine roles?

The implications of Hofstede's categories for business

Dimension	Implication
High Power Distance	• Managers make autocratic decisions. • Structures tend to be tall (many levels of managers and supervisors). • Status differences between managers and subordinates.
High Individualism	• Self reliance. • Autonomy. • Individual achievement (not achievement of group) important.
High Masculinity	• Status through high earnings. • Advancement value. • Challenges sought.
High Uncertainty Avoidance	• Formalised organisational structures. • Depend heavily on rules and regulations. • Do not like anything that deviates from accepted norms.
High Long Term Orientation	• Strong work ethic; emphasis on perseverance. • High value placed on education and training. • Respect for tradition.

Hofstede also looked at cultural differences in work related attitudes. These include:

Leadership – in some countries, such as those in Latin America, leaders are expected to take a strong personal interest in employees and appear at private social functions, such as weddings, whereas in other countries such as Germany such social contact is discouraged. In other countries, notably in Asia and Africa, public criticism is intolerable as the loss of self-respect brings dishonour to the employee and his family.

Motivation – the incentives for effective performance must match the culture. It is pointless offering individual bonuses to workers where there are strong group and company loyalties, as in Japan, or where loyalty to an individual's superior is paramount as in Turkey and the Near East.

Structure – research showed that French firms are bureaucratic with orders and procedures set from above whereas German work organisation relies more on the professional expertise, which derives from the trained knowledge and skill of the more junior employees.

Other cultural models

Trompenaars and Hamden Turner developed the 'Seven Dimensions of Culture Model' to analyse cultural differences and this also provides managers with some insight into the complexity of managing international teams.

The basic premise of the model is that an understanding of the underlying values of different cultures leads to greater respect for diverse ways of operating and to the desire and skills for reconciling cultural differences to achieve business performance.

Ronen and Shenkar attempted to cluster individual countries into groupings based on observed shared characteristics and affinities. For example, they created a set of clusters based on the analysis of four key characteristics:

- the importance of work goals
- job satisfaction
- the impact of managerial and organisational variables
- work roles and interpersonal orientations.

8 National Account Balances and Government Policy

8.1 Introduction

The decisions made by the government of a particular country will have a huge impact on any company that trades with, or within, that country.

The factors that companies need to consider include:

- growth in the economy
- the rate of inflation
- the exchange rate
- levels of unemployment
- the balance of payments, i.e. whether the country is a net importer or exporter.

8.2 Government policy

Typically, governments will have four macroeconomic policy objectives:

- **Economic growth** – how can productive capacity be increased? Growth can be measured by looking at an the increase in two figures:
  - Gross Domestic Product (GDP) = the total value of income/ production from economic activity within a country.
  - Gross National Product (GNP) = GDP + overseas income – income earned in the country by overseas residents.

- **Inflation** – how can we ensure that general price levels are kept relatively stable?

- **Unemployment** – how can we ensure that everyone who wants a job has one?

- **Balance of payments** – how should we manage our relationship and trade with other countries?

These are discussed in more detail below.

More detail on policy objectives

Stagnation and economic growth

Most governments want economic growth. Growth should result in the following:

- more goods being demanded and produced
- people earn more and can afford more goods
- more people should have jobs.

On the face of it, therefore, growth should result in an improved standard of living in a country and higher profitability for businesses.

However, growth is not without its problems.

- Is economic growth fast enough to keep up with population growth?
- Growth rates have to exceed inflation rates for benefits to arise (i.e. "real" growth has to occur).
- Growth may be in 'demerit' goods, such as illegal drugs.
- Growth may be at the expense of the environment or through exploitation of the poor.
- The gap between rich and poor may grow, as the benefits from growth are not evenly distributed.
- Rapid growth means rising incomes and this often 'sucks in' imports, worsening the balance of trade, rather than benefiting domestic producers.

Inflation

Most governments want stable prices and low inflation. The main reasons given include the following:

- Inflation causes uncertainty and stifles business investment.
- Not all incomes rise in line with inflation – the poor and those on fixed incomes suffer the most.
- In extreme cases of inflation, the function of money may break down, resulting in civil unrest.
- Inflation distorts the working of the price mechanism and is thus a market imperfection.

Note that high inflation can affect savings in different ways:

- inflation erodes the future purchasing power of funds so people may decide to save less but spend more now

- an alternative argument is that higher prices reduce individuals' real wealth and so they spend less. This could result in higher savings (the "real balance" effect).

Unemployment

Even in a healthy economy some unemployment will arise as people change jobs. However, mass unemployment is a problem due to the following:

- The government has to pay out benefits to the unemployed at a time when its tax receipts are low. This can result in the government having to raise taxes, borrow money and cut back on services.

- Unemployment has been linked to a rise in crime, poor health and a breakdown in family relationships.

- Unemployment is a waste of human resources and can restrict economic growth.

High unemployment could give firms higher bargaining power allowing them to pay lower wages to prospective employees.

Balance of payments

In the long-term, government seeks to establish a broad balance between the value of imports into, and exports from, the country.

To run a persistent surplus or deficit can have negative macroeconomic effects.

- A long-term trade deficit has to be financed. The financing costs act as a major drain on the productive capacity of the economy.

- A long-term trade surplus can cause significant inflationary pressures, leading ultimately to a loss in international confidence in the economy and a lack of international competitiveness

The government will aim to balance this range of economic factors through the use of either:

- Fiscal policy or
- Monetary policy.

8.3 Fiscal policy

Involves changes in:

- **Taxation** – the government raises revenue from individuals and businesses via taxes.
- **Government spending** – the way in which the government spends the money will impact the strength of the economy.

Illustration 14 – UK government spending cuts

In 2010 the UK government announced plans to cut £6.2 billion of what it calls 'wasteful spending'. The chancellor, George Osborne, argued that unless the government tackled huge public debt, it could derail the economic recovery. However, the reaction to these cuts has not always been warmly received by the public or opposition party.

Taxation policy

Governments raise revenue from individuals and businesses via a variety of taxes. The way they spend that money can have a significant effect on the strength of the economy.

There are two ways we can look at taxation. We can consider taxation to be direct (in which case it is deducted from earnings, either individual or corporate), or indirect, in which case it is levied on expenditure.

Direct tax

Direct tax is normally a percentage deducted from either earnings or profits. Invariably for businesses it is based on profits. Not all direct tax is levied on earned income and an individual may pay income tax on their salary but also a tax on dividends that they hold in a company unrelated to their work. This would be described as a tax on unearned income. Sometimes a special tax on individuals will be designated for a particular purpose, for instance a tax to provide for old age pensions.

Indirect taxes

Indirect taxes, sometimes called taxes on consumption, are levied on expenditure. This means that when we buy something the cost will have been inflated by a percentage which, when the vendor receives it, must be paid to the government. One of the advantages of this type of tax for the government is that they have to collect tax from fewer sources – there are fewer vendors in most economies than there are earners.

Types of indirect tax include:

- A **value added tax** – which can be levied on all goods, although a government may decide to apply different rates to different products to encourage (or discourage) patterns of consumption. For instance there is unlikely to be any VAT on this book – the government may want to encourage study – but if you have some chocolate whilst you are reading it, that will carry VAT since it is a luxury.

- **Hydrocarbon tax** – a tax on the fuel that people use in their vehicles. Again there is a motivation for government over and above the mere raising of revenue; they may wish to discourage the use of cars and so tax fuel heavily. We shall discuss that again when we discuss the environment.

- **Tobacco tax** – aside from the revenue raised, the higher the tax the more people are discouraged from smoking which will be good for the nation's health and, possibly, reduce the demands on the health provision in the country.

- **Import duties** – again governments will use this form of taxation to encourage or discourage particular patterns of consumption as we discussed earlier in the chapter.

For a government there are two further decisions to be made other than those implied in the decisions described above.

(1) Firstly they will need to decide whether the majority of the tax revenue should come from individuals or from companies.

Obviously businesses will consider the environment more favourable if there is a low level of corporate tax. If it isn't they may decide to relocate to a country with a more favourable tax regime.

Tax havens such as the Bahamas or Bermuda will have exceptionally low, or even no, income tax to attract foreign companies to set up branches there.

Governments may decide to have a threshold of income below which taxation is not paid by individuals, effectively helping the low waged to live. In the case of companies they may have a system of tax credits for particular industries to encourage investment in those areas.

The population would prefer the income tax levels to be low since they would prefer to keep the majority of their earnings to use as they see fit. Too high a level of taxation will not encourage people to work harder to raise their income levels.

(2) Secondly they will need to decide how much they wish to raise by taxing earnings compared to the amount the wish to raise via indirect taxation.

8.4 Monetary policy

Monetary policy refers to the management of money supply within the economy.

In particular, monetary policy may be concerned with:

- The **volume** of money in circulation – the stock of money in the economy (the 'money supply') is believed to have important effects on the volume of expenditure in the economy. This in turn may influence the level of output in the economy or the level of prices.

Illustration 15 – Quantitative easing

Throughout 2010, the UK's interest rate was 0.5%, (this is the base rate set by the Bank of England) the lowest level in history. The low rate was aimed at easing the credit crunch and getting banks lending again. However, this did not happen to the extent required and therefore the Bank of England has injected billions of pounds into the economy through a programme of 'quantitative easing'.

Quantitative easing is a method of pumping money into the economy through the bank's purchase of government and corporate bonds. The organisations selling these assets (e.g. banks and insurance companies) will then have 'new' money in their accounts which boosts the money supply.

- The **price** of money – the price of money is the rate of interest. If governments wish to influence the amount of money held in the economy or the demand for credit, they may attempt to influence the level of interest rate. A rise in interest rates should result in:
    - a fall in spending
    - a fall in investment
    - foreign funds attracted to the country
    - a rise in exchange rates.

Test your understanding 9

Explain how changes in monetary policy can influence a business.

8.5 Balance of payments

The **balance of payments** records all the transactions that have taken place between the residents of a country and overseas residents during the period of a year, e.g. payments for a country's export and import of goods and services.

The balance of payments

The balance of payments is split into three parts:

- current account (goods and services),
- capital account (e.g. buildings) and
- financial account (e.g. cash flows)

Exporting goods for cash would give rise to a debit in the financial account and a credit in the current account.(This is similar to sales being a credit in the income statement).

When discussing debits and credits we conventionally look at the current account, hence exports are a credit entry and imports a debit.

Balance of payments deficits

If a country is said to have a deficit on its balance of payments this means that there is a net outflow of funds from the country, for example through importing more than it exports. Clearly, this outflow cannot continue as a country cannot keep spending more than it earns in foreign currency – eventually it will run out of reserves and other countries will cease to be willing to loan it money.

Government can seek to reduce a balance of payments deficit in a number of ways. Traditionally the strategies that can be used are divided into:

- expenditure-reducing strategies
- expenditure-switching strategies.

Expenditure-reducing strategies

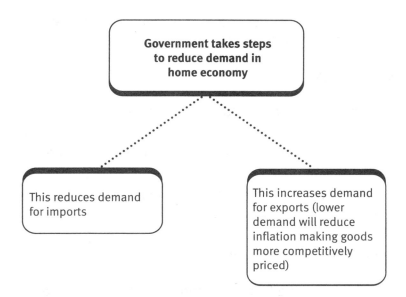

Expenditure-switching strategies

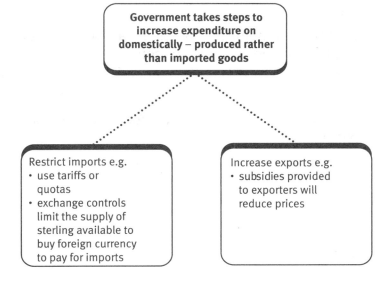

In this case the government seeks to change expenditure patterns of consumers by encouraging expenditure on domestically-produced rather than imported goods.

Import controls

Government could seek to restrict imports. This could be achieved by:

- direct imposition of tariffs or quotas

- or through exchange controls limiting the supply of domestic currency available to buy overseas currencies to pay for imports.

The imposition of trade barriers is highly controversial, however, and is likely to breach WTO regulations.

Boost exports

A government could seek to boost exports in a number of ways:

- Provide subsidies to exporters to allow them to reduce export prices.

- Extend export credit guarantees to more countries, reducing the risk for exporters of non-payment.

Weaken the exchange rate

- In the case of a fixed exchange rate this is referred to as a devaluation. Where exchange rates are floating it is referred to as a depreciation. This strategy has the effect of making imports more expensive and exports cheaper (in their own currency) to an overseas buyer.

- This policy has a number of problems associated with it often making it a last choice of government. These problems include:
  - It may not work if it results in competitive depreciations or devaluations.
  - It may not work as the rise in import prices triggers domestic inflation.

9 Chapter summary

```
┌──────────────────────┐  ┌──────────────────────────┐  ┌──────────────────────┐
│ Different economic   │  │ Free trade and           │  │ Emerging market multi-│
│ systems              │  │ protectionism            │  │ nationals            │
│ • Planned            │  │ • International trade     │  │ • Globalisation      │
│ • Mixed              │  │ • Liberalisation – free  │  │ • BRIC economies     │
│ • Free market        │  │   trade                  │  │                      │
│ • Transition         │  │ • Economic nationalism – │  │                      │
│                      │  │   protectionism          │  │                      │
│                      │  │ • Balanced trade         │  │                      │
└──────────────────────┘  └──────────────────────────┘  └──────────────────────┘

              ┌─────────────────────────────┐
              │ Introduction to the global  │
              │ business environment        │
              └─────────────────────────────┘

┌──────────────────┐ ┌──────────────────┐ ┌──────────────────┐ ┌──────────────────────┐
│ Country and      │ │ Outsourcing and  │ │ Cross-cultural   │ │ National account     │
│ political risk   │ │ offshoring       │ │ management       │ │ balances and         │
│ • Political risk │ │ • Outsourcing    │ │ • The Hofstede   │ │ government policy    │
│ • Country risk   │ │ • Transaction    │ │   model          │ │ • Government policy  │
│                  │ │   cost theory    │ │ • Other cultural │ │ • Fiscal policy      │
│                  │ │ • Offshoring     │ │   models         │ │ • Monetary policy    │
│                  │ │                  │ │                  │ │ • Balance of payments│
└──────────────────┘ └──────────────────┘ └──────────────────┘ └──────────────────────┘
```

10 Practice questions

Question 1

Risk relating to matters such as the political stability of a country, the social and economic infrastructure and the culture of the country is known as:

A   country risk

B   financial risk

C   accounting risk

D   political risk

(2 marks)

Question 2

In a free market economy, decisions and choices about resource allocation are determined by:

A   individuals

B   the government

C   a combination of individuals and the government

D   the money markets

(2 marks)

Question 3

Which of the following would NOT be a feature of a mixed economy?

A   private ownership of land

B   government control of interest rates

C   public ownership of all resources

D   the influence by the government on the private sector

(2 marks)

Question 4

The imposition of which one of the following would NOT act as a barrier to international trade?

A   quotas

B   tariffs

C   value added tax

D   embargoes

(2 marks)

Question 5

A country that has a culture where there are wide status differences between subordinates and managers would be said to have:

A   low masculinity

B   high individualism

C   high long term orientation

D   high power distance

(2 marks)

Question 6

Explain FOUR reasons why a UK insurance company may be concerned about offshoring its customer call centre to India.

(4 marks)

Question 7

Briefly explain the similarities and differences between the economic systems of the UK and the US.

(4 marks)

Question 8

X Company is a manufacturer of non-alcoholic soft drinks and has a well-established position and brand recognition in country Z. The potential for future growth in country Z is, however, limited, with the market reaching saturation. One option for expansion is to move into new markets in other countries offering its existing product range.

The business development team is evaluating this option and is currently working on proposals to sell the company's range of drinks in country Y. One possible strategy to achieve market entry that the team is investigating is through a joint venture with a company that is already established in country Y, and is in the drinks distribution business.

The Board of X Company has given the business development team the task of undertaking a feasibility study to explore the viability of the proposed strategy. The feasibility study needs to assess the cultural compatibility of the ways of doing business in country Y compared to how X Company currently operates in country Z.

Required:

Explain how Hofstede's research could be used to assess the compatibility of X Company's strategy with the culture of country Y.

(15 marks)

Question 9

POOL Publishing is a publisher of books with a listing on the stock exchange of the country in which it is based. POOL has a large number of customers. Almost five years ago, it outsourced its accounting to an external service provider, ITW. The accounting system is fully computerised, and is a bespoke system developed several years ago for POOL, and updated occasionally since that time.

The service from ITW has operated fairly well until recently, but ITW now appears to have difficulty in dealing with the rapidly-growing accounting requirements of POOL, as its business has expanded.

A decision has therefore been taken that the contract with ITW will not be renewed when it expires in six months' time. The accounting work will be given to a different outsourcing firm.

As management accountant and internal auditor for POOL, you have been asked to plan the changeover from ITW to the new outsourcing firm. In addition, in accordance with the contractual agreement with ITW, you will be required to carry out an audit of the accounts system before the changeover occurs.

Required:

Describe the potential risks that need to be considered in the changeover from ITW to the new outsourcing firm, and recommend measures to limit those risks.

(13 marks)

Test your understanding answers

Test your understanding 1

The best examples of planned economies are the (former) Soviet Union and China after World War 2. However, tremendous social and political changes in these countries since the late 1980s have resulted in an increase in free enterprise.

Test your understanding 2

- **Protection for infant industries** – industries in developing countries may need to be protected from competition if, say, they are too small to have gained economies of scale and have insufficient finance for investment.

- **Self sufficiency** – the country may wish to maintain self sufficiency, e.g. this may be important in times of war.

- **Prevents dumping** – a country may produce an excess of a product, e.g. beef, and may 'dump' it in another country at a low price. This country would be facing unfair competition.

- **To protect national culture** – for example, France has restricted the import of American culture through cinema and radio for a number of years and has media legislation in place restricting the amount of broadcasts in languages other than French.

- **To prevent import of harmful goods** – the import of goods, such as drugs or live animals (potentially carrying infectious diseases), may be banned.

- **Prevents establishment of foreign based monopolies** – competition from abroad could drive domestic producers out of business. The foreign company, now having a monopoly, could charge high prices for sub-standard products.

Test your understanding 3

- Low cost, efficient technology
- Convergence of lifestyles and tastes
- Increasing travel creating global networks
- Establishment of world brands
- Government drivers such as a reduction in trade barriers
- Increases in ownership of organisations by foreign acquirers
- Globalisation of financial markets
- Greater automation and improved production methods have freed up labour previously preoccupied with agriculture to work in service industries.

Test your understanding 4

(a) **Before the investment takes place**

- The company should take steps to understand the level and types of political risk.

- A decision to invest should only be taken if the potential economic return is sufficient to compensate for the political risk.

- The company should take out appropriate insurance prior to investment.

(b) **During the period of investment**

- Establish business relations – partnerships with local businesses and suppliers can help the company to learn local business customs and their advice should help to reduce the risks from nationalism and anti-foreign sentiment in the country.

- Set up a local operation – this should be headed by a local manager and should help to reduce risks from nationalist attitudes.

- Borrow in the local currency – the profit from the business can be used to repay loans. This reduces risks from currency conversion or from restrictions on payments out of a country.

- Develop government contacts – winning the support of government should help to reduce the risk of unhelpful political measures such as the refusal of planning permission.

> – Split operations between countries – this will reduce the incentive for the government to nationalise the business.
>
> – Set up a joint venture – risk is shared with another partner.
>
> (c) **After the risk has been realised**
>
> – Litigation or retaliation.
>
> – Implementation of a contingency plan.
>
> – Exit from market.
>
> – Insurance claim.

Test your understanding 5

Accountancy services are often outsourced in smaller companies, but it could be argued that they are critical to the performance of the organisation and may well drive the future of the company. Also there should be some managerial control in this area.

Test your understanding 6

Cost savings – one of the biggest advantages is cost savings. Companies have been able to reduce the cost of services by 30-40% by offshoring to India. These cost savings are due to:

- Lower wages – Indian workers are paid much lower wages than those in the UK.

- Lower capital expenditure – infrastructure costs are lower in India.

- Improved labour management – labour is only employed as and when it is needed for a project, rather than on a permanent basis, as in the UK.

Large talent pool – India has a large pool of talented and motivated professionals. There are 2.1 million graduates each year and this number is set to grow. As a result, UK companies are able to choose between a number of suitable candidates.

Technology – advances in technology and the falling price of technology has enabled UK companies to carry out activities overseas that would have previously been done in the UK.

Common language – India has the largest English speaking population in the world. This will ease communication between the UK and India.

Fast turnaround time – the time taken to carry out a task can be reduced by between 30–50% when offshoring to India. This is partly due to the efficiency of the Indian professionals but is also due to the zonal time differences, e.g. many IT projects have an onsite and offsite team. The offsite team can work on the project during the day in India. When the Indian team leaves work for the evening the onsite team can take over the project in the UK.

Test your understanding 7

c

Test your understanding 8

Although the points can be debated, and the culture is changing, Great Britain probably:

Individualistic

Low power distance

Masculine roles

Test your understanding 9

Changes in monetary policy will influence a business in a number of ways:

- **The availability of finance**: Credit restrictions will reduce the availability of loans. This can make it difficult for small or medium-sized new businesses to raise finance. The threat of such restrictions in the future will influence financial decisions by companies, making them more likely to seek long-term finance for projects.

- **The cost of finance**: Any restrictions on the stock of money will raise the cost of borrowing, making fewer investment projects worthwhile and discouraging expansion by companies. Also, any increase in the level of interest rates will increase shareholders' required rate of return. Thus, organisations are less likely to borrow money and will probably contract rather than expand operations.

- **The level of consumer demand**: Periods of credit control and high interest rates reduce consumer demand. Individuals find it more difficult and more expensive to borrow to fund consumption, while saving becomes more attractive. This is another reason for organisations to have to contract operations.

- **The level of inflation**: Monetary policy is often used to control inflation. Rising price levels and uncertainty as to future rates of inflation make financial decisions more difficult and more important.

- **The level of exchange rates**: Monetary policy which increases the level of domestic interest rates is likely to increase exchange rates as capital is attracted into the country. Many companies now deal with overseas suppliers and customers and can therefore not afford to ignore the risk associated with exchange rate movements.

Question 1

A

Question 2

A

Question 3

C

Individualism and Collectivism

Individualism and collectivism examines how much people prefer a tight-knit social framework based on 'loyalty' to an involvement based on individual cost and benefit. Some cultures are more cohesive than others, with Anglo Saxon cultures more individualistic than the collectivist cultures of South America.

- Individualism – individuals are expected to take care of themselves.
- Collectivism – individuals look after one another and organisations protect their members' interests.

If Y has high individualism, then X would have to encourage managers to demonstrate:

- self reliance
- autonomy
- individual achievement not the achievement of the group or community.

Masculinity/Femininity

Masculinity versus femininity looks at the degree to which 'masculine' values predominate: e.g. assertive, domineering, uncaring and competitive, as opposed to 'feminine' values such as sensitivity and concern for others. A masculine culture is one where distinctive roles between genders are large, with the male focus on work, power and success. Such cultures include Japan and Italy. Feminine cultures, such as Finland, have smaller differences in gender roles and success is likely to be regarded as a social, rather than personal activity.

- Masculine – value achievement, heroism, assertiveness and material success important.
- Feminine – value relationships, caring for the weak and quality of life.

If Y is a country with high masculinity, then X will seek to motivate staff by:

- recognising that status is often gained through high earnings
- offering the possibility of advancement
- ensuring staff are given challenges.

Long term orientation

This examines how much society values long term standing rather than short term values and traditions.

If Y has a high long term orientation, then X would have to encourage:

- a strong work ethic with a strong emphasis on perseverance.
- education and training.

Should X find that there are significant differences between its own culture and that of Y, then this could seriously undermine the chances of success of the proposed venture.

Question 9

A significant risk in switching from one service provider for accounting services to another is the risk of loss or corruption to data during the change. ITW will be required to supply up-to-date and accurate files at the end of its contract, either to POOL or to the new service provider. During this handover process, records might be lost from files, or entire files might be corrupted. For example, ITW might hand over out-of-date files, missing some recent transactions. POOL needs to be able to check that all the information has been properly transferred.

One way of dealing with this problem might be to arrange for a short period during which both ITW and the new service provider are maintaining accounting records for POOL. An internal (or external) audit can then carry out a check on the files in the two systems, to ensure that they appear identical (e.g. with the same total number of records and same control totals).

There might be technological or software difficulties if the accounts are moved from ITW's computer system to the system of another provider, and there might be difficulties in getting the system to operate properly on the system of the new service provider. The solution to this problem is also to have a period of time during which the two systems are running in parallel, so that any technical problems can be identified and resolved.

There is also a risk of unauthorised retention of files. An individual within the ITW organisation might retain copies of the accounts files of POOL. This would create a risk of file data about customers getting into the possession of another organisation. Alternatively, the individual retaining the file copies might subsequently use the information they contain for fraudulent purposes. POOL needs to check, if possible, that there are no duplicate copies of files that have been retained within ITW without authorisation.

This risk is difficult to deal with. However, ITW should be asked to demonstrate that after the handover of the files, copies have not been retained in ITW's computer system. If ITW is an ethical organisation, it should be willing to comply with this request, and demonstrate that it no longer holds files for POOL.

There could be operational difficulties in changing from ITW to a new service provider, particularly if ITW is unwilling to be helpful. ITW might have no incentive to give assistance to another company that has taken their contract with POOL. Inevitably, operational problems will arise, and the new service provider might need to ask questions. Unless ITW is willing to provide assistance, operating difficulties might arise.

The efficiency and success of the change to the new service provider depends on the goodwill of ITW for a number of reasons, and POOL might wish to consider offering a bonus payment to ITW after the change has taken place, provided this has happened in a satisfactory way, and with the full co-operation and assistance of ITW's staff.

It has been assumed that the same system operated on behalf of POOL by ITW will be used by the new service provider. This is not necessarily the case, and it might be the intention of POOL to switch its accounting system to a different accounting system that is better able to handle the growing volume of transactions and data. If a new system is required, all the risks associated with new system design, development and implementation will arise.

Governance and Regulation in the Global Business Environment

Chapter learning objectives

Lead	Component
A2. Analyse the relationship between the internal governance of a firm and external sources of governance and regulation.	(a) Explain the principles and purpose of social corporate responsibility and the principles of good corporate governance in an international context.
	(b) Analyse relationships between business, society and government in national and regional contexts.
	(c) *Note:* this is included in chapter 2.
	(d) Discuss the nature of regulation and its impact on the firm.

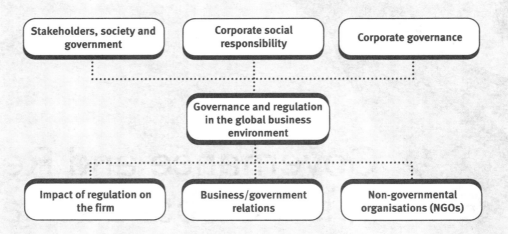

1 Stakeholders, Society and Government

1.1 Stakeholders

A **stakeholder** is a group or individual, who has an interest in what the organisation does, or an expectation of the organisation.

Managers should consider the stakeholders when setting the mission and objectives of the firms, for two key reasons:

- Stakeholder power – stakeholders can affect the success of a strategy, depending on whether they support or oppose it, e.g. a staff strike would disrupt a strategy.

- Organisational legitimacy – this view suggests that firms should be good corporate citizens and its decisions must consider the interests of stakeholders.

Stakeholders can be broadly categorised into three categories; internal, connected and external.

Internal stakeholders

Internal stakeholders are intimately connected to the organisation, and their objectives are likely to have a strong influence on how it is run. Internal stakeholders include:

Stakeholder	Need/ expectation
employees	pay, working conditions and job security
managers/ directors	status, pay, bonus, job security

Connected stakeholders

Connected stakeholders have a direct link with the organisation but function outside of it. They include:

Stakeholder	Need/ expectation
shareholders	dividends and capital growth and the continuation of the business
customers	value-for-money products and services
suppliers	paid promptly
finance providers	repayment of finance

External stakeholders

This group will have quite diverse objectives and have varying ability to ensure that the organisation meets their objectives. They include:

Stakeholder	Need/ expectation
community at large	will not want their lives to be negatively impacted by business decisions
environmental pressure groups	the organisation does not harm the external environment
government	provision of taxes and jobs and compliance with legislation
trade unions	to take an active part in the decision-making process

Further example of stakeholder management

R is a high-class hotel situated in a thriving city. It is part of a worldwide hotel group owned by a large number of shareholders. Individuals hold the majority of shares, each holding a small number, and financial institutions hold the rest. The hotel provides full amenities, including a heated swimming pool, as well as the normal facilities of bars, restaurants and good quality accommodation. There are many other hotels in the city, all of which compete with R. The city in which R is situated is old and attracts many foreign visitors, especially in the summer season.

The main stakeholders with whom relationships need to be established and maintained by management and the importance of maintaining these relationships is as follows.

Internal stakeholders

The employees and the managers of the hotel are the main link with the guests and the service they provide is vital to the quality of the hotel as guests' experience at the hotel will be determined by their attitude and approach.

Managers should ensure that employees deliver the highest level of service and are well trained and committed.

Connected stakeholders

The shareholders of the hotel will be concerned with a steady flow of income, possible capital growth and continuation of the business. Relationships should be developed and maintained with the shareholders, especially those operating on behalf of institutions. Management must try to achieve improvements in their returns by ensuring that customers are satisfied and are willing to return.

Each guest will seek good service and satisfaction. Different types of guests, e.g. business versus tourist, will have different needs and managers should regularly analyse the customer database to ensure that these needs are met.

Suppliers should be selected very carefully to ensure that services and goods provided (e.g. food and laundry) continue to add to the quality of the hotel and to customer satisfaction. Suppliers will be concerned with being paid promptly for goods. Maintaining a good relationship with suppliers will ensure their continued support of the hotel.

External stakeholders

The management of the hotel must maintain close relationships with the authorities to ensure they comply with legislation. Failure to do so, could result in the hotel being closed down.

Stakeholder conflict

Stakeholder conflict

The needs/ expectations of the different stakeholder groups may conflict. Some of the typical conflicts are shown below:

Stakeholders	Conflict
Employees versus managers	Jobs/ wages versus bonus
Customers versus shareholders	Product quality/ service levels versus profits/ dividends
General public versus shareholders	Effect on the environment versus profit/ dividends
Managers versus shareholders	Independence versus growth by merger/ takeover

It is important that an organisation meets the needs of the most dominant stakeholders, but the needs of the other stakeholders should also be considered – nearly every decision becomes a compromise. For example, the firm will have to earn a satisfactory return for its shareholders whilst paying reasonable wages.

Mendelow's power-interest matrix

If an organisation is having difficulty deciding who the dominant stakeholder is, they can use Mendelow's power-interest matrix.

		Level of interest	
		Low	High
Level of power	Low	Minimal effort	Keep informed
	High	Keep satisfied	Key players

By plotting each stakeholder according to the power that they have over an organisation and the interest they have in a particular decision, the dominant stakeholder(s), i.e. the key player(s) can be identified. The needs of the key players must be considered during the formulation and evaluation of new strategies.

1.2 The role of society

Until the 1970s, the role of society was seen as the ultimate producer and consumer of an organisation's goods and services.

However, in recent times, organisations have recognised that they owe a 'duty of care' to society and that being responsible could lead to payback for the firm. The concept of corporate social responsibility is explored in section 2.

1.3 The role of government

Similarly, until the 1970s, the government was treated by most organisations as a regulator and tax levying body.

However, public 'scandals' of the 1980s and 1990s (such as Maxwell and Polly Peck) led to governments recognising a new role – one of protecting other stakeholders from over-aggressive, negligent or even fraudulent directors and managers. This led to the development of corporate governance (see section 3).

2 Corporate Social Responsibility

Corporate social responsibility (CSR) refers to the idea that a company should be sensitive to the needs and wants of all the stakeholders in its business operations, not just the shareholders.

Stakeholder theory recognises that a company should be accountable to all stakeholders and not just shareholders.

A socially responsible company may consider:

- the environmental impact of production or consumption, e.g. due to the use of non-renewable resources or non-recyclable inputs.

- the health impact for consumers of certain products, e.g. tobacco and alcohol

- the fair treatment of employees

- whether it is right to experiment on animals

- the safety of products and production processes.

CSR encompasses four dimensions:

- **Economic** – does the company contribute to the development of the local economy in which it operates?

- **Legal** – does the company restrict its operations to comply with the law?
- **Ethical** – does society approve of the company's operations?
- **Philanthropic** – the extent to which the company makes voluntary contributions to society.

Distinction between business ethics and CSR

Although the two terms are often used interchangeably, they have distinct meanings:

Business ethics:

- Ethics is a set of moral principles that guide behaviour, based on what is 'felt' to be right.
- Comprises principles and standards that govern business behaviour.
- Actions can be judged to be right or to be wrong, ethical or unethical by individuals inside or outside the organisation.
- The judgement will influence society's acceptance or rejection of the actions taken.

CSR, however, refers to a firm's obligation to maximise its positive impact upon stakeholders whilst minimising the negative effects. As such, ethics is just one dimension of social responsibility.

Different understandings of CSR

A formal definition of CSR has been proposed by the World Business Council for Sustainable Development (WBCSD):

'CSR is the continuous commitment by business to behave ethically and contribute to economic development while improving the quality of life of the workforce and their families as well as the local community and society at large'.

WBSCD meeting in the Netherlands, 1998

From the same source, perceptions of CSR from different societies and cultures were given as:

- 'CSR is about capacity building for sustainable livelihoods. It respects cultural differences and finds the business opportunities in building the skills of employees, the community and the government' (Ghana).
- 'CSR is about business giving back to society' (Philippines).

We can see that there is no one definition, or theory, of corporate social responsibility. However, it is certain that there will be increasing pressure on organisations to play an increasing role in the solution to social issues. This will be particularly true of those that have a global presence. This means that multinationals and non governmental organisations (NGOs) will increasingly be expected to take a lead in addressing those issues where a national government or local firm has not been able, or willing, to arrive at a solution. With increasing globalisation, which we discussed earlier, the power of the institutions attached to the nation state (national governments, judiciary and police, for example) is declining.

Illustration 1 – British Petroleum (BP)

BP, primarily known as an oil company, launched its 'Beyond Petroleum' initiative in 2000 to address climate change. In 2005, it announced plans to invest $8 billion over the next 10 years in renewable energy. It is already the second largest solar-power producer in the world.

However, a number of incidents have damaged BP's image for CSR:

- In 2005 there was an explosion in its Texas City refinery in which 15 people were killed and over 150 people injured.

- In 2006 there was a serious oil leak from its pipeline in Prudhoe, in Alaska.

- In 2010 the Deepwater Horizon oil disaster spewed 4.1m barrels of oil into the Gulf of Mexico over 87 days, making it the biggest unintentional offshore oil spill in the history of the petroleum industry. The incident fouled hundreds of miles of coastline, cost at least $20bn (£12bn) and turned BP into one of the most hated enterprises in America.

There are accusations that lack of investment in safety, training and inspection were responsible for all of these incidents. Critics of BP have accused it of deflecting blame and 'greenwash', i.e. using environmentally friendly programmes to divert attention from other activities.

888.com

888.com is an internet gambling site that is listed on the London Stock Exchange. It is headquartered in Gibraltar and operates under a licence granted by the Government of Gibraltar. It has responsibilities to the following stakeholders:

- **Shareholders** – since it is listed on the London Stock Exchange it must comply with the rules of that exchange, including adopting the UK Corporate Governance codes.

- **Employees** – to be a good employer to all its members of staff.

- **Customers** – to offer a fair, regulated and secure environment in which to gamble.

- **Government** – to comply with the terms of its licence granted in Gibraltar.

- **The public** – the company chooses to sponsor several sports teams as part of strengthening its brand. The company also tries to address public concerns about the negative aspects of gambling, e.g. by identifying compulsive gamblers on their site and taking appropriate action.

Test your understanding 1

Voluntarily turning away business

Why should a gambling company like 888.com voluntarily choose to turn away certain business, e.g. known compulsive gamblers, gamblers who may be under-age, gamblers in certain countries, etc?

A closely linked idea is that of **sustainable development.** Companies should make decisions based not only on financial factors, but also on the social and environmental consequences of their actions. This area is explored further in Chapter 6.

The importance of CSR to an organisation's success

Traditionalists argue that companies should operate solely to make money for shareholders and that it is not a company's role to worry about social responsibilities.

The modern view is that a coherent CSR strategy can offer business **benefits** in the following ways:

- Differentiation – the firm's CSR strategy (e.g. with regards to the environment, experimentation on animals or to product safety) can act as a method of differentiation.

- High calibre staff will be attracted and retained due to the firm's CSR policies.

- Brand strengthening – due to the firm's honest approach

- Lower costs – can be achieved in a number of ways, e.g. due to the use of less packaging or energy.

- The identification of new market opportunities and of changing social expectations.

- An overall increase in profitability as a result of the above - project net present values will increase due to increased sales, lower costs, an extended project life and a lower level of risk (which will in turn reduce the cost of capital).

By aligning the company's core values with the values of society, the company can improve its reputation and ensure it has a long-term future.

The single-minded pursuit of short-term profitability will paradoxically always end in reduced profits in the longer-term, as customers drift away from the company if they no longer feel any attachment to it.

There is considerable evidence that the cost of CSR initiatives should be thought of as an investment in an intangible strategic asset rather than as an expense.

Illustration 3 – The importance of CSR

BAA plc

BAA owns and operates seven airports in the UK. BAA recognises that they are responsible, both directly and indirectly, for a variety of environmental, social and economic impacts from their operations.

Positive impacts: employing 12,000 people; allowing business people to travel to meetings, thus supporting the global economy; allowing tourists to enrich their cultural experiences; allowing dispersed families to visit each other.

Negative impacts: large consumption of fossil fuels; emission of greenhouse gases; noise affecting people living close to airports.

BAA sees its CSR programme as managing these operational impacts in order to earn the trust of their stakeholders.

For example, local people living near airports are sensitive to the noise of aircraft approaching and taking off. If BAA did nothing about this issue, local people could complain to politicians who could pass laws to curb the number of flights which would damage the company. As part of its CSR programme, BAA will therefore offer to buy the properties of local people concerned about aircraft noise, or will offer to pay for sound-proofing of the properties.

You should consider whether such expenditure is an expense against the company's profits, or an investment in building up a strategic asset of goodwill among the local community.

The development of CSR over time

Pressures from various stakeholders are likely to increase CSR over time.

The norms of corporate behaviour in Victorian Britain would seem totally unacceptable in Britain today. The long hours, child labour, appalling working conditions, lack of redress for grievances, the filthy conditions of the workplace, the smoke and other pollution pouring from the factories, are not only illegal nowadays, but are totally alien to the norms of society.

Developed countries tend to have a strong sense of CSR although there are differences in approaches. For example:

- **America** has a more **philanthropic** approach to CSR, e.g. companies focus on charitable donations to society. The problem with this approach is that donations tend to be one of the first items of expenditure to be cut when the company is facing more challenging times.

- The **European** approach tends to focus on a combination of **responsible business practices** and **investment in communities**. It may be argued that this is a more sustainable approach to CSR.

Many developing countries are still to embrace the practices of CSR, the ruthless forces of globalisation and non-representative governments conniving in the process of preventing the implementation of CSR practices.

Another factor contributing to the development of CSR is that activities that start as desirable but unprofitable, tend to become profitable as consumers come to expect firms to behave in socially responsible ways and punish firms that do not, by boycotting their products. Thus companies such as McDonalds, Nestle and Nike have been very concerned to 'clean up' their corporate image because of adverse publicity.

Nike and Gap, which produce much of their footwear and clothing in South-East Asia, have been accused of operating sweatshops in these countries with low wages and poor working conditions. Nike and Gap reply that, compared with other factories in these countries, pay and conditions are better.

3 Corporate Governance

3.1 Why corporate governance?

A number of high profile scandals over the last few decades have highlighted the need for guidance to confront the problems that can arise in an organisation's system of governance.

The separation of ownership and control

The need for corporate governance arises because, in all but the smallest of organisations, there is a separation of ownership and control.

The separation of ownership and control refers to the situation in a company where the people who own the company (the shareholders) may not be the same people as those who run the company (the board of directors).

Illustration 5 – The separation of ownership and control

The agency problem in a company

The directors of a large quoted company may hold a board meeting and vote themselves huge bonuses and salaries even if only modest profit targets are achieved and may also put contractual terms in place granting them huge compensation payments if they are sacked. Those votes are in the selfish best interests of the directors, and not in the best interests of the shareholders who own the company and whose interests the directors are meant to be looking after.

3.2 The meaning of corporate governance

Corporate governance is the set of processes and policies by which a company is directed, administered and controlled. It includes the appropriate role of the board of directors and the auditors of the company.

Corporate governance is concerned with the overall control and direction of a business so that the business's objectives are achieved in an acceptable manner by **ALL** stakeholders.

3.3 Systems of corporate governance

One of the main debates surrounding corporate governance regulation is whether it should be:

- A set of **best practice** guidelines – as in the UK with its principles based approach requiring companies to adhere to the spirit rather than the letter of the law.

- A **legal** requirement – as in the US with appropriate penalties for transgression.

3.4 Features of UK Corporate Governance codes

UK Corporate Governance codes (the Combined Code) include guidance on following:

Use of the AGM

The board should use the annual general meeting (AGM) to construct a dialogue with shareholders.

Chairman and Chief Executive Officer (CEO)

The positions of the chairman of the board and the CEO (the person in charge of running the company) should be separated. This is to ensure that no one individual has too much power within the company.

Non-executive directors (NEDs)

Directors who are involved in the execution of day-to-day management decisions are called **executive directors**. Those who primarily only attend board meetings (and the meetings of board committees) are known as **NEDs**.

Current guidance is that NEDs should as far as possible be 'independent' so that their oversight role can be effectively and responsibly carried out.

Typical recommendations include:

- At least half of the board (excluding the chairman) should comprise independent NEDs. A smaller company should have at least two independent NEDs.

- One of the NEDs should be appointed the 'senior independent director'. Shareholders can contact them if they wish to raise matters outside the normal executive channels of communication.

Among the independent NEDs at Sainsbury's is Anna Ford, a former BBC newsreader. She is well known to the public and of good reputation, so the public at large might see her as 'their' representative on the board and will trust her to put forward their point of view. Anna Ford, herself, may have little or no experience of big business, but again the public would not see that as a disadvantage in representing them on the board.

Test your understanding 2

Independent NED

Mr X retires from the post of finance director at AB plc. The company is keen to retain his experience, so invite him to become a NED of the company. Can he qualify as an independent non-executive?

Nomination committees

Appointments to the board should be made via a nominations (or appointments) committee. This is to provide some independence from the current board members and to ensure that all appointments are based on merit and suitability.

Remuneration committees

The board of a listed company should establish a remuneration committee of at least three (or two in the case of smaller companies) NEDs.

The remuneration committee should be responsible for setting the remuneration of all the executive directors and the chairman, including pension rights and any compensation payments.

Remuneration committee

Advantages of having a remuneration committee:

- It avoids the agency problem of directors determining their own levels of remuneration.

- It leaves the board free to make strategic decision about the future.

Disadvantages of having a remuneration committee:

- There is a danger that NEDs may recommend high remuneration for the executive directors in the hope that the executives will recommend high remuneration for the NEDs.

- There will be a cost involved in preparing for and holding the meetings.

Test your understanding 3

Remuneration of NEDs

On what basis should NEDs be remunerated for their service to the company?

Audit committees

An audit committee consists of independent NEDs who are responsible for monitoring and reviewing the company's financial controls and the integrity of the financial statements.

Auditors (both internal and external) have long had a problem – the people they report to and liaise with (the board) are often those people whose activities they report on.

The audit committee acts as an interface between the board of directors on one side and the internal and external auditors on the other side.

An audit committee should be comprised of three NEDs, and should be the first point of contact for auditors, improving the independence and the overall quality of the audit functions.

The role of the audit committee

- Being available for both sets of auditors (e.g. the audit committee meetings are likely to include both internal and external auditors).

- Executive directors to attend meetings if requested by the audit committee.

- Reviewing accounting policies and financial statements as a whole to ensure that they are appropriate and balanced.

- Reviewing systems of internal controls.

- Agreeing agenda for work for internal audit department.

- Receiving results for internal audit work.

- Short listing firms of external auditors when a change is needed.

- Reviewing independence of external audit firm.

- Considering extent to which external auditors should be allowed to tender for 'other services'.

Test your understanding 4

Composition of audit committee

Why are the members of an audit committee required to be NEDs rather than executive directors?

Test your understanding 5

Discuss the benefits of good corporate governance.

3.5 The US Sarbanes-Oxley Act 2002 (SOX)

The US Sarbanes-Oxley Act 2002 (SOX)

In 2002, following a number of corporate governance scandals such as Enron and WorldCom, tough new corporate governance regulations were introduced in the US by SOX.

SOX is only applicable in the US and for subsidiaries of US-based companies.

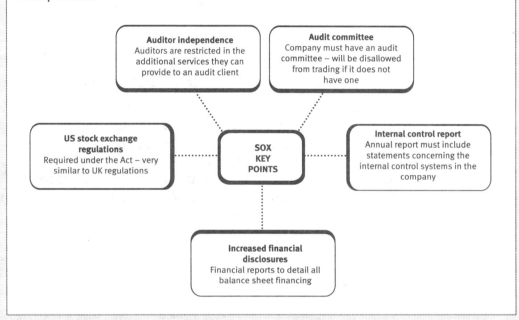

4 The Impact of Regulation on the Firm

4.1 Introduction

One of the roles of government is to act as a regulator.

Regulation is any form of government interference and is required to ensure that the needs of stakeholders can be met and that businesses act in the public interest.

Test your understanding 6

Identify some common examples of government regulation.

4.2 Efficient and effective regulation

Effective regulation will ensure that a safe and effective product or service is delivered, whilst not inhibiting the effective function of the business.

Efficient regulation is said to exist if the total benefit to the nation is greater than the total cost.

There are also schemes of **voluntary regulation**, e.g. corporate governance in the UK.

4.3 Impact of inappropriate regulation

Test your understanding 7

Briefly discuss the impact of inappropriate regulation.

Illustration 7 – Negative impact of regulation

A 2011 survey by the Institute of Chartered Accountants in England and Wales concluded that the number of small and medium enterprises that considered the current UK regulations and tax regime to be beneficial had fallen from 55% in 2010 to 38% in 2011. Small businesses had to deal with a number of changes in 2011, including the introduction of flexible working for employees who request it and the abolishment of the default State retirement age.

4.4 UK and international regulation

UK and international regulation

Regulation in the **UK** includes:

(1) **Regulation of the level of competition in the market**
   - The government wants to encourage competition in the market.
   - Competition drives down prices, encourages firms to be efficient with the use of their resources and improves quality.
   - Therefore, competition is in the best interests of the consumer.
   - Sources of regulation include:
     - The Competition Act
     - The Office of Fair Trading
     - The Competition Commission.

(2) **Regulation of externalities**

Externalities are costs or benefits of production experienced by society but not by producers or consumers themselves.

For example:

- an external cost may be cigarette smoke. The government may regulate this by taxing cigarettes to reduce consumption.
- an external benefit may be the health impact of vaccinations. The government may regulate this by offering free vaccinations.

(3) **Regulation of people in business**

The government will regulate the people managing a company to:

- prevent insider trading – it is a criminal offence to use privately held knowledge to make a profit or avoid a loss when buying or selling shares.
- to prevent trading if a company is insolvent.

Examples of **international regulation** include:

(1) **The US Sarbanes-Oxley Act 2002**
- The aim of the Act is to stop creative accounting.
- As mentioned in section 3 of this chapter, it was implemented as a result of huge corporate scandals, e.g. Enron and WorldCom.
- It has no impact on a UK company unless they are registered on the US stock exchange as well as the UK stock exchange.
- The main provisions of the Act were reviewed in Section 3 of this chapter.

(2) **International regulation of trade**
- The benefits of free trade were discussed in chapter 2.
- Free trade is supported by the World Trade Organisation (WTO).
- Regional trading organisations, such as the EU and NAFTA, allow free trade between specific countries.

5 Business/ Government Relations

5.1 Corporate political activity (CPA)

Corporate political activity refers to the involvement of firms in the political process, with the aim of securing particular policy preferences.

Corporate political activity can be an important element in any firm's effort to gain competitive advantage.

Illustration 8 – Corporate political activity

In the US the protection of domestic trade is among the most popular policies demanded by producers with US politicians being easily influenced by the generous donations made by US firms.

There are two types of corporate political activity:

- **Buffering** – proactive political actions on the part of firms, for example:
    - by employing lobbyists, who will put their case to the government to influence legislative or regulative processes.
    - by making donations to party funds. Obviously this is open to question; it could be seen as a form of bribery.

Illustration 9 – Donations to party funds

The problem of corruption continues to be strong in many developing countries. A cash-for-votes scandal overshadowed the presidential elections in Brazil in 2006.

- **Bridging** – a more proactive form of behaviour. For example, firms may track the development of laws and regulation, so to have compliance in place when the legislation is passed, or exceeding compliance levels for regulation.

Illustration 10 – President Obama's changes

In January 2009, President Obama implemented some of the toughest lobbying restrictions in US history, seeking to eliminate undue influence in American politics. New rules prohibit presidential appointees from accepting gifts from lobbying organisations and restricts appointees' ability to work on issues on which they recently lobbied while in the private sector. It will take time to see if this new approach has an impact on governance.

It is usually in the interest of a government to consult with the business sector when it is forming new policies:

- to widen its perspective
- and so that it can defend its actions politically.

5.2 Business/government relations in developed and developing countries

In most **developed** countries there is a strong business lobby consisting of individual companies and business-related organisations. They spend considerable amounts of money and are among the most prominent political players.

Very large companies are likely to be in frequent contact with government departments and parliament on an individual basis and many have distinct departments for government liaison.

Such departments will monitor and advise on political and governmental developments, make regular contacts with politicians and senior civil servants, organise representation and undertake lobbying operations in London, Brussels, Washington, Geneva etc, often assisted by non-executive directors and consultants.

Illustration 11 – Responsible business lobbying

Companies with statements on CSR must align their business activities with social responsibility. For example, mining companies making statements about responsible stewardship to the environment should not be found lobbying to dumb-down environmental legislation.

Business lobbying in the UK

In the UK, the business lobby consists of organisations such as the following:

- The Confederation of British Industry (CBI), representing the entire private business sector.

- The Federation of Small Businesses (FSB) and local Chambers of Commerce.

- The Institute of Directors (IOD).

- Several thousand trade associations and employers' organisations, representing particular industries and sectors.

In **developing countries**, CPA is far more overt. Politicians, or even whole governments, can be persuaded to introduce, modify or remove legislation fairly cheaply. Policy-making bodies are open to threats and bribery.

Influence of business on international organisations

It may be particularly important to try to influence the drafting process of organisations such as the European Commission and the WTO. Their regulations take priority over national law or more local arrangements and their decisions may be very difficult to change because they are only arrived at after long periods of international negotiation.

- There should be no delay. Firms should monitor the issues that are being dealt with by the governing body and make their views known as early as possible in the process. The governing body will probably publish a 'green paper' discussing proposed changes and inviting comment before issuing a 'white paper' and passing a statute, a treaty or a set of standards.

- Firms should collaborate with others in the same industry and encourage firms in other countries to lobby their own governments. An organisation's opinions will carry more weight if it can show that it is not just self-seeking but that those opinions are shared by others in the industry.

Government impact on business

Required:

List the possible ways that government can impact on business both as an aid and as an impediment.

Solution:

An aid to business:

- as large buyer
- as sponsor for research and development
- as the champion of free trade (or as protector against unfair trade in certain circumstances)
- as a controller of inflation, and inflationary influences
- by providing help for wealth creation, including skill training
- by providing assistance for the start up of businesses.

An impediment to business:

- as defender of the interest of the consumer
- as the guarantor of health and safety at work
- as the protector of the environment
- as regulator of business practices
- as the protector of minority groupings.

6 Non Governmental Organisations (NGOs)

6.1 Introduction

The term **'non governmental organisation'** or NGO can mean different things in different countries. However, NGOs are defined by the World Bank as "private organisations that pursue activities to relieve suffering, promote the interests of the poor, protect the environment, provide basic social services or undertake community development".

Given these definitions, NGOs may function at different levels of influence ranging from community, city, country or even internationally. The degree of influence can be significant, particularly for international NGOs. Some of the largest NGOs operate in the humanitarian sphere and include Oxfam, Amnesty International, The Red Cross, World Vision and Save the Children. World Vision, for example, had expenditure of over $3.5 billion in 2009, which is more than the GDP of some countries.

6.2 Types of NGO

- **Operational NGOs** – seek to achieve change directly through projects such as community development.

- **Campaigning NGOs** – seek to achieve change indirectly through the use of lobbying and public relations (PR) programmes to influence government.

6.3 The relationship between businesses and NGOs

NGOs could operate as partners with firms in lobbying governments for change or as opponents if the firm's activities are at odds with the NGO's mission.

Partnerships between businesses and NGOs
Companies and NGOs have discovered a number of reasons to partner: - Creating business value and environmental benefits. - Raising the bar on environmental performance. - Gaining skills and perspectives not available in the organisation. - Building respect and credibility. - Providing independent validation of a company's claim of environmental and social benefits from a project.

7 Chapter summary

Stakeholders, society and government
- Stakeholders
- The role of society
- The role of government

Corporate social responsibility
- Definition
- Benefits
- Approaches by different countries

Corporate governance
- Reasons for corporate governance
- Definition
- Systems of corporate governance
- UK corporate governance codes
  US Sabanes-Oxley Act (SOX)

Governance and regulation in the global business environment

Impact of regulation on the firm
- Definition of regulation
- Efficient and effective regulation
- Impact of inappropriate regulation
- UK and international regulation

Business/government relations
- Corporate political activity
- Business/government relations in developing and developed countries

Non-governmental organisations (NGOs)
- Definition
- Types of NGO
- Relationship between businesses and NGOs

8 Practice questions

Question 1

Anti-monopoly laws are based on the idea that the best way to achieve efficiency and to avoid excessive prices is through:

A   corporate governance

B   increased public ownership

C   regulation

D   an increase in corporate social responsibility

(2 marks)

Question 2

What is the definition of corporate governance?

A   The system by which companies are directed and controlled

B   The definition in the Sarbanes-Oxley Act 2002

C   A set of rules that a company must follow to continue being listed on the London Stock Exchange

D   A set of rules introduced as a result of several high-profile corporate collapses

(2 marks)

Question 3

Which of the following is NOT the job of a NED (non executive director)?

A   Contribution to the development of strategy

B   Scrutiny of management performance

C   Decisions on which suppliers to use for the company's raw materials purchases

D   Determination of executives' remuneration packages

(2 marks)

Question 4

JV limited manufactures cleaning chemicals at its factory in a small town in the Lake District. It employs 300 people, and is the largest employer within a 20 mile radius.

The factory is located on the side of a lake, at the end of a single track road.

Required:

Identify FOUR social responsibilities of this company.

(4 marks)

Question 5

An increasing number of companies have expressed their willingness to consider their wider social responsibilities. This often involves them voluntarily undertaking extra responsibilities and costs, for example:

- In order to reduce pollution, they may decide to treat waste products to a higher standard than required by legislation.

- They may decline to trade with countries whose governments they find objectionable.

- They may pay wages above minimum levels.

Required:

(a) Explain:
   (i)   whether the pursuit of a policy of social responsibility necessarily involves a conflict with the objective of shareholder wealth-maximisation
   (ii) the extent to which the existence of a conflict between a company's objectives is acceptable.

(8 marks)

(b) Explain how it is possible to encourage staff, particularly managers, to pursue and implement socially responsible policies.

(5 marks)

(c) Explain to what extent it is possible to include the requirements of all stakeholders when creating a plan for corporate social responsibility.

(7 marks)

(Total: 20 marks)

Question 6

Eastborough is a large region with a rugged, beautiful coastline where rare birds have recently settled on undisturbed cliffs. Since mining ceased 150 years ago, its main industries have been agriculture and fishing. However, today, many communities in Eastborough suffer high unemployment. Government initiatives for regeneration through tourism have met with little success as the area has poor road networks, unsightly derelict buildings and dirty beaches.

Digwell Explorations, a listed company, has a reputation for maximising shareholder returns and has discovered substantial tin reserves in Eastborough. With new technology, mining could be profitable, provide jobs and boost the economy. A number of interest and pressure groups have, however, been vocal in opposing the scheme.

Digwell Explorations, after much lobbying, has just received government permission to undertake mining. It could face difficulties in proceeding because of the likely activity of a group called the Eastborough Protection Alliance. This group includes wildlife protection representatives, villagers worried about the potential increase in traffic congestion and noise, environmentalists, and anti-capitalism groups.

Required:

Discuss the ethical issues that should have been considered by the government when granting permission for mining to go ahead. Explain the conflicts between the main stakeholder groups.

(15 marks)

Test your understanding answers

Test your understanding 1

Either you could argue that such action was ethically correct (with the company wanting to 'do the right thing'), or you could argue that a concentration on short-term profits is likely to store up problems in the longer term. If under-age gamblers are seen to be gambling on a particular website, then the public reputation of that site will be damaged and its long term profitability could be in jeopardy if governments or customers turn against it.

Test your understanding 2

It is very unlikely that Mr X can be independent since he has been an employee of the company within the last five years. If the board believes that Mr X is independent despite his recent employment then they must state the reasons for this determination.

Test your understanding 3

NEDs should be paid fees that reflect the time commitment and the responsibilities of the role, e.g. a fixed daily rate for when they work for the company. Share options should not be granted to the NEDs since this could detract from their independent judgement.

Test your understanding 4

NEDS have no day-to-day operating responsibilities, so they are able to view the company's affairs in a detached and independent way and liaise effectively between the main board and both sets of auditors.

Test your understanding 5

Good corporate governance:

- **Reduces risk** – corporate governance can help reduce the risk of fraud. It can provide a mechanism for reviewing and assessing projects.

- **Stimulates performance** – it institutes clear accountability and effective links between performance and rewards which can encourage organisations to improve performance.

- **Improves access to capital markets** – due to a reduction in the level of risk perceived by outsiders, including investors.

- **Enhances the marketability of goods and services** – due to an enhancement in reputation and public confidence.

- **Improves leadership** – the wider pool of knowledge and experience available to the board, through the inclusion of external members, helps the board to identify opportunities more readily.

Test your understanding 6

The government may regulate:

- prices
- wages
- pollution
- product quality standards
- employment conditions.

Test your understanding 7

Inappropriate regulation:

- Makes firms less likely to innovate and adapt the quality and mix of goods and services to changing customer needs.

- Can have an adverse effect on markets, making firms uncompetitive due to bureaucracy.

Question 1

C

Question 2

A

Question 3

C

Question 4

Many points can be included, such as:

- not polluting the lake with waste chemicals
- making sure employees use adequate protection when working with the chemicals
- complying with legislation regarding the use of hazardous chemicals
- minimising the impact of traffic on local roads
- minimising the visual impact of the factory on the area.

Question 5

(a) (i) About 20 or so years ago, the idea that profitability was overwhelmingly the principal objective of a business would have been uncontroversial. Today's climate is different: increased public awareness of the social impact of large organisations has broadened the range of objectives which businesses must aim to achieve. New factors to be considered include pollution control, conservation of natural resources and avoidance of environmental damage.

In the short term, the measures described in the question would reduce profits; all of them involve increased profits or revenue foregone. And reduced profits imply reduced shareholders' wealth in the form of dividends and capital growth.

However, this analysis, though relatively straightforward in the short term, may not be so clear-cut in the long term. Many commentators argue that the reputation and image of corporations will suffer if they do not respond to heightened awareness of social responsibility amongst consumers. Given that many companies are already taking steps along this path, and making good public relations out of their efforts, there is pressure on other companies to follow suit. Failure to do so may lead to long-term decline.

(ii) A conflict between company objectives implies a picture of managers pulling in opposite directions, some trying to meet criteria of social responsibility, others hell-bent on maximising profit. Given that all of the managers in a company are drawing on the same pool of resources this is a recipe for disaster.

However, this does not mean that companies are doomed to fail if they pursue more than one objective. The idea is to agree on a balance between conflicting objectives, and to settle on a strategy which satisfies both sets of objectives, to the extent that they can be reconciled.

(b) Part of the difficulty in pursuing aspirations towards social responsibility lies in the relative novelty of the concept. Managers brought up in a culture of profit maximisation may find it hard to appreciate the importance of other objectives, and to adapt their behaviour accordingly. To encourage managers to pursue and implement social responsibility involves, as a first step, making managers aware of the need for it. This may be achieved by:

- appropriate training

- dissemination of targets and measures related to social objectives

- formal incorporation of social objectives into the decision-making process

- collaboration with other organisations to launch a common approach

- appointment of external consultants to assess existing performance in this area and to recommend improvements

- monitoring achievement by logging and publishing of performance indicators

- appointment of a committee to review and implement social and ethical policies.

(c) An organisation's stakeholders include:

- owners/shareholders

- employees

- business contacts, such as customers and suppliers

- the general public

- the government.

Owners/shareholders will be interested primarily in profitability, but the analysis in Part(a) above suggests that long-term profitability may depend at least in part on the adoption of social objectives.

Employees obviously have a very direct interest in at least some social objectives: for example, the question mentions a policy of paying wages above national minimum levels.

Business contacts have a less direct interest in this issue. However, as a minimum, creditors will be impressed with an ethical policy of paying debts on time, and customers who themselves have social and ethical interests, may exert pressure on their suppliers to conform as well.

The general public, as already mentioned, have shown themselves increasingly aware of these issues, and are prepared to back their principles with direct action (such as refusing to invest in companies whose objectives they disapprove of).

The government must meet international obligations as well as satisfying the demands of their own electorate. Both factors mean that they will take an interest in the social and ethical policies of organisations.

Question 6

Ethics

Ethics are a code of moral principles that people follow with respect to what is right or wrong. General examples might include staying within the law, not engaging in bribery or theft or endangering other people.

Also a part of ethics is social responsibility; the duty towards the wider community or society in general which includes environmental issues, public safety, employment and exploitation of third world workers.

In this case, ethical issues which the government should have considered when granting permission for mining include:

- **Employment in the local area** – the government has a duty toward people to provide them with jobs. In Eastborough there is significant unemployment so it is particularly important to the government to generate jobs in the area. The effect of the mining on employment levels should therefore be considered.

- **The local economy** – the government has an obligation to the people of Eastborough to improve the wealth of the people there. This largely depends on a successful economy. The local economy of Eastborough has been performing badly despite various initiatives based around tourism. The effect of mining on the local economy generally must be considered (i.e. jobs create income which is then spent in local shops, demand for property increases and prices rise for all in the area).

- **Environmental concerns** – Eastborough has a beautiful coastline with rare birds nesting there. The government has a debt towards society generally to preserve areas of natural beauty for all to appreciate and enjoy, and a moral obligation towards other species on the planet to protect them from extinction. The effects of the mining operations on the rare birds, the beauty of the coastline and any pollution caused in the locality should therefore have been considered by the government.

- **Rights of local individuals** – Individuals have the right for their quality of life to remain high. While employment and an improved economy may enrich the quality of life of many, there may also be negative effects for some local people such as increased noise and traffic congestion. These broader effects on villagers are likely to have been considered.

- **Right to free operation of business** – Many capitalist countries believe in free trade and removing barriers to trade. This may be seen as a right of the business, and it may be considered as part of the decision to allow Digwell to open the mining operation.

Conflicts between stakeholder groups

Stakeholders are people who are affected or interested in some way by the mining operations.

In this case stakeholders include:

- national government
- local government
- local people
- wildlife protection groups
- environmental groups
- directors of Digwell
- employees of Digwell
- shareholders of Digwell.

The conflicts which may exist include the following:

- **National vs local government** – local government will be interested in Eastborough and its interests. National government have to balance those needs with the needs of all people of the country. There may be a conflict over the amount of funding available to support local initiatives such as help with starting up the mining operations.

- **Unemployed vs people based near mining operations/ working people** – unemployed people in the area will notice a direct benefit from the mining operations through increased jobs and are likely to support it. Other local residents may simply view the operations as disrupting their existing life (noise/congestion) and oppose the idea.

- **Shareholders/directors of Digwell vs environmental/wildlife protection groups** – both shareholders and Directors of Digwell wish to make profits from Digwell's operations. The mining operations will enable them to make full use of an asset they own (tin reserves) and hence increase profit. They will wish it to go ahead, and may have very little interest in the broader impact. Environmental groups aim to protect the environment and are likely to oppose any part of the mining operation which will affect the environment irrespective of profitability.

The Wider Business Context Within Which Information Systems Operate

Chapter learning objectives

Lead	Component
B1. Discuss the wider business context within which information systems operate.	(a) Identify the value of information and information systems organisations.
	(b) Discuss the reasons for organisations' increased dependence on information systems.
	(c) Discuss the transformation of organisations through technology.

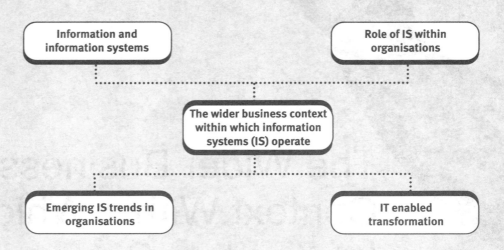

1 Information and Information Systems

1.1 Information and data

Introduction

Information is different from data.

 Data consists of numbers, letters, symbols, raw facts, events and transactions which have been recorded but not yet processed into a form that is suitable for making decisions.

 Information is data that has been processed in such a way that it has a meaning to the person who receives it, who may then use it to improve the quality of decision-making.

Characteristics of good information

The information produced by a system should have the following characteristics (identified by the acronym ACCURATE):

Accurate – sufficiently accurate to be relied upon.

Complete – managers should be given all the information they need, but information should not be excessive.

Cost effective – the value of information should exceed the cost of producing it.

Understandable – information needs to be clearly presented and displayed in an understandable form.

Relevant – the information should be relevant to its purpose.

Accessible – information should be accessible in an appropriate way, e.g. by email, verbally or by written report.

Timely – information should be provided in sufficient time for decisions to be made based upon that information.

Easy to use – the information should be clear and easy to use.

The value of information

- Collecting and processing information for use by managers has a cost.
- The value of the information to the business must be greater than the cost.

Value of information	Cost of information
Information may: • reduce unnecessary costs; • eliminate losses; • result in better marketing strategies; • assist in attaining competitive advantage.	• Design and development costs, e.g. system design, testing, capital cost of equipment. • Running costs, e.g. staff salaries, security. • Storage costs, e.g. for hardware.

Converting data into information

The process of turning data into information may include the following stages:

(1) Data **collection**: raw data is collected from both the internal (within the organisation) and the external environment (outside of the organisation).

(2) Data **evaluation**: collected data is filtered for relevance.

(3) Data **analysis**: different dimensions of the data are analysed, e.g. comparison with budget, with the historical record, with industry best.

(4) Data **interpretation**: meaning added to the data.

(5) Data **reporting**: information is disseminated to users.

1.2 Information technology and information systems

 Information systems (IS) refer to the provision and management of information to support the running of the organisation.

 Information technology (IT) is the supporting equipment (hardware) that provides the infrastructure to run the information systems.

Within a **factory** setting complex problems have been solved through the use of IS, for example:

- Computer aided design (CAD)
- Computer aided manufacturing (CAM)

CAD and CAM have resulted in innovative solutions to product design and can lead to the use of robots and computerised inventory management.

In the **office**, automation has been brought about by technology such as:

- Electronic data interchange (EDI) – replacing traditional paper based documents; it allows the computer-to-computer transmission of data contained in standard business documents such as customer invoices and purchase orders.
- The Internet
- Email
- Video and teleconferencing

2 The Role of Information Systems within Organisations

2.1 Introduction

An organisation's information systems serve two important purposes:

- processing, storing and reporting **day to day transactions**.
- supporting **managerial activities**, such as decision making, planning and control.

Test your understanding 1

Active First has grown rapidly over the past three years by acquiring a number of smaller gyms and health clubs. This strategy resulted in the organisation inheriting many different systems and it is now considering replacing these systems with a fully integrated, state of the art, organisation wide system.

Required:

Briefly describe the benefits to Active First of the implementation of the new system.

Role of IS within modern organisations

Information systems play a vital role in modern day organisations at a number of levels, for example:

- improving operations and manufacturing
- contributing to enhanced products and services
- offering the opportunity for cost reduction
- improving communication
- allowing managers to make better informed decisions.

2.2 Decision making

Introduction

Decision making is an important aspect of any organisation.

Three levels of decision making are normally identified; **strategic**, **tactical** and **operational**. Each results in different information requirements.

Operational (low-level) decisions occur most frequently (e.g. daily basis) but have a lesser impact on the organisation.

Strategic decisions are less frequently made but are more significant. For example, a UK based supermarket chain may put a strategic plan in place outlining its decision to expand into a number of other European countries. This plan is a long term plan and the development of new markets will have far reaching implications for the whole organisation.

Levels of information

Within an organisation, management information requirements can be classified into three different levels:

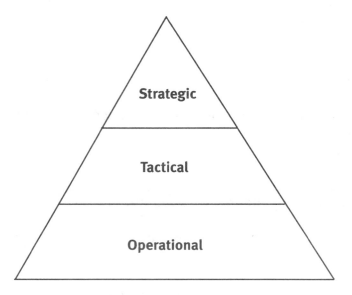

Strategic information is mainly used by directors and senior managers to choose between alternative courses of action, to plan the organisation's overall objectives and strategy and to measure whether these are being achieved. For example:

*   profitability of main business segments
*   prospects for present and potential markets.

Tactical information is used by managers at all levels, but mainly at the middle level for tactical planning and management control activities, such as pricing, purchasing, distribution and stocking. For example:

*   sales analysis
*   stock levels
*   productivity measures.

Operational information is used mainly by managers on the operational level such as foremen and section heads who have to ensure that routine tasks are properly planned and controlled. For example:

*   listings of debtors and creditors
*   payroll details
*   raw materials requirements and usage.

Decision making systems

A hierarchy of systems can assist in the decision making process:

- **Transaction processing systems (TPS)** – these major applications carry out essential, routine processing of day to day transactional data. They are sometimes referred to as data processing systems. Examples include payroll or stock control systems.

- **Management information systems (MIS)** – provide middle managers with information to monitor and control the organisation's activities and to report this to senior managers, e.g. budgeting and control systems.

- **Decision support systems (DSS)** – provide managers with information to support one off decisions. Uses complex mathematical models to allow managers to carry out complex 'what-if' analysis.

- **Expert systems** – a system that stimulates the problem-solving techniques of human experts, by applying human expertise and knowledge to a range of specific problems about a particular area of expertise.

- **Executive information systems (EIS)** – provide senior level managers with strategic level information to help them to make strategic decisions. Information can be presented in a user friendly format, e.g. graphs, pie charts.

Test your understanding 2

Identify the benefits of good MIS and EIS

2.3 Organisational dependence of information systems

Many organisations cannot function adequately without their information systems, e.g. airlines, travel agents, banks, insurance companies and even supermarkets.

Test your understanding 3

Many supermarkets have implemented an EPoS (electronic point of sale) system. This system includes a bar code scanner, touch screen technology, integrated credit card processing and pin pad device and records important information, e.g. sales information for inventory purposes and customer information for marketing purposes.

Required:

Explain the ways in which supermarket's operations have been transformed by the EPoS system.

3 Emerging IS Trends in Organisations

This section explores emerging IS trends in organisations including:

- enterprise-wide systems such as area networks and databases,

- knowledge management systems,

- customer relationship management systems such as e-business and Web 2.0 tools.

3.1 Enterprise-wide systems

An enterprise-wide system enables:

- communication between different geographical regions, e.g. between divisions located in different parts of the country or world

- the individual divisions to meet their specific processing requirements.

Examples include networks and databases:

Networks

A network is where a number of computers and other devices are linked in such a way that any one device can communicate with any other so enabling resource sharing between a number of users.

Most organisations connect their PCs and other computers together in local area networks (**LANs**), enabling them to share data and peripherals such as printers.

LANs can also be interconnected to create sophisticated, geographically dispersed wide area networks (**WANs**).

Databases

A **database** is a common file of data for many users and for a variety of purposes.

A database will be controlled by a **database management system (DBMS)**. It controls all aspects of:

- access
- maintenance
- security of data.

Advantages include:

- **Data independence** – multiple users can access the same data, at the same time for use in different ways.
- **Elimination of data redundancy** – i.e. the storage of data in more than one location. This problem will be eliminated since data is only stored once in the central database store.
- **Reduced storage costs** – again, since data is only stored once.
- **Improved data integrity** – by keeping only one version of the data, inconsistencies in the data should be eliminated and the organisation is more inclined to focus on the accuracy of this single version.

Disadvantages include:

- **Security risk** – a sophisticated DBMS is required to monitor access to and changes to data.
- **Data ownership** – this may be disputed and hence a dispute over responsibility for file maintenance may arise.
- **Contingency planning** – effective back-up is essential since data is only held in one location.
- **Cleansing of data** – data will need to be analysed and 'cleansed' before it can be integrated into the database.
- **Staff training** – may be required

Test your understanding 4

Your organisation is considering changing to a database system. List the issues it would need to consider.

3.2 Knowledge management systems

What is knowledge management?

Knowledge management is a relatively new approach to business in which an organisation gathers, organises, shares and analyses its knowledge to further its aim.

Where does the knowledge reside?

Knowledge resides in:

- **Human capital** – the knowledge, skills and experience possessed by employees.

- **Structural capital** – includes intellectual capital (e.g. patents) and client information (e.g. address lists and client records).

What is a knowledge management system?

A knowledge management system is any system that helps the organisation in its process of knowledge management.

Types of knowledge management system

- **Networks** – see earlier discussion in section 3.1.
- **Groupware** – this software helps teams to work together and collaborate on projects. Examples include:
  - A **calendar** allowing users to, for example, plan meetings and generate reminders of deadlines or meetings.
  - An **address book** allowing contact details to be accessed.
  - A **journal** for automatically recording interactions with people involved in a project, e.g. emails.

- **Intranet** – An Intranet is an internal organisational network that is based on Internet technologies and can only be accessed by authorised employees. One of the main advantages of an Intranet is that it allows confidential internal information sharing, e.g. corporate policies, training documents, telephone directories.

- **Extranet** – An Extranet is an extended Intranet. It links the organisation to business partners such as suppliers and customers and allows information to be shared. For example, an organisation could connect its purchase order system to the product catalogue database on a supplier's Intranet.

Test your understanding 5

A barrier to knowledge management is that many people believe that keeping knowledge secret gives them unique power. Knowledge management, however, requires that knowledge is uncovered and shared.

Required:

What arguments could be used to encourage individuals to freely give up and share information?

3.3 Customer relationship management (CRM) systems

CRM systems help the organisation to get to know their customers better and to use that knowledge to serve their customers better. Examples include:

- E-business
- Web 2.0 tools.

E-business

E-business is the transformation of key business processes through the use of Internet technologies (note: e-commerce is one part of e-business and refers to buying or selling products/services online).

Illustration 1 – Amazon and CRM

A number of individualised targeted products will be recommended to customers logging into the Amazon website. These products will be related to previous purchases or searches made by the Amazon customer.

Advantages of e-business include:

- Cost reduction, e.g. lower overheads, cheaper procurement.
- Increased revenue, e.g. due to online sales, better understanding of customers' needs.
- Better information for control, e.g. through the monitoring of web sales.
- Improved marketing, e.g. emailing customers with special offers.

Barriers to e-business include:

- Technophobia of managers/employees/customers.
- Security concerns.
- Set-up and running costs.
- Limited IT resource in house.
- Limited opportunities to exploit e-business.

Web 2.0 tools

Web 2.0 tools are one of the more recent developments in e-business.

Web 2.0 tools, or social networking tools, are changing the way that people share their perspectives, opinions, thoughts and experiences.

There are two key ways in which the tools can be used by businesses:

- To listen to customers by monitoring content.
- To influence customers by writing content.

Test your understanding 6

There are a number of Web 2.0 tools. Identify some of the more popular ones.

Illustration 2 – Listening to customers

Let's consider how an individual customer or potential customer may use Web 2.0 tools and how these could result in vast amounts of useful information which the organisation can harness.

Podcasting

James is considering buying a new games console. He downloads a podcast (i.e. a video or audio review) about the Nintendo Wii console, from a website such as podcast.net.

Blog

James decides to comment on this podcast on his Blogger blog. This is an online diary which other people can read and write comments on.

Social bookmarking

James decides that he wants more people to see and remark on his blog post. He could submit it to a social bookmarking site such as Digg. This site will organise submissions by allocating 'tags' to them. People searching for say, 'games consoles', could then easily find and read James' submission.

As more people read and comment on the blog, James will be said to be social networking.

How will this benefit Nintendo?

This process will result in a vast amount of information being written in relation to the Nintendo Wii and games consoles that compete with this product. Nintendo can use this to enhance the understanding of their customers' needs.

Illustration 3 – Influencing customers by writing content

Blogs

The website for Dove body products includes a number of celebrity blogs. These blogs include diet, fashion and lifestyle information. The writer of each blog and the contents of each blog has been carefully chosen to appeal to Dove's target audience and the blogs have enabled the organisation to serve their customers better.

Twitter

Some companies are using Twitter to post about company accomplishments and to distribute links that take people back to the corporate web page, press releases, and other promotional sites. For example, Starbucks posts new offers and also participates in threaded discussions to these offers with their Twitter followers.

Facebook

With over 200 million users worldwide, Facebook represents a huge opportunity for companies to acquire new customers. The company can set up a free Facebook page. This allows the company to interact with users and customers can be invited to join the network. The company can promote company blogs or their website by including extracts on Facebook. In addition to these free tools, the company can also pay for advertising. This advertising can be targeted towards specific customers, whose personal details are recorded when they register.

Generation Y

Addressing the 2008 CIMA Lecturers' Conference, Dr. Melodie de Jager profiled what she believed to be a new generation (generation Y) of potential students emerging in many Western countries.

Born between 1980 and 2001, the Y generation are:

- technology savvy (well used to ipods, facebook, blogs and YouTube) but have poor grammar and spelling due to over reliance of text, mms and sms.

- 95% of the generation own a computer and cell phone, and 76% own an instant messaging service: 34% use websites as the primary source of news, 28% author blogs, 44% read blogs and approximately one in two share and download with peers.

The implication of this is that a generation is emerging that is being actively shaped by current technology, possibly more than any other before it. This generation will not only be future customers of existing businesses but also form the workforce. Ignoring technology is not an option for any organisation.

Test your understanding 7

Discuss FOUR opportunities that Web 2.0 tools can offer to firms.

4 IT Enabled Transformation

4.1 Introduction

IT has enabled, and continues to enable complete organisational transformation. Organisational restructuring might accompany IT changes to take full advantage of technology.

Two significant changes include:

- An increase in teleworking.
- The emergence of virtual organisations and virtual teams.

Note: Technology is just one of a wider group of factors which will act as extreme triggers for change. These factors can be categorised using the PESTEL framework (i.e. political, economic, social, technological, ecological/environmental, legal).

4.2 Teleworking

IT developments have enabled employees to work at home rather than being based in an office. This is known as teleworking or homeworking.

Impact of teleworking on the organisation

The **advantages** of teleworking include:

- Increased employee motivation and productivity.
- Increased commitment to the organisation.
- Attracting individuals because of the availability of such conditions.
- Reduced absenteeism and staff turnover.

The **disadvantages** of teleworking include:

- Difficulties in co-ordinating staff.
- Loss of control of staff.
- Dilution of organisational culture.
- Less commitment to the organisation.
- Extra labour costs, e.g. providing employees with equipment.

Impact of teleworking on the employee

Test your understanding 8

Consider your own employment. Would you like or dislike working from home? Discuss the reason for your opinion on this issue.

4.2 Virtual companies and virtual teams

Virtual companies

A **virtual company** is an organisation that uses computer and telecommunications technologies to extend its capabilities by working routinely with employees or contractors located throughout the country or the world. Using e-mail, faxes, instant messaging, data and videoconferencing, it implies a high degree of working away from the office as well as using remote facilities.

Characteristics of a virtual company include:

- A virtual company is a business that operates with very little physical presence. The most extreme type of virtual company is one with only 'virtual employees' and no central office. Everyone works from home, including top management.

- Virtual companies use IT, e.g. the internet, email, faxes, videoconferencing and instant messaging, to enable the company to work with employees or contractors located throughout the country or the world.

Illustration 4

'Not on the High Street' is an internet based business selling luxury homeware, clothing and gifts. It has enjoyed rapid growth and success since it was launched in 2006.

The founders work with over 900 small British businesses. These businesses design, produce and deliver the products to customers. This enables Not on the High Street to sell a unique range of products to fulfil the needs of the demanding modern customer and to keep costs low.

- Virtual companies enable executives, scientists, writers, researchers and other professionals to collaborate on new products and services without ever meeting face to face.

- The important issue is that these organisations feel 'real' to the client, and meet their needs at least as adequately as the more 'traditional' organisations.

- A virtual company will outsource most or all of its functions.

Illustration 5

A firm manufactures wedding dresses. It could outsource:

- the design to a wedding dress designer;

- marketing to a specialist marketing firm;

- manufacture to a sub-contractor;

- delivery to a specialist logistics firm;

- collection of money from customers to a specialist debt collection company;

- tax returns and accounts to a specialist accountancy firm.

Discuss the benefits of adopting a virtual company strategy.

Drawbacks of virtual companies

- It may be difficult to negotiate a revenue sharing agreement between the different partners.

- Loss of control may result in a fall in quality.

- The partners may also work for competitors thus reducing any competitive advantage.

Virtual teams

A **virtual team** is a group of people who interact through independent tasks guided by a common purpose and work across space, time and organisational boundaries with links strengthened by IT.

They are essentially teams of people who are not present in the same office or organisation.

IT/ IS has enabled the formation of virtual teams:

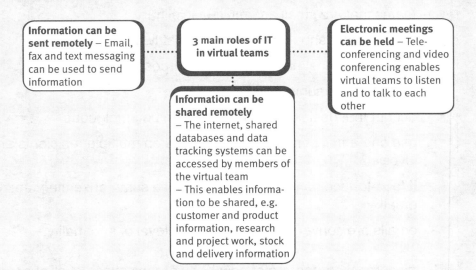

The following **challenges** face virtual teams:

- **Forming a team** – it may be difficult to establish a cohesive and trusting team.

- **Knowledge sharing** – may prove more difficult due to the absence of face to face contact.

- **Processes and goals** – it may be more difficult to establish clear decision making processes and goals.

- **Leadership** – this may be more difficult since employees will be working at different times, in different locations and in different ways.

- **Cultural differences** – team members will be from different backgrounds and cultural differences may make working together more difficult.

- **Morale** – some team members may find this way of working isolating.

Test your understanding 10

Identify the ways in which the challenges faced by virtual teams can be overcome.

Skyrme and Meall's work on virtual teams

Skyrme (1997) proposes certain principles for creating and maintaining innovative virtual teams. Some of the main principles are:

- high levels of trust

- being mutually supportive

- giving as much as you get, in terms of support, transfer of information and knowledge

- teams that are small and multi-disciplinary

- every worker should belong to at least two teams

- every team must have a sense of purpose

- frequent communication

- accept that decision-making will often be ambiguous

- use one email per topic, especially when multiple recipients are involved

- if face-to-face conversations take place summarise the meeting by email

- emails are conversations, so insert a level of informality.

The piecemeal harnessing of new IS by organisations of all shapes and sizes has, however, left many with a mixture of disparate and disconnected systems that do little to improve their efficiency or effectiveness. **Meall** (2004) reports that the accounting profession has been particularly hard hit, and the growing burden of bureaucracy threatens many.

5 Chapter Summary

Information and information systems

- Data and information
- Characteristics of good information
- Information technology (IT) and information systems

Role of IS within organisations

- Day to day and managerial activities
- Decision making
- Organisational dependence on IS

The wider business context within which information systems (IS) operate

Emerging IS trends in organisations

- Enterprise-wide systems
- Knowledge management systems
- Customer relationship management systems

IT enabled transformation

- Teleworking
- Virtual companies and virtual teams

6 Practice Questions

Question 1

A working definition of information would be:

A   facts you can work with

B   facts

C   facts useful to the production manager

D   facts useful to the decision maker

(2 marks)

Question 2

Blogs, podcasts and social bookmarking are all examples of:

A   enterprise-wide systems

B   web 2.0 tools

C   internet enablers

D   knowledge management systems

(2 marks)

Question 3

Explain how FOUR different developments in information technology could assist an organisation with a conventional structure to become a virtual organisation.

(4 marks)

Test your understanding answers

Test your understanding 1

- **Reduced duplication** of data and activities.
- **Improved system quality** of the new state of the art system.
- **Reduced costs** in the long term due to simplification of operation.
- **Improved accuracy** due to the use of just one data system.
- **Better control** because managers have all the information in one system.
- **Improved reporting and decision making** due to the speed and accuracy of the new system.
- Potential source of **competitive advantage** over rivals.
- Potential **improvement in security**.

Test your understanding 2

The value of having good **MIS** includes:

- Potentially more effective operations and improved management control.
- More complete information available to managers to improve decision making.
- Improved satisfaction and motivation amongst managers.
- Better information leading to improved budgetary control, stock control, improved forecasting etc.

The value of having good **EIS** includes:

- Ability to make informed and potentially significant, decisions of strategic value.
- Maintaining a competitive advantage over rival companies who do not make this investment.
- Improved ability to recognise opportunities or external challenges.
- Ability to track key performance indicators (KPIs) meaning that monitoring and control at strategic level is more effective.

Test your understanding 3

- **Cost savings and improved profitability** – costs associated with the staff daily cashing up, checking stock and placing orders for the next day's trading could potentially be eliminated. In addition improved stock control and better informed decisions on product lines should boost profits.

- **Stock management** – EpoS software can simplify stock and product ordering locally. EpoS eliminates staff errors on counting and so overcomes the risk of over ordering or product 'stock-outs'. EpoS also simplifies stocktaking and reduces the need for time consuming paper work to be carried out in stores.

- **Greater organisational control** – data will be received directly by head office allowing for greater control as well as common detailed reporting for marketing and management accounting purposes.

- **Alignment of corporate aims** – reporting through the EPoS system may be tailored to the particular business needs of the individual organisation.

- **More efficient use of management time** – EpoS can provide detailed reporting in real time, freeing managers from this burden and allowing them to redirect their time more productively.

- **Financial management** – with improved reporting efficiency the organisation should feel a real benefit as management accounting with be strengthened and reporting will be more accurate and timely.

- **Control of pricing** – EpoS can keep pricing consistent across stores and can change prices, e.g. to reflect a special 'buy one get one free' offer.

- **Product management** – should be improved. Data received through transactions in store can help inform on matters such as promotional campaigns and the future range of products that should be stocked.

- **Customer management** – if transaction data is linked to customer loyalty card information, customer buying habits can be identified and promotional activities targeted.

- **Operational efficiency** – user friendly touch screen terminals allow for faster processing resulting in increased customer satisfaction and improvements in employee motivation.

- **Effective management of staff and transactions** – EpoS will allow for closer control of staff (e.g. the monitoring of staff efficiency) and improved security of cash.

- **Attainment of industry standard** – an investment in EPoS will ensure the supermarket has equipment that is at least comparable to its rivals.

Test your understanding 4

- Specialist staff required (in implementing and running the new system, such as a database manager and administrators).

- Set-up costs of new software and possibly new hardware.

- Training costs.

- Security features.

- Possible disruption.

- Responsibilities.

- Contingency and back-up facilities.

Test your understanding 5

The following arguments could be used:

- If everyone shares their knowledge, each person should gain more than they give up.

- Organisations are often so complex that it is rare that one person can achieve much alone. Teamwork and sharing knowledge is the best way of assuring a safe future.

- Knowledge is perishable. If knowledge is not used quickly then it is wasted. If knowledge cannot be shared the chances are that it will become useless before it can be used.

- Knowledge management is vital to the success of many businesses. If an organisation uses knowledge creatively, the chances are that it will gain a competitive advantage. People within the organisation should not be competing with each other at the expense of the company.

Test your understanding 6

Some popular Web 2.0 tools include:
- MySpace
- YouTube
- Blogger
- Facebook
- Twitter
- Digg

Test your understanding 7

Advertising – for example, Starbucks is tweeting to customers and you can join their Facebook site to find out about its news and promotions.

Brand development – for example, Volkswagen uses Flickr to develop its brand. Individuals are able to post pictures of their Volkswagen Beetle or their camp-a-van on the site.

To listen to customers – sites where customers and potential customers discuss the products of the company and of its competitors can be vital, e.g. customer ratings on Amazon.com.

Communication – for example, Deloitte Australia have held employee performance reviews in World of Warcraft and BDO uses Second Life as an avenue for meetings, presentations and events for staff and for clients.

Test your understanding 8

Advantages

- Reduced travel time and hence cost savings.

- Reduction is stress due to the removal of the daily commute and the removal of the distractions of a busy office.

- Better work/life balance due to the removal of the daily commute and potential opportunities to work more flexible hours than the traditional '9 to 5'.

- Control – employees may feel an improved sense of control if they have more flexibility to decide their working patterns and hours.

- Employment opportunities for disadvantaged individuals, e.g. disabled people may now find it possible to work due to the removal of travel and the office environment.

Disadvantages

- May not suit those with poor personal motivation or who are not self starters.

- May be distracted at home, e.g. by family members.

- Loss of learning/sharing of ideas from face to face contact.

- Loss of social interaction and stimulation.

- Difficultly in separating home and work life – an inability to 'switch off' from work may lead to 'burn out' or damaged personal relationships.

Test your understanding 9

- **Can exploit opportunities** – a business may not have the time or resources to develop the manufacturing and distribution infrastructure, people competencies and information technology required to exploit new opportunities. Only by forming a virtual company, of all-star partners, can it assemble the components it needs to provide a world-class solution for customers and capture the market opportunity.

- **Look bigger than they are** – virtual companies can be made to look much bigger than they actually are, enabling them to compete with large and successful organisations and to win large and lucrative contracts.

- **Flexibility** – teams of experts can be formed to meet the specific needs of a project. This team can then be dissolved and a new team formed for the next project. The performance of each project team should be much better than those of non-virtual competitors.

- **Lower costs** – one of the main aims of virtual companies is to reduce costs. Investment in assets, e.g. land and buildings, is minimal. This should help to drive competitive advantage.

Test your understanding 10

The challenges faced by virtual teams can be overcome by:

- training in technology and teamwork;

- spending time getting to know each other, e.g. team identity, jokes, occasional face to face meetings, team trips out;

- clear roles and responsibilities;

- detailed and timely feedback between the leader and team members;

- regular and predictable communication matters. The benefits should be maximised, e.g. the use of email, video conferencing, social networking sites and blogs could all assist in overcoming some of the challenges. Time zone differences may mean that managers and employees may have to accept that response times may not be immediate;

- paying attention to cultural differences. This may require training in cross-cultural appreciation;

- choosing dependable and self-reliant employees but managers should still be on hand to offer support;

- valued staff should be made to feel wanted and a sense of loyalty to the firm instilled;

- managers may need to view their role differently, the emphasis being on co-ordination rather than leadership;

- clear communication from managers of information coming from higher up in the organisation to ensure that employees are fully informed and share the organisation's vision.

Question 1

D

Question 2

B

Question 3

The following developments in IT have made it easier to become a virtual organisation:

- Advanced telephone systems allow features such as call diversion, caller identification and conference calling. This means that individuals can change how they answer the telephone (referring to an organisation or project) and can also participate in 'meetings' without being in the same location.

- Websites allow even very small organisations to appear much larger than they actually are. Customers might visit a website that creates the image of a 'real' organisation, while actually belonging to a virtual one.

- Developments in e-mail mean that individuals can collaborate more easily. Detailed documents and communications can be exchanged almost instantly, so a virtual organisation is no longer at a disadvantage in terms of response times.

- Personal computer (PC) and workstation equipment is so cheap, and takes up so little space, that the individuals within a virtual organisation can each work from home. This reduces premises costs and allows the virtual organisation to be more price-competitive.

- The use of Intranets allows the individuals within a virtual organisation to access and share large volumes of data. There is no requirement to be in the same location as the database, as communication can be via the Internet of a virtual private network (VPN).

- Using the 'desktop publishing' capabilities of modern PC software, a virtual organisation can have many different corporate images or trading styles. These can be generated at relatively low cost, without the need for commercial printing. This allows a group of individuals or small organisations to operate as a large number of apparently different virtual organisations while maintaining a professional appearance.

(**Note:** Only four examples are required. Marks will be awarded for other relevant examples).

The Implementation of IS to Support Organisational Strategy

Chapter learning objectives

Lead	Component
B2. Analyse how information systems can be implemented in support of the organisation's strategy.	(a) Discuss ways for overcoming problems in information system implementation.
	(b) Discuss ways for organising and managing information system activities in the context of the wider organisation.

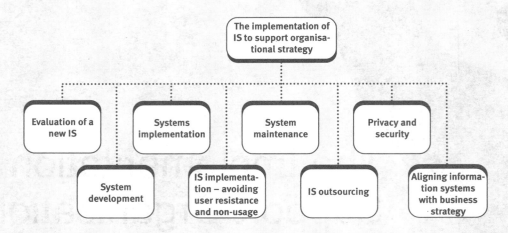

1 Evaluating a New IS

1.1 Introduction

When an organisation sees a possibility for introducing a new IS, an evaluation of the new system should be made to decide whether the potential benefits are sufficient to justify the costs.

Cost-benefit analysis (CBA) can be used to assess the expected costs and benefits of the IS.

The benefits of the new IS should be greater than its cost. If this is the case, the new IS is worth implementing.

1.2 Costs of a new system

Initial costs	Running costs
• Costs to design and develop system if software is bespoke.	• Cost of labour time to run the system.
• Purchase price of software if it is not bespoke.	• Cost of materials, e.g. replacement parts.
• Purchase cost of new hardware.	• Cost of service support, e.g. IT helpdesk.
• Cost of testing and implementation of the new system.	
• Training costs.	

1.3 Benefits of a new IS

These may be more difficult to quantify in monetary terms but could include:

- Enhanced efficiency and capacity – e.g. resulting in labour savings.
- Better quality of information – information may be more 'ACCURATE'.

- Better access to information – e.g. by means of an Intranet.

- Improved sharing of information – e.g. through the creation of a database.

- Improved communication – e.g. through the introduction of an email system.

- Better decision making and customer service.

The IS could be a source of competitive advantage.

Test your understanding 1

Discuss the potential disadvantages of a new IS.

Cost-benefit analysis

A sales director is deciding whether to implement a new computer-based sales system. His department has only a few computers, and his sales people are not computer literate. He is aware that computerised sales forces are able to contact more customers and give a higher quality of service to those customers. They are more able to meet commitments, and can work more efficiently with production and delivery staff.

His financial cost/benefit analysis is shown below:

Costs

New computer equipment:

- 10 network-ready PCs with supporting software @ $2,000 each

- 1 server @ $3,000

- 3 printers @ $1,000 each

- Cabling & Installation @ $4,000

- Sales Support Software @ $10,000

Training costs:

- Computer introduction – 8 people @ $300 each

- Keyboard skills – 8 people @ $300 each

- Sales Support System – 12 people @ $500 each

Other costs:

- Lost time: 40 man days @ $150 / day
- Lost sales through disruption: estimate: $10,000
- Lost sales through inefficiency during first months: estimate: $10,000

Total cost: $76,800

Benefits

- Tripling of mail shot capacity: estimate: $30,000 / year
- Ability to sustain telesales campaigns: estimate: $15,000 / year
- Improved efficiency and reliability of follow-up: estimate: $30,000 / year
- Improved customer service and retention: estimate: $20,000 / year
- Improved accuracy of customer information: estimate: $5,000 / year
- More ability to manage sales effort: $20,000 / year

Total Benefit: $120,000/year

2 Systems Development

Systems development follows a cycle called the systems development life cycle (SDLC). This is characterised by a number of stages:

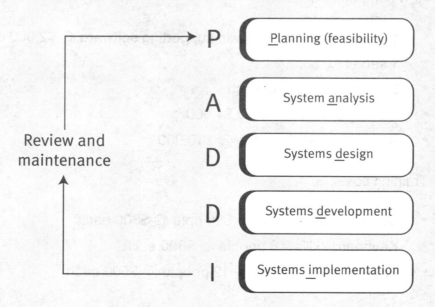

This chapter will focus on systems **implementation** and system **maintenance**.

3 Systems Implementation

3.1 Introduction

Systems implementation involves a number of activities that take the new system and brings it into full-scale use. These activities include testing and changeover.

3.2 Testing

A critical activity prior to changeover is testing the new system to ensure that it is working correctly before going live. Ultimate users should be involved in conducting tests.

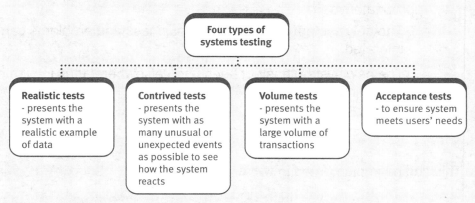

3.3 System changeover

System changeover is the change from operating the current system to introducing the new system operationally.

There are four approaches to system changeover, and the most appropriate approach will vary according to circumstances.

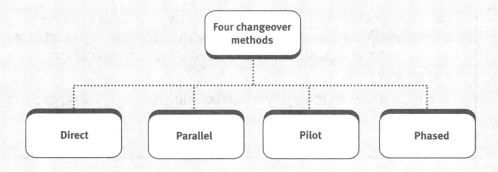

Direct

• The computer user ceases to operate the old system and switches completely to using the new system.

- Appropriate when:
  - The new system has been used elsewhere (for example, an off-the-shelf package) and there is confidence that it will function properly.
  - The problems for the computer user will be tolerable, even if the system fails to function properly.

Parallel

- The old system and the new system are both operated together for a while. If the new system performs to an acceptable level, a decision can be taken to stop operating the old system, and change entirely to the new system.
- Appropriate when:
  - The new system is critical to the business and problems can't be tolerated.
  - The new system has not been used elsewhere, thus implementation is high risk.

Pilot

This can be implemented in two ways:

- A retrospective data pilot operates the new system with old data. The results can be cross-checked to the existing system.
- A restrictive data pilot takes one whole part of the complete system and runs it as the new system. If this operates correctly then the remaining elements can be transferred gradually.

Phased

- Involves gradual implementation and is used in large systems projects or geographically dispersed organisations, e.g. an organisation may implement a complete information system but in one geographical region at a time.
- Appropriate when the system can be implemented in distinct parts.

Illustration 1 – Phased changeover

If a company introduces a new accounting system by phased conversion, it might begin by introducing the new sales ledger system, followed by the new payables ledger system, followed by the new inventory system, and so on.

Test your understanding 2

Identify the advantages and disadvantages of each of the four changeover methods.

4 IS Implementation – avoiding user resistance and non-usage

4.1 Reasons for project failure

There are a number of reasons for project failure. These include:

- Insufficient user involvement – the risk of project failure is increased if users are not involved in the implementation. New systems will bring about change, and users reject the system simply because they don't like the change, or the changes have resulted in loss of status or control. Insufficient user involvement is the major cause for failure.

- Lack of management support – little commitment to implementation or poor problem solving.

- Project is too complex for the organisation to manage.

- Poor planning and scheduling.

- Unrealistic deadlines being set.

- Poor monitoring and control.

- IT staff may have the technical skills but not the management skills required.

- Insufficient training for users.

Test your understanding 3

Identify **three** reasons why user involvement is so important when implementing a new system.

Test your understanding 4

Identify potential problems that might arise if there is inadequate or inappropriate user training following the introduction of a new system.

The 3Cs

Three broad conditions are necessary to implement IT successfully – commitment, coordination and communication.

Commitment

- It is important to get all users that are involved or affected by a project to become committed. The resources of the users will be necessary in the planning, development, testing and implementation stages of any IS project. Gaining their dedication and joint ownership of the project ensures that they are equally responsible for its eventual success or failure.

- Commitment must exist from top management and across all management levels. Commitment from senior management is shown by the allocation of resources in terms of people, money, time, information and technology.

Coordination

- A disorganised project will take considerably longer to achieve success, and normally at a greater cost than an organised one will. This increases the likelihood that such a project will never be completed.

- A disorganised project will have constantly moving targets, which are seldom attained.

- Coordination through planning and control of all the relevant factors will help to ensure that the right people are doing the right things in the right way, using the right resources at the right time.

Communication

- Through good relationships and communication with all interested parties, obstacles within, among and between them can be avoided in the planning and implementation of an information system.

- All stakeholders need to be kept informed and be encouraged to become actively involved throughout the whole process.

- IS projects often suffer severe communication chain problems between the various people involved. The chain is only as strong as its weakest link.

4.2 Overcoming user resistance

Kotter, Schlesinger and **Sache** identified six main methods of dealing with resistance:

Method	Advantages	Disadvantages
Education and communication	• Communication about the benefits of change should result in employees accepting the change.	• Time consuming. • Employees may not agree with benefits. • Usually used to reinforce another approach.
Participation	• Employees are more likely to support the change as they 'own' the change. • Utilises employee expertise.	• Time consuming. • Requires a strong relationship between management and the workforce.
Facilitation and support	• Techniques, such as counselling, will help employees overcome their fears and anxieties about change.	• Can't always address the reason for resistance, e.g. change may threaten job security.
Negotiation	• Conflict dealt with in an orderly fashion, preventing problems such as industrial action. • Since employees agree on the outcome it should encourage commitment and preserve morale.	• Time consuming. • Not always possible to reach a compromise.

Manipulation and co-optation (involves presentation of misleading information or buying off key individuals by giving them positions of authority).	• Quick. • Relatively inexpensive.	• May lead to future problems if individuals realise that they have been manipulated. • May raise legal/ethical problems.
Power/coercion (compulsory approach by management to implement the change).	• Speed. • Managers can implement required changes.	• Poor commitment. • Results in weak motivation • When employees enjoy a stronger position in the future, e.g. union representation, they are less likely to co-operate • May raise legal/ethical problems.

- The most appropriate approach will be dependent on the goals of the change programme and the likely reactions of the people involved.

- One of the problems of choosing the 'right' approach is that people will not always openly admit the real reasons for opposing change, e.g. the reason may be related to self-interest but is disguised as a 'technical objection'.

- In reality, managers may find it effective to use a combination of the approaches.

Test your understanding 5

If a manager discovers that there are instances of non-usage of a new system how might this be interpreted?

Lewin's Force Field Analysis

Lewin developed a technique for visualising the change process called force field analysis.

Force field analysis maps out the driving forces that are pushing towards a preferred state (i.e. the implementation of the new system) and the restraining forces, which are pushing back to the current state (i.e. continuing to use the old system).

Restraining forces

The first step of any successful change process is to identify the restraining forces and overcome them:

Potential restraining force	Potential method for removing restraining force
Fear of loss of control	Education, participation
Fear that there will not be enough time for training or to attend meetings or that the new system will be too difficult to use	Give employees the time required for training/ meetings and to learn the skills required
Doubt that the initiative will be properly implemented	Participation in the change process, education about benefits
Anxiety about job security	Reassure employees about job security
Employees don't feel the change is needed	Education regarding the benefits of change

Driving forces

Once the restraining forces have been addressed, the second step of the change process is to implement the new system. There may be a number of driving forces for this change:

- Management believe that the system will improve organisational performance.

- Competitors have implemented a new system and achieved significant improvements in productivity, quality and financial returns.

- Improved information.

- Difficult to maintain the current system.

- Reduced running costs.

- Fresh challenge in job.

These forces may be enough to drive the positive change. However, action can be taken to increase the strength of the driving forces, e.g. by providing exact figures regarding the increase in financial returns that could be enjoyed, and to introduce further driving forces, e.g. small rewards may be offered to staff who participate in the implementation of the new system.

Once the new system has been implemented, the final step of the change process is to reinforce the new behaviour. This may involve praising and rewarding those employees who embrace the new system.

5 System maintenance

System **maintenance** is the repair, correction or further enhancement of systems once it is in operation and can take several forms:

- **Corrective maintenance** – This relates to the need to correct technical difficulties that have arisen in the operation of the system. These include virus infection, hardware failure and file corruption as well as delaying response times due to systems overload.

- **Adaptive maintenance** – This relates to the need to make changes to the system in order to reflect the changing needs of the organisation over time. Such changes are inevitable given the changing nature of the business environment. Major changes will eventually lead to the need to replace the system entirely.

- **Perfective (preventative) maintenance** – This relates to general upgrades to both hardware and software in order to maximise the overall speed and functionality of the system, e.g. installing the latest version of an application. These improvements should prevent possible failures in the future.

6 IS Outsourcing

6.1 Introduction

IS outsourcing involves purchasing from outside the organisation the IS services required to perform business functions.

The scope of IS outsourcing can range from single system development to complete outsourcing of IT capability, i.e. systems development, maintenance, operations and training.

An organisation that has decided to outsource its IS function will need to address the following issues:

- **Communication with the workforce** – staff must understand the rationale for the decision and be aware of the timescale. Appropriate support should be offered if any redundancies/redeployment is anticipated.

- **Invitation to tender** – reputable contractors should be invited to tender for the work.

- **Choice of contractor** – the most appropriate contractor should be chosen based on robust criteria. A service level agreement (SLA) should be drawn up.

- **Establishment of relationships** – a strong client-contractor relationship should be established, e.g. through the use of an in house client contract manager.

- **Handover** – this may be done in a phased or direct manner.

- **Monitoring cost** – the budget needs to be carefully controlled and any additional costs accounted for.

- **Monitoring of standards** – the terms of the contract should be adhered to and user satisfaction should be evaluated. Any necessary steps should be taken to identify problems identified.

Illustration 2

In 2008, Shell agreed a $4 billion IS outsourcing deal with three companies; AT&T, EDS and T-systems. In a bid to minimise redundancies for its 3,000 IT staff, Shell negotiated that almost 99% of their staff would be transferred to the three companies.

6.2 Advantages and disadvantages of IS outsourcing

Test your understanding 6

Many organisations are taking the decision to outsource their non-core activities, such as IT. Identify the advantages and disadvantages of IT outsourcing.

Illustration 3 – Risks of outsourcing

Suppose that a regional hospital authority agrees a contract with a software company. The software company agrees to develop a new system that the hospital will use for maintaining patient records, communicating with patients at home, scheduling operations and charging the patients for services that are not free. After the system has been implemented, the software company will operate the system itself for a contract period of five years, and the hospital staff will only be involved with the system to the extent of providing the software company with the data for input.

The risks of the outsourcing agreement for the development and operation of this system include:

- The system might be imperfectly specified when system development work begins. If the hospital authority subsequently changes the specification, the software house might be able to increase its fee substantially.

- Since the software company will operate the system, it could be difficult for the staff of the hospital authority to test it.

- The software company will wish to make a profit from the contract, and will be reluctant to agree to changes, and might even argue against maintenance, unless it is paid for as an 'extra' cost.

- Once the system becomes operational, the hospital authority might have very little control over the communications between the software company's staff and the general public (the patients or 'customers').

- If the system creates bad publicity, due to errors in the system relating to scheduling of operations or invoicing, the hospital authority will have no control over the damage to its reputation.

- What happens at the end of five years? Will the hospital authority be forced to renew the contract with the software house because no one else understands the system? Alternatively, will the authority be obliged to abandon the system and buy a new system to replace it?

6.3 Managing the relationship

The use of contracted expertise raises the issue of establishing and maintaining strong client-vendor relationships.

When choosing a vendor, careful evaluation and selection processes should be followed, for example:

- background checks of vendor financial performance
- references
- litigation history.

Vendors should be chosen in accordance with pre-determined selection criteria. Relationships should be built on trust and mutual respect and so it would be helpful to:

- set out the terms and conditions of the outsourcing arrangement in a service level agreement (SLA).
- ensure the vendor understands, and will comply with, organisational ethical practices.
- ensure easy contact with the vendor by establishing relationships at various levels, e.g. key account managers, operators, executives.
- put in place mechanisms to periodically review and evaluate customer satisfaction and agree remedial action if necessary.

7 Privacy and Security

7.1 Introduction

There are two forms of IT/IS controls that exist to safeguard the privacy and security of data as well as ensuring complete and accurate processing of data:

General controls – ensure that the organisation has overall control over its information systems, e.g.:

- Personnel controls – includes segregation of duties, policy on usage, hierarchy of access.
- Access controls – such as passwords and time lock-outs.
- Computer equipment controls – to protect equipment from destruction, damage or theft.
- Business continuity planning – a risk assessment to decide which systems are critical to the business continuing its activities.

Application or program controls – performed automatically by the system and include:

- Completeness checks to ensure all data is processed.

- Validity checks to ensure only valid data is input/processed.

- Identification and authorisation checks to ensure users are identified and authorised.

- Problem management facilities to ensure problems are recorded/managed on a timely basis.

Test your understanding 7

Data integrity and security is a particular issue in a database. For data to have integrity, it must be accurate, consistent and free from accidental corruption.

Required:

What controls are required in a database to ensure that data integrity and security are maintained?

7.2 Privacy and security risks

Potential threat	Solution
Natural disasters – e.g. fire, flood.	• Fire procedures – fire alarms, extinguishers, fire doors, staff training and insurance cover. • Location, e.g. not in a basement area liable to flooding. • Physical environment – e.g. air conditioning, dust controls. • Back up procedures – data should be backed up on a regular basis to allow recovery.
Malfunction – of computer hardware or software.	• Network design – to cope with periods of high volumes. • Back up procedures (as above).

Viruses – a small program that once introduced into the system spreads extensively. Can affect the whole computer system.	• Virus software – should be run and updated regularly to prevent corruption of the system by viruses. • Formal security policy and procedures. • Regular audits to check for unauthorised software.
Hackers – deliberate access to systems by unauthorised persons.	• Firewall software – should provide protection from unauthorised access to the system from the Internet. • Passwords and user names – limit unauthorised access to the system.
Electronic eavesdropping – e.g. users accessing private information not intended for them.	• Data encryption – data is scrambled prior to transmission and is recovered in a readable format once transmission is complete. • Passwords and user names (as above)
Human errors – unintentional errors from using computers and networks.	• Training – adequate staff training and operating procedures.
Human resource risk – e.g. repetitive strain injury (RSI), headaches and eye strain from computer screens, tripping over loose wires.	• Ergonomic design of workstations should reduce problems such as RSI. • Anti-glare screens reduce eye strain. • Cables should be in ducts.

7.3 The UK Data Protection Act (DPA) 1998

The UK Data Protection Act (DPA) 1998

Privacy is the right of an individual to control the dissemination or use of data that relates to him or her.

Legislation relating to privacy varies considerably from country to country. Within this section, we use the example of UK law to illustrate typical principles.

The UK Data Protection Act (DPA) 1998

- Personal information can be misused much more effectively on a computer than on manual systems.

- The DPA gives individuals the right to know what information is held about them (provisions of the Act) and provides a framework to ensure that information is handled properly (principles of the Act).

- Failure by data users to comply with the DPA can result in seizure of data and unlimited fines.

8 Aligning Information Systems with Business Strategy

A **business strategy** is a major plan of action formulated to achieve the organisation's objectives. It is developed by senior management in response to organisational needs and will be used to guide the company through the next period of activity.

Business planning can be viewed as having three levels:

- corporate strategy (for example, which markets should we be in, which products should we have in our portfolio?)

- business strategy (for example, how to make a particular product more successful) and

- functional strategy. (for example, HR and marketing).

Using this hierarchy, IS would be viewed as a functional strategy designed to support the overriding corporate and business strategies. IS may act as a core competence and be a source of competitive advantage (i.e. an advantage over competitors gained by offering customers greater value, either by means of lower prices or by providing greater benefits and service that justifies higher prices).

However, developments in IT/IS can also be the trigger for new corporate and business strategy, such as the growth in e-trading, so the relationship is more than simply one of support.

Aligning information systems with business strategy

Clegg (2003) offers a number of insights into strategy development. He makes the point that an IS strategy is a plan for ensuring that information is effective (appropriate, accurate, available and timely). Strategy development might begin by either:

- reviewing all the information currently in the organisation, and then overcoming duplication or inaccuracies, or alternatively,

- taking the starting point as the organisation as a whole, and then deciding of the information it needs to operate effectively.

Secondly, strategy should not be left to IS experts; managers themselves know what type of information they need.

Boomer (2007) offers a checklist of issues to address in planning IS at both a strategic and tactical level as follows:

Strategic	Tactical
• What are the organisation's priorities (as expressed in the corporate plan)? • How might technology help meet corporate objectives? • What are the latest trends in and outside of our industry?	• What HR resources do we have, and what are their unique abilities? • How are our IS and IT resources currently managed? Should we outsource or staff internally? • What is the timeline and budget and other resources?

9 Chapter summary

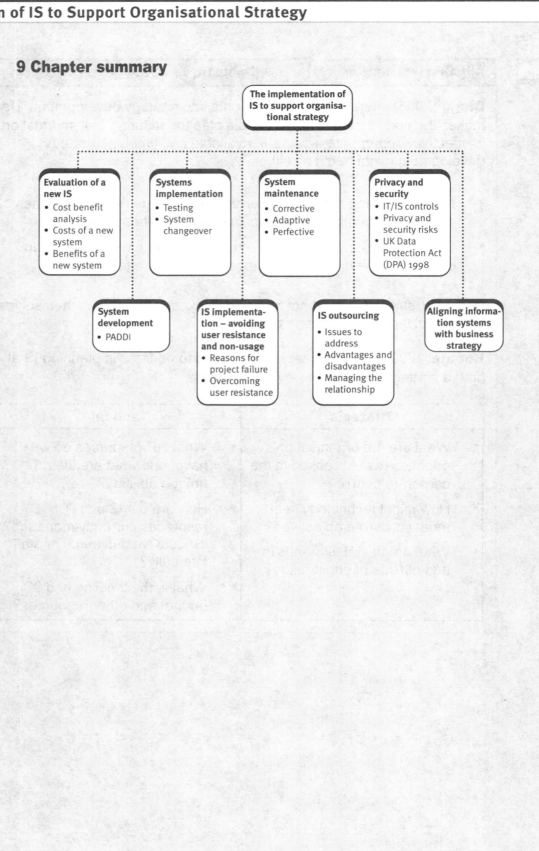

10 Practice questions

Question 1

Outsourcing can lead to:

A   reliance on a third party solicitor

B   increased reliance on internal departments

C   increasing staff numbers

D   retaining managers to monitor the contract

(2 marks)

Question 2

Identify FOUR tangible costs and FOUR intangible costs of a new information system.

(4 marks)

Question 3

Explain FOUR of the methods recommended by Kotter and Schlesinger for overcoming resistance to a new information system.

(4 marks)

Question 4

A manufacturing company has decided to replace its inventory control system. The current system was implemented 10 years ago but has restricted reporting facilities and a text-based interface. It is to be replaced with a Windows-based package which undertakes the same basic functions, but is easier to use, has flexible reporting facilities and interfaces easily with other Windows-based software. Both systems run on the same hardware.

The manager of the project is now considering the details of implementation. He has been advised that he should consider both 'parallel running' and 'direct changeover/direct conversion'.

Required:

(a) Briefly explain what the terms 'parallel running' and 'direct changeover' mean.

(5 marks)

(b) Briefly describe THREE advantages of 'direct changeover' over 'parallel running'.

(6 marks)

(c) Identify the main risk of direct changeover and suggest how this risk might be reduced for the manufacturing company's inventory control system implementation.

(4 marks)

(Total: 15 marks)

Question 5

The directors of DS are not satisfied with the GDC facilities management company, which was contracted two years ago to run the IT systems of the company. At that time, the existing in-house IT development and support department was disbanded and all control of IT systems handed over to GDC. The appointment of GDC was relatively rushed and, although an outline contract was agreed, no detailed service level agreement was produced.

Over the last few weeks, the number of complaints received from staff regarding the service has been increasing and the provision of essential management reports has not been particularly timely.

A recent exchange of correspondence with GDC failed to resolve the matter. Staff at GDC recognised the fall in standards of service, but insisted that it had met its contractual obligations. DS's lawyers have confirmed that GDC is correct.

Key features of DS's contract with GDC facilities management company:

- The contract can be terminated by either party with three months' notice.

- GDC will provide IT services for DS, the service to include:
  - Purchase of all hardware and software
  - Repair and maintenance of all IT equipment
  - Help desk and other support services for users
  - Writing and maintenance of in-house software
  - Provision of management information
  - Price charged to be renegotiated each year but any increase must not exceed inflation, plus 10%

Required:

(a) Explain, from the point of view of DS, why it might have received poor service from GDC, even though GDC has met the requirements of the contract.

(10 marks)

(b) Explain the courses of action now available to DS relating to the provision of IT services. Comment on the problems involved in each course of action.

(6 marks)

(Total: 16 marks)

Question 6

The Gort Organisation supplies industrial sewing machines to a variety of clients. Sales of machines and spare parts are made by sales representatives visiting each owner of a Gort machine, checking that machine for maintenance requirements and then ordering the parts upon their return to the office. Requirements for new machines are also discussed during the maintenance visit. While customers are generally happy with the service provided, there can be significant time delays in ordering parts for machines because sales representatives may not return to their office for several days. This delay has resulted in some loss of customer goodwill.

The Board of Gort has recognised the need to develop a new information system to support sales representatives. The new system will allow remote access to the Gort Ordering System via mobile computers, and also provide order status and expected delivery dates for customers who will be able to access the Ordering System via an Extranet connection.

The Gort Organisation has never maintained a large IT department and the Board are seriously considering outsourcing the development of this new system.

Required:

Discuss the benefits and drawbacks of outsourcing the new information system in the Gort Organisation.

(10 marks)

Test your understanding answers

Test your understanding 1

- Security problems, e.g. risk of unauthorised access or fraud.
- Failure of the system to meet its objectives.
- Redundant data, i.e. the system might produce a large amount of data which no one uses.
- Maintenance problems – maintenance may prove to be more difficult or more expensive than expected.

Test your understanding 2

	Advantages	Disadvantages
Direct	<ul><li>Quickest and cheapest changeover method.</li><li>Low risk if the system is already operating effectively elsewhere, e.g. competitor organisations.</li><li>The existing system may be too problematic.</li><li>Symbolic gesture of management's faith in the new system.</li></ul>	<ul><li>High risk – if new system does not function properly, the computer user will have no system at all.</li></ul>
Parallel	<ul><li>Low risk.</li><li>Old and new systems can be compared to verify the output of the new system.</li></ul>	<ul><li>Cost – additional resources required to operate two systems.</li><li>Slower than direct changeover.</li><li>Users may feel comfortable with old system and still rely on it.</li></ul>

Pilot	• Less risky than direct changeover since can check new system functions properly and deal with any problems before full implementation. • Less costly than parallel changeover.	• Slow. • Riskier than parallel changeover.
Phased	• Gives staff time to adjust to one part of system before introducing the next. • If new system results in job losses, there will be more time to deal with staff retraining or to prepare them for work elsewhere. • Less risky than direct changeover.	• Slow. • Links between parts of the system may make this difficult.

Test your understanding 3

User involvement:

- Ensures system meets requirements.
- Reduces resistance.
- Incorporates knowledge and expertise into the system.

Test your understanding 4

- Fear of the new system's effect on jobs.
- Fear of the unknown.
- Reluctance to use the new system.
- Errors in processing.
- Slower processing due to, say, lack of confidence or unfamiliarity.
- Staff turnover or absence arising from avoidance of the new system.

Test your understanding 5

Non-usage may be due to:

- An expression of resistance. In this case, appropriate influencing measures should be applied.

- A lack of confidence in the new system, in which case enhanced communication is required and system modification should be applied where appropriate.

- A lack of confidence in their own abilities to cope with the new system. In this case, training and other support mechanisms should be employed.

Test your understanding 6

Advantages

- Cost reduction: e.g. due to economies of scale since equipment is bought in bulk.

- Improved performance: management can concentrate on core competencies and suppliers used will be IT experts.

- Avoids problem of shortage of IT experts.

- Organisation can keep up with technological change.

- Cost control: creating a formal relationship tends to concentrate the focus on cost control which is sometimes lost when functions are performed internally.

- Flexibility to increase or decrease IT capacity.

- Time to market: outsourcing can accelerate the development and implementation of new IS.

Disadvantages

- Dependent on supplier – the supplier may not understand the business process and the organisation may lose control over its IS.
- Loss of confidentiality (outsourcing company may work for competitors).
- Locked into contract.
- Lose expertise.
- Loss of competitive advantage since the outsourcing company may work for competitors.
- Costs may be high, e.g. if the vendor keeps charging for updating the technology.

Test your understanding 7

- Control of access to workstations.
- User identification required for access by individual passwords.
- Users only see the icons for the functions where they have access rights.
- Restrictions on access to certain aspects of the database, e.g. using passwords.
- Users only to have access to those aspects that they need to do their job.
- Restrictions on use of functions or programs, e.g. writing off debts as bad debts.
- Transaction logs maintained automatically for checking and for back-up purposes.

Question 1

D

Question 2

Tangible costs	Intangible costs
Hardware and software costs	Downtime during implementation
Maintenance costs	Slower operating until users become more familiar with the new system
Training – initial and ongoing	Opportunity cost – money can't be invested elsewhere
Staff salaries	Training will take staff away from their normal work

Question 3

- **Education and communication** – communication about the benefits of the change should result in employees accepting the change.

- **Participation** – employees are more likely to support the change since they have bought into the process and own the change.

- **Negotiation** – conflict is dealt with in an orderly fashion preventing problems such as industrial action. Employees will agree with the outcome which will increase commitment and preserve morale.

- **Power/ coercion** – this is a compulsory approach to implementing the change. This approach may be required if rapid implementation of the change is necessary.

(**Note:** facilitation and support or manipulation and co-optation could also be mentioned).

Question 4

(a) Parallel running and direct changeover are both methods of systems implementation

With a parallel running approach, the old and the new systems are run together and the results and outputs are compared until the user has sufficient confidence in the new system to switch to it permanently and stop using the old system. Transactions are run through both systems and the outputs of one system are checked against the outputs of the other to check the accuracy and usability of the proposed new system.

With a direct changeover approach, the old system is removed on a specific date and operations switched, immediately and in full, to the new system. There is no period where the systems are operationally used together. The verification of the new system takes place during system and user acceptance testing.

(b) Possible advantages of direct changeover over parallel running include:

Cost and time savings

The direct changeover approach should be cheaper and less time-consuming than the parallel running approach. With parallel running, there is usually a significant cost in entering data twice (staff overtime, temporary staff) and checking the outputs of the two systems against each other. With the direct changeover method, data is entered into the new system only.

Increases commitment to the new system

Users of the system are usually very familiar with the operation and outputs of the current system. During parallel running there may still be a tendency to rely on the old system and not identify properly and investigate the differences between outputs from the current and the new system. As a result, significant problems may only be properly tackled when the parallel running period has ended and the old system is discarded.

Proper attention to system and user acceptance testing

Although the stages of system testing and user acceptance testing are formally recognised in an approach using parallel running, there may be a tendency to underrate their importance because users are aware that the current system will be available as a 'fail-safe' during the implementation stage. The immediate nature of direct changeover means that proper attention has to be paid to both system and user acceptance testing.

(c)   The main risk of direct changeover is that the system fails and there is no other system to fall back on to. As a result, the company may not be able to process the transactions required to carry on its business. This places it at considerable business risk and could create an exposure to claims from its customers for consequential damages.

This risk may be reduced in several ways:

–   Comprehensive systems and user acceptance testing prior to implementation. Strict testing requirements and acceptance criteria must be laid down and adhered to.

–   Effective training of users and operations staff before the new system goes live. Users will need familiarisation with the Windows style of interface with the enhanced reporting facilities, and with interfaces to other software.

–   Contingency plans that enable the business to process transactions manually while the new system is corrected and recovered.

–   A temporary increase in stock levels to reduce the risk of stock-outs while any problems with the new system are corrected.

Question 5

(a) From the point of view of DS, there are many reasons why it may have received poor service, even though the terms of the contract have been fulfilled. The terms are as follows:

(i) **Purchase of all hardware and software**. GDC may have a preference for hardware and software that they are familiar with and this may not be a suitable fit to the existing system. Unfortunately, hardware and software become obsolete very quickly and GDC may not have been replacing it fast enough to keep up with the demands of the company. It could be that they have bought software to upgrade the system and they have not trained staff sufficiently to maintain it. A similar situation could have occurred with networking and routing equipment. Problems can occur that are very difficult to sort out without available expertise.

(ii) **Repair and maintenance of all IT equipment**. This is a tall order for any company. When the equipment was purchased, DS should have arranged a maintenance service through the manufacturers themselves. There could easily be a misunderstanding over the type of maintenance required from GDC. Are they supposed to fix faults when they occur or do regular maintenance checks to ensure the smooth running of the equipment?

(iii) **Help desk and other support services for users**. Users often have an inadequate understanding of existing systems and develop unrealistic expectations. This means that they may generate unreasonable and unmanageable volumes of requests for change. GDC might suffer from high programmer turnover rates. Their employees may not have the necessary skills or motivation. Many programmers prefer development work to maintenance work and may be reluctant to get involved in help desk support.

(iv) **Writing and maintaining software**. Since the contract is vague and the scope so large, there are bound to be areas of poor service from GDC. Maintenance may be required to:

- correct faults;

- adapt the system to reflect the changing needs of the organisation;

- upgrade the system if product enhancements are released.

(v) **Provision of management information**. Unless the type, content and timing of the management report required is specified, then there is ample scope for poor service. A new person at GDC may be responsible for producing the reports and he or she may not know the full routine. The report may have been left in the wrong place, or delivered to the wrong person first. However, the problem may not be due to a fault at GDC. To obtain essential management reports, the information must be kept up to date by the staff at DS. If the employee responsible for maintaining the database is sick or the files containing the data get damaged or corrupted, then the production of reports is likely to be delayed.

(b) There are several options available to DS:

Re-write contract with the help of GDC

The first is to re-write the contract with the help of GDC so that there is some flexibility but no vague areas and each party knows what is expected from them. This could be done through negotiation while the existing contract is still running. The problems with this course of action is that DS are locked into the current arrangement and GDC will be aware of the problems it could cause by giving three months' notice and leaving DS. They would be in a very strong position to increase the price substantially or restrict their commitment to DS in any negotiations that might take place.

Obtain help in re-writing the contract

The second would be to obtain help in re-writing the contract and, when satisfied, give GDC three months' notice and ask them, and other facilities management companies, to tender for the new contract. The problems with this course of action is that DS might just be trading in one company that is giving poor service for another that they do not know. There is no guarantee that service standards will always be as expected.

End outsourcing agreement

The third option would be to revert to an in-house IT development and support department solution. This would require a lot of effort and expense and, if new staff have to be recruited, there will be a long period before they could understand the system and be in a position to do what GDC are already doing.

Question 6

Benefits

The benefits of outsourcing the new information systems will include the following:

- **Freedom to shop around for the best deal**
  Various suppliers can be asked to tender for the work, with the contract being awarded to the supplier providing value for money and hopefully relevant experience in designing this type of system.

- **Minimum diversion of management time and focus from core business activities**
  The core business of Gort appears to be provision of sewing machines and spares for those machines, not the maintenance or development of IT systems. Outsourcing this development will allow the Board of Gort to remain focused on their core business rather than have to manage an IT project where they lack appropriate knowledge and experience.

- **Advantages of contractual terms and conditions in times of dispute**
  The development of the new system will be governed by the terms of any service contract. If the outsourcing company do not deliver on a part of the contract, they can be asked to complete that phase without additional cost to Gort. Late delivery with in-house systems will normally mean having to allocate additional resources to the project, without any financial remedy from the IT department.

- **Access to the latest programming techniques as in house skills may be out of date**
  As there is only a small IT department in the Gort corporation, it is quite likely that the increase in IT skills will be out-of-date. Any programmers and analysts are also unlikely to have time to take on a significant development project. Outsourcing the contract will therefore provide the Gort corporation with the necessary skills.

- **Shorter delivery time**
  Outsourcing will result in a shorter delivery time because Gort will not have to interview and recruit additional staff to monitor the development.

- **Outsourcer may have experience of developing similar systems**
  Providing a central database with remote access and Extranet access is likely to be a relatively specialised task. However, the outsourcing company may be able to provide relevant experience in this area, which the IT staff at Gort will not have.

Drawbacks

The drawbacks of outsourcing may include the following:

- **Lack of understanding of business objectives**
  The outsourcing company are likely to focus on implementing the IT system. They may not understand fully the business objectives of Gort and so the system may lack some of the required functionality. Care will be required in defining the systems specification to ensure it meets the requirements of Gort.

- **Loss of confidentiality, which could be a source of competitive advantage**
  Provision of an enhanced service to customers may provide Gort with some competitive advantage. The outsourcing company will need to sign appropriate confidentiality agreements to ensure that loss of confidentiality does not happen.

- **Ransom hold of particular supplier for maintenance and upgrades**
  Given that Gort does not have the expertise in-house to implement the system, the outsourcing company will also be required to maintain the system for Gort. This could give rise to increased costs. Details of expected maintenance and service costs for say five years should also be included in the original quote for the system.

Introduction to Operations Management

Chapter learning objectives

Lead	Component
C1. Explain the relationship of operations management to other aspects of the organisation's operations.	(b) Explain the relationship of operations and supply management to the competitiveness of the firm.
	(c) Explain the particular issues surrounding operations management in services.
	(d) Explain the importance of sustainability in operations management.
C2. Apply tools and techniques of operations management.	(e) Describe ways to manage relationships with suppliers.

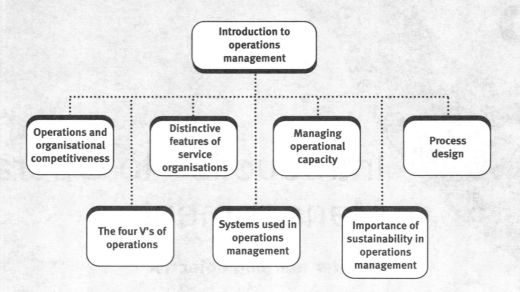

1 Introduction

During the eighteenth century the UK experienced dramatic change through what became known as the industrial revolution. It was during this period that the economy was transformed from agricultural to industrial and population migrated to towns from the countryside.

F.W.**Taylor** and others developed work measurement and applied 'scientific' methods to production from the 1890s onwards. These studies clearly show that the productivity of organisations depended both on the technology available and how key resources were managed. 'Good' management constituted an application of knowledge and skills of a 'scientific' nature, rather than intuition and guesswork. This thinking laid the foundation for the study of an area later referred to as **operations management**. At its simplest, operations management tries to ensure that organisations are run as efficiently as possible.

Definitions

Operations – this involves the transformation of inputs to outputs in order to add value.

Many of the principles of operations management were developed in a manufacturing context but later adopted by service organisation.

Operations management – refers to the activities required to produce and deliver a product or a service. It includes purchasing, warehousing and transportation.

 Operations strategy – as with other aspects of running a business, there is a strategic context to operations management. An organisation can achieve significant competitive advantage over its rivals through superior operating capabilities of its resources, e.g. assets, workforce skills, supplier relationships.

World class manufacturing

World class manufacturing is concerned with achieving significant improvements in quality, lead times, flexibility and customer satisfaction. Core features include:

- a strong customer focus

- a flexible approach to responding to customer needs.

Test your understanding 1

The O Company, founded in the early 1970s, manufactures electric pumps.

Required:

Describe the key activities in the operations function of an organisation such as O Company.

2 Operations and Organisational Competitiveness

2.1 Mintzberg's effective organisation

Mintzberg suggested that an organisation is made up of five parts. It is important that an organisation considers the relative balance of these elements in order to achieve their organisational goals and secure optimal competitiveness.

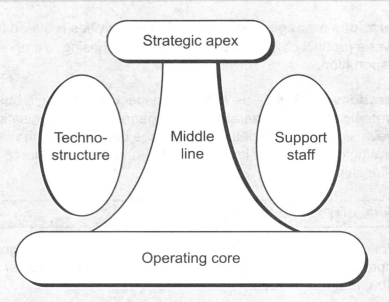

Operating core

Refers to those individuals who perform the task of producing the product or providing the service. In a small organisation this will represent nearly all of the organisation, but larger organisations will require more complex arrangements.

Strategic apex

Those individuals who formulate and implement strategy in order to serve the owners of the organisation.

Middle line

The hierarchy of authority from strategic apex to front line supervisors. Links the strategic apex to the operating core.

Technostructure

Concerned with co-ordinating the work by standardising processes, outputs and skills. Includes human resource (HR) managers and accountants.

Support staff

Provide assistance outside of operational workflow such as catering services, legal advice and press relations.

Test your understanding 2

Many organisations are now actively seeking flatter hierarchies, better quality and ways contracting out of non-core activities.

Required:

Briefly discuss the implications of this on Mintzberg's organisation.

2.2 Porter's value chain

Infrastructure					
Human Resource Management					
Technology					
Procurement					Margin
Inbound logistics	Operations	Outbound logistics	Marketing and sales	After Sales Service	

Porter developed his value chain to determine whether and how a firm's activities contribute towards its competitive advantage.

"Margin" looks at the difference between the cost of activities and their value. This helps the firm to determine whether or not best value products or services are developed.

The approach involves breaking the firm down into five 'primary' and four 'support' activities, and then looking at each to see if they give a cost advantage or a quality advantage.

'Primary' activities – directly concerned with the creation or delivery of a product/service.

Activity	Description	Example
Inbound logistics	Receiving, storing and handling raw material inputs.	A just-in-time stock system could give a cost advantage (see chapter 7).
Operations	Transformation of raw materials into finished goods and services.	Using skilled employees could give a quality advantage.
Outbound logistics	Storing, distributing and delivering finished goods and services.	Outsourcing activities could give a cost advantage
Marketing and sales	The mechanism by which the customer is made aware of the product or service.	Sponsorship of a sports celebrity could enhance the image of a product.
After sales service	All activities that occur after the point of sale, such as customer enquiries, returns and repairs/maintenance.	Marks and Spencer's friendly approach to returns gives it a perceived quality advantage.

Operations management is concerned with all of these primary activities apart from marketing and sales.

'Support' activities – helps improve the efficiency and effectiveness of the primary activities.

Activity	Description	Example
Infrastructure	How the firm is organised.	A firm could have a very "lean" structure at head office in contrast to competitors with more staff and more bureaucracy.
Human resource management	How people contribute to competitive advantage. Includes activities such as recruitment, selection, training and development and reward policies.	Employing expert buyers could enable a supermarket to purchase better wines than competitors.

Technology	How the firm uses technology.	The latest computer-controlled machinery gives greater flexibility to tailor products to customer specifications.
Procurement	Purchasing, but not just limited to materials.	Buying a building out of town could give a cost advantage over High Street competitors.

Operations management is directly concerned with procurement and some elements of firm infrastructure and technology development.

Illustration 1 – Value chain

Value chain analysis helps managers to decide how individual activities might be changed to reduce costs of operation or to improve the value of the organisation's offerings. Such changes will increase 'margin' – the residual value created by what customers pay minus the costs.

For example, a clothes manufacturer may spend large amounts on:

- Buying good quality raw materials (inbound logistics)
- Hand-finishing garments (operations)
- Building a successful brand image (marketing)
- Running its own fleet of delivery trucks in order to deliver finished clothes quickly to customers (outbound logistics).

All of these should add value to the product, allowing the company to charge a premium for its clothes.

Another clothes manufacturer may:

- Reduce the cost of its raw materials by buying in cheaper supplies from abroad (inbound logistics)
- Making all its clothes by machinery running 24 hours a day (operations)
- Delaying distribution until delivery trucks can be filled with garments for a particular request (outbound logistics).

All of these should allow the company to be able to gain economies of scale and be able to sell clothes at a cheaper price than its rivals.

The supply chain

More recently, organisations have started to consider supply chain partnerships. The **value system** looks at linking the value chains of suppliers and customers to that of the organisation. A firm's success depends not only on its own value chain, but on its ability to manage the value system of which it is a part.

A **supply chain network** is a group of organisations which relate to each other through the linkages between the different processes involved in producing the finished product.

- Traditionally, businesses within the supply chain operated independently.

- However, organisations are recognising that there are benefits associated with establishing links between the different companies in the supply chain.

- Co-ordination of the different firms within the supply chain should lead to better planned production and distribution which may cut costs and give a more attractive final product leading for increased sales and profit for all of the businesses involved.

- Competition is no longer on a company versus company basis but rather takes on a supply chain versus supply chain form.

- A **demand network** is the evolution of a supply chain network and involves the collaboration between buyers to influence what goods are supplied.

3 The Four Vs of Operations

Operations may vary according to:

- **v**olume

- **v**ariety

- **v**ariation

- **v**isibility.

Four Vs of operations

All operations involve a transformational process but they can differ in four different ways

Volume

Operations differ in the volume of inputs they process. High-volume operations are likely to be more capital-intensive than low-volume operations, and there is likely to be a greater specialisation of labour skills.

Variety

Some operations handle a wide range of different inputs, or produce a wide range of output products or services. Others are much more restricted in the range of inputs they handle or outputs they produce.

Variation in demand

With some operations, demand might vary significantly from one season of the year to another, or from one time of the day to another, with some periods of peak demand and some periods of low demand. Other operations might handle a fairly constant volume of demand at all times.

Visibility

Visibility refers to the extent to which an organisation is visible to its customers. When an operation is highly visible, the employees will have to show good communication skills and interpersonal skills in dealing with customers.

4 Distinctive Features of Service Organisations

The approaches to operations management discussed in this chapter have been most widely applied in manufacturing firms.

However, modern advanced economies are now dominated by service organisations and future economic growth also depends heavily on this sector. These service organisations may try to embrace the management philosophies and techniques that have proven successful in other sectors.

Service industries have certain distinguishing features that should be considered:

- Services are **intangible** and it is more difficult to measure their quality than it is for a physical product.
- Services are consumed immediately and **cannot be stored**.
- **Customers participate directly in the delivery process** (in contrast to a manufacturing organisation where production and purchase are usually physically separated).
- The customer when evaluating the quality of the service will take into account the **face-to-face contact** and the social skills of those providing the service.
- Service organisations tend to be **more labour intensive**.

> **Test your understanding 3**
>
> Identify a service that you use and analyse the way in which it has altered over the past ten years.

5 Systems Used in Operations management

A number of manufacturing systems have been developed in an attempt to improve the planning and control of operational capability.

5.1 Material requirements planning (MRP)

MRP is a computerised system for planning the requirements for raw materials, work-in-progress and finished items.

Functions include:

- Identifying firm orders and forecasting future orders with confidence.
- Using orders to determine quantities of material required.
- Determining the timing of material requirement.
- Calculating purchase orders based on stock levels.
- Automatically placing purchase orders.
- Scheduling materials for future production.

Benefits of MRP

- Improved forecasting.

- Improved ability to meet orders leading to increased customer satisfaction.

- Reduced stock holding.

- The MRP schedule can be amended quickly if demand estimates change since the system is computerised.

- System can warn of purchasing or production problems due to bottlenecks or delays in the supply chain.

- A close relationship tends to be built with suppliers (it is consistent with just-in-time – see chapter 7).

However, MRP will not be suitable if it is not possible to predict sales in advance.

5.2 Manufacturing resource planning II (MRP II)

MRP II is an extension of the MRP system. It integrates into the MRP system other processes that are related to materials planning. For example:

- Financial requirements planning.

- Equipment utilisation scheduling.

- Labour scheduling – particularly important for service operations

MRP II provides a central database that all functions will have access to, thus everyone is working from the same information.

5.3 Enterprise resource planning (ERP)

ERP is an extension of MRP II. It integrates all aspects of the business, including planning, manufacturing and sales.

- As with MRP II it ensures that everyone is working off the same information.

- Software companies like SAP and Oracle have specialised in the provision of ERP systems across many different industries and types of operation, including both production and service types.

Features of ERP systems

Features of ERP systems include:

- Allowing access to the system to any individual with a terminal linked to the system's central server.

- Decision support features, to assist management with decision-making.

- In many cases, extranet links to the major suppliers and customers, with electronic data interchange facilities for the automated transmission of documentation such as purchase orders and invoices.

Pros and cons of ERP

Advantages

- Can easily share data between departments and across the organisation.

- Better monitoring and forecasting.

- Lower costs.

- Improved customer service.

- Processes can be streamlined.

Disadvantages

- Cost may be prohibitive.

- May be too rigid to fulfil the needs of the organisation.

- Technical support may be inadequate.

5.4 Optimised production technology (OPT)

Optimised production technology (OPT) is a production improvement method based on bottleneck improvements. It concentrates on constraints and seeks to identify and then remove bottlenecks that hinder the flow of a system.

5.5 Just-in-time (JIT) system

Most inventory management systems assume that it is necessary to hold some inventory. An alternative view is that inventory is wasteful and adds no value to operations.

Just-in-time (JIT) is a system whose objective it is to produce or procure products or components as they are required by the customer or for use, rather than for inventory. This means that inventory levels of raw materials, work-in-progress and finished goods can be kept to a minimum.

JIT applies to both production within an organisation and to purchasing from external suppliers:

JIT purchasing is a method of purchasing that involves ordering materials only when customers place an order. When the goods are received, they go straight into production.

JIT production is a production system that is driven by demand for the finished products (a 'pull' system), whereby each component on a production line is produced only when needed for the next stage.

Illustration 2

Toyota pioneered the JIT manufacturing system, in which suppliers send parts daily – or several times a day – and are notified electronically when the assembly line is running out.

More than 400 trucks a day come in and out of Toyota's Georgetown plant in the USA, with a separate logistics company organising the shipment from Toyota's 300 suppliers – most located in neighbouring states within half a day's drive of the plant.

Toyota aims to build long-term relationships with its suppliers, many of whom it has a stake in, and says it now produces 80% of its parts within North America.

Requirements for successful operation of a JIT system

- **High quality and reliability** – disruptions create hold ups in the entire system and must be avoided. The emphasis is on getting the work 'right first time':
    - Highly skilled and well trained staff should be used.
    - Machinery must be fully maintained.
    - Long-term links should be established with suppliers in order to ensure a reliable and high quality service.

- **Elimination of non-value added activities** – value is only being added whilst a product is being processed. For example, value is not added whilst storing the products and therefore inventory levels should be minimised.

- **Speed of throughput** – the speed of production should match the rate at which customers demand the product. Production runs should be shorter with smaller stocks of finished goods.

- **Flexibility** – a flexible production system is needed in order to be able to respond immediately to customer orders:
  - The system should be capable of switching from making one product to making another.

  - The workforce should be dedicated and have the appropriate skills. JIT is an organisational culture and the concept should be adopted by everyone.

  - Management should allow the work teams to use their initiative and to deal with problems as they arise.

- **Lower costs** – another objective of JIT is to reduce costs by:
  - Raising quality and eliminating waste.

  - Achieving faster throughput.

  - Minimising inventory levels.

Illustration 3

The Impact of JIT

- Under JIT, a buyer can reduce the number of suppliers. GM, the US car manufacturer, reduced their suppliers by 50%.

- Westinghouse Electric Company has reduced their inventories by 45% and plant stockouts by 95%.

- The pharmaceutical company, Warner-Lambert has replaced its costly batch production by a JIT-based controlled process. Suppliers are also chosen because of close proximity to the plant. Long-term contracts and single sourcing is advocated to strengthen buyer-supplier relationships and tends to result in a higher quality product. Inventory problems are shifted back onto suppliers, with deliveries being as required.

- The luxury car manufacturer, Jaguar, when it analysed the cause of its customer complaints, compiled a list of 150 areas of faults. Some 60% of them turned out to be faulty components from suppliers. One month the company returned 22,000 different components to suppliers. Suppliers were brought on to the multi-disciplinary task forces the company established to tackle each of the common faults, establishing and testing a cure and implementing it as quickly as possible. Jaguar directors chaired the task force of the 12 most serious faults, but in one case the task force was chaired by the supplier's representative.

Test your understanding 4

Explain the advantages and disadvantages to an organisation of operating a JIT system.

Supplier relationships and JIT

As mentioned previously, many of the steps taken to improve the supply chain (and hence profitability) involve improving the relationship between the manufacturer and its suppliers.

This will be of particular importance in a company operating a JIT system.

The advantages to a JIT company of developing close supplier relationships are as follows:

- **No rejects/ returns** – a strong relationship should help to improve the quality of supplies. This should minimise production delays since there will be less inspection, fewer returns and less reworking of goods.

- **On-time deliveries** – the development of close working relationships should help to guarantee on-time deliveries of supplies.

- **Low inventory** – suppliers can be relied upon for frequent deliveries of small quantities of material to the company, ensuring that each delivery is just enough to meet the immediate production schedule.

- **Close proximity** – the supplier/ portfolio of suppliers will be located close to the manufacturing plant. This will reduce delivery times and costs.

Test your understanding 5

What is the main principle difference between MRP and JIT?

6 Managing Operational Capacity

6.1 Capacity planning

Capacity planning aims to balance customer demand with production capability. There are three possible approaches to capacity planning:

- Level capacity plan – maintains production activity at a constant rate. A simple approach but can result in a build up of inventory or in stock outs.

- Chase demand plan – matches production with demand. Will require a flexible approach to production and a good forecasting system.

- Demand management planning – attempts to influence demand to smooth variations above or below capacity e.g. supermarkets may offer discounted ice-cream during the winter period in order to keep demand stable.

Illustration 4 – Capacity planning at Ikea

In reality, most organisations combine several approaches when managing capacity. For example, the world's largest furniture retailer, Ikea:

- has large warehouses containing goods that have yet to be ordered

- extended opening times over the Christmas period to cater for an increase in demand

- uses price cutting in order to shift products that have gone out of fashion.

6.2 Systems used to manage operational capacity

There are a number of systems used to improve operational efficiency:

Computer-aided design (CAD) and computer-aided manufacturing (CAM)

CAD and CAM can help the organisation to:

- provide flexibility to meet customer requirements more fully

- eliminate mistakes

- reduce material wastage.

Computer-integrated manufacturing (CIM)

Integrates CAD and CAM. CIM directs data flow and the processing and movement of material.

Flexible manufacturing systems (FMS)

A **FMS** is a highly automated manufacturing system, which is computer controlled and is capable of producing a large number of parts in a flexible manner.

The main benefit is that dedicated output can be produced quickly in response to specific orders, giving a high level of customer focus and responsiveness.

The main features include:

- The ability to change quickly from one job to another.
- Fast response times.
- Small batch production.

The main disadvantage of a FMS is that there is a cost to the enhanced flexibility. Traditional production lines are very efficient at making single products cheaply and benefit from economies of scale and specialisation. However, developments in IT/IS have closed the gap in costs between the two approaches, making FMS more feasible.

6.3 Queuing theory

Queuing theory is a technique designed to optimise the balance between customer waiting time and idle service capacity.

- It applies in situations where obvious queues form, e.g. shops and bus stops, but it is also applicable in other areas, e.g. call centres, planes that circle before they land and in computing, where web servers and print servers are now common.

- Queuing theory concludes that throughput improves and customer satisfaction increases if one long queue is used instead of separate lines.

- The frustrations of getting in a 'slow line' are removed because one slow transaction does not affect the throughput of the remaining customers.

- Many banks, airport check-ins and large post offices have implemented this system.

7 The Importance of Sustainability in Operations Management

7.1 Introduction

- Companies are beginning to consider how their operations affect the environment and future generations.

- Sustainable development is about meeting the needs of the present without compromising the ability of future generations to meet their own needs.

- It is the practice of doing business in a way that balances economic, environmental and social needs.

7.2 How sustainability impacts operations management

Process design

The process should be designed to minimise waste, reduce energy use and reduce carbon emissions.

Product design

The product design should consider factors such as:

- Use of recycled inputs.

- Use of sustainable inputs.

- Ability to recycle product or dispose of it safely.

- Minimising wastage, e.g. unnecessary packaging.

Supply chain management

- **Purchasing**: Only products from a sustainable and ethical source should be purchased, e.g. a furniture manufacturer may purchase timber from sustainable forests only.

- **Supplier selection**: One of the key criteria to use when choosing between suppliers should be their adoption of sustainable development policies.

- **Location**: The distance between the supplier and the company should be minimised.

Quality management

Higher quality should help to improve efficiency and reduce waste.

Test your understanding 6

Explain the potential benefits of sustainability to a firm.

8 Process Design

Process design is the method by which individual specialists seek to understand business activities and ensure that these activities are designed to be as efficient and effective as possible. The design of processes will go hand in hand with the design of new products and services.

Processes may be improved through the operation of methods such as:

- TQM
- Kaizen
- BPR
- Benchmarking
- the use of process maps
- and improvements in supply chain management.

Some of these methods are discussed in more detail in Chapters 7 and 8.

Product and service development

Companies need to continually look for new or improved products or services, to achieve or maintain competitive advantage in their market.

Operations managers are not responsible for product/ service design but will offer advice and assistance in the process.

The stages of product/service development are as follows:

Stage 1: Consider customers' needs

The product/service should satisfy the needs of the customer, e.g. value for money, high quality, cutting edge design.

Stage 2: Concept screening

The new product/service concept should be vetted. It will only pass through to the design and development process if it meets certain criteria. For example, does the company think that the new product/ service will be profitable?

Stage 3: The design process

This may include procedures such as:

- Building a physical prototype or a virtual prototype (using computer aided design).
- Value engineering, i.e. ensuring that all components/ features add value.

Stage 4: Time-to-market

A short time-to-market is desirable since:

- New product/service may be released ahead of competitors.
- Developments costs may be lower.

Stage 5: Product testing

The new product should be tested before it is released to the market:

- Does it work properly?
- Do customers like it?

9 Chapter summary

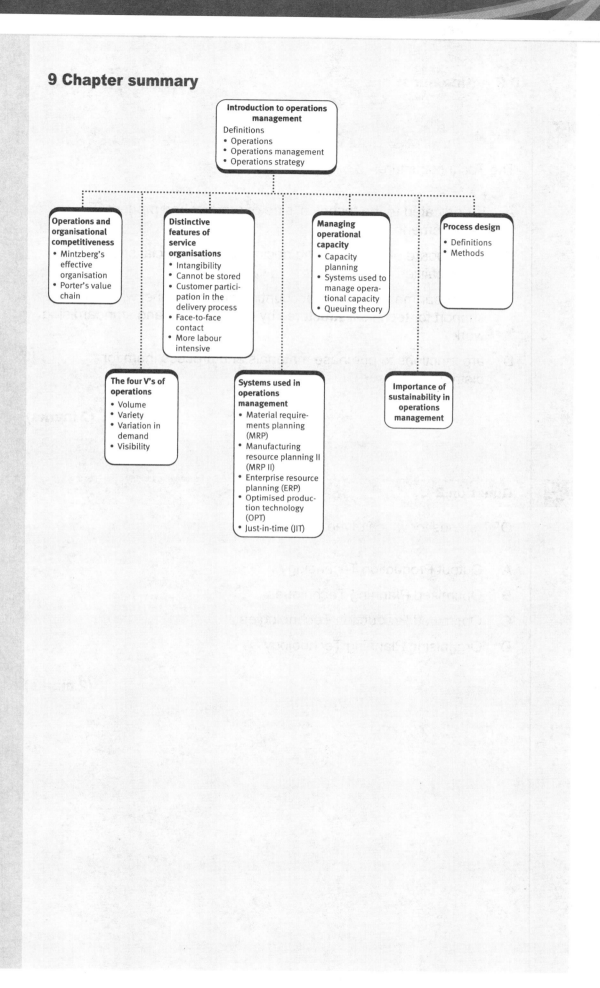

Introduction to operations management

Definitions
- Operations
- Operations management
- Operations strategy

Operations and organisational competitiveness
- Mintzberg's effective organisation
- Porter's value chain

Distinctive features of service organisations
- Intangibility
- Cannot be stored
- Customer participation in the delivery process
- Face-to-face contact
- More labour intensive

Managing operational capacity
- Capacity planning
- Systems used to manage operational capacity
- Queuing theory

Process design
- Definitions
- Methods

The four V's of operations
- Volume
- Variety
- Variation in demand
- Visibility

Systems used in operations management
- Material requirements planning (MRP)
- Manufacturing resource planning II (MRP II)
- Enterprise resource planning (ERP)
- Optimised production technology (OPT)
- Just-in-time (JIT)

Importance of sustainability in operations management

10 Practice questions

Question 1

The Technostructure:

A   is dedicated to the technical side of product and process development

B   is the board of directors who decide on the financial structure and technicalities of a business

C   are departments such as accounting and personnel which provide support for technical structures by co-ordinating and standardising work

D   are functions to purchase materials and process them for distribution

(2 marks)

Question 2

OPT stands for which of the following?

A   Output Production Technology

B   Optimised Planning Techniques

C   Optimised Production Technologies

D   Organising Planning Technology

(2 marks)

Question 3

Which of the following is a value-added activity?

A   Painting a car, if the organisation manufactures cars

B   The board of directors who decide on the financial structure and technicalities of a business

C   Storing materials

D   Repairing faulty production work

(2 marks)

Question 4

Which of the following is an advantage of a flexible manufacturing system?

A   A firm can make bespoke products in response to differing customer needs

B   The system allows management to identify and remove constraints within the system

C   The number of employees can be increased or reduced to fit with existing needs

D   It integrates data from all operations within an organisation

(2 marks)

Question 5

MRP II:

A   integrates data from all operations within an organisation

B   schedules production based on the capacity of the bottleneck

C   is a computerised system for planning the requirements of material

D   is a system that integrates all processes relating to materials planning

(2 marks)

Question 6

What is the first stage in product development?

A   Product design

B   Investigating the product offerings of competitors

C   Considering customers' needs

D   Investigating ways to reduce the time-to-market

(2 marks)

Question 7

Which of the following is not an example of a 'support activity' as described in Porter's Value Chain?

A   Technology development

B   Human resource management

C   Procurement

D   Firm structure

(2 marks)

Question 8

Explain the relationship between a JIT (Just-in-Time) system and cash flow management.

(4 marks)

Question 9

Explain, using examples, the meaning of JIT (Just-In-Time) purchasing and JIT production.

(4 marks)

Question 10

Distinguish strategic decisions from tactical decisions in the context of operations management.

(4 marks)

Question 11

Explain why it might be necessary to involve suppliers in a new product design and development process.

(4 marks)

Question 12

Explain the importance of sustainability in operations.

(4 marks)

Question 13

Woodsy is a garden furniture manufacturing company, which employs 30 people. It buys its timber in uncut form from a local timber merchant, and stores the timber in a covered area to dry out and season before use. Often this takes up to two years, and the wood yard takes up so much space that the production area is restricted.

The product range offered by the company is limited to the manufacture of garden seats and tables because the owner-manager, Bill Thompson, has expanded the business by concentrating on the sale of these items and has given little thought to alternative products. Bill is more of a craftsman than a manager, and the manufacturing area is anything but streamlined. Employees work on individual units at their own pace, using little more than a circular saw and a mallet and wooden pegs to assemble the finished product. The quality of the finished items is generally good but relatively expensive because of the production methods employed.

Marketing has, to date, been felt to be unnecessary because the premises stand on a busy road intersection and the company's products are on permanent display to passing traffic. Also, satisfied customers have passed on their recommendations to new customers. But things have changed. New competitors have entered the marketplace and Bill has found that orders are falling off. Competitors offer a much wider range of garden furniture and Bill is aware that he may need to increase his product range, in order to compete. As the owner-manager, Bill is always very busy and, despite working long hours, finds that there is never enough time in the day to attend to everything. His foreman is a worthy individual but, like Bill, is a craftsman and not very good at man-management. The overall effect is that the workmen are left very much to their own devices. As they are paid by the hour rather than by the piece, they have little incentive to drive themselves very hard.

Required:

(a) Explain what is meant by the terms 'value chain' and 'value chain analysis'?

(5 marks)

(b) Use a diagram to give a brief explanation of the two different categories of activities that Porter describes.

(5 marks)

(c) Analyse the activities in the value chain to identify the key problems facing Woodsy.

(5 marks)

(d) Based on your analysis, prepare a set of recommendations for Bill Thompson to assist in a more efficient and effective operation of his business

(5 marks)

(e)   Describe the stages in the development of new garden furniture.

(5 marks)

(f)   Explain the different aspects of design that Bill Thompson can consider for his garden furniture.

(5 marks)

(Total: 30 marks)

Test your understanding answers

Test your understanding 1

The operations function in manufacturing electric pumps is concerned with converting raw materials into a finished product and delivering them to the customer. Operations therefore covers the following areas:

- **Purchasing**. The purchasing department are responsible for obtaining raw materials and parts from suppliers.

- **Production**. The production function converts the raw materials and assembles parts and components into finished products. Without more information about the nature of the pumps that the company produces, it is not possible to suggest what type of production process the company uses.

- **Production planning and control**. This function is concerned with scheduling production, and making sure that the materials, labour, machinery and other resources are available to manufacture the pumps. Production control involves monitoring production flow and dealing with any problems, hold-ups and bottlenecks that might arise.

- **Product design or engineering**. There will probably also be a separate section within operations that provides technical expertise. These experts might be responsible for new product design.

- **Inventory management**. Raw materials and finished goods inventory must be stored or warehoused.

- **Logistics**. Manufactured pumps must be distributed to customers. The customers for pumps will be industrial buyers, and the task of delivering them will probably be included within the operations function.

Test your understanding 2

A clearer focus on the core activity and hence further importance attached to operations management.

Test your understanding 3

You may have identified factors such as:

- being less labour intensive
- more extensive use of IT
- being more centralised and global
- communication via the Internet
- trading via the Internet
- other online services.

A service such as banking is a good example.

Test your understanding 4

Advantages of JIT

- Lower stock holding costs means a reduction in storage space which saves rent and insurance costs.
- As stock is only obtained when it is needed, less working capital is tied up in stock.
- There is less likelihood of stock perishing, becoming obsolete or out of date.
- Avoids the build-up of unsold finished products that can occur with sudden changes in demand.
- Less time is spent checking and re-working the products as the emphasis is on getting the work right first time.

The result is that costs should fall and quality should increase. This should improve the company's competitive advantage.

Disadvantages of JIT

- There is little room for mistakes as little stock is kept for re-working a faulty product.

- Production is very reliant on suppliers and if stock is not delivered on time or is not of a high enough quality, the whole production schedule can be delayed.

- There is no spare finished product available to meet unexpected orders, because all products are made to meet actual orders.

- It may be difficult for managers to empower employees to embrace the concept and culture.

- It won't be suitable for all companies. For example, supermarkets must have a supply of inventory.

- It can be difficult to apply to the service industry. However, in the service industry a JIT approach may focus on eliminating queues, which are wasteful of customers' time.

Test your understanding 5

JIT is a pull-based system which responds to customer demand. In contrast, MRP is a push-based system which tends to use stock as buffers between the different elements of the system such as purchasing, production and sales.

Test your understanding 6

Sustainability may result in a number of benefits to the firm:

Improved operational efficiency

Practices associated with sustainability include reducing waste, improved energy and water consumption and the sale of by-products that were previously a cost of disposal. These practices will contribute to improved long-term performance.

External stakeholder support

Sustainable development should help the company to portray a positive image and can result in enhanced relationships with external stakeholders, e.g. the local community may view the operations more positively if sustainable practices are used.

Internal stakeholder support

Sustainability can enhance relationships with the organisation's workforce. The organisation may use its sustainability policy as a tool for attracting and retaining the best employees. Employee motivation may increase if employees are involved in sustainability discussions and a positive culture should be shaped.

Source of competitive advantage

Sustainability may result in competitive advantage if:

- new business opportunities are exploited
- market share increases due to customers' needs being met and brand loyalty increasing.

Required by legislation

Legislation/regulation has increased in recent years and has resulted in many companies implementing policies for sustainable development. For example, three new pieces of legislation were introduced in the UK in 2008; the Climate Change Act, the Energy Act and the Planning Act.

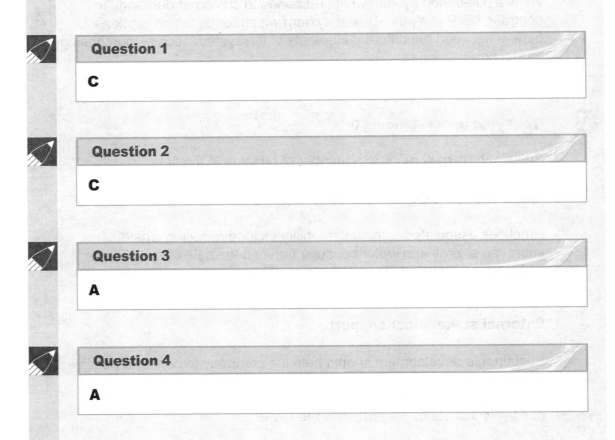

Question 1

C

Question 2

C

Question 3

A

Question 4

A

Question 5

D

Question 6

C

Question 7

D

Question 8

A Just-in-Time (JIT) system involves purchasing items from suppliers and the production of items only when they are needed to meet demand. A consequence of JIT should be a reduction in inventories of raw materials and components, and finished goods. Expenditure will therefore be incurred later than in a traditional operating environment and the 'cash cycle' should be shorter. This is the time between paying for expenses and receiving payments from customers. As a result, working capital should be lower and cash flows should improve.

Question 9

- **JIT purchasing** is a method of purchasing that involves ordering materials only when customers place an order. When the goods are received they go straight into production.

- For example, a customer may place an order for a new car. The materials required to make the car will only be ordered from the suppliers once a firm order is received from the customer.

- **JIT production** is a production system that is driven by demand for the finished products (a 'pull' system), whereby each component on a production line is produced only when needed for the next stage.

- For example, production of a new car will only begin when there is a firm order for the car.

Question 10

Strategy deals with how an organisation achieves its objectives. For example:

- Where is the business trying to get to in the long term (direction)?

- Which markets should a business compete in and what kind of activities are involved in such markets (markets; scope)?

- How can the business perform better than the competition in those markets (advantage)?

- What resources (skills, assets, finance, relationships, technical competence, facilities) are required in order to be able to compete (resources)?

- What external, environmental factors affect the business's ability to compete (environment)?

- What are the values and expectations of those who have power in and around the business (stakeholders)?

Tactics are the most efficient deployment of resources in an agreed strategy.

Tactics follow on from strategy.

Question 11

- It is probably not necessary to involve suppliers of standard raw materials or components.

- It might be necessary to check that the supplier is able to produce a part or component to the planned design specification.

- It might be necessary to discuss with the supplier how a part or component might be produced within a target cost limit.

- The supplier might be able to contribute ideas for improving the specification for the product.

Organisations might establish a long-term relationship with some key suppliers, and work together with those suppliers in new product design and development. The supply relationship is then a strategic relationship, with the organisation and the suppliers sharing common strategic business objectives.

Question 12

- It is important for a company to consider how their operations affect the environment and future generations.

- Sustainable development is about meeting the needs of the present without compromising the ability of future generations to meet their own needs.

- Sustainable development will not only benefit the environment but can also benefit the company:

  - The company can use sustainable development as a tool for attracting customers and the best employees.

  - Sustainable development can help the company to reduce costs, e.g. due to lower wastage.

  - Sustainable development can help the company to comply with legislation.

Question 13

(a) **'Value chain'** describes the full range of activities which are required to bring a product or service from conception, through the intermediary of production, delivery to final consumers, and final disposal after use. It is a way of looking at a business as a chain of activities that transform inputs into outputs that customers value. Customer value derives from three basic sources:

  - activities that differentiate the product

  - activities that lower its cost

  - activities that meet the customer's need quickly.

The value chain includes a profit margin since a mark-up above the cost of providing a firm's value-adding activities is normally part of the price paid by the buyer – creating value that exceeds cost so as to generate a return for the effort.

'Value chain analysis' views the organisation as a sequential process of value-creating activities, and attempts to understand how a business creates customer value by examining the contributions of different activities within the business to that value. Value activities are the physically and technologically distinct activities that an organisation performs. Value analysis recognises that an organisation is much more than a random collection of machinery, money and people. These resources are of no value unless they are organised into structures, routines and systems, which ensure that the products or services that are valued by the final consumer are the ones that are produced.

(b) Porter describes two different categories of activities.

Infrastructure					
Human Resource Management					
Technology					
Procurement					Margin
Inbound logistics	Operations	Outbound logistics	Marketing and sales	After Sales Service	

The primary activities, in the lower half of the value chain are grouped into five main areas:

- Inbound logistics are the activities concerned with receiving, storing and handling raw material inputs.

- Operations are concerned with the transformation of the raw material inputs into finished goods or services. The activities include assembly, testing, packing and equipment maintenance.

- Outbound logistics are concerned with the storing, distributing and delivering the finished goods to the customers.

- Marketing and sales are responsible for communication with the customers e.g. advertising, pricing and promotion.

- Service covers all of the activities that occur after the point of sale e.g. installation, repair and maintenance.

Alongside all of these primary activities are the secondary, or support, activities of procurement, technology development, human resource management and firm infrastructure. Each of these cuts across all of the primary activities, as in the case of procurement where at each stage items are acquired to aid the primary functions.

(c) The key problem areas are as follows:

- Inbound logistics – Woodsy has problems with the procurement of the raw materials, labour and machinery. The company is buying its raw materials two years in advance of using it. This must be tying up capital that could be used to purchase new machinery and tools. Storing the timber entails large amounts of money being tied up in stocks, which are prone to damage, restrict the production area and is very slow moving. The workmen are being paid by the hour rather than by the piece and this means that they have little incentive to work harder.

- Operations are concerned with the transformation of the raw material inputs into finished goods or services. At Woodsy, employees work at their own pace on the assembly of the garden seats and tables, using very basic tools. The production methods used make the finished product relatively expensive. The linkages between the support activities are also causing some problems. Both the owner and the foreman have no man-management skills. Technological development is non-existent and the company needs re-structuring.

- Outbound logistics are concerned with storing, distributing and delivering the finished goods to the customers. Woodsy does not seem to have a system for distributing and delivering its goods.

- Marketing and sales are responsible for communication with the customers e.g. advertising, pricing and promotion. This seems to be non-existent at Woodsy as, in the past, satisfied customers have passed on their recommendations to new customers. The company relies on its position on a busy road intersection to displays its products, for customers to carry away themselves.

(d) For Bill Thompson, the main task is to decide how individual activities might be changed to reduce costs of operation or to improve the value of the organisation's offerings. The recommendations would include the following:

- The business needs managing full-time. A new manager, or assistant manager, could encourage Bill to streamline the manufacturing process, introduce new technologies and new production and administrative systems. He or she could also negotiate new payment methods to give the workforce an incentive to work harder.

- To increase the production area, the alternative strategies that the company could explore include storing the timber elsewhere, or purchasing it after it has dried out and seasoned.

- Holding high levels of finished goods might give a faster customer response time but will probably add to the total cost of operations.

- The purchase of more expensive power tools and equipment may lead to cost savings and quality improvements in the manufacturing process.

- The company needs a marketing and sales department to research the market, inform the customers about the product, persuade them to buy it and enable them to do so. The product range may need to be extended and alternative outlets for the products sought.

(e) The development stages are as follows:

- Consider customers' needs – the new product should satisfy the needs of the customer. Bill must start by identifying these needs, e.g. value for money, high quality, cutting edge design or a wide product range.

- Concept screening – the new product should be vetted and will only pass through to the design and development stage if it meets certain criteria. For example, does Bill think that a new range of wooden sun loungers would be profitable?

- The design process – Bill may build a prototype and check that all the components add value.

- Time-to-market – Bill should minimise time-to-market in order to reduce development costs and increase competitiveness.

- Product testing – the product should be tested before it is released to the market. For example, do customers like the new sun lounger and does it work properly?

(f) The purpose of design is more than to improve the appearance of a product. It must also satisfy the customer in its performance, durability, simplicity of operation and cheapness. Bill Thompson can consider the following different aspects of design for his garden furniture:

- Design for function – value in use implies quality and reliability: the product must satisfy the customer in its purpose and give long service.

- Design for appearance – although products should please the eye to attract customers, the appeal of the product may not be solely visual. Other senses are also often involved and sometimes characteristics such as texture may predominate.

- Design for production – to ensure component parts are made easily and economically, so that they can be assembled and transported easily and sold at an attractive price.

- Design for distribution – to enable easy packing, reduction of storage space and packing costs.

The Supply Chain and Supply Networks

Chapter learning objectives

Lead	Component
C1. Explain the relationship of operations management to other aspects of the organisation's operations.	(a) Explain the shift from price-based to relational procurement and operations. (b) Explain the relationship of operations and supply management to the competitiveness of the firm.
C2. Apply tools and techniques of operations management.	(b) Explain process design. (e) Describe ways to manage relationships with suppliers.

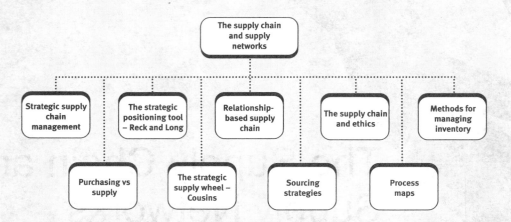

1 Introduction

The supply chain includes the entire process from extracting raw materials to delivering the finished product to the end customer. The supply chain will involve a number of separate companies that will all play a part in satisfying the needs of the end customer.

A **virtual supply chain** is a supply chain that is enabled through e-business links, e.g. the internet.

2 Strategic Supply Chain Management

Supply chain management is the management of all the activities aimed at satisfying the end customer in a way that maximises the effectiveness of the process.

Supply chain management has a strategic role within the organisation and can help the company to achieve competitive advantage.

Supply chain management
Supply chain management has three themes: • **Responsiveness** – firms must be able to supply customers quickly (this has led to systems such as JIT). • **Reliability** – deliveries must be reliable. • **Relationships** – members of the supply chain should develop a mutual understanding and trust through the development of collaborative relationships.

3 Purchasing vs Supply

Purchasing:

- concentrates on the day to day buying of goods
- emphasis is on the price, quality and accurate delivery of goods
- may be viewed as an out of date approach to supply chain management.

Supply – a more modern approach dealing with important issues beyond the day to day including:

- planning and implementing a supply strategy
- managing the overall supply process
- considering the appropriateness of outsourcing arrangements
- investigating whether strategic partnerships could be developed
- the number of suppliers it should use.

The key distinction is that supply is a strategic issue for firms. It is a vital means of gaining competitive advantage, especially considering most manufacturing firms spend more than 60% of their expenditure of purchasing goods and services.

4 The Strategic Positioning Tool – Reck and Long

The extent to which supply chain management is a strategic issue can be considered through **Reck and Long's** strategic positioning tool.

There are four stages of development that the purchasing function should pass through in order to attain a strategic status:

Stage 1 = The **passive** stage	• Purchasing is seen as an administrative task and attempts are made to get the best deal.
	• Purchasing has no strategic direction and passively reacts to requests from other departments.
Stage 2 = The **independent** stage	• Involves a more professional approach to purchasing, using the latest purchasing practices and technology.
	• Strategic direction is still independent from corporate strategy.
	• Emphasis is on price negotiations.

Stage 3 = The **supportive** stage	• Greater awareness that purchasing can affect the firm's strategic goals. The function supports the organisation's competitive strategy.
	• Emphasis is on better co-ordination between departments involving timely communication about changes in price and availability of materials.
Stage 4 = The **integrative** stage	• Purchasing is seen as a key part of strategic planning and is integral to the organisation's competitive strategy.
	• The emphasis is on developing relationships with suppliers, who are seen as vital partners.

5 The Strategic Supply Wheel – Cousins

Cousins' strategic supply wheel depicts the corporate supply strategy at the hub of the wheel and underlines the need for an integrated approach to supply strategy involving a balancing of all of the spokes of the wheel.

The model is useful for organisations that want to move to move away from 'purchasing' their goods to developing an organisational-wide supply strategy.

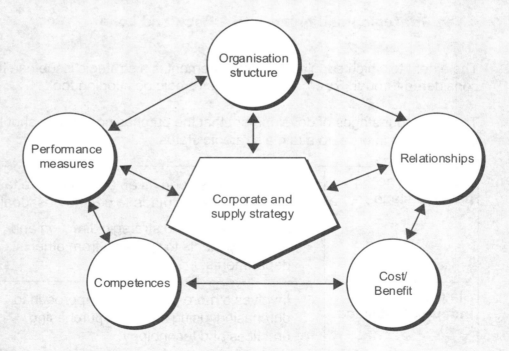

Spoke of wheel	Explanation
Organisation structure	The choice of structure (centralised, decentralised or a mix of these) impacts control and interaction. It should enhance rather than hinder supply strategy.
Relationships with suppliers	Relationships can be: • opportunistic/competitive – based on price deals, or • collaborative – a more positive relationship based on a joint quest to reduce costs and/or improve quality.
Cost/benefit	The cost of the strategic approach chosen must be less than the benefit. Cost/benefit analysis should be at the heart of any strategic decision.
Competences	Do the skills exist to achieve the strategy? For example, the development of long term supplier relations may require staff training.
Performance measures	Necessary for monitoring and controlling the strategy chosen. Measures should extend beyond price and should be aligned with the strategy.

Relationships

Cousins' strategic supply wheel depicts the corporate supply strategy at the hub of the wheel since the purchasing director should set goals and policies that are connected to those of the overall firm. For example:

- A firm that is cost focused will expect supply activity to deliver savings. Opportunistic relationships with suppliers will help to achieve short-term price reductions. The firm will not be interested in forming close working relationships with suppliers or implementing complex sourcing strategies.

- A firm that is differentiation focused, e.g. differentiates itself on quality or design, will review supply as strategic to their business. The firm will form close, collaborative relationships with suppliers.

6 Relationship-based Supply Chains

As mentioned in the previous section, Cousins identified two broad approaches to supplier relationships; competitive (also known as opportunistic) and collaborative.

Competitive (opportunistic)

In the past the supply chain was typically defined by competitive relationships.

- The purchasing function sought out the lowest-price suppliers, often through a process of tendering, the use of 'power' and the constant switching of supply sources to prevent getting too close to any individual source.

- Supplier contracts featured heavy penalty clauses and were drawn up in a spirit of general mistrust of all external providers.

- The knowledge and skills of the supplier could not be exploited effectively: information was deliberately withheld in case the supplier used it to gain power during price negotiations.

Hence, no single supplier ever knew enough about the ultimate customer to suggest ways of improving the cost-effectiveness and quality of the trading relationship.

Collaborative

It is now recognised that successful management of suppliers is based upon collaboration and offers benefits to an organisation's suppliers as well as to the organisation itself. By working together organisations can make a much better job of satisfying the requirements of their end market, and thus both can increase their market share.

- Organisations seek to enter into partnerships with key customers and suppliers so as to better understand how to provide value and customer service.

- Organisations' product design processes include discussions that involve both customers and suppliers. By opening up design departments and supply problems to selected suppliers, a synergy results, generating new ideas, solutions, and new innovative products.

- To enhance the nature of collaboration, the organisation may reward suppliers with long-term sole sourcing agreements in return for a greater level of support to the business and a commitment to on-going improvements of materials, deliveries and relationships.

7 Sourcing Strategies

Sourcing strategies refer to the way an organisation organises its supply process and these have strategic implications.

There are four main sourcing strategies available:

Strategy	Explanation
Single sourcing	The organisation chooses one source of supply.
Multiple sourcing	The organisation chooses several sources of supply.
Delegated sourcing	The organisation chooses one supplier (1st tier). This supplier then co-ordinates and works with other suppliers (2nd tier) to ensure the supply requirements are fulfilled.
Parallel sourcing	The organisation uses a mix of the three approaches

Test your understanding 1

State the advantages and disadvantages of:

(i)   Single sourcing

(ii) Multiple sourcing

(iii) Delegated sourcing

(iv) Parallel sourcing

Kyoryoku kai

In most countries, suppliers' associations are organised and run by the suppliers themselves. In Japan, there are supplier associations known as kyoryoku kai, which are organised by a major buyer/customer in the industry. For example, an association of suppliers in the automotive industry might be set up and organised by a major car manufacturer. The first such association was set up by Toyota in 1943. Its original purpose was to provide an assurance of business to suppliers who were suffering from the consequences of the war effort in Japan. Over time, the main focus of interest in these supplier associations has been:

- Improving quality
- Reducing costs by means of efficiency improvements throughout the industry
- Health and safety standards.

The benefit of having a supplier association organised by a major buyer is that the buyer is able to exert strong influence over its suppliers, and encourage the open exchange of ideas and information between suppliers.

8 The Supply Chain and Ethics

Organisations need to be aware of how effective supply chain ethics can help them to avoid costly product recalls and brand damage that results from an unethical supply chain decision.

Illustration 1 – Primark and ethics

Primark is an exciting, growing brand that provides consumers with value-for-money fashion items. The company has an effective supply chain bringing together manufacturing units in China, India, Turkey, Bangladesh and other countries, with retail outlets in Ireland, the UK and other parts of Europe.

A key principle of Primark's business practice is to make sure that it provides its consumers with value-for-money garments, whilst maintaining ethical manufacturing standards. This involves paying for independent audits of all its factories and working with suppliers to address issues in a sustainable manner.

By working with external agencies such as the Ethical Trading Initiative (ETI) and independent auditors, Primark helps to set and maintain standards. Its auditors work with suppliers over a period of time to help them meet the exacting standards set out by the ETI. This enables the supplier to become approved. Primark sees this as a programme of continuous improvement.

By making its ethical trade process transparent, Primark aims to demonstrate its commitment to responsible manufacturing. This helps to assure its customers that the goods they are purchasing are not only fashionable and good value-for-money, but also that they are ethically produced by workers who are fairly treated.

9 Process Maps

The workforce spend between 20% and 40% of their time dealing with waste issues. These might involve an individual rectifying things which have either not been done or were done badly. To regain control and to drive out waste, management must first understand the basic processes. One straightforward way of getting this understanding is through the use of process maps.

Process maps can be used to visualise the flow of material and information as the product makes its way through the supply chain.

It builds a flowchart of the process being analysed in order to:

- Standardise the process
- Find areas of improvement, e.g. eliminate unnecessary steps or duplicated steps
- Assist understanding of the process due to the visual representation
- Link the supply chain strategy to the corporate strategy.
- Allow employees to understand what their job is and how it fits into the whole process.

Process maps may be used in the redesign of business processes, i.e. process design (this was discussed in Chapter 6).

Example of a process map

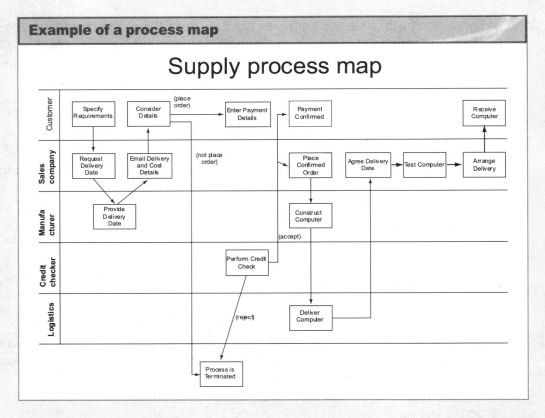

10 Methods for Managing Inventory

10.1 Introduction

The control of inventory is important for a number of reasons:

- Holding costs of inventory may be high

- Production may be delayed if the company runs out of raw materials

- Loss of customer goodwill if demand can't be fulfilled

- Obsolescence if inventory with a short shelf life is not used or sold

Therefore, it is important for a company to choose an appropriate inventory management system. There are three main types of system available. Each system will be reviewed in turn.

10.2 Continuous inventory system

A **continuous inventory system** keeps the level of inventory under continual review. Each new addition and withdrawal is recorded as it occurs. A pre-determined quantity of inventory is ordered when the inventory level falls to a re-order level.

The **economic order quantity** (EOQ) model can be used to establish the optimum re-order quantity:

- The model will minimise the total inventory costs.
- It is assumed that there are no price discounts available for larger-sized orders, and the total annual inventory costs therefore consist of:
  - Ordering costs, e.g. delivery cost, administration cost of placing and monitoring orders
  - Holding costs, e.g. finance cost of holding inventory, storage costs

EOQ model

Imagine that a firm sells A units a year and sales are constant. If it retails the product at a price p, its turnover will be pA. The firm purchases stock at a wholesale price of w, sells it and, when stock has fallen to zero, obtains more stock. If the firm orders an amount Q, the stock level of the firm will follow the profile shown in the diagram below, where Q has been assumed to be 10 and stock usage is one unit a period. From the diagram it follows that the average stock level will be Q/2, in this case five units.

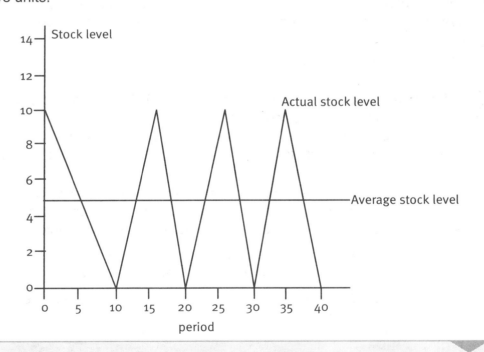

Total inventory costs are minimised when the combined cost of ordering inventory and holding inventory each period (each year) is minimised. To decide what to do, we must look at the demand and costs:

C = ordering cost per order event (fixed cost to place an order, not per unit)
H = holding cost per unit per unit of time e.g. per year
Q = is the reorder quantity
A = total sales per annum

The equation below, which you will not need to derive or use, is the so-called economic order quantity or EOQ

$$Q = \sqrt{\frac{2AC}{H}} = EOQ$$

10.3 Periodic inventory (or bin) system

The periodic inventory system does not keep inventory levels under continual review. Instead, inventory is checked on a regular basis and a variable order is placed depending on the usage during the period.

10.4 ABC system

The ABC system is based on Pareto's law. This law states that 80% of inventory usage can be accounted for by 20% of inventory items. By dividing a company's inventory into different classifications - A, B or C, managers can focus on items that account for the majority of the inventory.

- Category A – items of high value in terms of usage rate. Close monitoring of these items is vital as is the management of the supplier-buyer relationship. A stock-out would result in disappointed customers.

- Category B – items of medium value in terms of usage rate. Less important than category A and therefore require less control.

- Category C – the least used inventory items and require little management control.

11 Chapter summary

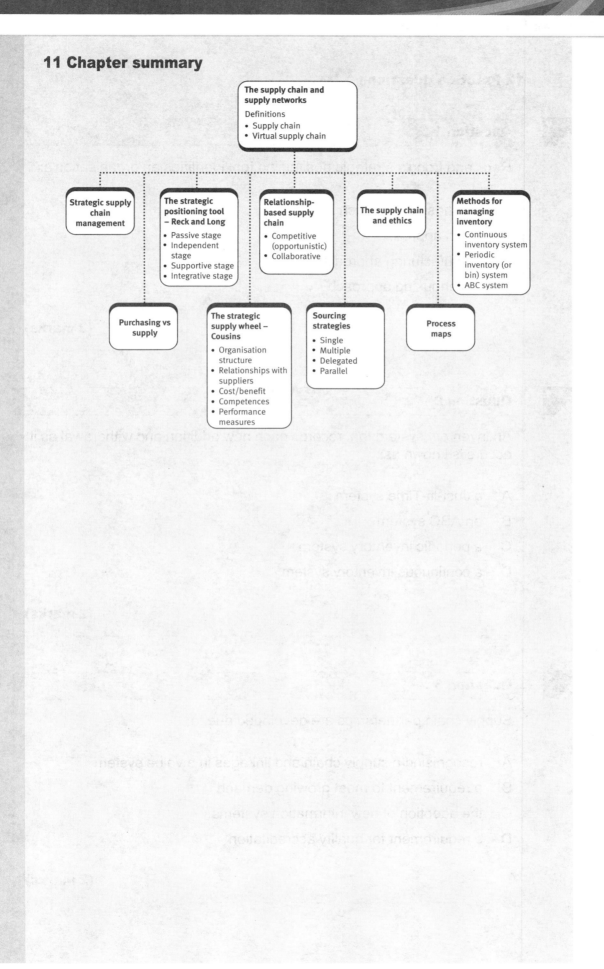

The supply chain and supply networks

Definitions
- Supply chain
- Virtual supply chain

Strategic supply chain management

The strategic positioning tool – Reck and Long
- Passive stage
- Independent stage
- Supportive stage
- Integrative stage

Relationship-based supply chain
- Competitive (opportunistic)
- Collaborative

The supply chain and ethics

Methods for managing inventory
- Continuous inventory system
- Periodic inventory (or bin) system
- ABC system

Purchasing vs supply

The strategic supply wheel – Cousins
- Organisation structure
- Relationships with suppliers
- Cost/benefit
- Competences
- Performance measures

Sourcing strategies
- Single
- Multiple
- Delegated
- Parallel

Process maps

12 Practice questions

Question 1

Reck and Long's strategic positioning tool identifies an organisation's:

A   purchasing approach

B   sales approach

C   manufacturing approach

D   warehousing approach

(2 marks)

Question 2

An inventory system that records each new addition and withdrawal as it occurs is known as:

A   a Just-In-Time system

B   an ABC system

C   a periodic inventory system

D   a continuous inventory system

(2 marks)

Question 3

Supply chain partnerships are developed due to:

A   recognising a supply chain and linkages in a value system

B   a requirement to meet growing demand

C   the adoption of new information systems

D   a requirement for quality accreditation

(2 marks)

Question 4

According to Cousins, which one of the following is a 'spoke' of the 'supply wheel?'

A   Corporate and supply strategy

B   Organisation culture

C   Purchasing

D   Relationships

(2 marks)

Question 5

An ABC system refers to:

A   an inventory management system that aims to eliminate or minimise inventory levels

B   accuracy, benefit and cost effectiveness of the inventory management system

C   an inventory management system that concentrates effort on the most important items

D   a system used to manage relationships with suppliers

(2 marks)

Question 6

Identify FOUR reasons why process maps may be used as part of supply chain management.

(4 marks)

Question 7

Overdrive Transmissions and Bearings (Overdrive) is a European manufacturer of gearbox and transmission systems for the car industry. Overdrive was formed in 1949 and is now one of the largest producers of such products in Europe. It has a turnover in excess of 300 million Euros and employs 2,000 staff in three large factories in its home country.

Gearbox and transmission systems are complex products, with each typically containing over 200 parts. Each part must be manufactured to stringent quality standards, as the operating temperatures and stress levels involved are very high. There are also potential safety implications of quality failure in any component supplied to the car industry. Overdrive's customers (the major car manufacturers) demand high standards of quality, reliability and service level. Under the terms of the contracts between Overdrive and their customers, the car manufacturers can charge severe financial penalties for any failure in delivery or quality. Such penalties can amount to many millions of Euro for each incident. Because of this, Overdrive has stringent quality control procedures.

While most of the parts and components used in Overdrive's products are manufactured by Overdrive itself, some components are bought in from other specialist manufacturers. One of these is component G4 – the gearshift selector assembly. Component G4 is used in most of Overdrive's products, and is currently bought from three small suppliers who each make the component to a design supplied by Overdrive. The suppliers are prohibited from supplying component G4 to any other organisation.

In a recent meeting, the purchasing manager of Overdrive said, '… the modern trend in managing inbound logistics is to enter into sole supplier agreements. We should consider this for component G4.'

Required:

(a) Explain what is meant by the 'inbound logistics' in Porter's value chain model.

(5 marks)

(b) Explain the types of decision regarding inventory management that the management of Overdrive need to take?

(5 marks)

(c) Explain the difference between continuous inventory and periodic inventory systems?

(5 marks)

(d) Explain THREE advantages to Overdrive of having a formal agreement with a single preferred supplier for component G4.

(5 marks)

(e) Explain THREE disadvantages to Overdrive of having a formal agreement with a single preferred supplier for component G4.

(5 marks)

(f) Outline the problems of applying the theory of JIT (Just-In-Time) to all industries in practice

(5 marks)

(Total: 30 marks)

Test your understanding answers

Test your understanding 1

		Advantages	Disadvantages
(i)	**Single sourcing**	• Better communication • Economies of scale • Better production quality, lower variability • Possible source of competitive advantage since can build relationship with single supplier.	• Risk to security of supply since rely on one supplier • Few competitive pressures may reduce incentive for supplier to perform well • The supplier is in a powerful position and may increase prices or reduce quality
(ii)	**Multiple sourcing**	• Greater security of supply • Pressure on suppliers to be competitive • Buyer remains in touch with supply market	• Economies of scale may be lost • This is a traditional price-based strategy but it may not result in good relationships • Suppliers may display less commitment/ quality may be poorer
(iii)	**Delegated sourcing**	• The 1st tier supplier may be able to negotiate economies of scale • May result in the optimum mix of suppliers being used • Organisation delegates responsibility to the 1st tier supplier thus freeing up staff time	• 1st tier supplier is in a powerful position • Organisation may have little knowledge with regards to the 2nd tier suppliers, e.g. quality, work practices
(iv)	**Parallel sourcing**	• May blend the best bits of each strategy	• Quite difficult to manage

Question 1

A

Question 2

D

Question 3

A

Question 4

D

Question 5

C

Question 6

Process maps are used to:

- standardise the process.
- find areas of improvement, e.g. eliminate unnecessary steps or duplicated steps.
- assist understanding of the process due to the visual representation.
- to link the supply chain strategy to the corporate strategy.

Question 7

(a) Inbound logistics in the value chain is the systems and procedures relating to the acquisition, movement and storage of inputs to the organisation. The buyer will study commodities, sources of supply, systems and procedures, inventory problems and market trends, methods of delivery, whether maximum discounts are being earned and the amount and use of waste materials. Inbound logistics also includes warehousing, stock control and transport. From the point of view of corporate financial strategy, storing inputs entails vast amounts of money being tied up in stocks, which are prone to damage and shrinkage and are perhaps slow moving. There is also the creation on the shop floor of a mentality that pushes components through to satisfy stocks (just in case) rather than pulling them through made to order (just in time). This means yet more stock is ordered and so on. While the choice of supplier is a 'procurement' function in the value chain, the management of the supplier relationship tends to be classified as inbound logistics, particularly when it comes to more closely integrating the organisation's purchasing systems with the sales systems of the supplier.

(b) There are two main types of decision for inventory management:

   – How much to order? When an order is placed with a supplier, what quantity should be ordered?

   – When to order? How frequently should inventory be ordered? Should it be ordered at regular intervals, or when the inventory level has fallen to a reorder level?

The trade off is:

Ordering more frequently	**Ordering less frequently**
Higher ordering costs	Lower ordering costs
Smaller average inventory	Larger average inventory

(c) Two methods of inventory control include the periodic review system and the continuous review system. In the **periodic review system**, the inventory position is reviewed at regular intervals (usually at the time of a scheduled re-order). The inventory is counted and the order quantity is calculated by subtracting the amount of stock on hand from the desired maximum inventory. A manager using this system determines the re-supply schedule by establishing a reorder interval (the number of months between orders), and places orders based on this schedule.

In the **continuous review system**, the inventory level is reviewed on an ongoing basis for every transaction in which stock is dispensed. When the amount of stock reaches a predetermined reorder level, an order is initiated. Each time the stock is replenished, it is for a standard quantity (usually for that amount which will raise the stock level backup to the desired maximum level). This system is based on stock levels rather than on time intervals

(d) The main advantages of sole supplier agreements are as follows: (Any three required)

– Overdrive should be able to negotiate lower initial prices due to the increased volume of business to be transacted with the supplier. The suppliers are all currently small organisations, so a trebling of the order quantities from any one of them should allow that supplier to exploit economies of scale.

– Overdrive should be able to gain better control over their inbound logistics through direct involvement with the supplier. Giving the sole supplier more attention and management time should improve the reliability of deliveries and also reduce the risk of quality failure.

– There is an opportunity to integrate the systems of Overdrive with those of the supplier, as mentioned above. For example, Overdrive could give the supplier access to production forecasts, which would allow the supplier to amend production plans for component G4 to meet forecast demand. This would allow a move towards just in time (JIT) logistics, and reduce (or eliminate) finished goods inventory at the supplier and component inventory at Overdrive.

– Overdrive should be able to ensure better quality due to the extent of the supplier's reliance on Overdrive. The supplier would probably not wish to disappoint such a major customer.

(e) The main disadvantages of sole supplier agreements are as follows: (Any three required)

– Once the agreement is signed, there is a risk over future price rises. It could be argued that the sole supplier agreement leads to increased supplier bargaining power over Overdrive, though this will depend on how well the relationship is managed.

– There is a significant risk in relation to possible delivery failure by the supplier. Overdrive has contracts with car manufacturers that include 'liquidated damages' clauses for late delivery. These would have to be written into any contract with a supplier, and a small supplier may not be able to afford the cost of such a high exposure to possible penalties.

- There is a risk of falling quality from the supplier if the relationship with Overdrive becomes too 'comfortable'. Overdrive must continually remind the supplier of its quality expectations. This is a big issue for Overdrive, as they are buying a high technology component that forms a key part of their product. There are also safety implications associated with product failure, and these could lead to legal action against Overdrive.

- If Overdrive only uses one supplier, they might miss out on future innovations in the industry. Overdrive should change their planning process to ensure that they take advantage of any future developments by other suppliers.

(f) Although it might be difficult to argue against the philosophy of JIT, there can be problems with applying the theory of JIT to all industries in practice.

- It is not always easy to predict patterns of demand.

- The concept of zero inventories and make-to-order is inapplicable in some industries. For example, retailing businesses such as supermarkets have got to obtain inventory in anticipation of future customer demand.

- JIT makes the organisation far more vulnerable to disruptions in the supply chain.

- JIT was designed at a time when all of Toyota's manufacturing was done within a 50 km radius of its headquarters. Wide geographical spread, however, makes this difficult.

- It might be difficult for management to apply the principles of JIT because they find the concept of empowering the employee difficult to accept.

8

Quality Management

Chapter learning objectives

Lead	Component
C2. Apply tools and techniques of operations management.	(a) Apply contemporary thinking in quality management.
	(c) Apply tools and concepts of lean management.
	(d) Illustrate a plan for the implementation of a quality programme.

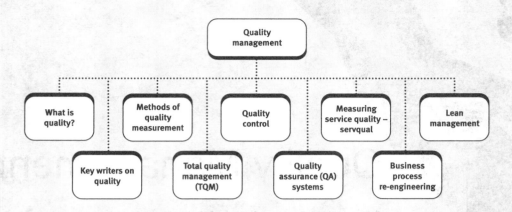

1 Introduction to Quality

Quality is one of the most important and far-reaching issues in modern organisations.

The term is difficult to define and often means different things in different organisations. However, the need to **satisfy customer's needs** is critical to most definitions of quality.

What is quality?

In order to control and improve quality, it must first be defined. Most dictionaries define quality as 'the degree of excellence' but this leaves one having to define what is meant by 'excellence'. Who defines what is excellent and by what standards is it measured? In response to this problem, a number of different definitions of quality have been developed.

In an industrial context, quality is defined in a functional way. Here, quality means that a product is made free from errors and according to its design specifications, within an acceptable production tolerance level.

Such an approach also emphasises that every unit produced should meet the design specifications, so the idea of consistency becomes important. Note that consistency is a key aspect of quality standards such as the ISO 9000 series.

This still leaves a problem, however. How should standards and specifications be set? Who decides what an 'acceptable' tolerance level should be?

An alternative approach to defining quality is thus to focus on the user.

- Japanese companies found the definition of quality as 'the degree of conformance to a standard' too narrow and consequently started to use a new definition of quality as 'user satisfaction'.

- Juran defines quality as 'fitness for use' (1988).

In these definitions, customer requirements and customer satisfaction are the main factors. If an organisation can meet the requirements of its customers, customers will presumably be satisfied. The ability to define accurately the needs related to design, performance, price, safety, delivery, and other business activities and processes will place an organisation ahead of its competitors in the market.

Taking these definitions together, Ken Holmes (Total Quality Management) has defined quality as 'the totality of features and characteristics of a product or service which bears on its ability to meet stated or implied needs'.

Quality is also normally seen in relation to price, and customers judge the quality of a product in relation to the price they have to pay. Customers will accept a product of lower design quality provided that the price is lower than the price of a better-quality alternative.

Test your understanding 1

Explain the reasons why quality may be important to an organisation.

The growth of global companies has resulted in dramatic improvements in the quality of products and services. Much of this impetus can be attributed to the efforts of Japanese manufacturing companies.

2 Key Writers on Quality

Much of the research on quality has arrived at broadly similar conditions in terms of what organisationally is required.

There are a number of key writers on quality:

Writer	Main contribution
W.Edward Deming	Believed: • managers should set up and then **continuously improve** the systems in which people work • managers should work with employees to gain feedback from those who do the job • workers should be trained in quality to identify what needs changing and how. Deming was credited with the creation of TQM in Japan.
Joseph M. Juran	• Drew on Pareto principle and stated that 85% of quality problems are due to the systems that employees work within rather than the employees themselves. • Therefore, need to develop key projects for dealing with quality problems rather than concentrating on employee motivation. • Also believed that anyone affected by the product is considered a customer, so introduced the idea of internal as well as external customers.
Phillip P. Crosby	• Introduced the concept of 'zero defects'. • Believed that prevention is key and that the importance of quality is measured by the cost of not having quality.

3 Methods of Quality Measurement

Despite Crosby's mantra ('prevention is free') there are four types of quality costs:

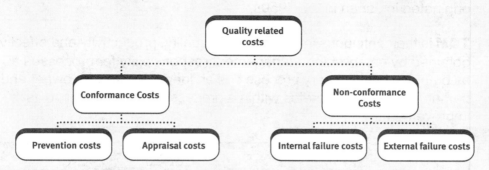

- **Prevention costs** – cost of preventing defects before they occur. For example:
    - Designing products and services with built in quality.
    - Training employees in the best ways to do their job.

- **Appraisal costs** – the cost of quality inspection and testing to ensure products/services conform to quality requirements.

- **Internal failure costs** – the costs arising from a failure to meet quality standards. Occurs **before** the product/service reaches the customer. For example:
    - Cost of re-working/scrapping parts.
    - Re-inspection costs.
    - Lower selling prices for sub-quality goods.

- **External failure costs** – the costs arising from a failure to meet quality standards. Occurs **after** the product/service reaches the customer. For example:
    - Costs of recalling and correcting products.
    - Cost of lost goodwill.

4 Approaches to Quality Management

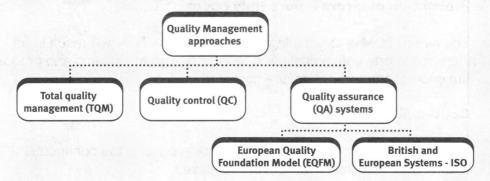

4.1 Total quality management (TQM)

4.1.1 Introduction

Total quality management (TQM) is a philosophy of quality management that originated in Japan in the 1950s.

TQM is the continuous improvement in quality, productivity and effectiveness obtained by establishing management responsibility for processes as well as outputs. In this, every process has an identified process owner and every person in an entity operates within a process and contributes to its improvement.

Illustration 1

A TQM success story

Corning Inc is the world leader in speciality glass and ceramics. This is partly due to the implementation of a TQM approach. In 1983 the CEO announced a $1.6 billion investment in TQM. After several years of intensive training and a decade of applying the TQM approach, all of Corning's employees had bought into the quality concept. They knew the lingo – continuous improvement, empowerment, customer focus, management by prevention and they witnessed the impact of the firm's techniques as profits soared.

An example of TQM failure

British Telecom launched a total quality program in the late 1980s. This resulted in the company getting bogged down in its quality processes and bureaucracy. The company failed to focus on its customers and later decided to dismantle its TQM program. This was at great cost to the company and they have failed to make a full recovery.

4.1.2 Fundamental features of TQM

Prevention of errors before they occur

The aim of TQM is to get things 'right first time'. TQM will result in an increase in prevention costs, e.g. quality design of systems and products, but internal and external failure costs will fall.

Continual improvement

Quality management is not a one-off process, but is the continuous examination and improvement of processes.

Real participation by all

The 'total' in TQM means that everyone in the value chain is involved in the process, including:

- Employees – they are expected to seek out, identify and correct quality problems. Teamwork will be vital.
- Suppliers – quality and reliability of suppliers will play a vital role (TQM and JIT often go hand in hand).
- Customers – the goal is to identify and meet the needs of the customer.

Commitment of senior management

Management must be fully committed and encourage everyone else to become quality conscious.

4.1.3 TQM Techniques

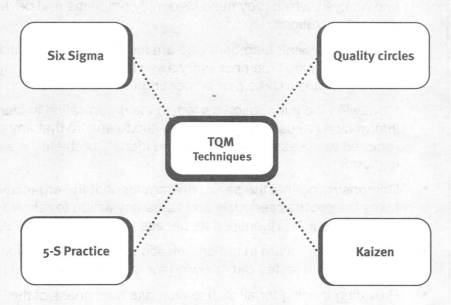

Quality circles

A **quality circle** is a small group of employees, with a range of skills from all levels of the organisation. They meet voluntarily on a regular basis to discuss quality issues and to develop solutions to real problems.

Advantages include:

- Improvements in quality, leading to greater customer satisfaction and improved productivity.
- A culture of continuous improvement is encouraged.

- Employees at operational level will form part of the quality circle. They often have a better understanding of quality problems than their superiors/ managers and their participation will increase commitment to and ownership of problems.

- The group approach helps to foster organisational unity.

- Using interdisciplinary teams helps staff to gain a better perspective of the whole organisation and their part within it.

Encouraging the development and use of quality circles

Putting the idea of quality circles into practice can be very difficult. There are a number of ways in which firms can encourage the development of the use of quality circles:

- Ensuring that there is high profile executive commitment to support the initiative.

- Ensuring that staff members have the training in problem solving and analysis which they need to identify problems and develop workable solutions.

- Ensuring that staff members who are involved in quality circles are free to spend the time necessary away from their day-to-day responsibilities to take part in meetings and activities.

- Reviewing the information system in the organisation to identify the information needs of quality circles, and to ensure that any data required to assess performance and identify problems is available to them.

- Demonstrating that the senior management of the organisation takes the process seriously and takes any action to resolve problems which is identified as necessary by quality circles.

- Developing a culture in the organisation that allows possible changes to be tested out, allowing for the possibility of mistakes.

- Providing training for all staff to increase awareness of the importance and value of quality circles.

Kaizen

Kaizen is a Japanese term for the philosophy of continuous improvement in performance in all areas of an organisation's operations.

Features include:

- Involves all levels of employees.

- Everyone is encouraged to come up with small improvement suggestions on a regular basis.

- Suggestions are not limited to a particular area, such as production or marketing, but look at all areas of the business.

- Setting standards and then continually improving those standards.

- Training and resources should be provided for employees in order for them to meet the standards set.

Illustration 2

Many Japanese companies have introduced a Kaizen approach:

- In companies such as Toyota and Canon, a total of 60–70 suggestions per employee per year are written down and shared.

- It is not unusual for over 90% of those suggestions to be implemented.

- In 1999, in one US plant, 7,000 Toyota employees submitted over 75,000 suggestions, of which 99% were implemented.

There are a number of Kaizen tools:

Tool	Explanation
Plan-Do-Check-Act (PDCA) cycle	A cycle that encourages key stages to continuous improvement: • Plan: Plan activities • Do: Implement the plan • Check: Check the results • Act: Improve the process

The fishbone diagram	• A cause and effect diagram used to analyse all the contributory causes that contribute to a single effect. • A line is drawn indicating a route of continuous improvement and off this line 'fish bones' will splinter indicating problems that may be encountered.
The Pareto rule	• Pareto identified that 80% of the country's wealth was held by 20% of the population. • Similarly 80/20 classifications occurred regularly in most other areas. • The 'rule' encourages a focus of effort on the important 20% in order to be effective.
The five why process	• Examine issues by constantly asking 'why' until the real issue is identified. • First developed at Toyota; it encourages employee problem solving.

5-S practice

The 5-S practice is an approach to achieving an organised, clean and standardised workplace.

- The 5-S practice is often part of a Kaizen approach.
- The 5Ss are Japanese words but can be translated as follows:

Word	Meaning	Example
Seiri	Sort	Eliminate unnecessary items, e.g. old, unwanted files.
Seiton	Organise	A structured filing system – 'a place for everything and everything in its place'.
Seiso	Clean	Clean work station regularly
Seiketsu	Standardise	Alphabetic filing system
Shitsuke	Discipline	Do not slip back into old habits.

The principle may appear simple, obvious common sense but until the advent of 5-S many businesses ignored these basic principles.

Six sigma

This quality management programme was pioneered in the 1980s by Motorola, a multinational telecommunications company now best known for its mobile phones and tablet pcs.

The aim of the approach is to achieve a reduction in the number of faults that go beyond an accepted tolerance limit through the use of statistical techniques.

The sigma stands for standard deviation. For reasons that need not be explained here, it can be demonstrated that, if the error rate lies beyond the sixth sigma of probability, there will be fewer than 3.4 defects in every one million.

This is almost perfection. Customers will have a reason to complain fewer than four times in a million.

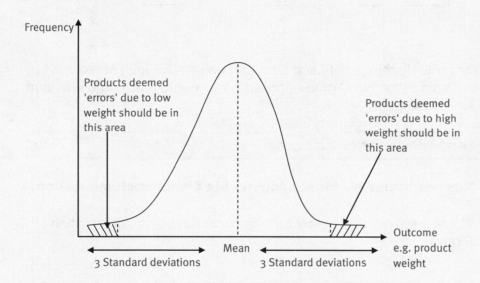

Statistical process control is the method used to continually monitor and chart a process whilst it is operating, to warn when the process is moving away from the predetermined limits.

- As per six sigma, the upper and lower limits will be three standard deviations away from the expected value (mean).

- All points outside the control limits should be investigated and corrective action taken.

For example, the following statistical control chart shows the size of a product (this may be an important aspect of product conformance) against time.

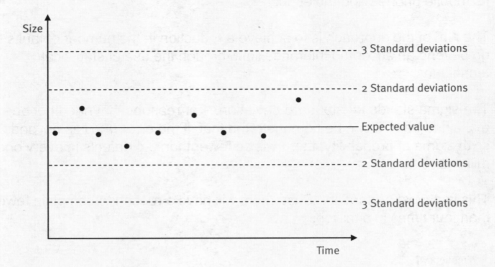

In order to do things right first time with no (or very few) defects, a key emphasis of the Six Sigma approach is to identify root problems and address them.

Further aspects of Six Sigma

Key requirements for successful Six Sigma implementation

There are a number of key requirements for the implementation of Six Sigma.

- Six Sigma should be focused on the customer and based on the level of performance acceptable to the customer.

- Six Sigma targets for a process should be related to the main drivers of performance.

- To maximise savings, Six Sigma needs to be part of a wider performance management programme which is linked to the strategy of the organisation. It should not be just about doing things better but about doing things differently.

- Senior managers within the organisation have a key role in driving the process.

- Training and education about the process throughout the organisation are essential for success.

- Six Sigma sets a tight target, but accepts some failure – the target is not zero defects.

Some criticisms and limitations of Six Sigma

Literature on Six Sigma contains some criticisms of the process and identifies a number of limitations as follows.

- Six Sigma has been criticised for its focus on current processes and reliance on data. It is suggested that this could become too rigid and limit process innovation.

- Six Sigma is based on the use of models which are by their nature simplifications of real life. Judgement needs to be used in applying the models in the context of business objectives.

- The approach can be very time consuming and expensive. Organisations need to be prepared to put time and effort into its implementation.

- The culture of the organisation must be supportive – not all organisations are ready for such a scientific process.

- The process is heavily data-driven. This can be a strength, but can become over-bureaucratic.

- Six Sigma can give all parts of the organisation a common language for process improvement, but it is important to ensure that this does not become jargon but is expressed in terms specific to the organisation and its business.

- There is an underlying assumption in Six Sigma that the existing business processes meet customers' expectations. It does not ask whether it is the right process.

4.1.4 Implementation of a TQM approach

The implementation of a TQM approach may involve the following steps:

Step 1: Senior management consultancy – Managers must be committed to the programme and should undergo quality training

Step 2: Establish a quality steering committee – The committee will guide the company through the process of implementing TQM

Step 3: Presentations and training – The steering committee should communicate the benefits of the change programme to employees in order to gain buy-in

Step 4: Establish quality circles – This will involve employees in the process of quality improvement

Step 5: Documentation – The actions carried out should be clearly documented

Step 6: Monitor progress – Actual results should be monitored against the standard set

Test your understanding 2

Discuss some of the common reasons for the failure of TQM programmes.

4.2 Quality control (QC)

Quality control (QC) involves a number of routine steps which measure and control the quality of the product/ service as it is developed.

The approach identifies production processes that are critical to quality and then establishes warning limits and tolerances measure any unacceptable variances.

Quality control

The use of quality control is an approach involving:

- establishing quality standards for a service or product

- designing a process to deliver the service or product to the required quality

- measuring the quality of the service or product

- comparing actual quality with planned quality

- taking remedial action where quality does not meet the standard

- reviewing the standard originally set and adjusting if necessary.

4.3 Quality assurance (QA) systems

A **quality assurance (QA)** system involves a review of the QC procedures, commonly by an independent third party. It aims to verify that the desired level of quality has been met.

Quality assurance

QA must account for:

- design of products and services

- materials of a consistently appropriate standard

- suppliers who are reliable and consistent in the supply of materials

- plant and machinery that is reliable

- staff that benefit from training and development so reducing the potential for human error

- the appropriate planning and management of operational procedures.

Two types of QA system will be reviewed here:

- British and European systems – ISO.
- The European Quality Foundation Model (EQFM)

British and European systems – ISO

The ISO 9000:2000 series of quality standards is the most recent set of ISO standards (published in 2000).

- A company registering for ISO 9000 certification is required to submit its quality standards and procedures for external inspection.
- Requirements include:
  - A set of procedures that covers all key business processes.
  - Keeping adequate records.
  - Checking output for defects.
  - Facilitating continuous improvement.
- If the company receives a certificate it can claim to be ISO registered/ certified and will be subject to continuing audit.

Test your understanding 3

Explain the advantages and disadvantages to a fast growing UK based mobile phone company of becoming ISO certified.

Accreditation of **ISO 14001** is closely linked with ISO 9000:2000. It specifies a process for controlling and improving a company's **environmental performance**.

ISO 140001

ISO 14001 covers:

- environmental policy
- planning
- implementation and operation
- checking and corrective action
- management review.

The European Quality Foundation Model (EQFM)

EQFM is one of the best known self-assessment models for business improvement. It:

- provides a structured methodology for organisations to measure their own performance in areas critical to the business

- should allow for improvement through this self-assessment

- includes a set of results, e.g. customer results, people results, society results and relevant enablers, e.g. leadership, strategy, processes.

EQFM

In the Basque Country, a region in Northern Spain, experience has been gained over many years into the implementation of the EFQM excellence model in the regional health care service, formed by 31 health organizations.

The project was started in 1995. Until 1999, only self-assessments were done. Since 2000, the most advanced organizations concluded external evaluations and have achieved quality awards from the Basque government.

Scores for most of the EFQM criteria improved, particularly in 'processes'. The overall patients' satisfaction was higher than 89% in all settings, in most of the cases it was higher than 95%, a significant improvement.

5 Measuring Service Quality – Servqual

A service company, e.g. a hotel, bank or restaurant, may wish to know more about customers' perceptions of its service, to compare these to what they had expected and to identify trends in perceived quality.

Servqual uses 22 questions to understand a respondent's attitude about service quality. Customers may be asked for their responses both before and after the service is consumed to compare their initial expectations of the service and their perception of the actual service delivered.

These questions are claimed to be reliable indicators of five distinct dimensions:

Dimensions	Examples for a restaurant
Tangibles	Appearance and taste of food, staff appearance, physical facilities such as bathrooms
Reliability	Order processed accurately
Responsiveness	Staff response to queries, e.g. information on specials, request for bill
Assurance	Waiting staff inspire confidence and trust
Empathy	Restaurant guests are treated as individuals

Test your understanding 4

Explain how the Servqual dimensions could be applied to an online environment, such as a company using a website to sell its products and to deal with customer concerns and queries.

6 Business Process Re-engineering (BPR)

Business process re-engineering (BPR) involves the fundamental re-thinking and redesign of existing business processes to achieve improvements in performance.

BPR involves focusing attention **inwards** to consider how the business processes could be redesigned or re-engineered to improve efficiency.

Hammer and Champy describe BPR in terms of:

Radical and fundamental

BPR assumes nothing; it starts by asking basic questions about why tasks are carried out and challenges traditional methods.

Dramatic

BPR changes should lead to quantum leaps in performance not just incremental benefits.

Process

The changing process can be defined in terms of:

- Combining jobs;
- Devolved decision making;
- Reduced checks and control with quality built in.

IT is an enabler or facilitator in the change process and a major contributor to BPR programs.

IT and BPR

Some of the key technologies that allow fundamental shifts in business operations to occur are:

- Shared database access from any location;
- Expert systems to devolve expertise;
- Powerful telecommunication networks for remote offices;
- Wireless communication for on-the-spot decision making;
- Tracking technology for warehouse and delivery systems;
- Internet services to re-engineer channels of distribution.

7 Lean Management

As the name suggests, lean management is a philosophy that aims to **systematically eliminate waste**.

In this section we will look first at manufacturing contexts but then we will consider how the same principles can be applied within service organisations.

Illustration 3

60 years ago, the cars that Toyota was making were uncompetitive in both cost and quality terms. In a bid to catch up with its American competitors, it developed lean production. Lean production helped Toyota to become what it is now – the biggest car manufacturer in the world.

7.1 Wastes to be eliminated

- **Inventory** – holding or purchasing unnecessary raw materials, work-in-progress and finished goods.

- **Waiting** – time delays/ idle time when value is not added to the product.

- **Defective units** – production of a part that is scrapped or requires rework.

- **Effort** – actions of people/ equipment that do not add value.

- **Transportation** – delays in transportation or unnecessary handling.

- **Over-processing** – unnecessary steps that do not add value.

- **Over-production** – production ahead of demand.

7.2 Characteristics of lean production

- **Improved production scheduling** – production is initiated by customer demand rather than ability and capacity to produce, i.e. production is demand-pull, not supply-push.

- **Small batch production or continuous production** – production is based on customer demand, resulting in highly flexible and responsive processes.

- **Economies of scope** – lean production is only achieved where 'economies of scope' make it economical to produce small batches of a variety of products with the same machines. This is in stark contrast with traditional manufacturing and its emphasis on economies of scale.

- **Continuous improvement** – the company continually finds ways to reduce process times:
  - A multi-skilled, trained workforce provides flexibility.
  - The machines, tools and people used to make an item are located close together.
  - Quality at source reduces re-working.
  - A clean and orderly workplace.

- **Zero inventory** – JIT purchasing eliminates waste.

- **Zero waiting time** – JIT production means that the work performed at each stage of the process is dictated solely by the demand for materials for the next stage, thus reducing lead time.

Illustration 4 – Reverse Engineering

IBM regularly compares part counts, bills of materials, standard versus custom part usage, and estimated processing costs by tearing down competitor products as soon as they are available.

Through such tear-downs during the heyday of the dot matrix printer, IBM learned that the printer made by the Epson, its initial supplier, was exceedingly complicated with more than 150 parts. IBM launched a team with a simplification goal and knocked the part count down to 62, cutting assembly from thirty minutes to only three.

7.3 The six core methods of lean manufacturing

- **JIT** (see earlier discussion)
- **Kaizen** (see earlier discussion)
- **5-S practice** (see earlier discussion)
- **Total productive maintenance (TPM)** – this engages all levels and functions of the organisation in maintenance. Workers are trained to take care of the equipment over its entire useful life.

Illustration 5 – TPM

Pulling the cord, called 'andcan', is part of Toyota's lean production system. An employee who notices a problem, pulls the cord to stop the production line. This will prompt fellow workers to gather round and to solve the problem.

Workers at the Toyota plant in Georgetown, Kentucky, pull the cord 2,000 times a week and their care is what makes Toyota one of the most desired and reliable brands in the US. In contrast, workers at Ford's plant in Michigan pull the cord only twice a week.

In 1998 it took Ford 50% more hours to make a car than Toyota. Toyota's lean system means that it has been able to produce cars more cheaply, and to a higher quality, than Ford.

TPM

The major factors that need to be considered in order to implement TPM are:

- training
- equipment maintenance
- planning
- having an adequate budget in place.

TPM should reduce equipment breakdowns, enhance equipment capability and improve safety and environmental factors.

- **Cellular manufacturing** – work units are arranged in a sequence that supports a smooth flow of materials and components through the production processes with minimal transport or delay.

- **Six sigma** (see earlier discussion).

7.4 Criticisms and limitations of lean manufacturing

- **High initial outlay** – It might involve a large amount of initial expenditure to switch from 'traditional' production systems to a system based on cellular manufacturing. All the tools and equipment needed to manufacture a product need to be re-located to the same area of the factory floor. Employees need to be trained in multiple skills.

- **Requires a change in culture** – Lean manufacturing, like TQM, is a philosophy or culture of working, and it might be difficult for management and employees to acquire this culture. Employees might not be prepared to give the necessary commitment.

- **Part adoption** – It might be tempting for companies to select some elements of lean manufacturing (such as production based on cellular manufacturing), but not to adopt others (such as empowering employees to make on-the-spot decisions).

- **Cost may exceed benefit** – In practice, the expected benefits of lean manufacturing (lower costs and shorter cycle times) have not always materialised, or might not have been as large as expected.

7.5 Application of lean techniques to services

Toyota pioneered the concept of a 'lean' operating system and it has now been implemented in countless manufacturing companies. Lean techniques can also be applied to service companies. The six core methods will still apply, although the use of the methods will be different.

With service operations, a lean approach often focuses on improving the customer experience.

In chapter 5 we identified certain distinguishing features that may make it difficult for service operators to reduce costs and increase quality. These same factors affect the application of lean techniques to services:

- Service organisations tend to be **more labour intensive**, so a lean approach to services could involve a mixture of cutting staffing levels, reducing wasted time and reducing mistakes.

  For example, a teller in a bank may spend only 6 out of 8 hours in day in direct customer service, and the remaining 2 hours are wasted in 1–2 minute segments. Rather than letting unplanned activities fill the void, a priority list of service support tasks such as restocking supplies, following a standardised procedure, can be used to not only reduce waste but also help eliminate other sources of poor service quality.

- Services are **intangible** and it is more difficult to measure their quality than it is for a physical product.

  Attempts to improve time efficiency may have an adverse effect on quality that could be difficult to quantify.

- Services are **consumed immediately** and cannot be stored.

  Matching staff levels to demand for services is critical to avoid wasted time.

- **Customers participate directly in the delivery process**, so firms must evaluate their services from the customer's perspective.

  The customer, when evaluating the quality of the service will take into account the face-to-face contact and the social skills of those providing the service. Again there is a danger that efficiency gains may compromise customer service.

Illustration 6 – Lean management in the NHS

Within the NHS in England lean thinking and Six Sigma have been used to reduce waiting times for patients.

Lean thinking looks to improve the flow in a patient journey and reduce waste while SIx Sigma has been used to uncover root problems to ensure things are done right first time.

NHS leaders and staff previously had not fully understood how patients and their information (referrals, appointments, X-rays, pathology specimens, reports, coding information etc) flowed through their organisations and departments. Managers and clinicians tried to optimise their organisational or departmental activity and costs, with no reference to the bottleneck in the system that governs the rate at which patients and information flow along the system or pathways of care.

Accident and Emergency (A&E)

For example, in A&E, lean management approaches identified the bottleneck as the rate of arrival of patients in ambulances and the rate at which junior doctors could assess them and initiate treatment plans. To address this patient journeys were analysed to identify common processes, skill requirements and cycle times. As a result patients were split into two groups:

- Patients with minor conditions have a huge variety and range of conditions but all require a quick simple process to sort them out by experienced staff with minimal equipment. Processing the majority of patients in less than 20 minutes improves the overall time in A&E for the vast majority of patients.

- The major injury and resuscitation patients are fewer in number, but require different skills and technology and have much longer cycle times.

Mixing minors with majors is like putting a lorry into the fast lane on a motorway. It slows the speed of the whole motorway.

Processing pathology specimens

In 2007, turnaround times in pathology at Hereford Hospital were reduced by 40% in 7 days by improving the flow of the specimens through the department and eliminating wasteful activities, such as unnecessary staff movements like searching for things. A key change here was having dedicated staff man the specimen reception. This enabled staff to start processing specimens as soon as they arrived, rather than waiting for someone from a lab to come and see if any had arrived.

The reduction in processing times resulted in estimated savings of £365,000 a year because inpatients could be discharged quicker, shortening length of stay and creating extra capacity in the hospital.

Test your understanding 5

Explain how the six core methods of lean manufacturing can be applied to a call centre.

The lean supply chain

The main objective of a lean supply chain is to completely remove waste in order to achieve competitive advantage through a reduction in costs and an improvement in quality. Other benefits are:

- reduced inventories (and thus increased cash flows and profits)

- shorter lead times, and thus faster deliveries to customers

- few bottlenecks, so better utilisation of resources, and further improvements in profit,

- few quality problems, so less re-work, lower costs of quality failures, and happier customers.

However, disadvantages include the potential for large, powerful customers to dominate the supply chain and an over-emphasis on cost reduction rather than quality improvement.

8 Chapter summary

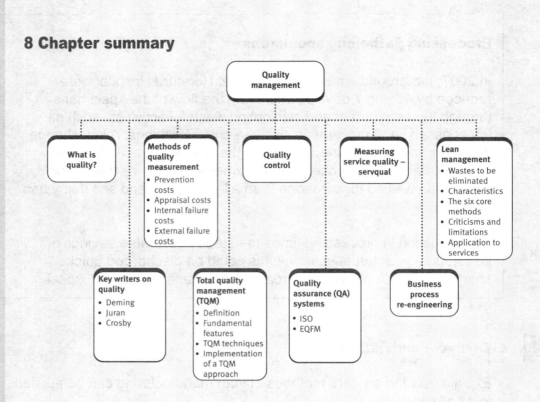

9 Practice questions

Question 1

Which of the following is not a benefit of quality accredited standards such as ISO 9001?

A   Excellent marketing tool

B   Better quality

C   Revenue reduction

D   Cost reduction

(2 marks)

Question 2

What are the main benefits of ISO 14001 accreditation?

Question 3

What is the likely error rate if it lies beyond the sixth sigma of probability?

A   1 defect in 100,000

B   3.2 defects in 600,000

C   3.4 defects in 1,000,000

D   4 defects in 6,000,000

(2 marks)

Question 4

Which writer on TQM advocated a zero defects philosophy?

A   Deming

B   Peters

C   Crosby

D   Juran

(2 marks)

Question 5

The six core methods of lean manufacturing include cellular manufacturing, six sigma, JIT, Kaizen, TPM and:

A   benchmarking

B   TQM

C   MRP

D   the 5-S practice

(2 marks)

Question 6

Describe the importance of quality management.

(4 marks)

Question 7

Explain how servqual can be used to measure quality in a hotel.

(4 marks)

Question 8

The production director in a large manufacturing company wants to introduce quality circles into the company's factories, because he has heard of their success in several Japanese companies. He asks for your advice about introducing a system of quality circles, and he tells you: 'My objectives in wanting to introduce these circles are to arrive at decisions for change in product designs and production methods and to get a maximum degree of acceptance. Quality circles can improve quality, productivity, interdepartmental communication, teamwork, team spirit. They can reduce costs and absenteeism and create more job satisfaction. I want them.'

Required:

The production director asks you to explain whether you can foresee any problems with introducing quality circles, and how you would set about implementing a programme for setting them up and using them.

(10 marks)

Test your understanding answers

Test your understanding 1

Higher quality can help to increase revenue and reduce costs:

- Higher quality improves the perceived image of a product or service. As a result, more customers will be willing to buy the product/ service and may also be willing to pay more for the product/ service.

- A higher volume of sales may result in lower unit costs due to economies of scale.

- Higher quality in manufacturing should result in lower waste and defective rates, which will reduce production costs.

- The need for inspection and testing should be reduced, also reducing costs.

- The volume of customer complaints should fall and warranty claims should be lower. This will reduce costs.

- Better quality in production should lead to shorter processing times. This will reduce costs.

Test your understanding 2

Tail off – after an initial burst of enthusiasm, top management fails to maintain interest and support.

Deflection – other initiatives or problems deflect attention from TQM.

Lack of buy-in – managers pay only 'lip service' to the principles of worker involvement and communication.

Rejection – TQM does not fit in with the organisational culture and is therefore rejected.

Test your understanding 3

Advantages

- **Overcoming internal weakness** – ISO 9000 is based on product standardisation and quality control and should therefore help to solve internal quality problems.

- **Continuous improvement** – the need to document every procedure and work instruction should act as a stimulus for continuous improvement.

- **Recognised standard** – the company's reputation for quality will be enhanced since ISO is a recognised international standard of quality.

- **Marketing** – ISO certification will act as an excellent marketing tool. It will help to differentiate the company, on the grounds of quality, in the customer's eyes.

- **Improved profitability** – fulfilment of the ISO criteria should help the company to improve quality. This, in turn, should reduce costs (e.g. due to the efficiency of standardised procedures) and increase revenue (due to an increase in new/returning customers).

- **International competitiveness** – ISO certification is becoming increasingly useful in international markets and may help the company to compete on a world stage.

Disadvantages

- **Cost** – fees are upwards of £995 depending on the size of the company.

- **Time** – documentation can be time consuming to produce.

- **Bureaucracy** – the scheme encourages bureaucracy with lots of form filling and filing rather than positive actions.

- **Rigid policies** – these may discourage initiative and innovation and may therefore hinder the quality process.

- **Not all embracing** – ISO certification will form a small part of a TQM approach.

Test your understanding 4

Tangibles

- The 'tangibles' heading considers the appearance of physical facilities, equipment, personnel and communications.

- For online quality the key issue is the appearance and appeal of websites – customers will revisit websites that they find appealing.

- This can include factors such as structural and graphic design, quality of content, ease of use, speed to upload and frequency of update.

Reliability

- Reliability is the ability to provide a promised service dependably and accurately and is usually the most important of the different aspects being discussed here.

- For online service quality, reliability is mainly concerned with how easy it is to connect to the website.

- If websites are inaccessible some of the time and/or e-mails are bounced back, then customers will lose confidence in the retailer.

Responsiveness

- Responsiveness looks at the willingness of a firm to help customers and provide prompt service.

- In the context of e-business, excessive delays can cause customers to 'bail-out' of websites and/or transactions and go elsewhere.

- This could relate to how long it takes for e-mails to be answered or even how long it takes for information to be downloaded to a user's browser.

Assurance

- Assurance is the knowledge and courtesy of employees and their ability to inspire trust and confidence.

- For an online retailer, assurance looks at two issues – the quality of responses and the privacy/security of customer information.

- Quality of response includes competence, credibility and courtesy and could involve looking at whether replies to e-mails are automatic or personalised and whether questions have been answered satisfactorily.

Empathy

- Empathy considers the caring, individualised attention a firm gives its customers.

- Most people would assume that empathy can only occur through personal human contact but it can be achieved to some degree through personalising websites and e-mail.

- Key here is whether customers feel understood. For example, being recommended products that they would never dream of buying, can erode empathy.

Test your understanding 5

JIT – planning and forecasting can be used to manage demand. This will ensure that there is an appropriate number of staff to minimise queuing times (these waste customer's time but also give them an adverse impression about the quality of the service) but that staff idle time is also kept to a minimum. Well trained staff should be able to meet the customers' needs effectively and efficiently and a well organised work area should be able to reduce the amount of time that customers are on hold for.

Kaizen – this might be used to reduce customer waiting times. Some call centres use electronic wall boards. These show information, such as the number of customers waiting, and can be used to reduce this waiting time for customers.

5-S practice – this model can be used to organise the surroundings of the call centre office. All of the materials the employee uses should be organised and within reach without having to leave the area. This should allow the call centre staff to talk on the phone, access the computer and view any other documents, all without moving from their desk.

TPM – call centre staff should be trained to take care of their equipment and will be able to solve common problems themselves, e.g. with their phone/ computer.

Cellular manufacturing – rather than placing pieces of equipment such as postage machines, photocopiers, fax machines and file drawers throughout the area for everyone to use (and wait on), consider placing these together in a U shaped cell to minimise movement.

Six sigma – It is more difficult to define a fault in a service company but it can be thought of as not fulfilling the needs of the customer. Well trained, experienced staff will have the ability to put the customer first and to achieve the low level of 'faults' required by six sigma.

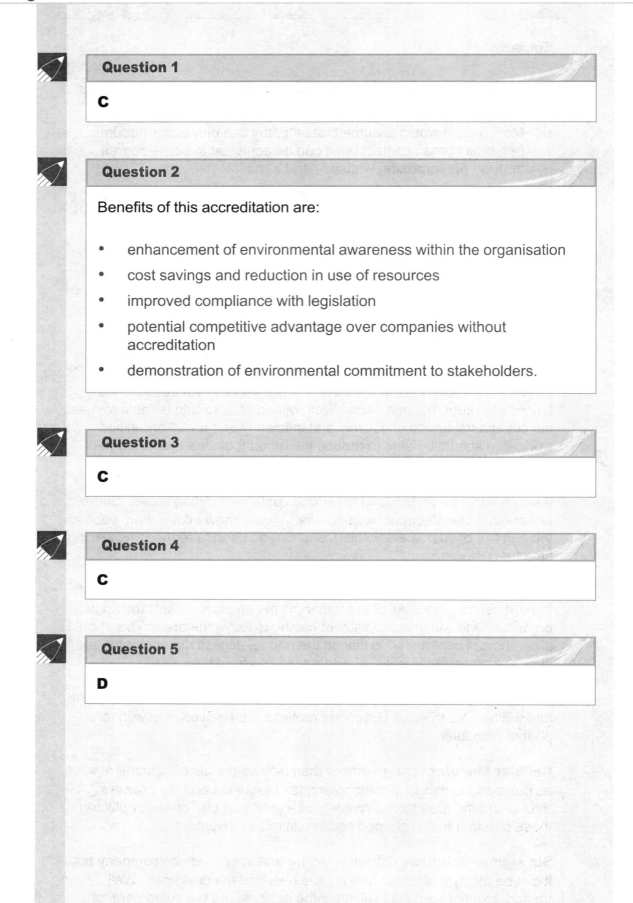

Question 1

C

Question 2

Benefits of this accreditation are:

- enhancement of environmental awareness within the organisation
- cost savings and reduction in use of resources
- improved compliance with legislation
- potential competitive advantage over companies without accreditation
- demonstration of environmental commitment to stakeholders.

Question 3

C

Question 4

C

Question 5

D

Question 6

- The management of quality is the function and responsibility of everyone within the organisation.

- Complex products require unique product specifications for demanding customers.

- Customer focus is important, giving value for money and quality and creating competitive value for the price paid. This requires a flexible approach to design procedures and requires supplier involvement at the design and production stages.

- Continuous improvement in both products and internal procedures is a critical factor in maintaining competitive advantage. A Total Quality Management programme (TQM) would instil quality throughout the organisation and ensure that service excellence and value are primary aims for the whole of the company.

Question 7

Servqual will use 22 questions to understand a respondent's attitude about service quality in the hotel. The questions are reliable indicators of five dimensions:

- Tangibles – for example, design of the hotel or cleanliness of the rooms.

- Reliability – for example, booking processed correctly or wake-up call received on time.

- Responsiveness – for example, staff respond to requests for directions.

- Assurance – for example, reception staff inspire confidence.

- Empathy – for example, each hotel guest is treated as an individual.

Question 8

Quality circles are a method of trying to encourage innovative ideas in production, and by involving employees they are likely to improve the prospects for acceptance of changes in products and working methods.

The production director should be advised that the nature of the changes recommended by the quality circle will depend on the range of skills and experience of the circle members. The wider their skills are, and the broader their experience, the more significant and far-reaching will be the changes they might suggest. Groups of workers with similar skills are more likely to make suggestions for limited changes, within the sphere of their own work experience. What range of skills should the circles have?

The 'terms of reference' of the circles should be made clear. Are they to recommend changes to senior management, or will they have the authority to decide changes, and make them?

Since the purpose of quality circles is to encourage innovation, the co-operation of employees will be crucial. The plans for setting up quality circles should therefore be discussed with the employees who will provide membership of the circles.

Possible problems with the introduction of quality circles might be:

(a) not enough support from top management.

(b) no co-operation from middle management.

(c) poor choice of circle leaders.

(d) insufficient training of circle members.

(e) unwillingness to participate among employees.

(f) individual talkers dominate the circle.

(g) poor communication.

The keys to a successful programme are:

(a) creating a proper atmosphere in which to launch them – a positive approach and good publicity.

(b) giving circle member adequate training in quality circle techniques.

(c) introducing circles slowly, one or two at a time, instead of setting up too many all at once. Learning from experience. Getting employees to accept the value of circles from their experience and observations over time.

(d) full support from top management.

(e) an enthusiastic 'facilitator' – a manager in charge of making the circles a success.

(f) setting up a good system for following up and evaluating proposals for change.

(g) giving recognition to circle members – for instance, rewards for successful changes.

Introduction to Marketing

Chapter learning objectives

Lead	Component
D1. Explain developments in marketing.	(a) Explain the marketing concept, and the alternatives to it.
	(b) Describe the marketing environment of a range of organisations.
	(e) Describe theories of consumer behaviour.

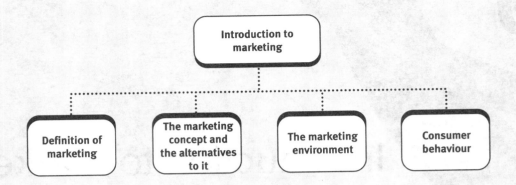

1 Introduction

- Organisations are increasingly recognising the importance of marketing's role and its contribution in achieving sustainable growth and profitability. It can be a key driver of competitive advantage. Marketing is not simply promotion but is a much broader concept.

- This chapter introduces what is meant by marketing. The following two chapters describe the marketing tools that an organisation may use to compete.

In the UK, the Chartered Institute of Marketing (CIM) defines marketing as:

"The management process responsible for identifying, anticipating and satisfying customer requirements profitably."

The organisation will first understand the needs of the customer and will then adopt a strategy producing products with the benefits and features to fulfil these needs.

2 The Marketing Concept, and the Alternatives to it

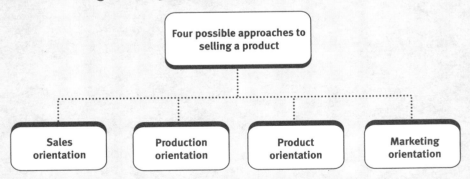

A marketing orientated business is one that has adopted a marketing concept (philosophy). However, a number of other 'orientations' – sales, production and product – may be adopted. Before explaining the marketing concept each of these alternatives will be introduced.

2.1 Sales orientation

- The major task of management is to use persuasive communication and aggressive promotional policies to entice the customer.
- The sales team and the sales manager are the focal point of the business.
- The belief is that a good sales team can sell anything to anybody.

Test your understanding 1

Explain the types of organisation that adopt a sales orientation.

Drawbacks of the sales orientation

- There is no systematic attempt to identify customer needs, or to create products that satisfy them.
- As a result, the organisation has to rely on intensive sales techniques.

2.2 Production orientation

The main focus is on production efficiencies and low costs.

Illustration 1 – Production orientation

In America and Europe, the production orientation was a popular approach until the 1930s. Up until then, there was a general shortage of goods relative to demand and a lack of competition resulted in a seller's market.

During periods of shortages, a production orientation sometimes returns to an industry sector. Normally the UK honey industry is typified by a marketing orientation (see below), where customer needs are prioritised. However, a poor summer in the UK in 2008 resulted in a honey shortage since worker bees don't forage as much in the rain or cold weather. This resulted in producers simply trying to harvest and produce as much honey as possible, a production orientation.

Drawbacks of the production orientation

- If production exceeds demand, too much may be produced and left unsold.
- The approach does not take account of customer preferences and the low cost may be associated with lower quality.

2.3 Product orientation

The business centres its activities on continually improving and refining its products, assuming that customers simply want the best quality for their money.

Drawbacks of the product orientation

The business concentrates on its products and, as a result, the product may or may not fulfil customer requirements.

Illustration 2 – Product orientation

Sir Clive Sinclair's business adopted a product orientation. Some of his products proved extremely popular. For example, The Spectrum computer released in 1981 was very cheap and powerful for its day.

Other products were not such a success: The Sinclair C5, a road hugging vehicle that could reach speeds of 15mph. When it was released in 1985, it was billed as the last word in futuristic transport. However, it was rumoured to be powered by a washing machine motor and was so small that driving it was dangerous. The product was consigned to the commercial scrapheap after just ten months.

2.4 Marketing orientation

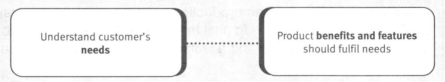

All of the approaches reviewed so far have potential drawbacks. The best approach that an organisation can adopt is a marketing orientation.

Benefits of the marketing orientation

Where an organisation is able to meet its customers' needs efficiently and effectively, its ability to gain an advantage over its competitors will be increased.

As CIM point out:

"It is all about getting the right product or service to the customer at the right price, in the right place, at the right time. Business history and current practice both remind us that without proper marketing, companies cannot get close to customers and satisfy their needs. And if they don't, a competitor surely will."

Test your understanding 2

Car manufacturers must adapt their strategy to reflect changing customer needs. For example:

- In the 1980's some car manufacturers targeted young upwardly-mobile professionals (yuppies).

- In the early 21st century, car manufacturers targeting families have had to recognise the changing needs of the modern family.

Using the example of a car, explain the needs of the two groups above. Describe what features and benefits manufacturers have included in their cars in order to fulfil the needs of these customers.

Who is responsible for marketing?

Satisfying customers is at the heart of marketing. Who then assumes responsibility for this important function? Possibly the marketing department or the sales force? True, such personnel can have an influence on customer satisfaction, but marketing as a philosophy is wider than this narrow group of employees. Employees outside the marketing department or sales force can also play an important role in determining customer satisfaction.

Marketing is more than a range of techniques that enables the company to determine customer requirements. It can be better understood as a shared business ethos. The marketing concept is a philosophy that places customers central to all organisational activities. The long-term strategies of an organisation might be centred on profit maximisation, market share growth, or growth in real terms but none of this can be achieved without satisfying customers.

Without customers there would be no business.

3 The Marketing Environment

3.1 Different levels in the marketing environment

The marketing environment is the content in which the organisation exists. The environment can have a considerable impact on the organisation and exists at three levels.

The macro environment

This includes all the factors that influence an organisation but are outside of their control. Organisations will need flexible marketing practices to respond to this dynamic environment.

Test your understanding 3

The factors in the macro environment are realistically out of the organisation's control, however is there any way an organisation may seek to exercise some influence?

The micro environment

This includes all the factors that can influence an organisation, but the organisation has some opportunity to exercise influence. It consists of the organisation's stakeholders, such as suppliers and customers.

The internal environment

This includes all the factors that are internal to the organisation and are therefore potentially all controllable including its human resources, finance available and assets.

3.2 PEST(EL) analysis

One popular technique for analysing the **macro** environment is PEST(EL) analysis.

This analysis divides the business environment into six related sub-systems – Political, Economic, Social, Technical, Environmental/Ecological factors and Legal. Each of these factors can be applied to the marketing function.

Political

Political factors can have a direct effect on the way a business operates. Decisions made by government affect our everyday lives.

For example, the instability of many governments in less developed countries has led a number of companies to question the wisdom of marketing in those countries.

Economic

All businesses are affected by economical factors nationally and globally. For example, within the UK, the climate of the economy can dictate how consumers behave within society.

Test your understanding 4

Describe the changes that may be made to the marketing approach of a supermarket if the country goes into recession.

Social

Forces within society such as family, friends and the media affect our attitude, interests and opinions and, in turn, will influence our purchases.

For example, within the UK people's attitudes are changing towards their diet and health. Over the last 10 years, the UK has seen an increase in the number of people joining fitness clubs and a massive increase in demand for organic food.

Social factors

According to Johnson and Scholes the following social influences should be monitored:

- **Population demographics** – a term used to describe the composition of the population in any given area, whether a region, a country or an area within a country.

- **Income distribution** – will provide the marketer with some indication of the size of the target markets. Most developed countries, like the UK, have a relatively even distribution spread. However, this is not the case in other nations.

- **Social mobility** – the marketer should be aware of social classes and the distribution among them. The marketer can use this knowledge to promote products to distinct social classes within the market.

- **Lifestyle changes** – refer to our attitudes and opinions to things like social values, credit, health and women. Our attitudes have changed in recent years and this information is vital for the marketer.

- **Consumerism** – one of the social trends in recent years has been the rise of consumerism. This trend has increased to such an extent that governments have been pressured to design laws that protect the rights of the consumer.

- **Levels of education** – the level of education has increased dramatically over the last few years. There is now a larger proportion of the population in higher education than ever before.

Technical

This is an area in which change takes place very rapidly and the organisation needs to be constantly aware of what is going on.

For example, new technology has resulted in the production of new products, such as hybrid cars. These cars have improved fuel economy and reduced emissions.

Ecological

These have become increasingly important in recent years and influence a marketing orientated organisation in a number of ways

For example, pressure on natural resources has influenced the products offered by some industry sectors, e.g. the fishing industry.

Legal

Regulations governing businesses are widespread; they include those on health and safety, information disclosure, the dismissal of employees, vehicle emissions, the use of pesticides and many more.

For example, the UK smoking ban in public places has resulted in UK tobacco companies exploring new products, such as the legal, electronic cigarette (these simulate the functions of a cigarette but without the harmful chemicals), and new markets outside of the UK.

4 Consumer Behaviour

4.1 Introduction

The marketing concept means that organisations need to understand their customers before marketing plans can be developed, or attempts made to improve customer satisfaction.

4.2 Factors affecting buying decisions

Lancaster and Withey concluded that there are three key factors that influence the purchasing decision:

Factor	Examples
(1) Socio/ cultural influences	• **Reference groups** such as school friends or work colleagues e.g. it is a bold person who reads the Sun in an office full of FT readers • **Role modelling** e.g. a young mother would be influenced to make certain buying decisions, such as a push chair, due to her role • **Family** e.g. the influence of 'pester power' may result in child dominant decisions. • **Culture** e.g. beliefs and values may influence whether or not meat is bought by a household.
(2) Personal influences	• Age • Family status • Occupation • Economic circumstances • Lifestyle e.g. a young single male in his 20s, with a high level of disposable income, is likely to purchase a different type of car to a man in his 30s with a growing family.
(3) Psychological influences	• Motivation • Perception • Learning • Beliefs and attitudes e.g. Individuals will be motivated by different needs. Some buyers may be motivated by superb customer service and would not return to a restaurant unless this is received.

Social interaction theory states that an individual's behaviour may depend on what he or she perceives others in society to be doing. The social influence of others therefore impacts on a person's buying habits.

4.3 The stages in the buying process

Lancaster and Withey concluded that customers go through a five stage decision-making process in any purchase. This is summarised in the diagram below:

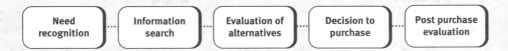

Stage 1: Need (problem) recognition

The consumer identifies the need or the problem and the firm must use appropriate promotional tools to convince the customer that their product could be the answer.

Illustration 3

Marketers have recognised that the cheap coffee that was once bought from a supermarket or a cafe is not going to satisfy the needs of increasingly discerning buyers who seek a coffee that suits their particular tastes, lifestyle and budget. In addition, a growing awareness of ethical trading and healthy living has contributed to the development of coffee to cater for these increasingly complex needs.

Starbucks is one company that has successfully understood these needs. Its cafes sell a huge range of coffees and other beverages and the company also sells its own-branded quality coffee in UK supermarkets.

Stage 2: Information search

Once a need has been recognised buyers will look for information regarding which products may satisfy their needs.

Test your understanding 5

Explain what information sources are likely to be used by a buyer when seeking out information about the alternative ways in which they can satisfy their needs.

Stage 3: Evaluation of alternatives

The consumer compares various brands and products in order to make a choice. The organisation needs to understand the basis of this choice (e.g. price, quality, design, branding etc).

Stage 4: Decision to purchase

This stage is where the customer actually makes a purchase choice.

The final decision to purchase may involve a large number of people, known as the decision-making unit (DMU). The DMU is made up of six groups:

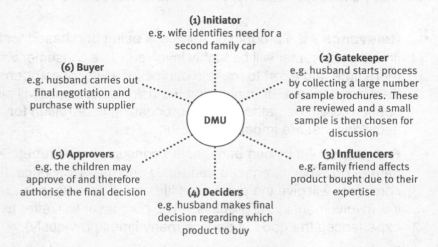

(1) Initiator
e.g. wife identifies need for a second family car

(2) Gatekeeper
e.g. husband starts process by collecting a large number of sample brochures. These are reviewed and a small sample is then chosen for discussion

(3) Influencers
e.g. family friend affects product bought due to their expertise

(4) Deciders
e.g. husband makes final decision regarding which product to buy

(5) Approvers
e.g. the children may approve of and therefore authorise the final decision

(6) Buyer
e.g. husband carries out final negotiation and purchase with supplier

DMU

Stage 5: Post-purchase evaluation

The consumer will assess whether they are satisfied with their purchase decision.

Satisfied customers will act as one of the best forms of promotion: a customer spending just $20 in a restaurant on a first visit could be worth thousands of pounds over the next few years.

The company may seek customer feedback.

Evaluation of 5-stage process

The five-stage model implies that customers pass through all stages in every purchase. However, in more routine purchases, customers often skip or reverse some of the stages.

For example, a student buying a favourite hamburger would recognise the need (hunger) and go right to the purchasing decision, skipping information search and evaluation. However, the model is very useful when understanding any purchase that requires some thought and deliberation.

4.4 Buyer behaviour

> ### Buyer behaviour
>
> Rationally consumer behaviour can be understood in terms of:
>
> - **Relevance** – if a product or service is being purchased for the first time the consumer will be highly involved. The consumer will take more time and effort to make a choice as a way of compensating for their inexperience or minimising the risk. Consumers will also spend more time gathering and processing information for decisions that are important for them.
>
> - **Frequency** – if by comparison, the consumption is repetitive by nature, possibly purchased frequently and has a low price, the consumer will give the purchase little conscious attention and have low involvement in the process. (The purchaser will, after all have experienced the good or service many times previously).
>
> - **Freedom** – a less voluntary or involuntary consumption. It may be seen as something unavoidable possibly if there is little choice between brands, for example the purchasing process is refilling a car with fuel.
>
> - **Influence** – here the issue is the susceptibility of the consumer to influence by others because the consumer might be purchasing on behalf of the family as a whole or the business they work for.

4.5 Theories of consumer behaviour

The following theories should help to guide marketing practices:

- **Cognitive paradigm theory** – the theory is based on the idea that a purchase is an outcome of problem-solving. The consumer receives and makes sense of considerable quantities of information before choosing between products.

- **The learned behaviour theory** – consumers learn from past satisfying or unsatisfying purchases and therefore make shortcuts with future routine/habitual purchases.

- **Habitual decision making** – consumers make decisions based on loyalty, inertia or satisfying behaviour (i.e. the first product is good enough even if a better solution exists).

4.6 Types of buyer behaviour

Buyer behaviour will be influenced by the type of consumer good:

Type of consumer good	Meaning	Factors influencing the purchase
Fast moving consumer good (FMCG)	• Relatively cheap • Purchased on a regular basis e.g. bread, baked beans	• Habitual purchases – often involves very little decision making by buyer • Advertising, branding and packaging will be important.
Durable goods	• Relatively expensive • Not purchased on a regular basis e.g. TV, computer, car	• Fashion • New technical features • Old product wearing out

5 Chapter summary

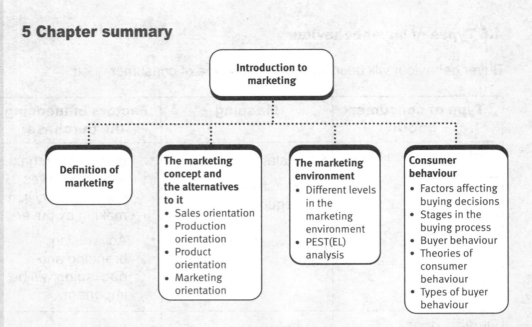

6 Practice questions

Question 1

A company that concentrates on using aggressive promotional policies to entice the customer is referred to as:

A   a production organisation

B   a learning organisation

C   a marketing organisation

D   a sales organisation

(2 marks)

Question 2

Which of the following is a drawback of the production orientation?

A   The business concentrates on its products but the product may not fulfil the customer's needs

B   The organisation relies on sales techniques to sell its products

C   Low cost may be associated with low quality

D   High volume production results in economies of scale

(2 marks)

Question 3

Which one of the following is not one of the accepted headings included in PESTEL analysis?

A   Economic

B   Taxation

C   Social

D   Technical

(2 marks)

Question 4

Harry is 12 years old. He is a keen Manchester United supporter and in his spare time he plays football for his local team and is a scout member. Which of the following would be least likely to be a reference group for Harry?

A   His teachers

B   One of the Manchester United players

C   The other members of his local football team

D   The other members of his scout group

(2 marks)

Question 5

Which of the following is an example of a durable good?

A   A games console

B   Milk

C   Tea bags

D   Shampoo

(2 marks)

Question 6

Distinguish socio/cultural influences from personal influences, giving examples of each.

(4 marks)

Question 7

List FOUR examples of fast moving consumer goods and FOUR examples of durable goods.

(4 marks)

Question 8

M Company began over a century ago as a small family-run business, selling its own-branded clothing, food and drink. The company has grown rapidly over the past 30 years and now has a prominent position on the high street of many of the country's towns and cities.

Until recently, the company had a strong reputation and was well known for quality products at affordable prices. However, the situation has changed dramatically as new entrants have taken market share away from M company.

Sales and profits have fallen over each of the three past consecutive years and there is concern that the company may make a loss in the forthcoming year.

After various attempts failed to improve matters, M company has recently appointed a management consultant to identify the reasons for the declining sales and the loss of customers.

The marketing consultant has concluded that the problem for M company is that it has never moved from being sales orientated to being marketing orientated and that is why it has lost touch with its customers. The consultant has recommended the adoption of a marketing orientation.

Required:

(a) Explain the difference between a company that concentrates on 'selling' its products and one that has adopted a marketing orientation. Explain the benefits to M company of adopting a marketing orientation.

(10 marks)

(b) Explain, using examples, how M company's marketing function may use PESTEL analysis to understand its external environment.

(10 marks)

(Total: 20 marks)

Test your understanding answers

Test your understanding 1

A sales orientation has been adopted by a number of business sectors. For example:

- Organisations selling double glazing
- Organisations selling timeshare holidays

These organisations rely on persuasive and aggressive promotional policies to entice the customer.

Test your understanding 2

	Needs of target customer	Product features	Product benefits
1980's - some car manufacturers targeted yuppies	• A fast car • Cutting edge design • Car should enhance image	• Sporty design • Turbo engine • Other features such as an electrically operated roof and leather upholstery	• 0-60 mph in six seconds • Superb road handling
Early 21st century - some car manufacturers target families but have had to recognise their changing needs	• Value for money • Safety • Environmental friendliness • Low fuel consumption	• Air bags • Economical engine • Designed for safety and space	• Good safety record • Low fuel consumption and CO_2 emissions • Room for child seats

Test your understanding 3

An organisation may seek to influence laws by political lobbying or by being part of a trade organisation.

Test your understanding 4

The changing needs of the population must be reflected in the product offerings. For example:

* The supermarket may reduce its range of luxury items in favour of lower priced, basic products.

* Special offers may be made on products, for example, discounts, buy one get one free offers, additional loyalty points on products.

* The supermarket may introduce more 'restaurant style' meals to reflect the trend that fewer people are eating out.

Test your understanding 5

* **Personal experience** – the buyer may already have used the company's products.

* **Word-of-mouth** – for example, recommendations from friends regarding a restaurant.

* **Internet** – for example, websites such as Trip Advisor include user feedback on a large number of hotels.

* **Reference groups** – rather than referring to people we know, we may use various other reference groups to guide us, for example, what kind of shoes is our favourite celebrity wearing at the moment?

* **Reviews** – newspapers and consumer review sources such as Which? magazine.

Question 1

D

Question 2

C

Question 3

B

Question 4

A

Question 5

A

Question 6

- Personal influences are specific to the individual and include factors such as age, occupation and family status.

- These personal influences will impact the needs of the individual. For example, a 35 year old professional male, who is married with a young family, may have a need for an estate car.

- However, the manifestation of these needs will be influenced by socio/ cultural factors, e.g. reference groups, role models, family and culture.

- For example, the colleagues of the 35 year old male may influence the model of estate car purchased.

Question 7

Durable goods	Fast moving consumer goods
Car	Bread
Washing machine	Washing powder
Fridge	Butter
MP3 player	Milk

Question 8

(a) Sales orientation

A company that concentrates on 'selling' its products is said to be sales orientated. M company currently adopts a sales orientation.

The major task of M's management will be to use persuasive communication and aggressive promotional policies to entice the customer to buy its products.

The sales team and the sales manager will be the focal point of M company. There will be huge investment in the sales department, the belief being that a good sales team can sell anything to anybody.

Techniques such as personal selling and product promotion will be used to emphasise product differentiation and branding.

Drawbacks of the sales orientation

M company is losing customers and its sales and profits have fallen for each of the past three consecutive years. These problems may be largely due to the adoption of a sales orientation since:

– There is no systematic attempt by M company to identify customer's needs, or to create products that satisfy these needs.

– As a result, M company is having to rely on intensive sales techniques but these do not appear to be working.

Adoption of a marketing orientation

This orientation addresses the problems highlighted above.

If M company were to adopt a marketing orientation, they would begin by understanding the needs of the customer and would then adopt a strategy producing products with the benefits and features to fulfil these needs.

Benefits of a marketing orientation

If M company adopts a marketing orientation it will put its customer's needs first. If it is able to identify these needs and meet the needs efficiently and effectively, its ability to gain competitive advantage will increase.

(b) If M company is to turn itself around, not only will it have to understand its customer's needs but it will also need to understand the opportunities, challenges and risks presented by changes in the external environment. PESTEL analysis can be used to analyse the external environment. Each of these factors can be applied to M company's marketing function.

Political

Political factors will have a direct effect on the way in which M company operates.

For example, the government in the UK is currently encouraging sustainability in operations and the adoption of a healthy lifestyle by individuals. This may influence a decision by M company to reduce the amount of packaging in its products or to improve product labelling to clearly show the sugar, fat, salt and calorie content of their food products.

Economic

M company will be affected by national and global economic factors.

For example, if the country moves into recession, M company may decide to focus on selling cheaper products rather than luxury products.

Social

Forces within society such as family, friends and the media will influence the choices that individuals make.

For example, within the UK consumer's attitudes, with regards to the source of products, is changing. Ethical sourcing is becoming more important to individuals, e.g. with an increased emphasis on fair trade, a reduction in air miles and fair treatment of suppliers all being considered important. These factors will all influence the decisions taken by M company.

Technical

This is an area in which change takes place very rapidly and it is important for M company to monitor and react to these changes.

For example, new technology may allow existing products to be made more quickly and hence prices can be lowered.

Ecological

These have become increasingly important is recent years and M company must react to any ecological factors. For example, pressure on natural resources may influence the types of fish that M company sell or include in their products.

Legal

Regulations on businesses are widespread, including those on health and safety, information disclosure, the dismissal of employees and many more. For example, M company must clearly display product information on its goods, such as a list of ingredients on its packaged food.

If M company understands its customer's needs as well as its external environment, there is a good opportunity for the business to be turned around.

10

The Market Planning Process and the Marketing Mix

Chapter learning objectives

Lead	Component
D2. Apply tools and techniques used in support of the organisation's marketing.	(a) Explain the relationships between market research, market segmentation, targeting and positioning.
	(b) Apply tools within each area of the marketing mix.
	(d) Describe the market planning process.
	(e) Explain the role of branding and brand equity.

1 The Market Planning Process

A company may currently have a sales/ production/ product orientation and may want to adopt a marketing orientation. In order to do this, it will need to implement a strategic marketing action plan.

The following components should be included in this plan:

Step 1: Situation analysis

A number of techniques can be used:

SWOT analysis – the organisation needs to understand its own strengths and weaknesses together with an appreciation of the wider environment in which it operates (opportunities and threats).

PEST(EL) analysis – the organisation should review the macro environment for opportunities that may allow it to further meet their customers' needs. It should also monitor its competitors' strategies.

Step 2: Review corporate objectives/mission

The organisation may already have a mission statement and a set of corporate objectives in place. However, these should be reviewed to ensure that they are still relevant for the organisation.

Step 3: Set its marketing objectives

Marketing objectives should be consistent with the company's overall mission and objectives.

Marketing objectives should be SMART – specific, measurable, achievable, realistic and time bound, e.g. to achieve a 10% growth in sales in Europe in the next 12 months.

Step 4: Devise an appropriate marketing strategy

The organisation should consider the following:

- Segmentation – the market should be segmented, e.g. by age, social class or income. The needs of each segment should be established using market research.

- Targeting – the most attractive segments in terms of profitability and growth should be targeted using an appropriate marketing mix.

- Positioning – an appropriate positioning strategy, e.g. differentiation or cost leadership should be chosen for each market segment.

- Marketing mix – the organisation should use the marketing mix to determine the correct strategy for product, price, place and promotion.

Market research will be required to understand the organisation's activities and to provide a basis for effective marketing decisions to be made.

Note: Each of these ideas will be explored in more detail in the remainder of the chapter.

Step 5: Plan the marketing mix

The organisation must then plan the specific elements of the marketing mix into a marketing action plan.

The marketing action plan will form an important component of any business plan. The business plan has many objectives including:

- Securing external funding
- Measuring business success.

Step 6: Implementation

The marketing action plan should then be implemented.

Step 7: Review

The plan should also be monitored to gauge its success and to identify any necessary changes.

2 Segmentation, Targeting and Positioning

2.1 Market segmentation

Market segmentation is the sub-dividing of the market into homogenous groups to whom a separate marketing mix can be focused.

A market segment is a group of consumers with distinct, shared needs.

Why segment the market?

- Market segmentation allows companies to treat similar customers in similar ways.

- Each segment has slightly different needs which can be satisfied by offering each segment a slightly different marketing mix.

- The key objective is to say that people falling into a particular segment are more likely to purchase the product than most.

- The company will choose a particular segment or segments to target.

Criteria for market segments

Kotler suggested that segments must be:

- **Measurable** – It must be possible to identify the number of buyers in each market segment so that their potential profitability can be assessed, e.g. the size of the segment of people aged 30–40, or who are married with children, can be accurately calculated but information about the number of people who are environmentally aware is not readily available.

- **Accessible** – It must be possible to reach the segment, e.g. some buyers in a market may be tied to suppliers by long-term supply contracts. Therefore, this market is not accessible.

- **Substantial** – The cost of targeting a particular segment must be less than the benefit. Small market segments may prove unprofitable.

Bases for segmentation

One form of segmentation may be enough, or a number of variables may be used, to define the target market exactly. Possible bases include:

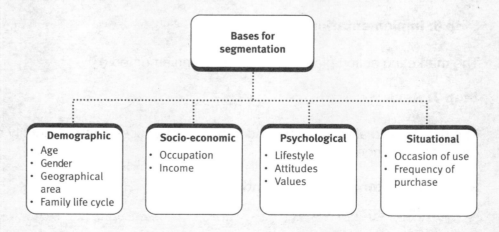

Bases for segmentation

Demographic

Market segments are frequently based on age, gender, geographical location or family life cycle.

This can be highly relevant with some products, for example, certain brands of breakfast cereal have regular sales to families with young children (e.g. Coco Pops), where as other brands (e.g. Bran Flakes) sell almost entirely to adults.

In other areas, demographic influences seem to have little effect. For instance, own-label products are believed to sell equally to high and low income families and single people and across all age groups.

Family life cycle segmentation divides customers by their position in the family life cycle:

Life cycle stage	Characteristics	Examples of products purchased
Bachelor	Financially well off. Fashion opinion leaders. Recreation orientated.	Cars, holidays, basic furniture, kitchen equipment.
Newly married couple	Still financially well off. Very high purchase rate, especially of durables.	Cars, furniture, houses, holidays, refrigerators.
Full nest (i)	Liquid assets low. Home purchasing at a peak. Little money saving.	Washers, TVs, baby foods, toys, medicines.
Full nest (ii)	Better off. Some partners work. Some children work part time. Less influenced by advertising.	Larger size grocery packs, foods, cleaning materials, bicycles.
Full nest (iii)	Better off still. Purchasing durables.	New furniture, luxury appliances, recreational goods.
Empty nest (i)	Satisfied with financial position.	Travel, luxuries, home improvements.
Empty nest (ii)	Drastic cut in income. Stay at home.	Medicines, health aids.

Socio-economic

One of the most widely used forms of segmentation in the UK is socio-economic.

Class	Social status	Job descriptions
A	Upper middle class	Higher managerial, administrative and professional
B	Middle class	Middle management, administrative and professional
C1	Lower middle class	Supervisory, clerical, junior management, administrative staff
C2	Working class	Semi and unskilled manual jobs
D	Subsistence	Pensioners, widows, lowest grade workers

While such class-based systems may seem out of date, the model is still widely used, especially in advertising. Socio-economic class is closely correlated with press readership and viewing habits, and media planners use this fact to advertise in the most effective way to communicate with their target audience.

Psychological

Lifestyle segmentation may be used because people of similar age and socio-economic status may lead quite different lifestyles. Marketers have segmented the market using terms such as 'Yuppies' (young, upwardly-mobile professionals) and 'Dinkies' (double income, no kids).

Attitudes and values can be harder to measure but can prove to be a useful basis for segmentation, e.g. individuals may have a value based on caution and therefore purchase a safe, reliable car.

Situational

Occasion of use – a product may be bought at different times for different uses. For example, workers may expect a lunchtime meal in a restaurant to be fast and good value for money, whereas those same individuals may be willing to pay more in the evening for a more relaxed dining experience.

Frequency of purchase – frequent buyers may be more demanding with regards to product features and may be more sensitive to price changes.

Test your understanding 1

Explain five variables that you think would be useful as a basis for segmenting the market for cars.

Industrial segmentation

Industrial segmentation is different from that used in consumer marketing. The following factors influence the way industrial customers can be segmented:

Geographic is used as the basis for sales-force organisations.

Purchasing characteristics – is the classification of companies by factors such as average order size or the frequency with which they order.

Benefit – industrial purchasers have different benefit expectations to consumers. They may be orientated towards reliability, durability, versatility, safety, serviceability or ease of operation. They are always concerned with value for money.

Company type – industrial customers can be segmented according to the type of business they are, i.e. what they offer for sale. The range of products and services used in an industry will not vary too much from one company to another.

Company size – it is frequently useful to analyse marketing opportunities in terms of company size. A company supplying canteen foods would investigate size in terms of numbers of employees. Processed parts suppliers are interested in production rate, and lubricants suppliers would segment by numbers of machine tools.

2.2 Targeting

Targeting is the process of selecting the most lucrative market segment(s) for marketing the product.

Having segmented the market, the organisation can now decide how to respond to the differences in customer needs identified and will reach a conclusion as to which segments are worth targeting.

When evaluating potential target markets, the following issues should be considered:

- Size of segment

- Growth potential

- Profit potential

- Degree of competition

- Accessibility

- Barriers to entry

2.3 Positioning

 Positioning involves the formulation of a definitive marketing strategy around which the product would be marketed to the target audience.

After the target market has been chosen, marketers will want to position their products in relation to the competitors for that segment. A variety of techniques are available.

For example, the market for package holidays can be split into a variety of different segments – the family market, the elderly market, the young singles market, the activity holiday market, the budget holiday market, etc.

It would be virtually impossible to provide one single holiday package that would satisfy all people in the above markets. Because the people in the different segments will have different needs and wants, a holiday company has a choice in terms of its marketing approach. It can go for:

- **Concentrated marketing** (sometimes referred to as niche or target marketing) specialises in one or two of the identified markets only, where a company knows it can compete successfully. For example, Saga holidays offers a variety of holidays for the older market niche only.

- **Differentiated marketing** (sometimes called segmented marketing) – the company makes several products each aimed at a separate target segment. For example, Virgin Holidays offers a variety of family holidays, honeymoon packages and city breaks, each of which is targeted at a different group. Many retailers have developed different brand formats to target different groups.

- **Undifferentiated marketing** (sometimes called mass marketing) – this is the delivery of a single product to the entire market. There is little concern for segmentation. The hope is that as many customers as possible will buy the product. When Henry Ford began manufacturing cars he offered any colour 'as long as it's black'.

Perceptual mapping

Perceptual mapping is used to chart consumers' perceptions of brands currently on offer and to identify opportunities for launching new brands or to reposition an existing brand. Marketers decide upon a competitive position that enables them to distinguish their own products from the offerings of their competition (hence the term 'positioning strategy').

The marketer would draw out the map and decide upon a label for each axis. They could be price (variable one) and quality (variable two), or comfort (variable one) and price (variable two). The individual products are then mapped out next to each other. Any gaps (strategic spaces) could be regarded as possible areas for new products. The analysis below illustrates a local grocery market.

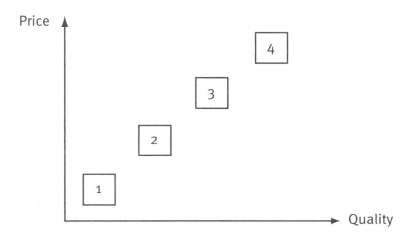

The two critical success factors here are price and quality. Of course, others, such as location, opening hours, marketing expenditure, and so on might be important too under some circumstances.

Group 1 are the price discounters. The business cuts cost wherever it can. Product ranges are restricted and there are few attempts to make the store decorative or service friendly.

Group 2 are the main market retailers. They compete on price, but offer more and better ranges, better customer service, and so on.

Group 3 offer a higher quality range, they do not attempt to compete on price at all.

Group 4 are delicatessens. They offer a superior service and specialist items. Prices are very high.

It is a great strategic mistake to try to position oneself where there are no customer groups. For example, several companies have tried to cross between groups 1 and 2, usually without success.

3 Market Research and Forecasting

3.1 Market research

Market research is the way in which organisations find out what their customers and potential customers need, want and care about.

It involves a number of data gathering techniques and methods of analysis:

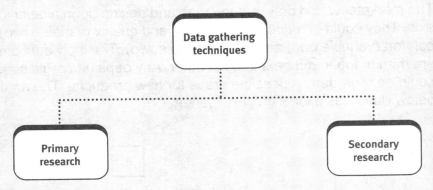

Primary research

This is collected for the specific purpose of the research in question. The organisation may enlist a specialist agency to carry out the research. Methods include:

- **Questionnaires** – A popular technique and can be done face to face, online, over the telephone or by self completion. Key information about the respondents will be obtained for segmentation purposes.

- **Focus groups** – consist of a group of approximately 8–10 people plus a trained moderator who leads a discussion on an issue about which the company wants to learn more, e.g. feedback on a new product.

- **Observation** – observational techniques can be used to understand behaviour, for example:
  - Many organisations will monitor their competitors through gathering brochures, monitoring websites and obtaining price lists. This will help the organisation to understand how its competitors are aiming to fulfil the needs of its customers.

  - In addition, the internet has allowed customer behaviour to be monitored, e.g. how many visits has a customer made to a website, have there been subsequent purchases, which pages did they review and in which order?

- **Interviews** – a similar approach to questionnaires but may be more detailed and open ended and may focus on a smaller group due to the time involved.

- **Experimentation** – similar to focus groups, in so much as users may discuss a product, but it does not require group discussion. For example, triad testing is where people are asked which of a given three items they prefer. If the three are brands of a given type, replies may show a great deal about which features of a product most influence the buying decision.

Data collection and analysis will be helped by the use of technology, e.g. the use of databases.

Secondary research

This is data that is already available and is therefore cheaper and quicker than carrying out primary research. However, the data may not be accurate and may not meet the exact needs of the organisation.

Test your understanding 2
Describe the sources of secondary research that may be available.

3.2 Forecasting

Forecasting will focus on sales potential.

The **sales potential** is an estimate of the part of the market that is within the possible reach of a product.

Estimates of sales potential are required to decide whether to invest money in the development or promotion of a new or improved product. The forecasting of sales potential can be based on:

- historical data, e.g. using techniques such as linear regression
- future demand, e.g. using:
  - a survey of buyers' intentions
  - sales force/other expert's estimates.

Forecasting

The determination of the future profitability of a chosen target segment is the critical element for marketing success. Sales forecasting may utilise a variety of sources, rely on hard facts and subjective views as well as use technology and gut feeling to reveal what is essentially an unknown future to the marketer.

Market demand (total market potential)

This approach uses a combination of variables in simple formulaic structure to determine the future market potential. Variables are:

- Size of customer group;
- Time period;
- Geographical area;
- Market environment.

Area demand (area market potential)

This is an identical approach but on a smaller geographic scale.

Industry sales and market share

Determination of industry size and the company's relative sales will provide an analysis of market share that can be used to extrapolate income based on projected growth in the marketplace over the future time period.

Survey of buyers' intentions

Survey of a small group of potential customers, and their reaction to a marketing mix provides some general indication of the likely uptake of a full marketing strategy in the future.

Sales force opinions

Since the sales team is close to the customer, they will provide an expert view on the potential future success of a new product.

Expert opinions

Independent experts offer an unbiased view of future environmental conditions, particularly economic change, that affects consumer confidence and buyer behaviour.

Past sales analysis

Trend analysis, including seasonal elements smoothed through time series analysis, could be used as the basis for forecasts.

Market tests

There are a variety of market tests including the launch of a trial product in a localised area or the use of market research to elicit possible buyer responses to a new product. This could be the same as a survey of buyers' intentions.

4 The Marketing Mix

4.1 Introduction

Once the positioning strategy has been arrived at, the marketing mix will be formulated.

By blending the different 'P's' of the marketing mix together the organisation aims to satisfy customer's needs profitably.

The traditional marketing mix (4P's):	Elements
Product	Quality, design, durability, packaging, range of sizes/ options, after-sales service, warranties, brand image.
Place	Where to sell the goods, distribution channels and coverage, stock levels, warehouse locations.
Promotion	Advertising, personal selling, public relations, sales promotion, sponsorship, direct marketing, e.g. direct mail and telephone marketing.
Price	Price level, discounts, credit policy, payment methods.
Additional 3P's for the service industry:	
People	Relates to both staff, who will have a high level of customer contact in the service industry (staff will need to be motivated to support the firm's external marketing activities), and customer's whose needs must be monitored (e.g. supermarkets use customer loyalty cards).

Processes	These are the systems through which the service is delivered, e.g. teaching methods used in a university, speed and friendliness of service in a restaurant.
Physical evidence	Required to make the intangible service more tangible, e.g. brochures, testimonials, appearance of staff and of the environment.

The extension of the traditional marketing mix to include the three additional P's acknowledges that there are fundamental differences between products and services (as discussed in Chapter 6) and therefore services marketing assumes a different emphasis to product marketing.

Features of service organisations

The main differentiating features of services are:

- The consumer is a participant in the service process.

- Services are perishable. If there is no sale on Monday, it cannot (like a tin of fruit) be sold on Tuesday; that sale is lost forever. Pricing will be mindful of the perishability of the service.

- Services are intangible, so communication is made more difficult when explaining the benefits.

- Services are people orientated and the characteristics of the workforce determine the effectiveness of the service. Promotion might emphasise personal selling.

- Output measurement is less easy to evidence.

Test your understanding 3

H Company, a High Street clothing retailer, designs and sells clothing. Until recently, the company was well-known for quality clothing at an affordable price, but the situation has changed dramatically as new entrants to the market have rapidly taken market share away from H Company.

One marketing analyst has commented that the problem for H Company is that it has never moved from being sales orientated to being marketing orientated and that this is why it has lost touch with its customers.

Required:

Explain how the management in H Company could make use of the traditional marketing mix to help regain its competitive position in the clothing market.

Link between the marketing mix and positioning

The marketing mix is essentially the working out of the tactical details of the positioning strategy. An organisation should ensure that all of the above elements are consistent with each other.

For example, a firm that decides to go for a strategy of differentiation through high quality, knows that it must produce high quality products, charge a relatively high price, distribute through high-class dealers and advertise in high quality magazines.

Each element of the traditional marketing mix will now be reviewed in turn:

4.2 Product

4.2.1 Introduction

A product can be a physical commodity, a service or an experience. It has two important roles in the marketing mix:

- It plays a key role in satisfying the customer's needs.
- Product differentiation is an important part of competitive strategy.

4.2.2 Product portfolio

A product portfolio is a collection of products or services an organisation provides to its customers.

After determining the main target markets and the type of product(s) it will offer, the organisation needs to determine the variety and assortment of those products.

The following are the elements of a typical product portfolio:

- **Product item**: This is the individual product, e.g. a specific model of phone or a brand of washing powder. The organisation will usually sell a variety of product items.

- **Product line**: This is a collection of product items that are closely related. For example, The Campbell Soup Company sells many types of soup.

- **Product mix**: This is the total range of product lines that a company has to offer. It consists of:
    - **Width** – the number of product lines. For example, Apple sell computers, i-pods, phones and accessories.
    - **Depth** – the number of product items within each product line. For example, Apple sell a large variety of i-pods.

Different ways of defining a product

The product can be viewed or defined in a number of different ways:

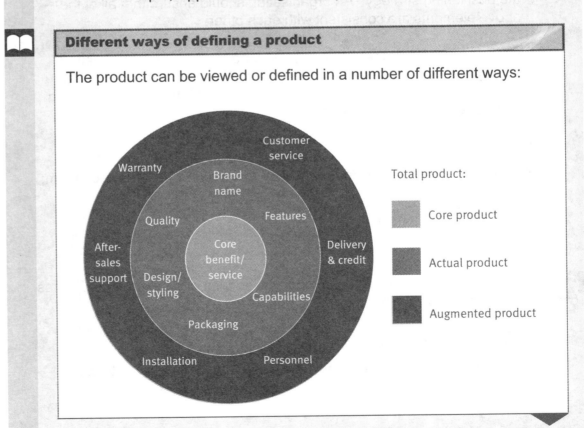

The core product – what is the buyer really buying? The core product refers to the use, benefit or problem solving service that the consumer is really buying when purchasing the product, i.e. the need that is being fulfilled.

The actual product is the tangible product or intangible service that serves as the medium for receiving core product benefits.

The augmented product consists of the measures taken to help the consumer put the actual product to sustained use, including installation, delivery and credit, warranties, and after-sales service.

An automobile offers personal transportation (core product), has many different features and attributes (actual product), and may include a manufacturer's warranty or dealer's discounted service contract (augmented product).

A product, therefore, is more than a simple set of tangible features. Consumers tend to see products as complex bundles of benefits that satisfy their needs. Most important is how the customer perceives the product. They are looking at factors such as aesthetics and styling, durability, brand image, packaging, service and warranty, any of which might be enough to set the product apart from its competitors.

The organisation will need to decide how much funding to allocate to each product, e.g. for promotion, further research and development, branding etc. The following models should help the organisation with these investment decisions:

- the product life-cycle
- the Boston Consulting Group (BCG) matrix.

Note: Branding is explored further in Section 5.

4.2.3 The product life-cycle

Most products go through a number of stages in their existence:

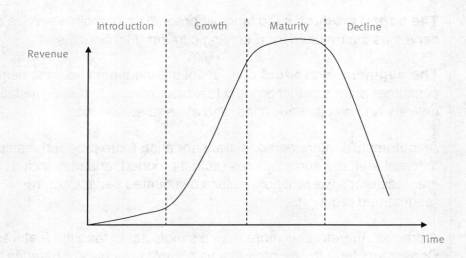

The marketing mix will change over time as the product goes into different stages of its 'life'. For example:

- When a product is in the 'growth' stage, the marketing mix may emphasise the development of sales outlets and advertising.

- In the maturity stage, there may be an increased emphasis/investment in product quality and design.

- To postpone decline, prices may be reduced and advertising increased.

Stage 1: Introduction – A small number of individuals will be prepared to pay a high price for a new, innovative product, e.g. the latest mobile phone model. High marketing costs are likely.

Stage 2: Growth – Revenue and profit grow as production and interest in the product increases. Prices may fall due to economies of scale and increased competitive pressure. The firm will seek to differentiate its product and brand.

Stage 3: Maturity – This is the longest and most successful stage of the life cycle. Purchases settle down into a pattern of repeat or replacement purchasing. Growth slows or halts due to high levels of competition. The price may be cut in order to attract a new group of customers.

Stage 4: Decline – Few people will purchase the product at the end of the life cycle as superior alternatives replace it and promotional activity will drop. The firm will look to exit the market and find profitable alternatives.

Note: An extra stage is sometimes included in the product life-cycle. This stage is called 'market shakeout' and comes between the 'growth' and 'maturity' stages. Sales growth begins to dip due to market saturation and the weakest products are 'shaken out' and exit the market.

A key aspect of product lifecycle analysis is products at different stages in the lifecycle have different implications for resource requirements, risk and strategy. This would emphasise the importance of portfolio management and suggest that a balanced portfolio of products is required, for example:

- Having too many products in the development stage will put a strain on finance as they will all require significant investment in marketing.

- On the other hand, if all products are at the maturity stage, then there may be a question mark over the firm's long term future – how long will it be before they move into the decline phase?

4.2.4 Product Portfolio Theory – Boston Consulting Group (BCG)

The BCG diagram plots all products in a portfolio according to the:

- growth rate of the market served and
- the market share held.

The matrix allows a firm to:

- visualise a diverse range of products together to consider the overall cash flow surplus or deficit within the portfolio
- to help to decide whether a change in the mix of products is required.

This analysis classifies products into one of four categories with the following implications:

Boston Consulting Group Growth / Share Matrix

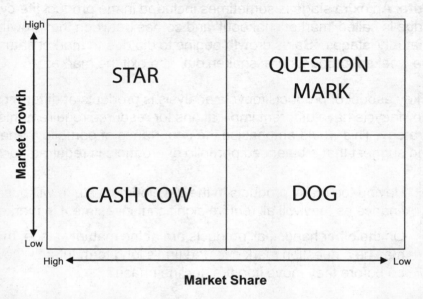

Cash cows (high market share, low market growth)

• These products generate cash for investment elsewhere in the portfolio.

• Investment tends to be low and the product is simply 'harvested' or milked of cash.

Stars (high market share, high market growth)

• Investment needed to maintain market share but is worth it since the market is growing.

• Will become tomorrow's cash cows.

Question marks (low market share, high market growth)

• Also known as a problem child. A choice must be made:
  – business may invest (e.g. in promotion, product modification) to increase market share or
  – may divest if insufficient funds are available and/or better investment decisions exists.

• Cash user overall.

Dogs (low market share, low market growth)

• Few growth opportunities so often divested as quickly as possible.

4.3 Pricing

Pricing includes basic price levels, discounts, payment terms, credit policy etc.

Factors influencing price; the 3 C's

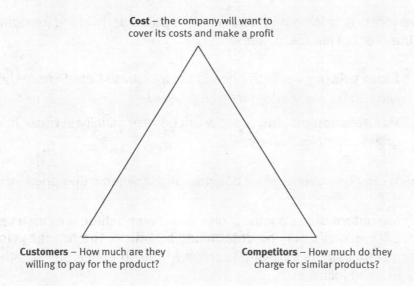

Cost – the company will want to cover its costs and make a profit

Customers – How much are they willing to pay for the product?

Competitors – How much do they charge for similar products?

Ultimately the organisation must address the issue of whether customers believe the price is fair and commensurate with the quality of the product or service.

Pricing strategies

The pricing strategy should not be made in isolation. It is important that the company considers:

- The **positioning strategy** – a large, well established business is better able to compete on price due to:

  - **economies of scale**, i.e. average unit cost falls as the scale of production increases

  - **the experience curve**, i.e. average unit cost falls due to learning from past experiences.

  For other companies, it may be more advisable to add value to their products so differentiating it from the competitors' offering.

- The products stage in the **product life-cycle**.

Two forms of pricing might be applied, particularly in the introduction stage of the product life-cycle, namely:

- **Skim pricing** – a high price is set initially to benefit from those who want to be early adopters of a product.

- **Penetration pricing** – a low price is set initially in order to gain rapid growth in market share.

There may be several other considerations when fixing price including:

- the nature of the competition – if the competitor is a price leader, pricing levels may be determined by **follow the leader pricing**. So, for instance, if the largest oil company cuts the price of fuel, others are likely to follow suit

- the nature of the market – for example, a company may find itself to be in the fortunate position of being the sole producer of a product due to a monopoly 'know-how', resources or raw materials. This company will therefore have more scope to charge **high prices** for its product

- pricing as a result of a promotion – this may lead to **loss leader pricing** (i.e. products are sold at a loss) of certain products in order to generate customer loyalty or more sales of other products. This is particular popular in pricing consumables in a supermarket

- pricing as a competitive weapon – **low prices** may be charged in order to crush competitors rather than achieve returns in revenue.

4.4 Promotion

Introduction

Promotion includes the tools available to communicate with the customer and potential customers.

The organisation must first attempt to understand what the customer sees as the main benefits of their product or service and will then focus on these aspects using promotion.

Communications can take many forms and generally operate at one of three levels:

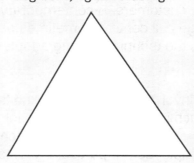

Mass Media - non personal and aimed at whole market segment, eg advertising

Personal and direct - typically one way communication with a customer, eg by letter

Personal and interactive - involves a one to one dialogue between the salesperson and the potential customer

Interactive marketing

Prof. John Deighton (1996) first defined interactive marketing as "the ability to address the customer, remember what the customer says and address the customer again in a way that illustrates that we remember what the customer has told us."

For organisations of any size to 'remember' what the customer has said and then 'communicate' with them is realistically only possible by use of the Internet. Thus IT allows customer information to be collected online and communication made either by e-mail or by 'remembering' when a customer logs on to the company website in future.

Developments in other communication technologies, specifically cable, satellite and digital technologies have also provided a platform for another form of home shopping via the television. Advantages over web-based selling include complete user familiarity with the equipment (the TV) and the ability to extensively demonstrate/advertise the products visually on a dedicated channel.

Telephone technology is not new but ownership is more widespread than ever. Within the UK, virtually all businesses, most homes and increasingly all teenagers and adults have a telephone. This provides the potential for contact to be made by telemarketing to stimulate product interest, sell directly or arrange for a visit to be made by a salesperson. There has, of late, been great emphasis in providing specialist training for telesales personnel including coaching on accent and responses to questions raised by customers. A contemporary trend is also the development of large call centres sometimes based overseas. ('M-marketing' refers to the technique being adopted using mobile telephones.)

This type of selling involves the initiative being taken by the vendor and is unsolicited. As such it may be unwelcome, intrusive even and naturally ethical concerns can surface. Impolite approaches or 'pushy' sales techniques being employed are particularly distasteful.

Promotional tools and the promotional mix

An organisation's **promotional mix** comprises the blend of promotional tools that a company uses to promote its products to existing and potential customers.

There are a number of promotional tools available:

- **Advertising** – e.g. using TV, radio, newspapers, billboards or the Internet.

- **Sales promotions** – e.g. product discounts, coupons, buy one get one free (BOGOF) offers.

- **Public relations** – news items in the media, e.g. a press release on the company's newest product.

- **Personal selling** – direct one to one contact with a potential customer, e.g. telesales.

- **Direct mail** – traditional mail or email sent to potential customers.

Test your understanding 5

Identify the advantages and disadvantages of following methods of promotion:

(a) Advertising

(b) Personal selling

(c) Public relations

(d) Sales promotion

(e) Direct mail

Advertising

There are two polar opposite views on advertising:

- Advertising is ineffective and a waste of money, only adding to company (and hence customer) costs. Brands such as Body Shop and Pizza Express do not see a need to use advertising in their promotional campaigns relying instead on other sources of information in order to form positive attitudes towards their products. In any case some might think that advertising demeans a particular product or company. In some cases, advertising may seem unethical. Lancaster and Withey (2005) conclude that some brands may be strong enough to sell on their own merits only if they are long established and have strong brand-loyal users.

- Advertising is so powerful and effective as to be essential. Consumers, it could be argued, will rarely purchase unadvertised brands so by not advertising, a company will be at serious disadvantage compared to its competitors. The results of advertising campaigns have been undeniably successful including those for brands such as Walkers Crisps, Strongbow cider and French Connection.

New forms of marketing communication

Three relatively new forms of marketing communication include viral, guerrilla and experiential marketing:

- **Viral** marketing – encourages individuals to pass on a marketing message to others, so creating exponential growth in the message's exposure in the same way computer viruses grow.

> **Illustration 1 – Viral marketing**
>
> A good example of viral marketing is a Nike video of footballer Ronaldinho putting on a new pair of boots and then juggling a ball for three minutes. The video was posted on YouTube and to date over 30 million people have got to know about the video and so have been exposed to Nike's promotion of their products.

- **Guerrilla marketing** – relies on well thought out, highly focused and often unconventional attacks on key targets.

> **Illustration 2 – Guerrilla marketing**
>
> A good example of guerrilla marketing is when a leading men's magazine projected the image of the model Gail Porter on the Houses of Parliament in London. It was a stunt that was talked about by a huge number of people. It was an attempt to get people to vote for the magazine's 'world's sexiest women' poll and the results were outstanding.

- **Experiential marketing** – an interactive marketing experience aimed at stimulating all the senses, e.g. road shows, street theatre, product trials. The next time the consumer sees the product, it should trigger a range of positive memories making it the first choice.

> **Illustration 3 – Experiential marketing**
>
> Dove body products has a long running campaign for real beauty, challenging the stereotypical model of beauty. This has included building an online sharing community, emotive photography, road shows and in store sampling.

E-marketing

The internet can be used as a method of promotion but can also be used in other parts of the marketing mix, e.g. it can act as a distribution channel in 'place'.

In recent years, there has been a huge increase in online marketing and a move away from traditional media

Advantages of using the internet to sell products	Disadvantages of using the internet to sell products
Global access to customers	Cost of set-up and maintenance
Internet presence not governed by organisational size	Possible credit card fraud
A new method of distribution	Possible virus infection
Information is delivered free to customers	Potential for hacking
Intimate customer relationship possible	Risk of losing confidential customer information
It provides sophisticated segmentation opportunities	Site may fail
	Inability to find site using search engine/ poorly designed site

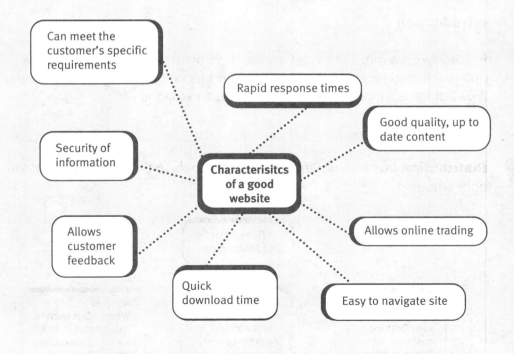

Illustration 4 – E-marketing

The Amazon.com (or Amazon.co.uk) site provides the following facilities, all of which can be linked to marketing and customer service, and that help Amazon to acquire customers, retain customers and increase income from them.

- Home delivery of books/CDs, etc. (place).

- Customers can write reviews and read other people's reviews of products (promotion).

- Based on previous buying habits, products are recommended (promotion).

- 'Customers who bought this product also bought these products…' (promotion).

- Order tracking

- Prices of new and used items are displayed. Prices of new items are usually lower than conventional shops (price).

- Very smartlooking interface (physical evidence).

- Search facilities (promotion).

- Emails if orders are delayed (processes).

4.5 Place

Introduction

Place involves more than just the location of factories, offices or sales outlets. It also includes distribution channels and coverage, stock levels, types of transportation vehicle, warehouse locations etc.

Distribution

Distribution involves getting the right products to the right people at the right time.

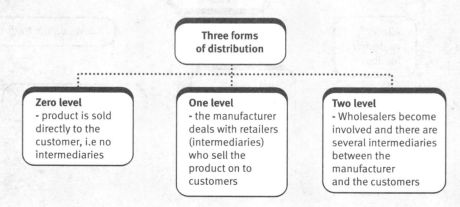

Direct marketing may be used for zero level distribution. One and two level distribution involve two types of marketing:

- A '**pull**' strategy means massive advertising to create consumer demand and this demand more or less forces the retailers to include this product in their assortment (not having this product in stock means disgruntled consumers that may go elsewhere to shop).

- A '**push**' strategy means that the producer does not try to create consumer demand through heavy advertising, but instead offers high margins to the trade channel members (retailers and wholesalers) and expects that in return they will actively promote and market the product.

Note: These strategies can also be called push and pull **promotion**.

5 Branding

5.1 Introduction

A **brand** is a name, symbol, term, mark or design that enables customers to identify and distinguish the products of one supplier from those offered by competitors.

Brands can vary from company names (e.g. Volvo) to logos (e.g. the Nike 'tick' symbol) to product names or even to the people themselves (e.g. David Beckham)

The Chartered Institute of Marketing (CIM) identify certain attributes of brands as follows:

- people use brands to make statements about themselves
- good brands reduce the risk of poor product choice
- brands can be a key asset for a business
- brands are the reason consumers choose one company over another
- although intangible, brands can be of substantial value
- strong brands can positively influence share performance
- brands can command higher prices

Brand equity is the premium that customers are prepared to pay for a brand compared to a similar, generic product.

Illustration 5 – Leading UK brands

The following is a list of the leading brands in the UK in 2008/09:

Brand	Rank	Category
Google	1	Internet – General
Microsoft	2	Technology – Computer hardware and software
Mercedes-Benz	3	Automotive – Vehicle manufacturer
BBC	4	Media – TV stations
British Airways	5	Travel – Airlines
Royal Doulton	6	Household – General
BMW	7	Automotive – Vehicle manufacturer
Bosch	8	Household – Appliances
Nike	9	Sportswear and equipment
Sony	10	Technology – General
Apple	11	Technology – Computer hardware and software
Duracell	12	Household – General consumables
Jaguar	13	Automotive – Vehicle manufacturer
Coca-cola	14	Drinks – Carbonated soft drinks
AA	15	Automotive – General
Lego	16	Leisure and Entertainment – Games & toys
Marks & Spencer	17	Retail – General
Thorntons	18	Food – chocolate and confectionery
Cadbury	19	Food – chocolate and confectionery
Hilton	20	Travel – Hotels and resorts

5.2 Characteristics of a strong brand

- **Consistency:** This is crucial to the development of the brand. For example, McDonalds manage to achieve consistency through standardisation.

- **A distinctive name:** The name should have positive associations with the product. For example 'Flash' sounds like it will clean thoroughly whereas the 'Nova' car was very unpopular in Spain since 'Nova', in Spanish, means 'doesn't work'.

- **Distinctive product features:** These will help to prompt instant recognition. For example, the Cadbury Chocolate Orange has a distinctive 'orange shape' design which makes it recognisable and Coca Cola has a distinctive image that is also instantly recognisable.

5.3 Brand management

Brand management is the development and implementation of a strategy with the long-term objective of putting a brand at the forefront of consumer's minds.

Developing and maintaining a brand can be expensive. However, a strong brand can enhance profitability.

The value of a brand is based on the extent to which it has:

- High loyalty.
- Name awareness.
- Perceived quality.
- Strong personality association.
- Other attributes such as patents and trademarks.

It is very important that brand value is protected:

- Low quality, counterfeit goods can erode the genuine brand's kudos and exclusivity

- There is a risk of some brands becoming a generic term – for example, aspirin and shredded wheat were once brands but were eventually declared to be generic terms.

- Adverse publicity can seriously undermine the values associated with a brand. For example, Body Shop will vigorously challenge any accusations that its products are not as ethical as they would like you to believe.

- Some firms have made the mistake of using exclusive brands on inferior goods hoping the brand would enhance perceived value. Unfortunately the reverse happened and the value of the brand was compromised.

Benefits of effective brand management

- **Improved profitability** – effective brand management should translate into improved profit potential.

- **Valuable asset** – although intangible, brands can be of substantial value.

- **Higher prices** – a strong brand will create the opportunity to create higher prices than competitors.

- **Method of differentiation** – a brand can distinguish an organisation from its competitors acting as a source of competitive advantage.

- **Way of connecting with customers** – brands can connect with customers in a deep way resulting in high levels of customer loyalty.

- **Assists with other marketing practices** – the brand should assist with other marketing practices, e.g. advertising by establishing a bond of trust which can be built upon.

- **Customer loyalty** – effective brand management should add to grand loyalty, repeat sales and habitual buying

Brand strategies (Kotler)

Kotler identified 5 brand strategies:

(1) Line extensions

- an existing brand is applied to new variants/products within the same product category
- e.g. Ford Fusion and Ford Focus are both small cars

(2) Brand extensions

- an existing brand is applied to products in a new product category
- e.g. Honda cars and motorcycles

(3) Multibrands

- having many different brands in the same product category
- e.g. Kellogs breakfast cereals include Cornflakes, Frosties, Special K, etc

(4) New brands

- new brands are created for new products and/or markets, usually because existing brands are not deemed suitable.
- e.g. when the banking arm of the Prudential expanded into internet banking they created a new brand, Egg Banking

(5) Cobrands

- two brands are combined in an offer so the brands reinforce each other.
- e.g. Dell Computers with Intel Processors

6 Chapter summary

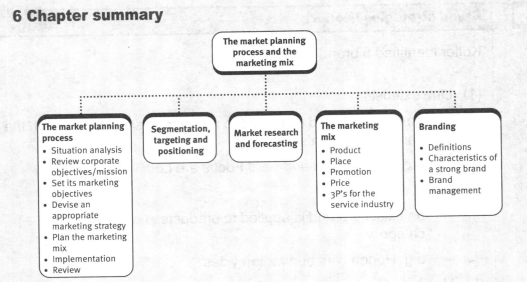

The market planning process and the marketing mix

The market planning process
- Situation analysis
- Review corporate objectives/mission
- Set its marketing objectives
- Devise an appropriate marketing strategy
- Plan the marketing mix
- Implementation
- Review

Segmentation, targeting and positioning

Market research and forecasting

The marketing mix
- Product
- Place
- Promotion
- Price
- 3P's for the service industry

Branding
- Definitions
- Characteristics of a strong brand
- Brand management

7 Practice questions

Question 1

In marketing 'skim pricing' reflects:

A   full recovery of costs only

B   a promotional device to entice customers into the store

C   high prices but low profit due to fixed costs

D   a competitive strategy to deny the competitors opportunities to enter a market

(2 marks)

Question 2

Undifferentiated marketing involves an organisation in offering:

A   products based on market research

B   a single product to the market as a whole

C   multiple products to the market as a whole

D   single products to segmented markets

(2 marks)

Question 3

Segmentation involves identifying target market which must be:

A   measurable, accessible and substantial

B   acceptable, feasible and suitable

C   undeveloped, undiscovered and undifferentiated

D   aligned to core competences

(2 marks)

Question 4

Companies with high costs will find it difficult to compete on the basis of price and would be well advised to:

A   compete on the Internet

B   develop brand loyalty amongst customers

C   employ high pressure sales techniques

D   develop new products

(2 marks)

Question 5

Which one of the following phrases explains concentrated marketing?

A   The company produces one product for a number of different market segments

B   The company introduces several versions of the product aimed at several market segments

C   The company produces one product for a mass market

D   The company produces one product for a single segment of the marketplace

(2 marks)

Question 6

A promotional pull policy will lead to:

A   high advertising costs

B   price reduction to entice customers

C   a focus on maximising channels of distribution.

D   product breadth and depth decisions

(2 marks)

Question 7

Quantum pricing relates to:

A   a $1.99 price tag

B   a variable price based on timing of use

C   a variable price placed on volume purchased

D   something to do with physics

(2 marks)

Question 8

(a) Explain the advantages that a company might hope to gain by targeting particular segments of the market.

(5 marks)

(b) Describe three variables you think would be useful as a basis for segmenting the market for clothing sold by a large retail chain, and two variables for segmenting the market in paint sold to other businesses by a paint manufacturer.

Explain your reasons for the choice of all five variables.

(5 marks)

(Total: 10 marks)

Question 9

Johnson, Halifax and Company are a long-established medium-sized training practice operating in a large industrial city, in the country of Wetland. The practice had developed a stable and profitable client base between 20 and 30 years ago providing advice on corporate presentations and media skills, along with the usual steady income stream from general staff training. During this period the practice's main clientele had been owner-managed manufacturing and retail businesses within the city and its suburbs. The partners had never actively sought out business and new clients had arrived on the basis of recommendations and personal contacts. In summary, the practice was seen to be the natural supplier of training services to the small and medium-sized business sector of the city. Over the years, Johnson, Halifax and Company have become conservative in approach and inflexible.

The last two recessions led to a massive shake-out in the manufacturing businesses in the city. Many of these businesses closed, and with restructuring in the manufacturing sector, there were numerous mergers and acquisitions. Understandably as headquarters were relocated and businesses were taken over, the practice began to lose clients as they moved to larger training practices in order to streamline their training. In addition, many of these companies ran their own training departments.

In response, Johnson, Halifax and Company attempted to attract new business by focusing on the smaller services sector. This approach brought them into direct conflict with the small training companies. The result was not the success they had hoped for. The very wide range of small clients did not present the opportunities for economy of delivery, and the intense fee competition was producing a large amount of smaller profit margin contracts.

By the end of 20X9, the partnership was only just breaking even financially. The long delayed economic recovery was not bringing them the rewards they had hoped for. Although the older partners recognised the problems they were undecided as to the way forward. The younger members of the practice were beginning to voice their discontent.

One in particular, Dominic Gower, was proposing a more proactive role for the firm. His main concern was that the partnership needed to go out and market itself. It was not enough to be technically proficient. It needed new and profitable business, particularly in the current turbulent and competitive environment. The managing partner agreed that something needed to be done urgently if the firm was to see prosperous times again and decided to encourage Gower to develop his ideas.

Required:

(a) Explain the need to adopt a marketing-orientated stance to the management of the partnership and suggest a possible approach to the development of a partnership marketing plan.

(10 marks)

(b) Explain the differences that are likely to arise between the marketing of consumer products and the marketing of services?

(10 marks)

(Total: 20 marks)

Question 10

Vitac Corporation is a medium-sized regional company producing and distributing fruit-flavoured, carbonated drinks. In recent years, it has seen a rapid decline in its sales to local stores and supermarkets. There are two main reasons for its poor performance. First, the major corporations who sell cola drinks have developed global brands which are now capturing the youth market in search of 'sophisticated' products. Secondly, the sales outlets are no longer willing to provide shelf space to products which are not brand leaders, or potential leaders, in the product category.

The managing director (MD) of Vitac believes that the company needs a drastic turnaround if it is to survive. The soft drinks industry has become too competitive, and the bottling technology too expensive to warrant new investment. However, the company feels that its greatest strength is its knowledge of and access to distribution channels, and therefore its opinion is that it should stay within the food and drinks industry.

Whilst on a fact-finding mission to the USA, the MD was attracted by a new chocolate confectionery product named 'EnerCan' which claims to provide high energy content but low fat. This seems to be a successful combination of attributes for those consumers, mainly active participants in sporting activities, who are concerned with their diet but enjoy an occasional treat. EnerCan has been developed and is owned by a relatively-unknown confectionery company in California. The company has agreed to provide Vitac with a licensing contract for manufacture and sale of the product within Vitac's own country.

The MD is convinced that the secret to success will be in the marketing of the product. The company has suffered in its drinks business because it did not develop a distinctive and successful brand. EnerCan is also unknown in Vitac's own country. In order to get national recognition and acceptance from the major retail outlets, the product will need considerable promotional support. As the company has very little experience or expertise in promotional activity it was decided to use a marketing consultancy to provide guidance in developing a promotional plan.

Vitac, being a medium-sized company, has only a limited budget. It will have to focus upon a new and national market instead of its traditional, regional stronghold. It has to develop a new brand in a product area with which it is not familiar. Before committing itself to a national launch of EnerCan, Vitac has decided to trial the product launch in a test market.

Required:

You have been appointed to act as business consultant in the marketing consultancy team assisting Vitac.

(a) Prepare notes for the management of Vitac recommending and justifying the types of promotional activity that could be used to support the new product launch.

(10 marks)

(b) Explain the factors which need to be considered to ensure that the test market produces results which can be reliably used prior to the national launch?

(10 marks)

(Total: 20 marks)

Test your understanding answers

Test your understanding 1

Gender

It would be useful to segment the market based on gender. Females may prefer a car that is smaller, is available in bright colours and comes with fashionable accessories. Males, on the other hand, may prefer a more masculine looking and powerful car.

Age

The age of the consumer will be of upmost importance. Teenage drivers may prefer a cheaper model, whereas drivers in their 20s, with more disposable income, may prefer a more expensive and stylish model.

Lifestyle

There may be a number of different lifestyles that could be targeted. Each group will have quite different needs, e.g. a leisure user may be more interested in the style and design of the car where as a commuter may want a safe, reliable car.

Income

The level of income will impact the make and the model that the user can afford and any optional extras that may be purchased.

Family life cycle

The life cycle stage will be important, e.g. bachelors may prefer a higher priced, sporty, stylish model where as those with a young and growing family may prefer a safe, reliable and family orientated people carrier.

- Market research agency data, e.g. Mintel produce periodic sector reports on market intelligence.

- The Internet.

- Universities typically have databases allowing for research and analysis of customer behaviour.

- Companies' Annual Reports and Accounts.

- Professional and trade associations.

- Trade and technical journals.

- National media.

Test your understanding 3

The marketing mix aims to match the products being sold by the company with the needs of the particular market segment that H Company have decided to target. The main elements of the mix are as follows.

Product

If H Company has already carried out some market research into what kind of products its customers want, these products should be available in its stores. For a clothes retailer this will include looking not only at what styles to offer, but also considering things like sizes, colours, fabrics, etc. An additional point is to note that these things are likely to change on a fairly frequent basis, so H Company should always be trying to look ahead.

Price

In the past, H Company has attempted to sell quality clothing at affordable prices. This may now have to be reviewed. The research carried out by the company may lead it to attempt to go upmarket, the higher quality/design of its clothes leading to higher prices, or it may go downmarket, by reducing innovative design/using cheaper fabrics with a consequent reduction in price if customers feel that the company is not offering them anything extra for their money.

Place

The place commonly refers to where the products are available to consumers. For a clothes retailer such as H Company, this would have traditionally been via retail outlets. Based on the results of market research, H Company will have to decide on the best way to retail their clothes. Various possibilities exist, amongst these are:

- Expanding the number of shops in the High Street.

- Expanding the number of shops on retail parks.

- Expanding the number of in-store displays in departments stores (within e.g. Debenhams etc.).

- Setting up an Internet website.

The place must be linked in with the other elements of the marketing mix, for example if H Company is trying to appeal to a more exclusive clientele then having its own range of shops in prestigious locations would be sensible. Alternatively, if the company wants to appeal to a more mainstream customer base then having the clothes sold in department stores would be more appropriate.

Promotion

The promotional part of the mix refers to how the potential customer is made aware of the products. The first consideration is looking at where to advertise. Clothes have traditionally been advertised through magazines and newspapers. If H Company goes down this route, then they should advertise in appropriate publications that are likely to be seen by their target customers. An increasingly popular approach particularly for clothes aimed at the upper end of the market is that of endorsement by celebrities. Clothes might be loaned/given to people in the public eye, thus generating positive publicity.

All of the above elements must be blended together so that the product, price, place and promotion appeal to the market segments identified by H Company.

Test your understanding 4

- **Introduction**

  High prices might be charged, because the product is new and supply is limited. Initial set up costs also need to be recovered.

- **Growth**

  Competition between rival producers intensifies so prices will reduce in the hope of penetrating the existing market and either retaining or increasing market share at the expense of competitors.

- **Maturity**

  Prices fall mainly in order to beat competitors but the experience curve and scale economies should come into play. Market segments are sought where higher prices can be charged.

- **Decline**

  The product declines into obsolescence so it may even be sold off below cost price to clear stocks and exit the market.

Two forms of pricing might also be applied, particularly in the introduction stage of the product life cycle, namely:

- Price skimming reflecting high prices but low profit due to high fixed costs.
- Penetration pricing, deliberately entering a market at a low price to build market share and pricing so as to deny the competitors those opportunities.

Test your understanding 5

	Method	Advantages	Disadvantages
(a)	Advertising	• Reach a large number of potential customers. • Low cost for each potential customer.	• Total cost can be very high. • Difficult to evaluate effectiveness.
(b)	Personal selling	• Can focus on needs of individual customer. • A talented salesperson can be very persuasive.	• Can be seen as pushy. • High cost per potential customer.
(c)	Public relations	• Low or no cost. • Can be targeted. • Unbiased opinion.	• Negative review may damage reputation.
(d)	Sales promotion	• Can help gain new users. • Counteract competition. • Clear out surplus stock.	• Can be costly. • May not win customer loyalty.
(e)	Direct mail	• Personalised targeting of an individual. • Test market before a full roll out. • Less competitor visibility.	• Negative associations. • Can be costly.

Question 1

C

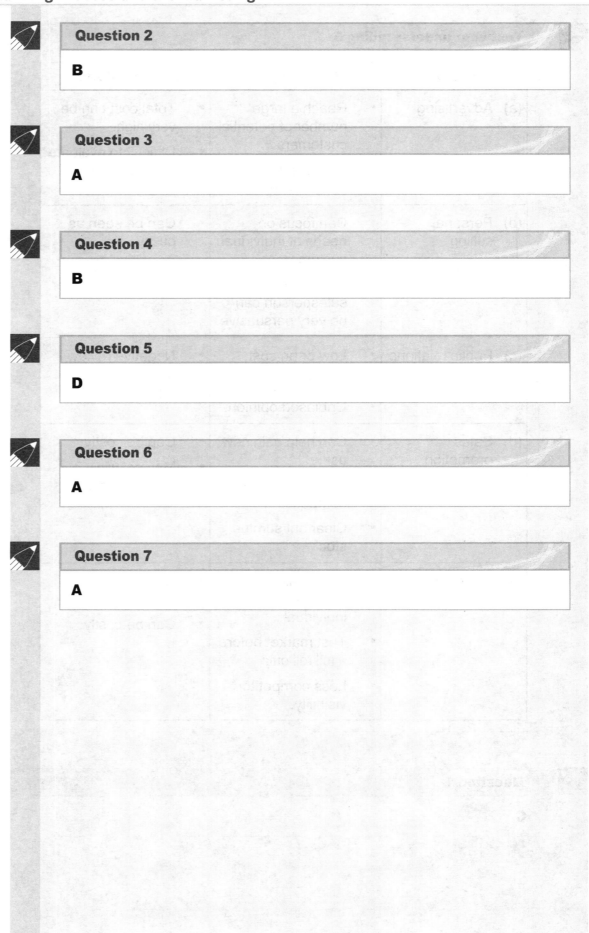

Question 2

B

Question 3

A

Question 4

B

Question 5

D

Question 6

A

Question 7

A

Question 8

(a) There are a number of different ways in which a company can aim marketing at people. One of these is known as undifferentiated marketing, which involves marketing the product in the same way to everybody. The obvious problem with this approach is that a lot of the marketing effort and cost will be wasted, by marketing products to people who are not interested in them.

An alternative would therefore be to market products individually to consumers; the obvious disadvantage here is that this would cost too much money and be impractical (an example of a company successfully carrying this out is Dell computers, which makes computer systems individually to customer specifications).

The solution most companies adopt is to undertake what is referred to as market segmentation. This means dividing the population into a number of segments. The population within each segment will have similar needs and the company can market their product in the same way to this entire segment. This approach should be cost effective as well as achieving desired sales levels.

An additional benefit of this approach is that the company may identify some segments that it is not interested in, or that the company knows will have no interest in the product. These segments can therefore be avoided to reduce wasted expenditure.

A final advantage of segmentation is that segments that are currently not catered for might be identified. The company can then develop products to satisfy the needs of these consumers. A good example is the rise in products and services aimed at young, single, professional people (particularly women) who have a high disposable income.

(b) There are many ways in which a company can segment its market. The variable it chooses will depend on the business it is in.

Clothes retailer

Gender

The first obvious variable is gender; clothes for men and women are clearly different and many shops will specialise in one type or the other (even if they sell both, the departments will be separated).

Use

Many clothes shops specialise in clothes for a particular use; good examples include shops specialising in sports clothes. At a more general level, some shops specialise in suits and other 'workplace' clothes whilst others specialise in leisure-wear clothes.

Age

One of the most distinctive differences between clothes shops is in the age group that they cater for. As people grow older their tastes in clothes will change and so retailers can specialise in clothes aimed at different age ranges.

Paint manufacturer

Price

The first thing to bear in mind is that a manufacturer is an industrial company, in other words, it does not sell products to consumers, but rather to other businesses. A key variable will therefore be the price the business is prepared to pay. For a construction company painting interior walls, a low price might be a key requirement, while a car manufacturer might be prepared to pay a higher amount.

Volume

Another key variable will be the amount of paint that the customer will require. The construction company mentioned above is likely to require a high volume, while the car manufacturer may require much smaller amounts. If the manufacturer cannot produce paint in large quantities, there is little point in trying to attract the construction company.

Question 9

(a) Adopting a marketing orientation

Johnson, Halifax and Company need to perform better and more cost-effectively than their competitors; forcing them to be more flexible and responsive to client needs. In order to satisfy them, the needs of the clients must be analysed and understood by the partnership.

Marketing plan for the partnership

Step 1: Situation analysis – an initial assessment of the current position of the partnership will be performed as part of the marketing plan. This will involve why and where there has been a deteriorating change in the client base in recent years. One reason is the economic downturn within the region that Johnson operates in.

Another reason may be that they are offering the wrong types of training, i.e. not meeting the demands of their customers. One of the main problems identified by the company is that it appears to be 'stuck in the middle': in other words, its services are not priced cheaply enough to appeal to small companies whilst at the same time it does not have the range of services required by larger companies.

Step 2: Set corporate objectives – the partnership did enjoy past success but there is no indication that there is a mission statement or set of corporate objectives in place. Even if there is, these should be reviewed to make sure that they are still relevant.

Step 3: Set marketing objectives – these should be set in relation to the marketing objectives.

Step 4: Devise an appropriate strategy – this will involve:

- Segmentation – the market should be segmented, e.g. by size of client, and the needs of each segment should be established.

- Targeting – the most profitable segment(s) should be targeted using an appropriate marketing mix.

- Positioning – a strategy of differentiation or cost leadership should be chosen for each segment.

Step 5: Marketing mix – a plan for the development of the marketing mix needs to be adopted for Johnson and Halifax to achieve its plans.

Product (i.e. the development of new services)

In the light of newly-established customer requirements, new products or services need to be developed, possibly forced by the changing requirements of the local economy. Johnson will need to carry out some kind of research in order to establish what these needs are and then segment the market to decide which training courses they will provide. These new services will have to be closely monitored and may have to be regularly updated.

Price

Prices charged by the firm will obviously have to be competitive but will equally have to be reflective of the business segment they are operating within, and its specific competitiveness. It may prove necessary to run free 'taster' courses so that potential clients can see what the company is like.

Distribution channel (i.e. place)

If the firm has a great deal of flexibility in its distribution of services, then it should gain a competitive advantage quickly. At the moment Johnson appears to be tied to its current geographical region.

The partnership should take advantage of any available IT systems such as the Internet to help gain a competitive advantage.

Promotional activity

The use of good quality communication will be crucial in an attempt to target appropriate clients. Media considerations are relevant (e.g. where and when to advertise), however it should be remembered that there may only be one person within a company who decides on the company's training needs, these people should be identified and contacted with a view to building a long-term relationship.

Step 6: Implementation and control – The marketing plan should then be implemented. The plan should also be monitored to gauge its success and to identify any necessary changes.

(b) Service industries face different problems to production industries for the following reasons:

Intangibility

In a service industry, it is difficult to judge quality because it is difficult to sample a service.

It is difficult for customers to examine a service in advance. However, in a production business, such as the manufacture of cars, the sampling will be achieved by test driving the vehicle. Steps can be taken to make the service more tangible, e.g. physical evidence such as brochures can be used.

Inseparability

The service is often inseparable from the individual delivering the service. Clients could easily become disappointed if they discover that the work carried out on their behalf is not performed by the person with whom the contract was negotiated. Partners therefore need to maintain enough interest in the work performed to ensure that personal contact with the client is maintained. The marketing of a product is different, as the item or goods will be purchased from the seller.

Heterogeneity

As a result of inseparability, the service will vary from one occasion to the next. To ensure consistency, the firm needs to maintain the training of personnel as well as ensuring quality standards are adhered to. However, in the production of, say a motor car, each vehicle will conform exactly to its specification.

Perishability

Services cannot be stored; sale and consumption take place at the same time. To ensure that assets are utilised effectively, steps can be taken to manage this problem, e.g. off-peak discounts or using temporary staff to solve the problem of fluctuating demand. Products, on the other hand, can be stored (even if only for a limited period).

Differentiation

As most training firms offer similar services to their clients it is important to gain a competitive advantage by offering a slightly different service which is relevant to the needs of the particular clients served. This could include aspects such as personal involvement by all staff, follow-up contacts, experience and the use of high technology equipment. The differentiation of a product refers to the specific attributes enforced by that firm and therefore is easy to undertake.

Ownership

Consumers may find it difficult to value a service since there is no transfer of ownership.

Question 10

(a) Introduction

The company has acquired an interest in a product that is new to the market, and is proposing to market this product via the major retail outlets to a specific target group, namely sports participants.

Promotional vehicles

The key objective during the trial period is to create awareness within the target market. The focus of the promotion will be on the different types and styles of promotion to be used to obtain the appropriate responses from the target market. These will vary from conventional advertising to sales and public relations.

With a limited promotional budget the company could concentrate on a 'push' strategy which influences the retail outlets to stock and display the products.

In attempting to influence the target consumers a key strategy would be to encourage them to try the product initially.

Due to the inherent high costs, it is not realistic to expect wide-scale consumer advertising on television and through the mass print media. This strategy would not be specifically targeting the chosen market segment.

The preferred choices would include a balanced selection of the following.

- **Advertising**. Dependent upon the budget available, advertising should focus on advertisements or editorials placed in one or two specialist magazines. These magazines would be those that are commonly read by the target market – sports enthusiasts. The advertising should be supported with point-of-sale material to draw potential consumers' attention and encourage trial purchase.

- **Sales promotions** could be both trade and consumer led.

- **Trade promotions**. It is essential that retailers both stock the product and provide excellent shelf display. To generate a 'push' approach to promotion, it may be possible to provide retailers with inducements in the form of customer prizes and discounts. Without retailer commitment, it is unlikely that the product launch will be successful.

- **Customer promotions**. This will need significant expenditure on sales promotional material which would include a mixture of the following:
    - In-store trials;
    - Coupon offers;
    - Initial price reductions.

All of the above might help to stimulate demand and make the product recognisable. Attractive packaging of the product will in itself help stimulate product interest and create brand awareness. The following could also be tried:

- **Public relations**. It could be beneficial to use one or two well-known sports personalities to recommend the product. Though it might appear to be expensive this could provide exposure significantly cheaper than could otherwise be obtained from conventional media. Additionally the product could be trialled at prestigious sports meetings, international athletics meetings, cycling events, tennis tournaments, etc. The product image would reach the target audience and it would be promoted in a superior environment

- **Sales**. The sales force will need to be sufficiently skilled and committed, being able to operate at a national level to obtain wide geographical coverage. Although this approach may be expensive it will be far more cost effective than attempting a nationwide television campaign. The sales force will have the task of persuading retailers to accept the product, and providing merchandising support. They will handle most of the problems at the product's launch.

Conclusion

With the restrictions of a limited budget, expenditure should be directed at those areas which will accurately reach the target market and encourage participation in the trial.

On this basis, the promotional emphasis should be on a 'push' strategy as opposed to a 'pull' strategy. To measure how well the campaign is progressing, control systems should be implemented. The systems should ensure that the use of the limited money available achieves the desired objectives.

(b) Definition of a test market

A test market is often used prior to the launch of fast-moving consumer goods. It enables the company to identify any operational problems that may occur and to fine tune its marketing activities.

The company has the benefit that it can save considerable amounts of money which would have been lost if the mistakes had occurred at the national level.

Factors to consider

The following factors should all be taken into consideration before deciding upon a test market area. If the test is to provide guidance for a future national launch, the results should be based upon reliable sets of data.

- **Comparable test areas**. The test market area should provide a good indication as to how the market throughout the whole country will behave. It would be of little use if the results from the test market misrepresented the true state of the total market. The test market area must be representative of the total market in terms of demographics – income, social class, age and any other parameter which would help determine purchase activity.

- **Comparable distribution channels**. The distribution channels, including the sales outlets, should be comparable with the rest of the country. It is pointless if small retailers dominate the test area whereas in the rest of the country the multiple supermarkets are dominant.

- **Isolation of test area**. The area should be reasonably isolated so that outsiders coming into the test area do not influence test results.

- **Comparability of promotional media**. If the national promotional emphasis were to be radio then there ought to be a local radio station available.

- **Control markets**. There should be a control market just in case extraneous activities might falsify the results, e.g. a strike at a major employer within the test area.

- **Test period**. The test period should be long enough to enable reliable results to be obtained, in this case time for a repurchase after the initial trial. However, the test period must not be so long that it alerts competitors.

11

Further Aspects of Marketing

Chapter learning objectives

Lead	Component
D1. Explain developments in marketing.	(c) Explain marketing in a not-for-profit context.
	(d) Explain the social context of marketing behaviour.
D2. Apply tools and techniques used in support of the organisation's marketing.	(c) Describe the business contexts within which marketing principles can be applied.

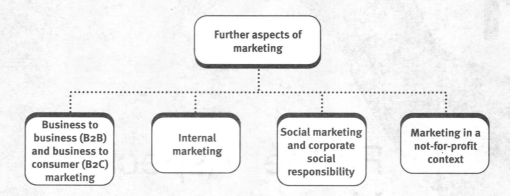

1 Business to Business (B2B) and Business to Consumer (B2C) Marketing

1.1 Definitions

- **B2B marketing** – targeting goods and services at businesses that will use the products to produce the goods or services that they sell.

- **B2C marketing** – the market for products and services bought by individuals for their own use or for their family's use. As mentioned in Chapter 8, consumer goods fall under two categories; durable goods and fast moving consumer goods.

1.2 Features of B2B marketing

- **Derived demand** – demand for the product is derived from consumer demand.

- **Fewer buyers** – the number of buyers for an industrial good is generally smaller than for a consumer good.

- **High purchasing power** – each industrial buyer tends to have a higher purchasing power than consumers.

- **Closer relationships between buyers and sellers** – this is because there are fewer buyers with higher purchasing power in B2B marketing compared to B2C marketing.

- **Technical complexity** – There is often a greater degree of technical complexity in B2B marketing.

Test your understanding 1

On what basis are B2B purchasing decisions made?

Buying decisions with B2B

Business-to-business (B2B) marketing differs from business-to-consumer (B2C) marketing in a number of key respects, not least the fact that the purchaser makes buying decisions for organisational rather than personal reasons. In addition, several individuals and groups are involved in the B2B buying decision including:

- **Initiators** who start the buying process. (For example, a department who identifies a need to replace a piece of equipment.)

- **Influencers** who affect the buying decision often based on their particular technical expertise.

- **Buyers** who raise orders and sanction payment, although they may enter into negotiation, they may be guided heavily by others in the organisation.

- **Users** who ultimately operate the equipment (using the earlier example).

There may be others (dependent upon the organisation) who will have further roles such as Deciders, Approvers and Gatekeepers.

2 Internal Marketing

This is the means of applying the philosophy and practices of marketing to the people who serve the external customers so that:

- The best possible people can be employed and retained.
- The employees will do the best possible work.

Internal marketing is essentially the process of motivating and training employees so as to support the organisation's external marketing activities.

Employee's efforts to achieve marketing goals should be recognised and rewarded.

Implications of internal marketing

- The company may have a strong marketing strategy but without their employee's support, it will not be effective.

- If advertising promises are not kept through the services and the products provided, eventually the company's reputation will suffer and the customers will stop buying.

- For the firm to deliver consistently high quality, everyone must practise a customer orientation. This will require investment in employee quality and performance.

- Internal marketing will be of particular importance in service companies which tend to be more customer-facing.

3 Social Marketing and Corporate Social Responsibility

3.1 Social marketing

Social marketing uses commercial marketing practices to achieve non-commercial goals, e.g. the solution of social and health problems.

Social marketing is based on the logic that if marketing techniques can encourage people to buy products such as a fizzy drink brand or a particular telephone handset, then it can also encourage people to adopt 'beneficial' behaviours for their own good and the good of others.

Merit goods are commodities that an individual or society should have on the basis that it is 'good' for them rather than ability or willingness to pay. Governments often provide merit goods 'free at the point of use' and then finances them through general taxation (e.g. in the UK access to health care is through the National Health Service).

Demerit goods are the exact opposite of merit goods and negative consequences can arise from their consumption for society as a whole, e.g. health implications of smoking, unwanted pregnancies.

Social marketing can be applied to promote merit goods and encourage society to avoid demerit goods, e.g. persuading people to give up smoking through the use of a powerful advertising campaign.

> ### Understanding social marketing
>
> According to the National Social Marketing Centre (2008) the following features and concepts are key to understanding social marketing:
>
> - A strong customer orientation with importance attached to understanding where the customer is starting from, their knowledge, attitudes and beliefs, along with the social context in which they live and work.
>
> - A clear focus on understanding existing behaviour and key influences upon it, and developing clear behavioural goals.
>
> - Using a mix of different methods to achieve a particular behavioural goal.
>
> - Audience segmentation to target efforts more effectively.
>
> - Use of the 'exchange' concept (understanding what is being expected of an individual, and the real cost to them).
>
> - Use of the 'competition' concept (understanding factors that impact on people and that compete for their attention and time).

3.2 Corporate social responsibility in a marketing context

As discussed, a marketing orientated firm will seek to produce and sell products that meet the needs of the customers. However, this policy may result in firms adopting policies which society, as a whole, view as irresponsible.

> ### Test your understanding 2
>
> Explain why a company may be deemed irresponsible for providing customers with products that meet their needs?

Social responsibility is the acceptance of an obligation towards the society in which the organisation exists. In a marketing context, the term initially highlights the needs for the organisation to accept that, in the process of pushing products towards individuals, it has the responsibility for the impact of those products on individuals and society overall.

Key questions include the following:

- To whom do we sell?

- Are our products of an appropriate standard, safe and produced to environmental standards?

- How do we advertise: is it fair, balanced and truthful?

- Do we have policies that address the concerns of dissatisfied customers?

- Is our pricing or advertising policy exploitive of any groups in society, etc?

The basis of social responsibility is the premise that an organisation enjoys certain benefits of society and, in return, should engage in practices that supports rather than exploits society.

Illustration 1

The following are some of the companies that will have a responsibility that goes beyond their own profit motive:

- Tobacco companies

- Alcohol producers and retailers

- Gas and oil companies

- Car manufacturers

- Drug companies

- Media companies

3.3 Advantages to a company for adopting a socially responsible approach

- **Unique selling point** – the market for a particular product may be highly competitive. The support of socially valuable causes may allow a company to develop a unique identity for its products.

  Starbucks, for example, has managed to create a strong brand and a unique selling point in what is a saturated market by only using 'Fair Trade' coffee and supporting community projects.

- **Increased sales** – customers may be willing to pay more for a product bought from a responsible company rather than an irresponsible one.

  In 2008, for example, a UK TV program saw celebrity chefs on a crusade against intensive chicken farming. As a result of this campaign, sales rocketed for the more expensive, free range chickens.

- **Change before new legislation is introduced** – some companies may put new practices in place before new legislation is introduced. This may help the company to gain from positive publicity.

  Some UK pubs and restaurants, for example, introduced a smoking ban before the UK legislation banning smoking in enclosed public spaces, was introduced in July 2007.

- **Can reduce company costs** – many companies wrongly believe that social responsibility will increase costs but it can actually reduce them.

Illustration 2 – Marks & Spencer

In May 2008 Marks & Spencer (M&S) introduced a number of initiatives aimed at improving their image as a socially responsible retailer. These included an initiative to reduce the number of plastic carrier bags used by customers:

- The introduction of a 5p charge for its single use carrier bags, in all of its UK stores.

- All profits (1.85p per bag) raised from the sale of the 5p bags will be invested in 'Groundwork', a charity which creates and improves greener living space in the UK.

- Any unwanted or unused M&S carrier bags can be returned by customers to any M&S store for recycling.

- M&S were the first major UK food retailer to use a standard carrier bag made from 100% recycled plastic.

- The steps taken have not only helped M&S's image as a socially responsible retailer but they have also enabled the company to reduce their costs.

4 Marketing in a Not-for-Profit Context

4.1 Introduction

The not-for-profit (NFP) sector incorporates a diverse range of operations including:

- private sector organisations, e.g. charities, sports associations
- public sector organisations, e.g. healthcare, education.

Many such organisations have now adopted (and adapted) a marketing orientation.

Whilst private sector organisations may try to understand and meet the needs of their customers, NFP organisations will have the challenge of needing to reach several groups with their marketing efforts, for example:

- contributors of money
- customers (may be referred to as clients, patients etc)
- volunteers and other supporters.

4.2 Marketing for charities

Charities must focus on the needs and wants of all different customer groups:

- beneficiaries (users, clients, members, etc.),
- supporters, and
- regulators.

With thousands of charities worldwide, competition for voluntary giving is intense. Those charities employing the most appropriate marketing practices are most likely to attract the generosity of peoples' time and money for their particular cause. Branding in particular is important in communicating a particular charity's core values, and distinguishing it from another.

Test your understanding 3

First run in 1994, Cancer Research UK's Race for Life, is the largest women-only fundraising event. Women are invited (for a fee) to walk, jog or run 5k at a choice of hundreds of Race for Life events taking place each year. The event has been a huge marketing success with over 6 million participants and £457 million raised to date.

Required:

Explain, using examples, how Cancer Research UK (a not-for-profit organisation) has been able to use the traditional marketing mix to increase the success of its running series.

4.3 Marketing for the public sector

- Within the UK, political reforms have pushed the public sector into a more commercial and managerial style meaning some managers need to make marketing decisions.

- Specialist companies have been enlisted to carry out market research, e.g. on behalf of public sector bodies.

- Social problems concerning (say) the elderly or disabled may call for information about their opinions and circumstances to help inform policy decisions.

4.4 Marketing for NGOs

NGOs play an important role in international development by directing development funds from donors and agencies to the point of need, unconstrained by profit or politics.

NGOs use marketing to:

- find a position for themselves within the market

- distinguish client and donors needs

- formulate and communicate NGO requirements

- gain new supporters.

5 Chapter summary

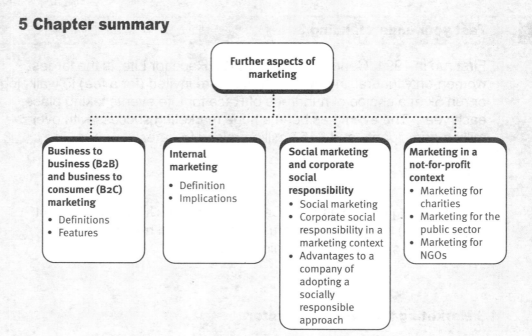

6 Practice questions

Question 1

Which of the following is not a feature of business to business (B2B) marketing?

A   Industrial buyers have a lower purchasing power than consumers

B   A closer relationship between buyers and sellers than compared to business to consumer (B2C) marketing

C   Fewer buyers than B2C marketing

D   Demand for the product is derived from consumer demand

(2 marks)

Question 2

Which of the following statements is false with regards to the not-for-profit sector?

A   Marketing is difficult because there is no marketplace within which customers can choose competing goods and services

B   A desire to meet customer's needs is constrained by the requirements to meet wider social goals

C   The not-for-profit sector will have a number of financial objectives and non-financial social objectives

D   The not-for-profit sector is unable to successfully adopt marketing principles

(2 marks)

Question 3

Internal marketing is about:

A   fulfilling the needs of employees and managers

B   ensuring employees are able to support the organisation's marketing activities

C   promoting the company's products to employees in order to increase sales

D   reducing expenditure on advertising

(2 marks)

Question 4

Explain why a fast food restaurant may decide to adopt a socially responsible approach.

(4 marks)

Question 5

Sam is the Chief Executive Officer (CEO) of T Inc, a tobacco company. He has traditional views about the purpose of business in general and his own organisation in particular. Though he is frequently pressured by a variety of groups and organisations that think he should run his organisation differently, he sticks firmly to the view that the overriding purpose of business is to make money for the shareholders. His son, Frank, who is being coached to take over the CEO role, takes a very different perspective. In his view, T Inc has a responsibility to a wide range of stakeholders.

Required:

(a) Explain how:

    (i)   Sam would justify his view that the overriding purpose of the business is to make money for the shareholders.

    (ii) Frank would justify his view that T Inc has a responsibility to a wide range of stakeholders.

(12 marks)

(b) Describe the stages Frank should go through in determining the priority of the goals of T Inc when he becomes CEO.

(8 marks)

(Total: 20 marks)

Test your understanding answers

Test your understanding 1

A mixture of

- Economic/task factors (price, delivery, location, quality, reliability, customer care, after care, etc.)

- Non-task factors (personal risk or gain, previous decisions, politics, those influencing the purchaser, perception, etc.)

As a result, significant B2B marketing mix features include quality assurance, reliability, delivery, price and after sales service.

Test your understanding 2

- **Environmental impact** – the product may deplete natural resources or emit harmful gases. In 2008, the DIY store B&Q decided to end the sale of patio heaters due to their environmental impact.

- **Harmful product** – products such as addictive drugs, alcohol and fast food may fulfil a customer's short term needs but could result in long term damage.

- **Vulnerable consumers** – marketers have a responsibility towards vulnerable groups such as children who are unable to fully evaluate decisions. For example, in the UK in 2007, TV advertisements for unhealthy food were banned during kids TV programs.

- **Deceptive practices** – for example, a customer may perceive that a certain mobile phone deal fulfils their needs. However, not reading or understanding the small print may mean that they don't know what they are committing themselves to.

- **Labour practices** – for example, a customer may buy a product because it fulfils their need for good value. However, they may be unaware that the labour used to produce the product are paid a poor wage and are subject to substandard working conditions, e.g. in 2008 Primark, the UK clothing company, were found to be using Indian suppliers who sub-contracted the work to smaller suppliers who, in turn, relied on child labour.

Test your understanding 3

Product

- Brand image is bright and consistent.
- The product fulfils many women's need to keep fit whilst also fulfilling a need to raise money for charity.
- The distance, 5k, is challenging but manageable for most.

Price

- The fee is affordable for most women.
- The fee is higher than an average race entry but most women will be willing to pay more since the money is donated to a good cause.
- Women will also be encouraged to raise sponsorship money.

Promotion

- The product is promoted using adverts on TV, in women's magazines and in gyms.
- The website is easy to navigate, branding is consistent, on-line entry is available and the site contains helpful advice with regards to training and sponsorship.
- Celebrity endorsement has been used. Many popular women celebrities have completed the race.

Place

- A wide choice of accessible locations.
- Scenic locations making the event enjoyable.

Question 1

A

Question 2

D

Question 3

B

Question 4

- **Unique selling point** – the market for fast food is highly competitive. The support of socially valuable causes can act as a unique selling point for the business and attract more customers to the business.

- **Increased sales** – customers may be willing to pay more for a product bought from a responsible company. For example, the fast food restaurant may have a policy of supporting British farmers. This may be important to consumers and they may be willing to pay more for these products.

- **Can reduce company costs** – social responsibility can actually reduce costs, e.g. due to less wastage.

- **Change before new legislation is introduced** – the business will gain positive publicity if they put practices in place before new legislation is introduced.

Question 5

(a) (i) Stakeholders are any people or groups that have an interest in a particular organisation. Although there are a large number of stakeholder groups that might have an interest in a company, the most important group is usually seen as the shareholders.

Sam would argue that there are a number of reasons for this:

The reason why a company exists is to make money for its owners, i.e. for its shareholders. The company belongs to them and so they should always be given the highest priority.

Although there are other stakeholders such as employees, suppliers, etc. they are given their rewards through items such as high wages, bills being paid on time, etc. It is only possible to do these if the company is profitable, i.e. this is the same goal as keeping the shareholders happy.

(ii) Frank would argue that the responsibility of the company stretches to more than just the shareholders. For example:

T Inc could increase profitability at the expense of its employees (by paying them lower wages) or suppliers (by taking extended credit). Although these are both of benefit in the short term to the profits of the company and therefore to the shareholders, it is unlikely that they will bring long-term benefits.

The company is operating in the tobacco industry and as such is high profile. If the company is seen to be acting irresponsibly it might be forced by government to adopt certain procedures, which will lead to increased costs. It is therefore more sensible to consider the environment and local community since it is more cost effective in the long term.

Frank would argue that any modern organisation must see itself as being in co-operation with a large number of other people: suppliers, customers, employees, etc. If it views itself as purely catering to shareholders and the pursuit of profit it will be unlikely to be successful in the modern business environment.

(b) The process that Frank needs to go through in determining the priorities of stakeholders is sometimes known as stakeholder mapping.

Firstly, Frank will need to draw up a list of all stakeholders from both inside and outside the organisation.

Secondly, Frank should identify what each group wants from T Inc. For example:

- Shareholders want increased profits and dividends.

- Employees want increased wages and working conditions.

- Government wants taxes and some contribution towards healthcare costs from both T Inc and from their customers.

- Action groups might want T Inc to stop targeting young people for advertising campaigns.

- Political groups might want to ban/limit the use of T Inc's products through smoking bans (as was introduced in 2008 in the UK).

It can be seen from the above list that it is not possible to meet the expectations of each group since some are in direct opposition to others.

Thirdly, Frank should look at how much influence and power each group has. For example, shareholders (particularly institutional ones) can sell their shares and depress the share price if they are unhappy with the decisions being made by T Inc. As such they are powerful. On the other hand, low-grade employees may not have many other job opportunities so they have much less power to influence decisions.

Finally, Frank will have to set goals and objectives that meet the expectations of those groups with the most power whilst meeting the minimum requirements of each group with some power.

HR Theories and Practices related to Motivation

Chapter learning objectives

Lead	Component
E1. Explain the relationship of human resources (HR) to the organisation's operations	(a) Explain how HR theories and activities can contribute to the success of the organisation.
E2. Discuss the activities associated with the management of human capital	(b) Discuss the HR activities associated with the motivation of employees.
	(c) Describe the HR activities associated with improving the opportunities for employees to contribute to the firm.

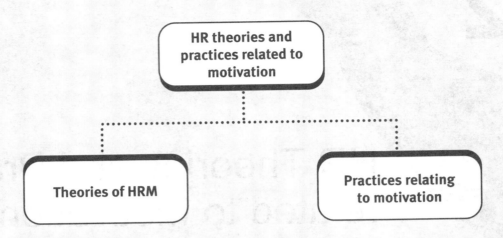

1 Theories of Human Resource Management

1.1 Introduction

There are a number of theories of human resource management (HRM) relating to ability, motivation and opportunity.

Theorist	Year	Theory
Taylor	1911	Scientific management – workers motivated by money
Mayo	1927	Hawthorne Experiments
Maslow	1954	Hierarchy of needs
Vroom	1964	Expectancy theory
Herzberg	1968	Two factor theory
Handy	1976	Psychological contracts
McGregor	1981	Theory X and theory Y
Schein	1990	Four categories of worker
Mullins	2007	Applied three classes to understand motivation

Eras in managing people

The table below summarises the development of thinking surrounding the management of people.

The Industrial Revolution 18th and 19th centuries	• Factory owners improved their methods of recruitment, training and other related activities by trial and error. • Early factories often characterised by the harsh treatment of employees. • Philanthropic employees contributed to improvements in working life by running 'model factories' and appointing industrial welfare workers to look after their employees. • 1881: University of Pennsylvania launched an undergraduate business education program so saving costs for the local steel company. • 1911: Taylor argues that there is only one correct way to perform industrial jobs.
First World War	• Large numbers of women in factory environments. • Thousands of women supervisors appointed to observe and regulate conditions of workforce. • At the end of the war in 1918, the establishment of the Industrial welfare officer reflected in the setting up of the 'Welfare Workers' association.
1918–1939 interwar	• Pressures to cut costs and increase efficiency encouraged the use of the ideas of scientific management and, later, the use of human relations techniques to secure the commitment and motivation of workers.
Second World War	• Demand for productivity maximisation led to a strengthening of personnel specialist roles.

1945–1980s	<ul><li>Personnel management established as a profession with own institute and examinations.</li><li>Growth and increasing influence of trade unions seeking to improve the pay and working conditions of their members.</li><li>Management of industrial relations and personnel issues dominate.</li><li>1956: General Electric open in-house leadership development 'school' in New York.</li><li>1959: Drucker describes the declining importance of manual labour and describes a new type of 'knowledge' worker.</li></ul>
The 1980s onwards	<ul><li>HRM became fashionable with more strategic thinking.</li><li>Less conflict with trade unions.</li></ul>
Mis 1990s onwards	<ul><li>The flexible workforce, managing contractors, HR as a strategic advantage.</li></ul>

Before reviewing these theories, it is useful to consider what motivates employees and why this is important to the employer.

Test your understanding 1

(a) What motivates you to go to work?

(b) Would you still work if you won £20 million in the lottery?

(c) Why do organisations care about their employees being motivated?

Illustration 1

There are a number of well documented cases about lottery winners who have returned to work after scooping the jackpot.

- Carl Prance and his family won £6.9 million in October 07. However, ten months after he became an instant millionaire, the railway worker is back to normal – getting up at 5 o'clock in the morning for a shift.

- Millionaire lottery winner Maria Murray could earn £75,000 per year interest on her winnings but she continues to serve fried breakfasts and cups of tea to factory workers every morning for the minimum wage per hour.

1.2 Content and process theories of motivation

There are two broad classes of motivation theory:

Content theories	Process theories
• Ask the question **'What'** are the things that motivate people? They are also referred to as **"need theories"** and assume that human beings have a set of needs or desired outcomes which can be satisfied through work.	• Ask the question **'how'** are people motivated. They attempt to explain how individuals start, sustain and direct behaviour and assume that individuals are able to select their own goals and means of achieving those goals through a process of calculation.
• Content theories assume that everyone responds to motivating factors in the same way and that there is one best way to motivate everybody.	• Process theories change the emphasis from needs to the **goals** and **processes** by which workers are motivated.
• For example, Maslow's theory, Herzberg's theory.	• For example, Vroom's theory.

1.3 Taylor's scientific management

- Taylor concluded that workers are motivated by obtaining the highest possible remuneration (money).

- He believed that by analysing work in a scientific manner, the **'One Best Way'** to perform a task could be found.

- By organising work in the most efficient way, the organisation's productivity will be increased and this will enable the organisation to reward its employees with the remuneration they desire.

Steps in scientific management

Taylor's scientific management consisted of four principles, each of which has relevance to the topic of operations as well as HR management:

- Work methods should be based on the scientific study of the task, i.e. they should be planned in a way to maximise productivity. This often involves breaking the work down into separate functions.

- Select, train and develop the most suitable person for each job, i.e. scientific management of staff.

- Managers must provide detailed instructions to workers to ensure work is carried out in a scientific way.

- Divide work between managers and workers – managers apply scientific principles to planning and supervising the work and workers carry out the task.

Taylorism today

With modern trends including the need for flexible working and multi-skilling, it would be easy to dismiss Taylorism as outdated. However, it is still relevant in many areas, e.g. call centres.

Pig iron study

Taylor suggested that if workers were moving 12.5 tonnes of pig iron per day, and they could be incentivised (by money) to try to move 47.5 tonnes per day, left to their own devices they would probably become exhausted and fail to reach their goal.

However, by first conducting experiments to determine the amount of resting that was necessary, the worker's manager could determine the optimal time of lifting and resting so that workers could lift 47.5 tonnes per day without tiring.

Interestingly, only 1/8 of pig iron workers were capable of doing this. They were not extraordinary people but their physical capabilities were suited to moving pig iron. This led Taylor to suggest that workers should be selected according to how well they are suited to a job.

1.4 Mayo

During his research scholarship at Pennsylvania University, Mayo became involved in some research in a spinning mill in Philadelphia. The mill had a labour turnover of 250% – that is nobody stayed in the job for more than five months – while the average for other parts of the company was 6%. After introducing rest breaks and other improvements in working conditions, Mayo and his colleagues found that within a year labour turnover fell to the average elsewhere in the company. Mayo concluded that **social factors** were a more powerful motivator in the workplace than financial rewards.

After this, he was invited to take part in a series of experiments at Western Electric's Hawthorne factory outside Chicago, for which he gained high profile recognition. Here the working conditions had been altered, as at the spinning mill in Philadelphia. However, there was one important difference. When, for instance, the level of lighting was increased, productivity rose, as was expected. However, when the lighting was dimmed, productivity also, unexpectedly, rose. Mayo concluded that the key factor was workers' feeling that they were being **involved in the changes** to their working conditions. **Group relationships and management-worker communication** were far more important in determining employee behaviour than were physical conditions or wage levels.

Mayo's work is still relevant today. Most recently in manufacturing there has been a move towards team working and groups.

1.5 Maslow's hierarchy of needs

Maslow's theory suggests that within each employee there is a hierarchy of needs and the individual must satisfy each level before they move onto the next. The employee will seek to satisfy the five hierarchical needs from bottom to top:

Maslow's heirarchy of needs

SELF-FULFILMENT

EGO

SOCIAL

SAFETY/SECURITY

BASIC/PHYSIOLOGICAL

Related aspects at work
- Challenging job
- Creative task demands
- Advancement opportunities
- Achievement in work

- Merit pay increase
- High status job title

- Compatible work group
- Friendships at work

- Job security
- Fringe benefits

- Basic salary
- Safe working conditions

Maslow's hierarchy explained

Maslow's theory may be summarised and simplified by saying that everyone wants certain things throughout life, and these can be placed in five ascending categories, namely:

- **Basic or physiological needs** – The things needed to stay alive: food, shelter and clothing. Such needs can be satisfied by money.

- **Safety or security needs** – People want protection against unemployment, the consequences of sickness and retirement as well as being safeguarded against unfair treatment. These needs can be satisfied by the rules of employment, i.e. pension scheme, sick fund, employment legislation, etc.

- **Social needs** – The vast majority of people want to be part of a group and it is only through group activity that this need can be satisfied. Thus the way that work is organised, enabling people to feel part of a group, is fundamental to satisfaction of this need.

- **Ego needs** – These needs may be expressed as wanting the esteem of other people and thinking well of oneself. While status and promotion can offer short-term satisfaction, building up the job itself and giving people a greater say in how their work is organised gives satisfaction of a more permanent nature. An example might be being asked to lead groups on a course.

- **Self-fulfilment needs** – This is quite simply the need to achieve something worthwhile in life. It is a need that is satisfied only by continuing success, for example opening and running a new office.

Test your understanding 2

Violet is the managing director of a successful design company. Assess her motivation using Maslow's hierarchy.

Implications for managers

In order to motivate their employees, managers must understand the current level of needs at which the employee finds themselves and take steps to ensure that these current needs and the subsequent higher needs are satisfied.

Test your understanding 3

(a) Explain the criticisms/ limitations of Maslow's theory.

(b) Why might a graduate starting a new job, who had already satisfied the basic needs on Maslow's hierarchy, seek to satisfy needs in a different order?

1.6 The Vroom expectancy model

Vroom believes that people will be motivated to do things to reach a goal if they believe in the worth of that goal and if they can see that what they do will help them in achieving it.

Vroom's theory may be stated as:

Force	= **valence × expectancy**
where	
Force	= the strength of a person's motivation
valence	= the strength of an individual's preference for an outcome, e.g. a promotion
expectancy	= the probability of success, e.g. the opportunities that exist for promotion

1.7 Herzberg's two factor theory

Herzberg's needs based theory identified two sets of factors on the basis that they "motivate" in different ways.

Hygiene factors must be addressed to avoid dissatisfaction and include:

- Policies and procedures for staff treatment
- Suitable level and quality of supervision
- Pleasant physical and working conditions
- Appropriate level of basic salary and status for the job
- Team working.

However, in themselves hygiene factors are not sufficient to result in positive motivation.

Motivators will not cause dissatisfaction by not being present but can increase motivation if present. They include:

- Bonus
- Sense of achievement
- Recognition of good work
- Increasing levels of responsibility
- Career advancement
- Attraction of the job itself.

Most are non-financial in nature.

Implications for managers

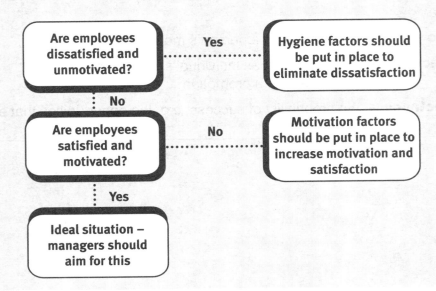

Herzberg went on to define three ways that management can attempt to improve staff satisfaction and motivation

- **Job enrichment** (sometimes called 'vertical job enlargement') – a deliberate, planned process to improve the responsibility, challenge and creativity of a job.

Illustration 2

Typical examples of **job enrichment** include delegation or problem-solving.

For instance, suppose an accountant's responsibilities for producing quarterly management reports ends at the stage of producing the figures. Job enrichment could involve extending the responsibilities so that they included the preparation of figures and submitting them to senior management. This alteration in responsibilities could not only enrich the job but also increase the workload, leading to delegation of certain responsibilities to clerks within the department, the cascading effect enriches other jobs as well.

- **Job enlargement** (sometimes called 'horizontal job enlargement') – widening the range of jobs, and so developing a job away from narrow specialisation. There is no element of enrichment.
- **Job rotation** – the planned rotating of staff between jobs to alleviate monotony and provide a fresh job challenge.

Illustration 3

The documented example of **job rotation** quotes a warehouse gang of four workers, where the worst job was tying the necks of the sacks at the base of the hopper after filling; the best job was seen as being the fork-lift truck driver. Job rotation would ensure that equal time was spent by each individual on all jobs. Herzberg suggests that this will help to relieve monotony and improve job satisfaction but is unlikely to create positive motivation.

Improving the opportunities for employees contribution

This section considers practices aimed at creating opportunities for employees to contribute to the organisation whether through job design, communications, involvement procedures or engaging in formal negotiating and bargaining.

A relatively recent concept of organisational citizenship behaviour (OCB) has grown up to describe the efforts of those who voluntarily undertake innovative, spontaneous tasks that go beyond their normal job role. Organ (1988) describes such behaviour as

…discretionary, not directly or explicitly recognized by the formal rewards system and that in aggregate promote effective functioning of an organization.

Clearly such behaviour is most apparent in organisations that have positive inclusive cultures that value team work and adopt supportive management approaches. The approach adopted by a particular manager can, in many situations, have a significant effect on efficiency, effectiveness and motivation. The potential impact of work groups on individual motivation has long been recognised and was famously illustrated by Mayo in the Hawthorne Studies.

This thinking naturally goes to the heart of job design and the methods by which team working is encouraged. Traditionally, jobs have been designed on the basis of the scientific management approach with a high degree of specialisation and strict controls. This is highly effective for bringing about conformity in many situations, but is hardly conducive to commitment. A number of other approaches to job design attempt to build more interest, variety, challenge and collaborative working into jobs.

Self-directed work teams have emerged from group technology developed by motor manufacturer, Volvo. The initiative arose as a result of recruitment and retention problems for production line jobs which involved repetitive working procedures.

Under cellular manufacturing methods, teams form a cell that jointly make a substantial proportion of the finished product rather than singly assemble one component of it. Cellular production often forms part of programmes of quality improvement. Indeed 'Total Quality Management', which seeks to move the emphasis away from detecting faults to preventing them, stresses employee involvement and team working as important ways of achieving this.

Job redesign can therefore be used to help develop individuals and groups within the workplace.

The job characteristics model sets out the links between characteristics of jobs, the individual's experience of those characteristics, and the resultant outcomes in terms of motivation, satisfaction and performance. The model also takes into account individual differences in the desire for personal growth and development (what Maslow called 'self-actualisation'). The heart of the model is the proposition that jobs can be analysed in terms of **five core dimensions** as follows:

- **Skill variety**: the extent to which a job makes use of different skills and abilities.

- **Task identity**: the extent to which a job involves a 'whole' and meaningful piece of work.

- **Task significance**: the extent to which a job affects the work of other organisation members or others in society.

- **Autonomy**: the extent to which a job gives the individual freedom, independence and discretion in carrying it out.

- **Feedback**: the extent to which information about the level of performance attained is related back to the individual.

These five core dimensions induce the **three psychological states** critical to high work motivation, job satisfaction and performance. These three states are defined as follows:

- **Experienced meaningfulness**: the extent to which the individual considers the work to be meaningful, valuable and worthwhile.

- **Experienced responsibility**: the extent to which the individual feels accountable for the work output.

- **Knowledge of results**: the extent to which individuals know and understand how well they are performing.

Jobs that have high scores are more likely to lead their incumbents to the experience of these critical psychological states than jobs that have low scores.

1.8 Handy's psychological contracts

The **psychological contract** outlines the perceptions of the employee and the employer regarding what their mutual obligations are towards each other.

- Unlike the employment contract, the psychological contract is highly subjective, not written down and not legally binding.

- Handy suggested that they cover the following:

	Employee	Employer
What do they want?	Want their needs to be satisfied	Want employee to work hard. Will have a set of expectations for each employee
What are they willing to give?	Will offer their energies and talents	Payment, benefits and other outcomes, e.g. a promotion

Implications for managers

- A psychological contract can exert a strong influence on behaviour because it captures what employees really believe they will get in return for what they give.

- If employees feel that the employer has broken promises, or violated the contract, employee reactions range from mild irritation or reduction in effort to handing in their notice.

- In order for managers to motivate and retain employees, they must understand the importance of the psychological contract.

Illustration 4

Kate has worked as a trainee accountant with the same company for the past two years. She is ambitious and enjoys her work. Her manager asks her to produce a report that is outside of her normal role.

The report turns out to be difficult and time consuming and she has to put in long hours to complete the report on time as well as carrying out her normal work.

She meets the deadline and sends the report to her manager. However, she receives no acknowledgement. The next day she finds out that her manager has successfully presented the findings of the report to his boss and has taken the credit for the report.

Kate is angry and has decided that she will never do any extra work for her boss again and has even started looking for another job due to the breach of her psychological contract.

Types of psychological contract

There are three types of psychological contract:

- **Coercive contracts** – which are not freely entered into and where a small group exercise control by rule and punishment. Although the usual form is found in prisons and other custodial institutions, coercive contracts also exist in schools and factories.

- **Calculative contracts** – where control is retained by management and is expressed in terms of their ability to give to the individual 'desired things' such as money, promotion and social opportunities. Most employees of industrial organisations 'enter into' such a contract.

- **Co-operative contracts** – where the individual tends to identify with the goals of the organisation and strive for their attainment. In return the individual receives just rewards, a voice in the selection of goals and a choice of the means to achieve such goals. Most enlightened organisations are moving towards such contracts but it must be emphasised that if they are to be effective, then the workers must also want them – if such a contract is imposed on the workforce, it becomes a coercive contract.

In all cases, the employees must know the results of their increased efforts and the management must understand the individual's needs.

1.9 McGregor's Theory X and Y

McGregor presented **two opposite sets of assumptions** made by managers about their staff.

Theory X assumptions:

- people dislike work and responsibility
- people must be coerced to get them to make an effort
- subordinates prefer to be directed, wish to avoid responsibility, have relatively little ambition, and want security above all.

Theory Y assumptions:

- physical and mental effort in work is as natural as play or rest.

- the average human being does not inherently dislike work, because it can be a source of satisfaction.

- people can exercise self-direction and self-control to achieve objectives to which they are committed.

- people can learn to enjoy and seek responsibility.

Test your understanding 4

Explain how management style should differ depending on whether individuals are theory X or theory Y type employees.

1.10 Schein

Schein identified four categories of worker:

- **Rational economic man** – self-interest and maximisation of gain are prime motivators.

- **Social man** – socialisation and acceptance at work are critical motivators.

- **Self actualising man** – challenge, responsibility and pride are key issues.

- **Complex man** – a blend of workers' expectations and whether the firm meets these is the motivator.

1.11 Mullins

Mullins identified three broad classifications that could be applied to understand motivation:

- **Economic rewards** – such as pay, security.

- **Intrinsic rewards** – derived, for example, from the nature of the work, interest in the job and self-development.

- **Social relationships** – such as friendships and being part of a team.

2 Practices Relating to Motivation

2.1 Reward systems

A **reward system** can help in keeping staff highly motivated in order to deliver high performance.

Types of remuneration structure

Type	Description
Graded pay	A sequence of job grades against which a payment range is attached.
Broad banded	The range of pay in a band is significantly higher than in a conventional structure. The structure usually covers the whole workforce from the shop floor to senior management.
Individual job ranges	Used when the content and size of jobs is widely different throughout the organisation.
Job family structures	Consists of pay related to jobs in a function or discipline such as financial specialists.
Spot rates	Allocation of a specific rate for the job.
Pay spines	Consists of a series of incremental points extending from the lowest to the highest paid jobs covered by the structure. Pay scales or ranges for different job grades may then be superimposed on the pay spine.
Integrated pay structures	Covers groups of employees who have all been paid under separate arrangements. There may be one grading system which includes all employees.

The aims of a reward system:

- **Motivation** – the reward scheme should encourage desirable behaviour and should recognise that different employees will be motivated by different factors.

- **Quality of staff** – the reward scheme should help to attract and retain the best staff.

- **Consistency and fairness** – the reward scheme should provide a fair and consistent basis for motivating and rewarding employees.

- **Reward performance** – the scheme should reward performance, e.g. by promotion through developed pathways.

- **Recognise factors other than job performance** – the reward scheme should recognise other factors such as the level of responsibility or additional tasks taken on.

- **To control costs** – it is important that the reward scheme assists in controlling salary costs.

- **To achieve organisational goals** – the reward scheme should assist the organisation in achieving its goals.

- **To comply with legislation/ regulation**

An **incentive scheme** links pay to performance. It can be tied to the performance of an individual or a team of employees. The scheme should ideally link performance to organisational goals.

There are four main types of incentive scheme; profit-related pay, piece rates, performance-related pay and non-financial rewards. Each of these is explained below.

Profit-related pay

Payments are made to employees in the light of the overall profitability of the company. Share issues may be part of the scheme.

Test your understanding 5

Profit-related pay schemes are not as popular as they once were. Briefly discuss the reasons for this.

Piece rates

A Taylorist philosophy based on paying employees on the basis of output alone.

This is suitable where output can easily be measured and mainly attributes to one individual.

Performance-related pay (PRP)

This is an appraisal based method where by the individual receives a bonus or an increase in pay based on achievements of the individual objectives (performance measures) set for them.

Performance measures for managers and employees should fulfil the SMART criteria:

- **S**pecific
- **M**easurable
- **A**chievable
- **R**ealistic
- **T**ime bound

In this way, managers and employees will be aware of the levels of performance they need to attain with absolute certainty.

Illustration 5

The Organic Juice Company has three divisions, the Fruit Juice division, the Smoothie division and the Fruit Cordial division. The market for smoothies is expected to grow by 20% over the next year and the Smoothie division expects to retain its share of the market. No other changes are anticipated.

The manager of the Smoothie division has been set a target to increase gross profit by 20% year on year.

This target fulfils the SMART criteria in that it is:

- specific – gross profit to increase by 20%

- measurable – it is possible to measure the annual change in gross profit

- achievable and realistic – the target seems achievable and realistic given that the market is expected to grow by 20%

- time bound – a year on year target has been set.

Benefits of PRP	Drawbacks of PRP
• Increased productivity.	• PRP not applied consistently.
• Method of rewarding and retaining most effective employees.	• Employees not aware of the level of performance they need to attain.
• Should promote greater employee involvement and commitment to organisational goals.	• Subjectivity in assessment.
	• Financial constraints restrict the amount of reward resulting in employee resentment.

Non-financial rewards

The use of non-financial rewards recognises that employees are motivated by factors other than pay. For example, Maslow's needs from bottom to top are:

- Physiological needs such as a competitive basic salary.

- Safety needs such as a good pension scheme.

- Social needs such as work nights out.

- Ego needs such as an opportunity for a merit pay increase.

- Self-fulfilment needs such as a challenging job and achievement in work.

A **total reward package (TRP)** draws together all the financial and non-financial benefits available to employees.

Test your understanding 6

Identify the advantages and disadvantages of a TRP approach.

2.2 Flexible working arrangements

Flexible working arrangements can be used to increase employee motivation. Flexibility in work patterns can be achieved in many ways:

Flexitime	The need to work a standard set of hours but less restriction on when these hours are worked;
Shift system	Working outside of normal working day patterns;
Compressed week	Standard hours within fewer days in a shift rotation;
Job sharing	Two employees share a standard hour week;
Part-time	Fewer hours than the standard weekly number;
Teleworking	Technology has enabled employees to work away from the office, usually at home.

Test your understanding 7

Explain the advantages and disadvantages for the **employer** of flexible working arrangements.

It is also important to consider the flexible working arrangements from the **employee's** point of view:

Advantages for the employee	Disadvantages for the employee
• Cost and time savings, e.g. because the employee works at home or does not travel to work at peak times.	• Increased costs, e.g. employees have to pay for additional utilities when working from home.
• Flexibility to fit work around family life and other commitments.	• Loss of social interaction, e.g. due to the flexible hours or working from home.
• Increased enjoyment of work since feel employer is listening to their needs.	• Lack of support, again due to the flexible hours or working from home.

2.3 Workforce flexibility

Flexible working arrangements encompass one type of flexibility within organisations. 'Workforce flexibility' is the term used to describe a much broader range of flexible working options:

- **Task or functional flexibility** – employees have the ability to move between tasks as and when is required. This will allow an organisation to react to changes in production requirements and levels of demand.

Achieving functional flexibility

Functional flexibility can be achieved by:

- Training staff in a wide variety of skills.

- Recruiting staff with a wider variety of skills.

- Introducing a programme of job rotation.

- **Numerical flexibility** – the use of non-core workers allows the organisation to adjust the level of labour to meet fluctuations in demand. For example:
  - Temporary workers

  - Part time workers

  - Overtime

- **Financial flexibility** – this is achieved through variable systems of rewards, e.g. bonus schemes, profit sharing. By linking rewards to performance, a number of improvements in performance should be realised.

- **Flexible working arrangements** – as discussed in section 2.2. Arrangements that result in a variability of labour work time, e.g. flexible hours or a compressed working week, are sometimes referred to as 'temporal flexibility'.

Handy's Shamrock organisation

Handy suggested the idea of a 'Shamrock' organisation. People linked to an organisation are said to fall into three groups. Each group will have different expectations and it is important that they are managed and rewarded in an appropriate way. The groups are:

- **The professional core** – includes managers and technicians. They should be rewarded through a high salary and benefits since they are essential to the continuity of the organisation.

- **The contractual fringe** – contracted specialists, rewarded with a fee.

- **Flexible labour force** – part time and temporary workers provide flexibility

2.4 Arrangements for knowledge workers

Knowledge workers are people who create knowledge and produce new products and services for the organisation to sell. For example:

- Research staff
- Chemists
- Architects

As we move from a traditional manufacturing economy to a service economy, it is recognised that knowledge is a primary source of competitive advantage.

Implications for human resource management

- **Selection criteria** – employees should be selected for their skills, i.e. knowledge, as opposed to their ability to do a particular job.

- **Sharing of knowledge** – encouraged by:
  - Team working
  - Job rotations

- **Retention of knowledge** – this can be achieved by:
  - Filling vacancies internally.
  - Ensuring there is a well defined career path to increase motivation and hence retention.

- **Performance appraisal** – the appraisal must:
  - Prioritise the development of knowledge skills if the employees are to believe that the organisation takes these seriously.
  - Encourage employee input into their own development, skills and careers.

Commitment of knowledge workers

Key contributing factors to employee commitment are:

- The degree of flexibility and autonomy within the workforce.

- An emphasis on performance-related pay. Performance could be measured by, for example, the amount of quality information about a product published professionally on a web site that will help sell more of that product. The more motivated the knowledge worker is, the more quality information he or she will create.

- Appraisal systems that monitor and reward knowledge contributions and application e.g. knowledge turned into information, into documents, into content.

- Profit-sharing or equity-based forms of reward. Quality information about a product published professionally on a web site will help sell more of that product. The more motivated the knowledge worker is, the more quality information he or she will create.

- Career progression – make it clear that those who contribute quality information on a consistent basis will move up through the organisation.

2.5 Employee involvement

Employees should be given the opportunity to contribute to the organisation. **High performance work arrangements** rely on all employees for their ideas, intelligence and commitment to make the organisation successful. Increased motivation and positive financial benefits can be gained from:

- Greater employee participation in job design – job enrichment, enlargement and rotation can all result in increased motivation.

- Open and honest communication.

- Empowered, involved and listened to employees.

- A willingness for the employer to compromise and bargain with employees.

3 Chapter summary

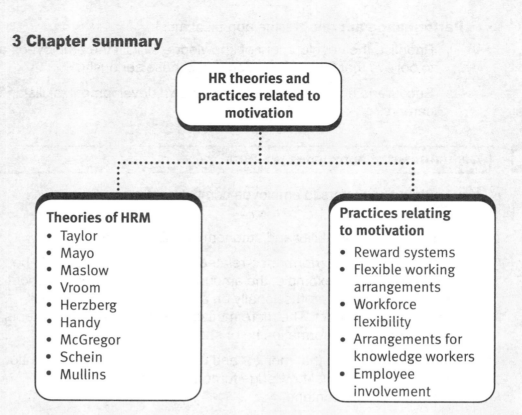

HR theories and practices related to motivation

Theories of HRM
- Taylor
- Mayo
- Maslow
- Vroom
- Herzberg
- Handy
- McGregor
- Schein
- Mullins

Practices relating to motivation
- Reward systems
- Flexible working arrangements
- Workforce flexibility
- Arrangements for knowledge workers
- Employee involvement

4 Practice questions

Question 1

In Frederick Herzberg's theory of motivation, basic pay is regarded as:

A   A motivator

B   A satisfier

C   A hygiene factor

D   A resource

(2 marks)

Question 2

When a performance appraisal scheme is ineffective, this may be due to:

A   a lack of objective criteria for the appraisal of personality

B   under-performing employees

C   excluding discussions about pay

D   a lack of objective criteria for the appraisal of performance

(2 marks)

Question 3

One example of a flexible work arrangement is a compressed work week. A compressed work week involves:

A   working for longer-than-usual hours on some days in exchange for a day off work

B   working for some days at home instead of in the office

C   allowing employees to choose their hours of attendance each day, provided that they work a full day

D   allowing employees to work less than the standard number of hours each week

(2 marks)

Question 4

Content theories of motivation tend to focus mainly on:

A   the needs of the group

B   feelings of complacency or dissatisfaction

C   the needs of individuals

D   the use of 'carrots' and 'sticks' as devices

(2 marks)

Question 5

A company pension scheme is an example of which need in Maslow's hierarchy?

A   Basic needs

B   Self-fulfilment needs

C   Safety needs

D   Retirement needs

(2 marks)

Question 6

Discuss the strengths and weaknesses of Herzberg's theory of motivation.

(4 marks)

Question 7

Explain the nature of a psychological contract between an individual and an organisation, and describe the three types of psychological contract identified by Handy.

(4 marks)

Question 8

Explain what is meant by hygiene factors and motivators and explain what action should be taken by managers if they identify that both sets of factors are absent in the organisation.

(4 marks)

Question 9

List the hierarchy of needs and examples of hygiene/ motivators. What parallels can you draw between the two approaches?

(4 marks)

Question 10

Harriet has just been appointed to take charge of part of an accounting department concerned with processing information from the operating division of a large company.

Based on her previous experience, she has determined that the running costs of the department are too high, due to absenteeism, lateness, low productivity and time spent in correcting errors.

Investigation of the design of the jobs in the department reveals that each employee is trained in a task which is made as simple as possible. The equipment used is maintained by a service department. Strict discipline ensures that clerks do not carry on conversations during working hours, and tasks are performed in exactly the order and method laid down.

Harriet has decided that performance can be improved by changing the job design.

Assume that Harriet's superiors approve the changes, that correct training is provided and that resistance by the clerks to change is properly overcome.

Required:

(a) Discuss the likely consequences for organisations and employees of designing jobs which are repetitive, routine and lacking in significant skill requirements.

(10 marks)

(b) Distinguish between job enrichment and job enlargement and give examples of these techniques in action.

(10 marks)

(c) Describe five changes that might achieve improved job satisfaction.

(10 marks)

(Total: 30 marks)

Question 11

CP is a small but successful company which specialises in selling car and home insurance to individuals. All sales are made over the telephone, and there are no personal callers to the company's offices. The company employs 25 staff, 22 in the telephone sales department and the remaining 3 running all the accounts and administration functions. As a consequence of its recent success in the market, CP is planning to expand its operations.

The company has been evaluating its cost structure and has discovered that the cost of providing office space for each worker is $3,500 per annum. New workers would require office space with a cost per worker of $4,000 per annum. This amounts to a significant cost in the company's operating budget. The Management Accountant has calculated that 90% of office costs can be avoided if the telephone sales staff worked from their homes. This idea has, so far, been discussed only at board level.

At present, employees appear to enjoy working in the office, where they spend most of their time using the telephone and computer system to sell insurance. Coffee and lunch breaks are normally spent in the rest area where staff also compare some notes and queries concerning their jobs. All the data that they need to perform their job is otherwise available on the computer system. This data includes:

- records on each customer;

- access to a value added network (VAN) providing costs of insurance from other companies which sell insurance;

- word-processing and other systems for producing letters and insurance quotes to customers.

The proposal to work from home was put to staff last week and this has met with some initial resistance although the Management Accountant stressed that this proposal was only a possibility.

Write notes to the Managing Director explaining:

(a) from the viewpoint of the staff, the potential benefits that will be gained by home working. Explain the concerns that staff may have over home working and whether the IT infrastructure can help alleviate these concerns.

(12 marks)

(b) what can be done to encourage staff to accept the proposed change.

(8 marks)

(Total: 20 marks)

Test your understanding answers

Test your understanding 1

(a) The answer depends on the individual. Factors that may motivate you to go to work include money, enjoyment of the work, challenge, opportunity to achieve something, enjoyment of the social side of work/ friends at work.

(b) Again, the answer depends on the individual. Some people would not return to work but others would. This leads us to believe that factors, apart from money, motivate individuals to go to work.

(c) Motivated employees are important to the organisation since:

– If individuals are motivated they will work more efficiently and productivity will rise.

– They may produce a better quality of work.

– Motivation may result in employees exercising their creativity and initiative in the service of organisational goals.

– Motivation will reduce staff turnover and the associated costs.

Test your understanding 2

Statements	Satisfied	Not Satisfied	Explanation
Self-achievement needs	✓		Self-achievement needs should be satisfied by the succuss of the business.
Ego needs	✓		Ego needs should be satisfied by being MD.
Social needs	✓		Social needs are met by being part of the Board of Directors (Note: you could have argued that some MDs may feel isolated and that the Board is against them.)
Safety/ security needs	✓		Security needs will be met by a generous pension scheme and a long notice period.
Basic/ physiological needs	✓		Basic needs are satisfied by a high salary.

Test your understanding 3

(a) The following are criticisms/ limitations of Maslow's hierarchy:

– Individuals have different needs and not necessarily in the same order.

– Individuals may seek to satisfy several needs at the same time.

– Not all of these needs are or can be satisfied through work.

(b) A graduate might then seek to meet social needs before worrying about job security and long term security of pension arrangements.

Test your understanding 4

Based on their assumptions, supervisors will adopt a corresponding management style:

- If you believe that you have Theory X workers, then you adopt an authoritarian, repressive style with tight control. Effectively the workforce are a problem that needs to be overcome by management.

- If you believe that you have Theory Y workers, then you adopt a participative, liberating, developmental approach. Employees will be viewed as assets who need to be encouraged and empowered.

Test your understanding 5

- The firm may 'massage' its year end profits.
- The tax implications of employee share schemes.
- Employees may resent the scheme if their actions do not directly impact the profit.
- Employees may resent the scheme if it is restricted to only a group of managers/ directors.

Test your understanding 6

Advantages	Disadvantages
• Helps to retain and motivate high quality staff. • Method of attracting talented staff. • Recognises that a combination of pay and non-pay benefits are essential for motivation. • Flexible approach allowing employees to pick and choose the rewards to suit their needs. • Projects a positive image to stakeholders.	• Cost may outweigh benefit. • Wouldn't work in isolation e.g. if poor recruitment practices exist. • Staff may be suspicious viewing package as a way to keep pay down. • Costly failure if design flaws.

Test your understanding 7

Advantages

Flexible working arrangements may fulfil the needs of the individual resulting in:

- Increased employee motivation and productivity;
- Increased commitment to the organisation;
- Attracting talented individuals because of the availability of such conditions;
- Reduced absenteeism and staff turnover.

In addition, the company may reduce costs, e.g. due to a reduction in office space if employees work at home or a reduction in the number of full time workers in favour of part time workers.

Disadvantages

Flexible working arrangements such as working from home or working non-standard hours may result in:

- Difficulties in co-ordinating staff;
- Loss of control of staff;
- Dilution of organisational culture;
- Less commitment to the organisation;

In addition, some costs may actually increase, e.g. due to the extra cost of providing equipment for employees to work from home.

Question 1

C

Question 2

D

Question 3

A

Question 4
C

Question 5
C

Question 6

The strengths of Herzberg's theory

The motivation-hygiene theory has clear implications for management. If this theory is correct then management, in seeking higher levels of performance, should give more attention to the job-content factors, such as opportunity for achievement, recognition and advancement: these are the motivating factors. The theory also points out that money may not be the most potent motivating force; and neither are the other content or hygiene factors such as fringe benefits and supervision. For managers, Herzberg's theory offers some clear ideas that may be translated into specific work-design policy.

The weaknesses of Herzberg's theory

In Herzberg's study, about 80% of the participants were motivated by the motivating factors he defined, and fewer than 70% were affected by the failure to maintain the hygiene factors. This shows that his ideas have a limited application to certain types of worker. In addition, his theory does not allow for:

- the differences in the type of employee;
- the workers who are principally motivated by financial reward;
- the skill levels required by the work;
- the challenges associated with the work.

Question 7

A psychological contract between an individual and an organisation is a 'contract' in the mind of the individual. In return for the organisation satisfying some of the individual's needs, the individual will give some of his/her energy and talent to the organisation.

Handy's three types of psychological contract are:

- **A coercive contract**: the individual is forced to work in the organisation without his consent. Examples are a prisoner in prison and, in some cases, a student at school.

- **A calculative contract**: control of the rewards that satisfy the individual's needs (pay, promotion, and so on) is in the hands of the organisation's management. The individual decides how much effort it is worth putting into the job to get the rewards.

- **A co-operative contract**: the individual identifies with the objectives of the organisation and works hard to attain them – in return for fair rewards, and a voice in the selection of targets or objectives and in the means of achieving them.

Question 8

- A hygiene factor is something that does not motivate employees but it will result in unmotivated employees, if they are not present.

- A motivator is something that, if present, will motivate staff but the absence of motivators will not result in unmotivated staff.

- Managers should begin by ensuring that hygiene factors, such as supervision and acceptable working conditions, are in place.

- Only once these hygiene factors are present, should the managers take action to ensure that motivators, such as a bonus scheme or opportunity for career advancement, are in place.

Question 9

Hierarchy of needs	Motivators	Hygiene factors
Self-fulfilment needs	Opportunity for advancement	Sports/ social facilities
Esteem needs	Acknowledgement	Working conditions
Social needs	Increased responsibility	Pension
Safety/ security needs	Work challenges	Pay
Basic/ physiological needs		

There is a clear relationship between Herzberg's 'hygiene factors' and the lower level of Maslow's 'Hierarchy of Needs.' Likewise there is a close relationship between the motivators and Maslow's higher needs.

Question 10

(a) **Consequences of routine, repetitive jobs**

McGregor concluded that there are two types of worker; theory X and theory Y. Theory X type staff dislike work, will prefer to be directed, avoid responsibility and have very little ambition. These types of staff would actually prefer a routine, repetitive and low skilled job.

However, theory Y type staff will enjoy and seek responsibility and want to be able to exercise self-direction and self-control. It is likely that the staff within the accounts department are theory Y type staff. For these types of worker, routine work results in subjective feelings of monotony and boredom and this in turn leads to less than optimum performance by the workforce.

Studies of workers in car assembly factories in various parts of the world have confirmed that a large proportion of the workforce dislikes the repetitive nature of assembly line work, and that it is strongly associated with above average levels of absenteeism, labour turnover and industrial action. These problems are most apparent in times of full employment, but their lack of visibility in times of high unemployment and job insecurity does not mean they disappear but that workers are less ready to risk their jobs by taking any form of industrial action.

All the problems which characterise low discretion, routine work, as highlighted by Harriet, inflict costs in terms of poor quality work, lower levels of production, costs of cover for absent employees, loss of output and damage to trust and cooperation between management and employees.

The kind of behaviour exhibited by employees required to carry out tedious work operations is often explained as arising from a lack of need fulfilment. Theorists such as Maslow and Herzberg, for instance, argue that routine, repetitive work does not meet the higher level social and self-actualising needs of people. Employees frustrated by the lack of self fulfilment in their work seek to avoid it by frequent absence from the organisation on the grounds of sickness or by seeking more interesting and challenging work elsewhere. Their readiness to take industrial action is explained in terms of yet another means of venting their frustration by striking for some socially acceptable reasons such as higher pay and/or better working conditions.

(b) **Job enrichment and job enlargement**

Job design is a method of redesigning jobs by taking into account the needs of individual workers as well as the objectives of the organisation. For the individual this can lead to greater job satisfaction and greater control over his/her work environment. It may also be a vehicle for increasing the participation of employees in the immediate work area. In an effort to improve the variety of work for employees, additional tasks are often added to those contained in the current job description.

Job enrichment (sometimes called vertical increase) – provides the employee with extra tasks that demand use of authority, skills, behaviour and decision-making at a higher level than that required in his or her normal job.

This gives the manager:

- more time to concentrate on higher level tasks.
- an opportunity to assess the potential of the employee.
- an opportunity to develop communication.

Employees have motivation factors provided, e.g. recognition, achievement, growth. They also have a chance to prove their potential and gain rewards and an opportunity to work with less supervision.

Examples include:

- a senior could be taken 'on site' by a manager/partner to gain experience and eventually be given an area of client visits that he/she alone would organise.

- a clerk could be given training on computer terminals and word processors so that he/she could carry out secretarial and machine room operations as well as the normal tasks.

Disadvantages of job enrichment include:

- the new jobs have to come from somewhere or someone, so there may be organisational problems. There can also be friction between colleagues when one of them is 'specially chosen'. Less capable employees may be worried about the additional skills required.

- there is the risk in certain areas that control by segregation of duties might be lost. For example, the cashier who opens the mail and writes up the books might be vulnerable to corruption if inadequately supervised.

Job enlargement (sometimes called horizontal increase) occurs when additional tasks are given to the employee essentially at a similar or lower level than his or her present job, giving the job a longer cycle time. This reduces the amount of repetition and may require the exercise of a wider range of skills.

Unfortunately, it is unlikely to be a positive motivator, but it does provide recognition and job variety.

This technique gives the manager the benefits of a busier workforce capable of carrying out a variety of tasks with the ability to assess potential or training needs.

The employee has job variety and can develop new skills and can show potential and develop positive attitudes.

Examples of job enlargement include the following:

- A salesperson, even if only a booking clerk or building society cashier could advise customers on more services/bargains available.

- Retail salespeople could become more involved in inventory control, and ultimately ordering/buying.

(c) **Changes that might achieve improved job satisfaction**

A range of measures is available to Harriet to try to reduce the level of dissatisfaction felt by the staff and to motivate them to work harder.

Several of these involve some form of job redesign. Much of the routine work that the clerks do is reminiscent of the scientific management approach to work design, which amongst other things, involves job simplification by breaking a job down into a number of very simple tasks which are easy to perform. It has been widely adopted because of its assumed efficiency. Workers become adept at completing the tasks quickly because of their constant repetition. Unfortunately, as already indicated, this kind of work leads to frustration and stress and workers behave in ways that detract from both their own performance and that of the organisation.

Job satisfaction might be improved if Harriet were to adopt the following five changes:

Job enlargement – aims to give employees greater variety in their work by adding extra tasks of the same level as before. This 'horizontal extension of the job', though criticised for not giving any real increase in responsibility, often works in practice to bring about improved morale and/or productivity.

Job enrichment – is usually applied to the 'vertical extension of job responsibilities'. It implies giving an employee more responsibility through the introduction of both senior (higher) and junior (lower) level tasks into their workload. This, in turn, acts to add interest and challenge to a job by giving people tasks through which they can gain a sense of achievement.

Job rotation – allows an element of variety to be introduced into a job by switching an employee from one undemanding job to another undemanding job. This is obviously not much of an improvement but it does involve a little more variety.

Work groups – involve employees working together in a self-organised, autonomous group, which is collectively responsible for reaching its own production targets. Tasks within each group are allocated by the members and each group is responsible for the rate and quality of its output. Reportedly first established in the British coal mining industry under the 'composite longwall method', subsequent developments have shown that autonomous work groups can help to improve job satisfaction and hence employee morale.

Quality circles – are small, voluntary groups of about eight to ten shop-floor employees who meet regularly to identify problems of quality, productivity, safety, etc., to set targets to improve the situation caused by problems and to implement any required changes. The latter point is significant because unlike other forms of employee participation, quality circles permit the employees themselves to implement changes agreed by the management, thus implying a degree of grass-roots decision-making, which is new to most shop-floor situations.

(**Note:** marks would be awarded for other relevant points).

Question 11

(a) **Potential benefits to staff**

- Less time wasted commuting and therefore there is more time to pursue personal interests.

- Less stress and expense incurred in travelling.

- A more relaxed dress code. Suits, collars and ties will be needed rarely.

- More flexible work patterns that can be fitted around family life and other commitments and interests.

- Fewer interruptions and less time wasted by the trivial matters that typically arise in most offices. The more peaceful and relaxed environment should mean that tasks are completed more efficiently and effectively.

- Assuming there are suitable communication links, staff will have more freedom about where they live and even how long they can be away during the holiday season as their business could be conducted from almost anywhere.

The concerns of staff

- Staff realise that the proposed change will have dramatic effects and are right to be concerned. The level of an individual's concern will vary, depending on how much they enjoy office life, their home circumstances and how comfortable they feel with advanced computer systems.

- Work plays a very important role in most people's lives. In addition to providing income, work can also help meet social, ego and self-fulfilment needs. Home working will greatly reduce social opportunities for staff and they will meet colleagues only occasionally; they may fear isolation. Ego needs (the need to be looked up to and respected) will be harder to fulfil in the relatively solitary world of the home worker.

- Staff may feel cut off from important information that they need.

- Learning and problem solving opportunities will be reduced. In addition to formal training, most employees learn a tremendous amount informally by watching and by discussing problems with colleagues. Often, employees will learn by listening in on discussions being carried on between two other parties.

- Working from home may have negative effects on home life. The equipment will have to be sited somewhere in the employee's house; work time may encroach on private time as there is no longer the formal cut-off of going home from work.

- Some employees may have more interruptions at home than they would have in the office.

- Home working may make career structures more limiting. More people are working on their own and there might be less management to carry out. Furthermore, promotion will be on fewer success criteria as the only results seen by head office will be sales; managerial and human qualities will be more difficult to display.

Use of the IT infrastructure

The infra-structure can help as follows:

- Email will provide easy communication (albeit written) between staff.

- Voice and video attachments will make it possible for staff to talk to and see each other. This will reduce their feeling of isolation.

- Communications equipment and software will allow access to data about customers and the value added network.

- Standard letters and forms can be used by the word processor to produce quotations and other commonly required documents.

- The provision of on-line help and electronic performance support systems will help staff learn on demand (just-in-time learning).

(b) **How staff could be encouraged to accept the proposed change**

- Participation in the decision making process and in the establishment of new work norms.

- It is unlikely that all work can be carried on from home without the need of meetings or visits to the office. Pointing this out should help to reduce fears about isolation.

- Emphasise the benefits that there should be (see above).

- Consider offering help to staff for the establishment of suitable work areas at home. At the very least, office furniture will have to be supplied. If a separate area is not available, the furniture will have to be carefully chosen so as to fit in with domestic furniture.

- Emphasise that CP will pay for the installation of an ISDN line which is equivalent to two additional phone lines. One line will be used for IT; the other as a conventional business line. Help towards additional heating costs may be appropriate as staff will now occupy their own houses most of the day.

- Additional efforts should be made to arrange out of hours social events to reduce feelings of isolation and loss of social contact.

- Instead of enforcing immediate changeover of all staff, many of whom may be reluctant to cooperate, it might be possible to ask first for volunteers. These people could be seen as a pilot operation from which, no doubt, both staff and the company will learn. Every effort should be made to maximise the success of this operation so that other staff members will also be encouraged to change.

- Staff will be aware that the company will save money and may expect some financial inducements to change their work practices.

Conclusion

Home working offers great potential benefits to this organisation but it represents a fundamental change in the culture and work practices of staff, who have legitimate worries. However, by addressing these worries and attempting to win their cooperation, staff concerns should be outweighed by the very considerable benefits which should be obtained by them.

13

Managing Human Capital

Chapter learning objectives

Lead	Component
E1. Explain the relationship of human resources (HR) to the organisation's operations	(b) Explain the importance of ethical behaviour in business generally and for the line manager and their activities.
E2. Discuss the activities associated with the management of human capital	(a) Explain the HR activities associated with developing the ability of employees. (d) Discuss the importance of the line manager in the implementation of HR practices. (e) Prepare an HR plan appropriate to a team.

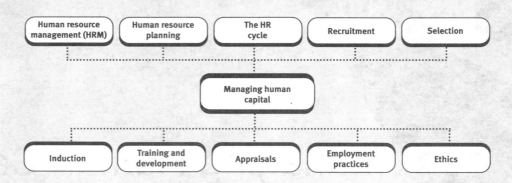

1 Introduction

Human resource management (HRM) can be viewed as a strategic approach to acquiring, developing, managing and motivating an organisation's key resource. This should help the organisation achieve its stated objectives through the best use of its employees.

Note that HRM is not simply a renaming of old "personnel" departments but a radical change in emphasis:

The role of personnel versus the role of HRM

Personnel	HRM
• The **traditional** approach to managing human resources.	• The **modern** approach to managing human resources.
• Concerned with **operational** matters, e.g. recruitment to fill a current vacancy.	• Concerned with **operational and strategic** matters, e.g. training to fulfil the current and future needs of the organisation.
• Employees seen as **costs**.	• Employees seen as **assets**.
• Employees motivated by **payment and coercion.**	• Employees motivated by **consent and involvement**.
• Line manager's role is more **transactional** with an emphasis on **negotiation**. Key managers are seen to be personnel and industrial relations specialists.	• Line manager's role is now one of **transformational leadership** with an emphasis on **facilitation**. Line managers are seen as key within a HR emphasis.

The Guest model of HRM

A HR strategy can only make sense when related to business objectives. One model that clearly demonstrates the relationship between HRM activities and strategy was proposed by David **Guest** (1997) and comprised six components:

(1) HRM strategy

(2) HRM practices

(3) a set of HRM outcomes

(4) behavioural outcomes

(5) a number of performance outcomes

(6) financial outcomes.

The central idea of the model is that HRM practices should be designed to lead a set of positive outcomes including high staff commitment and quality, and highly flexible employees. The main features are:

- a goal of binding employees to the organisation and obtaining behavioural outcomes of increased effort, co-operation, involvement and organisational citizenship

- high quality employees, involving workplace learning and the need for a capable, qualified, skilful workforce to produce high-quality services and products

- flexibility concerned with ensuring that workers are receptive to innovation and change and operation.

Outcomes 3–6 focus on the link between HRM and performance. According to the model, only when all three HRM outcomes, of commitment, quality and flexibility, are achieved, can behaviour change and superior performance outcomes be expected. These HRM goals are a 'package' and each is necessary to ensure superior performance and financial outcomes.

2 Human Resource Planning (HRP)

The organisation's **HR plan** is a strategy developed within the context of the organisation's corporate strategic plans.

- Its aim is to define and close the gap between the demand for labour and the supply of labour within the organisation.

- A typical HR plan looks forward 3–5 years and is a cyclical process.

Reasons for creating a HR plan

(1) To rationally plan recruitment;

(2) To rationally forecast future costs to assist in budgeting and control;

(3) To smooth change management in redeployment, redundancy etc.;

(4) To assist in planning the education, development and training needs of staff;

(5) To adapt more quickly to ever changing circumstances.

The stages of HRP are as follows:

Stage 1: Strategic analysis
- The organisation's strategic objectives will have implications regarding the number of employees and the skills required over the planning period (e.g. development of a new product or expansion into a new market)
- The broader strategic environment should also be considered (e.g. trends in population growth, pensions, education and employment rights of women)

Stage 2: Internal analysis
- An 'audit' of existing staff should be carried out to establish the current numbers and skills
- Also consider:
  - Turnover of staff and absenteeism
  - Overtime worked and periods of inactivity
  - Staff potential

Stage 3: Identify the gap between supply and demand
- Shortages or excesses in labour numbers and skills deficiencies should be identified

Stage 4: Put plans into place to close the gap

Adjustments for shortfall
- Internal: Transfers, promotions, training, job enlargement, overtime, reduce labour turnover
- External: Fill remaining needs externally. Consider suitability and availability of external resource

Adjustments for a surplus
Consider use of natural wastage, recruitment freeze, retirement, part time working and redundancy

Stage 5: Review
Measure the effective use of the human resource and their contribution towards the achievement of the organisation's objectives

Stage 4 of the HR plan

In stage four of HRP a number of plans will be created and used:

Recruitment plan	Numbers and types of people, when required, recruitment programme
Training plan	Number of trainees required and training programme
Redevelopment plan	Programme for transferring staff
Productivity plan	Setting targets and developing incentive schemes
Redundancy plan	Location, selection process, package details
Retention plan	Career development programmes

Test your understanding 1

Describe **four** problems in implementing the HR plan.

Test your understanding 2

How can an organisation plan rationally in an unstable environment?

Line managers and human resource practices

Organisational HR practices inevitably vary dependent upon the individual size and culture of the organisation and availability of specialist HR or personnel managers to support management in carrying out their duties.

The need to respond to a fast moving environment has led to organisations moving from traditional hierarchies to adopting more flexible organisational structures including fluid matrix or project-based firms. Alongside these virtual or networked firms have grown up. Inevitably these non-traditional structures have presented new HR challenges and required managers to adapt traditional approaches to these local contexts.

Clearly HR thinking and practice needs to evolve in responses to these challenges of flexibility and environmental uncertainty, specifically in the areas of:

- planning horizons

- staff appraisal where there may be no formal supervisor/subordinate reporting relations

- remuneration strategies where outputs are not easily attributable to individuals alone

- the structure of the workforce and the use of consultants and contractors

- development, promotion and succession planning.

New forms of organisation have resulted in changing HR needs. For example:

Project based teams

Employees are organised into work teams, e.g. for a particular project or customer group. HR implications:

- Multi-skilled employees are required.

- Intensive training will be needed.

- A movement away from traditional hierarchies to flatter structures.

Virtual organisations

Technology has resulted in the development of virtual organisations. Virtual teams work together using the World Wide Web, networked computers and teleconferencing.

This can bring huge benefits for the employer in terms of the flexibility to recruit the most talented individual for a particular role. However, it can also bring additional challenges with regards to HR since geographical spread will make all elements of HR (i.e. recruitment, selection, inductions, appraisals and training and development) more difficult.

3 The HR Cycle

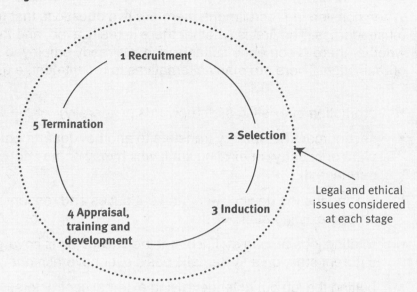

Each of these activities will be reviewed in turn.

4 Recruitment

4.1 Introduction

Recruitment involves attracting a field of suitable candidates for the job.

The best recruitment campaign will attract a small number of highly suitable applicants, be cost effective, be speedy and show courtesy to all candidates.

The recruitment plan includes:

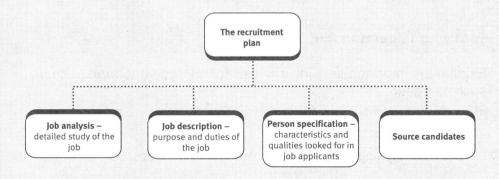

Assessing the need to recruit

When considering recruitment, there are two questions that managers must address. The first is whether there is really a job, and the second is whether there is someone suitable who is already employed by the organisation. There are many alternatives to recruitment, e.g.

- promotion of existing staff (upwards or laterally)

- secondment (temporary transfers to another department, office, plant or country) of existing staff, which may or may not become permanent

- closing the job down, by sharing out duties and responsibilities among existing staff

- rotating jobs among staff, so that the vacant job is covered by different staff, on a systematic basis over several months

- putting the job out to tender, using external contractors.

4.2 Job analysis

Job analysis is 'the process of collecting, analysing and setting out information about the content of jobs in order to provide the basis for a job description and data for recruitment, training, job evaluation and performance management. Job analysis concentrates on what job holders are expected to do.' **Armstrong**

Such an exercise is frequently necessary since all too few organisations have a precise picture of the work that people do to achieve organisational objectives.

Test your understanding 3

Explain the importance of job analysis for a large supermarket chain, such as Tesco.

Methods of analysing and defining roles would include:

- interview with existing post holder or supervisor

- direct observation

- questionnaires

- manager trying the job.

4.3 Job descriptions

After a full job analysis has been carried out, a job description can be drawn up identifying the precise nature of the job in question.

Test your understanding 4

Prepare a job description for a London based role as a Finance Director in an internet media company which is about to become a public company.

Job descriptions

Most job descriptions include all of the following points.

- The title of the job and the name of the department in which it is situated.

- The purpose of the job, identifying its objectives in relationship to overall objectives.

- The position of the job in the organisation, indicating the relationships with other jobs and the chains of responsibility. For this purpose, many firms refer to existing organisation charts.

- Wage/salary range.

- Principal duties to be performed, with emphasis on key tasks, and limits to the jobholder's authority. Usually included under this heading is an indication of how the job differs from others in the organisation.

- A further breakdown of principal duties is made identifying specific tasks in terms of what precisely is done and in what manner, and with some explanation, both in terms of quantity and quality.

- Aspects of the 'job environment' should be considered. Descriptions should be made of how the organisation supports the job, in terms of management and the provision of key services. The working conditions should be considered in terms of both the physical environment and the social environment (is the job part of a group task?). The opportunities offered by the job should be identified; these are especially important in a recruitment exercise.

- No job description is complete without a full identification of the key difficulties likely to be encountered by the jobholder.

Most of the content of a job description will be generated by the line manager. However, an HR department can help through the use of standardised templates, discussions over grading and salary and the position of the role in the wider organisation.

4.4 Person specifications

The **person specification** defines the personal characteristics, qualifications and experience required by the job holder in order to do the job well. It therefore becomes a specification for the attributes sought in a successful candidate for the job, a blueprint for the perfect person to fill the role.

Rodgers recommended that the following categories should be covered in a person specification:

Category	Example
B – Background/ circumstances	Details of previous work experience and circumstances, e.g. family background, criminal record.
A – Attainments	Details of qualifications and any relevant experience.
D – Disposition	The individual's goals and motivations, e.g. where do they see themselves in 5 years time?
P – Physical make-up	Appearance, speech, health and fitness may be important.
I – Interests	General interests and hobbies will be important, e.g. being a member of a football team demonstrates teamwork skills.
G – General intelligence	Not necessarily academic qualifications but may refer to practical intelligence, e.g. problem solving ability.
S – Special attributes	Skills such as the ability to speak another language or IT skills.

As with job analysis and job description, the prospective line manager is usually in the best position to construct a person specification but many managers will appreciate assistance here from HR specialists who may have more experience.

Fraser's 5-point plan

A similar blueprint was devised by **Fraser**. He referred to it as the Five Point Plan, to include the following considerations:

- **F**lexibility and adjustment – emotional stability, ability to get on with others and capacity for stress.
- **I**mpact on other people – appearance, speech and manner.
- **R**equired qualifications – education, training, and experience.
- **M**otivation – determination and achievement.
- **I**nnate abilities – 'brains', comprehension and aptitude for learning.

Illustration 1

Care must be taken not to transgress one of the laws relating to discrimination, as in the case of a job advertisement seeking 'a female Scottish cook and housekeeper', which was barred both on the grounds of race and sex discrimination.

Test your understanding 5

Are there any circumstances when discrimination on the basis of physical make-up is acceptable?

4.5 Source candidates

It is important to know where suitable candidates may be found, how to make contact with them and to secure their application. The following sources are available:

Source	Comment
Job centre	Free but may not find a suitable candidate.
Recruitment consultant	Reduces burden on employer and may be a source of expertise but expensive and may not understand the organisation's needs.
Job fair	Can meet people face to face but may not attract enough suitable candidates.
National press	Good coverage for national jobs but advertisements are expensive and short-lived.

Local newspaper	Useful for local staff and cheaper than national but may not attract sufficiently qualified people.
Internet	Good as long as target people are frequent internet users.
Radio and TV	Expensive but sometimes can produce a large number of suitable candidates.
Specialist journals	Already degree of selection but may contain many similar advertisements.

Sourcing candidates usually involves the HR department unless the firm is particularly small. Partly this is to ensure that any advertisements comply with any legal requirements on diversity and discrimination, but also because the HR department will have more experience of recruitment consultants and the different advertising media.

5 Selection

5.1 Introduction

Selection is aimed at choosing the best person for the job from the field of candidates sourced via recruitment.

Any selection process needs to ensure:

Reliability	to give consistent results;
Validity	as a predictor of future performance;
Fairness	selection in a non-discriminatory way;
Cost effectiveness	in terms of managers' time and other options available

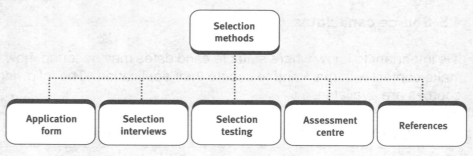

5.2 Application forms

Application forms are used to obtain relevant information about the applicant and allow for comparison with the person specification of the job. They should also give the applicants some ability to express themselves beyond the limited factual remit of the form. Their usefulness includes:

- eliminating unsatisfactory candidates
- saving interview time by selecting only the most suitable candidates for interview
- forming an initial personal record for an employee.

Application forms are likely to be standardised to some extent and hence will be produced by HR professionals with input from the line managers.

5.3 Selection interviews

Once a shortlist has been drawn up, the most common way of selecting a candidate is by interview. Their purpose is to:

- find the best person for the job (research shows that an interview used in isolation is unreliable as a selector but when used with other selection methods greater reliability is achieved)
- ensure the candidate understands what the job is and what the career prospects are
- make the candidate feel that they have been given fair treatment in the interview.

Line managers would normally expect to be part of the interviewing panel for new employees for their departments.

> **Individual or one to one**
> **-** good for establishing a rapport between the interviewer and candidate but can be subject to bias

> **Tandem**
> **-** uses two interviewers per candidate. Reduces rapport but also bias

> **Interview options**

> **Panel**
> **-** a number of people interview the candidate simultaneously. Allows comparison of the candidate in real time but one panel member may dominate and it may be more suited to confident candidates

> **Sequential**
> **-** the candidate undergoes several one to one interviews. Allows a number of opinions to be reached about candidates but their opinions may vary

Advantages of selection interviews

- Places candidates at ease
- Highly interactive, allowing flexible question and answers
- Opportunities to use non-verbal communication
- Opportunities to assess appearance, interpersonal and communication skills
- Opportunities to evaluate rapport between the candidate and the potential colleagues/bosses

Test your understanding 6

The validity of a face-to-face interview as a means of gauging a person's ability, character and ambition is regularly challenged. Briefly explain the main shortcomings of the interview technique.

5.4 Selection testing

Cognitive tests
Include
- Intelligence tests, eg IQ tests
- Aptitude tests, eg clerical or numerical ability

Psychometric tests
- Contain features of all other types of test
- Quality of tests varies

Selection Tests

Personality tests
- Reveals a candidates true characteristics
- The Cattell 16PF (personality factor) test provides 16 basic dimensions, eg extrovert/introvert, along with scores from 0 - 10

Many of the above techniques would lie outside the expertise of the line manager and so specialists would be called in to carry out the testing and feed back.

Psychometric testing

In the following extracts from an article by Bryan Appleyard the growth and usefulness of psychometric testing is reviewed:

Welcome to the weird world of psychometrics. If you want to work for a big company there's at least a 70% chance that before being given a job you will be subjected to a personality test by one of the big four – MBTI (Myers-Briggs Type Indicator), 16PF (16 personality factors), OPQ (occupational personality questionnaire) or Hogan – and an ability exam measuring verbal reasoning and numeracy.

These are basically IQ tests by another name...according to the Association of Graduate Recruiters, it's because nobody trusts university degrees any more. It has just issued a report saying degree standards are inconsistent and, as a result, companies are turning to psychometrics. But Ceri Roderick at occupation psychologists Pearn Kandola adds two other reasons. 'Companies want to know things like the motivational characteristics of recruits and the technology is now available to do these things.' There's also a fourth reason: the need to compete for quality recruits. 'There's a war for talent,' says Professor David Bartram of the British Psychological Society (BPS), 'companies are fighting to get the best people.' All of which means there is now a rapid proliferation of psychometrics consultancies, most of them offering candidates the chance to do all the tests online. . . .

Sceptics think the whole enterprise is misguided. In America a book – The Cult of Personality by Annie Murphy Paul – has cast doubt on the intellectual credibility of psychometrics…

In support of Paul's book the author Malcolm Gladwell questions the very idea of measuring personality: 'We have a personality in the sense that we have a consistent pattern of behaviour. But that pattern is complex and that personality is contingent: it represents an interaction between our internal disposition and tendencies and the situations that we find ourselves in.'. . .

But are Gladwell and Paul right to question the whole theory on which they are based? The history of psychometrics marches hand in hand with the history of IQ testing. Alfred Binet, the French psychologist, produced the first modern IQ test in 1905 and Walter Dill Scott subjected 15 engineering graduates to the first psychometric test in 1915. Both ideas were inspired by the conviction that there could be no reason why the human mind should be impervious to scientific investigation. . . .

Psychometrics works, but only if the tests are properly applied, rigorously interpreted and accompanied by traditional interviews. This means that they do not necessarily speed up the recruitment process. They might, however, help weed out unsuitables in advance, a huge benefit at a time when all companies are swamped with applicants for attractive jobs.

Source: Appleyard, B. (2007) Want a job? Let's play mind games. Sunday Times, 22 July.

5.5 Assessment centres

- The idea of the assessment centre grew out of the obvious shortcomings of the selection interview and other selection techniques.

- Assessment centres, usually provided by external consultants unless the firm is particularly large, allow the assessment of individuals working in a group or alone by a team of assessors, who use a variety of assessment techniques.

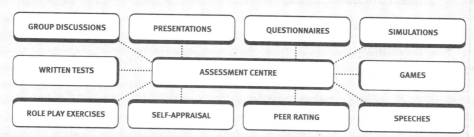

- Groups of around 6–10 candidates are brought together for one to three days of intensive assessment.

- The assessment centre can be designed so as to test the applicant's competencies against the criteria set out in the person specification.

Test your understanding 7

Explain why assessment centres are part of a competency-based selection process used by many major employers when recruiting staff for their graduate training scheme?

Drawbacks of assessment centres

- The assessment centre must be rigorous or else there is a temptation to select the person who just seems the most sociable or likeable.

- The cost of setting them up, administering them, staffing them and producing results can be extremely high.

5.6 References

The purpose of references is to confirm facts about the employee and increase the degree of confidence felt about information given during the other selection techniques.

References should contain two types of information:

- Straightforward factual information. This confirms the nature of the applicant's previous job(s), period of employment, pay, and circumstances of leaving.

- Opinions about the applicant's personality and other attributes.

Content of references

A standard form to be completed by the referee might pose a set of simple questions about:

- job title
- main duties and responsibilities
- period of employment
- pay/salary
- attendance record.

Problems with references

Opinions should obviously be treated with some caution. Allowances should be made for:

- prejudice – favourable or unfavourable
- charity – withholding detrimental remarks
- fear of being actionable for libel

5.7 Employment offer and negotiation

- **Offer of employment** – once an eligible candidate has been found, an offer can be made, in writing or by telephone, subject to satisfactory references and medical checks.
- **Negotiation** – it may be necessary to reach a mutually agreeable compromise over some aspects of the employment contract, e.g. pay, hours of work or holiday allowance.

Offer of employment

An effective offer of employment must not contain anything that cannot be delivered and should contain the following elements:

- Must be a written document – a written statement is a legally binding document, which should help to seal the offer. A telephone call to break the good news to the successful candidate is fine, but should not go into too much detail about the offer in conversation.

- Must contain sufficient detail – must contain the job title and location with details of pay, benefits, hours of work, holiday as well as the terms and conditions of employment, including notice period, sickness payment schemes, pension scheme details, disciplinary and grievance procedures and an outline of the probationary period where one is in force.

- Should offer an opportunity to make further contact before a final commitment is made – a clear but informal opportunity for further discussion, which may lead to negotiation on terms and conditions of employment.

6 Induction

The purpose of an induction is to ensure the most effective integration of staff into the organisation, for the benefit of both parties.

The **benefits** of a good induction programme include:

- Quick and effective assimilation into organisational life

- A well planned programme will reassure employees. This will aid motivation and improve performance

- Increased commitment since it can provide a positive reflection of the organisation while the employee is still comparatively receptive and has not been subject to negative views

- Reduces staff turnover and associated costs

Induction programmes may focus on company wide issues, in which case they will usually be designed and run by the HR department, and/or focus on departmental practices and procedures, in which case they may be set up by the line manager.

Illustration 2

In 2008 the average UK employee turnover rate was 17.3% and the average cost of employee turnover was £5,800 for each employee. A major reason why employees leave within the first six months to a year is a poorly planned induction process. Therefore, there are significant savings to be made from implementing an effective induction process.

A good induction programme would typically include:

Pre-employment	• joining instructions • conditions of employment • company literature
Health and safety	• emergency exits • first aid facilities • protective clothing • specific hazards
Organisation	• site map – canteen, first aid post etc • telephone and computer system • organisation chart • security pass and procedures
Terms and conditions	• absence/sickness procedure • working time including hours, breaks and flexi-time • holidays • probation period • discipline and grievance procedure • internet and email policy
Financial	• payment date and methods • benefits and pension • expense procedures
Training	• discuss training opportunities and agree training plan • career management
Culture and values	• organisation background • mission and objectives

7 Training and Development

7.1 Learning

Learning is a complex process that underpins development, education and training.

Kolb's experiential learning cycle

Kolb suggests that learning is a series of steps based on **learning from experience**. He suggested that classroom learning is false and that learning should be an active process if it is to be effective.

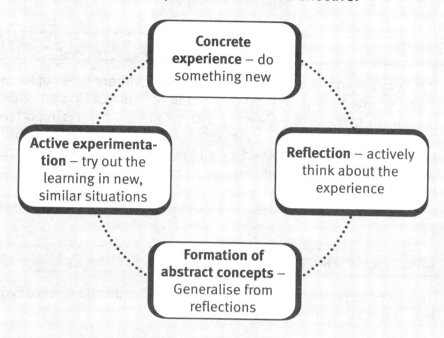

Honey and Mumford's learning styles

Honey and Mumford suggest there are four different learning styles:

Learning style	Explanation
Activists	Involve themselves fully and without bias in new experiences. They are open-minded, enthusiastic, constantly searching for new challenges but are bored with implementation and long-term consolidation.
Reflectors	Prefer to step back to ponder and observe others before taking action. They are in general cautious, may be perceived as indecisive and tend to adopt a low profile.
Theorists	Adapt and integrate information in a step-by-step logical way. They prefer to maximise certainty and feel uncomfortable with subjective judgements, lateral thinking and anything flippant.
Pragmatists	Are keen to try out new ideas, theories and techniques to see if they work in practice. They are essentially practical, down-to-earth people, like making practical decisions, act quickly on ideas that attract them and tend to be impatient with open-ended discussions.

Test your understanding 8

State the most effective learning methods for each of Honey and Mumford's learning styles.

Illustration 3

It is generally agreed that a combination of different types of learners will make an effective team in an organisation. In discussing an issue, the most likely question the Reflector will pursue is 'Why it is important'; the Theorist, in contrast, will be interested in 'What it is all about'; the Pragmatist will be concerned with 'How it can be applied in the real world'; and the Activist will be keen to know 'What if we were to apply it here and now'.

Effective learning programmes

The following general principles can guide the design of effective learning programmes:

- Participants should have both the ability to learn and the required skills/knowledge and the motivation to learn.

- It usually helps to provide an overview of the tasks to be learned before dealing with particular, specific aspects.

- The availability of timely, accurate feedback greatly enhances the effectiveness of most forms of training.

- There should be positive rewards or reinforcements when activities are carried out correctly. These rewards may be internal (e.g. a feeling of accomplishment) and/or external (e.g. the issue of a certificate, a compliment from the trainer, etc).

- Active involvement is usually associated with more effective learning rather than simply listening or reading.

- Most training will involve a learning curve which may be initially very flat as the learner struggles to acquire basic competence or in other cases quite steep when the skills required for modest competence are learned more quickly, but all learning will involve periods when there seems to be no improvement in performance (a learning plateau).

- Training should be as much like the job as possible to minimise problems of conceptualising theory to the workplace.

7.2 Management development

Management development (or simply development) is a realisation of a person's potential through formal and informal learning to enable them to carry out their current and future role. The process is seen as one of self-development.

Illustration 4 – Development

The importance of self-development is reinforced by the emphasis many professional bodies (including CIMA) places on continuing professional development (CPD), which recognises that being admitted to a professional body does not guarantee proficiency forever. Individual members of the profession must take responsibility for their own post qualification continual development and updating. In this way individuals can ensure they remain up to date in a rapidly changing world and can facilitate career planning.

7.3 Training

Training is formal learning to achieve the level of skills, knowledge and competence to carry out the current role (note the contrast with management development which focuses on the current and future role).

Training delivery can be provided:

- **in house** – e.g. through the use of on the job training, open learning (i.e. learning at a time, place and pace to suit the individual learner) or through using external trainers.
- **externally** – e.g. through local colleges, universities or specialist training companies.

Test your understanding 9

Identify the advantages and disadvantages of in-house training.

The use of IT in training

Information technology, and particularly the Internet and Intranet systems, has provided new opportunities for training and development at relatively low cost.

The stages of the training process

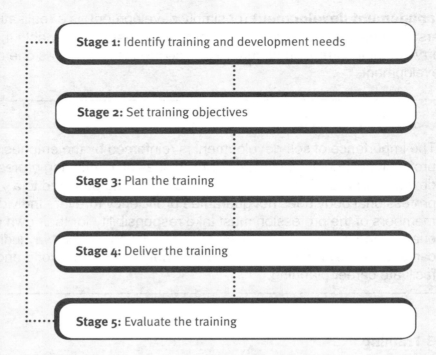

Stage 1: Identify training and development needs

Stage 2: Set training objectives

Stage 3: Plan the training

Stage 4: Deliver the training

Stage 5: Evaluate the training

Stage 5: According to **Kirkpatrick** there are four levels at which training can be evaluated:

(1) **Reaction** – did the participants like the training?

(2) **Learning** – did the participants learn the principles, facts and theories covered in the training?

(3) **Behaviour** – did behaviour change as a result of the training?

(4) **Results** – what benefits (e.g. reduced costs, better quality) resulted from the training?

Stages in training and development

- **Identifying training needs** – this could include an investigation into the organisation's current performance as well as mapping the corporate skills base. It should drill down to the level of the individual to target specific needs.

- **Setting training objectives** – as with all objectives these should have clear, specific, measurable targets in relation to the standard of behaviour required in order to achieve a given level of performance.

- **Planning the training** – this covers who provides the training, where the training takes place and divisions of responsibilities between trainers, line managers or team leaders and the individual personally.

- **Delivering/implementing the training** – a combination of formal and on-the-job training programmes will be used.

- **Evaluating training** – assessment of cost versus benefit using feedback forms, end of course tests, assessment of improved performance in the work place and impact on corporate goals.

7.3 Career/succession planning

Career/succession planning is the process for identifying and developing internal people with the potential to fill key business leadership positions in the company.

Traditionally, it was viewed as the process which allowed able employees to move up a pre-defined career ladder.

The advantage of career/succession planning is that it increases the availability of experienced and capable employees that are prepared to assume available roles. However, it is not without its problems:

- Operational issues – staff may feel that vacancies arise too slowly or at inconvenient times.

- Too rational – the high level of planning may not be appropriate in a fast moving business environment.

- Insularity – the policy ignores the possibility of more capable candidates outside the organisation.

- Career trends – the modern trend is for employees to take responsibility for their career development and to move between organisations.

- Emergence of flatter structures – this has removed some of the traditional career paths.

8 Appraisals

Appraisal is the systematic review and assessment of an employee's performance, potential and training needs.

8.1 Benefits of appraisal

Benefits for the employer	Benefits for the employee
• **Feedback and objective setting** – the appraisal is an opportunity for the employer to give feedback and to set the employee's objectives for the following period.	• **Feedback and objective setting** – the appraisal is an opportunity for the employee to receive feedback and to set the objectives for the following period.
• **Promotion** – it provides a formal system for assessing the performance and potential of employees, with a view to identifying candidates for promotion. This will assist with HRP.	• **Future prospects** – a formal appraisal system offers employees an opportunity to discuss further prospects and ambitions.
• **Training** – it provides a system for identifying training needs, in order to raise the level of efficiency and effectiveness.	• **Training** – appraisals can be used to identify and agree further training, to improve employee competence.
• **Improved communication** – if well managed, communication and hence working relations can be improved between managers and staff.	• **Pay and rewards** – the appraisal can be used as a basis for considering pay and rewards.
• **Career planning** – discussions concerning longer term development and career planning can be had and appropriate action taken.	• **Voice concerns** – appraisals can provide a platform for staff views and to voice concerns.

Effective appraisal systems

The following factors should be present in an effective appraisal system:

- Careful planning which ensures the purpose and objectives of the system are widely understood.
- Skill in carrying out the appraisal interview.
- Selecting the most appropriate method of appraisal.
- Setting challenging targets which the appraisee can influence.
- Adopting a participative system that enables those being appraised to have a meaningful input into the system.

8.2 The stages of performance appraisal

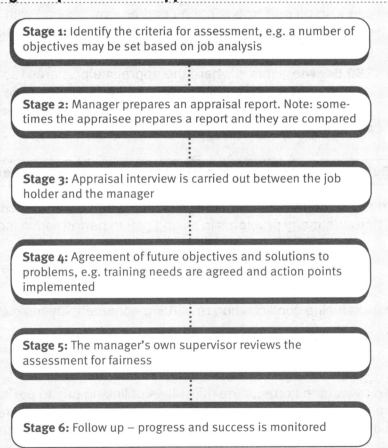

Stage 1: Identify the criteria for assessment, e.g. a number of objectives may be set based on job analysis

Stage 2: Manager prepares an appraisal report. Note: sometimes the appraisee prepares a report and they are compared

Stage 3: Appraisal interview is carried out between the job holder and the manager

Stage 4: Agreement of future objectives and solutions to problems, e.g. training needs are agreed and action points implemented

Stage 5: The manager's own supervisor reviews the assessment for fairness

Stage 6: Follow up – progress and success is monitored

8.3 Types of appraisal

Setting objectives as part of performance appraisal involves agreement on SMART objectives. A system of 'management by objectives' (MBO) is helpful if the employees are participants in their own objective setting.

A number of types of appraisal exist:

- **Self-appraisal** – this often takes place in preparation for a supervisor/appraisee meeting. This can save managerial time but the value of an individual appraising themselves may be questionable.

- **Supervisor/appraisee** – the manager or supervisor who carries out work or allocates priorities carries out the appraisal. In some cases where there are many workers this may not be possible.

- **180 degree** – often managers collecting anonymous or named views of colleagues can solve the problems of poor supervisor appraisals. This can also be performed in the open groups session with the emphasis on first how the group performed and then the individuals' contribution (or lack of it).

- **360 degree** – this is where the appraisee prepares feedback on the appraiser as well as getting 180 degree feedback from colleagues. Problems include potential conflicts, power, influence issues, time and bureaucracy.

Relationship between appraisal and the reward system

In many organisations there is a link between performance and pay. There are many problems in linking pay to performance including:

- employees concentrating on goals that have a definite link to the reward system

- inducing conflict when rewarding some employees more than others

- financial constraints due to recessionary factors, or poor company results

To overcome some of the difficulties of linking pay to performance it is necessary for those carrying out the appraisal to be well trained and skilled at carrying out the process. Schemes need to be uncomplicated, free from bias and subjectivity, and perceived to be fair by those who are to be appraised.

8.4 The barriers to effective appraisal

Lockett suggests that appraisal barriers can be identified as follows:

Confrontation	• Differing views regarding performance. • Feedback is badly delivered.
Judgement	• Appraisal is seen as a one-sided process – the manager is judge, jury and counsel for the prosecution.
Chat	• An unproductive conversation. • No outcomes set.
Bureaucracy	• Purely a 'form filling' exercise. • No purpose or worth.
Annual event	• A traditional ceremony, carried out once or twice a year.
Unfinished business	• No follow up. • Points agreed are not actioned.

8.5 Appraisal and career development

Appraisal has a clear link to career development. Career development sees the interaction of three concepts:

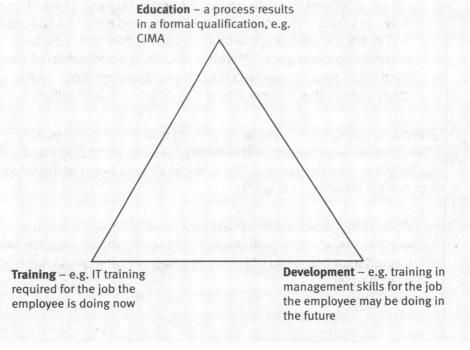

Education – a process results in a formal qualification, e.g. CIMA

Training – e.g. IT training required for the job the employee is doing now

Development – e.g. training in management skills for the job the employee may be doing in the future

Career planning and development

Career planning has traditionally been viewed as an organisation-driven activity that enables human resource managers to concentrate on jobs and building career paths so providing for logical progression of people between jobs. These career paths, particularly for people such as management accountants, have tended to be mainly within one specialised function and represent ladders on which individuals could progress within their functional specialism. Organisational career planning suffered severe setbacks from the layoffs during the recession of the late 1980s and early 1990s.

In addition these core concepts have increasingly been challenged due to a number of other developments including:

- Non-traditional organisational structures emerging. These flatter organisation structures have removed some career paths entirely and reduced opportunities in other areas. Additionally these structures imply a need for multi-skilling and teamwork at the expense of promotion 'ladders' found within traditional hierarchies. Increasingly workers are seeking to be 'multi-skilled' often developing a good understanding of more than one function rather than specialising.

- The development of general management skills and the concept of cross-functional career paths long been accepted as the norm in Japanese firms.

- Increasingly, career development has become led by the individuals themselves. An individual philosophy of building a portfolio of experience qualification and networks arose in order to develop a career outside a single organisational structure. This individual career planning focuses on individuals' goals and skills. It considers ways in which each individual might expand his or her capabilities and enhance career opportunities both within and outside a particular organisation. (Within the UK the Association of Graduate Recruiters recently warned that career paths no longer exist: only crazy paving that the individual lays himself or herself!)

Given this background, it is unsurprising that succession planning as an alternative to external recruitment may be seen as of decreasing HR significance. Problems have in any case always been associated with succession planning, including:

- Retention. Unlike other assets that have received investment, employees who are well trained (especially those who are were trained in anticipation of future developmental moves) are highly marketable.

- Individual failure. A failed assignment damages the individual, the company and the working relationships. 'Failure' may be attributable to one of a number of HR defects including poor control or managerial judgement, the over-promotion of individuals, and defective appraisal monitoring systems.

- Timing. One person failing to move because of personal circumstances can hold up the development of others unless some other kind of arrangement can be made. Slow promotion or development can lead to frustration and (for instance) graduate staff leaving shortly after becoming useful to the organisation. As the process depends on political expediency, many talented staff find that their present manager is reluctant to release them.

- Size of organisation. For a multi-national organisation, extensive relocation can be financially costly and for the family potentially distressing, demotivating and stressful. For many in small organisations a feeling of 'waiting for dead people's shoes' (as the old expression has it) may exist.

- Overseas postings. The issues of combining multi-cultural groups and three types of employee (the parent country nationals (expat), the home country nationals and the third country nationals) may prove problematic. Planning the correct combination of these staff is virtually impossible because of competing priorities and so many firms merely rely on the ability of all employees to 'mutually adjust' to each other and the new situation.

9 Employment Practices

9.1 Dismissal

Dismissal is termination of a worker's employment with or without notice by the employer.

Dismissal without notice is usually wrongful because it breaches the contract of employment. When analysing whether dismissal is fair or a breach of contract, a number of issues are relevant:

- **Conduct** – a well documented and fair disciplinary procedure should be in place.

- **Capability** – the employer must demonstrate how the employee failed to meet the standards set for them and should detail formal/informal warnings and any remedial action it tried to take, e.g. extra training or transfer to another (more suitable) role.

- **Breach of statutory duty** – dismissal would be considered fair if continuing employment would breach statutory duty, e.g. health and safety legislation.
- **Some other suitable reason** – e.g. dishonesty, refusal to transfer within the organisation.
- **Redundancy** – see Section 9.2 below.

Constructive dismissal

This involves an employee resigning because the employer has made matters so difficult for them which equates with having in effect terminated their contract of employment.

9.2 Redundancy

A dismissal of the grounds of redundancy may be justified on any of the following grounds:

- cessation of business
- cessation of business in the place where the employee was employed
- cessation of the type of work for which the employee was employed.

In the UK, legislation demands that redundancies are fair and consultation must take place, e.g. with employees and trade unions. However, redundancy should always be viewed as the last resort.

Test your understanding 10

Identify the alternatives to redundancy that a good employer should consider.

Redundancy is unpleasant both for the individual and for the organisation. A good employer may consider:

- offering redundancy payments above the statutory minimum
- telling employees using the best method, usually face to face
- giving employees reasonable time off work to look for another job
- inviting local employment agency advisers to come to the premises
- providing good counselling service support.

10 Ethics

10.1 Introduction

Ethics is a set of moral principles to guide behaviour.

Illustration 5 – Ethics and morals

'**Ethics**' is used interchangeably with the word 'morals'. However, it is worth noting that very occasionally there will be a conflict between moral judgement and ethical duty, e.g. a management accountant may have access to confidential information regarding big bonuses paid to the managers of a department that is under the threat of redundancy. Morally, the accountant may feel that they should inform employees/other stakeholders about these big bonuses but this would be a breach of confidentiality or professional ethics.

10.2 CIMA's ethical guidelines

Ethical reasoning is not something that can be learned through practice since ethical dilemmas come up rarely.

Illustration 6 – Ethical dilemmas

The following ethical dilemmas may arise:

*   A rival company creates the legally permitted maximum of toxic waste. Your company has a range of expensive systems that keep waste to much lower levels. Not using these would reduce costs, and there is increasing pressure from industry analysts to increase the return on investment.

*   A young, talented and ambitious team leader wants you to dismiss a member of his team, who is much older than the rest and does not really fit in. However, the worker in question has worked at the company a long time with a good record of service.

*   You are forced to make redundancies in a department. The Human Resources manager has said, off the record, that it must not seem that gender or ethnicity is an issue, so you must make it look fair. However, this would require you to keep some weaker individuals, and lose some good ones.

CIMA's Code of Ethics seeks to help management accountants in their day to day role. It helps management accountants to identify areas where ethical pressures may exist and provides a recommended course of action for their resolution.

In order to achieve the objectives of the accounting profession, professional accountants have to observe five fundamental principles:

Fundamental Principle	Interpretation
Integrity	Integrity means being straightforward, honest and truthful in all professional and business relationships.
Objectivity	Objectivity means not allowing bias, conflict of interest, or the influence of other people to override your professional judgement.
Professional competence and due care	This is an ongoing commitment to maintain your level of professional knowledge and skill so that your client or employer receives a competent professional service. Work should be completed carefully, thoroughly and diligently, in accordance with relevant technical and professional standards.
Confidentiality	This means respecting the confidential nature of information you acquire through professional relationships such as past or current employment. You should not disclose such information unless you have specific permission or a legal or professional duty to do so. You should also never use confidential information for your or another person's advantage.
Professional behaviour	This requires you to comply with relevant laws and regulations. You must also avoid any action that could negatively affect the reputation of the profession.

10.3 Dealing with ethical dilemmas

If you are faced with an ethical dilemma at work, then you should follow the following process:

(1) Obtain further information – do you have firm evidence to support concerns?

(2) Follow established internal procedures (e.g. whistle blowing help-lines)

(3) Consult with direct line management

(4) Escalate issue to higher levels of management

(5) Escalate to audit committee

(6) Seek advice from professional institute (e.g. CIMA ethics department)

(7) Finally, consider withdrawing from the engagement / situation.

Test your understanding 11

You are a recently qualified management accountant and have just accepted a new post as management accountant in Black Pearl Co, a company specialising in the provision of credit and loans to wealthy individuals. You report to Mr. Sparrow, the senior management accountant and your duties involve performing credit checks on new customers through to the preparation of monthly management accounts and cash and profit forecasts for the company.

An initial review of the receivables ledger shows one debt from Miss Swan is quite old; there have been no loan repayments for the last six months, and the outstanding balance has risen to nearly $150,000 with accrued interest. When queried, Mr. Sparrow suggests not making a provision for this amount because to make a provision would decrease profit and cash flow by an unacceptable amount.

After leaving work for the day, you go for a drink at the Parlez wine bar with the junior management accountant, Will. After a few drinks, Will informs you that Mr Sparrow is a personal friend of Miss Swan, which may be a reason Mr Sparrow does not want to make a provision at this time.

Required:

Identify which, if any, of the fundamental principles within the CIMA ethical guidelines Mr. Sparrow has broken and describe possible actions that you should take in response.

11 Chapter summary

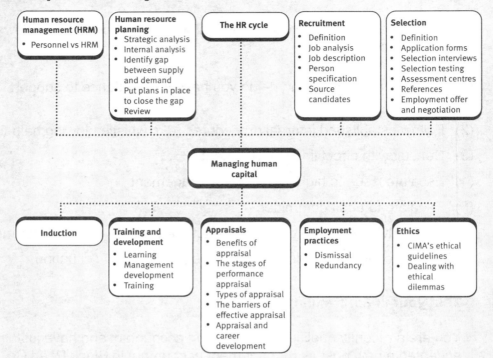

Human resource management (HRM)
- Personnel vs HRM

Human resource planning
- Strategic analysis
- Internal analysis
- Identify gap between supply and demand
- Put plans in place to close the gap
- Review

The HR cycle

Recruitment
- Definition
- Job analysis
- Job description
- Person specification
- Source candidates

Selection
- Definition
- Application forms
- Selection interviews
- Selection testing
- Assessment centres
- References
- Employment offer and negotiation

Managing human capital

Induction

Training and development
- Learning
- Management development
- Training

Appraisals
- Benefits of appraisal
- The stages of performance appraisal
- Types of appraisal
- The barriers of effective appraisal
- Appraisal and career development

Employment practices
- Dismissal
- Redundancy

Ethics
- CIMA's ethical guidelines
- Dealing with ethical dilemmas

12 Practice questions

Question 1

Aptitude testing is most frequently used:

A   As part of a selection process

B   As part of an appraisal process

C   As part of a process of training and development

D   As part of an exit interview process

(2 marks)

Question 2

HR selection tests that accurately predict future performance are said to be:

A   Valid

B   Equitable

C   Reliable

D   Stable

(2 marks)

Question 3

Development can be defined as:

A   The creation and maintenance of an individual

B   The progressive alteration to the individual

C   Growth and change in the individual

D   The growth or realisation of a person's ability and potential

(2 marks)

Question 4

A test used in the selection of individuals for jobs might ask questions about their likes and dislikes, attitudes, and what they would do in certain non-work situations. This type of selection test is:

A an intelligence test

B an aptitude test

C a personality test

D a situational test

(2 marks)

Question 5

An employer has decided to offer a job to a candidate following a selection process, but still has some doubts about whether the individual will be well-suited to the job. Which of the following options would be the most effective way of dealing with these concerns about the individual's aptitude for the job?

A Making the employee redundant if he/she fails to perform well

B Offering the job initially for a probationary period

C Offering the candidate a low rate of pay until he/she has demonstrated the ability to do the job well

D Dismissing the individual for incompetence if he/she does the job badly

(2 marks)

Question 6

The use of standard questions in job interviews helps ensure:

A   fairness

B   validity

C   reliability

D   completeness

(2 marks)

Question 7

The purpose of a person specification is to provide details of:

A   organisational size and diversity of activity

B   the types of responsibilities and duties to be undertaken by the post holder.

C   personal characteristics, experience and qualifications expected of a candidate

D   individual terms of engagement and period of contract

(2 marks)

Question 8

Which one of the following is a part of the recruitment rather than the selection process?

A   Job analysis

B   Interviewing

C   Testing

D   Assessment centres

(2 marks)

Question 9

Briefly describe Kolb's experiential learning cycle.

(4 marks)

Question 10

Identify FOUR ways in which a training system would benefit the accounting function.

(4 marks)

Question 11

Discuss any FOUR factors that should be taken into account when deciding upon whether to use recruitment consultants.

(4 marks)

Question 12

Identify the objectives of performance appraisal from the viewpoint of:

(a) the individual

(4 marks)

(b) the employer

(4 marks)

Question 13

(a) Explain what is meant by the selection interview and explain the purpose of the selection interview.

(3 marks)

(b) Discuss the problems associated with using the interview as a selection technique.

(6 marks)

(c) Explain how inexperienced interviewers damage the effectiveness of selection interviews?

(5 marks)

(d) Explain FOUR key skills needed to carry out the selection interview successfully.

(4 marks)

(Total: 18 marks)

Question 14

(a) Explain why it is necessary for chartered management accountants to adhere to a professional code of conduct.

(10 marks)

(b) Describe the steps that both professional accountancy bodies and organisations more generally can take to ensure that their members take seriously the ethical principles included in their organisations' codes of conduct.

(10 marks)

(Total: 20 marks)

Test your understanding answers

Test your understanding 1

- People resources are costly and should therefore be carefully planned.
- Knowledge, expertise and skill requirements are constantly changing and it can be difficult to keep up with these changes.
- Rapid social and technical changes also make planning difficult.
- All types of forecasting will be open to uncertainty.

Test your understanding 2

- By staying flexible.
- By taking greater account of external factors.
- By more sophisticated monitoring and control mechanisms.
- By planning in shorter time frames.

Problems in achieving plans might to a degree be predictable and in the past have also centred on:

- retention, especially when employees are well trained or have specialist skills
- slow promotion leading to staff turnover
- unexpected vacancies arising in senior positions or vital skills areas.

Test your understanding 3

- Effective recruitment depends on accurate job analysis, e.g. if the exact nature of the job is known, then it facilitates precisely worded adverts, which will assist in attracting a suitable field of candidates.

- It may eliminate the need for recruitment, e.g. the job may no longer be necessary or could be shared elsewhere in the organisation.

- To assist in determining the most appropriate method of selection.

- To help identify the need for training and the most appropriate training method.

- To establish differences between jobs so that wage and salary differentials may be determined.

Test your understanding 4

- Finance Director required **(Title of the job)**

- At least five years post qualified experience **(special requirements)**

- Experience of a dynamic industry **(special requirements)**

- Understanding of investor relations and pre-floatation requirements **(special requirements)**

- Ability to manage change and form own department **(special requirements)**

- Role includes **(brief description of role):**
  - Planning, monitoring and control of business and financial strategy.
  - Reporting and accounting as per the legal requirements
  - Management of strategy for and liaison with stock market business press and the business analyst community

- Excellent package including competitive salary and share options **(remuneration)**

- Responsible for a growing team of 18 people **(number of staff directly supervised)**

- Report directly to the Managing Director **(responsible to)**

- Located in London with approximately 20% travel to other European locations **(location and special attributes, e.g. shift systems, willingness to travel)**

Test your understanding 5

Discrimination may be acceptable in certain circumstances, e.g.:

- Army soldiers must be fit, healthy and be able to carry heavy kit.

- Firemen must be a certain height so that they can reach the equipment.

- An Italian restaurant can choose to recruit only Italian waiters and waitresses.

Test your understanding 6

Shortcomings of selection interviews include:

- too brief to 'get to know' candidates

- interview is an artificial situation

- 'halo' effect from initial impression

- contrast problem – an average candidate following an awful one will look very good

- qualitative factors such as motivation, honesty or integrity are difficult to assess

- prejudice – stereotyping groups of people

- lack of interviewer preparation, poor questioning, poor retention of information

- environmental factors, e.g. an unsuitable location, noise, lack of time

Test your understanding 7

- An assessment centre uses a wide range of assessment methods and it is therefore argued that the approach is more thorough and therefore more successful than the more traditional approaches. If nothing else, the process takes longer and allows the potential employer to see the candidates over a longer period of time. The opportunity to get to know a potential employee could prove to be invaluable. This contrasts well with the very time-constrained, artificial interview situation.

- It has been shown that they are much better at predicting a successful match between the selected candidate and the employer. The wider the range of techniques used, the more successful the result in terms of reliability and validity.

- Avoidance of single–assessor bias.

- The development of skills in the assessors, which may be useful in their own managerial responsibilities.

Test your understanding 8

Activists – they enjoy learning through games, competitive teamwork, tasks, role-plays and on-the-job training.

Reflectors – the reflector prefers learning activities that are observational such as carrying out an investigation or work shadowing.

Theorists – the theorist prefers learning to be structured, allow time for analysis and provided by other theorists, e.g. classroom based courses.

Pragmatists – the pragmatist prefers learning activities that are as close as possible to direct work experience. They will only engage in formal training, such as lectures or computer based training, if it reflects their actual job.

Advantages	Disadvantages
• Course content and timing can be tailor-made to the organisation's needs. • An organisation's specific technical equipment, procedures and/or work methods can be used. • Cost effective. • Easily monitored. • Can involve expert sessions from senior managers or staff. • Can generate a team spirit and develop culture. • Can be linked to specific outcomes that are then monitored by participants. • Can be enhanced by incorporating work-based projects.	• Participants are not exposed to outside influences. • Participants may be called away at short notice to deal with work problems. • Participants are more likely to withdraw at short notice. • Inhibits open discussion if immediate colleagues or bosses are present.

Test your understanding 10

Alternatives to redundancy include:

- reduced overtime
- limiting future recruitment for vacancies that arise or putting a total freeze on recruitment.
- retraining for new roles
- transfers to jobs in other departments
- job-sharing between two or more people
- a shorter working week
- retirement
- more effective HR planning in the future.

Test your understanding 11

Identifying the ethical dilemma

Mr Sparrow appears to be basing business decisions on his friendship with other people. In this sense the following ethical principles may have been breached:

- Firstly, *Integrity* – members should be honest and straight-forward in all personal and business relationships.

- Secondly, *Objectivity* – members do not allow bias or conflict of interests in business judgements.

It certainly appears that Mr Sparrow has been less than objective. Without the friendship with Miss Swan, it appears that the customer would have been sued by now to recover the outstanding money. The action also appears to lower the integrity of Mr Sparrow because the level of trust you have in his actions will now be lower – you can no longer be sure of his motivations.

Action

You now have a possible reason for Mr Sparrow not pursuing Miss Swan for the outstanding debt; although to be clear this is only hearsay and may yet be determined to be incorrect. To progress matters, you could ask Mr Sparrow if there are any other reasons he can think of as to why the debt from Miss Swan remains unpaid – this gives him the chance to explain that Miss Swan is a personal friend.

If Mr Sparrow denies knowledge of friendship, then there is simply his word against Will's – it will be difficult to report the case to CIMA's ethics committee for lack of objectivity because there is no breach of principles that can be proven.

However, there is still the issue of the outstanding amount from Miss Swan. You can suggest that a provision is made, although again Mr Sparrow may reject this assertion.

Other options available to you therefore include:

- Reporting directly to the board on the issue,
- Taking advice from CIMA's ethics department.

It appears no further action can be taken due to lack of any firm evidence.

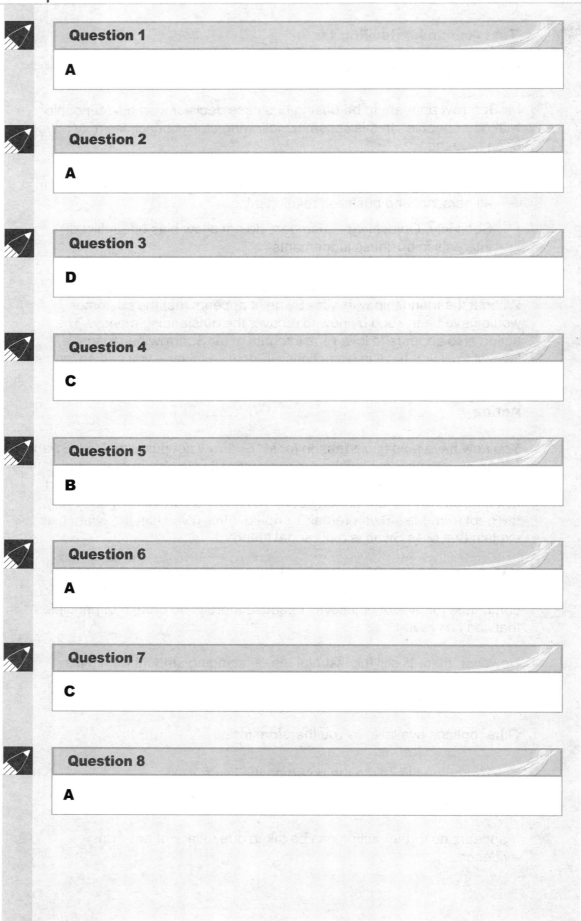

Question 1

A

Question 2

A

Question 3

D

Question 4

C

Question 5

B

Question 6

A

Question 7

C

Question 8

A

Question 9

Kolb suggests that learning is a series of steps based on learning from experience. He believes that classroom learning is false and that actual learning comes from real life experiences. Experiential learning comes from 'doing', thus ensuring that learners actually solve problems. Kolb's experiential learning cycle (shown below) identifies the four steps:

- The first step is where the person is learning something new,
- then the experience is reviewed,
- then the experience is accepted or rejected, and
- the fourth step is when the person calculates how and when to apply what has been learned.

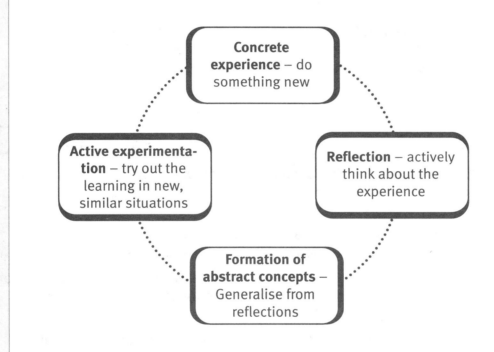

Question 10

The most likely benefits of a training system for the accounting function of an organisation are:

- more efficient use of staff resources as staff understand their duties more clearly, so that, for example, difficult accounting entries will be dealt with more intelligently.

- greater flexibility of operation as more staff acquire more skills, allowing for replacement of those concerned with maintaining one set of records by those working on others if workload or absences demand it.

- greater ease in introducing new techniques as a training system will exist to help with the changeover, particularly useful if the accounting records are being computerised.

- improved staff morale and greater capability for dealing with staff turnover as the training programme automatically provides for career succession.

Question 11

Any organisation which is considering the use of external recruitment consultants would make its decision upon the following:

- The availability, level and appropriateness of expertise available within the organisation and its likely effectiveness.

- The cost of using consultants against the cost involved in using the organisation's own staff, recognising the level of the vacancy or vacancies against the consultant's fee.

- The particular expertise of the consultants and the appropriate experience with any particular specialised aspect of the recruitment process.

- The level of expertise required of potential employees and therefore the appropriate knowledge required of the consultants.

Question 12

(a) **The objectives of appraisals from the viewpoint of the individual**

- It compares the individual's performance against a set and established standard.
- It identifies work of particular merit done during the review period.
- It provides a basis for remuneration.
- It establishes what the individual has to do, regarding the objectives of the organisation.
- It determines the future employment of the individual e.g. to remain in the same job, be transferred, promoted or retire early.
- It determines whether the individual is in a job where proper use is being made of his or her skills and talents.
- It establishes key results which the individual needs to achieve in work within a set period of time.
- It identifies training and development needs.

(b) **The objectives of appraisals from the viewpoint of the organisation**

- It monitors human resource selection processes against results.
- It identifies candidates for promotion, early retirement etc.
- It helps to identify and provide a record of any special difficulties/hazards surrounding the job, perhaps not previously realised.
- It identifies areas for improvement.
- It provides a basis for human resource planning.
- It helps formulate the training plan.
- It improves communication between managers and the managed where the organisation adopts the joint problem-solving approach in their appraisal system.

Question 13

(a) The selection interview is a formal discussion where an employer assesses an applicant for a job, and where an applicant decides whether he or she wants to take it.

The purposes of the interview are:

(i) to find the best person for the job;

(ii) to make sure the candidate understands what the job itself entails, and the career prospects associated with it;

(iii) to make the candidate feel that they have been given fair treatment during the interview.

The main limitations of the selection interview are that they fail to provide accurate predictions of how a person will perform in the job, partly because of the nature of interviews, partly because of the errors of judgement by interviewers.

(b) The following problems are often associated with poor selection decisions:

(i) **Scope**

An interview is too brief to 'get to know' candidates in the kind of depth required to make an accurate prediction of work performance.

(ii) **The 'halo' effect**

A tendency for people to make an initial general judgement about a person based on a single attribute, such as being neatly dressed or well spoken. This single attribute will colour later perceptions, and might make an interviewer mark the person up or down on every other factor in their assessments.

(iii) **Contagious bias**

The interviewer changes the behaviour of the applicant by suggestion. The applicant might be led by the wording of a question or non-verbal cues from the interviewer, and changes what he or she is doing or saying in response.

(iv) **Stereotyping**

Stereotyping groups people together who are assumed to share certain characteristics, for example, women or vegetarians, then attributes certain traits to the group as a whole. It then assumes that each individual member of the supposed group will possess that trait.

(v) **Incorrect assessment**

Qualitative factors such as motivation, honesty or integrity are very difficult to assess in an interview.

(c) Inexperienced interviewers are one of the main reasons why the selection interview is often ineffective. Inexperienced interviewers might:

(i) be unable to evaluate the information they obtain from a candidate;

(ii) fail to compare a candidate against the requirements for a job or a personal specification;

(iii) plan for the interview inadequately;

(iv) avoid taking control of the direction and length of the interview;

(v) have a tendency either to act as an inquisitor and make candidates feel uneasy or to let candidates take over the interview;

(vi) show a reluctance to probe into fact and challenge statements where necessary.

(d) The skills of interviewing involve those of:

(i) planning and preparing for the selection interview. Information gathering and research are the primary activities involved in selection interviewing and form the basis of an effective selection interview;

(ii) analysing the application form and other information about the candidate to decide on the main areas of questioning. An interviewer should have a very clear idea of the applicant in terms of their knowledge, skills, and experience, and be aware of the personal situation of the applicant;

(iii) questioning the candidate in an appropriate way. Focused and relevant questioning is vital for the interviewer to obtain the necessary information on which to base the selection decision;

(iv) evaluating the candidate by objectively analysing and evaluating the information which has been obtained from the interview.

Question 14

(a) CIMA have a professional code of conduct which, amongst other areas, includes:

- keeping client matters confidential;

- a requirement to serve the public interest (which overrides the point noted above);

- to behave with objectivity and integrity;

- to maintain technical competence.

The main reason for this code is that the role of the management accountant (MA) within the organisation is that of a provider of information. If the MA were to provide false or misleading information (through technical incompetence or not being objective) this might lead to senior managers making incorrect decisions. This would then have an impact on stakeholders of the company such as shareholders and creditors.

At the present time accountancy in most countries is self-regulating. This means that the conduct of accountants is left to the professional bodies rather than being legislated. Because of this CIMA (and the other professional bodies within the UK) must be seen not only to have a code of conduct but also to enforce it.

The accountants within any organisation are in a crucial position in that they have access to confidential information. Employers must be confident that this information will be kept confidential to the organisation. Although an employee being a member of a professional body does not guarantee this it should provide some assurance.

Finally, it is important for MAs to comply with a code of conduct since if they did not it would damage the entire profession.

(b) The reason why a code of conduct is required is because instances will arise in which an MA will face conflicts between what is good for the organisation and what is good for them personally.

From the point of view of the professional body, the code of ethics must be enforced rigorously. This means investigating suspected cases where the code has not been followed. If the allegations are proved then the offender will be punished either financially or, in extreme cases, struck off the register of members.

As far as individual organisations are concerned there are a number of steps that can be taken to try and ensure that employees act in an ethical manner.

The simplest and most effective method would be to employ the right kind of staff in the first place. Recruiting staff who have high personal ethical standards should mean there will be no ethical problems in the future. The obvious drawback to this approach is in identifying these qualities in applicants.

Many organisations will formalise ethical behaviour through procedures and rules that must be followed (and that carry disciplinary action if they are not). The drawback with this approach is that it is almost impossible to draw up guidelines on every single circumstance and so some measure of personal responsibility will always remain.

An increasing number of organisations have instituted ethics committees which oversee the working practices and procedures in an organisation. If these are to be successful they need to be high-profile and set up at a high enough level within the organisation. The drawback with this approach is that it can give general but not specific guidelines.

From the above, it can be seen that there is no single approach which will ensure that all employees behave ethically all of the time.

Pillar E

E1 – Enterprise Operations

Specimen Examination Paper

Instructions to candidates

| You are allowed three hours to answer this question paper. |
| You are allowed 20 minutes reading time **before the examination begins** during which you should read the question paper and, if you wish, highlight and/or make notes on the question paper. However, you will **not** be allowed, **under any circumstances**, to open the answer book and start writing or use your calculator during the reading time. |
| You are strongly advised to carefully read ALL the question requirements before attempting the question concerned (that is all parts and/or sub-questions). The requirements for questions 3 and 4 are contained in a dotted box. |
| ALL answers must be written in the answer book. Answers or notes written on the question paper will **not** be submitted for marking. |
| Answer the ONE compulsory question in Section A. This has ten sub-questions on pages 2 to 4. |
| Answer the SIX compulsory sub-questions in Section B on page 5. |
| Answer the TWO compulsory questions in Section C on pages 6 to 8. |
| The list of verbs as published in the syllabus is given for reference on page 9. |
| Write your candidate number, the paper number and examination subject title in the spaces provided on the front of the answer book. Also write your contact ID and name in the space provided in the right hand margin and seal to close. |
| Tick the appropriate boxes on the front of the answer book to indicate the questions you have answered. |

E1 – Enterprise Operations

TURN OVER

SECTION A – 20 MARKS

[the indicative time for answering this section is 36 minutes]

ANSWER *ALL* TEN SUB-QUESTIONS

Instructions for answering Section A

The answers to the ten sub-questions in Section A should ALL be written in your answer book.

Your answers should be clearly numbered with the sub-question number and ruled off so the markers know which sub-question you are answering. **For multiple choice questions you need only write the sub-question number and the answer option you have chosen.** You do not need to start a new page for each sub-question.

Each of the sub-questions numbered from **1.1** to **1.10** inclusive, given below, has only ONE correct answer. Each is worth two marks.

Question One

1.1 A deliberate addition of new, stimulating requirements to a person's job normally carried out by someone more senior is called

A   job enrichment.

B   job enlargement.

C   responsibility 'creep'.

D   multi-skilling.

(2 marks)

1.2 Employers wishing to attract and retain talented employees by bringing together pay and non pay elements and emphasising a positive organisational culture are said to operate a

A   benefit scoping strategy.

B   total reward package.

C   talent strategy package.

D   a consolidated remuneration package.

(2 marks)

1.3 Which of the following does NOT represent a 'spoke' in Cousins' strategic supply wheel?

A   Performance measures

B   Organisational structure

C   Organisational culture

D   Cost/benefit analysis

(2 marks)

1.4   Customers' direct participation in the delivery process is a feature of

A   cellular production.

B   the value chain.

C   the service industry.

D   lean product manufacture.

(2 marks)

1.5   An operations management programme involving a series of long term continuous development practices is referred to as

A   queuing theory.

B   a sustainability program.

C   optimised production technologies improvement.

D   stakeholder engagement strategy.

(2 marks)

1.6   The acronym/phrase/term 'BRIC' is normally associated with

A   a Japanese quality development technique.

B   a stock control method.

C   supplier development through buying, relating, investing and collaborating.

D   the emerging combined economies of Brazil, Russia, India and China.

(2 marks)

1.7   Organisations engaged in off-shoring

A   have some operations carried out in a different country.

B   diversify their operations.

C   brand themselves as 'global'.

D   maximise competitive advantage by being based in a particular country.

(2 marks)

1.8   Which of an organisation's competences should NOT be outsourced?

A   Allied competences

B   Core competences

C   Complementary competences

D   Residual competences

(2 marks)

Section A continues over the page

TURN OVER

1.9 A formal definition of a level of service to be provided is usually found in

A documented quality assurance arrangements.

B a marketing plan.

C a corporate strategy.

D a service level agreement.

(2 marks)

1.10 A country's earnings from investment abroad is included in its

A Gross Domestic Product.

B Gross National Product.

C Relative Trade Balance Index.

D Quality of Life Index.

(2 marks)

Reminder

All answers to Section A must be written in your answer book.

Answers or notes to Section A written on the question paper will **not** be submitted for marking.

End of Section A

Section B starts on the opposite page

SECTION B – 30 MARKS

[the indicative time for answering this section is 54 minutes]

ANSWER *ALL* SIX SUB-QUESTIONS IN THIS SECTION - 5 MARKS EACH.

Question Two

(a) Explain the benefits a collaborative process of Human Resource planning might bring to an organisation.

(5 marks)

(b) Explain what types of costs are associated with internal failure costs and the significance of these for an organisation with a reputation for quality.

(5 marks)

(c) Describe the features and benefits of SERVQUAL to organisations where it might be relevant.

(5 marks)

(d) Identify the key issues for a manufacturing organisation considering adopting Six Sigma philosophy.

(5 marks)

(e) Explain why a business with shareholders might take into account the interests of a wider group of stakeholders when considering a policy decision.

(5 marks)

(f) Identify the nature and effects of risks for an organisation considering doing business in a country that has a government and political system that it is unfamiliar with.

(5 marks)

(Total for Section B = 30 marks)

End of Section B

Section C starts on the next page

TURN OVER

SECTION C – 50 MARKS

[Indicative time for answering this section is 90 minutes]

ANSWER *BOTH* QUESTIONS IN THIS SECTION – 25 MARKS EACH

Question Three

CW is an established charity based in the capital city of the developed country of Statesland. It raises funds locally to finance clean water and sustainable agricultural projects in some of the poorest areas of the world. CW relies heavily on the work of unpaid volunteers and prides itself on low operating overheads and directing a large proportion of its income to 'on the ground' projects. CW's sources of income involve donations from the public and the operation of charity shops in the north of the country selling unwanted clothes and household items. Recently however, a downturn in the economy, 'charity fatigue' and competition from other causes has made fund-raising more difficult. It is clear that CW needs to either reduce the level of projects it currently funds or increase income.

The Chief Executive of the charity has convinced her Board of Trustees that the charity needs to professionalise its operations, be more 'outward facing' and employ modern marketing practices. Consequently, an independent consultancy firm with expertise in this area has been engaged to advise the charity. Trustees are supportive of the Chief Executive but are worried that certain marketing practices, particularly promotional activities, might be seen as unethical and damage the good reputation of the charity.

In the first meeting between a partner of the consultancy firm and the Board of Trustees, a number of areas were covered including
  • a discussion of the application of the marketing mix to the charity, and
  • market research options for CW.

A second meeting has been arranged. You work for the consultancy firm and have been asked to produce some briefing notes for the partner to help him with this second meeting.

Required:

Prepare briefing notes for the partner that addresses the following questions:

(a)   Explain what aspects of marketing could be helpful to CW. (Do not include matters covered in the first meeting or segmentation and targeting.)

(10 marks)

(b)   Explain the processes and implications of market segmentation and targeting to CW.

(10 marks)

(c)   Identify two types of promotional activity and for each explain the ethical concerns that might arise for CW using them.

(5 marks)

(Total for question three = 25 marks

Section C continues on the opposite page

Question Four

The S1K group has grown from a single optician's shop in a provincial town into (what it describes as) a 'lifestyle retail group'. S1K's policy is to buy existing shops in fashionable city centre shopping malls which it believes are 'underperforming'. In addition to traditional services offered by opticians, S1K offers eye correction (laser) treatment, designer sunglasses, cosmetic tinted contact lenses and, for certain spectacle frames, a range of complementary jewellery. S1K also plans to sell own-brand 'augmented' products and treatments such as eye creams and drops, make-up, etc. at premium prices from its premises. S1K is due to expand from thirty to thirty five geographically diverse shops in the south of the country within the next year.

The Board of S1K recognises the challenges ahead and has recently appointed a new Chief Executive who has a background in both retail operations and information solutions. He has just completed an initial review of systems and technology within S1K. His main findings are highlighted below:

- The opportunities for the use of information technology (IT) need to be grasped, particularly in the implementation and running of the information system network in support of management operations both in shops and in the main functional areas of S1K's headquarters.

- Systems are generally weak and the benefits of modern software applications lacking. The accuracy and completeness of information received by headquarters from shops needs to improve and there needs to be better coordination of activities. Through its acquisition policy S1K has 'inherited' a series of shops operating independent systems of varying sophistication and effectiveness. Several different systems are used and some are very inefficient. (For example, the equivalent of over 40% of a full time workers time is spent manually analysing and searching for information in shops.)

- Internet possibilities are being missed and there is no virtual network.

- Common computerised stock records will also be required when new products and treatments are sold.

- Some shops still use manual systems, others use basic stand-alone computers, but none take full advantage of software capabilities and most only use basic software functions. The financial system is the only shared system.

- The existing financial system is struggling to cope with the rapid growth of the group. Replacement software is due to go ahead within the next six months. Although the software does not fit existing business processes exactly, it has the clear advantage of giving S1K access to an industry best practice system and is identical to that used by all its main competitors. As such, it is a good choice. The least problematic implementation approach is a phased approach, and a programme of events for implementing was drawn up by the previous project manager who has now left S1K. A replacement project manager from within S1K needs to be appointed to oversee the introduction of the project as a matter of priority.

The requirement for this question is on the next page

Required:

(a) Identify the ways in which information technology and information systems might improve S1K's operations.

(10 marks)

(b) Discuss the Chief Executive's analysis of ways of overcoming potential problems in the implementation of the new financial system.

(10 marks)

(c) Identify the main individuals and groups S1K's Human Resources Department should target first for training and whether training provision should be made in-house or not.

(5 marks)

(Total for Question Four = 25 marks)

Total marks for Section C = 50 marks)

End of Question Paper

LIST OF VERBS USED IN THE QUESTION REQUIREMENTS

A list of the learning objectives and verbs that appear in the syllabus and in the question requirements for each question in this paper.

It is important that you answer the question according to the definition of the verb.

LEARNING OBJECTIVE	VERBS USED	DEFINITION
Level 1 - KNOWLEDGE What you are expected to know.	List State Define	Make a list of Express, fully or clearly, the details/facts of Give the exact meaning of
Level 2 - COMPREHENSION What you are expected to understand.	Describe Distinguish Explain Identify Illustrate	Communicate the key features Highlight the differences between Make clear or intelligible/State the meaning or purpose of Recognise, establish or select after consideration Use an example to describe or explain something
Level 3 - APPLICATION How you are expected to apply your knowledge.	Apply Calculate/compute Demonstrate Prepare Reconcile Solve Tabulate	To put to practical use Ascertain or reckon mathematically To prove with certainty or to exhibit by practical means Make or get ready for use Make or prove consistent/compatible Find an answer to Arrange in a table
Level 4 - ANALYSIS How you are expected to analyse the detail of what you have learned.	Analyse Categorise Compare and contrast Construct Discuss Interpret Prioritise Produce	Examine in detail the structure of Place into a defined class or division Show the similarities and/or differences between Build up or compile Examine in detail by argument Translate into intelligible or familiar terms Place in order of priority or sequence for action Create or bring into existence
Level 5 - EVALUATION How you are expected to use your learning to evaluate, make decisions or recommendations.	Advise Evaluate Recommend	Counsel, inform or notify Appraise or assess the value of Propose a course of action

Enterprise Pillar

Operational Level Paper

E1 – Enterprise Operations

Specimen Paper

Tuesday Morning Session

The Examiner's Answers – Specimen Paper
E1 - Enterprise Operations

SECTION A

Answer to Question One

1.1   A

1.2   B

1.3   C

1.4   C

1.5   B

1.6   D

1.7   A

1.8   B

1.9   D

1.10   B

SECTION B

Note: The answers that follow in Sections B and C are fuller and more comprehensive than would have been expected from a well-prepared candidate. They have been written in this way to aid teaching, study and revision for tutors and candidates alike.

Answer to Question Two

Requirement (a)

Human Resource planning is an organisational activity that will culminate in the production of an HR strategy to support corporate activity and aspirations. Critically, it will involve wide consultation within the organisation.

A means of gaining a realistic, strategic perspective. The process of Human Resource planning will provide a framework for clearly and rationally agreeing upon organisational challenges and obstacles that will arise in the future. Participants in the process will, as a consequence, be better able to face such challenges when they occur.

Agreement on priorities. The collaboration and discussions involved in the process should act as a focus for discussion, agreement and an establishment of common ground. In so doing, a shared focus on organisational priorities should emerge. This should in turn help define operating and functional priorities.

Commitment and ownership of the plan. A sense of ownership of the ultimate plan and a commitment to its accomplishment should be achieved through collaboration and communication.

Underline the value of people to the organisation. The intense focus on people issues should confirm the importance of people in delivering corporate aspirations. Hopefully, it will also assist defining necessary specific staff development activities essential for organisational success.

Overcome departmentalism. The collaborative nature of the process should help overcome departmentalism and provide a basis for stronger future working relationships. It should also help in strengthening or positively shaping an organisational culture.

Motivation and personal development. The inclusion of individuals within the process may prove to be a source of motivation by offering participants a better understanding of corporate issues and an opportunity to participate in a strategic process.

Suggest a plan of action. The actions arising from the process should be clearly understood by those involved and allow a smooth transition for the organisation rather than hurried responses to environmental and other factors.

Help match future organisational activity with its human resources. The process will ultimately allow for an identification of potential solutions to a particular need:

- Increasing supply of human resources to meet increased organisational demand. (Through for example, retraining / re-skilling; increased use of IT; outsourcing; recruitment & selection; etc.)

- Reducing supply of human resources to meet reduced organisational demand. (Through, for example, early retirements, redundancy, short-time working, sabbaticals, job-sharing, more flexible working patterns, etc.).

Requirement (b)

Internal failure costs are costs associated with finding and correcting sub-quality products before they reach the customer.

Types of costs:
- time to rework inspection rejects,
- materials to replace/rework inspection rejects,
- time to repair faulty machines,
- scrap / lost materials,
- excessive inspections/checking,
- lost income from the sale of cheaper goods marked as 'seconds'.

Significance:
If the organisation wishes to protect its reputation for quality these costs are preferable to external failure costs as they occur before they reach the customer. The organisation should see these costs as necessary but may wish to reduce their incidence through processes aimed at creating quality rather than detecting quality failures.

Requirement (c)

Contribution of SERVQUAL

SERVQUAL represents a structured means of assessing quality where the service is intangible by nature and rubrics used in manufacturing (such as rejects, returned goods, scrap, etc.) are not available. SERVQUAL is a quality measurement technique used by some service and retail businesses.

Organisations benefitting:
- Potentially any non-manufacturing organisation
- The concept is widely applied in areas such as healthcare, banking, finance and education

Features of SERVQUAL

Organisationally driven. SERVQUAL is instigated by the organisation itself because it has a commitment to quality and staying close to the customer.

Customer focused. SERVQUAL is based on a scale which takes account of customer attitudes in order to obtain measurements.

An established methodology and framework. SERVQUAL offers an established methodology and a comprehensive framework. The framework indicates differences between a customer's expectations for a service and their feelings of how the service was received. It involves customers answering questions about (both) their initial expectations and their perceptions of the actual service delivered.

Conceptually straightforward and seen as relevant. SERVQUAL is a straightforward concept, and is easily explained and understood by key stakeholders such as the workforce.

Identifies areas for future attention. SERVQUAL can be used to produce a checklist for future attention in order to improve service quality. Gaps will emerge between customer expectation and perception of the quality they receive. These will suggest service gaps that need to be remedied. Such gaps will arise where:

- the organisation does not understand what the customer wants, or
- the organisation is unwilling to meet customer demands, or
- the organisation fails to meet these demands despite its best attempts, or
- the customer may have gained an unrealistic perception of the organisation's service (possibly through false or misleading promises).

Inherent limitations in methodology. Virtually all approaches to quality contain limitations and SERVQUAL is no different in this respect. SERVQUAL can be complex to administer and maintain. In addition, the methodology is only pseudo-scientific by nature and results can be subjective, statistically unreliable and require interpretation.

Requirement (d)

Like TQM, Six Sigma is more than a quality enhancement programme; it represents instead more a business philosophy. The aim of Six Sigma is that processes are carried out to near perfect levels, through the elimination of defects and a tackling of production variations.

The costs and the benefits involved

The Six Sigma philosophy is only one of many approaches to quality management an individual organisation might choose to adopt. The organisation concerned should therefore review the alternative approaches in order to determine whether Six Sigma is the most appropriate for them. Six Sigma requires a high level of commitment and potentially a great deal of organisational upheaval, so it is important that the organisation is aware of this before choosing it as an option.

Cultural fit

The organisational culture needs to be receptive to the philosophy. Six Sigma can be considered to be a combination of measure, target and philosophy and these should be central to the way in which the organisation operates. If the culture is unreceptive, significant change may be necessary as Six Sigma strives for near perfection in order to 'delight' the customer. Six Sigma is very task oriented and demands high volumes for statistical methods to achieve significant results; as such, it may prove culturally unsuitable.

Top management commitment

Successful implementation of Six Sigma will require the full commitment from the top management of the organisation. Arguably, the culture of the organisation is created and managed by this group and the case has already been made that a sympathetic culture needs to be created and maintained.

The tools necessary

Improvements 'tools', including process mapping and problem-solving techniques, need to be adopted. As such, they need to be taught to the workforce and embedded within normal working practices.

Training
Much dedicated training is necessary to introduce Six Sigma. This might begin with convincing the workforce of the benefits of the approach, explaining the implications and then undertaking training in the tools and necessary metrics.

Monitoring and control metrics
Six Sigma aims for six standard deviations between the mean and the nearest specification limit in any process. To achieve Six Sigma, a process must not exceed 3.4 defects per million opportunities. Clearly, measurement and monitoring systems need to be established to allow organisations to do this.

Requirement (e)

Corporate social responsibility
The concept underpinning this thinking is known as 'corporate social responsibility' (CSR) or 'corporate responsibility'. CSR encourages businesses to balance financial profits, economic value addition and social good. This represents an ongoing commitment by a business to behave ethically, contribute to economic development and, at the same time, improve the quality of life of others (e.g. its work force and their families, the local community, society in general, etc.) CSR has been defined as having four dimensions: economic, legal, ethical and philanthropic. The thinking is as follows:

Validity of other stakeholder groups' claims on a business
Shareholders with their economic goals form one important group within a wider group of stakeholders. However, other individuals or groups also have a legitimate stake in the business and have goals, and these deserve to be taken into account when considering a policy decision. Business practices should be built around stakeholder analysis and engagement and reflect the needs and aspirations of society as a whole.

A need for a stable operating environment
If business trading is not to be disrupted, organisations need a stable social environment within which to operate. This stability helps provide a predictable climate. It follows that individual businesses understanding and responding to society's expectation is vital to maintaining such stability. (A programme of sustaining the environment for future generations might be seen as an investment in the future of the business).

Interdependence of business and society
Business cannot exist without society and society exists best with business. It follows that business must take full account of the societal expectations e.g. social and environmental concerns when making policy decisions. (A company's ultimate customer is after all a member of society).

CSR makes good business sense
Certain policies that take account of wider stakeholder groups can make good 'business sense'. Examples of where this may apply might include (for instance) the promotion of an appropriate work/life balance amongst the workforce which can reduce absences through ill health and increase productivity.

Better balanced decisions
Policy decisions that take a longer-term view combining social, environmental and economic considerations are more likely to be fully considered, balanced and soundly based.

Source of competitive advantage / relationship building
Policies based on principles of operating with integrity, being respectful of human rights and the environment, etc. might provide certain businesses with a form of advantage over competitors that are less sensitive to these issues. (Such considerations are also key in the management of relationships with governments and regulatory agencies, NGOs, etc.)

Requirement (f)

An organisation considering doing business in a country that has a government and political system that it is unfamiliar with should investigate the associated risks in terms of nature and potential impact.

Unstable trading conditions

The political system may be unstable or could easily become so, leading to social and economic upheaval in that country. This might lead to social unrest which could disrupt business. At the extremes, this unrest might involve armed conflict, riots, terrorism or the operation of anarchist groups (possibly targeting foreign businesses). Possible effects include:

- threat to organisational property
- endangering organisational personnel
- general disruption to business activity
- delays in moving goods through customs

Unfavourable Government policies

If the organisation is unfamiliar with the political system there is a clear risk. The existing or likely future government of that country may:

- give preference to local firms, or alternatively,
- more general government policies (whilst not directed specifically at foreign businesses) might create unfavourable trading conditions.

Possible effects include:

- increased taxation and other financial penalties, etc. so reducing profitability,
- making getting new business difficult due to preference given to local firms,
- reduced freedom to trade freely,
- revision of contracts gained,
- more stringent product and process requirements, restricting operating freedom,
- exchange rate fluctuations,
- technical product adaption to meet government requirements,
- difficulty in recruiting locally if the organisation is viewed unfavourably by government.

Totalitarian Government policies

From the prospect of government policies being unfavourable, policies may instead become discriminatory and harmful if a ruling group is likely to act in a totalitarian fashion. Possible effects include:

- expropriation of assets (with or without compensation),
- loss of ability to repatriate profits,
- cancellation of existing contracts,
- a use of indigenisation policies to make the organisation fit the local culture (contemporary examples might include the Zimbabwe regime which requires foreign-owned firms to transfer majority shareholding to local individuals or groups).

Lobbying and vested interests

The organisation would do well to understand the strength of political lobbying and the influence of such lobby and pressure groups within the target country. The vested interests of other stakeholders (e.g. local business people) also needs to be considered. Possible effects include:

- retaining existing business difficult,
- getting new business made more difficult.

SECTION C

Answer to Question Three

Requirement (a)

The proliferation of charitable causes and the competition between them combined with a downturn in the economy, and "charity fatigue" has made fund-raising more difficult. It is likely that those charities employing the most appropriate marketing practices will succeed in levering the greatest contribution of peoples' time and money for their particular cause.

Marketing concepts can be adapted and certain techniques and approaches used by the charity in order to maximise the generosity of supporters. (This support includes both the time of volunteers and the monetary donations of others). It is apparent from the scenario that the charity's operations are not very professional and that modern marketing practices are not currently being employed.

Become customer focused

The marketing concept is based on identifying and satisfying customer needs and being customer focused generally. CW's own customers are a different grouping from those enabling the service to be provided. A basic principle of marketing is that an organisation should satisfy customer needs but in this case CW should seek to get close to both groups. Charities, including CW, have to improve their focus on the needs and wants of all different customer (stakeholder) groups through marketing, including:

- contributors (of money and unwanted items for resale in the charity shops),
- customers of charity shops,
- beneficiaries (in this case those benefitting from the clean water and sustainable agricultural projects in some of the poorest areas of the world), and
- volunteer workers and other supporters.

Conduct a strategic review

CW would do well to conduct a basic strategic review of its current position including a simple SWOT analysis and a scan of its external environment. In this way CW will become more 'outward facing'. This process should reveal:

- positive internal strengths to build upon and opportunities that might be seized through marketing practices, and
- internal weaknesses that need to be remedied and external threats that need to be avoided or minimised through marketing practices.

In terms of potential income levels and streams, at the moment income only comes from two sources (donations and charity shops) so there is an opportunity to develop new income streams based on the strengths CW already possess. The operation of these shops and the process of obtaining donations could also be reviewed in order to improve income levels.

A concentration on external factors might usefully lead to a consideration of the activities and initiatives of competitors (other charities). How CW might respond to these initiatives and what might be learned from their operation are valuable areas of consideration.

The possibilities thrown up by this review process will need careful debate and research and should ultimately benefit the charity.

Branding

With so many charities, competition for voluntary giving is intense. Branding is particularly important in communicating a particular charity's core values, and distinguishing it from others. A belief in the worthiness of CW as evidenced by the work of unpaid volunteers and the core values that will be articulated from analysis, organisational strengths (as part of the SWOT) need to be agreed upon and a strong brand image promoted based on this thinking. In the case of CW, this is likely to emphasise the value of its clean water and sustainable agricultural projects to those who are far less fortunate than those who happen to live in Statesland. Although costs will be involved in brand development and promotional activities, the value of the CW brand if correctly communicated, should help in a number of ways:

- By overcoming suspicions that CW's charitable income will be wasted,

- By giving a reason why a donor or volunteer worker may choose CW over other charities,
- By providing a 'shorthand' image of the charity when communicating with stakeholder groups.

Relationship marketing

Relationship marketing involves an organisation seeking to develop a long term relationship with key customers in order to retain their loyalty and increase sales. This concept could be easily adapted to the charity's requirements. CW should look to identify its main donors, capture this information (possibly on a database) and keep in touch in some way. This might be achieved through newsletters and updates (either through traditional mail or emailed). One-off appeals, thanks for past support and explanations of some of the worthy projects financed by the charity should strengthen the donor/charity relationship and produce greater income flows. (It is acknowledged that an investment in IT and systems might be a necessary precursor to this). The charity also needs to recognise that it relies heavily on the work of unpaid volunteers and that an investment in strengthening these relationships is needed if continuing support is to continue.

Cause marketing

At the moment charitable donations from CW are received solely from individuals and CW might want to consider how they might obtain support from businesses and other organisations. This may prove difficult in times of economic downturn but it is an option worthy of consideration. Cause marketing involves the cooperative efforts of a business and a charity for mutual benefit. Relationships are established with a specific business (possibly local to CW's base) and would go much further than the organisation merely making a charitable donation. The organisation would 'adopt' the charity. It may make the relationship known in the media and might (for instance) collaborate and allow workers to participate in the running of events, promotions and certain aspects of the charity. The business would receive good public relations and CW would gain obvious benefits.

Requirement (b)

Implications for CW

The reality is that every market (whether industrial, domestic or charitable) consists of potential buyers/customers/donors with different needs, and with differing decision making and behaviour. Market segmentation is a technique based on recognition of this fact. The different variables within the market such as attitudes may be grouped into distinct **segments** or parts of an entire market. This then gives the possibility of a different marketing approach being taken for each market segment. The organisation itself may, however, consider that it is either undesirable or impractical to **target** every segment in this way and may make decisions accordingly.

For CW, the implications of market segmentation and targeting is that it needs to analyse its market and make rational decisions as to how it addresses itself to its customers and potential customers.

Quite apart from the outcomes of the analysis, one valuable result of the process is that CW will, for the first time, build a mental picture of who the customer currently is and who it might be in the future.

In common with all organisations, CW is offering its market a mix of product, promotion, price and place. (CW is possibly doing this at the moment without much thought). This mix is, however, powerful as it represents a set of available tools or ingredients from which effective marketing strategies can be developed and customer needs satisfied. The implication for CW is that by undertaking segmentation and targeting it can, for the first time, adopt a more sophisticated marketing approach and the appropriateness of its existing mix reviewed in order to better meet the needs of the target segment(s).

Process of segmentation

Market segmentation involves subdividing a total market into distinct subgroups of customers, where any subgroup can be selected as a target market to be met with a distinct marketing mix of product, promotion, price and place. For CW this will involve subdividing the total potential market for charitable support in Statesland.

The value of market segmentation to CW is that, although within the total market, widely different groups may exist. Each group consists of people (or organisations) with common needs and preferences, which perhaps react to a certain marketing mix in a similar way.

Segmentation can take place on virtually any basis but CW might identify the following variables as relevant:

- *Geographical area:* It seems that the current target is the region around the north and capital of Statesland but other areas (and indeed neighbouring countries) may also have potential.
- *Age:* The age profile of potential donors.
- *Gender:* The choices to be made in terms of gender are to focus marketing on males, females or both.
- *Income:* The income profile of potential customers.
- *Business/Individual:* Currently income comes solely from individuals but the potential for corporate 'customers' should not be excluded.

Other segmentation variables might be identified as relevant including occupation, social class, lifestyle, etc.

Process of targeting

Once the process of segmentation has been completed, targeting follows on naturally. At this stage the choice is made over which of the identified market segments the charity should target with its marketing efforts. This will involve weighing up the potential of one segment against another and realistically considering the ability of CW to serve such segments.

A narrowing down of *potential* segments should take place in order to establish a viable, *practical* focus on potential customers. Marketing wisdom suggests that since the purpose of these processes is to identify target markets, segments must be:

- *Measurable.* (Meaning that abstract segmentation by 'personality' for example might be elusive and difficult to measure. A segment identified as 'those with a belief in charitable giving' might present less difficulties in measurement.)
- *Accessible.* (The segment must be 'reached' by the charity without any undue difficulty through (for instance) promotion.)
- *Substantial.* (The likely revenue streams from the segment must outweigh the effort in reaching the segment or segments.)

It is highly likely that national statistics exist that indicate levels of charitable giving and may indicate sources (either geographical or corporate versus individual) and the potential of a segment might be gauged. This is, of course, only relevant so long as CW can access the segment concerned.

Any market segment can become a target market, requiring a unique marketing mix in order for the organisation to exploit it successfully. Recognition of market segments will enable any organisation to adopt a more refined marketing approach to a given group of potential customers. These same principles apply to CW, and like any organisation they have potentially three main targeting strategies available to them:

- *Undifferentiated:* Targeting the whole market with one marketing mix (something arguably they may be doing already by default).
- *Differentiated:* Targeting several segments with distinctive mixes unique to each segment (which can be expensive and complicated if many segments are targeted).
- *Concentrated:* Targeting a single segment with a single mix.

Once this process is completed and target segments identified, precise marketing mixes will need to be determined in order to position the charity to its potential customers.

Requirement (c)

Trustees are supportive but worried that certain practices particularly promotional activities might damage the good reputation of the charity. Having targeted a particular segment, CW needs to consider and avoid promotional practices that might be considered unethical.

Promotion of charities involves engaging in persuasion, more specifically engaging in ways of convincingly communicating the benefits of the charity to supporters and potential supporters. There are potentially many individual promotional tools available, but the following represent those most likely to be considered by CW:

Advertising

Advertising is a non-personal promotion of ideas and is targeted at a specific market through some media channel such as TV, radio, newspapers, posters, billboards, fliers, on-line advertising, etc.

Ethically questionable practices:

TV and radio advertising are expensive media and these may be seen as inappropriate for a charity that prides itself on low overheads and directing a large proportion of its income to "on the ground" projects. The big ethical dangers are, however, potentially overstating claims in promoting the charity or not applying money raised in the way 'promised' in the advertising material.

Sales promotion

Sales promotion is impersonal and short term by nature and involves offering incentives to encourage sale of products by stimulating consumer purchasing. Sales promotion might therefore be used in CW's charity shops.

Ethically questionable practices:

The difficulty of this is that if promotions such as special offers, discounts, BOGOFs (buy one get one free) are used donors may feel 'let down considering that donated products could have been sold for much more. An additional downside is that stocks could be depleted as a result of the activity.

Personal selling

Personal selling is an option that involves a direct, often one to one contact with potential customers. The salesperson verbally presents the benefits of the charity in the hope of gaining a donation. This may take the form of telesales or 'cold' calling by salespeople knocking on doors, or stopping members of the public in the street.

Ethically questionable practices:

This approach could be expensive as the costs of employing salespeople needs to be 'covered'. It would also go against what CW prides itself on, namely low overheads and directing income to 'on the ground' projects. In addition, tactics that pressure vulnerable members of the public or the application of undue pressure to get a donation are dangers (particularly where bonuses to sales people are based on income attracted).

Direct mailing

Direct mailing involves widespread distribution of promotional literature and brochures, through traditional mail systems or emails.

Ethically questionable practices:

The danger of this is that the literature and messages are seen as junk mail or SPAM and the efforts could be counter productive if recipients are irritated by the approach. If the approach is seen as invasive or bullying then it is clearly ethically inappropriate.

Answer to Question Four

Requirement (a)

It is clear from the scenario that S1K's operations might be improved considerably through both information technology and information systems.

Use of information technology

The new Chief Executive believes that the opportunities for the use of information technology (IT) needs to grasped, particularly in the implementation and running of the information system network and in support of management operations. The opportunities that IT offers are evident in a number of ways including the following:

- *Strengthening current operating and managing systems.* S1K's systems are generally weak and clearly these need to be improved upon and developed. In theory, it would be possible to have effective information systems without using information technology (IT). The size and complexity of the group means that IT is the only practical delivery option for meeting S1K's expanding information needs arising from an expanding product range and (soon) 35 geographically diverse shops.

- *Standardising operations.* IT would allow S1K to operate a number of different types of systems each designed to assist management, group coordination and decision-making. This will involve a move from the current stand alone applications to common integrated technology and systems.

- Offering a platform for greater accuracy and completeness of information through the introduction of IS.

- *Increasing operating efficiencies.* Currently the equivalent of over 40% of a full time workers time can be spent manually analysing and searching for information. IT can offer the platform to perform these functions in a less time hungry fashion. The time released should enable more value adding activities to be undertaken and potentially allow for a speedier answering of telephone and customer queries.

- *Simplifying procedures.* S1K's shops operate independent systems of varying sophistication and effectiveness, some based on manual systems rather than information technology. IT and the associated IS applications offer the potential to simplify and ensure consistency of operations.

- *Offering a platform for further system enhancement.* With appropriate information technology in place, the opportunity is then open in the future to introduce further information system networks and systems to support management operations and ensure greater group cohesion.

Use of information systems

- *Internet access.* The installation of internet access in all shops would enable email systems which offer speed and versatility, allowing easy communication, and the facility to send electronic attachments, so making returns to S1K's head office more efficient.

- *Maximising the benefits of a website.* Many organisations now use the potential offered by websites. By investing in a well designed web site, S1K could:
  - use it as a means of advertising and staying in touch with customers,
  - develop an online booking system for optical and other appointments.

- *Operating a network*, where a number of computers and devices are linked. As S1K operates throughout the south of the country the most appropriate computer systems configuration would be through a wide area network (WAN). Operations can be improved through the use of such a network in the following ways:
  - Speeding up communication between S1K's central management and headquarters functions and individual shops.
  - Improving inter-shop collaboration. A WAN would provide e-mail access and easier inter-shop communication and cooperation. This would allow resource and information sharing between S1K's growing number of shops.

- *New financial system software.*
  - ○ The new financial systems software will be able to cope with the size and complexity of the group in a way that the existing software cannot.
  - ○ This software has the clear advantage of giving S1K access to an industry best practice system and is identical to that used by all its main competitors.

Requirement (b)

The existing financial system is struggling to cope with the rapid growth of the group and replacement software is due to go ahead within the next six months. Based on his past experience, the Chief Executive has analysed potential implementation problems and solutions.

The potential problems appear to be as follows:
- Mismatch of software and business processes
- The implementation approach to adopt
- The current absence of a project manager

Mismatch of software and business processes

The new software does not fit existing business processes exactly. Despite this, the Chief Executive believes the software is 'a good choice'. This is based on two reasons identified in the scenario:
- It would give S1K access to an industry best practice system
- It would mean that S1K has the same opportunities as all its main competitors who use identical software

Realistically, given the timescale, an additional point is that S1K has already committed itself to take the software, will already have incurred some costs and will probably be contractually obligated to take the software.

The software is an 'off the shelf' package designed to perform specific financial functions of the business. As such, it is less expensive than a bespoke option. A bespoke solution would require some expertise to carry out software development and it is probable that S1K may need to employ outside sources for the purpose. Thus, such a process might be lengthy and costly.

Changing the business processes to correspond with software requirements represents a change initiative that staff may respond to negatively. Negative responses should be challenged. Competitors are using the software already and it is reasonable to assume that it will encapsulate industry best practice. The indications are, that because of its rapid growth and acquisition policy, S1K may operate in an inconsistent and possibly inefficient fashion, so a change in practices might be a positive thing.

The implementation approach to adopt

There are several potential implementation approaches S1K could adopt. Again the Chief Executive has backed previous decisions made by S1K, in this case those made by the previous project manager who has drawn up a staged programme of events for implementation.

The Chief Executive believes this approach to be the 'least problematic' for S1K. This staged approach allows for a degree of pilot testing to be carried out prior to full implementation across the organisation. The phased approach is often used in large system projects or in organisations that are geographically dispersed (like S1K). This might involve implementing a complete system in one geographical location at a time. If the system operates as expected then a further transfer can be made with existing systems retired in an orderly, staged way. Currently staff are likely to be experiencing 'change fatigue' from the instability caused by takeovers and a change of Chief Executive and this staged approach looks eminently sensible.

The phased approach is less risky given that the project manager would be new to the role and risk will be reduced as issues found in small-scale use of the new system can be remedied in time for wider software roll-out.

Alternatives S1K may have considered include:

- *Direct approach.* Under this approach, at a predetermined point in time all old systems cease and the new financial system becomes operational. This approach has the highest risk, as there is no opportunity to validate the new system's output with the old.
- *Parrallel approach.* This approach involves both old and new systems processing the same current data together for an agreed time (e.g. for a month). The outputs of the new system would be compared with those from existing systems to determine whether the new system is operating as expected. The downside of this approach is that implementation of the new system is delayed. This might indicate to S1K's workforce that management does not have complete confidence in the new system. Furthermore, additional time and effort would be taken in operating both old and new systems together.
- *Retrospective pilot.* This approach involves operating the new system with 'old' data (e.g. last month's financial data). The results produced by the new system can then be crosschecked with the results already processed by the existing systems. If there are no difficulties the old systems can then be withdrawn in favour of the new system. Like the parallel approach, additional time and effort would be taken in operating both old and new systems together to obtain duplicate output.

The absence of a project manager

The project manager who was overseeing project implementation has now left S1K. Clearly the introduction of such an important project as this needs to be properly managed and must not be left to chance. The Chief Executive's judgment that a replacement project manager should be appointed as a matter of priority seems well founded. However, he feels that the appointment should come from within S1K. The advantage of this is that the individual would have a good local knowledge. On the downside, there is no indication as to whether anyone within the group possesses the necessary expertise. Indeed, the system deficiencies within S1K suggest that little IS project management experience exists. This may be an error of judgment and a better option might be to buy in the services externally from a specialist IS project manager on a short term contract.

Requirement (c)

Main individuals and groups to be targeted

New project manager: Project management skills

Effective project management is crucial to the successful implementation of this important system. For the S1K employee who is appointed to oversee the introduction of the financial system it is likely that training in the technical skills of project management will be needed. If the appointee is inexperienced, or unfamiliar with what is required of a project manager, then this training is a priority. It is best provided by placing the individual on an externally facilitated training event.

Senior S1K managers: behavioural considerations

Support from the top is crucial for any significant change. In this case, senior management must be seen to support the new software initiative. They should understand the Chief Executive's analysis and a general overview of the system and its benefits could help, possibly through executive training seminars. This training is best provided in-house, possibly in conjunction with the Chief Executive (if possible) and the new project manager.

Central headquarters finance staff: training in all aspects of the new system

The new software is an 'off the shelf' package designed to perform specific financial functions of S1K's business. Finance staff will need to understand all aspects of the new package. This staff group will require regular returns from shops and, if properly trained, they can act as a source of advice and guidance to users in shops. Often software suppliers offer training options either as part of the contract or for an additional fee. Alternatively, as the software appears to be widely used within the industry, private training courses might already operate. The most convenient means of training staff would, however, be onsite but externally facilitated if this can be arranged.

System users in shops: general training in computer systems
Some shops still use manual systems, others use basic stand alone computers, so it is conceivable that some staff will not have sufficient confidence or experience to use any new application. Targeting further technical training might be beyond such staff without ensuring they first obtain a degree of computer literacy. S1K may have sufficient expertise in-house to provide such basic support and tuition for such individuals.

System users in shops: training in specific aspects of the new system
Detailed user instructions on how to operate the new system in shops will be needed (including procedures, commands and data-entry requirements, etc.). On-the-job training while staff are actively using the new system would be most appropriate. As shop users make returns to headquarters, appropriately trained headquarters staff could be used for the purpose. User manuals, 'help lines' and dedicated support teams might also be needed to support this process. Later, updates as users become familiar with the system may help consolidate growing knowledge and skills.

Users' managers: behavioural considerations
S1K's shop managers will be called upon to help ensure that potential disruption caused by the introduction of the system is kept to a minimum. Successful user acceptance is vital and local managers are also best placed to achieve local buy-in. Users' managers should therefore be made aware of the benefits of the system and the reasons for its introduction. In addition, an outline understanding of the elements of the system for which they are responsible should also be given. This training could be carried out by in-house staff through seminars and workshops, etc. Managers participation in such events could help get their full commitment and engender feelings of 'ownership'.

Index

Index

Index

Index

Index

Index

Africa
Fashion

Published to accompany the exhibition *Africa Fashion* at the Victoria and Albert Museum, London, from 2 July 2022 to 16 April 2023

Africa Fashion has been generously supported by

with additional support from

Designer: Aaron Yeboah Jr. | 2dots Space
Copy-editor: Linda Schofield
Origination: DL Imaging
Index: Nic Nicholas
New photography by Sarah Duncan and Kieron Boyle, V&A Photographic Studio
Printed and bound in China by C&C Offset Printing Co., Ltd.

Front cover illustration: Orange Culture ensemble, 'Peacock Riot' collection, Spring/Summer 2022. Photograph: Adebayo Jolaoso
Back cover illustration: Imane Ayissi dress, '*Tseundé*' collection, Spring/Summer 2021. Photograph: Douce d'Ivry for *Amina* magazine
Bled details: pp.82–3 detail of no.51; pp.160–1, detail of no.96

First published by V&A Publishing, 2022
Victoria and Albert Museum
South Kensington
London SW7 2RL
vam.ac.uk/publishing

Distributed in North America by Abrams, an imprint of ABRAMS
ISBN 9781 83851 027 5

10 9 8 7 6 5 4 3 2
2026 2025 2024 2023 2022

A catalogue record for this book is available from the British Library.

V&A Publishing
Supporting the world's leading museum of art and design, the Victoria and Albert Museum, London

Africa
Fashion

Edited by Christine Checinska

With contributions from Omoyemi Akerele, Amine Bendriouich, Gus Casely-Hayford, Sunny Dolat, Bonnie Greer, Monica L. Miller, Elisabeth Murray, Njoki Ngumi, Hadeel Osman and Roslyn A. Walker

V&A Publishing

CONTENTS

III

DIRECTOR'S FOREWORD

Africa Fashion celebrates the vitality, creativity and accelerating global impact of African fashions, which are as dynamic and multifarious as the continent itself. Ambitious in its scope, it is the UK's most extensive exhibition on the subject to date, giving a platform to African fashion creatives from over 20 countries across a broad spectrum of aesthetics. The fashions, textiles, photographs and everyday objects such as *Drum* magazines, posters and record albums featured here are catalysts from which to tell layered stories about the richness and diversity of the continent's myriad histories and cultures.

The staging of *Africa Fashion* at the V&A coincides with a period when the need to reimagine the practice of the museum along more equitable and encompassing lines could not be more apparent. Museums are not only about objects, they are also about the histories of people manifested through material culture. They are and always have been codified spaces and, necessarily, places of controversy through acts of omission or inclusion. Today, we appreciate more and more how certain peoples' histories have been hidden or misrepresented. The *Africa Fashion* exhibition and accompanying book reflect the V&A's broader commitment to focus on work by African and African diaspora creatives. From the project's inception we have drawn on expertise from the various communities in question, acknowledging that this comes in many forms, from the fashion creatives themselves, and academics and researchers based in the region, to community representatives, audiences and wearers. This centring of multiple African voices and perspectives not only gives this project its unique flavour but also exemplifies our emphasis on collaboration and storytelling as a way forward.

As a world-leading cultural institution, we have a part to play in the pressing debates of the day, providing space and a platform in the museum for those with often differing and under-represented views. By continually updating our core values of democratic, civic engagement and applying them creatively to the present, we can together develop collections and exhibitions of relevance to people across all cultures, all sectors of society, all perspectives. With this thought in mind, *Africa Fashion* lays a foundation for future projects, demonstrating that the V&A is more committed than ever in its aim of showcasing the very best of art, design, performance and creativity.

I am grateful to V&A Curator Christine Checinska and her team who have organized this spectacular exhibition. Thank you to all of the lenders, and to our supporters Gregory Annenberg Weingarten, GRoW @ Annenberg, and Merchants on Long. Without your generous support this exhibition would not have been possible.

Tristram Hunt
Director, V&A

1
Designed by Kofi Ansah
Ensembles for the wedding of
Ashley Shaw-Scott Adjaye and
David Adjaye
Ghana, 2014
Photographed in London in 2014
by Robert Pairer

SPONSOR'S FOREWORD

As an artist I was intrigued when I learned of Christine Checinska's proposal to 'spark a renegotiation of the geography of fashion'. I knew I wanted to support that philosophy and movement, which ultimately led to my supporting the *Africa Fashion* exhibition.

The visionary curator behind this exhibition, Christine Checinska shares the deep interest I have as a philanthropist in helping to recognize and redefine cultural influences and practices that impact us all. By turning our attention to the expansive grandeur of this rich continent we are acknowledging the diverse perspectives of our global culture.

Through our philanthropic initiative, GRoW @ Annenberg, we assist global communities by supporting true innovators who tackle challenges with their own vision and agency. I am therefore honoured to support the V&A in providing space for fashion creatives to construct new dialogue and continue to expand the parameters of fashion and culture.

In addition to thanking Christine Checinska, we at GRoW want to thank the board and staff at the V&A for their leadership and dedication. I hope this exhibition inspires others – not just in the fashion world – to continue to recognize, uplift and celebrate voices from around the globe.

Gregory Annenberg Weingarten
Founder, GRoW @ Annenberg
Vice President and Director, Annenberg Foundation

2
Sindiso Khumalo,
Detail of *Miss Celie* dress,
printed cotton
Cape Town, South Africa,
Spring/Summer 2020
V&A: T.2437–2021

PROLOGUE

Bonnie Greer

Africa Fashion.

What is it?

Imagine:

A man walks into a museum in Britain.

This museum holds the objects of his ancestors.

The images of these ancestors are on the shirt and the suit he is wearing.

He has designed these clothes himself, using cloth from his ancestral home.

In Africa.

His jewellery is from another part of Africa, and partly, too, from the *banlieue*. The banned place.

His shoes, made by a cousin in Brooklyn, were cobbled in the way shoes used to be made: on a bench with a hammer. That hammer: from Jamaica.

He is coming to the museum to have tea, and coming, too, to see the African statues whose calm faces, full of mystic cool, are his own.

He is not wearing the shirt to honour them, to remember them.

There is no memory of them as such.

Because Spirit is not there.

Spirit never got on the boat. Or in the knapsack of the foreign soldier.

The statue is here.

But Spirit does not travel against Its will.

Never taken.

Never can be.

What the statue helps to create is the African Imaginarium, an immense space of imagination; creativity; healing, daring, survival. Beauty.

A constant dialogue between Then and Now.

Taking tea inside of a museum with The Ones Not There, dressed in clothing adorned by the faces of those who lived before you.

Facing Now. Even when it encompasses The Past because that is a Now, too.

The African Imaginarium.

At the Parthenon Museum in Athens, I once saw a shield with the face of the Medusa on it.

This was the face that had the power to cause an army to flee in terror. A rout.

Medusa petrifies. When Perseus gently put her down on a bed of algae near the beach they turned into corals.

'A sea change into something rich and strange.'

I have always seen this face in books, shown as that of a raging woman, a harridan dragged out of a nightmare. A monster.

This is what a museum is for: to see.

To have your own, personal encounter; to read the descriptions, if you like, but a description only gives you information. The Encounter is what matters.

I looked at the face on the shield.

It was the face of a woman. With dreads.

An African woman.

The glass case that contained the mask reflected back to me my own face, staring in shock and wonder, and my face and the mask were together.

In that moment of reflection comes futurism.

Or better yet: The Futuristic...the portal through which Something Else can not only be imagined. But lived.

Africa Fashion is always a kind of Futurism. It takes you forward.

3
Designed by KISUA
Curated capsule collection to commemorate
the centenary of the birth of Albertina Sisulu:
anti–apartheid activist, freedom fighter
and nurse
South Africa, 2018
Photographed by Marijke Willems[1]

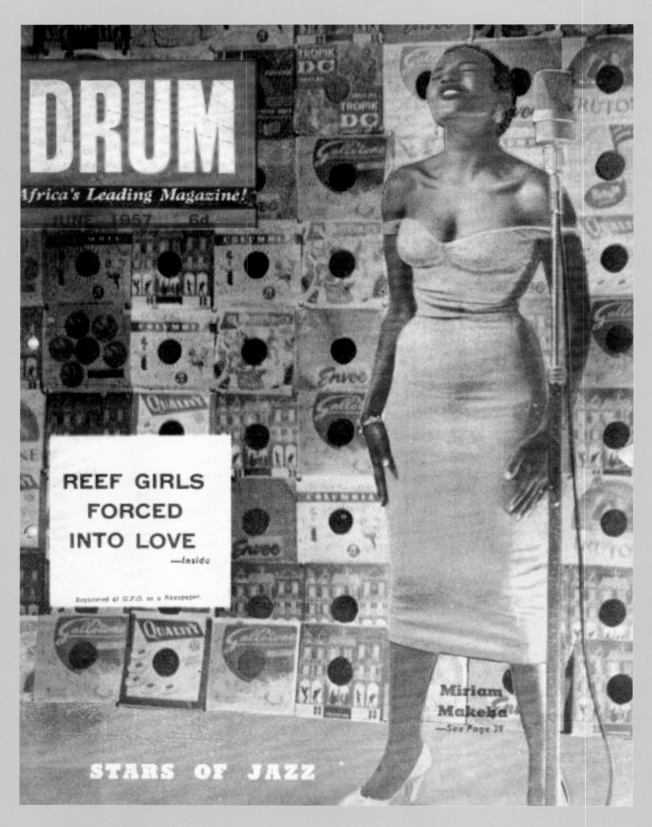

4
Miriam Makeba on the front cover of
DRUM Magazine
South Africa, June 1957

The present contemplating itself within the narrow parameters of oppression and repression.

The boldness of Africa Fashion is the complete act of will of it and the drive to creation. The insistence on this.

This insistence is the release of Imagination from when it, too, was condemned to be fettered like the body.

It is agency at its highest because it creates a future in which African people are not defined by anyone except ourselves. By. Ourselves.

The power of reordering the world, of remaking history, can give the maker of fashion another way of seeing Africa. Now.

This way of seeing I call Meta Africa. It is non-reactive vision in that it does not look back in order to mourn.

It is not punitive.

It is not nostalgic.

Africa Fashion takes the materials of the past and the present with the intention of seeing Africa Now.

Normal. Not: In Trouble. Centre: as Europe or America are assumed to be the centre.

Meta Africa steps back and allows this Afrocentrism to be.

On the surface, Africa Fashion can look assertive, maybe even deconstructive.

But at a deeper level, it has another gaze. It is not reaction. But action.

Materials usually made for ceremonies and rituals are fashioned to subvert their original intention.

Contrast is used as a blueprint by which this Meta Africa, sometimes fantastic, can be constructed.

I say the word 'future' because Africa Fashion is The Future, wearing and displaying itself.

You can wear it. In the act of doing that, in the act of other people seeing it…the future begins.

This is The Dare: that The Future – so long constrained by colonialism, enslavement, all of the elements emerging from it, and the oppression of our algorithmic present – becomes open, possible. Then what do you do?

Africa Fashion does not create a binary universe, even though on the surface this may appear to be the case.

What it does is releases Imagination, frees up the possibilities; mixes up the tropes and Things Assumed.

You can put the conundrums on your body. It can BE your body.

It can be Beauty. One of the highest values.

The kind that makes you know everything right away. And nothing. The conundrum and the challenge of Africa Fashion.

Africa Fashion takes our minds beyond the banal; even the political. It creates new roads of travel, posits new theories, makes new dreams, exposes the genius of the competencies forged out of oppression.

Competencies like Shoreline Thinking: my phrase for that capacity created out of the genius of the enslaved, to survive the dehumanization of colonialism and slavery.

And to do more than that: to make a contribution to human advancement itself.

Africa Fashion takes Shoreline Thinking and makes it wearable.

Makes it possible to make visible all the planes of existence that being African is. The melding and the weaving, the subtlety of Africa.

Even in a bold and colourful dress, there is also the quiet of a coming together.

That possibility that we, all of us, can know one another.

One major component of Africa Fashion is its Trickster

Knowledge: wit; insouciance.

Like cruisewear for a holiday. In Zanzibar. Like ladies-who-lunch in glorious dresses, topped with a 'Black Lives Matter' attitude.

Fists raised; faces set and serious. Styling Parisian haute couture. For the purposes of doing what African art does in all its transmutations: Just A Little Bit More. Just Go A Little Bit Further. Raise The Game.

African agency, African wit, African beauty. In and of itself. Africa Fashion is also invisible, hidden in the fashion of other people.

It can be and is appropriated and not acknowledged, but you know. It can be hidden in plain sight. Buried in the work of those not African; you can see it if you look. You don't have to look too hard.

Look.

There it is: in total command of the space. Built in. An African Continuum.

The Beautiful Assemblage, the weaver of words into whole cloth. It extends out to its children abroad, too: to Meta Africa, that assembly of genius fuelled by survival.

To me, 'Diaspora' is much too dainty a word for those of us who have survived and thrived outside of the continent. Who know deep inside ourselves that Africa Fashion is us, too...

Call and Response.

Response to itself.

Africa Fashion does not constantly refer to enslavement, colonialism, oppression. Although, in some form, they are there. In irony; or comment; or testament; or all of these at once and more.

You cannot narrow Africa.

The Imaginarium takes reality, knows it; acknowledges it; wears it. Take a hat. A thing for the skull; an adornment for the head.

Africa Fashion as African Imaginarium renders that hat a map. Study it closely for the texture and layering. For its witness and cool.

Study the Shape Shifter, Trickster, aspects of what appears to be a dress or a handbag or a pair of shoes, and what Africa Fashion does is take you beyond the materials. Not in a demanding way. In a whisper. Even when it is brash, Africa Fashion is subtle.

The African Imaginarium.

It faces everything. Directly. Yet searching, too, out of the corner of the eye.

It is the door to Ambiguity. That is one of the Shape Shifter aspects of it.

Like my first week in London, a few decades ago, and not knowing why I had left New York City for a subway system that had a curfew, I turned a long, endless corner and there was Meta Africa. The African Continuum. Not even in African clothes, but there were the eyes of the woman who had descended from centuries of Shoreline Thinking, of that special consciousness born of The Boat across the passage. That poster of Naomi Campbell made me know that I belonged here in this African city of London, and that Africa Fashion can be in the way you wear something, as well as what you wear. And when you choose to wear it.

When I was a child Miriam Makeba became the foundation deity of my African Imaginarium.

In my mind's eye she appeared on television in a white, slender dress. Like a Greco-Roman goddess. But my memory lied. What her style transmitted to me was a metaphor that played back to me through my proper-

Catholic education. It played back to me only the stuff that I knew at the time. She was such a shock in her Africa Fashion, beauty and grace. I knew that my hair was going to be like hers.

Miriam Makeba, that night on television, was definitely not dressed like some Greek goddess, but in a shape-shifting kind of elegance. That can make you see other things and even be in love and empowered by what is not even in your face.

It can be and is history.

And it is present.

And it is.

Africa Fashion had given me my first corrective in the way to be. It continues to do so.

Africa Fashion approaches life and death with the acknowledgment of elegance.

Even going to court to hear the possible death sentence of a loved one involved in a struggle for freedom. Even then. Elegance.

Elegance is power.

It is refutation of The Power.

And, too, in a real sense, it is confirmation of Our Power, Our Authority, handed down by the Elders who fashioned our souls and our minds. Who we cannot shake, from Day One of our existence.

'Be clean,' my Elders said.

Always be clean.

Africa Fashion is: Clean.

The Clean That Makes You Seen.

Enslavement, colonialization, cultural appropriation are ultimately acts of erasure. They are the principal grand attempt at re-remaking and forgetting. Forget your name; your god; your mother.

Africa Fashion undoes these acts of erasure with cloth and its mighty assemblage; with sewing and weaving and more.

Africa Fashion builds: links up the past, present, future, and that nether space where Spirit dwells. And you can feel and see Them if you're lucky enough.

So Africa Fashion goes in the opposite direction of erasure: not only in remembrance.

Not just that.

But to Memory. It creates and sustains Memory. The African man taking tea in the clothes bearing the faces of his ancestors does not wear these fashions to remember them, but to create Memory itself. And sustain it.

He does so with extension, comment and flair.

Take flair.

It can seem like a trivial thing, a vanity thing.

But allow me to go back to Africa America, Africa's child-in-exile and present the word: 'fly'. 'Fly' says everything.

To say that someone's attire or demeanour is 'fly' is to acknowledge and expose its ability and nerve to be lighter than air.

To be 'fly' is to dare to have wit in the very face of hell, and go even further than that: 'fly' flies.

It escapes into lightness; transcendence; steadiness and cool.

'Fly' comments, always in the most appropriate way. It challenges injustice and oppression with the lightest and wittiest touch. It is 'well-dressed'.

'Well-dressed' speaks well of your mother and your father; of your ancestors and the time and the place. Africa Fashion is ALWAYS well-dressed.

Even as it addresses politics: the hard and the cruel and the injustice of it all. To turn up slovenly, as I implied earlier, is to lose.

That is to lose, and to be back in those chains waiting for you just the other side of the Void, trapped in a space in which they do not call you by your right name.

To see only the façade of confidence that Africa Fashion sometimes seems to project is to not understand its nuance.

Africa has always been a site of projection.

We people of African descent outside of Africa spend more of our unconscious time, too, projecting on it. More than we know. Because it was denied us in its fullness and its truth. So it has become a well-spring of dreams.

The brilliance of Africa Fashion is that it plays this back, unabashed. It heals, too. Because it makes you stop and listen. Yes, I said listen. To the ancestors, the recent and the past.

Africa Fashion knows that Spirit can reside anywhere It chooses, and at the same time, in a particular space. It is fashion that can look like everything else, but that is because Spirit leaves and comes as It wills. It dares to turn and face you with a quiet blankness, questioning, defying you to say where it is at any point in time.

It can take a contemporary slogan, a theme, a moment, and make it stretch beyond an individual time and space. In order to extend agency.

On one level, of course, it is bound by its temporal restraints: by nation; by finance; by the skill of the maker of the fashion. But when it is 'fly', when it is 'funky', it lifts off and cannot be caught.

To this extent, Africa Fashion plays with extravagance, even in its most sombre moments. It insists that we look at it, not as static, but as fluid.

There is always the insistence on being 'correct', in Africa Fashion, because this is a quality of Spirit.

Pristineness is necessary in order for Spirit to live, for the Imaginary to grow. The African Imaginarium does not allow for 'otherness', because pristineness is always whole, complete; nothing is excluded.

Africa Fashion may look like ordinary clothing; may be copied by designers not African etc., but the real thing conjures.

It exists in the concrete but it also takes you to another plane.

It is not wise to think of assemblage as just putting things together, trying to make do.

This is a fashion that is the rearrangement of reality in action; a deep dive into Spirit is what this entire art form commands.

Yes, I say Spirit a lot because this fashion exists on both heaven and earth.

Best to approach it in this way to get the full flavour and more...the mystic cool of it.

The ordering of space and reality of it.

The love and the philosophy of it.

Music is to be taken as a given here.

But not the music you hear or buy.

Africa Fashion is human music. Inside us all.

Africa Fashion is fashion that talks back. It is in dialogue with itself and with the world simultaneously. Because it must be that.

It is the root, and opens up the world.

Africa Fashion is not new. It has never been 'discovered'. 'Discovery' is a word constantly associated with the southern regions of Africa.

Africa Fashion is inside of a museum.

It walks its own catwalk, taking bits and pieces of other cultures if it chooses, reshaping; and remaking, always making.

The African Imaginarium.

Museums, to me, are an agora of constant storytelling and re-storytelling; the meeting of history: stripped down and re-rewritten.

Always re-rewriting, assemblers of the 'trace', in the physics sense: the evidence of something that was once there. The museum holds the evidence. It is we who build. Who truly assemble.

Africa Fashion, its essence, is not to be pinpointed; it is nothing one can lay one's greedy hands on. But something beyond that you can receive: beauty, elegance, joy, dignity, and behind it, spirit (or Spirit).

In this deep knowledge of assemblage as healing and knowledge, Africa Fashion brings joy. What's called Black Joy.

Way beyond itself.

'Ancient to the Future', the motto of great jazz group AACM.

'Ancient to the Future.'

5
J.D. 'Okhai Ojeikere
Untitled, HG-457-04 from 'Headties' series
Nigeria 2004, printed 2012
Supported by the National Lottery through
the Heritage Lottery Fund
V&A: E.229-2013

INTRODUCTION

Christine Checinska

'Fashion allows us to speak about the continent in the way we know it.'

Awa Meité, December 2020[1]

'I am not African because I was born in Africa, but because Africa was born in me.'

Kwame Nkrumah, All African People's Conference, Accra, Ghana, 1958

A willowy model, cocooned in a calf-length egg-shaped coat crafted from Ghanaian *kente* cloth, strides across the floor: the epitome of *savoir-vivre* but also the embodiment of a synthesis of many cultural influences, an emblem of contemporary cosmopolitanism. The ensemble, created by designer Imane Ayissi, is completed by a simple shell top worn with a matching pair of burgundy ankle-skimming peg trousers. These underpinning pieces draw the eye back to the showstopping coat, with its rich tones of terracotta, lime, olive, orange and plum. A pair of mustard-yellow spike-heeled shoes and a single elongated feather earring add the finishing touches. Ayissi's dazzling *kente* coat is met with a ripple of applause from the audience and a flurry of flashing lights from the cameras of the international press who have gathered to witness this mix of elegance and quiet activism (no.6).

This distinctive ensemble featured in Ayissi's Spring/Summer 2017 Paris ready-to-wear collection *Asseulènn*, which means 'crossings' in Ewondo, his mother tongue. His aim with this collection was to choreograph a metaphorical dance between Africa, Asia and Europe through his choice of fabrics, playing with common motifs such as squares. He elegantly brought together vintage kimono fabrics from Asia, *kitas* from Côte d'Ivoire,[2] and local Cameroonian cottons, as well as tie-and-dye and *kente* cloths from Ghana, all sourced from collectors. Ayissi's shows reveal an aesthetic and sense of style that challenge understandings of what African fashions are

and can be: as he observes, 'cultural mixing is the world we are living in'.[3] While African textiles, cultures and histories are a constant source of inspiration, in conversation Ayissi stresses that 'creativity has no borders' and that his ultimate wish is to dress women of all cultures.[4]

These oversized *kente* coats have become a signature of Ayissi's brand, changing in mood and feel depending on the cloth used. The polyrhythmic piecing together of stripweave cloth – mustard-yellow against plum, against lime juxtaposed with terracotta – could be seen as a metaphor for the richness and diversity of the contemporary African fashion scene itself. Contemporary African fashions in turn are as eclectic and varied as the African continent, which consists of 54 countries and more than 1.3 billion people. Africa is the world's second largest continent by geographic area and population. From Tunisia to Lesotho, Senegal to Somalia, it is a place of multiplicity. To attempt to define and discuss all fashions from such a vast and complex region would be impossible. They are shaped by diverse histories, cultural backgrounds and influences, inspirations and desires. What does unite the fashion creatives from the corners of the continent represented in this book – the designers, stylists, photographers, e-tailers and industry leads – is their demand for and exercising of agency, a drive to create a sustainable fashion ecosystem and a cultural syncretism born out of historic and contemporary culture clash and entanglement. This book and

6
Imane Ayissi
Kente coat, '*Asseulènn*' collection
Paris, France, Spring/Summer
2017

the associated exhibition at the V&A offer a compelling glimpse of the glamour, politics and history of what is an ever-evolving and globally influential twenty-first-century fashion scene.[5] Both are inspired in part by the theatre of fashion with its narrative potential: the crafting and performance of identities through props such as a pair of Hassan Hajjaj babouche Nike slippers (no.8), or a gravity-defying *gèlè* (no.5), or a neatly fitting embroidered cap (no.7). Fashion's potential to tell stories and to transform is mesmerizing, particularly in the hands of Africa's fashion creatives.

The long story of African fashions

The cosmopolitan roots of the contemporary fashion scene go back thousands of years. African people have always travelled, criss-crossing internal and external borders, carrying with them tools of self-fashioning and self-expression, such as handworked cloths, beads and shells. Archaeological finds dating from 82,000 and 75,000 BCE in Morocco and South Africa reveal shells with holes bored through, suggesting that they were strung together to create jewellery.[6] Examples of domestic stripweave cloths have been found dating as far back as the eleventh century, in Mali.[7] In the past, North Africa was largely closed off from the regions south of Senegal in the west and Ethiopia in the east, physically separated by the desert terrain with the exception of established trade routes connecting them. The Sahara Desert, though seemingly uninhabitable, has been and remains home to nomadic groups such as the Tuareg. Crossed by established trans-Saharan caravan routes, North Africa engaged with the southern regions in the trade of products such as dyestuffs, ivory and spices, alongside the trade of people. Islam and Christianity came to West and Central Africa via these routes. Islam advanced south from North Africa during the eighth century. Christianity reached North Africa as early as CE 60, slowly spreading throughout the continent after that. These foreign religions brought significant changes in ways of dressing and fashioning the body. Islam and Christianity demanded modest fashions for men and women. Before the arrival of Islam, for example, the humid climate of certain regions dictated that body coverings were kept to a minimum. Early adopters of modest fashions were of the leadership classes, including the traders themselves. This led to imitation by those who desired the associated status signalled by such dress. Thereafter emerged the male gown, turban and loose easy trousers

favoured by men of the Muslim faith in the north, men of the predominantly Christian faith in the south, and men of neither faith who wanted to dress in what became a more traditional, conservative way of fashioning the body.[8] Archetypal West African styles such as the *boubou*, *agbádá*, *riga* and caftan have their genesis in eighteenth-century Islam.[9] Similarly, classic women's ensembles like the West African *kaba* are thought to have originated with the modest dress promoted by Christian missionaries, the term itself stemming from the coastal pidgin trade language for the English word 'cover'.[10]

The raw materials used to manufacture cloth in Africa include bark, bast, cotton, raffia, silk and wool.[11] Increasing demand for woven cloth generated by modest dress in the more densely populated southern regions could not be met by imports from North Africa, Asia and Europe. Trade with Europe in West Africa from the mid-fifteenth century onwards similarly increased the demand for and variety of locally produced cloths. There was also now a desire for African woven cloths, or 'country cloths', from a different region to one's own, cloths that could be acquired through seaborne traders. Country cloths from the West African interior were sold to the British, Dutch and Portuguese stationed in forts along the Ghanaian coast, who were then able to trade them on. It was in the eighteenth century that the Dutch, taking Java by force, introduced the now familiar wax-resist cloth, often referred to as African-print, into the region.[12] To this day the Dutch company Vlisco remains a world leader in the production of wax-resist print cloth.[13] It is important to note the inspiration and impact of Africans who historically adopted this cloth, transforming a colonial product into an art form through which one can trace historical moments of negotiation and protest.[14] In the southern regions, fashions made from imported and locally woven textiles allowed the requirements of modest dress to be readily met. For example, Indian block-prints were embraced in East Africa, alongside locally produced cloths woven on Asian-style looms.[15]

Between the sixteenth and eighteenth centuries, European traders and travellers noted the shifting aesthetics brought to bear on textiles and adornment in southern regions.[16] Consumers had discerning eyes and expected changing designs. African innovators took up and reworked Western styles, creating new local fashion looks.[17] Dutch traders even

7 (right)
Cap, cotton embroidered
with silk
Nigeria, 1900s
V&A: T.249–1966

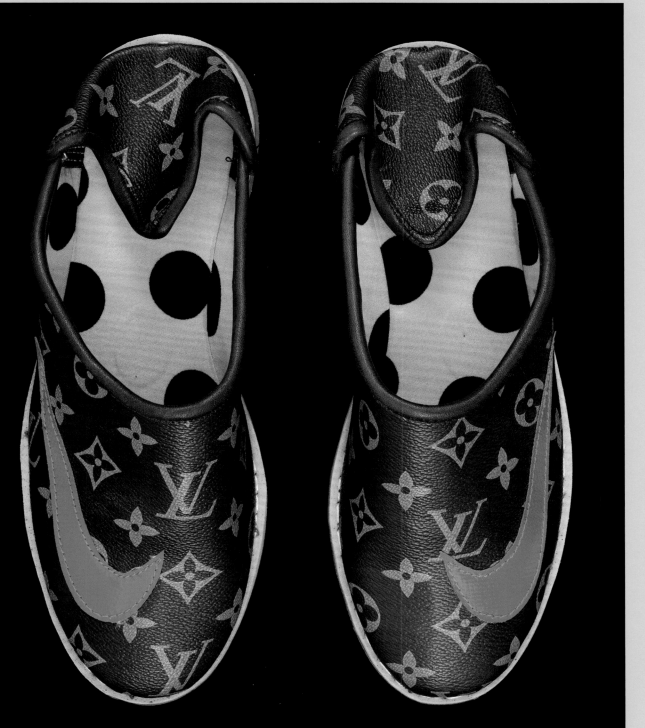

8
Hassan Hajjaj
Babouches
'Andy Wahloo' line, faux Louis
Vuitton x Nike design,
PVC, leather
Marrakesh, Morocco, 2020
Jameel Endowment
V&A: ME.17–2021

reported that Asante weavers unravelled silk cloths obtained from them, reweaving them into designs that suited local tastes.[18] From the mid-nineteenth century, European cloth producers actively sought to infiltrate potentially lucrative African markets. English 'Manchester print' cottons found a market in Southern Africa and West Africa catering to local trends. In the twentieth century machine-woven, block-printed *kangas* emblazoned with Swahili proverbs became popular in East Africa. Decorative beads were imported from Indian merchants in Zanzibar or else from Christian missionaries. As *bògòlanfini* from Mali caught the imagination of fashion trendsetters in the West, clothing tastes of the local elite shifted once again.[19] This process of trade, conversion, culture clash and imitation provided great stimulus to the continent's fashion producers.

In sum, the history of fashion in Africa, as everywhere, evolved from centuries of layered cross-cultural exchange, appropriation and transformation. Yet African fashions have been subjected to misrepresentation through the play of stereotypes that have historically presented African styles of dress either as unchanging, emerging from an essentialized monoculture, or as an exoticized source of inspiration for designers of the Global North. Through popular culture, they have all too often been reduced to the realm of the 'other' within histories of fashion, particularly those written from perspectives rooted in reductive Global North thinking. African fashions are either conspicuous by their absence, or their histories are not voiced by Africans themselves. The will to adorn and the will to innovate are universal, yet this has not always been recognized in an equitable way. Traces of European colonization remain, in spite of recent publications that have gone some way to redress the balance. Among the latter are Victoria L. Rovine's *African Fashion, Global Style* (2015), Helen Jennings's *New African Fashion* (2011), and Suzanne Gott and Kristyne Loughran's *Contemporary African Fashion* (2010). Contemporary African fashion creatives exhibit a high level of sophistication and cosmopolitanism, taking a multilingual approach to design, making and self-fashioning often through the adoption of 'hypersampled' references.[20] Contemporary African fashions are diverse, always in flux, always shirking classification.

Africa and the Global North

While this book does not set out to define a unifying African fashion aesthetic or identity, it is important to clarify why some terms are being used and not others, and what is meant by the terms that have been adopted. Centring Africa is a guiding principle of the *Africa Fashion* project. But there are different ways of thinking about Africa. The continent could be viewed either as a physical or a psychological space.[21] The Africa that is referred to here is characterized by multiple, at times interrelated, at times contradictory, histories, cultures and creative expressions. Consequentially, notions of what it is to be African, and fashionable, are represented through a wide range of voices and perspectives. Blackness is just one strand of African-ness being featured, and by that I mean Blackness in the political sense, as to focus solely on pigmentation would simply reduce what Africa is.[22] The fashion creatives fore-grounded in this book are engaged in a renegotiation of both Blackness and African-ness: some actively do so; others do so intuitively. By simply drawing on our own frames of reference to make work, rather than practising from behind the veil of Global North fashion systems and the corresponding white gaze, new ways of doing fashion are continually emerging.[23] It is as though contemporary fashion creatives are declaring this is the view of fashion *from* Africa. But this renegotiation of Blackness and African-ness is underpinned by a new pan-Africanism, informed by a continental sensibility and a cosmopolitanism that seeks to include rather than exclude. It is shot through with the expansive 'shoreline thinking' that Bonnie Greer references in the Prologue to this book. Tensions and flows between the myriad views, concerns and aesthetics are temporarily held by these inclinations and the desire to build a thriving and sustainable fashion industry.

Africa's worldwide cultural impact is hidden in plain sight. It is there in everyday products like sugar and cotton. It is there in the markers of luxury such as diamonds and other gems. But it is also there in the people around us. Traces of Africa are embodied by those who, like me, are of the diaspora; in my case British born of African heritage via the Caribbean. Being of the diaspora is different from being from the continent. Different cultural frameworks and therefore priorities apply, yet, as Bonnie Greer so eloquently points out in the Prologue, there is a connection. Issues associated with Blackness, for example, are less of a primary concern in the majority Black countries on the continent. The creolized African Caribbean outlook that I have inherited, with its multiple cultural reference points underlined by ancestral links to West Africa, inevitably informs my approach. This is not unusual since, as curators and editors, we all bring something of ourselves to every project. Subsequently, this publication aims to tell stories from across the continent, beyond it and in relation to it. Regarding our title, the phrase 'African fashion' is far too small, too constrained to capture such complexity, nuance and reach. It cannot describe the diversity of influences and aesthetics deployed by the fashion creatives of Global Africa (that is Africa and the African Diaspora). In contrast, the fluidity and ambiguity of 'Africa Fashion' allows for the open-endedness that this entangled subject dictates.

The term Global North generally refers to the north–south division of the earth along socio-economic and political lines. The Global North incorporates China, Japan, the USA and most of Europe, including the former colonial powers. In the main it correlates with the West and, in a similar manner to the way in which the concept of the West operates, can be seen as a matrix that represents wealth and power, as well as being a geographical region on some maps. Meanwhile, Africa sits within the Global South, which also encompasses Latin America, Asia and Oceania. The terms north and south, though contested, mark an attempt to eradicate cultural marginaliza-tion. Both are increasingly used within fashion studies as the old Euro-Western canon that left certain races and cultures out has begun to be slowly deconstructed by fashion scholars and practitioners across the globe.[24] It is therefore adopted here.

Africa's relationship to the Global North, particularly the former colonizing nations, is complicated. As Europe colonized the African continent, it brought its languages, philosophies, belief systems and cultural expressions with it. Europeans tried to read and represent Africa from their own viewpoints, squeezing the continent into narrow frames of reference. The 'colonial library' relegated African cultural expressions to the realm of the unchanging and the under-developed.[25] Africa became associated with lack. As unacceptable as this might seem to contemporary sensibilities attuned to the common humanity of all people, it is not unusual since we all draw on what we already know and understand to describe and define that which we do not. However, systematic widespread coloni-zation set in motion structures of evaluation and representa-tion that continue to inform societies' invisible borders based on hierarchies of value rooted in negative readings of racial and cultural difference. Colonization did not end, nor true independence begin, with the lowering and hoisting of flags. The pasts and presents of those of us of African heritage are, to a certain extent, haunted by the spectre of racism that became ingrained through European empire-building. The tightly woven relationship between colonization, racism and whiteness has long been critiqued by numerous scholars, from W.E.B. DuBois and James Baldwin to bell hooks, Reni Eddo-Lodge and many others. Latterly, critical studies of whiteness situated within current moves towards racial and social justice and the cessation of all forms of colonization have scrutinized the invisible way that whiteness operates alongside the systems that support it, perpetuating issues of innocence and guilt, denial and privilege, biases and blind spots.[26] Nevertheless, the white gaze still holds the power to batter us down with metaphorical tom-toms, to invoke philosopher Frantz Fanon.[27] It still holds the power to fix us as 'other', to dictate our entry into the global fashion arena.

In all societies fashion can be used to maintain and to contest such imbalances of power. This is an accepted truth. However, it is easy to fall into the trap of assuming that all African fashions and ways of fashioning the body are always deliberate acts of creative agency. Or that all African fashions have hidden political meanings rooted in issues associated with race. This is not the case. Some fashion creatives just want to make beautiful clothes. Some want to be part of the European haute couture system. Who are we to deny that choice? Clearly, there is more to the African fashion scene than first meets the eye. It is a complex scene of contradictions made more so by the uneasy relationship between fashion, culture and race surfacing from the entangled histories of colonization and decolonization.

Syncretism and fashioning the body

There are many ways to read fashion, from historical and cultural studies approaches, through to the social and psychological aspects of clothes and more. This book sets fashion within the wider context of art and culture. Fashion is therefore presented as a form of art and design, as a cultural expression, a way of speaking about oneself and one's place in the world, but it is also presented as a catalyst for social change. In colonial societies new cultural forms inevitably

9
Designed by Maison ARTC
Ensemble, 'Beautiful Sadness'
collection
Marrakesh, Morocco, 2018
Photographed in Addis Ababa,
Ethiopia, by Artsimous

emerged from the cross-cultural exchanges taking place at the meeting point, or borderlands, between each group, as people set up home often cheek by jowl. It is now widely accepted that all cultures are mixed, none are pure, none are static and unchanging.[28] Syncretism used here refers to the cross-cultural exchanges and coalescence instigated by the colonization of Africa. Imagine the borderlands as an in-between space, a space of colliding cultures, tensions and conflict but also, if we consider the border the point at which something begins rather than ends, a space of possibility.[29] Colonization was brutal; it did involve the fracturing of African histories, identities and psychologies.[30] However, it also set in motion new possibilities, new cultural expressions. The cultural expressions, ways of thinking and being of Europeans as well as Africans were irreversibly changed by these colonial encounters. In this scenario cross-cultural interweaving is in part made visible through the fashioning of the body. We also witness it in music genres such as High Life in South Africa, in spiritual practices like Vodun in West Africa, in dance forms like the Cake Walk performed by the enslaved on American plantations before the Civil War (1861–5) and after emancipation. Syncretism provides us with a departure point from which to consider aspects of twentieth- and twenty-first-century fashions and self-fashioning in Global Africa, an expression that alludes to a connectedness that transcends geographical separation, and so will be used strategically throughout this book.[31] It is not the only recurring characteristic of African fashions, but it is a thread that binds the fashion creatives in this book and the associated exhibition.

Local and global cross-cultural influences intertwine in the work of the fashion creatives featured in the following chapters. Designers like Bubu Ogisi of IAMISIGO, who is based between Lagos, Nairobi and Accra, and Laduma Ngxokolo of MAXHOSA AFRICA, in Johannesburg, draw on African cultures other than their own, cutting and mixing them with inspirations from elsewhere (pp.144–7). Such entanglement manifests in differing aesthetics that depend on each individual creative but is related to the cosmopolitanism and common systems of colonization outlined above. Minimalist designers such as Moses Turahirwa, creative director of Moshions, Rwanda (p.158), and mixologists, or bricoleurs, such as Artsi Ifrach at Maison ARTC, Morocco (no.9), have opposing aesthetics but still adopt syncretic approaches in the development of their collections. In explaining syncretism, it is useful to picture a

length of *kente* once again. As we have seen, cultural enmeshing happens when two or more aspects of different cultures come together in a contact zone creating a new idea, custom or philosophy. Syncretic forms, like the fashions presented here, are those that have been produced from a weaving together of different cultural traditions to generate a unique and harmonious whole. But there are tensions between the components, just as there must be tension between warp and weft, between each narrow strip of cloth, if we are to devise a distinctive design. Notice the plethora of colours, stripes and geometric effects in no.10, overleaf. Each element is distinct but also in dialogue with the next. In the case of Ayissi's cocoon coat (no.6), a Ghanaian weaving technique is placed in dialogue with European tailoring traditions to create an innovative twenty-first-century look. Both Parisian couture and Ghanaian artisanal weaving are reinscribed in the process.

Fashion is vitally important to Global Africa; it is not something to be taken lightly. The writer Ishmael Reed notes that it is 'as fundamental to Black cultural tradition as drumming'.[32] Meanwhile, the cultural critic Stuart Hall wrote that many cultural expressions stemming from Global Africa evolve around music, movement and the body, where style becomes 'the subject of what is going on'. From his point of view, the body is 'the only cultural capital' we have had.[33] It is as though the body is a canvas on which to re-present not only oneself but also the African continent of our heritage as cosmopolitan, assertive, possessing vitality and relevance. Aligned to this idea, artist and curator Leora Farber, drawing on fashion historian Monica L. Miller's observations, writes that the fashions of Global Africa sit within a broader context of 'movement culture', whereby ever-emergent identities are articulated through style.[34] This is a reminder of the close connection between fashion, music, dance and gestures such as striking a pose or walking with laid-back elegance. All are embodied practices, everyday cultural expressions that are woven into performances of nuanced identities. Fashion within movement culture operates via a constantly changing vocabulary of clothing and adornment, demeanour and gesture that 'fashion' the body, artfully crafting and expressing identities that are continually shifting.[35] So, self-fashioning can become a means by which to visually declare who we are, what our beliefs and values are, and how we want to be read at any point in time, from individual and collective perspectives.[36]

In essence, the process of fashioning the body can become a 'self-defining art form' that realigns our sense of self and articulates who we are, or, perhaps more accurately, who we are becoming.[37] To think about fashion in this way invokes a crucial expression of agency in Global Africa and so is an underlying theme in this book.

Ultimately *Africa Fashion* tells a story of the richness of the African continent, its people, cultures and histories, through the lens of fashion. It is a story of unbounded creativity, abundance and modernity told from multiple Global Africa perspectives. To that end this book consciously celebrates the vitality, innovation and cosmopolitanism of a contemporary African fashion scene saturated with diverse inspirations, aesthetics and motivations, mapping its history and giving a glimpse of glamour and politics along the way.

10
Cloth, cotton, woven in various techniques, loom embroidery
Ghana, 1900–49
Given by J.W.F. Morton, Esq
V&A: Circ.766-1967

I

LIBERATION AND POST-INDEPENDENCE FASHIONS

Christine Checinska

Sankofa

Twi, meaning return (*san*), go (*ko*), take (*fa*);
there is great worth in taking inspiration from the past.

'It was the time of Fela, and Wole Soyinka's plays... It was a time of Nigeria evolving. We were bringing in new ideas...Arts and culture were very rich. Lagos was swinging!'

Shade Thomas-Fahm, March 2021[1]

In 1957 Ghana became the first West African country to free itself from Britain, its former colonizer. Morocco and Tunisia, in the north, had gained independence from France a year earlier. In 1960 alone, 17 African countries declared independence from colonial rule. It soon became known as the Year of Africa.[2] This era signalled a reawakening. It heralded a new sense of pride in being Black and African. These were heady days. The radical social and political reordering that took place sparked a cultural renaissance throughout the continent, as creative artists across many disciplines contemplated their relationship to the new nation states, to the African continent and to a world increasingly divided by the Cold War (1947–91). Fashion, music and the visual arts drew on formerly marginalized traditions creating innovative forms that looked towards future self-rule with an unforgettable independence of spirit.

The female figure in the foreground of the black-and-white photograph of a group of young male and female fashion models taken by Mohamed 'Mo' Amin (1943–1996), in Nairobi in 1972 (no.11), captures an unmistakable zest for life that has come to characterize the African liberation and post-independence years. She laughs as she leans against a post outside a modernist mid-century building. Her slim physique is clothed in a sleeveless printed minidress. In the background, to her left, a young woman in a wax-resist print dress, equally thigh-skimming, looks directly at the camera and smiles. To her right, a woman wearing a *gèlè* and *dashiki* is deep in conversation with a tall slim man with a closely cropped afro.

The sartorial markers of what would later become the Black Power Movement – the afro, the *dashiki* – point to future equity for Black people across and beyond the continent. The work of artists and designers, including the continent's fashion creatives, was vital to the process of decolonization, the establishment of an 'Afro-Modernity' presented in Amin's photograph, and the beckoning in of Afro-Futurism.[3] Pan-Africanism, the engine that powered the independence and liberation movements, sought both political autonomy and a self-assuredness that manifested itself in the experimental nature of African creative arts. The minidresses are of the moment from a global fashion perspective. Taken in Nairobi nine years after Kenya gained its independence, there are echoes of the now familiar celebratory images of liberated youths by photographers such as Malick Sidibé (1935–2016) and Jean Depara (1928–1997). These photographs are forms of self-representation that made pride in being Black and African visible on our own terms.[4] The fashions being worn allowed us to show ourselves to the world as we knew ourselves to be: individuals with diverse beliefs, values, styles and identities. The minidresses, *gèlès*, *dashikis* and so forth demonstrated a sense of agency, as youthful as the new nations themselves. The fashionably dressed young men and women in these photographs represented visually our emerging, newly independent identities. They show the capacity of fashion to reaffirm one's sense of self. This *is* fashion as a self-defining art form.

The African liberation and independence years from the mid- to late 1950s to 1994 are foundational to the narrative of *Africa Fashion* because the political and social reordering that took place galvanized a long period of unbounded creativity culminating in an African cultural renaissance. To attempt to identify the moment when the cultural renaissance reached its zenith would be ill-advised. However, Senegal's poet-president Léopold Senghor's ambitious staging of the 1966 First World Festival of Black Arts, in Dakar, embodied the jubilation and hope of the era, although it was not without its critics. Senghor, like the other leaders, saw art and culture as central to defining independent Africa's role in the global arena. The festival ran for three and a half weeks, the participant list reading like a 'who's who' of Global Africa creatives and intellectuals across all genres, for example Duke Ellington, Frank Bowling, Aimé Césaire, Wole Soyinka and Katherine Dunham.[5] Part 1 of *Africa Fashion* looks at this compelling time, placing fashion into this context. The first chapter, written from a personal and philosophical perspective by Gus Casely-Hayford, explores the cultural renaissance through the lens of fashion. On the day that Ghanaian independence from British colonial rule was announced the cabinet, including Casely-Hayford's uncle Archie, gathered around, dressed in ancestral attire, while Kwame Nkrumah delivered a speech that marked an iconic occasion in the decoupling of Africa from the West. Most photographs of Nkrumah taken prior to this show him wearing a Savile Row-style tailored suit. Similarly, *kente* is a conduit that links the past and the future; in this moment the material that heralded a new path to be forged by African nations. It points to a political awakening in the 1960s that was mediated by images and objects that tell our stories. An awareness of the power of clothing to convey identity connects a community of people, a global diaspora, back to their African heritage in a way that feels tangible, as Casely-Hayford discusses in what he characterizes as an 'ambient' history of the period.

Prior to these pivotal years, the African continent had been arbitrarily divided among the European colonial powers between *c.*1884 and 1891. No attention was paid to existing cultural and societal boundaries. The 'scramble for Africa' was driven by a combination of greed and political posturing, led by Britain, France, the Netherlands (or Holland), Portugal and Spain, who had been present on the continent for some time, alongside Germany and Italy.[6] Through a brutal process of empire-building, Europeans brought their languages, belief systems, ideas and cultural expressions to the continent. They attempted to fit the African nations into their cultural framework, to read and represent each country from their narrow viewpoints. The lack of what Europeans regarded as clothing was deemed a marker of cultural poverty. In some instances, European dress codes were forced upon local people. In Namibia, for example, the 1800s saw Herero women adopting Victorian-style floor-length cloth dresses supported by layers of petticoats that they continue to wear, regarding them now as traditional. Prior to colonization they would have worn leather garments.[7] Similarly, the farthingale entered the fashion vocabulary of the Efik women of Nigeria.[8] Meanwhile, men's accessories such as nineteenth-century-style top hats and bowlers are still worn by chiefs in some coastal West African and southern Nigeria communities.[9] Colonization generated certain modes of thinking, systems of representation, standards of comparison or ways of articulating difference, and set in motion hierarchies of value that ultimately fixed African creativity outside of modernity. Racial and cultural differences became over-simplified.

During decades of colonial rule, African people and their creative expressions were represented as subhuman, something other than civilized, by the European colonizing forces. Nevertheless, Europe's civilizing mission failed to halt identity formation and cultural production underpinned by local sensibilities, including creative self-expression through fashioning the body. Fashion is indeed part of the process through which we experience the unequal distribution of power within society (consider the Herero women, above).[10] However, fashioning the body is also a means through which one can challenge or reaffirm one's position within the social order. The liberation and post-independence years saw new syncretic ways of dressing that provided us with a means with which to refashion our newly negotiated African identities. In these post-colonial moments of shifting power dynamics, cultural identities were refashioned out of the strategic and subconscious interweaving of cultures and performed through the manipulation of dress.[11] It is as though the fashions of the day both set and kept pace with the rhythms of freshly independent lives. The body became a site of transformation and representation, a primary symbol in the 'performances through which modernity [was] conceived, constructed

11
Mohammed Amin
Models taking a break from rehearsals
for a fashion show in downtown
Nairobi, 1972

and challenged in Africa'.[12] The idea that fashion might be a self-defining art form became a reality once more.[13] The notion of fashion as an expression of everyday activism re-materialized.[14] The wrapping of the body in a particular cloth, the donning of a tailored garment chosen with discernment, marked a point in the continent's history that is as significant as emancipation – both a *sankofa*-style return to pre-colonial potency and the embracing of Afro-Modernity.

Artist Sonya Clark's observation that cloth is to the African what monuments are to Westerners underlines the centrality of cloth to this book and to the fashion creatives featured within it.[15] The V&A collection is home to a seemingly insig-nificant strip of printed seersucker cotton (no.12). A closer look reveals the open palm of a hand and the words 'freedom in my hand I bring'. Manufactured in Manchester *c*.1960, the

khaki, lime-green and yellow cloth also bears the Ghanaian coat of arms. This distinctive insignia was originally designed by the artist Nii Amon Kotei and was introduced on 4 March 1957. The piece of seersucker is in fact a commemorative cloth created to celebrate Nkrumah's independent Ghana. The detail of Kotei's multicoloured design has been simplified so that it can be easily rendered for mass production. The central shield, the supporting eagles and the star, perhaps the most emotive elements, are still clear to see despite the reduction in colour and line detail. In the original, the flash of red found in the ribbons around the necks of the eagles and in the text symbolizes the blood of those who had died in the independence struggle. The gold usually used to depict the eagles, the garland, portions of the shield and the outline of the star symbolizes Ghana's mineral wealth. The black star is a universal symbol of African emancipation. These sentiments are not lost in the crinkle of this mass-produced Manchester print. Commemorative cloths such as this, manufactured mainly overseas prior to independence, are a visible expression of community concerns as well as identities, be they national, communal or individual. They typically commemorate important historical moments, people or events, artfully bringing together social commentary and creativity. It is intriguing to imagine how this cloth might have been worn. Perhaps it was used to make a trendy minidress like the one worn by the woman in the Amin photograph or perhaps a more conservative style such as *kaba* and *slit*. What is certain is that the wearer would have made an eye-catching statement about her- or himself, and about the renewed agency of the African nations on the international political stage during this period.

In chapter two, Roslyn Walker delves more deeply into the subject of cloth. It is not a comprehensive history of cloth in Africa, as clearly that would be impossible in the space available. Starting with textiles from the V&A collection such as *àdìrẹ* and commemorative print cloth, Walker explores aspects of the role of cloth, its significance across the continent, and in particular the impact of Malian *bògòlanfini* on haute couture and interior design in the Global North. Cloth, passed from generation to generation, seen in different contexts, worn and used for different occasions, has the power to unlock memories and to tell our stories. Traditionally *bògòlanfini* was deemed to have magical properties through the geometric symbols used in its patterning and was originally worn by hunters as a form of protection and by young women undergoing initiation into adulthood.[16] It is now an international fashion fabric, initially repurposed and popularized by designer Chris Seydou (1949–1994).

The third chapter brings to the fore the designers working in Africa during the liberation and post-independence years, the first wave of groundbreaking designers to gain attention both across the continent and globally. The work of pioneers Victoria Omọ́rọ́níke Àdùké Fọlashadé 'Shade' Thomas-Fahm (b.1933), Juliana Norteye (1932–1993), Kofi Ansah (1951–2014), Sidahmed Alphadi Seidnaly (b.1957), Zina Guessous (1925–1998), Naïma Bennis (1940–2008), Tamy Tazi (b.1930) and Chris Seydou, alongside their peers, provides a focal point to explore how certain fashions produced during this era not only reflect the social, political and cultural movements of the day, but

also facilitated a reimagining of the past and the future (nos 13–15). They allowed us to revalorize and integrate aspects of our histories, our cultures and ourselves, their seasonal collections echoing our processes of becoming. The new sartorial languages they created constituted different tones of a syncretic non-verbal 'nation language';[17] a language of fashion deployed in the creation and communication of our proudly independent Black and African selves; a language of fashion that expressed a modernity and cosmopolitanism crucial to the newly decolonized African nations. These mid-twentieth-century designers attracted international consumers, not least those of African heritage, awakened by the Black Power Movement's slogan 'Black is Beautiful' (nos 16, 17).

Throughout the struggle for liberation and post-independence, dressing in fabrics and fashions connected to one's cultural history constituted a highly political statement. At home and abroad politicians and first ladies adopted richly patterned handwoven cloths such as *kente*, beads, embroidered and draped garments, sending a powerful visual statement to the rest of the world – a statement readily transmitted via international newsreels, newspapers and magazines. Frantz Fanon observed that, in the post-colonial moment, the rediscovery of one's cultural identity becomes an urgent matter, the object of 'passionate research'.[18] The reason for such 'passionate research' in his view is that colonization 'turns to the past of oppressed people, and distorts, disfigures and destroys it.'[19] However, this research goes beyond an unearthing of pre-colonial histories in the manner of an archaeological dig, but rather what takes place is a *retelling* of the past; its rediscovery was a creative act. This is a defining feature of many art forms and cultural expressions produced in the years following liberation and independence, in the midst of Africa's cultural renaissance. Fashion was no exception.

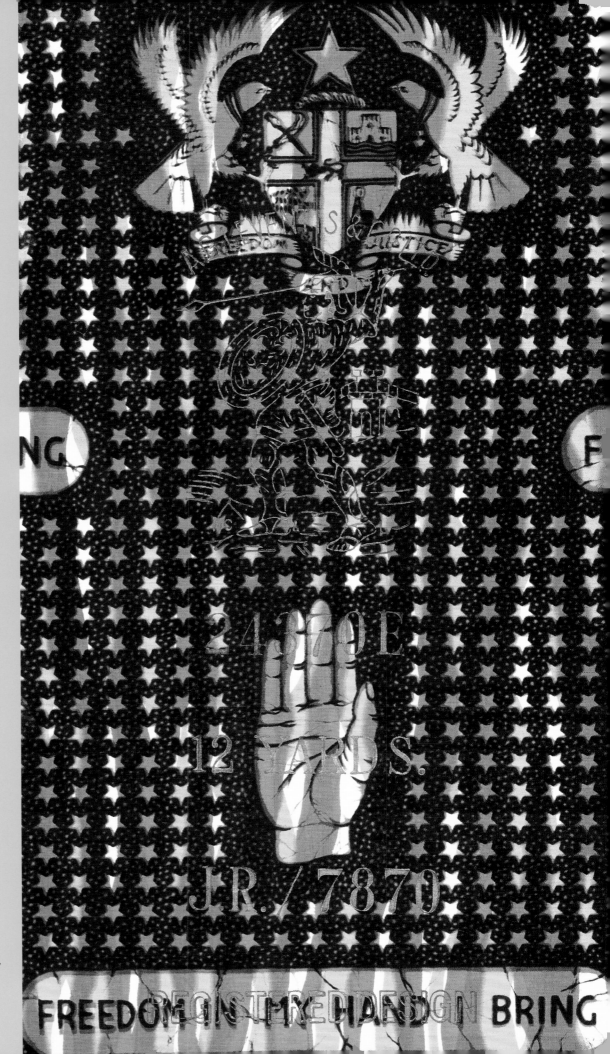

12
Manufactured by A.G. Leventis & Co.
'Freedom in my hand I bring', dress fabric,
printed cotton
Manchester, England, *c.*1960
Bequeathed by Miss Mary Kirby
V&A: Circ.299–1964

13
Designed by Chris Seydou
Bògòlanfini ensemble
Mali, 1991
Photographed in Grand–Bassam,
Côte d'Ivoire, by Nabil Zorkot

14
Shade Thomas–Fahm
Group wearing Nigerian print fabric
Nigeria, 1960s

15
Designed by Alphadi
Jacket
Niger, 1993
Photographed by Loïc Quentin

17
Shade Thomas-Fahm
'Olowu dudu' aṣọ-òkè dansiki with flat
stitched embroidery
Nigeria
Photographed in the USA, *c.*1972

16
Kwame Brathwaite
Grandassa models, part of the 'Black is Beautiful'
movement, alongside founding members of the
African Jazz-Art Society and Studio
New York City, USA, 1968

Many of us growing up in the diaspora recall snapshots of fashionably dressed uncles, aunties and cousins from back home. Whether black-and-white or colour, these treasured photographs passed from person to person, continent to continent, telling stories not just of the changing fashions but also of an aspirational modernity and cosmopolitanism. The democratisation of photography through the emergence of cheaper cameras and keenly priced film made self-representation on a grand scale possible.

These family portraits are a selection shared with us through a public call-out for post-independence images, with the majority of respondents hailing from Nigeria and Ghana. Each photograph captures the beauty, elegance and stylishness of the sitter. And each has the power to trigger personal memories of what we wore when and why. – *CC*

Opposite, left to right, top to bottom:

18 Princess Abioye Sherfiat Balogun nee Ojora, Olowogbowo, Lagos Island, 1976

19 Sheri Ajayi, Ebute Metta, Lagos, 1978

20 Prince Ajibade Ojora with Kehinde Danmol, Ebute Metta, Lagos, 1978

21 Monica Mbeledogu and friends, Enugu, Nigeria, *c.*1950s

22 Monica Mbeledogu and friends, Enugu, Nigeria, *c.*1950s

23 Dinah Osei (left) and friend, Kumasi, Ghana, 1967

24 Elizabeth Teteh, Dora Photo Works, Cape Coast, Ghana, 1969

25 Dinah Osei (right) and friend Kumasi, Ghana, 1967

26 Esther Suwaola, Akure, Ondo, Nigeria, 1960

27 Bright Owusu-Boateng (left) and his friend Agyeman, Accra, Ghana, 1957

28 Mary Kufuor and sister Rose Owusu-Boateng (both née Abrokwah), Accra, Ghana, 1966

29 Rose Owusu-Boateng, Accra, Ghana, 1968

30 Lawumi Ojesina, Ibadan, Nigeria, 1986

31 Rachel Adesida (left), Alice Beckley (right), Ibadan, Nigeria, 1984

32 Nora Ablordeppy, Birmingham, England, 1960s

33 Philip Osei-Baidoo, Cape Coast, Ghana, 1970s

WE FACE FORWARD

Gus Casely-Hayford

There were shouts of 'silence', but they were simply ignored. There was an occasional stern 'shush' from the front but voices, though palpably tired and discernibly hoarse, were defiant and the sounds of celebration continued. Every so often there was a momentary lull and then, spontaneously, laughter, calls and cheers erupted again, echoing out across the Accra rooftops. This night had been long planned, hoped for, prayed for. The irresistible tension was a long time in the building. After years of waiting, decades of petitioning, generations of campaigning, this evening of 6 March 1957 was the culmination of an interminable process of Bills and legal deputations, of international congresses and coalitions, of lost lives and broken hearts, of setbacks and sacrifice. That wait was now at an end. It was the close of a chapter of the African colonial story in which hundreds of thousands were forcibly enslaved, millions killed in wars and resistance struggles and the continent's populace put to work to fuel the empire machine. Although international business had colluded in the reconfiguration of the continent's industries to the benefit of others, and although the world had turned a blind eye to the systematic undermining and dissolution of cultural infrastructure, and the investment in racist theory – here, in a few brief minutes, that axis of commercial and political interests was arrested, and a new story began.

From the darkness at the side of the stage emerged half a dozen men, silhouetted before they found the light at the apex of a rickety podium (no.34). There was a roar and then for the first time that evening there was sustained silence, a colony's, a continent's inhalation of air before the words started, before the delivery of one of the most important passages of oratory ever spoken on African soil. 'At long last the battle has ended...' began Dr Kwame Nkrumah, the first president of Ghana.[1]

The USA had sent Vice President Richard Nixon and the civil rights leader Dr Martin Luther King; the Duchess of Kent represented Queen Elizabeth II; the Soviet Union sent a telegram – an open invitation to the first African leader of a post-colonial state in the southern regions – but Nkrumah stared out beyond them all. On this evening he was not here to court the world powers, but rather to renegotiate his continent's relationship with itself. As he defined it, this was not just a political, economic and constitutional rebirth, but also a spiritual renaissance, an occasion on which to reveal a new national anthem, a new flag, a new cultural optimism. Nkrumah's independent Ghana would look neither East nor West but towards the future. Its greatest ally would be time, both this fledgling nation's destined glorious future, but also the past. The new president wanted to rally his people around Africa's systematically maligned but beautiful heritage. Martin Luther King described it as 'a new order coming into being...of the universe being on the side of justice'.[2] Nkrumah, the Osagyefo ('the redeemer'), named his new nation Ghana after the pre-colonial African kingdom, a state untarnished by the colonial blight, and went on to say, 'we have a duty to prove to the world that Africans can conduct their own affairs with efficiency and tolerance and through the exercise of democracy. We must set an example to all Africa.'[3] The podium shook with his passion, reverberations that would be felt beyond West Africa, a clarion call that would touch a diaspora divided by oceans, inspire a race united on this night by hope that this was the long-awaited moment of change. It felt appropriate, therefore, that the men at the core of this pioneering cabinet were dressed not by Savile Row, but in the clothing of West Africa, in the attire of their ancestry, in the cloth of their magnificent new Ghana. It was only right that the future, like the past, was one of the *agbádás, dashikis* and *boubous* of their African forefathers.

My uncle, Archie Casely-Hayford (standing on the extreme left of the photography overleaf), was a lawyer and strategist who had helped establish the Convention People's Party, earning the nickname 'defender of the veranda boys' over years of bailing out his friends and political allies in colonial courts. Here that middle-class, internationally educated band of brothers, who had plotted and planned this moment on the verandas and in the bars of Accra's gentlemen's clubs (institutions with strict dress codes), looked into the face of destiny dressed in African clothing. Archie, Cambridge-educated, his crumpled tailored shirt probably made in London, his horn-rimmed spectacles likely to have been acquired in Europe, wore upon his back and across his shoulders a traditional *agbádá*. Like the whole inner circle of government, these men, more often seen in brogues and Bond Street suits, chose when it mattered African attire. They calculated the particular power of African cloth to be as eloquent as any speech in creating the appropriate visual link on this highly significant occasion. They saw the potential for post-colonial Africa to forge emotional touchpoints that might reach out across geography and generation, but to be rooted in Africa.

This was a sartorial strategy developed over decades of political campaigning. Archie Casely-Hayford would have seen his own father, Joseph (also a Cambridge-educated barrister), one of the pioneering African nationalists, adopting both traditional *kente* and lawyers' gowns to navigate his early career (nos 36, 37). He used *kente* to forge support among traditional political allies, while his suits, wing collars and barristerial gowns offered the visual gravitas that colonial civil servants could read. These men understood the necessary cultural compromises, but they had also learned when to draw the line. In 1924 Archie's father had defended the exiled and incarcerated Asante king, Prempeh I, whose utter submission and humiliation at the hands of the British had been catalytic

in galvanizing the development of this new nation. The Asante king, regarded by many as a living deity, a man whose ancestors had ruled the most powerful kingdom in the region, had been forced to grovel publicly, to beg 'for pity and mercy'.[4] To make matters worse, the British governor, Sir Frederick Mitchell Hodgson, had not only ignored the king's requests for clemency, but also demanded that, as governor, he be gifted the golden stool of Asante, one of the most venerated symbols of state, so that he might sit upon it in public. This strangely spiteful British strategy, designed to force the local population to yield to the imperial yoke, ironically became a recruiting sergeant of anti-colonial sentiment. Interpreted as acts of wilful disrespect, the British tactics inadvertently conferred an added resonance upon traditional cultural symbols, inspiring a wave of West African nationalism. The people had lost their king; they could not now give up on their golden stool. They would not lose their traditions of dressing, or indeed their fight for freedom. And so, a generation after King Prempeh's humiliation, Archie joined Nkrumah and his 'veranda boys' with particular pride, casting an eye towards a future rooted firmly in an African past. Ghana, then, as the first country in the southern regions to gain independence, became not just a forerunner but somehow a template for the nations that followed.

But alongside the future-thinking independence was a need for time for mourning, for truth and reflection: it was essential for Africa to have a moment to look back at what had been so ruthlessly taken and what might be saved, to consider how Britain's African colonial endeavour had stunted, broken and damaged so much of what it left behind. The therapeutic space required to deliberate upon colonial horrors was considerable. Much of the rage was suppressed; so much anger was sublimated and refashioned into acts of creativity to be played out through music, writing and fashion. The conversation

34
President Kwame Nkrumah delivering his speech at
the Ghanaian Independence ceremony, with Archie
Casely-Hayford, Komla Agbeli Gbedemah, Kojo
Botsio and Krobo Edusei, wearing *agbádás*, *kente* and
dashikis, Accra, Ghana, 6 March 1957

about how Africa might navigate the post-colonial cultural
arena became the constellation of concerns that concentrated
the minds of a creative generation. How could a continent build
upon such profound damage? It was a novelist who captured
it best.

Chinua Achebe had grown up in colonial south-east Nigeria,
his father a teacher, his mother a farmer. He had seen the
corrosive impacts of the imperial programme upon traditional
life and the cost upon the psyche of its subjects. In his 1958
novel *Things Fall Apart* he crafted a forensic and unforgiving
examination of a family and community divided by colonialism,
and of the complex collateral damage of such momentous
change (no.41). There are no heroes in Achebe's tale. Okonkwo,
the troubled protagonist, is a wrestling champion, an unrecon-
structed bully who kills a young boy placed in his care. It is an
act so perverse and appalling that it seems to disrupt natural

causality, to tip the universe off its footings, triggering a slow,
but inexorable unravelling of everything he values, a cascade
of terrible events that trip and collide one upon another,
reconstituting the world around him. His son is pulled out
of his sphere of influence, and control is leeched from every
area of his life, as the tightening clamp of alien cultures and
colonialism choke away freedom, pride and eventually heritage
and voice. The novel captures the complexity of impacts of
empire, of the cultural costs and corrupting void left in its
wake. It describes an alienation that many recognized. It was
this acculturated trauma that President Nkrumah's thesis of
African pride sought to address. The pain, dysfunction and loss
would need to be fashioned into something new.

Many, particularly the young, did not wish to spend any longer
than absolutely necessary looking back. The emancipation of
a continent, the founding of nations, heralded new freedom

35
J.E. Casely Hayford in suit and tie
Gold Coast (now Ghana), *c.*1915

36
J.E. Casely Hayford wearing *kente*
Probably Sekondia, Gold Coast (now
Ghana), *c.*1905

and opportunity in numerous unexpected areas. As the
colonial mantle rolled back, so did many of its associated social
values. The stuffy colonial clubs with their rules and mores,
frequented by 'veranda boys', began to feel old-fashioned.
The young wanted bars and music halls; to flirt and drink
and dance and to dress up. When the jazz musician Louis
Armstrong toured West Africa in 1956, 10,000 fans greeted
him at Accra airport and 100,000 more attended an open-air
concert. Young people wanted to let go, to embrace the
possibilities of continental culture, of global style, of Africa
fashions. Alongside the political tumult, their lust for cultural
renewal demanded seismic change. They longed to enjoy
fashion and all the sartorial choices that they felt denied. They
needed to document this moment of liberation and they found
the perfect mechanism to do so.

Of course, African portrait photography was not new, but in
the late 1950s it was completely remade as a craft. A generation
of African photographers began to make new kinds of images,
photographs that were not conceived just to be hung on
parlour walls. These were testing, daring pictures loaded and
encoded with risqué narrative and nuance: images that young
men carried in wallets, that young girls hid at the back of their
top drawer. The ambient atmosphere of liberation shifted
sexual politics, emboldening the young and changing the tone
of West African studio portrait photography – and with it,
fashion. Fast shutter speeds, cheap development processes
and new studios all meant that portraiture no longer needed
to record a lifetime. These were celebrations of the briefest
and most personal of moments, capturing style and previously
un-photographed attitudes – this was fashion and all that
fashion would come to represent. We did not only want to know
who he was, but where he bought that jacket, those glasses,

that sophisticated attitude – we simply wanted to know him (no.37). The choice of the light linen suit, the uniform of the colonial civil servant, is here utterly subverted by its wide lapels and tapering lines. This is not someone preparing for a day's work, but for an evening of flirtation. The flower, the fountain pen, even the glasses – not the horn-rimmed tools of study, but frames through which we might see the honest almost vulnerable look in his eyes. The best photographers, like Seydou Keïta, understood what this time of liberation required and created through their photography the platforms for a new kind of fashion. And they delivered.

In the period after independence Jamestown, one of the oldest parts of Ghana's capital, a stone's throw from the seat of government, attracted a constellation of new photography studios. They housed an exceptional generation of artists who were as creatively radical and conceptually revolutionary as the moment itself. They pushed Keïta's project further, wanting to upturn the tables of their art and not just capture the truth of everyday lives, but to use their lenses to hold the great and the good to account. James Barnor's Ever Young Studio, James Koblah Bruce-Vanderpuije's Deo Gratias Studio and Mrs Felicia Abban's Day and Night Quality Art Studio offered a vérité honesty, providing a platform upon which the previously invisible were afforded rightful attention, and charting the big, globe-altering events that were changing West African politics.

These studios captured Nkrumah's early successes in galvanizing pan-African unity as new African governments and intra-continental alliances began to take shape. Nkrumah acted as the convener. In late 1958 he gathered some of the continent's political superstar heads-of-state-in-waiting to craft a pan-African road map. The delegates shared ideology and history, but they navigated their cultural choices very differently, something that manifested itself powerfully through their wardrobes. Kenneth Kaunda, Zambia's president-in-waiting, arrived in Accra in his characteristic safari suit and a silk cravat. It was an idiosyncratic take on a well-worked tropical look, but Kaunda's suits were cut to speak to this historic moment: sophisticated yet practical, with V-shaped flaps above each breast pocket resembling an army officer's tunic, light colours drawn from the colonial civil service, gently flared trousers with a civilian profile. It was an outfit that balanced a variety of conventions, but it sent a

message of practicality, modernity and readiness to act. The other star of the gathering was the 34-year-old Patrice Lumumba, president of the Congolese National Movement, young, brilliant, dashing and immaculately dressed: he wore bespoke, fitted suits, finished with perfect crisp white shirts (no.38). Lumumba would have looked at home on the executive floor of a Fifth Avenue advertising agency, but he cut his look with a thin bow-tie or a leopard-skin smoking cap. This was a man whose outfits flamboyantly rejected military aesthetics; his clothes suggested he was someone with a hinterland. Every detail of Lumumba's wardrobe seemed researched, considered, curated. He did not wear the wide-brimmed fedora of the district commissioner or a long-peaked cap to suggest military gravitas. He wore the least practical hat imaginable: a smoking cap (originally donned by Victorian dandies seeking to protect their hair from tobacco smoke) but re-crafted in leopard skin.

In the company of such charismatic peers, Nkrumah may have realized that he lacked something of their style and cosmo-politan ease. It is said that when Nkrumah heard that Louis Armstrong was coming to West Africa, he was reported to have asked, 'Is it that boxer?'[5] Although he exhibited incomparable political instinct, it could be argued that his awareness of shifting ambient cultural attitudes was more limited. Even in the earliest months of his administration some felt that he was not keeping up with his people's appetite to quicken the pace of change. He would not respond with words, but instead he would turn to the photographer Felicia Abban, not to offer a veneer of coolness, but to reveal to his people something of his particular humanity.

This young photographer was offered special access to record this chapter of Ghana's history from within. She found a way to give the political elite the approachable intimacy that they perhaps did not project. Abban told the story of the inner world of the president and his cabinet, humanizing a figure who had realized the impossible. Her obvious affection and respect for Nkrumah, caught in avuncular visual vignettes, introduced Ghana to another side of the father of the nation, a man equally comfortable in traditional *kente* or casual Western shirts. It was Abban's photography that revealed a more emotionally intelligent and thoughtful Nkrumah. Abban turned the lens back upon herself in a series of nightly self-portraits, taken

37
Seydou Keïta
Untitled (Young Man with a Flower),
Mali, 1958 (photographed), 2001 (printed)
Gelatin-silver print
Given by Hackelbury Fine Art Ltd.
V&A: E.1419-2001

38
Patrice Lumumba, first President of the
Democratic Republic of the Congo,
wearing his trademark leopard print
hat, 1960

as she was about to leave to attend functions alongside the great and the good (no.39). These self-portraits tell the story of this new nation's ferocious political and social dynamism, but, as the 1960s arrived, her choices of fabric also reflected Ghana's exposure to a torrent of international cultural influences. Abban's shifting hemlines and silhouette captured Africa's changing sexual politics and renegotiation of its relationship to tradition. Her wardrobe embodied the growing confidence of women and their style. Fashion had become the bellwether of a blooming continent; it exposed a gap between the complex expectations of Africa's populations and what the new governments would and could deliver. Young people increasingly looked beyond the continent for their role models, their influences and answers. Fashion crafted a cultural space in which the momentum of a meta-revolution could strengthen alongside the forces of decolonialization. The pace of these developments was now in the wind, beyond geography and politics, an energy building through shared music, media and film into a force that would touch the young of every nation.

As the domino effect of toppling colonial regimes swept beyond West Africa to impact the east, north and central regions of the continent, Southern African colonies simply tightened their grip upon their populations and began to turn their backs on the world. But even the psychotic fanaticism of these Southern African regimes could not extinguish the ambient desire for change. It would be in the cultural arena that illegal topics could continue to be explored. Miriam Makeba grew up in a Johannesburg township, discovering music through school choirs. Her earliest professional performances were as part of a group inspired by the swing of the Andrews Sisters, but she made those harmonies into something all her own. By the late 1950s Makeba and her Skylarks had become one of the most successful South African vocal groups, known for mixing boogie-woogie with the four-part harmonies that originated in the Zulu mining communities. It was music that did everything that apartheid abhorred, beautifully and seamlessly mixing varied cultural influences and acting as a potent advert for a different kind of nation. The Skylarks slipped between English, Xhosa and Zulu, their joy transcending the barriers that their government had invested a huge amount of energy constructing. Makeba made her music with such zest that she became a billboard for stunning African fabrics and for dresses crafted into exquisite shapes that came alive as she performed (no.4). She flaunted her glamorous looks and African identity in ways that felt incendiary to the authorities, wrapping her hair in printed cloth or braiding it into long locks. She was fearless with it all, unafraid to speak out about the beauty of Black bodies, or when necessary, the moral bankruptcy of the government. She became a symbol of defiance and hope, young women copying her style and wardrobe, young men echoing the sentiment of Black pride. As she left South Africa to attend the Venice film festival in 1959, the government simply locked the door behind her, barring her return. But as she proved again and again, this kind of challenge only inspired her creativity and deepened her commitment to justice. She had demonstrated how culture, how fashion, could have a role in servicing African democracy, holding the powerful to account, and how clothing could help build meaningful continental connections between people, to offer voices to the marginalized that would not be silenced easily.

Over the course of the 1960s the dream of a coalition of independent African nations was severely tested. Nkrumah, 'the pan-African redeemer', was driven by a coincidence of Shakespearean circumstance to supply troops to the UN to help unseat his friend Lumumba within months of the young president taking office, ultimately facilitating the assassination of Congo's first president. A comparable constellation of internal and external forces subsequently combined to overthrow Nkrumah himself. While visiting China on a mission to petition for an end to the Vietnam War, Nkrumah was informed by Premier Zhou Enlai that his government had been toppled by a cabal of mid-ranking Ghanaian army officers. Although the ultimate momentum towards African independence was unaffected by these and similar events, it was more than evident that the reality of post-independence Africa would not resemble the dream. It was apparent that the tentacles of the Old-World order remained as strong and insidious as ever, and the potential for those that surrounded these fledgling African governments to be corrupted by money and power was equally potent.

It was, again, a musician who spoke truth to power most effectively. After being released from prison in 1989, Fela Kuti detonated an electrifying album upon Africa. *Beasts of No Nation* condemned the post-independence generation

39
Felicia Abban
Self-portrait wearing *kente* and lace
Accra, Ghana, *c.*1960

of lost politicians, lamenting the missed opportunities and broken lives (no.40). Kuti caught the mood, with tracks that cut through the bull with his particular clarity; it was time to listen, it was time to wage 'war against indiscipline, ee-oh/ Na Nigerian government, ee-oh/ Dem dey talk ee-oh'.[6] Kuti's call to arms was not a lone cry in the darkness. The album tapped into the wider cultural backdrop of the continent's crippling frustrations and bitter disappointment with its politicians and business communities, but it also reflected the indefatigable energy of Africa's creative sectors and their irrepressible drive to create beautiful things in the face of unimaginable challenges. In claiming fellowship of 'No Nation', Fela embraced the disenfranchisement that many felt, arguing that it was in creativity that the pan-African dream lived, that it was through culture that the sense of diasporic connectedness was experienced most palpably, and that it was so often artists who captured the mood of the people most affectingly. And, as Christine Checinska shows in her essay highlighting the role of mid-century African fashion designers (p.64), without doubt the arena in which ordinary Africans achieved that connectivity most accessibly was fashion. Through cloth and textile, through cutting and tailoring, through affordable brilliant street fashion, the continent's citizens uncompromisingly pushed back, reaching out and building links across geography and difference in celebrating the infectious irrepressible genius of Africa fashions.

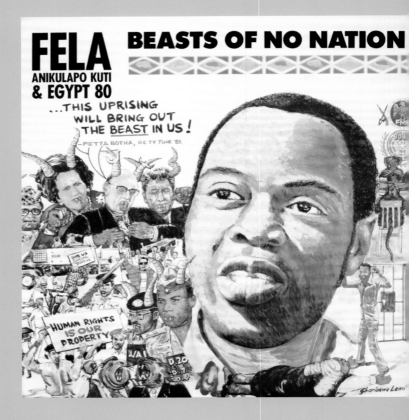

40
Fela Kuti
Beasts of No Nation,
Album cover artwork by Lemi Ghariokwu
Shanachie Records, 1989

50th Anniversary Edition

THINGS FALL APART

Chinua Achebe

41
Chinua Achebe
Things Fall Apart, 1958
Cover artwork by Edel Rodriguez
This edition, 2009

FIVE FRAGMENTS OF AFRICAN TEXTILE HISTORY

Roslyn A. Walker

'Cloth is to the African what monuments are to Westerners'

El Anatsui citing Sonya Clark, 2003

Among the Victoria and Albert Museum's millions of objects are clothing and textiles that reflect the tastes of African people and the methods by which they have made and decorated cloth for hundreds of years. Drawing on the collection, this text discusses five objects that exemplify some of the textile traditions and foreign cloths that have become the foundation and inspiration for contemporary fashions designed by African and other couturiers. They are documents of African textile history: small fragments of a rich history that incorporates hundreds if not thousands of textile techniques from across the continent.

Wax print

'Fancy print', 'wax print', 'Dutch wax print' and 'African trade cloth' are among the names for European manufactured cloths that have been sold in the southern regions of Africa for more than a century but are now produced on the continent and in China.[1] The history of this type of cloth begins in the Netherlands in 1846 when factory-printed reproductions of *batik* cloth from Java failed to sell in markets in the Dutch East Indies (modern Indonesia). The venture was unsuccessful because the mechanical process, which replicated the Javanese wax-resist technique, had an unintended technical fault. As the resistant resin dried up, it cracked and inadvertently made small veins and spots on the cloths. The Javanese did not like the crackling effect and refused to buy the cloth. The Dutch subsequently marketed the cloth in West Africa where it was successful because the 'marks of imperfection' made each cloth unique, a desirable quality. By the late nineteenth century, European manufacturers had created special departments dedicated to studying African tastes and styles

in order to design, manufacture and market the new fabric in Africa. Ideally, the imported cloths would replace those made locally.[2] Brown Fleming Ltd was one of the most successful textile factories that exported wax prints to British-controlled territories in West Africa from the late 1880s to 1912. It was founded by Ebenezer Brown Fleming (1858–1912), a Scottish merchant, who, through contacts with Gold Coast Colony missionaries, such as at the Basel Mission, learned about Africans' desire for superior-quality textiles, their tastes, and the role textile design played in projecting their social status, beliefs and other information they wished to convey to viewers. He also increased the dimensions of the cloths for taller African customers. Fleming initially had his cloths manufactured by HKM (Haarlemsche Katoen Maatschapprj) in the Netherlands, but established his own company in 1895 in Glasgow and obtained trademarks for his own designs and others he had appropriated.[3]

This wax print sample (no.42), thought to be skirt fabric, was designed in 1909 and sold on the Gold Coast (mostly modern Ghana) markets. Boldly drawn dresses, alternately inverted and separated by two *batik* crackle-effect white or ochre weft bands, are drawn flat on a dark blue 'indigo-coloured' ground. Consistent with the current fashion in Britain, the dresses have high collars and whittled waists. The designs on the dresses include images of hearts in medallions, black and white hands shaking in greeting within opposing hearts connected by three chains, and gold chain links with heart pendants. Cloth with such designs would have been attractive to African members of fraternal orders (such as the Freemasons, the Orange Order and the Oddfellows) who would have understood them to be

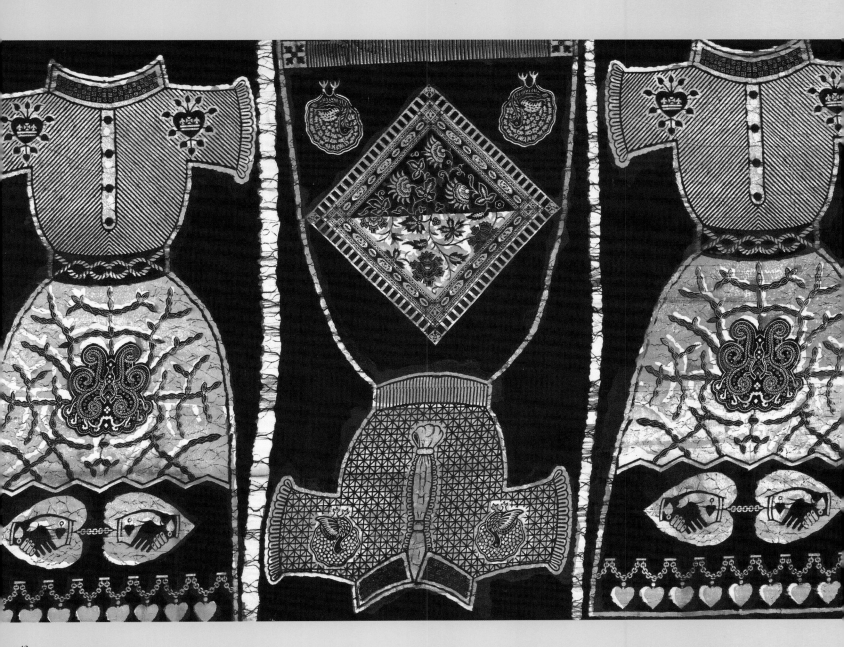

42
Brown Fleming Ltd (merchant)
Sample of printed cloth, cotton
Netherlands/Great Britain/Switzerland, designed 1909
V&A: T.167–2004

symbols of friendship, love and truth.[4] The peacocks, according to Christian belief, symbolize eternal life. It is likely that a skirt made of this wax print would have identified a Gold Coast woman as the spouse of a member of one of these fraternities and therefore projected her family's aspirations and affiliations under British colonial rule.

Commemorative cloth

Factory-printed commemorative cotton cloth is made to order by roller printing or, currently, rotary-screen printing. It was and continues to be made to celebrate and document significant events such as milestone anniversaries, to promote new ideas that will benefit society, and to celebrate the election of local and select foreign politicians (for example, Baraka Obama, the first African American president of the USA) and the inauguration of traditional rulers and heads of state.[5] While I cannot cite with certainty the first African political commemorative cloth, it is probably one from Ghana, the first of Britain's African colonies to gain independence in 1957. Within borders of black stars and framed with bunting is a central medallion with a silkscreened black-and-white portrait of Kwame Nkrumah on a green ground. The banner beneath the portrait reads: 'First Prime Minister Doctor Kwame Nkrumah'. Above the lower border are the Ghana coat of arms with a banner reading 'Freedom and Justice' alternating with two crossed Ghanaian flags and a banner reading 'March 6, 1957, Ghana Independence'.[6]

The commemorative cloth shown here (no.43) was made in the early 1990s following the release of Nelson Mandela, a co-organizer of the African National Congress (ANC) Youth League and soon to be South Africa's first Black president. The design of the cloth follows that of earlier ones with top and bottom borders, a central medallion, and national crests or party symbols. Narrow bands of black, green and yellow from the ANC flag appear above a repeat pattern of wheels that symbolize industry and moving forward. Beneath the wheels and floating on a green ground with a *batik* crackle-effect, a series of ANC slogans are displayed in capital letters: 'A BETTER LIFE FOR ALL · WORKING TOGETHER FOR JOBS, PEACE AND FREEDOM'. Flanking Mandela's silkscreened portrait in the central medallion, which is surrounded by solid green, are the ANC logo of a shield with a right hand holding the party's flag flying from a spear, and pairs of large

and small wheels. The wide bottom border displays a series of conjoined ANC logos above the manufacturer's symbol on the lower selvedge.

Àdìrẹ

Àdìrẹ is a resist-dyed cloth that has been made by the Yorùbá of south-western Nigeria since at least the nineteenth century. It was originally associated with the towns of Abeokuta and Ibadan, which were renowned for *àdìrẹ* made exclusively by women and used to make women's wrappers and men's sleepwear. The word *àdìrẹ* literally means 'to tie' (*adi*) and 'dye' (*re*), but it is applied to any technique that protects certain areas of the fabric from being penetrated by the dye to create patterns on a solid colour background. The Yorùbá practice four *àdìrẹ* techniques: *oniko*: 'the one-with-raffia', where the cloth is tied, pinched or folded with raffia thread; *eléso*: 'the one-with-seeds', where seeds are tied into the cloth to create circular patterns; *aláḅẹ́rẹ́*: 'the one-with-a needle', where stitches are made by hand with raffia thread or a sewing machine with cotton thread to resist the dye; and *eléko*: 'the one-with-corn-pap', where a starchy paste (originally made with corn but now with cassava) or candle wax is applied to the cloth to block the dye.[7] Once the exclusive preserve of women, men now engage in the practice but use zinc stencils to create the designs, which is less laborious than painting freehand.

According to tradition, mothers or older female relatives taught girls how to make *àdìrẹ* and to colour it with dye prepared from leaves of wild indigo plants, resulting in deep shades of blue after repeating the steps of dipping, oxidation, drying and rinsing. Some *àdìrẹ* makers sent the cloth to an *aláró*, 'the owner of the dye', who had special knowledge of the long and painstaking process. Both European cotton cloth and synthetic indigo were introduced in the 1920s. While the imported cloth was accepted because it took the dye better than the domestic cloth, the synthetic dye was initially met with resistance in favour of the local product.

The popularity of *àdìrẹ* has risen and fallen over the decades. Prior to the 1960s, *àdìrẹ* was commonly made by women who had no formal education and spoke only Yorùbá. These women usually belonged to families, often Muslim, that were involved in the cloth trade. To the educated middle classes that were evolving within the context of British colonialism, *àdìrẹ*,

43
Nkosi Traditional Fabrics CC
ANC Nelson Mandela commemorative cloth,
printed cotton
Akasia, South Africa, 1991
Given by Christine Checinska
V&A: T.2418–2021

traditional clothing and the makers represented backwardness. However, this negative attitude changed in the early 1960s when a group of Nigerian and expatriate avant-garde young men began to wear shirts of *àdìrẹ*, thereby making the cloth fashionable among educated people.[8] Today, *àdìrẹ* fashions can be found on runways both as hand-painted or factory-printed cloth.

The superb example of an indigo-dyed *àdìrẹ elẹ́kọ* cloth overleaf (no.44) was produced in Ibadan during the early 1960s by an *àdìrẹ* artist whose signature, a scorpion, is drawn on the underside of the cloth. The cloth was made into a woman's wrapper and is composed of two lengths of cloth that, after being dyed, were sewn together along the wider dimension. The maker painted the patterns with cassava starch paste on one side of the cloth, probably using a brush of chicken feathers and the midrib of a palm leaf to draw lines of different thicknesses and matchsticks to create dots. She divided each length of cloth into 28 rectangles and filled them with representational or stylized images of trees, leaves, fowls, reptiles, umbrellas and Ifa divination trays, among other objects.[9] This entire cloth has a total of 56 designs, seven of which are repeated four times, seven twice, three that appear twice on one half of the cloth and once on the other, and five that appear only once.

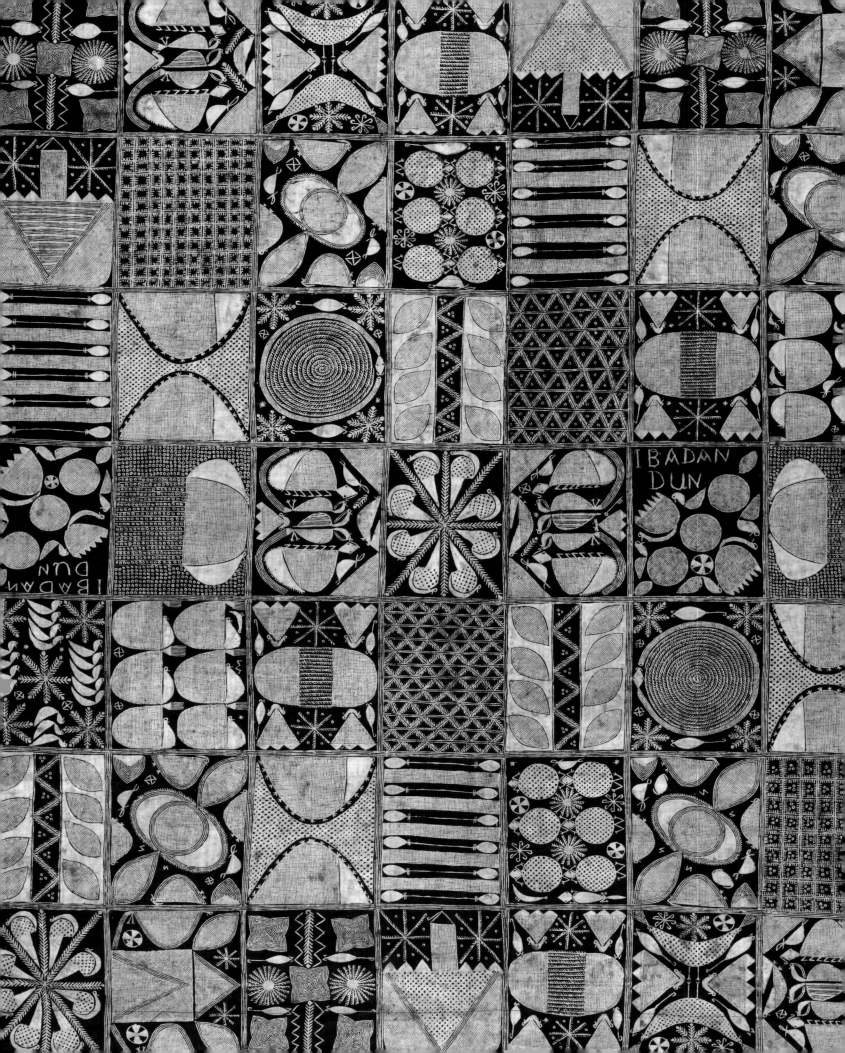

44 (opposite and left)
Àdìrẹ ẹlẹ́ckọ cloth in *Ibadan Dun* pattern
Cotton, natural indigo, replica top and *gèlè*
Ibadan, Nigeria, 1960–7
V&A: CIRC.588–1965
Styled in consultation with Shade Thomas-Fahm

45
Detail of textile, strip-woven
Ghana, Ewe, mid-twentieth century
Cotton
Bequeathed by Miss Mary Kirby
V&A: CIRC.321–1964

Like all older *àdìrę* cloths, this one has a name: *Ibadandun* (or *Ibadan Dun*), which means 'Ibadan is sweet (pleasant or good)' in Yorùbá and is written on the cloth in capital letters. This is the most complex of all the *àdìrę* cloths. The cloth's name refers to one of the squares of the design filled with a series of pillars from Mapo Hall, a colonial landmark built in 1925–9 on a prominent hill in Ibadan, as well as to spoons or pestles used for pounding food in a mortar. It was created during a period of prosperity when there were many successful harvests and a robust cocoa market.[10] This cloth is distinguished from others by the unprecedented number of times – four – that the Mapo Hall square is repeated and its depiction with five pillars and six spoons. At the time it was made, the quality of such cloths was judged according to the number of spoons alternating with the pillars. The best ones had five spoons, with four being the average and only three on cloth sold to tourists.[11] Unlike most artists, the maker of this extraordinary cloth did not replicate on the second length the placement or even the designs and patterns from the first one.

Kente

To most people, eye-dazzling *kente* cloth is only associated with the Asante of south-central Ghana. However, *kente* is also woven by the Ewe, who came from the east to settle in the Volta region of east-central Ghana and neighbouring Togo during the seventeenth century. In both societies, men wove the cloth on handlooms that produced narrow strips of cloth which were cut and sewn selvedge to selvedge to make a cloth large enough to wrap around a man or a woman. Both Asante and Ewe *kente* cloths feature complex designs made with supplementary horizontal weft floats on the vertical warp strips. While Asante weft float designs are usually geometric, those on Ewe cloths are representational, commonly depicting birds, animals, insects, stools, humans, lettering and the like. However, in contrast to the Asante, who are known as weavers of silk, the Ewe weave mostly cotton yarns and in a wider range of colours. The entrepreneurial Ewe weavers produce silk *kente* on commission for royal customers, including Asante royals. The Asante have one weaving centre at Bonwire, but the Ewe have

four of them in Ghana and Togo, each with a distinctive style. Until *kente* became the national dress in the 1960s, wearing *kente* was the prerogative of the elite leadership. This was not the case among the Ewe, whose chiefs and ordinary citizens alike could commission and wear the cloth.[12]

The *kente* textile above (no.45) comprises 19 narrow strips, enough for a man's wrapper. The dark red/maroon warp strips are decorated with weft float designs of single leaves alternating with blocks of variegated colours achieved by twisting two or more different colours together. This feature is unique to Ewe *kente*. As with Asante *kente*, Ewe patterns are meaningful and may relate to a historical event or a proverb. In Ewe thought, the leaf motif means 'I will survive if I am plucked from the tree'.

Bògòlanfini

Bògòlanfini is the Mandé word for mud cloth. *Bogo* means 'earth' or 'mud', *lan* means 'with' or 'by means of', and *fini* means 'cloth'. It is a discharge-dyed textile made by a number of people in Mali and Burkina Faso but most associated with the Bamana of Mali, especially those living in the towns and rural villages of Beledougou, north of Bamako, the capital.

Precisely how long ago the Bamana began weaving and dyeing cloth is not known, but hundreds of fragments of strip-woven and dyed cotton textiles dating from the eleventh to the sixteenth century have been found in Bandiagara burial caves of the Tellem civilization of Mali.[13] Originally, *bògòlanfini* was used to make tunics for hunters and warriors, and wrappers for teenage girls and women. Bamana women wore the wrappers during important periods of transition that involved their blood, for example, excision, the consummation of marriage, childbirth and passing to the afterlife. The graphic patterns on the cloth were not merely decorative but were believed to have protective properties that kept individuals safe.[14]

46
Nakunte Diarra, *bògòlanfini* artist
of the Beledougou region
Mali, 1992
Photographed by Tavy D. Aherne

While weaving and sewing the strips together to make the desired yardage was men's work, women traditionally cleaned, carded and spun locally grown cotton into thread. They learned as young girls the complex process of dyeing, designing and painting the cloth from highly skilled female specialists – mothers or other highly skilled women – through long apprenticeships. A woman's wrapper comprises six, seven or eight strips about 15 to 20 cm wide and typically divided into five sections with four bands framing a larger central field. According to some scholars, this grid framework is derived from Islamic amulets or amuletic cloths dating to the time of Bitòn Coulibaly, a Ségou king who reigned in the early eighteenth century. Some ritual patterns are thought to have stayed the same since at least 1900.

Before the cloth could be decorated with geometric motifs, the mud dye had to be prepared. It was made from iron-rich mud collected from large ponds that had evaporated during the dry season and been fermented in jars for several months to a year. First the artist washed the cloth and dried it in the sun. She then dyed the cloth with an infusion of mashed and boiled leaves from the n'gallama (*Anogeissus leiocarpa*) and n'tkemlara (*Combretum glutinosum*) trees, which produced a yellow colour. Next, sitting on a mat on the ground, she draped the part of the cloth on which she would be working on an inverted calabash on her lap and applied fermented dark mud to one side of the cloth with a metal spatula, painting around the designs. After drying, the cloth was washed to remove the mud. She repeated this step until she achieved the desired colour, from gray to reddish-brown or black. The yellow design was removed by retracing it with a concoction made by mixing together then heating peanuts, caustic soda, millet bran and water. After allowing the cloth to dry in the sun for several days, she washed off the soda mixture to reveal a white design on a dark ground.[15] According to one scholar, this dyeing technique, which was unknown in Europe until the beginning of the nineteenth century, required 'considerable scientific or empirical knowledge'.[16]

The V&A's exemplary dark brown and white *bògòlanfini* wrapper (*tafe*) (no.49) was made by an accomplished but unknown *bogolan* artist around 1960. It comprises seven strips sewn together and divided into five sections with two broad and two narrow bands framing the larger central field. It was made before *bògòlanfini* became popular outside of Mali, when the local women commissioned made-to-order cloths rather than buying generic ones at the market. They chose designs to decorate the cloth that are geometric/stylized forms of animals and other objects drawn from the natural world. The designs on this cloth include drums for *griots* (oral historians), a dot within a circle (reference to a particular stream), a cross at the centre of a diamond (a Mauritanian woman's cushion), zigzag lines (twisted roads or legs of a cricket) and others that may refer to Bamana history, mythology, religion and medicine. The designs were known locally, but the patterns created with them formed the owner's personal coded message.

Changes in society brought about by European colonization resulted in a rejection by the educated elites of Yorùbá *àdìrẹ eléko* cloth and *bògòlanfini*, which were associated with rural life, animist practices and a lack of formal education.[17] Attitudes would change over time as some influential individuals of the avant-garde encouraged their countrymen and women to wear traditional fashions as expressions of ethnic pride and national identity. Since the 1970s (some scholars cite the 1980s), *bogolan* designs have become more popular among Malians and have been adapted – sometimes appropriated – by international fashion designers. Among the noteworthy are American couturiers Norma Kamali and Oscar de la Renta (1932–2014).

Where did the designers find inspiration? Did they visit Mali? Europeans had become aware of *bògòlanfini* in the late nineteenth century and examples were eventually acquired by the Musée de l'Homme, Paris, in the 1930s.[18] Perhaps they viewed the *bògòlanfini* tunics and wrappers on display in European museums or in the groundbreaking 1972 *African Textiles and Decorative Arts* exhibition at the Museum of Modern Art in New York.[19] Whatever the source, Kamali was motivated to create her famous African 'Mudd Print' womenswear collection in the early 1980s, which included play clothes, kaftans, blouses, midi-length pencil skirts, and a two-piece ensemble of a sleeveless dress with a T-shirt back and a long bias-cut skirt with a handkerchief hem and a matching long-sleeved jacket (no.47). Neither Mali nor *bògòlanfini* nor *bogolan* is mentioned in connection with her fashions. All garments were made of brown and white cotton and silkscreen-printed. The repeat pattern comprises three designs. Similarly, the short after-five dress that de la Renta designed in 2008 features an enlarged and lively arrangement of the black, white and brown designs found on some *bògòlanfini* wrappers (no.48).

Kamali and de la Renta were not the first fashion designers to be captivated by African design. For example, in 1923 Jessie Franklin Turner (1881–1956), the resident designer for Bonwit Teller in New York City, designed dresses with printed fabric inspired by cut pile and embroidered raffia textiles made by Kuba women in the then Belgian Congo (modern Democratic Republic of the Congo) that were on view at the Brooklyn Institute Museum.[20] Numerous other examples can be cited, including a dress designed by Coco Chanel (1883–1971) in 1930 with Kuba patterns.

Bògòlanfini designs are printed on upholstery fabrics and home furnishings, cookery book covers, book bags, T-shirts and the like, dating from the end of the twentieth century and into the twenty-first century. The popularity of the designs does not wane because they are constantly rediscovered by younger generations.

In Mali in the 1970s *bògòlanfini* began to thrive in contemporary society thanks to the efforts of some local pioneers: Kandioura Coulibaly (1954–2015) and a group known as Bogolan Kasobané, among others.[21] Coulibaly, then a student at the Institut National des Arts de Bamako, became interested in traditional women's methods of dyeing cloth and wrote a thesis on the subject in 1974. He partnered with artist Lamine Sidibé and engaged in the practice. Later Sidibé taught *bogolan* techniques to young people in Mali.

Another *bògòlanfini* activist was Seydou Nourou Doumbia, aka 'Chris Seydou', whose work is discussed further in the next chapter (pp.69-70). The first African fashion designer practicing in Paris, by 1979 Seydou had successfully incorporated traditional dress elements of Malian and other West African cultures in his couture.[22] This important and symbolic act was a turning point in his career, which he continued upon returning to Mali in 1990. He used *bogolan* cloth bought at the tourist market or had plain cloth painted by local Malian artists according to his specifications, to simplify the designs. One of his designs (no.54) is a European-style ensemble composed of a miniskirt, a jacket and a pillbox hat, which presents an artful display of coordinating contrasts. He chose three patterns from the mud cloths, which are painted on grids on the jacket. The bold design of opposing chevrons within nested rectangles on the sleeves is repeated on the skirt. A different set of patterns is featured on the pillbox hat. Seydou reportedly expressed dismay at the adaption of *bògòlanfini* patterns by fabric designers in the USA, including Kamali.[23] He continued to be productive until his death in 1994 and is revered by Malians.

In the early 1980s a group of six artists who had met as students at the Institut National des Arts in Bamako in the mid-1970s formed the Groupe Bogolan Kasobané and began contributing to the revival of traditional dyeing. They established themselves in Ségou where they studied *bogolan* and found ways to improve the dyeing technique for their purposes, which included film-making, stage productions, interior decoration, costume and set designs, and the creation of large-scale paintings for sale in art galleries.[24] They continue to pursue their quest for intellectual and artistic ideals of beauty and cultural preservation.[25]

Textiles are non-verbal records of the various aspects of African life, including the politics, religious practices and social life of groups and individuals; they reveal what was important at the time. Thanks to modern technology and publications like this one, contemporary fashion designers have access to amazing historic textiles that can be integrated into their own designs or inspire them to create something new. One only hopes they will name the source of that inspiration and give credit where credit is due.

47
Norma Kamali
Two-piece ensemble, screen-printed Cotton Tabby
USA, 1980–4
Royal Ontario Museum, Toronto, 2001.79.25.1

48
Oscar de la Renta
Bògòlanfini design dress
New York, USA,
Spring/Summer 2008
Photographed for Saks 5th Avenue

49
Detail of *Bògòlanfini* wrapper,
cotton, natural dye
Mali, probably Bamana, *c.*1960
V&A: CIRC.497–1968

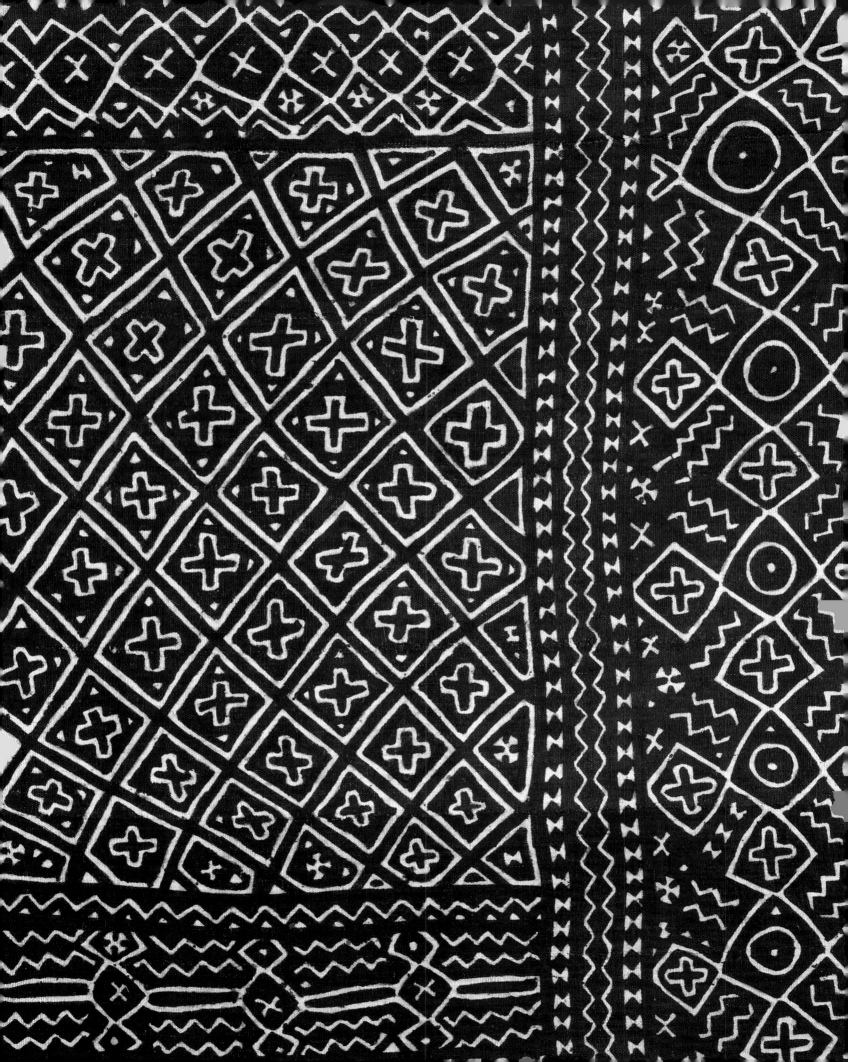

MID-CENTURY DESIGN: SHORELINE THINKING AND CROSSING BORDERS

Christine Checinska

'A boundary is not that at which something stops but... the boundary is that from which something begins its presencing.'

Martin Heidegger, *Poetry, Language, Thought* (1971)

'In the world through which I travel, I am endlessly creating myself.'

Frantz Fanon, *Black Skin, White Masks* (1967)

In the Prologue to this volume, Bonnie Greer proposes the idea of 'shoreline thinking' to encompass the expansive inner lives and ways of being that connect Global Africa across geographical boundaries. If, as she implies, unity is somehow submarine, then could the shoreline be a setting of cultural interaction and intermingling, a site of crossing, of new beginnings?[1] Could the sea be a metaphorical carrier of histories and memories, the ebb and flow of the tides a reflection of ongoing cross-cultural exchange?

Just as artists, writers and intellectuals of the African liberation and post-independence era travelled, living abroad before returning home to help rebuild their nations, so too did fashion designers such as Victoria Omọ́rọ́níke Àdùké Fọlashadé 'Shade' Thomas-Fahm, Juliana 'Chez Julie' Norteye and Seidnaly Alphadi Sidhamed, known as Alphadi.[2] The historical criss-crossing of the Atlantic by African people, whether involuntarily through the Triangular Trade or voluntarily through migration, had for centuries facilitated continual cross-cultural exchanges between Africa and Europe. What we see post-independence is a galvanization of creativity, cultural interaction, and economic and political will that provided the perfect context for the emergence of each of these designers, and consequently the building of a modern fashion industry in Africa.[3] By the 1960s West African women were spending up to 19 per cent of their yearly income on textiles, demonstrating the importance of the presentation of self.[4] African-produced goods also made economic sense to the newly independent nations. In Ghana, for example, President Kwame Nkrumah doubled the import tax on printed textiles to encourage local production, presenting a direct challenge to European wax-resist print companies like Vlisco.[5] In East Africa, factories such as the Urafiki Textile Mill, built in 1966, were set up under the endorsement of the government. Meanwhile, at grassroots level, making and wearing fashions and textiles produced on the African continent became a political act, signifying a new affirmation of cosmopolitan African identities (no.50).

The negotiation of geographical and metaphorical borders is a characteristic of Global Africa experiences. Crossing borders destabilizes ways of thinking and being.[6] The diasporic experiences we create when we set up home elsewhere are defined by a subliminal homelessness that is open to fluidity and diversity,[7] a sense of existing either beyond borders or within the 'borderlands'.[8] This is a conception of cultural identity that is rooted in syncretism. It is precisely this state of flux and intertwining of influences emerging from diasporic 'shoreline thinking' that enriches the work of designers in this period, confounding one-dimensional definitions of African fashions. Instead, the fashions produced by them could be

50
James Barnor
Untitled #2 (Two friends dressed
for a church celebration)
Accra, Ghana, 1970s

seen as different tones of a syncretic 'nation language'[9]: tools with which to express modernity, cosmopolitanism and pride in oneself on African terms.

Thomas-Fahm and her peers drew on past traditions, recovering and reinventing them, strategically putting them in dialogue with European fashion cultures to create a new sartorial language that matched the mood of the moment.[10] Travel to the European metropole was not motivated by a need for approbation, but rather Global North knowledge and cultural expressions were a resource, tools that could be employed in the making of an African modernity and the professionalization of the fashion industry. Travel to Europe was not about the Westernization of their designs, but rather their relationship to European fashion cultures echoed Henry Louis Gates's notion of 'signifyin''[1] – overseas fashions were there to be 'sampled', riffed upon, used to widen one's sartorial vocabulary and business know-how.

Colonial societies were such that European cultures were known but from a distance. Travel precipitated engagement of a different register since migration changes one's perception of self and others, and shifts ways of thinking. These vanguard designers have come to represent what was a vibrant mid-twentieth-century African fashion scene. Alongside fellow designers such as Tetteh Adzedu, Oumou Sy and Lamine Badian Kouyaté, founder of Xuly.Bët, they could be viewed as the forebears of the contemporary scene.[12] This chapter explores their creative practices, the diversity of their backgrounds, aesthetics and concerns, the connections and differences between them, and their impact.

Shade Thomas-Fahm (b.1933) – Nigeria's first fashion designer

Thomas-Fahm arrived in Britain in 1953 with a view to training as a nurse under the sponsorship of the British Council. These plans were abandoned after she saw fashionably dressed mannequins on London's Edgware Road, while out walking with a friend. She determined there and then to study fashion instead. This switch led her to take an evening class to gain her National Diploma, immediately afterwards enrolling at Saint Martin's School of Art to study fashion.[13] Her exposure to the world of fashion shows, exhibitions, histories of fashion and the arts proved to be foundational to her practice.[14] The seeds

of her aesthetic, 'a wonderful weaving in of tradition and new ideas',[15] began to blossom during these years.

Thomas-Fahm recalls:

It was a remarkable time! We Nigerian girls were eager for opportunities – and we were told that opportunities abounded abroad. At that time, I was extremely focused. If I set my mind on something it would be done, no ifs, ands, or buts...The drive to succeed, to earn, and come back home with the 'golden cup' – it drove my appetite.

Being away from home was always a temporary situation for me...From the day I arrived I started preparing for my return home, whether it was in paying for sewing machines that I wanted to ship back home, or whatever...[16]

Her 1960 return coincided with Nigerian independence from Britain. She initially opened a store, Maison Shade, later Shade's Boutique, at the Federal Palace Hotel and a factory on the Yaba Industrial Estate to produce her contemporary reimaginings of local Nigerian garments and textile techniques. Her experiences in London were her guide:

I modeled my factories in Yaba, and later in Broad Street, and then in Sandgross, Simpson Street, after the factories I worked in, in London's West End. The layout of any garment factory that I had worked in was 2 rows of machines...facing each other, with a long well in the middle for finished garments.

She soon had over 40 staff in her factory, sewing, finishing, embroidering, pressing, dyeing and weaving. She even had a clocking-in machine to log workers' movements. This professionalization of the burgeoning fashion industry, alongside the natural flair evidenced in her ingenious creations, is what earned her the title of Nigeria's 'first fashion designer'.

Shade's Boutique became the go-to place for 'highly cultured and affluent' men and women of style in Lagos.[17] Thomas-Fahm counted Nigerian royalty, diplomats and professionals among her regular clientele. Former client Professor Lalage Bown, who taught at the university in Ibadan, Nigeria, at the time of independence, describes Thomas-Fahm's aesthetic as 'elegant', 'imaginative', somehow

52
Shade Thomas–Fahm
Dress and hat, synthetic velvet,
lurex thread
Lagos, Nigeria, 1977
Given by Professor Lalage Bown
V&A: T.2418–2021

51
Shade Thomas–Fahm
Bùbá, ìró, ìpèlé and *gèlè, aṣọ-òkè*
Lagos, Nigeria, 1970s
Given by Shade Thomas–Fahm
V&A: T.2438–2021

'Nigerian as well as international' (no.52).[18] Her handwriting also caught the eye of elite overseas customers. Signature to her look was the innovative use of what was previously seen as traditional in silhouette and fabric. She favoured muted colours (no.51) rather than the flamboyant tones typically adopted for wax-print fabrics, which she felt allowed Nigerian fashions to be dismissed.[19] Instead, she pioneered the use of Nigerian fabrics like *aṣọ-òkè*, *òkènè and akwete*. As far as she was concerned such fabrics were far too versatile to be consigned to just the *ìró*. Her notable designs include the *boubou*, a simple, pared-down style for women adapted from the men's flowing *agbádá* robe, and the pre-tied *gèlè*. She famously inserted a zip into the *ìró* making it more suitable for independent women on the go during this period: 'the zip enabled women to move around quickly and more freely, to get things done'.[20] The *ìró* would previously have needed adjustment during the day: there was a risk of showing your *tòbí* underneath, which would have been highly embarrassing. Innovations such as this epitomize Thomas-Fahm's creation of an aesthetic that visually expressed nationhood, modernity and cosmopolitanism from newly decolonized Nigerian perspectives, while also contributing to the development of a fashion ecosystem that was directly informed by what she experienced overseas.

Juliana 'Chez Julie' Norteye (1932–1993) – 'The girl from Paris'

In 1961, just four years after Ghana gained its independence from Britain, the young Norteye returned to Accra from Paris, having received a scholarship that had allowed her to study fashion at the École Guerre-Lavigne, one of France's oldest schools; the headline in the local news read 'Julie – The girl from Paris'. Nkrumah had put in place initiatives such as this that enabled promising young Ghanaians to develop skills that could be deployed in the building of the nation on their return. After graduation but before going home in 1961, Norteye visited England, Germany, Austria, Belgium and Switzerland, absorbing the various fashionable styles in each and broadening her sartorial vocabulary.

When Norteye returned, there was already a buzzing fashion scene in Accra, comprising multiple overlapping local and global, or 'glocal', tendencies that echoed the cultural complexity of the former colonial society. Colonial societies could themselves be seen as borderland spaces, that is, spaces

53
Chez Julie
Kente kaba as photographed for the exhibition 'Kabas and Couture: Contemporary Ghanaian Fashion' 2015
Samuel P. Harn Museum of Art, University of Florida, Gainsville: Gift of Edith François

of tension and conflict but also of cross-cultural exchange and enmeshing. The coexistence of people of radically opposing cultures living within the colonies opened up the possibility of cultural hybridity. These in-between borderlands formed the interstices between fixed identifications, where the collective and individual experiences of nationhood and cultural value were shaken, renegotiated and performed through dress. In elite circles, it would not have been unusual to see fashionably dressed women wearing European tailored styles as well as fashions local to Accra or from Asia, for example saris, or indeed ensembles inspired by an amalgam of these influences. Contradiction, paradox, duality and ambivalence were ongoing features of colonial societies. This was reflected in the fashioning of the body.

Norteye established her brand 'Chez Julie' in 1960 and this is how she subsequently became known. What we witness in her work during the post-independence era is a knowing deployment of multiple cultural influences to create a unique representation of an Afro-Modernity stemming from a particular historical process through cloth and silhouette. She was among the first designers to use the wax-resist prints manufactured by the government-endorsed Ghana Textiles Printing Company Ltd (GTP). Her most significant styles were the *akwardzan* and the tailored *kente kaba* (no.53), which grew out of an interweaving of culturally specific inspirations while maintaining a link to historical Ghanaian techniques of self-fashioning. Chez Julie's reworked *akwardzan* is reminiscent of Thomas-Fahm's ingenious revisiting of the *ìró*. Chez Julie took the original garment, a man's uncut cloth, and tailored it, splicing a neckline and armholes into it but keeping enough cloth to replicate the flow of drape and wrap. Her *akwardzan* for men and women were easier to wear. Her tailored *kente kaba*, which challenged the accepted use of what was a precious family cloth, was similarly easy yet chic. Both were fashionable hybrid styles that allowed the intermingled influences that she encountered at home and abroad to be realized in her designs.[21]

Chris Seydou (1949–1994) – A bridge between cultures

Syncretic post-independence fashions in Mali are exemplified by the pioneering designs of Chris Seydou. Born Seydou Nourou Doumbia, in Kati, Seydou's creative practice was rooted in his upbringing. Here, Seydou was introduced to the fashions of Dior and Balenciaga through the French fashion magazines that his mother, a seamstress, and her clients drew on for inspiration.[22] His mother's embroidery work and the fabrics gifted to him by local tailors provided an outlet for his childhood foray into fashion. There then followed an apprenticeship with a tailor from whom he acquired his foundational skills, allowing him to finesse the garments that he was already making for himself. A year later, aged 16, he began making clothes for friends. This period marked the coming together of the influences that would define Seydou's aesthetic, connecting the three strands of his work: the daywear, the eveningwear and the *bògòlanfini* collections.

Seydou opened his first store in Ouagadougou, Burkina Faso, in 1967. The following year he moved to the cosmopolitan city

54
Chris Seydou
Skirt suit and hat,
bògòlanfini
Probably Mali, 1991
Emmanuelle
Courrèges Collection

of Abidjan in Côte d'Ivoire, expanding his client base. The early 1970s saw him relocating to Paris where he spent several years working for a number of different fashion houses. It was while in Paris that he changed his name to Chris. It is often reported that this was done in honour of the French couturier Christian Dior (1905–1957).[23] However, Seydou model and close friend Lydie Ullmann recalls discussing names with Seydou, around 1974, after her husband said to him: 'you will never make it in Paris with this name, we need to Christianize that'. Between them they decided on 'Chris'. Keeping 'Seydou' allowed him to bring the two cultural influences present in his aesthetic – the Malian and the European – into his professional persona. Being in Paris enabled him to study European couture at first hand. For silhouette, styling and mood, 'it was very important [for him] to…be in the cafes and look at what was happening in the street. And then once he had conceived everything… he would lock himself [up] for 10 days and come out with a collection.' He held a vision of the world he was trying to create, the story that he was trying to tell, in his mind. In Paris, his aim was to eclipse Yves Saint Laurent (1936–2008) and to show the elegance of African women, so eveningwear became the focus.[24]

Seydou spent some 20 years away from Mali, in Burkina Faso, Côte d'Ivoire and France. These years proved to be pivotal to his creative practice.[25] His self-imposed exile provided an opportunity for him to look at Malian culture from a distance just as he had, as a colonial subject, looked at and known French culture from a distance. This physical distance allowed him to see French and Malian ways of dressing in a new light. Seydou had started working in *bògòlanfini* while in Paris between 1975 and 1976. After a visit home, in 1973 or 1974, he discovered several lengths of the cloth in his suitcase. They had been gifted to him.[26] Naturally he knew the cloth from Kati. This encounter with a familiar cloth in an unfamiliar setting prompted him to re-evaluate its aesthetic potential on his return to Mali in 1990. The making and wearing of *bògòlanfini*, a cotton or wool mud cloth print fabric, has its roots in Bamana cosmology and ritual practices, customs and beliefs. It is thought to offer protection to the wearer, whether young women during initiation ceremonies, or young men out on hunting expeditions.[27] The cloth is created by a lengthy handworked process that begins with the carding, spinning and weaving of the chosen base cloth before preparing it for dyeing with mud (no.46). Narrow strips of cloth are stitched together

to form a wider usable piece. After soaking in an infusion of water and n'tkemlara (*Combretum glutinosum*) and n'gallama (*Anogeissus leiocarpa*) leaves, the cloth is dried over calabash gourds and the negative spaces of the geometric pattern are hand-painted using mud harvested locally and applied with brushes, sticks and stencils. Once the mud has penetrated the cloth sufficiently, the cloth is rinsed. The tannin in the mud creates the pattern.[28] A length of cloth can take several weeks to produce. The simplicity of the patterning masks the complexity of the process.

Seydou saw *bògòlanfini* simultaneously as a cultural root for his work and the raw material with which to fashion cutting-edge designs. He simplified familiar local patterns to suit a tailored garment as opposed to the traditional wrapped silhouettes. His bell-bottom pants, motorcycle jackets, bustiers and tight miniskirts made of *bògòlanfini* (nos 54, 55) caused a stir in Mali and drew attention to his work abroad among international designers including Paco Rabanne. During the 1990s he worked in partnership with Industrie Textile Du Mali (ITEMA) to develop commercially produced *bògòlanfini*. In an uncut garment the issue of having to match the print does not occur, whereas it would be unthinkable not to have the pattern match down the centre front or back of a tailored garment. It is also usual to cut sleeves as a pair so that they match. Seydou would have known this. In traditional *bògòlanfini*, no two sections of the cloth are the same. Patterns were therefore modified, motifs simplified and put into repeat, making them easier to tailor. Seydou would also have known that the symbols used to adorn ceremonial *bògòlanfini* carried specific and readily recognizable meanings since they were typically based on local myths, proverbs and histories. He is reputed to have not been comfortable with cutting into ceremonial cloth due to its association with private rituals and the spiritual realm.[29] Simplification of pattern, or decoding, came out of respect for Malian belief systems and luxury tailoring traditions. He believed in keeping local crafting techniques alive by exposing them to contemporary international markets, an approach that we see echoed in the work of contemporary designers like Awa Meité, in Mali. Seydou's use of *bògòlanfini* as a luxury fashion cloth and his ability to bridge cultures have secured his place in global fashion histories.

55
Chris Seydou
Dress, silk and lurex
Paris, France, 1983
Courtesy of Lydie Ullmann

Kofi Ansah (1951–2014) – The enfant terrible

Known as the 'enfant terrible' of Ghanaian fashion, designer
Kofi Ansah propelled Ghana onto the international catwalks.
Born into an artistic Ghanaian family, the son of a photographer and exponent of classical music, Ansah considered
himself a pan-Africanist, 'one of Nkrumah's children', with
a 'forward-looking global ethos'.[30] His career spanned three
phases: London, Ghana and global markets. Moving to London
was an inevitability for him since he knew that he would have
the world at his fingertips in terms of inspiration, fabrics and
tailoring expertise. His plan was to contribute to the London
scene and then to bring back what he had learned to help build
up his nation.[31]

Studying fashion design at Chelsea School of Art between
1973 and 1977 exposed Ansah to the work of David Sassoon (of
Bellville Sassoon) from whom he learned to cut.[32] He excelled at
drawing the female form and modelling on the figure, 'always
with the pin in the corner of his mouth and observing how the
garments draped'.[33] Visiting lecturers included designers Bill
Gibb (1943–1988) and Ossie Clark (1942–1996) who helped to
nurture his talents. Like Seydou, Ansah was a keen collector
of *Vogue* and *Harper's Bazaar*, the pages of which he avidly
consumed. During this period, he worked as a tailor for the
ready-to-wear store Cecil Gee. This experience, alongside
designing for Guy Laroche (1921–1989) after graduation, gave
him an invaluable understanding of various sectors of the
industry.[34] Ansah needed to demonstrate couture techniques
while in London to prove he could 'play by their rules'.[35] By 1981
he was ready to deploy these techniques in the creation of his
own brand.

56
Designed by Kofi Ansah
Ensembles for 'Blue Zone' collection
Shoot for *Revue Noire* magazine
Accra, Ghana, 1996
Photographed by Eric Don-Arthur

Having built up his London-based label over several years,
1987 saw the launch of Ansah's 'Blue Zone' collections, which
hit the runway at the Dorchester Hotel, London, under the
sponsorship of the Côte d'Ivoire Embassy. Ansah used Yorùbá
àdìrẹ cloths in new ways for 'Blue Zone' (no.56). In 1988, just
before launching the second collection, he was incorporated into the British Couture Collections (BCC).[36] Finding
inspiration in all things, Ansah had noticed a denim jacquard
fabric being used by a Japanese designer, a contemporary of
his. She had unwanted excess stock which Ansah took to cut
his first 'Blue Zone' styles. Unique to Ansah is the use of both
sides of the cloth thereby creating additional texture. In an

instant he had effectively turned an everyday fabric, denim,
into a covetable high-end commodity, selling in fashionable
boutiques such as Rich Bitch on Marylebone High Street,
London.[37]

Ansah returned to Ghana in 1992, following a commission
to design uniforms for Ghana Airways the year before. He
quickly established himself as a leading designer through his
company Artdress. Praised for his use of richly textured and
boldly coloured local fabrics, and for exhibiting the spectacular
and intriguing, he attracted a strong following at home and

abroad. A parallel can be drawn between the cross-pollination of influences in Ansah's creations and the use of *bògòlanfini* in Seydou's aesthetic, or the *aṣọ-òkè* embraced by Thomas-Fahm. As with these contemporaries, local and global fashion priorities intertwine in the glamour and wit of his designs. That same year Ansah created a range of *kente* jeans: a once regal cloth cut into a once utilitarian garment. This necessitated a collaboration with the weaver Spintex to develop *kente* cloth in wider widths suitable for manufacturing his contemporary styles. During the late 1990s Ansah applied his creative eye to Ghana Textiles Printing Company Ltd (GTP), advising the company on design and marketing, and producing his own wax-resist prints and weave designs through them.[38]

By the final phase of his career, Ansah was moving further into ready-to-wear, selling to local and global markets in Europe and the USA. Meanwhile, Kofi Ansah Couture continued to flourish, showing at Alta Roma in 2009. His *African Desert* and *European Couture* collections from this phase, predominantly using black and white along with silver and black *kente*, are especially striking. He aimed to bring *kente* into the twenty-first century. At the time of his death in 2014, he had set up a new factory to produce collections for Saks Fifth Avenue and retailers in Milan. Ahead of the sustainability curve, Ansah was working with the Ethical Fashion Initiative and Simone Cipriani.[39] He founded a weaving centre, instilling in young people the need for mass-produced 'Made-in-Ghana' textiles. He repeatedly asked: 'Why can't the initial creation be here?' He advocated for a more circular system. Seeing education as a route to fulfilling this ambition, he wanted students to gain an understanding of design, of dyes, of thread: that is, the entire design, development and production process, thus enhancing the employability of emerging talents and securing the skills needed to build the Ghanaian fashion industry of the future. The pan-Africanist within him realized that his approach could become a template for the rest of the continent.[40]

Ansah's legacy, therefore, lies not only in his head-turning cut-and-mix fashions but also in the up-and-coming creatives that he mentored: those with whom he shared his pride in being African and his demand for exactingly high standards of innovation and professionalism, those to whom he imparted the idea that, 'West is not always best' and 'inspiration is all around you'.[41]

Alphadi (b.1957) – The magician of the desert

Born in Timbuktu, Mali, on the eve of independence, Sidahmed Alphadi Seidnaly hails from a nomadic ancestry, which is reflected in a worldview that does not see borders. He routinely travels back and forth between Niger, Morocco and France to create his extravagant collections, which are infused with the spirit of the Tuareg, Songhai, Bororo, Haoussa, Peulh, Bambara, Arab and the Maasai. His creative practice, with its layered cross-cultural references, brings to life the notion of 'shoreline thinking'.

Alphadi moved from Mali to Niger with his family at a young age. The Niger of his youth was a crucible in which the traditional and the cosmopolit]an came together through an influx of people and wealth generated by the growing uranium industry. Elite circles were populated by the stylish, who readily combined historic dress forms with up-to-the-minute global fashions.[42] His interest in fashion was ignited by a childhood spent in the company of his Tuareg mother, aunts and sisters, who took pride in their self-fashioning. The Tuareg men he encountered, particularly those wearing flowing robes and the *tagalmust*, a distinctive turban and veil, paid equal attention to the styling of their bodies.[43] It is no surprise that he describes a childhood surrounded by beauty, elegance and an appreciation of different cultures.

Alphadi's vocation began when, aged seven, he was apprenticed to a master couturier, Mister Ouseman Chirfi.[44] Although fashion was in his blood, it was the move to France that brought him back to his calling in the late 1970s. He had relocated to Paris originally to study tourism. However, through his well-connected network of friends, he began helping backstage at catwalks shows during Paris Fashion Week. He went on to study at the Atelier Chardon Savard, one of the city's most prestigious design schools. Through this period, he worked with Kenzō Takada (1939–2020), Yves Saint Laurent and Paco Rabanne, who became his mentor. He learned the process of designing and the meaning of art.[45] This led to the release of his first couture line in 1985. His designs initially caught the eye of the first wave of independent Africa presidents. His client base soon expanded to France, Spain and the USA, and his ready-to-wear line and the Alphadi Gallery followed.[46] His sophisticated womenswear collections, then and now, are resolutely feminine and employ a range of local

57
Alphadi
Jacket, *kuba* cloth, cotton, linen
Niger, 1993
Given by Alphadi
V&A: T.2439–2021

and globally sourced fabrics such as leather, silver and bronze, cotton, silk, raffia and barkcloth (no.58). Like all designers whose careers span several decades, Alphadi's work continues to evolve, but his approach to design, the mix of cultural influences to create something new and relevant to today's context of intermingled cultures, remains. Recurring shapes include the bustier, for example those presented in his 2004 Paris Haute Couture collection, which consisted of silver plates engraved by Tuareg craftspeople. Repeating symbols include the Agadez cross.[47] Similarly, intricate artisanal embroideries and print fabrics abound.[48] For men, jackets and waistcoats that combine traditional textile techniques, such as *kuba* cloth, with European tailoring, have become a signature of his collections (no.57).

But fashion is much more than clothes to Alphadi. It is a vehicle for unity and prosperity throughout the continent and a route to achieving global peace. This belief motivated him to become a founding member of the Fédération Africaine des Créateurs in 1993, alongside Seydou, Ansah, Ainé Pathé Ouédraogo (Pathé'O), Katoucha Niane, Mickaël Kra and others. Alphadi took on the role of president the following year. This philanthropic leaning then led to the launch of Festival International de la Mode Africaine (FIMA) in 1998, supported by UNESCO and the Organisation Internationale de la Francophonie (OIF), in the Tiguidit Desert, in Niger.[49] Alphadi's vision of Niamey as a fashion hub was built on the optimism of the nationalist politics of the independence and liberation years. His pan-Africanist sensibilities were brought to bear on the curation of FIMA events and a range of designers from Global Africa show their collections there.

Participants of the early editions included Seydou, Pathé'O, Katoucha, Oumou Sy, Ly Dumas, Christian Dior and Kenzō. Some 50 designers from 52 different countries came to the first event, and about 120 models and more than 5,000 people flew into the desert to witness Alphadi's fashion, art and culture extravaganza.[50] It is also thought to have contributed to the 1998 peace settlement in Niger.[51] Subsequent humanitarian work has included bringing electricity to the villages of Gorou Banda and Boubon, as well as providing education for emerging fashion talents and creating infrastructures that support local artisans, introducing a level of professionalism.[52] Peace in Niger is fragile at best, elusive at worst. The 2013 edition opened amid escalating violence. Alphadi hosted the evening event 'Fashion for Peace', encouraging festivalgoers to dress in white. In recognition of this ongoing work to change lives and the fortunes of the region through FIMA, UNESCO named him 'Artist for Peace', in 2016.[53]

Throughout his career Alphadi has been driven by the desire to promote culture, peace and development in Africa, as well as to showcase the continent's cultures and histories through fashion. He has said:

> *It was important for me to show the beauty of the African continent...[to] show the diversity of our cultures and the strong history of each of them...to show our roots and the power of our colors and how our history, the pattern, the fabric, they all have meaning expressing something deep, powerful, strong and beautiful.*[54]

The breaking down of societies' hierarchies based on race and culture through syncretism is second nature to Alphadi's design philosophy and his approach to humanitarian work, being so rooted in his nomadic Tuareg heritage, which is continually reinvigorated by travel around the continent and to Europe. The elan of fashion, the richness of multiple cultures and the drive towards social justice are expertly woven together in his hands.

Zina Guessous (1925–1998), Naïma Bennis (1940–2008) and Tamy Tazi (b.1930) – Women of Independence

Not all designers working in the liberation and post-independence period followed a leave-and-return pattern. Some worked across social borders built on gender norms. In Morocco, for example, Zina Guessous reinvigorated couture in ways that stunned what was then a conservative society.[55] She and fellow designers Naïma Bennis and Tamy Tazi were inspired by new ideas of what was possible.[56] The urban elite to which these women belonged were already used to wearing Global North fashions, since they were readily available from the European department stores that opened in cosmopolitan Casablanca earlier in the twentieth century. For many, however, local fashions were still preferred for religious and ceremonial occasions.[57] Guessous, Bennis and Tazi's aesthetics, though varied, followed a similar syncretic impulse that reinterpreted local self-fashioning and textile techniques,

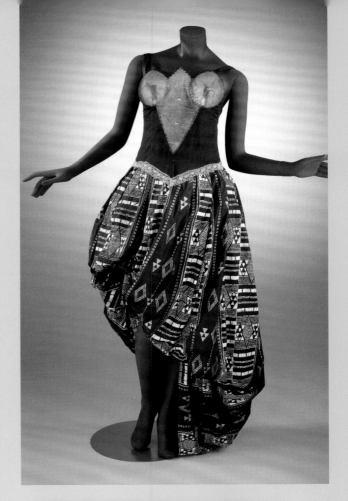

58
Alphadi
Dress, cotton and brass
Niger, 1988
Given by Alphadi
V&A: T.2440–2021

placing them in dialogue with European trends. Guessous and Tazi travelled outside the continent; Bennis did not. But they share a story of fashioning the feminine by borrowing from the traditional male wardrobe.

Guessous, born Zineb Salah Rachid, the daughter of Lalla Kenza, a member of the Moroccan royal family, had a progressive upbringing. She travelled abroad and was an early adopter of European fashions, appearing in public without a veil. Moroccan fashions traditionally consisted of weighty fabrics, such as velvets and brocades, often heavily embellished with metallic threads,[58] and voluminous layered looks. This did not suit the newly liberated lifestyles of privileged women such as Guessous, whose creativity came to be fuelled by this disconnect. She spent a crucial year, which undoubtedly influenced her work, in Paris as the first Moroccan to learn French couture at Maison Balmain. Her first boutique, Kenz, opened in the Royal Mansour Hotel in Casablanca in 1964, selling contemporary fashions and jewellery. She started to push the definitions of what a *qef-tan* could be, redesigning it for daywear and eveningwear in cotton, lace, jersey, silk prints, organza and striped voiles.[59] A 1965 meeting with US *Vogue* fashion editor Diana Vreeland (1903–1989) led Guessous to show her collection in New York alongside designer Emilio Pucci (1914–1992) the following year. Her mini-caftans – particularly one in cotton worn over a bikini and one in white wool trimmed with gold – enthused the crowd at Lord and Taylor's 1966 Mediterranean Odyssey show. Other designs included a purple-and-white-striped linen *djellaba*, a gold lurex hand-knitted coat worn over draped trousers, and silk velvet caftans with deep side splits.[60] The wafts of voluminous gleaming silks used for her more classic styles were sourced in Paris.

It is often said that timing is everything in the fashion world. Guessous's aesthetic spoke to the growing Global North fascination with Morocco and the trend for what were then seen as 'bohemian' fashions. Her significant designs include the mini-caftan, essentially a modernized version of the *qef-tan*, and the *gendura*, originally a man's garment, for women.[61] In May 1968, under the title of 'Mini-Caftans Highlight of the Moroccan Party', the fashion editor of Washington, DC's *Evening Star*, Eleni, wrote, 'if you are on the road to Morocco be sure to pick up a mini-caftan', with

reference to Guessous's designs.[62] Betty Beale, writing in *Womenswear Daily*, described Guessous as the 'top caftan designer of Morocco'. Beale notes that her collections include 'every type and shape of Moroccan feminine garb, from the richly ornamented, full length trailing gowns...to the simplest modernized version of the sleeveless street length slipover with the braid extending only to the bosom'.[63] Guessous's *bernouses*, or hooded capes, made stylish evening wraps, as did her new zippered versions of the *qef-tan*, which historically would have been fastened with dozens of tiny buttons and rouleaux loops. Beale also notes the way in which fashionable avant-garde Moroccan women seemingly shifted overnight from 'maxi-concealment' to the 'mini'.[64] These comfortable loose and lightweight, boundary-crossing innovations spoke to women of the jet-set wanting to embrace a freedom of movement that matched an independence of spirit and symbolized the *joie de vivre* of the era.

A small selection of garments and accessories by Guessous, housed in the V&A collection, gives a window into this moment of refashioning the feminine, redefining couture elegance and the birthing of a professional fashion industry in Morocco. The pieces were donated by her daughter Karima (Kouki) Guessous in 2014, and show Guessous's expert use of draping that lets the cloth flow around the body in a luxurious and sensual way. She created a new form of languid luxury, moving away from the tailored uptight silhouettes that had for decades been the couture norm. The ivory-coloured bolero and draped trouser ensemble (no.59) typifies her overall work: the borrowing from the male wardrobe, the revisiting of traditional embellishments and the referencing of Global North fashions. The colour coordination of the layers within the outfit, a subtle change that could easily go unnoticed to contemporary eyes, had not been seen before. The whole has an unmistakeable sophistication and sensuality that dispel the image of the veiled Moroccan woman. The synthetic jersey crepe cloth, a new intervention, is exploited to its full potential, the manufactured fibres allowing the drapes and folds of the trousers to hold their shape. The handworked gold metal embroidery and vegetable silk belt are fashioned using a passementerie technique (couched plaited cord) that is characteristic in shape for Moroccan traditions. Conceived in Morocco and made in Paris, the black leather and velvet evening bag, a reinterpretation of a traditional Moroccan purse (no.60), also displays a

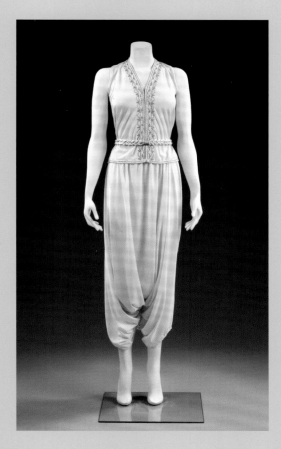

59
Zina Guessous
Bolero and trousers, synthetic material, metal
thread embroidery and vegetable silk belt
Morocco, 1960–80
Given in memory of Zina Guessous by Karima
Guessous-Niard
V&A: ME.9-2015

60
Zina Guessous
Black velvet and leather evening bag
with gold embroidery
Morocco, 1960–80
Given in memory of Zina Guessous
by Karima Guessous-Niard
V&A: ME.11-2015

61
Roll of labels, Naïma's Caftan,
Rabat-Hilton-Maroc, 1960–80
Given by Mouna Lotfi
V&A: NCOL.1163-2021

passementerie technique known as Bershman. There is a time-lessness about these pieces that highlights the way in which certain items like the caftan and the draped trouser have become global fashion classics now worn by everyday women and revisited by designers as diverse as Halston (1932–1990), Gnyuki 'Yuki' Torimaru and Yves Saint Laurent in the 1970s, alongside Donna Karan, for her *Urban Zen* collections, and Rick Owens in the 2000s.[65]

Naïma Bennis opened her first boutique in 1966, in Rabat, promoting the lifestyle brand Naïma's Caftan – Hilton Rabat, which extended to jewellery, crafts and perfume. Her atelier was situated behind the shop, where a number of seam-stresses brought her designs to life. The reel of simple yet stylish labels shown here (no.61) gives a sense of the level of business that she built and the quality of her clientele. The signing of her garments with her brand name through these labels, marked her out as a designer rather than an anonymous local seamstress or tailor.[66] As with Guessous, Bennis brought her own innovations to traditional embellishments, textile techniques and fashions. For example, her ability to synthesize the old and the new in one piece saw her applying antique passementerie decorations from old *qef-tan* onto new garments. Her use of *bzioui*, a fine woollen cloth traditionally reserved for male garments, and her transformation of the *bernous,* a man's cape (no.62), into an elegant womenswear piece to wear over a caftan or evening dress, are especially noteworthy.

In 1976 Tami Tazi took over the department store Joste in Casablanca, which had been influential in introducing European fashions to Morocco since its opening in the mid-1950s.[67] She simultaneously gained the rights to represent Dior and Yves Saint Laurent, giving her first-hand access to the Parisian couture salon shows, which in turn influenced her own work. Her entrée into designing her own fashion line was facilitated by the garments that she made for herself and her high-society friends. Her own collections were imbued with cross-cultural references from her travels, in France, Turkey and India. Local design inspirations included Berber and Jewish embroideries and needle lace previously found on men's garments.[68] She reworked familiar items of clothing like caftans, *djellabas* and *takchitas* by manipulating proportion and introducing new ornate embellishments. In this way Tazi built

up an aesthetic that married French fashions with Moroccan heritage, crossing gender and cultural divides to become the ambassador for style that she remains today.

The boundary-crossing creations of Guessous, Bennis and Tazi challenged conceptions of gender by expanding the fashion choices of women to suit their modern lifestyles. In their hands languid luxurious fashions became instruments in the refashioning and performance of the feminine. The Moroccan inspiration triggered by them and found in inter-national fashion magazines such as *Vogue* (no.63) broke down the then sterile rules of taste that existed for women. Guessous, Bennis and Tazi each fused aspects of traditional male dress and handcrafted detailing with elements of European couture to do so. This parallels the synthesis of cultural references in the work of Thomas-Fahm, Chez Julie, Seydou, Ansah and Alphadi, for whom geographical border crossings were and are a common catalyst to innovation.

Where Guessous, Bennis and Tazi engaged in metaphorical journeys across society's invisible borders to ignite the creative spark within, Thomas-Fahm, Chez Julie, Seydou, Alphadi and Ansah embarked on geographical journeys that irreversibly shaped their aesthetics and approaches to fashion. The rhythm of leave-and-return typified by them continues in the lives and work of contemporary designers such as Katungulu Mwendwa, Brian Kivuti and Ami Doshi Shah. But those mid-century designers who travelled to the metropole and came of age in the post-independence era did so with the express desire of returning to rebuild and dress their newly independent nations. This took the form of the professionalization of the industry, the nurturing of emerging talents and the setting up of pan-African organizations such as FIMA aimed at showcasing African fashions to global audiences. In this context, syncretic fashions, shaped by the resilience and openness of 'shoreline thinking', not only made ongoing cross-cultural exchanges visible, but also affirmed and articulated notions of modernity and mid-century cosmopolitanism from African perspectives. Each of the designers featured here engaged in conversations across the space between cultures, each stitch, fold, drape and line making connections between Global Africa and beyond.

62
Photograph of velvet cape
by Naïma Bennis
Morocco, *c*.1970
V&A: ME.4–2015

63
Spread from US *Vogue*,
July 1966

THE BEAUTIFUL PEOPLE IN CAFTANS

Here are the most becoming fashions ever invented: the languor of the seraglio clings to them; leisure and repose emanate from them. The classic robes of the Near East, they're now, suddenly, all over the contemporary map—inspiration of great dressmakers and every woman's discovery in beauty. . . . Go anywhere. Step out on a terrace in New York; walk along the beach at Marbella; enter a country house in Sussex; a villa in Rome; a ranch in Montecito—and what do you see? Women relaxing into caftans; into caftan-like jibbas, yeleks, djellabas . . . nothing is more completely feminine.
Mrs. Giancarlo Uzielli, left, the former Anne Ford—blond, blue-eyed, modern good looks, in a traditional Moroccan caftan of handwoven azure silk embroidered with gold and green leaves—on a terrace above Central Park.
Lady Antonia Fraser, far left, in a gold-bordered green velvet caftan from Morocco; she wears it, here—with an Ethiopian dollar on a long, heavy gold chain—in the indoor amaryllis garden of the Frasers' London house.
Mrs. Richard de la Mare, above, her yellow-silk hair spilling over red-white-black striped organza—a caftan from Liberty's, for summer parties here in London or at the De la Mares' villa beyond the hills of Florence.
Comtesse Michel de Ganay, above right, at the family Château de Fleury, wears an Egyptian caftan of blue-and-white striped cotton; her waist-length blond hair is plaited up in one thick braid, clasped in a gold ring.
Donna Allegra Caracciolo di Castagneto, right, looks across Rome from her parents' terrace; the toga-caftan, lemon-yellow crêpe lapped by Parma violet—Forquet's free-flowing and beautiful translation from the Arabic.

II

CONTEMPORARY CREATIVES

Christine Checinska

'West is not always best. Inspiration is all around you.'

Kofi Ansah, quoted by his son, Ryan Ansah, March 2021[1]

The contemporary African fashion scene has an unmistakable vitality and dynamism that is shifting the geography of global fashion. African fashion creatives working on the continent and beyond are charting their own course, pushing boundaries, breaking down stereotypes around culture, race and gender, ultimately challenging assumptions about what African fashions are, can and should be. Often, they are doing so simply by drawing on their own frames of reference, visual vocabularies and ways of thinking and being, informed by their own histories and cultures. There is a new pan-Africanism in the air, set to become a driving force behind the African-ization of the global fashion scene from designers to models, stylists to photographers, celebrity ambassadors to everyday people. There is a sense of unity despite cultural and historical differences across the continent: differences that are natural given the 54 countries that make up this vast geographical region, each with diverse people, cultures and histories within them. The divergent backgrounds, practices, aesthetics and influences are held together by a continental sensibility that infuses creativity and frames the common vision for a future in which we all flourish. But this is not confined to the continent. The impact of Global Africa creative visionaries at the helm of establishment fashion magazines and brands in the Global North cannot be underestimated. Virgil Abloh, (1980-2021), artistic director of the Louis Vuitton (LV) menswear collection from 2018 to 2020, was one such visionary.

The May 2021 issue of American *Vogue* features the poet and activist Amanda Gorman swathed in a printed *kente* cloth gown designed by Abloh (no.64). A close look at the cloth shows that he artfully fused the distinctive LV logo with familiar geometric stripweave patterning to create a twenty-first-century symbol of luxury and power. American *Vogue* editor-at-large André Leon Talley (1948–2022) describes this iconic cover as 'a soaring moment in the history of Condé Nast – it is a cover that all mothers and grandmothers and aunties of any color would want their young daughters to see and experience'.[2] It is the first time that a poet has been featured on a *Vogue* cover. Crucially, the choice of Gorman speaks volumes about the historical context leading to this soaring moment. Gorman reached international acclaim following the reading of her poem 'The Hill We Climb' at the inauguration of Joe Biden as president of the USA. There are echoes of President Kwame Nkrumah's 'We Face Forward' address in Gorman's now famous poem, not least the look towards a future in which we all thrive, where there is equity but also Black agency. Just as Nkrumah adopted *kente* to refashion his identity as the newly appointed leader of independent Ghana, Abloh's *kente* becomes Gorman's royal robe. Draped over one shoulder, cinched in at the waist by a heavily embellished gold belt, the cloth falls softly to the ground creating a pool of fragmented stripes, exposing her bare leg as it does so. This is another contemporary twist on Ghanaian tradition, this time at the hands of independent stylist and contributing editor Gabriella Karefa-Johnson, who takes the historical draped-over-one-shoulder male garb and turns it into a statement womenswear look. The *Vogue* article was entitled 'The Rise and Rise of Amanda Gorman, Poet, Activist, Phenomenon'. Past, present and future collide in this powerful image through the revaluation of an instantly recognizable textile form. There is a

64
Amanda Gorman on the cover of US *Vogue*,
May 2021
Cloth by Virgil Abloh, styled by Gabriella
Karefa-Johnson, photographed by Annie Leibovitz

sense of returning to the source since historically *kente* was a royal cloth reserved for only the most prestigious of occasions, worn by the Ghanaian elite. Gorman steps into her role as the voice of a generation, but she does so carrying our shared African heritages with her. Of her choice of cloth Karefa-Johnson says:

> *I subscribe to this idea of Pan-Africanism and the idea of cultural unity that exists between [all] people who live on the continent and people throughout the diaspora. Kente has always been a visual signifier of that idea to me – it means something to a lot of people who aren't always spoken to on the cover of powerful magazines.*[3]

The image-driven nature of contemporary life ensures that fashion images in all their variations readily infiltrate mainstream consciousness, influencing understandings of identity, shaping tastes, mapping and informing social and political histories. Therein lies the power of the Gorman/Abloh cover shot to make an assertion that goes against the mainstream grain in the Global North.

Abloh designed the cloth for his Louis Vuitton Autumn/Winter 2021 menswear collection, where it was shown draped around a grey melange hoodie emblazoned with the words 'tourist vs. purist' (no.65).[4] The look was inspired by a photograph of Abloh's grandmother, effectively a returning to heritage in order to reimagine the future that parallels the work of the vanguard designers Shade Thomas-Fahm, Chez Julie, Zina Guessous, Chris Seydou, Kofi Ansah and Alphadi. Abloh, like Karefa-Johnson, used his platform to centre Blackness, whether drawing on his personal story for inspiration or collaborating with a roster of other Black creatives to produce work that communicated their world views. His deployment of a range of cultural references was seen as groundbreaking by some audiences, but familiar by others that share his heritage. Of his collaboration with stylist Ib Kamara, Abloh observed, 'we have built this language of expressing ourselves through the styling and creation of my shows'.[5] He spoke of such work as a 'homecoming experience', where a 'new picture of Africa' is being painted, a necessity since 'the original pictures were erased', to which I would add skewed. Pondering the Karefa-Johnson cover, Abloh described engaging in an act of call-and-response through his Spring/Summer 2020 LV collection,

65
Virgil Abloh for Louis Vuitton
Ensemble for Autumn/Winter
2021 collection

which reflected on issues around race and the undervaluing of Black people. This act has been embraced and taken further by Karefa-Johnson. Global North majority perspectives on gender norms, male and female attire, masculinities and what constitutes the feminine, gender fluidity, and sensuality are temporarily destabilized by Gorman's image.

It is not only traditional *kente* that was repurposed by Abloh; the hoodie, arguably a symbol of contemporary Black urban youth, was also reclaimed. One cannot look at the grey melange hoodie chosen as the garment over which the LV *kente* is draped without remembering Trayvon Martin. Martin was a young Black African American boy from Florida who was shot and killed by George Zimmerman while on his way home from a nearby convenience store in February 2012. A photograph of Martin wearing a grey melange hoodie was seen all over social media, in news broadcasts and on news-stands. Zimmerman was tried and acquitted of second-degree murder and manslaughter in July 2013. Martin's murder sparked protests and much-needed debates about racial profiling and 'stand your ground' laws in the USA. Abloh founded his high-end streetwear brand Off-White in the same year in which Martin's life was taken. He described the brand as existing in 'the grey area between black and white'.[6] Off-White products are easily recognizable by Abloh's use of striking but stark embellishments such as quotation marks, hazard-tape symbols and large-scale fonts, essentially new forms of graphic patterning. Abloh displayed an acute understanding of the power of fashion – high fashion and vernacular fashion – to push against societies' invisible borders rooted in hierarchies of value and negative readings of cultural, racial and gendered difference. His use of quotation marks is said to signify a detachment from social norms. For a 2017 collection Abloh collaborated with neo-conceptual artist Jenny Holzer to create a line that critiqued the growing wave of neo-national rhetoric in the USA under President Donald Trump by emphasizing the positive aspects of immigration and cultural exchange. Of course, cultural exchange is not new to fashion. In the Global North, as Karefa-Johnson reminds us, the predominant representation is Italian and French culture, repackaged and sold in the USA. Fashion creatives in the Global North have historically looked towards African cultures for inspiration, appropriating cultural symbols, borrowing aesthetics; consider the wealth of Egyptian cultural signifiers that became foundational to 1920s Flapper style and Art Deco with the opening of King Tutankhamun's tomb in the Valley of the Kings in 1922. But the common denominator has been whiteness. Blackness and African-ness, indeed Global Africa creativity itself, are subjected to and consumed by a white gaze. Abloh's pictures of Africa are therefore distorted.

The picture being painted by young fashion creatives across the continent and beyond is one that places Africa at the centre from which to tell a range of multiple, layered narratives from many perspectives. It is a picture that challenges assumptions about African fashions, while reaching across boundaries of geography, culture, race and gender, at a time when divisions are becoming entrenched. It is a picture that responds to the exclusion of Global Africa perspectives in crucial debates led by the Global North about sustainable and ethical fashion. But

it is also a picture that sets out new definitions of beauty and elegance. The work produced by the contemporary creatives featured in this book expands the imagination. Some, like Adeju Thompson, for their brand Lagos Space Programme, Amine Bendriouich, and Magdalene Afia Sakyi for her brand Aphia Sakyi (nos 66, 140-4, and pp.194-200), channel the long story of African fashions, operating at the intersection of spirituality, creativity and the suturing of fragmented cultural histories, which could be viewed as a form of social repair. Others, such as Katungulu Mwendwa, use forms of experimental cutting to construct sophisticated architectural forms. And still others, like Theresia Kyalo, who manipulates metals into continuous line drawings that contour the face (no.67), fashion familiar materials into sculptural body adornments.

In contemporary fashion photography and styling, African practitioners are applying their creativity to reframe long-established representational tropes and to break free from stereotypes of Black African people. Photographers such as Stephen Tayo and Daniel Obasi blur the boundaries between art, fashion and documentary photography. Curator Antwaun Sargent's important book, *The New Black Vanguard* (2019),[7] sets out the work of African heritage photographers who are forcing us to rethink the fashion image: Awol Erizku and Tyler Mitchell, Campbell Addy, Arielle Bobb-Willis, Micaiah Carter, Nadine Ijewere, Quil Lemons, Namsa Leuba, Renell Medrano, Jamal Nxedlana, Ruth Ossai, Adrienne Raquel, Dana Scruggs, Stephen Tayo and Daniel Obasi. Each of them draws on the everyday to explore what a fashion image can do, what statements can be made through it, how it can reflect differing perspectives, how it can cause harm, how it can potentially heal. All of us who work in fashion are ultimately embroiled in a process of building self-worth and the projection of self-esteem at an individual and collective level. As Sargent writes, the images created by this group 'carve out a space for Black beauty, a long-contested notion in the mainstream that is known fact before the lens of a Black photographer.'[8] But such images also present fluid and intersectional identities. They portray the nuances, the myriad differences within difference. They depict a multiplicity of stories that can be read in numerous ways. It is as though the camera is as much a tool of self-fashioning as the garments, accessories, hair and make-up applied by the stylists and supplied by the designers. The group's images are artistic celebrations of themselves and our wider selves, breaking down decades of misrepresentation. Since the era of Western imperialism, the transatlantic slave trade and subsequent colonization of Africa, images of the Black male body have not only adorned advertisements for so-called 'exotic' colonial produce such as tea, coffee, sugar and tobacco, but also the surfaces of objects employed in the ritual of dressing, such as boxes of bleaching agent, tins of shoe polish, hairpins, snuffboxes and trinkets. As early as the sixteenth century fashionable members of the English aristocracy donned black masks at courtly functions and, in some instances, painted themselves black as Moors. By the eighteenth century, the image of the Black male body, partly through its association with expensive products, had become a marker of status, wealth and style. It was also a sign of ownership. But could the misrepresented Black male body, now an object of desire, ever be deemed beautiful? How does the work of contemporary African photographers and stylists destabilize certain notions of beauty in the Global North? How does their work challenge assumptions and misrepresentations of Black masculinities?

Cultural critic Kobena Mercer writes that Black masculinities are 'confined to a narrow repertoire of "types", the supersexual

66
Magdalene Afia Sakyi for Aphia Sakyi
Winnie Mandela necklace, 'Embrace' collection
Ghana, 2018
Photographed by Keelson Studios

stud and the sexual "savage" on the one hand, or the delicate, fragile and exotic "oriental" on the other'.[9] Meanwhile Stuart Hall, commenting on the recurring misrepresentations of the Black male body, notes that for each depiction of the savage and the slave there exists a less threatening image of the Black as a docile servant and ever-merry minstrel or clown.[10] Furthermore, the Blackamoors, noble savages and Mungo Macaronis present in some contemporary fashion media are little more than manifestations of the savage, the slave, the servant and the clown, revealing traces of the ambivalent historical colonial fantasies that remain in popular culture.[11] Such representations have their roots in eighteenth- and nineteenth-century ethnographic and anthropological images of African people, for example, the cartes de visite that were circulated across the globe during the years of European imperialism. Each one is a form of 'blackface' that renders the individual invisible. These images are informed by and reinforce hierarchies of value, based on racial, gendered and

67
Designed by Theresia Kyalo
Uso Mzunguko (surrounding face) piece, 'Body Pieces' collection
Kenya, 2019
Photographed by Ngure Muchang

cultural difference. They reflect the underlying concerns or biases of both image-makers and consumers. As historian and theorist Paul Gilroy writes, 'the glamour of difference sells well'.[12] Within the fashion industry, particularly in the Global North, imagery and text laden with racialized codes and stereotypical visual cues are all too often disguised by being seen as demonstrating creative vision or an edgy quality that excites the viewer. But how do these images relate to everyday performances of Black masculinities and the fashion images created by contemporary African practitioners? The topic of fashioning African masculinities by African designers is picked up by Monica L. Miller in the essay that follows, through her close reading of clothing and accessories brand Orange Culture, which celebrates the gentler side of manhood.

Stylist and photographer Daniel Obasi re-presents local Nigerians in ways that reveal complex queer and feminine subjectivities, while reversing the relegation of Black beauty and elegance to the margins of the global fashion worlds. His work has been featured in such magazines as *i-D*, *Nataal* and *Niijournal*. In the 2019 photograph *Baff Up*, Obasi dressed his model Olasunkanmi Abayomi in a sumptuous draped one-shoulder top designed by Lisa Folawiyo, and a pair of emerald-green skinny satin trousers (no.68). Abayomi appears seated on a throne-like yet threadbare armchair that would not have looked out of place in a fashionable 1970s living room, with its russet and brown swirling floral cover and dark wooden trim. He looks directly at the viewer, but there is a softness to his face. His expression is calm. His head is crowned with a tomato-red cap, reminiscent of a fez. A large gold hoop earring hangs from each of his ears. For those schooled in the historical misrepresentation of Black men, the presence of the red cap immediately transports the mind. It conjures up derogatory but familiar images of happy smiling Africans, caricatures created to sell products such as Banania, the French milky banana drink found in many kitchen cupboards (no.69). Interestingly, a fading advertisement for Luna evaporated milk provides the backdrop for Obasi's photograph. The staging of this photograph, the elegant styling of Abayomi's body, Obasi's use of the tomato-red cap, could be seen as a form of counter-gaze able to temporarily overturn the invisibility of the individual that occurs in stereotypical views of Black men. Obasi's image characteristically presents a nuanced masculine identity that breaks free of the stereotypes

to which Mercer and Hall alert us. Through camera and stylist's eye, via the glint of the gold hoop earrings, the sumptuous satin fabrics against the threadbare upholstery and the soft vulnerability of Abayomi's face, the possibilities of how to be Black and male open out. The use of such jewellery and cloth do not collapse into exoticism or ostentation, or into what might be deemed feminine. There is a subtlety to the image. The concept of what Black masculinities are and can be is rewritten, made more complex.

Obasi has said regarding the genesis of his work, 'when you don't naturally fit into what is the masculine ideal, you're the one who's the problem. I found myself in the visual, working towards a visual style that I could connect with'. He effectively channels his first-hand experiences to 'unravel a well tied up knot' of misguided and confused information about queerness, womanhood, African-ness and what it is to be human. From his point of view, it is time to tell more visceral stories through fashion photography, stories that make us question the direction in which humanity is going. The use of symbolism and metaphor in his recent work comes from his desire to challenge the current carelessness and disregard for human rights that he sees resulting from misinformation. To that end, he views beauty as a form of activism. Beauty is not only about physicality and composition; it is also about emotion – what emotion does the image prompt? Does *Baff Up* make you feel haunted, soft, unsettled, for example? The Folawiyo draped one-shoulder top worn in the photograph was first featured in an Ibo-inspired collection, styled on a female model in the associated catwalk show. But, as Obasi points out, an Ibo man would traditionally wear a draped one-shoulder garment: 'the cut is how our ancestors dressed'. It is as though Obasi is asking through the image: where does this leave the media's fascination with gender fluidity and the presentation of male beauty through fashion?

The use of the street as a backdrop in Obasi's photography is deliberate. Evanescent graphics, like the Luna advertisement mentioned above, simultaneously ground his images and reference the charm of nostalgia.[13] But, seeing beauty in the way that he does, the street also provides him with a platform from which to orchestrate elegant protests. This parallels the use of the street as the setting for sartorialists' performance of identity and beauty, through dandy-esque discernment in dress. The idea of fashion as both a self-defining art form and an expression of everyday activism is taken to the max by the self-styling of those for whom fashion is a way of life (nos 70-2).

Parallel stereotypical views of Black women abide in popular visual culture. There is often a vast chasm between the way that we are represented and the way in which we see ourselves. From the maid to the matriarch, from the supersexual to the superwoman, Black women are all too often dually subjected to racism and sexism.[14] These issues are explored in the work of artist Mary Sibande, through her muse and alter ego Sophie. In her bright blue Victorian gown and white apron Sophie represents the archetypal Black woman as maid, but Sibande casts her in various scenarios that pull apart the image of invisibility and powerlessness portrayed by this stereotype (no.73). In the fashion world of the Global North there is a history of models from Africa, like Iman, being portrayed as 'dusky maidens', 'dipped in chocolate',[15] erotic, exotic, 'strange'.[16] Such depictions are equally reductive. African women have for decades critiqued their misrepresentation and raised the issue of the tightly interwoven relationship between racism and sexism. In 1976, for example, at the international conference on the theme of Women and Development at Wellesley College, Boston, Massachusetts, novelist Nawal El Saadawi, from Egypt, and sociologist Fatema Mernissi, from Morocco, vocalized their disdain at Western-centric feminist attempts to define global feminism.[17] Beyond the continent, author Alice Walker coined the term 'Womanism' six years later in 1982, to shed light on the intersection between these two 'isms' and to allow space for Black women to speak and be heard within and outside the then feminist movements of the Global North. bell hooks's seminal work *Ain't I a Woman* (1981) had similarly challenged the view that race and gender are two separate issues. hooks made a key point relevant to and reflective of contemporary thinking. To paraphrase, she wrote that equity for Black women has significance only if there is equity for all people. This echoes activist and poet Molara Ogundipe-Leslie's call for African feminisms rooted in West African historical, geographical and cultural specificities.[18] Latterly, feminist scholars have embraced the concept of intersectionality to consider race, gender, class, culture and geography together.

The increased number of Black female models gracing the pages of glossy magazines and appearing on fashion websites

68
Daniel Obasi
Baff Up
Egbeda, Lagos, Nigeria, 2019
Photograph published in *Nataal*, no.2,
April 2019

69
1950s advertisement for
Banania chocolate drink

70
Cedric Nzaka
Photograph for Everydaypeoplestories
Kramerville, Johannesburg, South Africa,
2020

71
Cedric Nzaka
Photograph for Everydaypeoplestories
Braamfontein, Johannesburg, South Africa,
2020

72
Cedric Nzaka
Photograph for Everydaypeoplestories
Newtown, Johannesburg, South Africa,
2019

across each market sector is there for all to see. However, some contemporary fashion images that seem to align with diversity and inclusion policies can reveal a subliminal strategy of 'exclusion by inclusion'.[19] There is a narrow inscription of what constitutes acceptable beauty and elegance, for example. Particular skin tones, hair textures and body types are seen as favourable. There is a Global Africa presence, but that presence is often circumscribed. *Vogue* editor-in-chief Edward Enninful and pioneering diversity advocate and former model Bethann Hardison are breaking this repeating pattern. Meanwhile, contemporary home-grown fashion media like *Nataal* and *Afrostylemagz* present African women in all their diversity and do not shy away from addressing issues around race, beauty, elegance and the feminine in their editorials and fashion spreads.

Anyone engaging with the contemporary African fashion scene cannot fail to notice the astounding number of inspiring women shaping the culture of the industry. Some strategically align themselves to forms of feminism, while others do not. But what they all do, through innovative business practices and their appreciation of the power of fashion to effect change, is expand understandings of the many ways in which we can be our integrated selves as women. To attempt to capture all their stories would be like 'trying to catch a flowing river in a calabash'.[20] Instead, let us consider two designers with contrasting aesthetics, Aisha Ayensu and Sindiso Khumalo, and a lifestyle brand and social enterprise, Studio One Eighty Nine. Aisha Ayensu, through her Ghana-based Christie Brown luxury brand, presents a head-turning image of femininity through her cinched-in waists, hourglass silhouettes and billowing layers of wax-resist print cloth (no.74). The brand aesthetic revisits local artisanal textile techniques, applying them to tailored ensembles that celebrate the female form. Wax-resist prints in sensual earth tones are pieced and patched together with unexpected fabrics such as shimmering brocades. Proportions are exaggerated. Flounces are sculptural. Lace cutwork is geometric and assertive; chic and grown-up. Ayensu takes familiar sartorial symbols of femininity – the curvaceous corseted forms and full skirts that emphasize the waist, the tailored peplum tops and long narrow skirts that visually reference the *kaba*, emphasizing the hips – as media through which to explore female power. The signifiers of old-school passive femininity are used to make a feminist

statement. Ayensu's collections are tantamount to power dressing for the twenty-first century. Gone are the skirt suits and shoulder pads of the 1980s, replaced by a look that marries female empowerment, independence and sensuality through fabric, form and ornament. Ayensu's fine detailing, deftly chosen embellishments, rich colours and womanly silhouettes operate in a similar fashion to artist Sibande's folded and looped Victorian-style gowns, used to challenge the disavowal of Black female agency.

Sindiso Khumalo's eponymous South African brand achieves similar ends but via a different aesthetic. Khumalo's research-based collections celebrate historical female activists like her own mother and the African American freedom fighter Harriet Tubman (see pp.136–7).[21] Fictional female characters such as Alice Walker's Miss Celie, the central protagonist in *The Color Purple* (1982), also provide starting points for her designs. Values and concerns that mirror those of Walker, for example equality and agency, are woven into Khumalo's collections. She is interested in the way that Black women are represented, and how she can reverse our misrepresentation through cut and cloth. Silhouettes therefore reference turn-of-the-twentieth-century women's clothes, with pie-crust frills and leg-of-mutton sleeves. Conversational prints, like the French eighteenth-century *toile de Jouy* style, are given a makeover by the inclusion of Khumalo's family and scenes from her remembered and imagined past. New forms of commemorative cloth are created through patchwork techniques, reminiscent of bell hooks's mobilization of the crazy quilt to map fragmented Global Africa histories.[22] In this approach, layered stories begin to be told: colonizer and colonized, European and African histories are no longer separated, compartmentalized; rather, they are shown to be tightly interwoven. Khumalo's collections actively yet subtly raise issues around race, gender and the way that power operates.

Since 2011, Rosario Dawson and Abrima Erwiah, co-founders of the fashion lifestyle and social enterprise brand Studio One Eighty Nine, have been fine-tuning an innovative business model that sits at the intersection of many of the themes discussed in this book. Through headquarters in Ghana and the US, the two produce fashion and home goods in collaboration with artisans based across the African continent who specialize in a number of craft techniques such as natural plant-based

73
Mary Sibande
Her Majesty Queen Sophie, 2010
Archival pigment ink on cotton rag paper

74
Designed by Christie Brown
Wax-print dress and metallic bustier
Accra, Ghana, Autumn/Winter 2020
Photographed by Duke Tetteh-Quarshie

indigo dying, hand-drawn batik, *kente* weaving, goldsmithing and engraving, and much more. Dignity, education (particularly for women and girls), sustainability and good design are placed at the heart of their organization. Dawson and Erwiah recognize and are motivated by the power of fashion – conscious, slow, respectful and Africa-centred – to effect lasting change at an individual, collective and environmental level. Working like this, they suggest alternative ways of producing and consuming fashion. On consumption Erwiah notes: 'It is critical to design with circularity in mind and to consider the effects of everything that we buy and make on the planet and on people.' By insisting on good design and the best quality of make, standards associated with luxury products, the duo and their team challenge expectations of what African fashions are. As Erwiah states:

We need to consistently be telling robust and multifaceted stories that show a wide range of the diversity and the beauty on the continent and its diaspora. And we need to be able to allow the work to be treated equitably and give the same opportunities for success as comparable goods in other countries.

By allowing artisans to make choices and to take ownership of their products, the studio also disrupts ideas of what developmental work might look like. The concept of the collective, whether building communities through fashion or networks between creatives and their customers, is a characteristic feature of the African fashion scene, one that is exemplified in Dawson and Erwiah's visionary work. Regarding this distinctive culture of fashion and the future of the broader industry, Erwiah summarizes the work of Studio One Eighty Nine: 'our mission is to work collectively and collaboratively to build a fashion industry that has more impact than aid and that shows the world and ourselves the power of craft, creativity, and our potential'. She stresses that the centrality of the collective and the proclivity to care is at the base of African cultures and values: 'One of my favourite West African *adinkra* [sayings] is "*Boa Me Na Me Mmoa Wo*" ("Help me and let me help you"), a symbol of inter-cooperation and interdependence'.[23] The idea of fashion as a medium to enact lasting change is further explored by the fashion creatives themselves through a series of illustrated personal reflections that form the main body of this part of the book. More than twenty contemporary practitioners have been carefully selected by Elisabeth Murray to show a

range of geographies, working practices and points of view. Each featured fashion creative exhibits a level of innovation that impacts the contours of global fashion. Each challenges understandings of what African fashions are and can be, while simultaneously critiquing assumptions about race, culture and gender. They all embrace fashion as a means through which we might create a future where we – that is the broader global inclusive 'we' – all flourish. Through photography and styling, Sibande, Obasi and the sartorialists show us that fashion can be a form of everyday activism, able to break down damaging stereotypes. Dawson and Erwiah, Ayensu and Khumalo are illustrative of the wealth of female leaders that are currently shaping the culture of fashion on the continent, effecting lasting change through economic growth, promoting empowerment through education, and instigating working practices grounded in sustainability and a respect for artisanry. These fashion creatives are just a small selection of the practitioners who are painting new pictures of Africa through fashion, to borrow Abloh's phrase. Foregrounding multiple and varied voices from the continent is a guiding principle of the *Africa Fashion* project as a whole since, as fashion photographer Tayo has said, 'everybody should be in charge of telling their own story. Because there is power and dignity in that'.[24]

75
Contemporary ensembles by MAXHOSA
AFRICA, IAMISIGO and Imane Ayissi
(see nos 123, 127, 89)

ORANGE CULTURE:
ONCE UPON A TIME, IN NIGERIA...

Monica L. Miller

*I had folded it carefully when I put it into the bag,
and now I smoothed the square it made in my lap. It was
deep blue, like what I imagined falling into the sea would
look like if you kept trying to find the bottom. There
were red hibiscus flowers splashed all over it, yellow dots
quivering at the stamens. They hadn't been printed to
scale; these hibiscus were smaller than real ones would be,
so more of them could fit into the blue. It had been Vivek's
favorite dress...*

*In the picture, Vivek was wearing the dress, a wraparound
tied on the left of his waist. The neckline fell into a V,
showing the bone of his sternum. His hair was down
and falling around his face. Juju had combed and plaited
it with gel into a hundred small plaits, then let them dry
and released them into many small waves cascading
down his body...*

*I remembered the first time I saw him in that dress;
I was surprised at its long sleeves and shoulder pads.
It would have been almost demure if not for the
neckline, which he would cover with his hair.
But he spun around to show it off, and for once
he looked happy and not tired...*

– Akwaeke Emezi, *The Death of Vivek Oji* (2020)

Once upon a time in Nigeria, Vivek became Nnemdi, who they truly were. This becoming was possible in and by means of a garment, a blue dress, printed with vibrant and brilliant hibiscus flowers, a dress with a deeply cut neckline that simultaneously exposed and concealed the skin. When Vivek became Nnemdi, the dress also became something else, a vehicle for a different kind of living in this skin, the beginning of a new and unexpected story. When Vivek became Nnemdi, the demand that he 'toughen up', stop being so soft and sensitive,

disappeared along with the fact that he 'was never one [a man] to begin with, anyway'.[2] As he 'spun around to show it off', the wraparound dress created its own environment, open to and for happiness.

What Nigerian writer Akwaeke Emezi shares with fellow Nigerian fashion designer Adebayo Oke-Lawal is an understanding of the way in which a garment, or clothing in general, can itself be a vehicle for the difference between living and being alive. Emezi's novel *The Death of Vivek Oji* begins with the knowledge of an ending – Vivek's death – but ends with the presence, however fleeting, of what Emezi might call themselves. Much more than the fabric from which they are made, clothes enable us to tell different stories with and on the body as they have the capacity to enable and support 'aliveness', especially a vitality that is dependent on expansiveness and a lack of actual and metaphorical boundaries and binaries.

In the novel, the dress with the hibiscus flower print serves as a material memory and talisman of a life lived evanescently. Never quite of, or even in, the place in which he was born, Vivek feels not just out of place, but actually otherworldly as a young boy growing up. His own recollections, seemingly from beyond the grave, interject the story that others are telling about him:

*I am not what everyone thinks I am. I never was. I didn't
have the mouth to put it into words, to say what was wrong,
to change things I felt I needed to change. And every day
it was difficult, walking around and knowing that they were
wrong, so completely wrong, that the real me was invisible to
them. It didn't even exist to them. So, if nobody sees you, are you
still there?*[3]

Vivek 'didn't have the mouth to put it into words'; instead, he let his appearance say what he could not articulate or announce. His cousin and lover Osita remembers their boyhoods together, conjures memories of a more elemental Vivek when looking at a photograph of him as a child:

Picture: the boy, shirtless, placing necklaces against his chest, draping them over his silver chain, clipping his ears with gold earrings, his hair rambling over his shoulders. He looks like a bride, half naked, partially undressed…

'I would give anything', he said, after Vivek's burial, 'give anything to see him like that just one more time, alive and covered with wealth.'[4]

Like Vivek, Adebayo Oke-Lawal also understood himself as incongruous, saying:

I grew up different to most boys…I was going to an all-boys school, a very hyper-masculine all-boys school, and I was very tiny and I had big glasses. People would say 'talk louder', 'talk like a man', 'do this', 'do that'. There was always aggravation towards me just because of the way I presented myself. So I was bullied a lot.[5]

Harassed by his peers, Oke-Lawal found the words to describe himself and his purpose when prompted by a teacher to write an essay about the colour orange. A combination of red and yellow and across the colour wheel from the primary colour blue (a traditionally 'masculine' colour in the West), orange is created out of and signals other muddy, indistinct possibilities. Oke-Lawal's essay, 'The Orange Boy', described a boy who was 'an individual; he was unique, he didn't really fit in, but he celebrated it despite this'.[6] Moved and impressed by the essay's honesty and power, Oke-Lawal's teacher arranged for it to be published online. The essay soon went viral, as it 'mused on feelings of otherness, acceptance, and vulnerability in Nigeria's patriarchal culture, and triggered an overwhelming response from people who, like Oke-Lawal, felt like outsiders'.[7] Letters poured in addressed to 'The Orange Boy'; here were expressions of connection and support, as well as threats and continued harassment at the daring of Oke-Lawal's masculine heresy. Nevertheless, 'The Orange Boy' was determined to be seen and manifest his presence, to continue his story. Oke-Lawal soon founded Orange Culture, which is much more than a clothing brand. It is a movement, born in and promoting a narrative exploration of truth-telling and power, vulnera-

bility and strength, resulting in an aliveness that can be created in the frisson between body and cloth, with fashion and style.

'The Orange Boy' story was necessary, resonated, and created its own path through and beyond the ways in which masculinity, gender and sexuality more generally are seen and experienced as part of self-fashioning in Nigeria. According to Ayodeji Rotinwa, writing on gender, fashion and style in contemporary Nigeria, 'Nigeria remains politically, socially, and religiously conservative. Men and women dress accordingly. In loose-fitting garments made from vivid traditional textiles (brocade, *àdìrẹ, ankara*) and Western-style business attire… much of their clothing is stylish, but is also meant to attract little attention.'[8] Given that 'these sartorial norms are upheld by institutions and social groups', the self-expression and desires of an 'Orange Boy' could and would be read as a provocation at best, or an indication of actual or perceived criminality at worst.[9] Dressing outside of expectation, openly 'appearing gay', will get you harassed by the police and the public.[10] From its beginnings, Orange Culture and Oke-Lawal defied gender norms. Even before he gave a name to his iconoclastic character in secondary school, Oke-Lawal spent his childhood exploring other ways in which to express himself that were beyond expectation. Interested in fashion from a very young age and inspired as a designer by watching his mother and her friends, who hailed from Enugu state, dress up in clothes full of colour and pattern, he is self-taught and learned to sew by watching videos. He would race home from school each day, pull out his sewing machine, and learn stitching and patterning via VHS. He preferred sewing to football, much to his father's disdain.[11] Internships with local designers all over Lagos during secondary school and university taught him what the videos could not. After a short career in finance, he launched Orange Culture, 'an emotional string of socially aware stories and expressions cut into clothing'. Orange Culture's own promotional material proudly declares that 'we believe that fashion can and should save lives'.[12]

Orange Culture's first collection 'was bold and featured a lot of red, and skirts over trousers'; upon its release, Oke-Lawal was greeted with both gratitude and death threats. Even as Orange Culture gained followers, he was told that his creations were 'demonic'.[13] When starting out, he designed for 'men' because he needed to establish a kind of legibility in order to

76
Designed by Orange Culture
Ensembles, 'S.E.N.S.E.S' collection
Nigeria, Autumn/Winter 2016
Photographed by Travys Owen

'We believe that fashion can and should save lives'

Orange Culture

make an impact on a specific design aesthetic that was about suits, tailored menswear, silhouettes that fit within a particular box. Therefore, Orange Culture's first 'stories' were about edgy menswear, about colour and fabric exhibiting another set of desires, about men expressing themselves however they might choose. Soon, though, the clothing became increasingly genderless and fluid enough to break out of that mould; a kind of androgyny developed within and around the designs.[14] Now making clothes that are described variously as gender-fluid, gender-neutral, androgynous, unisex and containing no binaries, Orange Culture says that 'we believe that clothing should be fluid and worn by any- and every-one'.[15]

Gender play in fashion design has a long history, but when this history intersects with the politics of race, Blackness and African-ness in fashion, the narrative changes, the play takes on other meanings. In a recent article, 'Can Fashion Be Truly Subversive When it Comes to Gender?', Georgia Illingworth questions the relationship between gender justice and two recent fashion world 'trends': the increasing prominence of non-binary and trans models, as well as the challenges these models make to the very traditional and seemingly hard and fast line between clothing for men and for women, the binary upon which the fashion industry is based. Noting that the rise of a fashion 'trend' is often its own demise, and that fashion's dependence on capitalism means that trends are trends only to the degree to which they 'sell', Illingworth argues that 'fashion has a history of responding to shifts in our cultural consciousness, co-opting and repackaging counter-culture with an alarming lack of meaningful consideration towards the people or ideas that are being appropriated.'[16] Referencing Yves Saint Laurent's Le Smoking, Coco Chanel's trousers and Giorgio Armani's power suit, Illingworth wonders, along with transgender model Hari Nef, if it is possible to disrupt, rather than merely play with, gender boundaries? Can gender binaries, represented here by boyfriend jeans and 'power' suits, be truly disordered without, for example, recourse to an uninspired, neutral colour palette and shapeless silhouette, seen in a recent unisex 'ungendered' line by fast-fashion giant Zara? Might the fashion designers and the industry have something to learn from brands that have a 'modern under-standing of gender' and which can express that understanding in a dynamic way? Illingworth mentions New York-based design collective Vaquera, which, like Orange Culture, would

like 'our clothing to be worn by any person of any gender', as a brand approaching these ideas.[17] We can also think of Black designer Telfar Clemens who has similarly 'been preaching the gospel of inclusivity for fifteen years', making clothes 'not for you, for anyone'.[18]

Telfar Clemens and Orange Culture share not only a commitment to liberatory design in terms of gender, but also link this commitment to racial equity and sustainability in their business practices. Clemens, a Liberian American, owns his business outright; once wanting to have the reach and capital of Michael Kors, he now eschews investors and controls all of his own sales. In her profile on the way in which Clemens's business thrived during the pandemic, Vanessa Friedman says that 'everything he has always stood for – financial, racial and gender inclusivity; community – is everything the fashion establishment, in the midst of economic upheaval and a long-overdue racial reckoning, is now desperate to embrace'.[19] Similarly, Oke-Lawal and Orange Culture have made a strong commitment to their own economic sustainability as well as environmental justice, in addition to the development and longevity of Nigerian and African fashion more generally. Orange Culture sources all fabric ethically and locally, and manufactures all of its clothing in Lagos; its manufacturing principles are designed to minimize waste and patrons are also encouraged to 'bring a garment back for updates'.[20] It runs a mentorship programme for young designers, hoping to provide and expand a knowledge base for the fashion industry in Nigeria.

Orange Culture and Clemens have both arrived at this deter-mination and commitment due to the historical exclusion and underdevelopment of Black and African fashion designers from the fashion system writ large. Clemens recognizes that 'for years we were treated like the sideshow to the actual industry...Now...their stance is, "No, we are the actual industry".'[21] Survival, it turns out, is not just linked to change and innovation, but to a radical, intersectional revisioning of the totality of the practice of getting dressed.

Fashion is about identity: as Orange Culture takes on Nigeria's culture of hyper-masculinity, a culture that Oke-Lawal describes as toxic and disabling, the movement also wants to challenge cliches about Africa and African fashions at the same time. When asked, 'What is masculinity to you?' and 'What is femininity to you?', Oke-Lawal has the same answer to both questions: 'a word that I do not think about or allow to limit my expression'.[22] He has a similar disdain for stereotypical thinking about Africa and Africans, insisting, with irony, that 'it is not all about malaria'.[23] If African masculinities are thought of as hard, unemotional and hyper-rational, then Orange Culture endeavours to enable the portrayal of vulnerability, softness and sensuality to challenge not only gender norms, but also misperceptions about African identity and possibility. In its collections Orange Culture materializes this desire for difference and modernity via a mix and mash-up of the typically feminine and masculine, as well as the African and Western. Diaphanous fabrics are worn with opaque cottons; designs based on or using traditionally African fabrics and shapes are paired with original patterns and prints. The innovative cut and drape of the clothes recall both Western and African dress, and contrasts and complements of rich, deep, bright and bold colour abound. Oke-Lawal knows that 'people want clothes that speak about culture, combat political backwardness, and pass on emotions. This allows me as a fashion designer to truly be an artist and to use art to fight, push for love, and to ward off ridiculous stereotypes'.[24]

Each Orange Culture collection is not just named thematically, but almost in/as a character, as a description, if you will, of 'The Orange Boy' and the importance of this alternative story about fashion, gender and culture. *Quirks Invasion* (Spring/Summer 2013) was followed by *Intrepid* (Resort 2014), which gave way to *The Feeling* (2014). *Pretty* (Autumn/Winter 2017) followed *School of Rejects* (Spring/Summer 2017). Most recently the Orange Boy seems to be giving advice and words to live by in collections like *Don't Look Under My Skirt* (Autumn/Winter 2019) and *Honest* (Autumn/Winter 2021). Consistent across these collections is a design aesthetic that maps the label's liberatory narrative impulse onto and within the very construction of the clothing. Nearly every collection features cut-outs, deep necklines and sheer fabrics (organza, pleated chiffon); texturing that pivots between the soft drape of, for example, silk or viscose, and harder materials like leather; as well as vibrant colour and colour contrast, across pattern and prints that themselves tell specific stories important to the openness and narrative tensions of the work and its culturo-political context.

Pretty (Autumn/Winter 2017) is about love and romance, according to Oke-Lawal, a manifestation of 'the full spectrum of what it means to be young, which encompasses the carelessness of love, the angst of failure, and also the delicateness of hurt'.[25] Across the collection, Oke-Lawal endeavours to visualize what it might feel like to experience love's excitement and warmth, as well as 'own [the] hurt' that often also accompanies it.[26] One observer finds that 'in some sense, it is a collection of rebirths – the moment after, the sense of journeying along, despite it all, and the idea of being broken to become beautiful.'[27] The colour story captures the attention first: *Pretty* is a study of browns, deep reds, maroons and yellows set off against jewelled tones of green and blue and, of course, fittingly burnt orange. Evoking the beauty and many hues of Black and/or African skin, 'pretty' is seemingly about loving the self as much as another, a possible pathway from hurt back to love. Brown and orange turtlenecks printed with a crying face or a person's legs from a body seemingly thrown down on the ground, pair with wide-leg brown leather trousers that eschew a typical waistband for a gathered leather ruffle (no.79); here we have contrasts of despair and whimsy communicated in the juxtaposition of the form-fitting knit with the more voluminous leather, the 'sadness' of the shirt with the gaiety of the trousers.

The *Pretty* collection is also a story of moments, as layering dominates many of the looks: a black crop shirt with the words 'Be True' appears over a long white tunic, and these top layers are worn over a pair of split-leg black trousers. The ingenious circular cut-outs on a yellow parka – one where a pocket could be, another on the shoulder – or the triangle cut-out on a longer white tunic, positioned where the heart would be, act as places of access, vulnerability. We also see this 'pretty' person on the other side of this emotional journey, luxuriating in love in a series of oversized, velvet suit pieces beautifully constructed for shape and movement (no.78). Rendered in a glorious solid, shimmering deep purple, or in a green velvet burnout fabric, these suit jackets, one short, the other long, frame the bodies of the models wearing them differently, but each exudes a sense of satisfaction. The shapes of the garments and the fabrics in which they are made, as well as the styling of this collection, invite any and all in: some of the cotton shirts have side ties, like wrap dresses, and the ruffles at the waist of the leather trousers are repeated on the shirt cuffs, blending 'masculine' and 'feminine' into unrecognizability. What matters here is not 'what piece for what person', but tone and mood – what is most important is romance, love, the highs and lows of a deep, intimate, emotional connection to another and/or to the self.

As the Orange Culture movement has matured and entered into the European and American fashion arenas, Orange Culture and Oke-Lawal are becoming even more articulate and clear about the importance to the movement of the interwoven nature of fashion, story, imagination and liberation. Orange Culture continues to commit to disruptive thinking about gender, masculinity, African-ness, and to visualizing that thinking within its collections in ever more subtle and blatant ways. It does not merely disrupt in order to critique and destroy, however; Orange Culture's design aesthetic also centres on repair, renewal, the process of deconstruction, building up and beginning again. Over the years, this portrayal of identity as a violent and beautiful process, as well as a sometimes circular emotional journey, has led to the brand being known for a radical iconoclasm, manifesting a tough sensuality or vulnerable strength that is increasingly appealing within Nigeria and also legible as such on the international market. As one outré stylista in Lagos, Charley Boy, opines, 'When you do something long enough, even if you have unbelievers in the beginning, they turn to converts.'[28] In recent years Oke-Lawal has worked to address both his loyal local audience as well as his new audiences abroad about the breadth of the Orange Culture project, giving interviews in high-profile places such as *Vogue*, and continuing to design clothes that articulate how Orange Culture manifests local histories that resonate beyond borders.

When speaking about Orange Culture in relation to one of his most recent collections, *Faces in the Cloud* (Spring/Summer 2021), Oke-Lawal says:

It is a powerful story not just about identity and survival, but of resilience that comes from a feeling of oneness. No story sits by itself. Our stories are woven by the fabric of our shared humanity. Yet it is often the case, this idea that one is not only marginalized but their story is seen as alien, something odd and deserving of exclusion. I have always understood clothing through stories and for me this was a way of peeling back, of

thinking how we exist in relation to what was before us. The pieces are deliberately soft, almost fragile, representing an understanding and thus caution, that the hurt we do to others, we also do to ourselves. For me, now more than ever, it is important to highlight that we have a human ability to rescue ourselves from violence.[29]

In order to embody this story in the *Faces in the Cloud* collection, Oke-Lawal called upon the character of Area Scatter, a genderqueer figure that takes Orange Culture's project into this historical and reparative territory. Area Scatter was an actual person, an Igbo man from south-east Nigeria, who, legend has it, disappeared for seven months and seven days, re-emerging 'spiritually and physically reborn' as a more feminine figure with 'preternatural musical gifts'.[30] He took on the name 'Area Scatter' or 'one who comes to disorganise a place, to shock and to reclaim; [he was] an eccentric fellow who has come to cause problems and change dynamics. And Area Scatter was true to her new name.' A 'gender-nonconformist', Area Scatter released an album, appeared on national television and was the subject of a now lost documentary; in short, they were 'embraced' by the late 1970s, post-civil war Nigerian scene. Orange Culture's decision to use Area Scatter as inspiration for the collection recovers a genderqueerness that existed before the current conservatism of Nigerian society and gestures back and forward to a time of increased freedom. Paying homage to this transformative life and thinking about them as a 'face in the clouds', evanescent, omnipresent and watching over, the collection's pieces are at once a combination of seeming contradictions that ultimately cohere into something new, something to be known by a new name. Indicating that 'the fabrication is soft, but deliberately charged against a few hard pieces', Oke-Lawal understands that 'this collection exalts form and textures as more than a decision to be different. It is an answer to surviving.'[31] A signature of the collection are its distinctive prints: ethereal white clouds on a background of a dramatic purple, blue, grey sky, shot through with bright orange bursts of colour; and a print of multiple curious, wide-open eyes, looking at and recognizing the viewer and body in the clothes (no.80).

This impulse to reclaim and begin again goes even further and is more personal in Orange Culture's latest collection, *Honest* (Autumn/Winter 2021), which takes this historical and

77
Designed by Orange Culture
Ensemble, 'Honest' collection
Nigeria, Autumn/Winter 2021
Photographed by Mikey Oshai

spiritual work home, literally (no.77). Focused on Oke-Lawal's turbulent relationship with his own father, who did not always understand or support his son's identity exploration or sartorial aspirations, the collection celebrates their recent reconciliation. As a child who eschewed sports and wanted to paint his nails, Oke-Lawal knows that he was a challenge to his father. Recently, however, everything changed when his father asked him about where the business was going and Oke-Lawal realized that this interest and curiosity signalled acceptance.[32] The collection plays with and modernizes the design aesthetic of his father's 1970s wardrobe, which inspired his work at its inception: 'His journey started at home. Portraits of his very stylish parents, now in their 50s, inspired his looks. His father wore printed shirts and shorts at a time when Nigeria was less conservative.'[33] Again the prints – which are few, but pivotal – are the key to the poignance of this collection. The 'Father's Love' print, a drawing of a father with a flower in his mouth, 'representing acceptance and tenderness', graces a sheer knit white turtleneck top; 'Held', a drawing of two intertwined hands, is rendered in white on a bright blue jacket; 'Flower Cave', which the campaign literature calls 'a mix of vibrant color contrasts that complicates the idea of monotone living experiences', is made into a duster coat, layered and floating over a shirt and slim trouser combination in the same fabric.[34] Taken together and spread across the collection, these prints tell a story of Oke-Lawal as a designer invested in trying to find as many ways as he can to recover and renew, for himself and for the culture.

The flowers in Orange Culture's *Honest* collection bring us back to Akwaeke Emezi, Vivek's hibiscus print dress and Nnemdi's liberation. As a critic, historian and theorist of gender who tells his story via fabric and fashion, Oke-Lawal endeavours to take as many as he can on a journey towards beauty, to infuse each and every person with the kind of wealth visible in the remembered photo of Vivek/Nnemdi. In the novel Vivek explains what a sense of beauty would or could mean for them, when contemplating a treasured book, a narrative of wholeness:

I kept the book for that title [The Beautyful Ones Are Not Yet Born], for how it was spelled. Beautyful. I had no idea why that spelling was chosen, but I liked it because it kept the beauty intact. It wasn't swallowed, killed off with an i to make a whole

new word. It was solid, it was still there, so much of it that it couldn't fit into a new word, so much fullness. You got a better sense of exactly what was causing that fullness. Beauty.

Beauty.

I wanted to be as whole as that word.[35]

Orange Culture is an ongoing story, a continual and continuous narrative of self-fashioning, a book with many chapters. Once upon a time, in Nigeria...

79
Orange Culture
Ensemble, 'Pretty' collection
Nigeria, Autumn/Winter 2017

78
Orange Culture
Ensemble, 'Pretty' collection
Nigeria, Autumn/Winter 2017

80
Designed by Orange Culture
Ensembles, 'Faces in the Cloud'
collection
Nigeria, Spring/Summer 2021
Photographed by Mikey Oshai

AGENTS OF CHANGE

Elisabeth Murray

'Don't ever forget. Know who you are'

Lukhanyo Mdingi

The work of contemporary African creatives disrupts by design, gently challenging the pervasive narrative that African fashion is singular and uniform. Beauty, luxury, minimalism all become politically charged concepts, challenging notions of what African fashion is and can be. Through their practice, African fashion creatives are agents of change, using their work to speak, putting to bed old stereotypes and looking forward, creating a better future. These narratives and provocations are multilayered and complex, and unique to the individual creatives. Yet among this diverse choir of voices certain notes resonate again and again: visibility, beauty, culture, community.

The practice of fashion exists across the world, as does the fashion industry in a multitude of forms. For many African fashion creatives the global fashion system is peripheral to their practice, the view or opinion of the Global North immaterial to everyday production and design. Yet for others it is important to change misconceptions about the continent. For Imane Ayissi, showing his work at Paris Couture Week is a provocation. In his reflection on page 120 he notes, 'luxurious contemporary garments made of textiles woven by craftsmen in Cameroon, Ghana or Nigeria is for me the best way of showing that African know-how is just as sophisticated and as valuable as artisanship in the rest of the world'. Visibility is the goal, but so is beauty. His work celebrates the plurality of the continent, glimpsed through combinations of raffia fringing and glossy silk or Cameroonian barkcloth flowers. Through his combination of materials Ayissi gives voice to the undeniable abundance of the continent, with diverse histories, cultures and material traditions. These provide a rich well of inspiration for African creatives, along with inspiration drawn from all elements of life and across the world, which can manifest in an incalculable number of ways.

Fibres and fabrics are the starting point for many, with textiles like *àdìrẹ*, *aṣọ-òkè*, barkcloth, *bògòlanfini*, *kanga* and *kente* providing rich sources of inspiration. In February 2020 Kenneth Ize made his debut at Paris Fashion Week with a collection created almost entirely from *aṣọ-òkè*, a handwoven cloth historically produced by the Yorùbá. *Aṣọ-òkè* is a staple of Ize's work, transformed into sharp tailored ensembles. For Ize, *aṣọ-òkè* is more than a fabric; it is a national resource and part of Nigeria's cultural heritage: 'What drives me now is passing down our story through fashion.'[1] Implicit in Ize's work is the challenging of notions about African fashion: 'Luxury is not a new thing that Africa has. There is a lot of luxury here. We had kings and queens and even now township men, who are a part of a really rich culture, very excessive, and extravagant.'[2]

Subtle challenge and notions of luxury are also found in the work of Lukhanyo Mdingi, which is a celebration of South African mohair. A fabric or fibre made from the hair of the Angora goat, mohair has been produced in Southern Africa since 1838, and South Africa, in particular the Karoo region, produces around 50 per cent of the world's mohair today.[3] In his Autumn/Winter 2019 *Perennial* collection, Mdingi worked with textile designer Stephanie Bentum to create felted wools from a mix of kid mohair and merino wool. The luxurious designs, in warm tawny gold and soft fluffy white, provide a distinct contrast to the colourful print cloth most associated with the continent by the Global North.

For Lisa Folawiyo, however, print cloth – or *ankara* as it is often known in Nigeria – is to be celebrated, and using it in her designs is a way of commemorating her cultural heritage. Introduced to West Africa in the mid- to late nineteenth century by European traders, its history is steeped in colonialism, but also agency. Local sellers and customers would regularly give feedback to the European merchants on the patterns and colours, influencing the development of the designs. Over time, specific patterns and designs gained local significance, commemorating an event, or speaking to a theme such as education or marriage. For Folawiyo, *ankara* is part of West African culture and central to her design aesthetic: 'Our mothers, grandmothers and probably great-grandmothers have worn this fabric.'[4] Yet culture is not static, and while Folawiyo's designs pay tribute to the history of *ankara*, they also place the fabric firmly in the current moment, with her designs mixing colours and prints, and often hand-embellished with beads and sequins. The pieces are far removed from Nigerian fashions of decades past. Fashion is constantly changing, and textile traditions evolve and adapt to meet the needs of the present. While fibres and fabrics serve as a starting point for many creatives, this does not mean that African fashion is uniform. Through their work creatives show there is no one way to *be* African and no single African aesthetic. The contemporary African fashion scene is as diverse and dynamic as the continent itself, and crucially always has been.

Narrative fashion is a foundational part of the contemporary African fashion scene: histories and cultures are woven into designs and translated into pattern and cut. For Thebe Magugu, each collection is an opportunity to explore a new story, from sexism and misogyny in his Autumn/Winter 2018 *Home Economics* collection to the changing face of African spirituality in his Autumn/Winter 2021 *Alchemy* collection, bringing together past, present and future. In the Spring/ Summer 2021 *Counter Intelligence* collection he explored the role of female spies in the apartheid government. Models were styled with navy leather holsters and leather satchels that could only be opened with a password. Mirroring the secretive nature of espionage, the details of this collection were hidden

in plain sight: a seemingly innocuous polka-dot print was, on closer inspection, a design created from the fingerprints of the former spy Olivia Anne Marie Forsyth.[5] Jackets featured a subtle screen-printed wire microphone on the lapel. Through his work Magugu shines a light on complex and often difficult pasts and presents.

Similar provocation can be found in Adeju Thompson's work for Lagos Space Programme. Thompson draws inspiration from a wide variety of sources, from pre-colonial knowledge systems, to workwear, architecture and Yohji Yamamoto. Detailed research is a fundamental part of Thompson's process, yet their work is not a homage to the past, but a prompt to look forward, 'continuing the conversation of culture'.[6] *Àdìrẹ*, a woven indigo-dyed cloth historically made by the Yorùbá, is a staple of Thompson's work. Their *Post-Àdìrẹ* project explored the future of this textile, translating it into knitwear and creating new graffiti-like motifs, speaking to today and the future, rather than emulating the past. Thompson's work is also a medium for exploring their identity, their designs mediated through a Nigerian lens. Thompson's last collection, *Project 5*, looked at the centuries-old gender-fluid Gélédé rituals of the Yorùbá. Speaking of the collection Thompson noted, 'Maybe my ancestors don't think of it as gender bending, but I can draw parallels with these ceremonies and the ballroom scene in New York in the 1980s.'[7] Thompson uses their work to call for better: 'I'm very proud of my identity as a queer man. I live in a society where you're policed for who you are and my work is a resistance to that policing.'[8]

The desire to use fashion as a medium for enacting change binds together creatives across the continent. Born out of the 2011 revolution in Egypt, Mariam Hazem and Hend Riad founded Reform Studio with the ambition to bring about positive social and environmental change.[9] Central to this mission is Plastex, a new fibre created by Hazem and Riad from discarded plastic bags mixed with cotton, prolonging the lifespan of a plastic bag from an average of 12 minutes to many years. Reform Studio's vision has expanded to also focus on revitalizing the Egyptian weaving industry, helping to protect knowledge of local weaving forms and to support weavers in rural areas so that they can earn a sustainable income from this craft. This approach is echoed by Awa Meité, whose work starts and ends with cotton, of which Mali is one of the biggest producers. The cotton industry employs around 40 per cent of the rural population, often living in sub-optimal conditions. For Meité the goal is to make pieces that celebrate the beauty of cotton, and through this to promote, support and actively create a thriving cotton industry in Mali, with a better working environment for those involved in cotton production.

This work is part of the much larger conversation around sustainability and sustainable practice. For many creatives sustainable practice is ground zero. Reuse, slow production, ethical working, local sourcing and circular production are all important elements in building a better future and a better society. In this, community is fundamental. Today, the African fashion industry is estimated to be worth $31 billion and contemporary creatives are determined to see this reinvested at a local level.[10] 'Made-in-Africa' is part of this, whether it is drawing on the rich natural resources of the continent, as with Mdingi or Meité, or manufacturing locally to create work.

Operating in Stone Town, Zanzibar, Tanzanian designer Doreen Mashika buys the cloth for her designs from local markets, noting that while it is more expensive than ordering wholesale, it is a way of giving back and contributing to the community.[11] Sarah Diouf follows a similar model for Tongoro, purchasing cloth in markets in Senegal, which are then transformed by local tailors into designs best known for being worn by Beyoncé. Due to limited cloth supply, the designs are made in small batches, which, as Diouf remarks, is challenging, but adds exclusivity to each garment. For Orange Culture's founder Adebayo Oke-Lawal, community is about encouraging the next generation, and he set up a mentorship programme, 'Painting Your Dreams', to empower and inspire young people through art.

Communities of fashion creatives across the continent are supported by the ever-evolving digital world, which plays an import role in connecting creative and manufacturer, designer and seller, wearer and maker. Creatives in Africa today are using this opportunity to explore new ways of working and thinking, contemplating their role as creatives and practitioners and their impact on society. Possibility abounds. The rich, diverse, pluralistic nature of the contemporary African fashion scene is both obvious and awe-inspiring. In this chapter, reflections by a number of creatives give a glimpse into the glamour and politics of this scene, and the agency and drive that are so fundamental to its community.

81
Orange Culture
Sweatshirt and skirt,
'S.E.N.S.E.S' collection, wool
Nigeria, Autumn/Winter 2016
V&A: T.2345-2021

Akosua Afriyie-Kumi
AAKS

I grew up around basket bags as a child in Ghana. I gave them as gifts and used them for storage. I remember having a lot of 'I wish it was more like this, I wish it was more like that' moments. Building on this idea I started researching into bag designs and fibres.

In 2015, after studying fashion at Kingston University in London, I embarked on my journey to Ghana to make this happen. I established AAKS, a luxury accessories brand that creates handcrafted quality bags in modern styles while maintaining the spirit and culture of Africa through traditional methods of weaving with bright exuberant colours. Ghana is a burgeoning creative hub, with a kaleidoscope of influences and inspiration that is unique and which I can tap into on my doorstep.

A central tenet of AAKS's philosophy is to preserve traditional techniques by combining them with modern design and utility. Our design philosophy prioritizes attention to detail, authenticity of technique and ethical values to shape truly unique pieces. Each collection silhouette tells a different story through detail, colour and shape. Our signature design, the Baw Pot Bag, takes its inspiration from earthenware pots usually used for cooking in the open air in many Ghanaian homes and of which I was very fond when growing up.

The artisans with whom I work use a traditional basketry weaving technique to create the shape of each bag. Weavers manoeuvre the strands between their fingertips, skilfully handling the fibres until the bags take shape. This technique has been passed down through generations in Ghana's Northern Region. There are no machines used in the weaving process. Because the bags are handwoven from raffia, each one retains an inherent uniqueness and this is what our handcraft entails.

We have an impact on the community in that we provide employment and encourage weaving to be valued as a major income earner for many in the cooperative. I hope that AAKS will go some way towards contributing to the revival and sustainment of weaving as a thriving art.

82 (above and below)
Weavers manoeuvring strands of raffia between their fingertips.

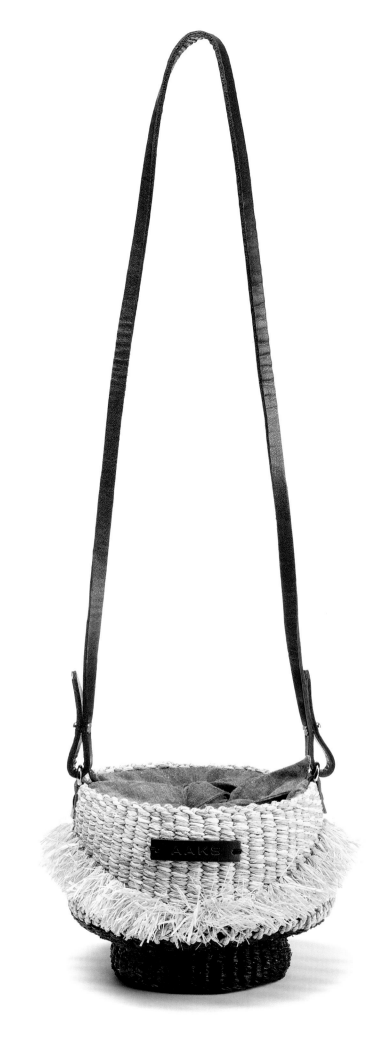

83
AAKS
Baw Pot Natural Cross Body Bag,
raffia, leather and linen
Ghana, designed 2014, made in 2021
V&A: T.116–2021

Gouled Ahmed

What drives me as an artist is the very immediate need to document and archive bodies in the Horn of Africa living on the margins: bodies deemed to have 'failed' society's expectations of worth, of usefulness, of care, of beauty. My work is a response to systems created to erase people who are seen as transgressive or deviant by moving us from the periphery, normalizing our difference, celebrating and dreaming of all the endless possibilities offered by a world that accepts all gender expressions. I am compelled by the need to bring a sense of freedom into the work that I produce and to allow all who interact with it to feel a sense of their own greatness. Art in all of its iterations is a site of disruption, a space of investigation and open curiosity. It allows us to contend with our own understandings of freedom, to test the limits and the barriers of our selfhoods. I attempt to embody this ethos in the images that I create.

Through my work as a costume designer, stylist and photographer I attempt to push back against the lack of nuance in the depictions of non-binary Black Muslims. If our starting point is invisibility, if our starting point is erasure, what modes and what modalities can we employ to prove that we exist, that we are here, alive and still breathing?

In my series *These Names Will Be Ours and Our Earth Will Remember Us Again Someday* I use self-portrait photography as a tool to reclaim agency over how my narrative is told, as well as to revolt against ingrained hegemonic cultural norms. I mix intricately textured garments from the Horn of Africa with contemporary, everyday materials, playing with the notions of the veil, of being masked and unmasked, and with shape and form.

My work seeks to dissect history and envision equitable aesthetic futures, as well as to create conceptual frameworks and a visual vocabulary to interrogate and reshape how structures of power have established the ways in which the 'other' is seen and understood in the Horn of Africa.

84
Styled and photographed
by Gouled Ahmed
Reclaiming Nostalgia
Addis Ababa, Ethiopia, 2018

85
Styled and photographed
by Gouled Ahmed
Golden Illusions
Addis Ababa, Ethiopia, 2019

86
Styled and photographed
by Gouled Ahmed
Addis Foam
Addis Ababa, Ethiopia, 2017

Imane Ayissi

I have been interested in fashion since I was a child, no doubt influenced by the elegance of my mother, the first Miss Cameroon, and the women in my family. At that time the political dimension of fashion was completely hidden for me, but it already sounded like a way to imagine a bigger, more wonderful world.

I moved to Paris in 1992 to work as a dancer and then quite quickly as a model, which allowed me to enter the big luxury fashion houses that I had dreamed of, like Yves Saint Laurent (1936–2008) and Pierre Cardin (1922–2020). Then I understood that fashion would be my way to tell African stories and show another version of African cultures. That is why, after several years, joining the official Haute Couture calendar became my goal, because haute couture can be considered the highest level of luxury fashion. For me it is an opportunity to change the world's vision of African fashion and, more generally, of African cultures. Africa has become 'trendy' in the fashion industry but in the Global North, and certainly for the majority of African people, associating Africa with luxury, refinement and preciousness remains problematic.

Showcasing, under the golden crown moulding of a Parisian building during Haute Couture Week, luxurious contemporary garments made of textiles woven by artisans in Cameroon, Ghana or Nigeria is for me the best way of showing that African know-how is just as sophisticated and as valuable as artisanship in the rest of the world, but also that African cultures fit perfectly in our modern times and can speak to the whole planet.

It is also an opportunity to reflect on the path that Africa can take to change the future of the fashion industry. Of course, the textile and fashion industry must be modernized on the African continent – but traditionally made-to-measure (therefore without overproduction), handmade African fashion using natural materials can be a starting point for imagining and rebuilding a future fashion industry that is more respectful of nature and human beings, in contrast to the fast-fashion industry and the environmental and societal damage it causes.

87
Imane Ayissi
Ensembles, 'Akouma' collection
Paris, France, Spring/Summer 2020

88
Imane Ayissi
Dress, 'Amal-Si' collection
Paris, France, Autumn/Winter 2020

89
Imane Ayissi
Detail of dress, 'Akouma' collection,
silk, hemp and barkcloth
Paris, France, Spring/Summer 2020
Given by Imane Ayissi
V&A: T.2434–2021

Maxwell Boko & Mmuso Potsane
MMUSOMAXWELL

For the longest time, Africa has been viewed and perceived by much of the world through a stereotypical lens. By creating MMUSOMAXWELL, we wanted to challenge that narrative and dismantle the idea of what African-inspired fashion should be or look like. Even though our work is inspired by our heritage, we are still individuals living in a modern age, influenced by the technology and science around us.

The nuances of our Xhosa and Sotho cultures are tacitly reflected in signature details, from border patterns to asymmetric illusion layering, while retaining a modern echo.

At the core, MMUSOMAXWELL is a ready-to-wear high-end womenswear brand, ethically creating garments inspired by African heritage and contemporary culture with a particular emphasis on tailoring to complement the modern woman: accentuating detail, practicality and wearability through a well-considered and sustainable design process that gives a sense of value and quality.

From the inception of the brand, we created as one of its missions an environment that is not only safe for the people and artisans we work with, but one that is also encouraging and kind. MMUSOMAXWELL is a small brand, so to enforce these practices is relatively easy now, but the aim is to grow with them intact and intertwined with our brand's DNA.

With South Africa producing approximately 50 per cent of the world's mohair, this industry is of immense value to the local economy. However, most of that raw material is not processed and finished locally. Therefore, it is imperative for us to utilize and promote this natural resource to create much-needed employment opportunities throughout the value chain.

90
MMUSOMAXWELL
Dress and trousers, 'Imbokodo' collection, wool
Johannesburg, South Africa, Spring/Summer 2021
Purchase funded by Diana Quasha
V&A: T.118–2021

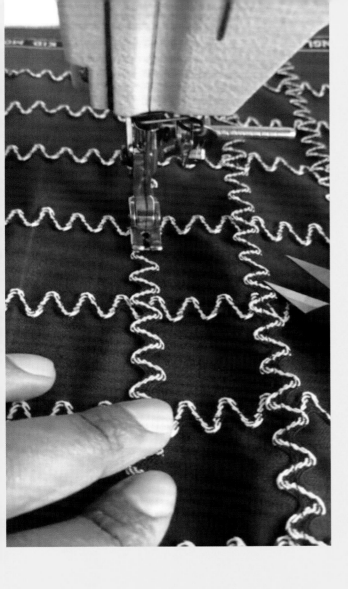

91
MMUSOMAXWELL
Top and skirt, 'Imbokodo' collection, kid
mohair, wool and beads
Johannesburg, South Africa, Spring/
Summer 2021 (detail of fabrication above)
V&A: T.117–2021

Lafalaise Dion

Native of Man, a town in north-western Côte d'Ivoire, I am a proud Dan / Yacouba. I became inspired by Dan culture thanks to the closeness I share with my grandmother, who would tell me countless stories about my foremothers. Such stories mesmerized me and I developed an unconditional admiration for the TéMaTé, a group of traditional dancers who dressed themselves with cowries before performing. Misconceptions, superstitions and leaving home meant I drifted away from my passion for dance until I reconsidered my place in this society. The more I researched African cultures and spirituality, the more I was drawn to cowries.

It all started in August 2018: I wanted to create a unique piece made of cowrie to wear at the Chale Wote Festival in Accra, something that would represent my culture and myself. My first headpiece, the *Queen of Cowries V*, was handcrafted with precious cowries, beads and a fishing line. The cowries represented the heritage that my ancestors gifted me, the gift I decided to share with future generations.

Lafalaise Dion is more than just a brand; it is a message I share. I want to promote the richness of my culture. We use cowries to communicate with our ancestors, to praise the Lord, to customize garments. They are the way that I reconcile myself with African spirituality. They are also an activist expression; all of my creations are messages to my fellow Africans, asking them to accept and embrace their story. Each piece is a different experience. It is a process of reflection, a message to get across, lots of research, a meeting, a conversation between the divine and us. Initially, not everyone understood my vision. Some were sceptical and afraid of the mystical side of cowries. But I kept going because I believed in myself and my story. Three years later, I can see how my work has influenced many people around the world. Young Africans are proud to claim their cultural heritage. We want to tell and write our own stories.

My ambitions for Africa fashion continue to grow. I want to be able to:

Bring about a change of mentality through my art
Encourage young designers to go back and embrace their roots
Promote African fashions and cultures
Show the world our greatness and make the ancestors proud
Create a real industry in fashion for the next generation

92
Lafalaise Dion wearing her jewellery,
Abidjan, Côte d'Ivoire, 2020

93
Designed by Lafalaise Dion
Jewellery, 'Tankë' (Dance) collection
Abidjan, Côte d'Ivoire, 2019
Photographed by Christian Goue

94
Designed by Lafalaise Dion
Jewellery, 'Tankë' (Dance) collection,
Abidjan, Côte d'Ivoire, 2019
Photographed by Christian Goue

Sarah Diouf
Tongoro

Whether artfully tying their *gèlè* (Nigeria) or draping themselves in a hand-dyed *bazin* (Mali), it is the regal aura emanating from the presence of whoever is wearing a garment that I believe to be the very essence of luxury: something priceless, timeless and intangible.

Africa's colonial history has delayed the continent in joining the global fashion dance over the last century, a gap furthered by a lack of investment in what could have been one of its most lucrative creative sectors.

In most African countries, tailoring is an inherent part of the culture and aesthetic. In Senegal, you are unlikely to walk two hundred metres in any neighbourhood without coming across a tailor's boutique; everyone has their own dedicated tailor, and whether we like to admit it or not, they are the true agents of the visible part of the culture and the vectors of local trends. However, outside the cultural festivities that provide most of their income, the activity is not lucrative enough for the average tailor to make a decent living.

Prior to launching Tongoro, I took the time to observe the African fashion scene and market, talked to Africans and non-Africans about their perceptions and consumption of African retail, had discussions with local tailors, and collected data I believed would help me develop a new formula. I started by asking myself why in all this time we haven't managed to create an African brand accessible enough in price to attract a large customer base, produced in a way that challenges perceptions about quality whilst telling an authentic story, and most importantly, benefiting all actors in the chain by keeping as top priority the hands who make the garments.

Tongoro was born out of my conviction that the 'Made in Africa' label could one day have as much cachet as any other, with a focus on quality, global resonance and local impact. Producing in Africa comes with its challenges but starting from scratch makes the possibilities endless in a space where everything is a first. If culture shapes the world, stories move it, and the internet and social media have allowed digital-native brands like mine to take the global stage, telling a story of the Africa of tomorrow, of the importance of cultural agents, visible and non-visible, and of pride in our identity, which remains the foundation of it all.

95
Designed by Tongoro
Ensemble for the 'Sama Gentu Maam' campaign,
Senegal, Spring/Summer 2021
Photographed by Sarah Diouf

96
Tongoro
Jama jumpsuit,
polyester satin
Senegal, 2021
V&A: T.2390-2021

97
Designed by Tongoro
Fifth Anniversary collection
Senegal, 2021
Photographed by Trevor
Stuurman

Ami Doshi Shah

As a child, I found comfort in the hours I spent outside digging for rocks and unearthing 'fossils'. There was something captivating about the silt-covered stones I clutched in my hand. What they represented about the earth's prehistory was something innately tactile and yet seemingly ethereal. And so began a lifelong obsession with the storytelling ability of a material or object (even in its rawest form) drawn from nature.

Away from the body, a piece of jewellery is an inanimate object, albeit beautiful. It is from this intersection between the human form and object that I derive the most joy and catharsis. How can I work with scale and texture and boldly connect with the human body, narrating in a more unexpected or even subversive way? How do the materials I use help me to do that and also root themselves in Kenya and our immense natural and human legacy?

The opportunity to make and produce in Kenya (and Africa in the wider context) inadvertently necessitates a slow and considered approach to design and production. Without cheap and easy access to complex supply chains and machinery, resourcefulness, human hands and ingenuity are part and parcel of crafting objects here. Sustainability is an ethos and methodology that makers on the continent have been practising for decades and it is the 'Global North' that is now striving for a way of producing and consuming that Africans have been compelled to adopt since the end of colonization.

I think the terms 'African Design' and 'African Designer' are huge misnomers. We are a continent of 54 countries, each with our own national, tribal, individual identities. I am a third-generation Kenyan of South Asian heritage with a Western/European education. Like anyone else, who I am and what I create are products of thousands of visual, human and cultural experiences, and with the globalized world that we live in, this is ever more magnified.

Each designer on the continent is carving out their own aesthetic, and collectively we exhibit the plethora of styles, craftsmanship, religious and cultural backgrounds that constitute 'Contemporary African Design'. It is this diversity that lends itself to broader understanding and review globally.

99
Designed by Ami Doshi Shah
Necklace, 'Salt of the Earth' collection, brass, sisal, borax salt
Kenya, 2019
Photographed by Sunny Dolat

98
Designed by Ami Doshi Shah
Earring, 'Closure' series, brass, ebony off-cuts, hair-on-hide leather
Kenya, 2018
Photographed by Maganga Mwagogo

100
Designed by Ami Doshi Shah
'Salt of the Earth' collection
Kenya, 2019
Photographed by Sunny Dolat

Lisa Folawiyo

I have always found fashion to be a multifaceted and fulfilling medium, where dreams and reality can coexist. We are subconsciously transported into heightened states of otherworldliness as we consciously mark times past, the present and the future. I draw inspiration from my Nigerian and West Indian heritage, the culture, traditions and ways of life. I am also influenced by my childhood memories, my moods, mindset, spiritual beliefs, sociopolitical convictions, my travels, the amazing personal style of women I have great admiration for, and so much more. Design serves as an art form without words through which I am able to fully express thoughts, feelings and ideas.

As a slow fashion brand, I am constantly motivated by new conscious methods of production that challenge us to reflect on our ecological footprint. We have tailored our techniques to heal the earth, while simultaneously celebrating our traditional craft and artisans. Through my designs, I am able to speak out and take ownership of a narrative: the story not only of who I am and where I am from, but also who I represent. With each garment created, culture and history are preserved, and through the work of our gifted artisans, such as weaving, beading and dyeing, knowledge and skill are transferred and communities are empowered.

Ankara, perhaps Nigeria's most loved and popular fabric, was also my first love. The company itself started with eight yards of *ankara* fabric, which we retexturized with intricate beading and embellishment. This one idea was instrumental in changing the way people viewed *ankara*: it added a certain glamour and luxury to what had always been perceived as an everyday fabric.

Oh, the joys in the art of design! To behold an idea become an actual piece worn by an actual person. The trials and failures and then the wins! The colours, the prints, the clashes and merges, the fabrics, the textures, the embellishments; the entire creative process is quite excruciating but most rewarding. The desire is to make every woman feel most beautiful and most confident. But, ultimately, it is for her to feel most herself, with most love for herself.

101
Lisa Folawiyo
The Maze shirt and shorts,
'Col 2 2021' collection
Lagos, Nigeria, 2021

102
Lisa Folawiyo
Shirt, 'Col 2 2021' collection
Lagos, Nigeria, 2021

103
Lisa Folawiyo
Ensemble, 'Col 2 2021' collection
Lagos, Nigeria, 2021

Mariam Hazem & Hend Riad
Reform Studio

Our story started ten years ago, directly after the first revolution in Egypt. We were excited to be part of the great changes around us, eager to make a stand, to make a difference. Our aim is to design for a cause, for a better quality of life: 'We turn trash into cash'. Every year Egypt produces millions of tons of waste, which ends up on the streets, in landfill, the sea or, even worse, is burned. Every minute, globally, around nine million single-use plastic bags are given out free to the public, making them the second most wasted item in the world. And the saddest thing is that each plastic bag is used, on average, for just 12 minutes. We knew we had to do something about all of this, so we created a unique material known as Plastex.

Plastex is a new eco-friendly handmade fabric made from wasted plastic bags interwoven with cotton threads. Plastex was officially tested at the National Research Centre, and it was proven to be strong, durable and water-resistant. We now have our own workshop that collects, stores and sorts the plastic bags before turning them into threads and weaving them on handlooms. We are committed to supporting the revival of the handweaving industry in Egypt that was on the brink of extinction, and to encouraging craftsmanship and empowering local communities, especially for under-privileged women with limited resources and education.

What made Plastex successful is not just the idea behind it, but how it has been designed. We have designed hundreds of patterns with a huge number of different applications for everyday products but with higher sustainable value, and we have also moved into fashion and accessories, an important step for us.

In 2020 we created the 'Rebel' collection, which was part of an active movement to support sustainable change in our world today. We were very careful while designing this collection to hang a label from each bag, allowing the owner to express herself, her own identity. The black-and-white labels, which deliberately contrast with the block colours of the bags, proudly proclaim the number of plastic bags that have been woven into the fabric. We want to encourage you to give back, make a statement and be rebellious, whether you are a he or a she or an it: 'IT'S TIME TO ACT AS ONE!'

104
Reform Studio,
Detail of Rebel Tote Bag (opposite)

105
Weaving with Plastex on the
loom at Reform Studio
Cairo, Egypt, 2021

106
Reform Studio
Rebel Tote Bag, orange
and pink Plastex
Cairo, Egypt, designed
2020, made in 2021
V&A: T.2391–2021

Nisha Kanabar

Once upon a time not too long ago, I thought a cookie-cutter fashion career was the validation I needed to offset my unconventional background as an Indian-heritage Tanzanian-born-and-raised woman with no real 'belonging' in fashion. Through my work in publishing at numerous Condé Nast houses, I cultivated a knack for both storytelling and design thinking, and a reverence for the role contemporary media played in a market's cultural identity and aesthetic ambassadorship. But I soon observed that fashion was an industry transforming quicker than it knew how to adapt – particularly in the advent of digital and e-commerce. It is undeniable that my continent has had a global perception problem. The Africa I know is diverse and pluralistic, brimming with stories of provenance, innovation and resilience. These are the stories I sought to tell, from within, through the lens of fashion, and the conversations I wanted to ignite through thoughtful commentary and real context.

In 2018 I designed *Industrie Africa*, a global destination for African luxury fashion, culture and community, to elevate the entire ecosystem – addressing its dissonance by coupling it with a world-class shopping experience, tackling consumer misconceptions of luxury from Africa, and ultimately creating a source of access, education and exposure to the region from the inside out. Interweaving consumer and industry ideals into one seamless online platform unlocks a sense of consciousness, and speaks to the new consumer in a way that aligns their patronage with their values.

As the climate evolves, we consider the strength of our voices in the future of fashion and the role we play within the global fashion system. Our regional fashion industry has made game-changing strides in the past few years alone towards increased creative and intellectual pan-Africanism. This barrier-breaking collectivism is the key to a greater sense of self-reliance – combined with accelerated digitization and regional trade. While today this idea is still relegated to modern niches, my hope for the region is to see this happen on a mainstream scale: an independent continent with a more robust intra-continental manufacturing and skills sector, where the consumer respects and shops local, and which offers better access to education and vocational training for the next generation of creative talent, especially in our smaller markets.

107
Industrie Africa campaign; Emmy Kasbit jacket, Emmy Kasbit skirt, Crystal Birch hat
Cape Town, South Africa, Spring/Summer 2020
Photographed by Ulrich Knoblauch

108
Industrie Africa campaign. Left to right: NKWO jacket,
Sidai Designs earrings, Shekudo shoes; KikoRomeo
jumpsuit, Pichulik earrings, Shekudo shoes; NKWO
jacket, Lisa Folowiyo cropped trousers and jacket set,
Shekudo shoes.
Cape Town, South Africa, Spring/Summer 2020
Photographed by Ulrich Knoblauch

109
Industrie Africa x Lisa Folawiyo
for Imprint Editorial
Lisa Folawiyo lookbook for
Spring/Summer 2020
Graphic Designer: Juan Carlos
Verdejor

Sindiso Khumalo

'Honouring women, past and present' is at the forefront of my practice. Inspired by the lineage of enduring and powerful Black women in history, our collections celebrate historical female figures such as South African activist Charlotte Maxeke, Sarah Forbes Bonetta (Yorùbán princess and god-daughter of Queen Victoria) and American abolitionist Harriet Tubman.

I hope to amplify their voices through the storytelling in our collections. The *Miss Celie* dress is a cornerstone and staple of my designs. Its name pays homage to and is inspired by the character in the 1982 novel *The Color Purple* by Alice Walker. An unassumingly simple A-line-cut dress, this garment combines the humble nature of an early 1900s smock or apron with soft femininity. Both decorative and understated, the dress challenges the aged notion that a feminine silhouette cannot also be utilitarian. The 'Zulu Princess' print featured in our dress was an illustration created by my friend, artist Alex Fox, to portray traditional Nguni life and homestead. The illustration is one of my mother on my wedding day, wearing a traditional traditional Zulu headdress called an *Inkehli*.

As a designer I work in the medium of textiles and print for my storytelling. We are currently working with NGO Embrace Dignity from South Africa on an initiative to uplift young Black women who have been previously trafficked and exploited. We teach them hand-embroidery, quilting and crochet, and their textiles are a big feature in our collections. We also work with artisans in Burkina Faso in making handwoven fabric. The input from both these initiatives are a big feature in our collections and in our business as a whole. As a sustainable designer, I believe sustainability is about people. Through all our individual projects, our goal is to create positive social and economic impact with the different communities, and in turn create real change in our African continent. Fashion as a form of social activism.

110
Sindiso Khumalo
North Star suit
Cape Town, South Africa,
Autumn/Winter 2021

111
Sindiso Khumalo
Miss Celie dress, 'Minty' collection,
printed cotton
Cape Town, South Africa,
Spring/Summer 2021

112
Sindiso Khumalo
Dress, 'Minty' collection
Cape Town, South Africa,
Spring/Summer 2021

Doreen Mashika

While worldwide many customs are in transition, I firmly believe that the bedrock of traditional cultures in Africa is still a powerful force, and one that I – and all of us – should celebrate! What is not to love about the uniqueness and splendour of African fashion?

My heart has always been in Tanzania and I knew I would return after living in Switzerland for a few years. When I did, I decided to start a business that would give back to my community. Fashion is such an effortless way to communicate your individual style, as well as your own views and ideas. I partner with women's groups in local villages who make the goods largely by hand, using traditional African techniques. Fair pay is just the beginning. I visit the village so I can meet my crafters and build relationships that cultivate high levels of mutual appreciation, respect and trust. From the first day of the brand, sourcing *khangas* for our collections has been exclusively open to smaller traders. Although access to larger factories is possible, it is my mission to see the brand empower households that need the income most. This way I can flourish together with the community, and such action also plays a part in reducing poverty while making women look confident and beautiful in Zanzibar contemporary fashion.

Proud to be making exclusively in my native Tanzania, I use traditional techniques and fabrics in an innovative way, combining big patterns with intricate detailing. In 2019 I had the wildest idea of incorporating handwoven grass into garments, which stemmed from a visit to Paje on the south-east coast of Zanzibar. Paje is famous for its seaweed farming. Watching these resilient women go to work, I noticed three things: vibrant dresses, woven baskets and working tools. I decided to launch the 'Mikono' collection, which involved a larger number of village women in the weaving of grass and in so doing was one of my most empowering collections. Expanding our customer base in Zanzibar, Europe and the USA, this collection found new customers in countries such as Kuwait.

Zanzibar – with its crosswinds and old colonial trading routes – has for centuries been a cosmopolitan and multicultural melting pot. It is precisely this essence of combined flavours – my Western design philosophy melding beautifully with African traditions, patterns and techniques – that inspires my work.

113
Designed by Doreen Mashika
Top and skirt, 'Nyota' collection
Zanzibar, Tanzania, Spring/Summer 2020
Photographed by Rogers Ouma

114
Designed by Doreen Mashika
Ensemble, 'Mikono' collection
Zanzibar, Tanzania, 2020
Photographed by Jacques Weyers

115
Industrie Africa x Doreen Mashika
The *Tamu* dress and the *Amani* dress
Zanzibar, Tanzania, Spring/Summer 2020

Lukhanyo Mdingi

The premise of our label stems from consideration and love. I do not mean this necessarily in a romantic way, but the essence of our label is based on collaboration and working with key artisans who are exceptionally passionate about their craft – primarily in textile development.

Our aim is to create a hybrid of artisanal craft and modern design. Having had the opportunity to work with each individual, I have come to realize that there is a mindfulness and soulful kind of spirit that gets woven within the fabric of select textiles. The intimacy of the human hands becomes an extension of that love and consideration that I speak of. It is evident within each piece; it is something honest, steady and strong. These become the key elements that we want people to feel, the human and artisanal part that becomes the provenance of our pieces.

Working with human beings is never a straight road. However, our movements and processes are always intentional and driven by reaching our fullest potential in the most honourable way. Using our time, our talent and the spirit of communication is the only way that we can achieve a level of excellence that is an extension of the previous body of work created. The idea is to be forever keeping our eyes on the motive and using that to get the job done in the most respectful and honourable way.

The power of the collective is far greater than that of a single person. Our key relationships are with our textile developers, pattern makers and seamstresses, essentially the hands that have given our label its honesty. I truthfully believe that this essence is woven within the fabric of our collections. The creation of a space of trust where individuals are able to use their time and their gifts within our label has contributed to who we are today.

We believe in human beings, their spirit and their ingenuity. Given the discordant place that the world is currently in, we need a sense of steadiness, consideration and mindfulness within the practice of design.

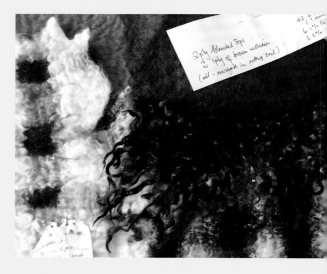

116
Lukhanyo Mdingi
Felted samples
Cape Town, South Africa, 2021

117
Lukhanyo Mdingi
'Don't Ever Forget'
Cape Town, South Africa, 2021

118
Lukhanyo Mdingi
Ensemble, 'Perennial' collection, mohair,
merino wool and silk
Cape Town, South Africa,
Autumn/Winter 2019
Collection of Lukhanyo Mdingi

119
Lukhanyo Mdingi
Ensemble, 'Perennial' collection,
mohair, merino wool and silk
Cape Town, South Africa,
Autumn/Winter 2019
Collection of Lukhanyo Mdingi

Awa Meité

Creativity and fashion allow us to write our own narratives. They are spaces for people who have a vision for the continent and who want to show its strength and its immense humanity, its beauty, and its material and non-material resources. This gives full meaning to the emergence of African and Black creatives, inspiring present and future generations. The recognition of African talent locally and internationally shows to the world the face of an Africa in which we believe.

I am committed to promoting local production in order to have an impact on the society in which I live. Healing cotton has become the image of my brand. Mali is one of the most important cotton producers in Africa. This sector creates millions of jobs for people locally in Mali, but the living conditions of both producers and other players in the sector remain precarious. Our fight is to transform cotton as much as possible locally in order to create real added value, instead of just being exporters of raw cotton.

The collections I create are in shapes and colours that are comfortable and can be worn in all seasons. Our fabrics are used season after season, recycled into the new collections. Preserving what we make is important because we want it to be timeless. Africa has no lesson to learn when it comes to slow fashion and environmental protection. We have been upcycling for decades: the clothes of the elders are well maintained so that the younger generation can inherit them.

The rich imagination of Africa is an inexhaustible source of inspiration for African creatives. The confidence we have in our contribution to global wealth makes us aware that we have an important place to occupy and that we have to force the doors that do not open to us.

Covid-19 has prompted a period of searching for alternatives, as the dominant model has reached its limits. Africa must be at the heart of new proposals, because its strength is its ability to reinvent itself through creation while giving hope to the world. Creativity and fashion must be at the centre of this process of rewriting a common narrative.

120
Awa Meité
Koloni ensemble
Mali, Spring/Summer 2020

121
Awa Meité
Yeleen ensemble
Mali, Spring/Summer 2020
Photographed by FINIMOUGOU

Laduma Ngxokolo
MAXHOSA AFRICA

MAXHOSA AFRICA was born out of my thesis project, looking for knitwear design solutions that would be suitable for *amakrwala*, initiates from the Xhosa people of the Nguni group, a cultural group primarily from Southern Africa.

Traditional Xhosa beadwork patterns, symbols and colours were a rich source of inspiration. My approach is very technical and rooted in anthropology. It leads me to study old artworks and research how regal people used to dress in the olden times. I reinterpret this in today's design language and make it cool for younger kids and the upcoming generations. It is very important to know that clothes are functional items, yet also express moods, feelings and personality.

Fashion has always been in my life. My mother, Lindelwa Ngxokolo, was a fashion designer; she filled our home with art and took us on museum excursions. My mother is affectionally known as the founder of the brand. She made a revolutionary move when she opted to purchase a knitting machine instead of a TV. I used it to design and knit my first jersey as a teenager. Her buying that knitting machine changed my direction in life forever. I believe art was always what I was destined to do; fashion became the canvas with which I showcase my art. I would now call myself a pattern designer and my outputs are fashion and lifestyle products.

I design to express feeling. I believe design is a state of mind: when you are happy, design; when you do not feel well, design. My latest collection showcased 'luxury as the new happiness', which I approached with the mindset that art and design make people happy, even with all the negative things happening in the world.

I believe I have shifted the paradigm around culture and luxury, along with the mindsets of people who saw African designs or culture as primitive. Not only is our African culture now beginning to be seen and celebrated by the global world, but it is also heralded as forward-thinking. I would like to think we have contributed to this, and to Xhosa cultures study and research. I believe we have shifted the mindsets of people who saw African designs or culture as primitive.

122
Laduma Ngxokolo, Johannesburg,
South Africa, 2016

124
MAXHOSA AFRICA
Dress, 'Apropriyeyshin' collection,
knitted wool,
Johannesburg, South Africa,
Spring/Summer 2017
Donated by MAXHOSA AFRICA
V&A T.2431–2021

123 (left and above)
MAXHOSA AFRICA
Shawl jacket and shorts, 'Camagu' collection,
knitted wool and knitted silk,
Johannesburg, South Africa, Autumn/Winter 2015
Donated by MAXHOSA AFRICA
V&A: T.2432–2021

Bubu Ogisi
IAMISIGO

I grew up in multiple cities: born in Lagos, spending holidays in London, with family, and later studying in Accra and Paris. Now I live between Lagos, Accra, Abidjan and Nairobi and IAMISIGO is based between these places.

Founded in 2009, we create wearable art pieces from unconventional materials such as barkcloth, plastic, hemp or raffia and use heritage textile traditions that are learned through in-depth research with remote African communities in different parts of the African continent. Our work primarily focuses on how fashion and textiles can not only keep history alive but also pass on information for the future through the preservation of techniques and expression through materials. Using the ultimate canvas – the human body – clothing becomes a vehicle of communication. By conveying lost historical stories and transforming this found 'data' into garments and fibres, we create a form of silent protest against post- and neocolonialism, portrayed through textile art, space installations, visuals and film.

The ideas of rawness, anti-'finishing' (and therefore anti-Eurocentrism) and functionality exist as strong conceptual design threads throughout my work. By exaggerating texture, structure and space I am able to break and transform the rules and expectations of what textiles are to conjure a sense of transient humanity. For me, the authentic African aesthetic is one that has no borders and is free in its form of expression: we do not often use zips; we create our own closures at IAMISIGO or create pieces that do not need closures, fine-lined seams or hemming.

My work focuses on decolonizing the mind thoroughly, by engaging with sociopolitical questions relating to religion, gender, traditions, symbols and scripts, tribes and magic, as well as issues affecting the future of our ecosystem. How do we embrace our histories as having passed, and now move forward?

As an agent of change my ideology is to highlight and promote cultural crossover where no identity is negotiated, bringing together multiple cultures to create free-minded pieces. Our work is 100 per cent artisanal and handmade, focusing on ancestral techniques while incorporating waste to show the importance of preserving handmade processes and fighting against environmental degradation.

126
IAMISIGO
Ensemble,
'Land of Gods' collection,
recycled polyester and beads
Nigeria, Spring/Summer 2021
Photographed by Chris Okoigun

127
IAMISIGO
Ensemble, 'Gods of the Wilderness' collection,
wool dress, recycled polyamide net and wool
veil and polyester velvet slippers
Nigeria, Spring/Summer 2019
Purchase funded by Lorraine and Steve Groves
V&A: T.2337–2021

125
IAMISIGO
Ensemble, 'Chasing Evil' collection,
palm leaf raffia and cotton
Kenya, Autumn/Winter 2020
Photographed by Maganga Mwagogo

Adebayo Oke-Lawal
Orange Culture

I launched Orange Culture in 2010/11, after having worked for several Nigerian designers. I wanted to turn my own vision and passion for fashion into reality. Orange Culture is more than just a brand: it is an emotional string of socially aware stories and expressions cut into clothing. We believe fashion can and should save lives. It is a 'movement' that covers universal silhouettes with an African touch, translating into a mixture of Nigerian-inspired print fabrics, colour and contemporary androgynous clothing. We believe clothing should be fluid and have the ability to be worn by any- and everyone.

We are known for exploring unusual fabrication methods and experiment with them on every and any gender. From organza on men in 2011 to pleated chiffons in later years, the brand is not and will never be limited by societal stereotypes of masculinity.

I grew up with a passion for confronting societal norms and I want to use fashion to combat hyper-masculinity, injustice and suppressed expressions of Africanism. Orange Culture's garments answer to just about anyone interested in telling a story with the way they present themselves. All pieces are manufactured in Lagos, using ethically sourced fabrics from local Nigerian fabric makers. We take our staff through rigorous training processes and offer them the opportunity to attend skill-acquisition initiatives.

I am also very concerned with youth and have launched a Corporate Social Responsibility project called 'Painting your Dreams', which aims to use art to inspire young people to believe in themselves; and we run an Orange mentorship programme, which provides knowledge exchange sessions led by industry practitioners to help aspiring designers within the continent and beyond. I believe in reducing waste and have introduced that into our practices, with zero to little waste in manufacturing procedures and fabric-sourcing methods, and through revamp programmes that allow customers to bring a garment back for updates. I believe the highest form of sustainability is community development and my focus is on using Orange Culture as a conduit to do just that. I teach, mentor and create spaces and manufacturing practices that gives back to the community on a regular basis.

128
Designed by Orange Culture
Shirts, 'D.Y.T.M.' collection
Nigeria, Spring/Summer 2018
Photographed by William Ukoh

130
Orange Culture
Shirt and shorts, 'Flower Boy' collection, cotton
Nigeria, Autumn/Winter 2020
Purchase funded by Lorraine and Steve Groves
V&A: T.2347-2021

129
Orange Culture
Blouse and trousers, 'Shadow Man'
collection, organza and polyester
Nigeria, Spring/Summer 2020
V&A: T.2346-2021

Nkwo Onwuka
NKWO

It all started for me with an obsession with dolls and a mother who taught me how to sew. I earned a degree in Psychology but the love of making dolls' clothes out of the scraps from my mother's cutting table has evolved into an artisanal brand at the forefront of the sustainable fashion movement in Nigeria. My brand has its very own philosophy – THE PHILOSOPHY OF LESS – which asks, 'What is the point in creating more than we can use if it causes us to live less of a life?' It addresses the issue of waste and what to do with it. With the conservation of natural resources and the environment as my core values, I focus on the issue of textile waste and how it can be reduced by using it as a resource.

My constant exploration and experimentation with ways to use waste as a raw material have led to the invention of a new African textile called DAKALA CLOTH. I developed a technique for stripping scraps of fabric and sewing them back together to form a new piece of cloth.

The experimentation did not stop there and over time I have added new dimensions to this ethical waste cloth in a bid to achieve 100 per cent zero waste garment production. With DAKALA WEB, for example, the waste scraps are stripped into yarn that is used to weave exact shapes, such as a sleeve, on traditional looms (another radical technique I developed). These pieces are then taken off the loom and coupled together, creating absolutely no waste at all!

It is my way of bridging the gap between textile waste reduction and the preservation of our traditional textile craft skills.

The hope is that by working closely with artisans and local makers I can create meaningful change on the continent by involving them in a new way of working that is more mindful, and celebrates and preserves the art of creation. Through innovation, our local crafts can move from a mere subsistence activity to become scalable and profitable businesses.

131
NKWO
Festival jackets, 'GEREWOL'
capsule collection
Abuja, Nigeria, 2020

132
NKWO
Strips of denim to be used for DAKALA
CLOTH

133
NKWO
DAKALA CLOTH ensemble, 'Who
Knew' collection, denim
Abuja, Nigeria, Spring/Summer 2019
V&A: T.115-2021

Neo Serati Mofammere
Nao Serati

Nao Serati is my 'Sasha Fierce'. She is the girl with the platinum blonde hair and platform heels putting everyone's joy at the centre of it all.

After studying art as a teenager at the National School of the Arts, Johannesburg, I wanted to choose a career for myself where I would get to create and share ideas.

Fashion was a creative language that I could use to have conversations and observe people working and living with my art form.

After a failed attempt at a fashion competition, I got the people's ears and eyes in South Africa, being invited to show after show!

This allowed me to stretch my feet and imagine a South Africa where you could wear a short skirt, sheer tops and dress African men in pink!

It was a freedom protest, asking, 'Now that we've got it, what do we plan on doing with it?'

With making clothing, I have learned the value of people's hands and hearts. I have learned that people want to share in projects that spark joy and conversation. I have learned that with a well-cut skirt we can discuss freedom, love and exploration.

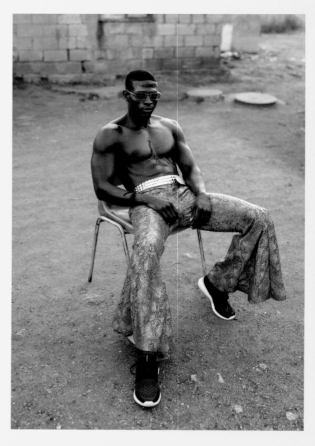

134
Designed by Nao Serati
Trousers
Johannesburg, South Africa, 2017
Photographed by Tatenda Chidora

135
Designed by Nao Serati
Ensemble
Johannesburg, South Africa, 2017
Photographed by Tatenda Chidora

Laure Tarot & Baay Sooley
Bull Doff

137
Bull Doff
Ensemble
Photograph at Africa Fashion
Week, London, 2012

Dakar is not one of those towns people tell stories about. Everything ends up falling into the sea there – genius, rumour and that vast wintering sun that holds the town in dazzling mystery. – Oumar Ndao, *Dakar L'ineffable* (2011)

It is an elusive town, but one that proves to have a gift of meaning written into the chaos. Dakar – or etymologically speaking *dëkk-raw*, 'the refuge' – is an invitation to travel: sounds, shapes, scents and images punctuate the colours of this ever-changing place. Dakar unfolds before you like a performance on an urban stage: the *thiaaf* (roasted nut) seller setting up at the foot of the building; the harmattan winds swelling the loose-fitting, coloured *boubous* and dumping the sand of desert dunes on the pavements; the shoeshine boy polishing up his footstool in the hope of attracting a customer with a keen ear. Dakar transports you like a never-ending trance. In 2010 it was from this evanescent whirlwind, this producer of ideas and desires, this everyday street life that the natural source of our inspiration came. And from our creative instinct came the idea of taking the fabrics, graphic elements and codes that surround us in a new direction by celebrating them in day-to-day clothing. The need to tell stories through our collections has always acted as a driving force, giving both aesthetic and narrative meaning to each of our textile architectures. These are artefacts that meld and merge with the urban setting, creating a universal encounter between fashion and the street.

Like any populated place, Dakar is inhabited by the silhouettes of figures that, like a mirror, reflect the intrinsic nature of their society, on a cultural, economic, social and indeed political level. Reflecting the contemporaneity of Africa, they are unconcerned by outside perceptions, by those too often stigmatized visions, rooted in a stereotyped image of a fashion considered as exotic or, worse still, as simple and nothing more. This is an Africa that is made of those and that which inhabit it – young and modern, deeply rooted and yet, at the same time, groundbreaking. For us today, the act of creation through fashion is an opportunity to showcase and express the immutable and indeed inviolable riches of this continent. It is not about identifying fashion in terms of different geographic areas. It is natural that each of us should remain attached and connected to our own roots, but fashion is now part of some kind of universality in which stylistic crossbreeding becomes the thread that holds it together.

138
Bull Doff
Ensemble
Photograph at Africa Fashion
Week, London, 2012

139
Bull Doff
'Tales & Legends – Djinn de Timis'
Senegal, 2013
Photography and visual design by
Fabrice Monteiro

Adeju Thompson
Lagos Space Programme

Lagos Space Programme is a non-binary fashion design project and multi-disciplinary art practice exploring the overlooked traditions of Yorùbá culture. The name of the label reflects the ethos behind my creative process; a name grounded in my roots, but still looking outwards. By reviving cultural knowledge in the objects I design, I identify overlooked potentialities for the present and create fashion archives that store cultural memories for the future. Over the course of my career, the concept of decolonizing design has informed my evolution and my practice. Through my work, I highlight an alternate side of the African narrative.

With my *Post-Àdìrę* exploration – an ongoing investigation of storytelling via traditional techniques using resist-dyeing with natural indigo – I collaborated with Alexandra Weigand and a community of women dyers in south-western Nigeria. Within these collaborations, the jointly created contemporary forms and objects reanimated traditional crafts through layered narratives.

My *Project 5* collection, entitled '*Aşọ Lànkí, Kí Ató Ki Ènìyàn* / We Greet Dress Before We Greet its Wearer', deconstructs myths around gender roles and identity by highlighting the gender-bending ritual of the Gélédé, through which the Yorùbá people celebrate female ancestors, deities and the community's elderly women – all embodied by men.

The collection explores the romance found in the ritual of dress, the way Yorùbá people have presented themselves for centuries: the drama of the folding and draping of sensuous fabrics made of stories, time-intensive labour, coded colours and varied textures. I also worked with a seventh-generation bronze caster, in collaboration with Swiss artist Dunja Herzog, to develop and design objects that highlight the aesthetic and spiritual significance of bodily adornments in Yorùbá culture. I collaborated with the London-based artist David Gardner to design the Gélédé mask.

It is very important that through my practice I deconstruct misconceptions about contemporary African life, especially notions about gender and queerness. There is a common misconception that this is a Western construct, and by exploring design through a cultural lens I aim to educate and highlight Africa's progressive pre-colonial past.

140
Designed by Lagos Space Programme
Ensemble, '*Aşọ Lànkí, Kí Ató Ki Ènìyàn* / We Greet Dress Before We Greet its Wearer' collection
Lagos, Nigeria, 2021
Photographed by Kadara Enyeasi

141
Designed by Lagos Space Programme
Accessory, '*Aşọ Lànkí, Kí Ató Ki Ènìyàn* / We Greet Dress Before We Greet its Wearer' collection
Lagos, Nigeria, 2021
Photographed by Kadara Enyeasi

142
Designed by Lagos Space Programme
Accessories, 'Aṣọ Lànkí, Kí Ató Kí Ènìyàn / We Greet
Dress Before We Greet its Wearer' collection
Lagos, Nigeria, 2021
Photographed by Adedamola Odetara

143
Designed by Lagos Space Programme
Dyeing fabric for Aṣọ Lànkí,
'Aṣọ Lànkí, Kí Ató Kí Ènìyàn / We Greet Dress
Before We Greet its Wearer' collection
Lagos, Nigeria, 2021
Photographed by Adedamola Odetara

144
Designed by Lagos Space Programme
Ensemble, 'Aṣọ Lànkí, Kí Ató Kí Ènìyàn /
We Greet Dress Before We Greet its Wearer'
collection
Lagos, Nigeria, 2021
Photographed by Kadara Enyeasi

Moses Turahirwa
Moshions

Imagination and design have been woven into every chapter of my life. Growing up, I was always playing with objects that I put together from what I found around me. I invented patterns from plants, drawing colour palettes from fresh and dried banana leaves, from lush green to dark khaki. I decorated my room with an evolving collection of items that I found aesthetically appealing.

Oblivious then to the concept of fashion, I now look back and see that the desire to create beauty was in me from childhood. I was obsessed with my mother's hand-embroidered tablecloths. Flowers and birds, delicate threads and colours, building little worlds on fabric. I loved watching my aunts as they hand crocheted, and I studied the neighbourhood women as they wove their intricate baskets. At my childhood ceremonies such as christening and birthdays, we were put in tailor-made clothes, and I soon began discussing my design ideas with the tailors, creating outfits for both myself and my sister.

In conceiving Moshions I wanted to pay homage to the incredible cultural aesthetics found in Rwanda and all across the African continent: meticulous artisanship, detail and design ken go into all these rich visual statements – from wickerwork to print techniques, and the hand-beadwork that forms patterned embellishments known as *amaraza*, *amatana* and *ibaba*, among others. My collections pay tribute to the symbolic attire that Rwandan royalties wore at special gatherings. For example, I often reconstruct the traditional *umushanana* – a ceremonial outfit with a wrap skirt and a draped sash – with contemporary new silhouettes. They also speak to the beauty, creativity and diversity found in ancient generations from all over the continent.

As one of Africa's many young creatives and agents of change, I believe that we have an immense opportunity and true responsibility to tell our stories and shape the African narrative as a new type of leader within fashion. We are in the process of redefining the meaning of luxury. We are shaping both the story and the purpose through our rich heritage and our desire to usher in a new era of slow, thoughtful fashion.

145
Designed by Moshions
Dress, 'Intsinzi' collection
Rwanda, Spring/Summer 2018
Photographed in 2020 by Awamu Moja

146
Moshions
Beadwork detail
Rwanda, 2018

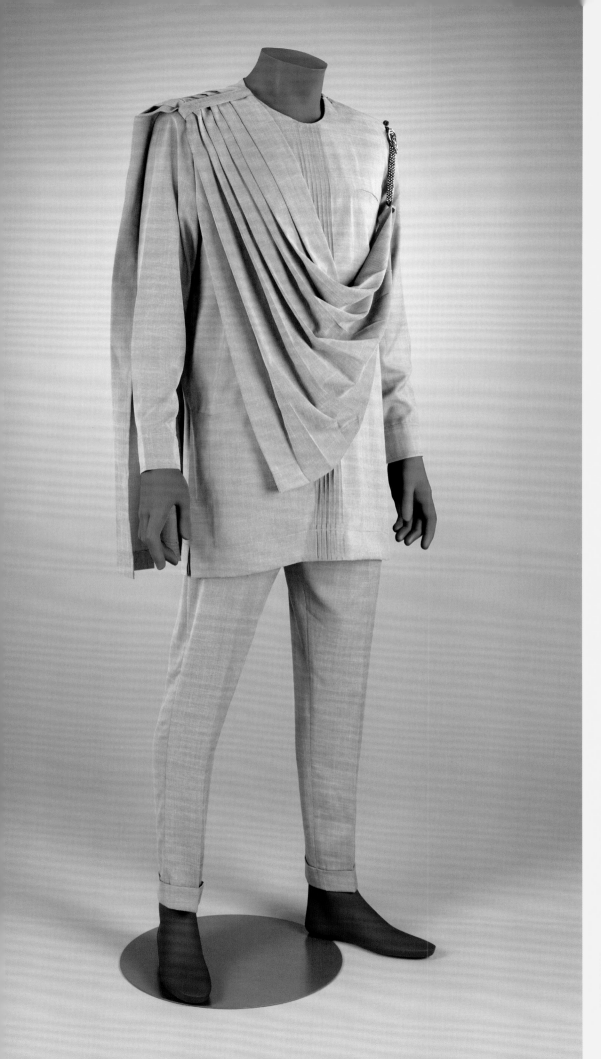

147
Moshions
Top and trousers, 'Intsinzi' collection,
wool and viscose blend, glass beads
Rwanda, Spring/Summer 2018
V&A: T.119–2021

III

AFRO-FASHION FUTURES

Christine Checinska

'Awaken your feet to the wisdom of the earth

Open your head to the wisdom

Of the heavens

Listen to the whispers

Of the fragrance

Of the survivors.'

Ben Okri, *Invocation for the Shrine* (2019)

Global conversations around sustainable and ethical fashions have gained increasing momentum. As consumers and fashion creatives, we have all become aware that the fashion industry has been killing the world for decades and is now among the largest global polluters.[1] The facts are undeniable. Each year the fashion industry releases 1.2 billion tonnes of greenhouse gas into the environment in the production and shipping of 100 billion garments. Every second the equivalent of a lorryload of clothes is either burnt or sent to landfill. On average only a paltry 1 per cent of clothing is recycled.[2] Linear fast-fashion systems typically take from the natural environment without giving back. Consider the excessive amounts of water used to make denim: around 8,000 litres to manufacture one pair of jeans. In addition, human exploitation remains a cruel by-product of the quest for the latest trends and lowest prices. Sustainability is now non-negotiable. Ethical practices are a must. We all need to unlearn our wasteful fast-fashion habits.

Circular and conscious fashion, sustainable and ethical practices, zero waste, upcycling, recycling and the prizing of artisanry are characteristic of today's fashion futures thinking in the Global North. Yet, they have always been central to vernacular African fashion systems. Local environmental, cultural and social concerns have also always been a priority. However, the contemporary African fashion scene struggles to keep ahead of the sustainability curve, largely because of the flooding of the lower end of the clothing market with cheaply made goods from China and second-hand items from the Global North. Second-hand clothes at first glance may seem like a positive story about recycling, but the prevalence of second-hand clothes in Africa inevitably has a devastating effect on local garment manufacturing. In the pages that follow, creative director, stylist and mentor Hadeel Osman, who is based in Sudan, urges us to rethink the second-hand clothing market. Instead, she invokes a future where sellers select the products they sell, tailoring them to their own aesthetics, exercising agency as entrepreneurs. In contrast, at present, goods produced by the sustainable and ethical brands that do exist can prove costly to bring to market. Often showing the mark of the hand in their manufacture, the sustainable collections created by designers such as Awa Meité, based in Mali, are a reminder of the true cost, and value, of clothes. Nevertheless, the promotion of locally produced textiles and garments, made-to-order models that limit wasteful consumption, as well as the use of local natural fibres such as barkcloth, mohair and merino wool, constitutes a revalorizing of vernacular systems that put fashion futures thinking into practice. The concept of Afro-Fashion Futures, grounded in African histories, cultures and philosophies, potentially offers a counterbalance to the destructive practices of global fast fashions.

Drawing on the expansive definitions of what it is to be African outlined in the introduction to this book, Afro-Fashion Futures are future fashion systems fed by the retention of African roots, which in turn nurture our relationship to the self, the collective and the environment. The sustainable nature of African vernacular fashions is being ignored by the Global North. Brushing against Afro-Futurism's blend of technology with elements of Black history and culture to reimagine a future in which Black people thrive, Afro-Fashion Futures embrace local knowledge and 'glocal' new technologies to invoke a future in which we – that is the broader 'we', – and the planet all thrive.

Pioneering organizations such as Orsola de Castro and Carry Somers's Fashion Revolution, the fashion activism movement founded after the 2013 Rana Plaza disaster in Bangladesh, have a global reach that incorporates over 100 countries, including 16 from the African continent.[3] Advocates of the movement prioritize people and the environment over profit and mindless consumerism, promoting dignity, equity, restraint and respect instead. They work with artists, businesses, governments and members of the public to re-educate and to lobby for change in the industry. However, African voices and perspectives are often absent from mainstream discussions about sustainability and ethical practices, even though African people have historically lived in harmony with their environments and have held cloth in high esteem, as something to be cherished and passed on. Looking after and repurposing what we own, indeed challenging the very notion of ownership through the honouring of the landscape and the prizing of the collective or the community, has for centuries been part of our heritage. The 2020 Future of Fashion indaba, hosted by the company Rewoven, was an important intervention that challenged this pattern of exclusion. The term 'indaba' comes from the Zulu and Xhosa languages. It refers to an important community meeting, but it also implies taking ownership of the issue or problem in hand. Here it describes an intervention into the global conversation about fashion futures while, importantly, exercising one's agency by centring multiple African perspectives. Entitled *African Sustainability – Our Way of Being*, it provided a platform from which to share insights into sustainable practices, calling into being an 'ethical and future-fit' industry from a wealth of local know-how.[4]

Nevertheless, there still appears to be little room for equitable collaboration and knowledge exchange within the global field of fashion futures with its Eurocentric bias. The economist Felwine Sarr suggests that Africa should go its own way. *Afrotopia* (2019), his meditation on an Africa that does not measure itself against the Global North, prompts us to ask what kind of fashion future we can imagine and solicit if we were to take as our departure point African sacred systems,

aesthetics and vernacular ways of making. If, as he proposes, we were to rehabilitate and apply African cultural values such as *jom* (dignity), *kersa* (modesty) and *ngor* (honour) to future fashion systems, might we naturally create sustainable and fair industries?[5] Omoyemi Akerele, founder and art director of Style House Files and Lagos Fashion Week, puts forward multiple strands that, in her view, must bind together if we are to reverse the detrimental impact of the fashion industry on people and on the environment. Overall, she emphasizes the need to work collectively to co-create a respectful and responsible industry that acknowledges, celebrates, understands and values difference.

Sarr writes that 'the future is a site that does not yet exist, but which one can already shape within a mental space'.[6] In his view, present-day signs formed within the creative spaces of the arts, including fashion and textiles, and the natural and urban landscapes, call the future into being. The syncretic practices, or 'remix culture', of designers like Alphadi (no.149),[7] originally from Timbuktu, Mali, and Selly Raby Kane, working in Dakar, Senegal, signpost a future, or futures, nourished by real and imagined African heritages. The cultural synthesis that characterizes their work brings a common humanity into view. Some creatives living within the diaspora 'also dream and fantasize about Africa' from the 'elsewhere of their exiles'.[8] Here Sarr references the work of writers such as Abdourahman Waberi and Léonora Miano whose creative practices have an Afro-Futuristic tone. From the point of view of fashion, these observations are a reminder of creatives such as D. Denenge Duyst-Akpem, currently based in Chicago, (no.148), who explores Afro-Futurism, Afrofuturity, African art, sacred systems and the urban landscape through projects like the *Camo Coat* collection and *AFRIFUTURI 02022020*; the artist-historian's first monograph launched with a runway show on the numerological portal 2 February 2020. The monograph details experimental works and writings on 'Afrofuturity', a term coined by Duyst-Akpem to encompass Global Africa futurisms through time and place beyond US-based Afro-Futurism. The critical and timely *Camo Coat* collection arose from urgent concerns around protection and healing for Black people within the African diaspora in urban landscapes, considering how fashion and design respond directly to the needs of the moment, employing new technologies and design strategies

148
D. Denenge Duyst-Akpem in the Original Camo Coat
Lurie Garden, Millennium Park, Chicago, Winter 2018
Photographed by Hilary Higgins for *Chicago Tribune* article
highlighting a course, 'Take Root Among the Stars: The Legacy
of Octavia Butler, Surviving the 21st Century & Beyond'

149
Designed by Alphadi
Ensembles for FIMA 2018
Photographed by Vincent Boisot
in the desert near Dakhla, 2018

such as camouflage in nature, organic bulletproof materials and protection within the garment's form itself.[9]

These elements combine to explore a scientifically advanced and hopeful future in which Black people thrive, nourished by our shared African roots, which in turn rehabilitate our relationship to the self, the collective and the environment. The notion of rehabilitation is taken up by Njoki Ngumi and Sunny Dolat of The Nest Collective, an interdisciplinary arts collective in Kenya, in a joint reflection on the place of Black collective joy, solidarity, excitement, tragedy, grief and shared identities in crafting African-centric fashion futures. In considering the future of the African fashion industry as an important element in defining and expressing Black and Global Africa freedoms, they rightly argue that it is crucial to incorporate economic strategies alongside cultural roots. For example, within an equitable and conscious system there must be room for us to have a choice between locally and globally made fashion goods and services, whether new or used. They set out a convincing argument for the same freedoms that have been afforded fashion creatives and consumers elsewhere. Furthermore, echoing Sarr, they suggest that we should determine what the future looks like for ourselves, and what success looks like, whether through paths already charted or through new ones that we create together. In a sense, the fashion future that they describe pivots on the decolonization of minds, the need for which thinkers and activists such as Frantz Fanon and James Baldwin alerted us to.[10]

The closing reflection, written by designer Amine Bendriouich, circles back to where this book began, weaving together many of the narrative threads shared along the way. Bendriouich, in his deeply personal essay, takes Marrakesh, the Moroccan city of his birth, a city that sits at the crossroads between Africa and Europe, to offer a lyrical counterpoint to Bonnie Greer's notion of 'shoreline thinking'. The traversing of borders is internalized; leave-and-return takes place within the imagination. Yet Africa – the physical and psychological space with all its richness and vitality, complexities and contradictions, with its refusal to be pinned down, with its long story of fashion – is the heartbeat of both, just as it is for the *Africa Fashion* project as a whole, just as it is for Sarr. Afrotopia is Sarr's vision of the future that is already being invoked. Springing from contemporary cut-and-mix and trusting in the continent's capacity

for renewal, the African fashion scene, glimpsed through these pages and read against his writings, is neither a copy nor a victim of the Global North; rather, it is an inspiration to it. If Africa is the birthplace of humanity, then Afrotopia, and that which emerges from it, is the place of its rebirth.

150
M.AROC: Mehdi Sabik
and Artsi Ifrach
Future Hope ensemble,
Marrakesh, Morocco, 2021

THE PLACE WE CALL HOME: ECONOMIC AND CULTURAL RECLAMATION OF AFRICAN FASHIONS

Sunny Dolat and Njoki Ngumi
The Nest Collective

The creation of Black collective joy, solidarity, excitement, tragedy, grief and vision in a shared identity, which then distils into what can be called a group ego, is a ritual of call and response. An offering is made to the universe, whether it be an act of supreme beauty or genius, or a gesture with a more immediately relevant, temporal weight. It could be American artistic gymnast Simone Biles's unimaginably dangerous, graceful leaps across a rubber-floored gymnasium,[1] or Kenyan chess champion and TikTok sensation Elsa Majimbo's peals of laughter as she falls back on a couch, crisps crackling, changing global definitions of performed comedy.[2] The offering can also spring from tragedy, such as the international grief at the murder of security officer George Floyd by Minneapolis police officers,[3] or at the still unresolved kidnapping by Boko Haram of 276 school-girls in Chibok, Borno State, Nigeria, many of whom are still missing.[4]

As a collective, we laugh together at Elsa, sharing every video. We reflect on and protest the global nature of police brutality, after George Floyd was viciously stolen from his family and community. This has happened whether we are 5 m across the street, or 50,000 km away over land and water. In every call and response, we recreate and galvanize the sense that we are indeed a 'we', as we have done at numerous points in the continued struggle for Black liberation everywhere.

African fashions are a tangible contribution to the repair and strengthening of this collective ego project. Firstly, when considering the future of African fashions as a key element in defining and expressing African and wider Black freedoms, it is crucial that the economic perspective is taken into account. This is because the ability to create and transfer value speaks to the autonomous involvement of Africans in deciding what we wear and why. This further extends into the opportunity to invite others to engage in our cultures by trade and other exchanges. Secondly, any insights on the future of African fashions have an irreversibly cultural point of view, strongly resonant with Black identity and Black life.

Economic Reclamation

The role of garments and apparel is crucial in delineating the similarities and differences between cultures. One of the first signifiers of the victory of colonialism in Africa was clothing. The garments that the diverse peoples of Africa already wore, made from resources already in their networks, and tailored for their work, climate and wider context, were reframed by white missionaries as primitive and demonic (see p.20). This was in order to pressure people through guilt and fear to take on European ways, and was incentivized by ensuring that those who went to these missionaries' churches enjoyed highest access to healthcare and education.[5] This was even further enforced by laws that had to be obeyed on pain of punishment by fines, imprisonment, beatings, torture and more.

The colonialist enterprise was heavy on administration and had to make money to sustain itself. It thus necessitated the forced conscription of Africans as free or heavily subsidized labour (again, encouraged by the unjust laws of the time, such as a demand for taxes that meant that people had to earn money in pre-determined ways).[6] From an economic perspective, this resulted in the destruction of African value chains of productive work. From a fashion, garments and apparel perspective, people were no longer available to make and trade in their own indigenous clothing. They could not generate the needed raw materials, process material into fibre, or carefully skin hides for leather preparation. In turn, those materials could not be made into garments and traded to others, who could wear them in exchange for other goods or services. When we consider the future of the African fashion scene, then, it must be with this concerted assault in mind, and an under-standing of how it has transferred into our present. One of the consequences of fast fashion's takeover in the Global North, which has resulted in affordable (for them) fashion, has been an increase in fashion waste when these clothes become dated and 'unstylish'.[7] This used to be defined by seasons, changing every three months, but is now reduced to just a number of weeks, as the large fast-fashion emporiums have much shorter cycles. These clothes, mostly dumped by donation or sold for pennies, take up a massive amount of space and must be moved quickly. Arriving in Africa, they make up a significant portion of fashion retail here.

There are those who would argue that this makes a strong case for global sustainability, and positive ways of taking creative control over this influx are explored by Hadeel Osman in the next chapter. However, there is a clear inequality when one population is given the job of re-wearing and re-using old items, which is the actual labour of sustaining, while others continue to glory in a never-ending supply of the new. There is a strong dignity implication in who gets to be the first to wear an item of clothing, and in wearing new clothing. Even something as small as taking the price tag off a new garment can be read as a statement about your position in the world, and your ability to quite literally put clothes on the backs of yourself and your family. Evidence of this dignity conundrum can be seen in some of the older names used for second-hand clothing; one of these was '*marehemu George*',[8] a Swahili phrase which translates to 'clothes of the late George' (there is ongoing debate on whether this makes any reference at all to King George VI, who was monarch before Queen Elizabeth II took the throne at his death during the colonial period in Kenya). A lot of class stigma used to be attached to people who wore second-hand clothing, as this was seen as a public statement about an unfortunate lack of economic well-being. While the immediate violence of this stigma has lessened over time, the name remains a cultural archive of many complex consid-erations around ethics, international relations, and power dynamics.[9] In addition, the possibilities for local production remain slim. There is no local industry that can pay fair wages and taxes while also competing with the price of imported second-hand goods, where a pair of decent-quality used jeans can go for as little as one or two US dollars.

The impact of multiple factors on economic conditions in Africa mean that most of us can only wear clothes that Americans or Europeans have worn previously. In so doing, Africans are still being denied the opportunities, just like before, albeit in different circumstances, to process our own raw materials, as well as make and trade our own fabric and clothes. This translates to massive losses in terms of jobs; spaces for knowledge acquisition and transfer; the start-up, growth and success of businesses; and contributions to the economic growth of people, households, communities and countries. Meanwhile, the same global entities whose governments took from Africans so long ago continue to experience unchallenged growth in these arenas. These truths are inextricably and tragically linked.

The future of African fashion, therefore, must include a space where many Africans can have the opportunity to have home-grown, quality garments when they are new. We should have the true choice between locally made fashion goods, and imported ones, whether new or used, if the market in this sector is ever to be called free.

151
Designed by Katungulu Mwendwa
Dress, 'Everyday Superheroes' collection
Nairobi, Kenya, 2021
Photographed by Sunny Dolat

Cultural Reclamation

Over the past decade, the democratization of media via platforms such as Tumblr and Instagram has been an important catalyst for the growth of the collective Black ego and esteem. The prevailing stories of Blackness and African-ness have always been forcibly whitened, first by explorers, then missionaries, then colonialists. We seem to have somehow cycled back to explorers again, as observed in the phenomenon of thousands of young white Global North citizens coming to Africa with only a suitcase, a tourist visa and a dream. These dreams are brought to quick fruition via their ability to raise millions in white venture capital funding, for startup and experimental projects across sectors.[10] These are resources that Black entrepreneurs and experts have little to no access to, despite years of learning, grassroots work, lived experience, and relevant data with the potential for high impact and returns.

The Black ego is attacked, therefore, in two ways: our stories are whitened, and our opportunities are appropriated, in the service of capitalistic interest from outside African communities. Modern post-colonial remixes of older narratives continue to re-establish white domination and victory at Black expense, which dehumanizes Africans, depicting us as 'less than', and as people who deserve to be owned, traded and colonized. This does not mean that all the healing and restorative work being done is in vain; the fact that Black people consider themselves worthy of care, repair and respite, constantly, despite what anyone else says, is a testament to the eternal life of this ego.

Because 'African-ness' and Blackness have been demonized and belittled for so long, this opportunity to own our narratives, to portray ourselves and each other with dignity, honour and respect, has been an important act of reclamation. Part of this has involved re-engaging with vernacular knowledge systems and traditional ways of making, which, because of being pre-industrial, were designed to be inherently sustainable. One great example of this is in the work of Nigerian fashion designer Nkwo Onwuka, and her eponymous brand NKWO, whose famous dakala cloth is handwoven from upcycled denim in a process that echoes the weaving of aṣọ-òkè, one of several prestigious handwoven textiles of the Yorùbá people in Nigeria (see nos 132, 133). African designers

have therefore begun to reflect on what it really means to run a fashion business in this day and age: while it is possible to opt for an industrial cut-make-trim factory operation, designers are increasingly choosing more complex models and processes that are slower and gentler on the planet and her people, such as those that allow for working with artisans, or using plant-derived dyes.

This return is also giving rise to a new wave of pan-Africanist expression, providing designers with the opportunity to celebrate a more continental African-ness, via inspiration from the cultures and practices outside their borders. Kenyan designer Katungulu Mwendwa's collection *Everyday Superheroes*, for example, combines the geometric markings and shapes typical in Rwandan Imigongo art with the patterns commonly featured on the mud cloth of Mali (no.151). These are juxtaposed with the convergence of acute angular points reminiscent of Nairobi's ever-broadening skyline, with towering skyscrapers seen from a ground up perspective.[11]

In her approach to this collection, as well as in her work more broadly, Katungulu has given herself permission to look beyond Kenya, and to marry concepts from different African aesthetics: a gentle summoning and glorious intermarriage of diverse African-ness, as it were. Besides the end product of beautiful garments, knowledge about her process and inspirations arouses curiosity in her clients and audiences, who leave her atelier or even just her social media more educated about different cultures than they were before. The borders between nation states are colonial lines, drawn to contain and control white access to African resources and people. Black designers and artists like Katungulu and others all over the continent and the Black diaspora are making aesthetic returns to skinfolk and kinfolk far and wide, serving as a concerted resistance to the artificial walls put up to separate us. This act has long resonated with the collective yearning in many to learn about their roots, to respectfully reconnect in both old and new ways, to build bridges to each other, and to chart new futures together. Fashion can be instrumental in depicting and expressing many parts of this healing.

As such, when we start to imagine what the future of African fashion might be, there are multiple possibilities. Some of these are far away, and others are closer to home. Beyond the

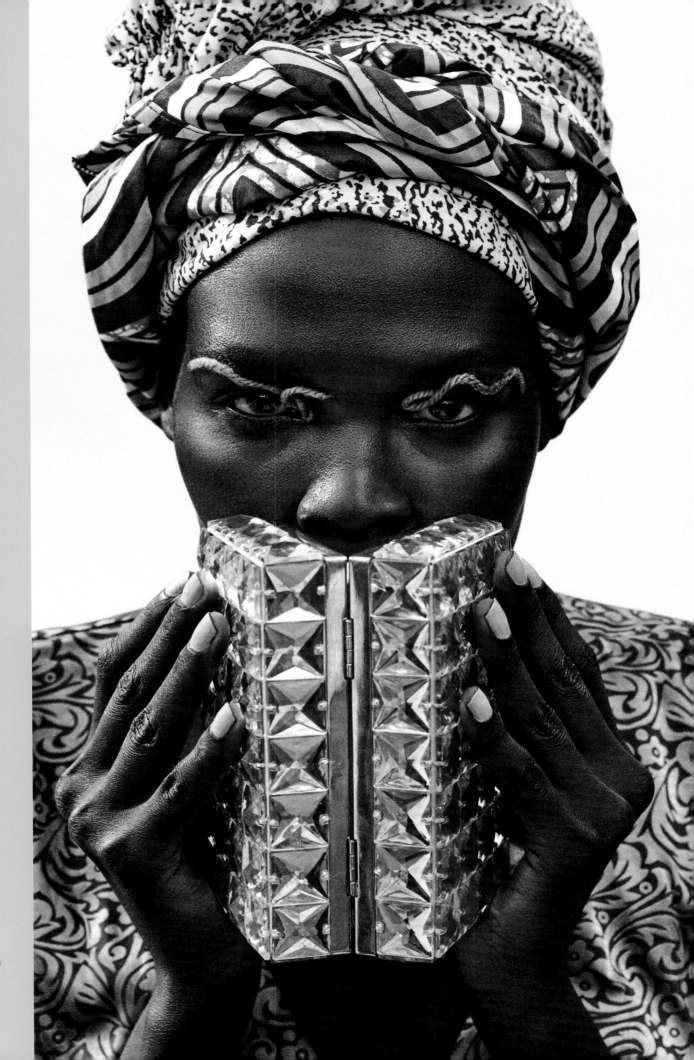

152
Designed by Aachera
Ensemble
Nairobi, Kenya, 2017
Photographed by
Thandiwe Muriu

continent, more African design talent could work at and take over the helms of European heritage brands, while conglomerates like LVMH and Kering might begin to buy into a new generation of heritage brands from Africa. More African brands could supply massive global stores, such as Harrods and Bergdorf Goodman. Although these possibilities are informed by, and aspire to, the widely peddled economic trajectories from the Global North brands, it is important that whatever paths and trajectories Black and African designers want to embark on are open to them.

It is important that our local definitions of success are as broad and diverse as the place we call home, so that they may honour the spectrum of designers, creative directors, tailors, made-to-order businesses, artisans and makers who contribute to this mega industry. There are those who have studied fashion to the highest possible formal education levels, while others have learned via apprenticeship, or long evening hours from YouTube videos and magazines, or deconstructing then reconstructing second-hand clothing. Due to this wide range of skills, entry points and possibilities, there are tremendous innovations happening in fashion spaces, such as communal production spaces and designer collectives. These tend to be more common in this part of the world, and indeed much of the Global South, because there isn't the same kind of support, industry infrastructure and business policy regulatory environment that exists in the Global North. Such approaches offer us glimpses into what the future of fashion could look like, not just in Africa but across the world. With proper holistic investment in infrastructure, regulations, and more, the path to African fashion success could therefore be travelled as easily in African urban and rural areas, by people of all tribes, genders and identities, exploring infinite possibilities of Black expression wherever they are, for audiences large and small.

The future of African fashions can hence only be charted with full awareness and honesty about what has caused the artificial economic and cultural rifts between African designers and their success, both at home and internationally, and the steps being taken to bridge these gaps. What is certain is that all Africans deserve exactly the same freedoms that have been afforded everyone else, to determine what this future looks like for them, and what success looks like for them, whether through paths already charted or new ones entirely.

153
Designed by Kapoeta by Ambica
Ensemble
Nairobi, Kenya, 2019
Photographed by Sunny Dolat

REIMAGINING SECOND-HAND MARKETS IN AFRICA

Hadeel Osman

When dissecting the different aspects of the global fashion industry, we seldom remember the active role played by second-hand markets. Often the forgotten links in the fashion supply chain, they are not seen as true contributors to the overall garment trade. However, it is important to note that in East Africa alone, second-hand garments are estimated to be worth over $200 million, so we can only imagine their overall continental impact.[1] In fact, with the consistent decline in locally mass-manufactured clothes across the continent since the early 1990s, second-hand clothes have come to dominate most of the markets and street stalls in Africa.[2] Considering that second-hand markets have become the main method by which clothes are sold, it is clear they will have a massive stake in terms of innovating the traditional trade cycle and contributing to the reinvention of clothing design.[3]

Sustainability in the fashion industry has become a main topic of discussion in recent years, as the not-so-secret practices of fast fashion have been revealed to the world. The appeal of easily accessible, affordably priced clothes fades with increased knowledge of the social, ethical and environmental impacts of this way of working.[4] Consumers who have armed themselves with awareness and education about one of the world's most polluting industries are naturally turning away from this model and relying more heavily on thrift markets and predominantly purchasing second-hand.

In Africa this is nothing new. Although markets flooded with second-hand goods further perpetuate poverty and what is called 'waste colonialism', they have also become an integral part of the culture of consumption over the past 30 years or so. It is no secret that hundreds of thousands of people have found jobs by informally selling garments that have entered the continent's borders, whether under the guise of charity donations or as wholesale trade deals from the United States, Canada and Europe.[5] Becoming a vendor is quite straightforward – you start by purchasing one bale, which is about 45 kg of clothes – and this means that independent job creation is constantly on the rise.

With the ubiquity of second-hand goods in many cities and towns, African consumers have developed a preference for these items. It is the combination of their mostly high quality and the fairly inexpensive price tag that keeps them buying. Therefore, we need to take a look at this trade with the future in mind. For second-hand traders to find longevity in an evolving market, they need to study the behaviours of their consumers. By seeing what people gravitate towards and taking note of what they are choosing to wear vendors can capitalize on these preferences. When vendors take the lead, they are actively reshaping how we, the consumers, view the market. This will bring about a sense of ownership that is currently missing, since most vendors are focused on numbers rather than a methodology of operation. A niche could be formed, allowing each trader to look at what makes them stand out from the rest. They might then be empowered to target different demographics, even if they still operate as small stalls within overflowing markets.

It would also be worthwhile for traders and sellers to consider specializing in specific goods, thereby making a name for themselves. This classification obviously makes for easier market browsing, which in turn ushers in more eager shoppers. For instance, some stalls might sell only vintage silk scarves or graphic T-shirts, while others could house a plethora of sports shoes, and some could even turn into emporia of everything denim. This method of market segmentation could become the blueprint for the evolution of these market stalls into specialized boutiques, or a new twist on the concept of malls. Malls traditionally have a variety of shops offering a wide range of products and so these second-hand markets could develop into a fully functional shopping space, changing how people view the products and adding to their shopping experience. Traders and street vendors will no longer be limited to just purchasing bales of miscellaneous garments to be sold so they can afford to pay their bills and put food on the table; they could become fashion curators. They will be the trend forecasters, picking and choosing what works in relation to the climate and culture. Through observation and investment, they will gain in-depth knowledge about garment materials and available brands, sorting clothes more efficiently and pricing items in a competitive manner. They could also provide mending, tailoring and maintenance services as an essential part of their businesses, thus expanding and functioning as alternative ateliers.[6] From their starting point as average sellers in local markets, they will end up shaping and transforming the ways in which Africans choose to shop, dress and express themselves.

This sort of influence can also move into the online space. With the current rise in social-media thrift shops, such as Never New in South Africa, Nguonzuri.254 in Kenya and Thrift Store Ghana, the future is looking bright. Having an online presence is a great way to provide a product without the additional expenses of renting a market stall and having to pay hefty government-issued fees or bribes. The only cost incurred once the bales are acquired is the payment of delivery fees and even that can be avoided by issuing customer-pick-up-only policies.[7] On the web, we could look into creating e-commerce platforms specifically for African sellers of second-hand clothing, enabling them to double their income if they choose to operate in both the offline and online spheres.

These platforms could be native to each country, incorporating a map of who sells what and where, while giving traders the opportunity to create profiles for their businesses and engage new demographics. Across the continent, there is a major lack of coordinated online documentation. To have a directory that also functions as an income stream would change the perception of the market and the people. Fashion tourism could also be a by-product of this online system, encouraging those travelling to and within the country to support small stalls and boutiques.

The future of second-hand clothes also lies within each item of clothing we see in the market. These can be regarded as the raw material, the fabric of which can be remodelled and made into new items.[8] Refashioning clothes and upcycling are integral parts of the circular fashion model, heavily reducing waste. This provides designers, students and fashion enthusiasts with a unique material with which to experiment and innovate. Not only is it cheaper to buy second-hand clothes than new fabrics, but also the range of materials, colours and patterns is much larger than that of pre-consumer deadstock fabrics, as this is less costly and more environmentally conscious than cotton farming.

Speaking of African textile production, this part of the fashion industry could start looking into textile recycling, repurposing the large volume of second-hand clothes that, if not sold, might otherwise end up in landfill.[9] The method involves sorting piles of garments by material and colour, then shredding them into threads, to be used as yarn. This could be used to make new clothes, home goods and furniture from scratch. Textiles may also be used across different industries, for insulation or stuffing, for example.[10] Since the clothes are already dyed and prepared, African designers and fashion practitioners

154
Nakasero second-hand Market,
Nakasero Road, Kampala, Uganda,
1 September 2017
Photographed by
Mariya Sukhoveyko

155

Vendors selling second-hand clothing
on street, Lusaka, Zambia, 2008
Photographed by Thomas Cockrem

could skip the dyeing process, which would be cost-effective and reduce the burden of water waste and chemical pollution. Traditional sewing techniques could also be embraced with a modern twist, showing that although heritage is vital, it can be adapted to current times.

The future of second-hand clothes in Africa could involve sustainable job creation and economic growth, all while embracing environmental consciousness and most importantly adapting innovative solutions for Africans, by Africans. Since enforcing large tariffs and trade regulations on the Global North to reduce or stop the import of second-hand clothing in Africa has proven to be a hard task, with trade and economic sanctions being imposed by the other side, Africa can have the upper hand by transforming what is considered waste into the main material for clothing creation. Second-hand markets are already flooded with clothes that need new homes or creative adaptations. Fabric does not necessarily need to be grown from the earth and spun into yarn in the traditional sense; it can be remade from existing garments and given an identity close to home.

156
Wholesale second-hand clothing
export bales, *c.*2010s
Photographed by Martin de Jong

IT TAKES A VILLAGE

Omoyemi Akerele

When we think of sustainable living what comes to mind is a Euro-American representation of what it should be, which is often only accessible to people who can afford it. However, there are many communities across Africa and beyond who have been living in harmony with their environment for thousands of years. For these communities, sustainable living has always been a way of being stemming from the belief that everyone and everything matters.

While the global fashion industry is fundamentally extractive of both natural and human resources, the concepts of recycling, repurpose and reuse are not alien to the African people. Whether subconsciously or deliberately, our communities have always had a focus on environmental impact, which is inextricably linked to socio-economic impact. 'We do not inherit the earth from our ancestors, we borrow it from our children': a quote attributed to the Maasai who can be found in Kenya, and whose culture and lifestyle have influenced countless designers globally including Kim Jones for Louis Vuitton.

A question that often comes up is: how can we adopt technology to support processes without dehumanization, considering innovation is key to the future? Mass customization – a hybrid of mass production and customization – has been proffered as a solution for meeting increasing demand, but the challenge has always been scalability. How do we innovate without losing the very essence of what makes 'African fashion' unique?

They say productivity gains come through a combination of specialization and mechanization, but I often wonder, how sustainable is African fashion's reliance on artisanship and its dependence on valuable resources or skills like embellishment, embroidery, weaving, spinning and customization? These are all techniques that make our fashions special because they have been touched by the human hand. When Lagos Fashion Week launched over a decade ago, it was very important to me that our focus should be on artisanship, the heartbeat of African fashion. It has become increasingly critical for us to protect this aspect of our heritage as some of those in a globalized post-colonial world seek to position other creators at the forefront of benefiting from the African fashion narrative rather than the African creators themselves. They might refer to it as a 'trend' or 'inspiration', but ultimately, it is who we are. How can we ensure African fashions preserve their essence? Automation is quickly replacing traditional skills and techniques. How can we balance the designers' need for scalability without upsetting the fragile ecosystem that is dependent on uniqueness? How can we protect our cultural power and symbolism, as expressed through the work of our designers?

Part of the answer lies with the creatives who depend on the availability of natural resources and valuable human skills to make the ecosystem function and thrive. They must be encouraged to source materials and labour across Africa and must be willing to continue to invest in the communities from which they source. Sourcing from Africa can create more opportunities for cross-cultural exchange that is beneficial to the participating communities. Brands like Lukhanyo Mdingi and IAMISIGO have championed this approach, which is already a part of what organizations like Ethical Fashion Initiative seek to broker by enabling communities of artisans in Burkina Faso to collaborate with heritage luxury brands like Loewe. Collaborations, I find, are still slightly more tilted in favour of the dominant partner than the communities they seek to support. They must support the livelihoods of the people in those communities and ensure they are well compensated for; this should be the starting point for our creative process.

157
Akwete Weavers,
Nigeria, 2017
Photographed by Kosol
Onwudinjor

158
Models holding hands,
Lagos, Nigeria, 2019
Photographed by Stephen Tayo
for Lagos Fashion Week

'Africa's population is estimated to be approximately 1.2 billion, spread across 54 countries. Our designers are currently being encouraged to explore intra-African trade with a mission to target and access a micro fraction of the population.'

Omoyemi Akerele

159
Sandstorm Kenya for Lagos Fashion
Week – Bag-making in process,
2018
Photographed by Mark Stephenson
for Lagos Fashion Week

Africa's population is estimated to be approximately 1.2 billion, spread across 54 countries. Our designers are currently being encouraged to explore intra-African trade with a mission to target and access a micro fraction of the population. However, the movement of goods and people across Africa involves a complex web of visas, routes and ratifications of trade agreements. In the absence of continent-wide luxury store franchises, logistics infrastructure must be in place to ensure efficient delivery and accessibility of goods in different African markets. We currently rely on bricks and mortar to create luxury retail experiences, which should be preserved, but we must explore how to replicate these experiences online to provide opportunities for designers to tap into a wider demographic. African brands must speak the retail language of today: omnichannel. Our main goal with distribution should be to embrace circular business models such as recommerce, rework, retool and possibly rental options through platforms like Style Rotate, a Cape Town-based rental platform. After all, we have a culture of passing clothes down from one generation to the next. We must also take advantage of the AfCFTA (African Continental Free Trade Area) to ensure that it is beneficial to our creators.

With regard to funding, traditional funding structures abound but they are not well equipped to support the sector. Lending rates might sound appealing but fashion requires long-term investment for sustainable growth, so there is a need for a deeper understanding of the nuances of the business between the lender and borrower. We need to invest heavily in research and development for the purpose of promoting innovation, supply chain capabilities and possibly scaling up new natural fibres.

Creative exchange is integral to preservation. Collaboration, co-creation and community are crucial to creative exchange. A Centre for Sustainable Fashion initiative brought together universities, businesses and NGOs from around the world and from diverse areas within fashion by allowing partici-pants to interact in ways not usually experienced either in the classroom or workplace. London College of Fashion students joined with STADIO Higher Education (formerly LISOF) students and the Buotemelo women's cooperative in South Africa to collaborate on a creative exchange that was set up at South Africa Fashion Week in 2007. Models like this should be revived with multiple opportunities for exchange across the continent.

The world has become one global community and we need to represent the community we serve. Yet a failure of representation has been declared throughout the ethical supply chain, where people of colour are constantly pushed into the background. How do we drive people towards the benefits of ethical systems if there is no change in the internal structure at the top of the pyramid? It is upsetting that there is a lack of recognition of this within the industry, which constantly amplifies other voices, particularly from the Global North, who profit from it while the originators are reduced to inspiration. Regardless, our creative community is strong in its resolve to keep going, keep telling our stories and keep creating. I am aware society makes it seem like people of colour always want to emphasize race, but the more pressing question is why not? Why should we not lead with our identity? Why do you want to adopt our human resources while remaining nonchalant about its impact on humans? Why does the Global North want to feed off our culture, while seeming sceptical about our people benefiting from it?

Change within the sector can be reinforced significantly at management level where decision-making power is mostly constituted. There has to be a new sense of awareness beyond press releases and performative activism on social media. We have to go back to examining structures of supply thought-fully and meaningfully so as to benefit both craftspeople and the environment. I constantly tell myself I have to be careful, so I do not end up being the token representative from my community. It is not enough to raise awareness about these issues; we have to create accountability and possibly sanctions against companies with unethical supply chains and extensive carbon footprints.

All of us have a duty to raise the bar, to ensure that leadership structures in our organizations are as diverse as the communities we serve or want to serve:

> We have to be empathetic.
> We have to be role models.
> We have to teach.
> We have to raise the bar of expectations.
> We have to influence conversations.

There must be a significant increase in technical expertise, funding and education across our existing value systems to curate the future we hope to see. We cannot do this without a collective mindfulness to co-create solutions that work for us. We will need the legislation and infrastructure to create the perfect enabling environment for this model of responsible fashion to thrive.

In the final analysis, African countries have a rich natural ecosystem that contributes significantly to creating today's fashion masterpieces. We all have a role to play in contributing to this beautiful legacy that has been passed down to us by preserving it for the next generation.

We have our differences; the future is not about erasing them but rather acknowledging, celebrating, understanding and valuing them as we journey together to build lasting structures to strengthen an ecosystem where everyone matters. Yes, everyone matters, every voice counts, thus every hand should benefit. As the African proverb tell us: 'It takes a village to raise a child'.

CHOOSE OUR OWN SEASONS, CROWN OUR OWN HEROES

Amine Bendriouich

When you are born in Marrakesh, in the Moroccan Kingdom, in the lands of North Africa – at any given time in history – you have access to one of the busiest and most interesting crossroads on the planet. You are exposed to an endless variety of cultures, cultures that mingle together in that magic, unique space for you to contemplate, appreciate or not, and sometimes even understand, if you are lucky. All of these emotions and information are enhanced by the blazing sun, trance rhythms, spice smells and the fog of kif and hashish. From a thieves' den to a major caravan stop, to the capital, to the richest city in the region, to the bastion of resistance against colonization in the south of the kingdom, to the City of the Seven Saints, to the birthplace of the late painter Abbès Saladi: a few of Marrakesh's 1001 lives. You may have the privilege of laying your eyes on a real Saracen's gold armour, on the pillars of a tenth-century mosque, on Roman artefacts, on the last Mecca cover produced under Ottoman rule; and lose yourself in the light of a Jacques Majorelle painting, in the curves of a stolen Pablo Picasso sculpture or in a Salvador Dalí sketch from the 1970s found in the medina; or to touch the caftan of a real princess and smell the clothes of a real king that was.

Being born in Marrakesh in the 1980s gives you all of these privileges, but the temporality of that context also solidifies in the concrete reality that you can never leave Marrakesh, Morocco: that colonialism and its outcomes rendered your passport unworthy of the freedom you grew up experiencing, naturally believing that everybody could travel everywhere and tell their stories, wear the apparel or bring the objects that make you long for those faraway lands. After all, Africans have always been natural-born creatives with a strong, unique and spontaneous style that cherishes life and what it gives you, and which aims always to make the best out of it. The youth confronting this reality started looking for alternatives

to physical travel: travel through your imagination, travel without leaving your spot, travel with your soul a thousand times around the globe and returning into your body. Luckily the ancestors on the continent left enough wisdom, knowledge, history and *baraka* (spiritual force) for us new generations to feed from, and preserve our most precious treasure: our deep, true FREEDOM that allows us to achieve these alternatives.

For myself, I found my salvation and protection in the tales of my grandmother about my grandfather, who was said to be one of the most renowned exorcists and imams of his times; I was soaked in stories and fables that make Harry Potter look like a sorcery YouTube fan. I found them in the sci-fi, supernatural and spy novels from Egypt sold in the vintage book market in Bab Doukkala. In the encyclopaedias I used to read from cover to cover like novels in my uncle's library. In the mangas of Akira Toriyama that I waited every summer to get on VHS from my cousins coming from France, or the new *Dragon Ball Z* film I hunted for in the neighbourhood after hearing that someone I knew knew someone that might have it, asking random people if they had heard of that person, and if ever I found them, convincing them to trust me and lend me the cassette. In the music of Michael Jackson, Nass El Ghiwane, Jimi Hendrix, in the music-video-watching sessions at the house of my only friend who had cable, on some German music channel, so that I only understood the music and the images. That is how I discovered graffiti, how I discovered hip-hop and baggy clothes, rock 'n' roll and ripped jeans and washed T-shirts, punk and full leather looks, Jean-Michel Basquiat, Andy Warhol, Missy Elliott...then came electronic music and psychedelic paradises, and the doors of perception that opened with them. All of these elements and influences turned the young boy I was into a mini reproduction of Marrakesh itself: a place bursting with all these cultures, tales, encounters that dance

160
Designed by Amine Bendriouch
Ensemble,
'Djellabas & Tricks' collection
Marrakesh, Morocco, 2020
Photographed by Sarah Nadjar

and mingle on the same beat that looks messy from afar, but the more you dive into it the more you understand the leading rhythm, and then the harmonies, a whole that constitutes a new form of expression of each one of these elements and a possibility and evolution of what Marrakesh/Morocco/Africa/humanity is and can be.

During my teenage years this creative substitute for travel and freedom chose to express itself through fashion. I could only afford to dress in the clothes that my parents chose for me, so I started drawing the clothes I would like to wear. As a way to express my love for a girl I would make a logo out of her name and design a collection inspired by her. In the early stages of my career, my professional and creative choices were not met with seriousness: my father believed I was gay, I was asked repeatedly what I would really do for a career and to survive financially, I was asked to reconsider my choices many times. I was told that I was just a passing trend, that I would fade away with time, that I would disappear from the scene when I cut my hair. An editor-in-chief of an important publication, who had written about me, told me once that he believed I was dealing drugs, as he could not understand how it would be possible otherwise to live from fashion in Morocco (and especially my kind of fashion). And, of course, all the time I was met with the assumption that if I really was a fashion designer then I must be making caftans, as if every Japanese designer makes kimonos or Senegalese designers *boubous*. Luckily all of this just made me grip harder onto my faith, and made me act like a mad man pushing the accelerator without caring about the fire bursting out of the engine, moved by my fear of never wishing to stop where they expect me to be, or take the place they chose for me.

The reactions to my first collection in Casablanca in 2007 were: 'It's beautiful, but I could never wear it' and all sorts of generic compliments. I could not understand this. I thought: the sky is beautiful, the trees are beautiful, but what I was trying to say through my work was something else, and I had so many things to say and a strong need to be understood. This made me realize two things: people need to understand where I am coming from and the culture I belong to, and that I cannot complain about the environment I find myself in as a result of a cosmic accident, but in order to thrive and survive I need to create the reality I want for myself that was not available around me. The fact that I was creating it in this specific place in the world made a lot of sense, as it is more needed than in other places where the battles have already been fought. As soon as I freed myself from the need to please and belong to an industry that did not know or care about my existence, things started to shift, as if the universe was responding and telling me that I was doing it right.

What I believe was the first step on this path was the creation of Contemporary Moroccan Roots: a multidisciplinary event/show where I presented my collection in the middle of an exhibition I curated showcasing the artists who inspire me, or artists that I wanted to add to my crowd whose art did not have a place in the official institutional platforms, topped by concerts and performances of the most progressive underground artists of the time. The audience was incredibly mixed: artists, designers, politicians, the mayor, ambassadors, sometimes even ministers. For me this was my answer to those who were saying that my work and my style were a product of imported culture, and also a way to open up my world to the people in order for them to understand me and my work. Once they loved the art, the music, the vibe, they wanted to have the clothes that went with them, and I started to get clients: a pharmacist, a lawyer, an accountant, a banker. Little by little I started shifting from 'the crazy dude we should invite to parties', to 'the designer that we need to get clothes from'.

From that moment on, when I realized that it was all possible, that it was working, and I saw the real advantage of being in Morocco, two ideas came to me very clearly. The first: when there is nothing, then there is everything to do. The second: I need to succeed in my own way in order to become living proof to all the kids out there who come from the same backgrounds as me, facing the same obstacles, that they still can make it. They do not need to be born in a rich country, or to a rich family to succeed, to live up to their dreams, as the future can be built by their own hands, assisted by nothing but strength of faith and the power of love.

Gradually, my path started to cross those of the people I had always met in my daydreams – magical, enchanting encounters of different kinds: encounters with teachers who corrected my trajectory when I needed to; men who had my back; women who saved my life; fabrics that are hidden gems veiled from

161
Designed by Amine Bendriouich
Carpet Space Suit
Casablanca, Morocco, 2013
Photographed by Christian Rinke

the public for years that chose to reappear before me; master artisans who saw in me a possibility of evolution for their craft, and trusted me with opening the doors of their knowledge. Cities that opened wide their arms for me and showed that I can be myself anywhere in the world, not only at home. Masters who taught me to follow my heart, befriend my fears and mistakes, and gave me the strength to never give up. Joys that kept my hopes alive, hardships that made me recognize the joys.

What I realized was that the only way available to me, that I thought I was obliged to take, turned out to be the best one for me. Spontaneous choices imposed by the lack of means were revealed as blessings. My personal convictions started becoming trends, my ideas transforming to seeds in other people's minds, giving birth to new projects. My idols started showing up in both my professional and personal life, blessing me with their guidance, support and love: one day Kehinde Wiley, another David Byrne, Naomi Campbell, Massive Attack, Madonna, Will Smith and so many more that I had the honour to work with and be touched by their grace. And then one day I was contacted by American *Vogue*, telling me I had been selected for the *Vogue* 100 – the 100 most influential creatives in fashion and street style – and that they had been observing me for a long time and knew everything about my career. The foolish dreamer boy from the medina made it to *Vogue* despite the waves of mockery, inexistence of a fashion industry, lack of support, lack of money, lack of exposure, and attracted the attention of the fashion gods from his enclosed home in Africa.

All of this that I have spoken about serves to explain what led me to the following observation: our main problem as African creatives is our knowledge and perspective *on* fashion in Africa, as you need to know where you come from to know where you are going. Fashion in Africa is not something that recently came to life, nor was it discovered by white men. It has always been there as an important form of expression of the countless civilizations that existed on the continent over thousands of years. That is why it is something that has been always embedded within the culture and tradition, and which we never felt the urge to make a fuss about, and why most Africans have this effortless sense of style. Fashion, its culture and trade in Africa, has an ancient history. In order for it to evolve and thrive, it should be considered as such, with all its specifics,

particularities, its ties to art, music, dance, religion, tradition, environment, natural resources, geography, politics. As I said above, when there is nothing, there is everything to create. So, we Africans have the chance to create our own systems and platforms that are sensitive and open to our particularities and needs, with our own rules based on the immense heritage and wealth we have. Instead of stressing and struggling to be part of a system that cannot fully understand us – not because it hates us or does not want us, but simply because it was built on other needs and ideas – we need to build a system that can integrate a newly conceived production process that is based on both industrial and artisanal skills, as the latter is a fundamental part of our being, and one cannot evolve while leaving a part of one's body behind.

This will lead to the full integration of different parts of society and make fashion impact directly on the lives of many more people, therefore giving it a stronger and wider popular basis and increase the need for it by revealing the potential of wealth and the importance it has for culture. I believe that only in this way will our work as African designers and creatives make sense in the contemporality of our times, and gain the respect and recognition we deserve from our occidental counterparts as independent, whole and fearless creative powerhouses with a lot to offer, shifting from the image of poor Third World wannabe designers who need help and exposure to be recognized by the world and begin to exist.

The best way to support African fashion is not to try to integrate it into an existing system that has already proven to be corrupt and starved of new gateways and inspiration, but to back African fashion as it builds its own channels, finds its own benefits, chooses its own seasons, establish its own trends, and crowns its own heroes, in order to gain its full strength, and become a truly beneficial force.

This, for me, is just a beginning, but the beginning of something that could finally touch the stars that once filled our eyes when we were the free children of Mother Africa.

162
Designed by Amine Bendriouich
Ensemble, 'A DNA' collection
Marrakesh, Morocco, 2018
Photographed by Marwane Pallas

NOTES

Prologue

1 Sisulu was banned for 18 years, longer than any other person in apartheid South Africa; the first woman detained for 90 days without trial and imprisoned multiple times thereafter. Meanwhile, her husband, Walter Sisulu, was serving a life sentence on Robben Island alongside Nelson Mandela. A strong believer in the collective power of women, Sisulu famously declared 'It is the women who will liberate this country'. Albertina Sisulu was an organiser of the historic 1956 August 9th, 20,000-strong women's march on the South African capital. Never one to seek the limelight, she was an active organizer with the ANC Women's League, the Federation of South African Women (FEDSAW) and the United Democratic Front (UDF) in the three decades of protests that culminated in the crumbling of the apartheid government. Albertina Sisulu held this 'VICTORY IS OURS' poster at a Women's Day picket in 1980.

Introduction

1 Awa Meité, interview with Christine Checinska and Elisabeth Murray, 4 December 2020.

2 *Kita* is a narrow handwoven cloth that originates from the Baule of Côte d'Ivoire, West Africa. The Baule are a subset of the Akan people of the Asante kingdom, i.e. Ghana. See Leila Walter, 'The Strip Woven Handloom Textile of Central Côte d'Ivoire', *Crosspolynations* (2020), crosspolynations.com/2020/05/04/baule-kita-of-cote-divoire/ (accessed 22 March 2021).

3 Emmanuelle Courrèges, 'Imane Ayissi and the African Textiles', *Vogue Italia* (19 October 2016), vogue.it/en/vogue-talents/news/2016/10/19/imane-ayissi-cameroon-africa-paris/ (accessed 22 March 2021).

4 Christine Checinska and Elisabeth Murray, interview with Imane Ayissi, 8 October 2020.

5 The V&A *Africa Fashion* exhibition aligns with Okwui Enwezor's 2001 show *The Short Century: Independence and Liberation Movements in Africa*, 1945–1994 and Simon Njami's 2004 show *Africa Remix*, in its cross-discipline approach to the prolific creativity of African people and the enmeshed nature of art, culture and politics across the continent.

6 Eicher 2010, p.x.

7 Gillow 2003, p.12.

8 Ibid., pp.10–11.

9 Jennings 2011, p.9.

10 Susan Gott, 'The Ghanaian Kaba: Fashion That Sustains Culture', in Gott and Loughran 2010, pp.11–27, p.13.

11 Picton and Mack 1989, p.23.

12 Gillow 2003, p.12.

13 Jennings 2011; Jessica Hemmings, 'Dutch Wax-resist Textiles: Roger Gerards, Creative Director of Vlisco, in Conversation with Jessica Hemmings', in Hemmings 2015, pp.66–91.

14 Françoise Vergès, 'The Invention of an African Fabric', in Kouoh 2013, pp.39–43, p.40.

15 Gillow 2003, p.13.

16 Gott and Loughran 2010, p.3.

17 Victoria L. Rovine, 'African Fashion: Design, Identity, and History', in Gott and Loughran 2010, pp.89–103, p.90.

18 John Picton, 'What to Wear in West Africa: Textile Design, Dress and Self-Representation', in Tulloch 2004, pp.22–47, p.38.

19 Gillow 2003, pp.13–14.

20 'Hypersampling' is a term describing the fast-paced and layered process of simultaneously drawing on multiple influences, often consumed via digital platforms by urban Generation Z fashion creatives in South Africa. See *Hypersampling Identities, Jozi Style*, an exhibition convened by VIAD in association with Nicola Cooper and Daniela Goeller, FADA Gallery, University of Johannesburg, 30 September – 2 October 2015. See also viad.co.za/hypersampling-identities (accessed 22 March 2021). Leora Farber defines 'hypersampling' as 'the remixing, reappropriating, reintegrating, fusing, conjoining, interfacing and mashing-up of often disparate elements gleaned from a multiplicity of online and offline sources to produce new fashion styles.' See Leora Farber, 'Hypersampling Black Masculinities, Jozi Style', *Image & Text: A Journal for Design* (9 January 2015), vol.26, no.1, p.122.

21 Sims and King-Hammond 2010, p.10. Bonnie Greer, in the Prologue to this book, uses the term Meta Africa to define the idea of Africa as a psychological space.

22 This definition of Blackness touches against its use in Britain during the 1980s to refer to African, African-Caribbean

and Asian people who, though central to the redevelopment of the UK after the Second World War, were marginalized.

23 In using the words 'behind the veil', I am referencing, or signifyin' on, W.E.B. DuBois' seminal work *The Souls of Black Folk* (1903), a meditation on Blackness. My use of the term signifyin' references Henry Louis Gates Jr's concept outlined in his groundbreaking book *The Signifying Monkey: A Theory of African-American Literary Criticism* (1988) where the term is shorthand for repetition that takes the form of critique or opposition, or as in this case, an occasion where a writer is pointing to a previous and well-known oppositional assertion.

24 The work of Erica de Greef and Lesiba Mabitsela, co-founders of the African Fashion Research Institute (AFRI), is just one example. AFRI seeks to decolonize fashion: the curricula, and the industry at a global level, by foregrounding voices and perspectives of critics, practitioners and wearers from the Global South. The Research Collective for Decoloniality & Fashion (RCDF), an international group of academics of which De Greef is also a founding member, similarly works towards a decolonized, equitable fashion arena.

25 Valentin-Yves Mudimbé, quoted in Sarr 2019, pp.12–27, p.14. The expression refers to European thinkers, writers, explorers, anthropologists and ethnologists such as G.W.F. Hegel, David Hume, Jean-Jacques Rousseau and Rudyard Kipling who constructed particular stories and beliefs about Africa.

26 See Hunter and Van der Westhuizen 2022. Hunter and Van der Westhuizen take an interdisciplinary approach to the critique of whiteness and the burgeoning field of Critical Whiteness Studies, incorporating multiple voices and perspectives from the Global South and the Global North in this timely and important publication.

27 Fanon 1986, p.112.

28 Bhabha 1994, pp.1–18.

29 Martin Heidegger, 'Building, Dwelling, Thinking', in Heidegger 1971; Bhabha 1994; Anzaldúa 1987.

30 Fanon 1986.

31 Lowery Stokes Sims and Leslie King-Hammond coined this term for the exhibition and publication of the same name. It is used here in the *Africa Fashion* book to denote the connection between those of us of African heritage that not only transcends geographical and political boundaries but also the fracturing of enslavement and colonization.

32 Ishmael Reed quoted in Wales Bonner 2019, p.25.

33 Hall 1993, p.109.

34 Farber attributes this to Miller, but this is not the case. Nevertheless, the concept of 'movement culture', with Farber's expansion of it, is a useful and pertinent one in relation to my reading of African fashions. See Leora Farber, 'Asserting Creative Agencies through the Sartorial: (Re) Fashioning African and African Diasporic Masculinities', in Farber 2017, pp.1–17, p.2. Note that Miller uses the expression 'Atlantic diaspora' (2009), whereas I use Global Africa.

35 See also viad.co.za/hypersampling-identities (accessed 22 March 2021).

36 Christine Checinska, 'Spinning a Yarn of One's Own', in Harris 2020, pp.235–55.

37 Miller 2009. Stuart Hall defined cultural identity as a process of becoming; see 'Cultural Identity and Diaspora', in Rutherford 1990, pp.222–37, p.225.

Liberation and Post-Independence Fashions

1 Folashade 'Shade' Thomas-Fahm, interview with Christine Checinska, 22 March 2021.

2 The number of independent African countries rose from 9 to 26 in 1960 alone, gaining their independence from Belgium, France and the UK. The phrase 'year of Africa' was coined by O.H. Morris of the British Ministry of Colonies.

3 Afro-Futurism is a cultural aesthetic and a philosophy that imagines the future from Black perspectives by integrating Global Africa histories and cultures with technology. The whole is framed by science fiction and fantasy. Fashion creatives drawing on Afro-Futurism include Selly Raby Kane and D. Denenge Duyst-Akpem in this volume. Within the visual arts they include artists such as Xenobia Bailey, known for eclectic crochet creations, and Wangechi Mutu, known primarily for painting and collage, and in music, Sun Ra (1914–1993), and George Clinton and Funkadelic, formed by Clinton in 1964.

4 The term Black is used here in a political sense that is not tied solely to those with black skins. Rather it refers to those who have been subjugated by white privilege, who sit outside the

NOTES

white mainstream. It is a reclamation of political Blackness as identified by Stuart Hall. See Hall 1993, pp.104–14.

5   Murphy 2021, pp.1–4. Dakar spawned other world festivals such as PANAF in Algeria, and FESTAC 77 in Nigeria. See also Tobias Wofford, 'Exhibiting a Global Blackness: The First World Festival of Negro Arts', *New World Coming: The Sixties and the Shaping of Global Consciousness* (2009), pp.179–86, academia.edu/25141247/Exhibiting_a_Global_Blackness_The_First_World_Festival_of_Negro_Arts (accessed 17 July 2021).

6   Chamberlain 2004, p.5.

7   Joanne B. Eicher and Doran H. Ross, 'Introduction: The Study of African Dress', in Eicher 2010, pp.3–9.

8   Eicher 2010, p.ix.

9   Victoria L. Rovine, 'African Fashion: Design, Identity, and History', in Gott and Loughran 2010, pp.89–103, p.90.

10 Barnard 1996, p.39.

11 Christine Checinska, 'Every Mickle Mek a Mockle: Reconfiguring Diasporic Identities', in Hutnyk 2012, pp.135–52.

12 Hendrickson 1996, p.13.

13 Miller 2009, p.7.

14 Christine Checinska, 'Disobedient Dress: Fashion as Everyday Activism', TedxEastEnd Ted Talk (22 February 2016), youtube.com/watch?v=63-9YIVAhpI (accessed 18 October 2021).

15 El Anatsui citing Sonya Clark in 'The Essential Art of African Textiles: Design Without End', metmuseum.org/exhibitions/listings/2008/african-textiles/el-anatsui (accessed 23 November 2021).

16 John Picton, 'What to Wear in West Africa: Textile Design, Dress and Self-Representation', in Tulloch 2004, pp.22–47, p.31.

17 Brathwaite 1984, p.5; Christine Checinska, 'Every Mickle Mek a Mockle: Reconfiguring Diasporic Identities', in Hutnyk 2012, p.139.

18 Fanon 1990, p.169.

19 Ibid.

We Face Forward

1   Inaugural speech made by Kwame Nkrumah in Accra on 6 March 1957.

2   Martin Luther King, radio interview by Etta Moten Barnett in Accra, Ghana, 6 March 1957.

3   Kwame Nkrumah, first session of Ghana's parliament, 6 March 1957.

4   Prempeh I, to H.E. the Governor of Seychelles, October 1913, in the correspondence book of King Prempeh I, alias Kana Kwaku Duah III (Nana Agyeman Duah), while in Seychelles Island (1912–21), Volume II, p.6.

5   Jimmy Moxon, Georgetown University, findingaids.library.georgetown.edu/repositories/15/resources/12290 (accessed 10 May 2021).

6   Fela Kuti, lyrics, *Beasts of No Nation*, 1989.

Five Fragments of African Textile History

1   See Suzanne Gott and Kristyne S. Loughran, 'Introducing African-Print Fashion', in Los Angeles 2017, pp.23–49, p.32.

2   Helen Elands, 'Dutch Wax Classics: The Designs Introduced by Ebenezer Brown Fleming circa 1890–1912 and Their Legacy', in Los Angeles 2017, pp.53–61, pp.54–5.

3   Ankersmit 2010; Halls and Martino 2018; Helen Elands, 'Dutch Wax Classics: The Designs Introduced by Ebenezer Brown Fleming circa 1890–1912 and Their Legacy', in Los Angeles 2017, pp.53–61, pp.55–9.

4   Halls and Martino 2018, pp.248–9.

5   Newark 1982–3.

6   See British Museum, Af1993,15.2 and UCLA Fowler Museum, X97.36.39; Newark and Los Angeles 1998, pp.164–5.

7   Oyelola 2010, pp.24–6.

8   Barbour 1970, p.365.

9   See Okunadaye 2017, pp.8–19; Chief Nike Davies-Okunadaye, 'An Overview', in Simmonds, Oyelola and Oke 2016, pp.73–8; Picton and Mack 1989, pp.155–8.

10 Okunadaye 2017, p.32.

11 Barbour 1970, p.372.

12 Adler and Barnard 1992, pp.99–110; Barbican Art Gallery 1995, p.24.

13 See New York 2020, pp.162–3.

14 Imperato and Shamir 1970; Brett-Smith 2014; Rovine 2001.

15 Adapted from Imperato and Shamir 1970; Polakoff 1980, pp.134–45; Picton and Mack 1989, p.161; and New York 2020, p.241.

16 Trowell 1966, p.37.

17 Barbour 1970, p.365.

18 De Zeltner 1910, pp.224–7; Clouzot 1931, n.p., plates I–V.

19 New York, Los Angeles, San Francisco and Cleveland 1972–3, p.208.

20 Mears 1998.

21 Pauline Duponchel, 'Bogolan: From Symbolic Material to National Emblem', in London 1995, pp.36–7.

22 Rovine 2015, pp.123–8.

23 Rovine 2001, p.116.

24 Doumbia 2006.

25 Janet Goldner, 'Group Bogolan Kasobane' (2017), janetgoldner.com/projects/groupe-bogolan-kasobane_ (accessed 25 July 2021).

Mid-Century Design: Shoreline Thinking and Crossing Borders

1 I am referencing Kamau Brathwaite's assertion that 'unity is submarine' as it brushes against Bonnie Greer's concept of 'shoreline thinking', helping us to imagine the flow of ideas and cultural expressions that travel across the Atlantic just as people do; Brathwaite 1975, p.1. Both Brathwaite and Greer allude to a common drive and capacity to resist the dehumanization of the colonial project and its legacies through creativity. See also Checinska 2018, pp.118–25, on the metaphor of the border, the coastline and the ocean in the creation of creolized cultural expressions. Creolization specifically refers to an African-Caribbean context but is viewed here as a form of syncretism.

2 It is important to recognize the limitations of this chapter. Certain pioneers such as Oumou Sy working in Dakar, Senegal, and Lamine Badian Kouyaté of Xuly.Bët, originally from Bamako, Mali, but now based in Paris, France, although featured in the accompanying exhibition via an audiovisual installation, are not included here. This should not suggest an undervaluing of their contribution to the histories of fashion; rather, it suggests and encourages further research. The designers that are featured here speak to the leave-and-return and the professionalization of the African fashion narrative. This chapter also aims to write women back into the history of global fashions.

3 Fashion designers existed prior to this; however, many did not self-identify as designers. Consider if you will the work of local dressmakers and tailors who co-created bespoke ensembles for their clients. Made-to-order is still a vibrant cutting-edge part of the African fashion scene yet the designer/makers go unrecognized. Christopher Richards addresses this topic: see Richards 2022.

4 McKinley 2021, p.154.

5 Ibid., p.153.6 Anzaldúa 1987; Bhabha 1994; Christine Checinska, '(Re)-fashioning Identities', in Anim-Addo and Scafe 2007, pp.54–70; Checinska 2018.

7 Christine Checinska, '(Re)-fashioning African Diasporic Masculinities', in Gaugele and Titton 2019, pp.74–89, p.77.

8 The 'in-between' space where borders meet. Anzaldúa 1987; Bhabha 1994.

9 Brathwaite 1984, p.5.

10 Thomas-Fahm, Ansah, Seydou and Alphadi each spent time overseas in Europe, as did many other artist and intellectuals from Africa and the Caribbean during the colonial era. The view of home from abroad informed their practices.

11 Gates 1988, pp.49–56.

12 Thomas-Fahm, Guessous, Seydou, Ansah, Alphadi and their peers could be viewed as the forefathers and mothers of the twenty-first-century African fashion scene. However, it must be acknowledged that the history of African fashions, and therefore the roots of the current fashion scene, reaches much further back than the twentieth century. Their creative practices mark a moment in a long history of creativity and cultural expression through cloth. With regards to fashioning the body, as early as the sixteenth century travellers documented changing trends in adornment, textiles and hair. See Gott and Loughran 2010, p.3.

13 Now Central Saint Martins (CSM), London.

14 Ezinne Chinkata, interview with Thomas-Fahm, 17 March 2017. See 'The Friday Column: Mrs Sade Thomas-Fahm', *Zinkata* (17 March 2017), zinkata.com/the-friday-column-mrs-sade-thomas-fahm/ (accessed 22 March 2021).

15 Christine Checinska and Elisabeth Murray, interview with one of Thomas-Fahm's clients, Professor Lalage Bown, who

NOTES

taught at the university in Ibadan, Nigeria, at the time of independence, 20 April 2021.

16 Christine Checinska, interview with Thomas-Fahm, 22 March 2021.

17 Ibid.

18 Christine Checinska and Elisabeth Murray, interview with Professor Lalage Bown, 20 April 2021. Thomas-Fahm started making bespoke garments but soon added ready-to-wear, 'off the peg'. She supplied department stores like Kingsway Stores and UTC Stores, as well as her own boutiques. The business names she worked under and incorporated were: Ola Ayo, Lady Shade and Shade's Boutique Ltd. Each had their own label, which were sewn into the garments for the different customers they attracted.

19 Elisabeth Murray, interview with Fauzi Fahm, 6 January 2021.

20 Christine Checinska and Elisabeth Murray, interview with Thomas-Fahm and her son, Fauzi, 26 August 2020.

21 Richards 2016, pp.8–21.

22 Victoria L. Rovine, 'African Fashion: Design, Identity, and History', in Gott and Loughran 2010, pp.89–103, p.94.

23 Helen Jennings, 'A Brief History of Postcolonial African Fashion', in Gaugele and Titton 2019, pp.104–13, p.105.

24 Conversation with Lydie Ullmann, 24 June 2020.

25 While in Paris he co-founded several important international forums for African designers, including Fédération Africaine de Prêt à Porter (African Federation of Ready-to-Wear Designers), in collaboration with Alphadi and Kofi Ansah.

26 Victoria L. Rovine, 'Chris Seydou', fashion-history.loveto-know.com/fashion-clothing-industry/fashion-designers/chris-seydou (accessed 20 June 2021).

27 Rovine 2015, p.123.

28 See africa.si.edu/collections/objects/19617/cloth (accessed 17 February 2021).

29 Victoria L. Rovine, 'African Fashion: Design, Identity, and History', in Gott and Loughran 2010, pp.89–103, p.94.

30 Christine Checinska, interview with Ryan Ansah, Kofi Ansah's son and founder of the Kofi Ansah Foundation, 25 March 2021.

31 Ibid.

32 Ansah studied at Chelsea School of Art at the same time as the London-based tailor Charlie Allen. Allen, who is from a family of tailors, studied painting and screen printing at that time. He went on to complete an MA in menswear design at the Royal College of Art, graduating in 1982.

33 Christine Checinska, interview with Ryan Ansah, Kofi Ansah's son and founder of the Kofi Ansah Foundation, 25 March 2021.

34 Meij 2002, p.42.

35 Christine Checinska and Elisabeth Murray, meeting with Makeba Boateng Utip, Fashion Forum Africa, and Ryan Ansah, Kofi Ansah's son and founder of the Kofi Ansah Foundation, 28 October 2020.

36 Meij 2001, pp.44–6.

37 Christine Checinska, interview with Ryan Ansah, Kofi Ansah's son and founder of the Kofi Ansah Foundation, 25 March 2021.

38 Meij 2001, pp.46–50.

39 Christine Checinska and Elisabeth Murray, meeting with Makeba Boateng Utip, Fashion Forum Africa, and Ryan Ansah, Kofi Ansah's son and founder of the Kofi Ansah Foundation, 28 October 2020.

40 Christine Checinska, interview with Ryan Ansah, Kofi Ansah's son and founder of the Kofi Ansah Foundation, 25 March 2021.

41 Ibid.

42 Gilvin 2014, p.43.

43 Ibid., p.42.

44 Christine Checinska, interview with Alphadi, 17 March 2021.

45 Ibid.

46 Ibid.

47 Agadez is the largest city in central Niger. Historically it was a hub for trans-Saharan trade connecting a number of West African cities like Timbuktu and Kano. The four points of the cross are said to represent the four points of a compass – north, south, east and west – and protect your travels across the vast expanse of desert sands of the Sahara. But it is also said to symbolize love. Legend has it that a young girl fashioned the first cross from the Tamazight word for love, *t(i)r(i)*, written in the Tifinagh script as +O, as a way of sending a secret message to a Tuareg warrior whom she loved; see menasymbolism.com/2019/04/19/tuareg-cross/

(accessed 24 June 2021).

48 Christine Checinska, interview with Alphadi, 17 March 2021.

49 Although motivated by the desire for peace, economic advancement and African pride, Alphadi's staging of FIMA with its glamour and what could be perceived as excess, could be seen as incongruous, at odds with the needs of a country in which a large proportion of the population is poverty-stricken, and many of whom are practising Muslims observing the rules that dictate modest dress. Indeed, there has been some local grassroots resistance to the staging of it throughout its history.

50 Christine Checinska, interview with Alphadi, 17 March 2021.

51 Rovine 2015, p.246; Gilvin 2014, p.48.

52 See Victoria L. Rovine, 'Runways in the Desert: FIMA and the Future of African Fashion', *Africultures* (9 March 2010), africultures.com/runways-in-the-desert-fima-and-the-future-of-african-fashion-9307/ (accessed 1 August 2021).

53 Elisabeth Murray, interview with Lalla Seidnaly, Alphadi's daughter, 8 January 2021.

54 Christine Checinska, interview with Alphadi, 17 March 2021.

55 Scant documentation exists about the creative practices of the pioneers of the Moroccan fashion scene. As far as we are aware archives and foundations do not exist. Archives are yet to be discovered. This has inevitably impacted the research into their work.

56 Maria Angela Jansen, 'Three Generations of Moroccan Fashion Designers: Negotiating Local and Global Identity' (2013), academia.edu/5079765/Three_Generations_of_Moroccan_Fashion_Designers_Negotiating_Local_and_Global_Identity (accessed 25 February 2021).

57 Maria Angela Jansen, 'Casablanca: Past, Present, and Future as Fashion Capital' (2012), academia.edu/2560604/Casablanca_Past_Present_Future_as_Fashion_Capital (accessed 23 June 2021).

58 Ibid.

59 Eleni, Washington, DC, *Evening Star*, 11 May 1968.

60 *New York Times*, 24 April 1966

61 Maria Angela Jansen, 'Casablanca: Past, Present, and Future as Fashion Capital' (2012), academia.edu/2560604/Casablanca_Past_Present_Future_as_Fashion_Capital

(accessed 23 June 2021).

62 Elena, Washington, DC, *Evening Star*, 11 May 1968.

63 Betty Beale, *Womenswear Daily* (no date on cutting).

64 Ibid.

65 Considering global fashion history prior to this period, Guessous could be seen as part of a fashion lineage that stretches back to Madame Grès (1903–1993) when it comes to the use of draping in high-end fashions. Grès opened her first couture fashion house, La Maison Alix, in Paris in 1932.

66 The concept of a fashion designer did not become embedded into Moroccan culture until the mid-1980s and 1990s, with the establishment of fashion schools and the advent of lifestyle press respectively. See Jansen 2015.

67 Maria Angela Jansen, 'Casablanca: Past, Present, and Future as Fashion Capital' (2012), academia.edu/2560604/Casablanca_Past_Present_Future_as_Fashion_Capital (accessed 23 June 2021).

68 Maria Angela Jansen, 'Joste – Tamy Tazi – Yves Saint Laurent: A Story of Cultural Appropriation, Otherness and Self Definition' (November 2015), academia.edu/19334899/Joste_Tamy_Tazi_Yves_Saint_Laurent_A_Story_of_Cultural_Appropriation_Otherness_and_Self_Definition (accessed 23 June 2021).

Contemporary Creatives

1 Kofi Ansah, quoted by his son, Ryan Ansah, in an interview with Christine Checinska, 25 March 2021.

2 André Leon Talley Instagram post, 8 April 2021.

3 vogue.com/article/virgil-abloh-louis-vuitton-amanda-gorman-vogue-cover-dress (accessed 24 April 2021).

4 Ibid.

5 *Vogue Runway* conversation, ibid.

6 See http://web.pdx.edu/~allstott/hypebeasthistory/offwhite.html (accessed 1 August 2021).

7 Antwaun Sargent, *The New Black Vanguard* (New York 2019), accompanies the exhibition *The New Black Vanguard: Photography between Art and Fashion*, Aperture Gallery, New York, 2019–20.

8 Ibid., p.11.

9 Mercer 1994, p.113.

10 Stuart Hall, cited in Mercer 1994, p.174.

NOTES

11 The concept of the noble savage is an amalgam drawn from representations found in classical mythology and the writings of Renaissance ethnographers. The term denotes an essential goodness, innocence and an innate wisdom that does not come from civilization. It suggests a oneness with nature. The second archetypal image, the Mungo Macaroni, references Julius Soubise, the son of an enslaved African, who in 1764, aged 10, was given as a present to the Duchess of Queensbury, Catherine Hyde. Later, his appearance on the London scene as a bewigged and perfumed Macaroni saw him ridiculed and celebrated in equal measure, the term Mungo Macaroni becoming shorthand for ostentation, folly and extravagance. The Blackamoor could be seen as a close cousin of the Mungo Macaroni. See Checinska 2009.

12 Gilroy 2004, p.250.

13 Christine Checinska, interview with Daniel Obasi, 21 June 2021.

14 Hill Collins 1991, pp.67–90.

15 Supermodel Iman recalled a white fashion magazine editor, referring to her beauty, describing her as like a white woman 'dipped in chocolate'. See Carole Cadwalladr, 'Iman: I Am the Face of a Refugee', *Guardian* (29 June 2014), theguardian.com/fashion/2014/jun/29/iman-i-am-the-face-of-a-refugee (accessed 10 June 2021).

16 1960s model Donyale Luna was described as 'strange'. She was also described as a 'Masai warrior, Gauguin-esque, Nefertiti reborn'. See Dream Cazzaniga, 'Remembering Donyale Luna, the First Woman of Colour Ever to Appear on the Cover of Vogue', *Vogue* (19 April 2019), vogue.co.uk/article/donyale-luna-model-vogue (accessed 10 June 2021).

17 Aili Mari Tripp, 'How African Feminism Changed the World', *Africa Arguments* (8 March 2017), africanarguments.org/2017/03/how-african-feminism-changed-the-world/ (accessed 10 June 2021).

18 Carmen McCain, 'Molara Ogundipe-Leslie: Teacher, Writer, Poet, Activist', *Beyond the Single Story* blog (2017), beyondthesinglestory.wordpress.com/2017/12/13/molara-ogundipe-leslie/ (accessed 10 June 2021). Molara Ogundipe-Leslie combined literature, theory and activism. She had a firm belief in the power of creativity, specifically literature, to change women's lives. Stiwanism is an acronym for Social Transformation Including Women in Africa. Stiwanism, as a movement, highlighted the fact that women's independence had been left out of African independence and that the Euro-American feminist movements had also left them out. Ogundipe-Leslie argued that there could be no true liberation of Africa without the liberation of women. She suggested that all Black men should be feminists, pre-dating novelist Chimamanda Ngozi Adichie's influential TED Talk, 'We Should All Be Feminists'. Ogundipe-Leslie decolonized feminist theory by recentring Africa in her writings. Her seminal work, *Re-Creating Ourselves* (1994), is a call to action. awid.org/whrd/molara-ogundipe (accessed 20 June 2021).

19 Bucknor 2005, pp.i–xliii.

20 Busby 1992, p.xxix.

21 Christine Checinska and Elisabeth Murray, interview with Sindiso Khumalo, 14 January 2021.

22 bell hooks, 'An Aesthetic of Blackness: Strange and Oppositional, Aesthetic Inheritances: History Worked by Hand', in Livingstone and Ploof 2007, pp.315–32.

23 Christine Checinska, interview with Abrima Erwiah, 29 June 2021.

24 Marina Azcárate, 'Beyond Labels: Stephen Tayo's Photography Tells a Story', *thenextcartel* (24 March 2021), thenextcartel.com/discover/stephen-tayo-photography (accessed 1 August 2021).

Orange Culture: Once Upon a Time, in Nigeria...

1 Emezi 2020, p.230.

2 Ibid., p.31.

3 Ibid., p.38.

4 Ibid., p.10.

5 Amy Frearson, '"People Are Afraid to Talk About Toxic Masculinity" says Orange Culture's Adebayo Oke-Lawal', *Dezeen* (31 May 2019), dezeen.com/2019/05/31/orange-culture-adebayo-oke-lawal-toxic-masculinity-fashion-diversity/ (accessed 15 February 2021).

6 Ibid.

7 Max Grobe, 'Nigeria's Orange Culture is Challenging

Masculine Stereotypes', *High Snobeity* (2018), highsnobiety.com/p/orange-culture-utr/ (accessed 15 February 2021).

8 Ayedeji Rotinwa, 'What It Means to Dress in Lagos', *New York Times* (1 December 2018), nytimes.com/2018/12/01/style/nigeria-lagos-fashion-experimental.html (accessed 30 April 2021).

9 Ibid.

10 Ibid. This sentiment is echoed by Nick Remsen in *Vogue.com*: 'The way society is in Lagos…we're used to specific ways of seeing things. Gender is an exact way of thinking back home and has been for a very long time.' Oke-Lawal says that Orange Culture has been accused of 'feminizing our men': 'If you have a problem with a man wearing jewelry or an oversize blouse or painting his nails, that's your problem. It's not Orange Culture's!' See Nick Remsen, 'Orange Culture's Adebayo Oke-Lawal Brings His Vision of Nigeria to New York City', *Vogue.com* (11 September 2019), vogue.com/vogueworld/article/orange-culture-nyfw-nigeria-adebayo-oke-lawal (accessed 30 April 2021).

11 Monica L. Miller, interview with Adebayo Oke-Lawal, 3 March 2021.

12 Orange Culture promotional materials for *Honest* collection, Autumn/Winter 2021.

13 Barclay Bram Shoemaker, 'Orange Culture Is the Unisex Brand Challenging What It Means to Be a Man in Nigeria', *i-D* (7 December 2017), i-d.vice.com/en_uk/article/595gpz/orange-culture-nigeria-interview (accessed 8 February 2021).

14 Monica L. Miller, interview with Adebayo Oke-Lawal, 3 March 2021.

15 Orange Culture promotional materials for *Honest* collection, Autumn/Winter 2021.

16 Georgia Illingworth, 'Can Fashion Be Truly Subversive When It Comes to Gender?', *Not Just A Label* (6 January 2021), notjustalabel.com/editorial/can-fashion-be-truly-subversive-when-it-comes-gender (accessed 15 March 2021).

17 Ibid.

18 Vanessa Friedman, 'The Year of Telfar', *New York Times* (29 March 2021), nytimes.com/2020/12/21/style/telfar-clemens-designer.html/ (accessed 30 March 2021).

19 Ibid.

20 Orange Culture promotional materials for *Honest* collection, Autumn/Winter 2021.

21 Vanessa Friedman, 'The Year of Telfar', *New York Times* (29 March 2021), nytimes.com/2020/12/21/style/telfar-clemens-designer.html/ (accessed 30 March 2021).

22 Ooooota Adepo, 'Interview with Adebayo Oke-Lawal of Orange Culture', *Vogue.cz* (Czech Republic) (1 August 2020), vogue.cz/clanek/vogue-cs-in-english/ooooota-adepo/interview-with-adebayo-oke-lawal-of-orange-culture (accessed 15 March 2021).

23 Channing Hargrove, 'How Orange Culture is Using Fashion to Combat Harmful Stereotypes About Africa', *Refinery 29* (12 September 2019), refinery29.com/en-us/2019/09/8407584/orange-culture-spring-2020-collection (accessed 15 February 2021).

24 Max Grobe, 'Nigeria's Orange Culture is Challenging Masculine Stereotypes', *High Snobeity* (2018), highsnobiety.com/p/orange-culture-utr/ (accessed 15 February 2021).

25 BellaNaija Style, 'Orange Culture Presents Autumn Winter 2017 Collection "Pretty"', *BellaNaija* (18 March 2017), bellanaija.com/2017/03/orange-culture-presents-autumn-winter-2017-collection-pretty/ (accessed 15 March 2021).

26 Ibid.

27 Ibid.

28 Ayedeji Rotinwa, 'What It Means to Dress in Lagos', *New York Times* (1 December 2018), nytimes.com/2018/12/01/style/nigeria-lagos-fashion-experimental.html (accessed 30 April 2021).

29 Ooooota Adepo, 'Interview with Adebayo Oke-Lawal of Orange Culture', *Vogue.cz* (Czech Republic) (31 July 2020), vogue.cz/clanek/vogue-cs-in-english/ooooota-adepo/interview-with-adebayo-oke-lawal-of-orange-culture (accessed 15 March 2021).

30 Emeka Joseph Nwankwo, 'The Gender-Nonconforming Spirit: Identity, Disruption and Performance in Igbo Culture', *Adda: The Online Magazine of New Writing from around the Globe* (Commonwealth Writers) (22 February 2019), addastories.org/gender-nonconforming-spirit/ (accessed 18 May 2021).

NOTES

31 Ooooota Adepo, 'Interview with Adebayo Oke-Lawal of Orange Culture', *Vogue.cz* (Czech Republic) (31 July 2020), vogue.cz/clanek/vogue-cs-in-english/ooooota-adepo/ interview-with-adebayo-oke-lawal-of-orange-culture (accessed 15 March 2021).

32 Monica L. Miller, interview with Adebayo Oke-Lawal, 3 March 2021.

33 Ayedeji Rotinwa, 'What It Means to Dress in Lagos', *New York Times* (1 December 2018), nytimes.com/2018/12/01/ style/nigeria-lagos-fashion-experimental.html (accessed 30 April 2021).

34 Orange Culture promotional materials for *Honest* collection, Autumn/Winter 2021.

35 Emezi 2020, p.49. *The Beautyful Ones Are Not Yet Born* (1968) is a novel by Ghanaian writer Ayi Kwei Armah.

Agents of Change

1 Antwaun Sargent, 'How to Save a Dying Art with Nigerian Designer Kenneth Ize', *Ssense* (24 February 2020), ssense. com/en-us/editorial/fashion/how-to-save-a-dying-art- with-nigerian-designer-kenneth-ize, accessed 11 May 2021).

2 Ibid.

3 'Sector Overview', South Africa Mohair Cluster, samohair- cluster.co.za/sector-overview/ (accessed 23 April 2021).

4 'Lisa Folawiyo', *Business of Fashion*, businessoffashion.com/ community/people/lisa-folawiyo (accessed 14 May 2021).

5 Thebe Magugu, 'The "Counter Intelligence" Collection TM. SS2021', thebemagugu.com/collections/ss-2021 (accessed 11 May 2021).

6 Elisabeth Murray, interview with Adeju Thompson, 13 April 2021.

7 Violet Conroy, 'Lagos Space Programme: "I'm Trying to Break Down the Misconception that Queerness is a Western Construct"', *SHOWstudio* (18 May 2021), showstudio. com/news/lagos-space-programme-im-trying-to-break- down-the-misconception-that-queerness-is-a- western-construct, (accessed 24 May 2021).

8 Tommy Dennis, 'Lagos Space Programme', nataal.com/ lagos-space-programme (accessed 24 May 2021).

9 'Hend Riad & Mariam Hazem | Reform Studio | Plastex', *Guiltlessplastic* (28 November 2020), guiltlessplastic.com/ reform-studio/ (accessed 24 May 2021).

10 Robb Young, 'Tapping the \$31 Billion Africa Opportunity', *Business of Fashion* (10 May 2015), businessoffashion.com/ community/voices/discussions/what-will-it-take-for- africa-to-join-the-global-fashion-system (accessed 27 April 2021).

11 Elisabeth Murray and Donata Miller, interview with Doreen Mashika, 21 April 2021.

Afro-Fashion Futures

1 The observation that the fashion industry has been kill- ing the world for decades knowingly invokes the work of journalist Lucy Siegle whose 2011 book, *To Die For: Is Fashion Wearing Out the World?*, clearly outlined the human and en- vironmental costs of fast fashions in a way that spoke to our generation of fashion creatives and wearers in the Global North. Each chapter considers everyday wardrobe staples, forcing the reader to question their shopping habits.

2 globenewswire.com/news-release/2020/10/28/2116073 /0/en/Sustainable-Fashion-Market-Analysis-Shows- The-Market-Progress-In-Attempt-To-Decrease- Pollution-In-The-Global-Ethicalfashion-Market-2020.html (accessed 11 May 2021).

3 See fashionrevolution.org/about/ (accessed 9 May 2021).

4 See rewoven.africa/masterclasses (accessed 19 June 2021). Rewoven was founded in 2018 by Tshepo Bhengu, Esethu Cenga and Lonwabo Mgoduso, based in Cape Town, South Africa, and operates at the intersection between sustainable fashion and well-being.

5 Sarr 2019, p.118.

6 Ibid., p.99.

7 Conscious of the need to create sustainable fashion sys- tems in Africa, Alphadi founded the International Festival of African Fashion, held every two years, to encourage young African designers of the future.

8 Sarr 2019, pp.99–102.

9 See denenge.net/ (accessed 1 August 2021).

10 See Fanon 1986 and 1990; Baldwin 2018.

The Place We Call Home: Economic and Cultural Reclamation of African Fashions

1 'Team USA: Simone Biles Stuns with New Triple Double on Floor', Youtube (2019), bit.ly/2XAqkrX (accessed 20 August 2021).

2 Karin Eldor, 'The Real Queen's Gambit: How Elsa Majimbo is Winning Over a Global Audience, One Move At A Time', *Forbes* (7 December 2020), bit.ly/2UxaFZt (accessed 20 August 2021).

3 Robyn Mowatt, 'The Nation and George Floyd's Family are Still Mourning his Death, a Year Later', *OkayPlayer* (May 2021), bit.ly/3svzoK1 (accessed 20 August 2021).

4 Amanda Holpuch, 'Stolen Daughters: What happened after #BringBackOurGirls?', *Guardian* (22 October 2018), bit.ly/3gdl18w (accessed 20 August 2021).

5 Seggane Musisi and Nakanyike Musisi. 'The Legacies of Colonialism in African Medicine', *World Health Organization*, bit.ly/3geJRoi (accessed 20 August 2021).

6 Maria Fibaek and Erik Green, 'Labour Control and the Establishment of Profitable Settler Agriculture in Colonial Kenya, c.1920–45', *Taylor and Francis Online* (10 April 2019), bit.ly/3gdJ1bC (accessed 20 August 2021).

7 Abigail Beall, 'Why Clothes are So Hard to Recycle', *BBC Future* (13 July 2020), bbc.in/3y1TQDm (accessed 20 August 2021).

8 James Mwangi, 'If it were not for "Mtush", Many Kenyans would be Naked', *The Standard*, Kenya (2015), bit.ly/2WcRDIo (accessed 20 August 2021).

9 For further reading, see Said Adejumobi, 'Second-hand Cult Debases Africa' *New African* (11 January 2018), newafrican-magazine.com/20297/ (accessed 20 August 2021).

10 Roble Musse, 'White Tech Startup Founders Are 50,000% More Likely To Get Funded In Kenya Than In The USA', *Medium* (5 February 2020), bit.ly/37WJtGz (accessed 20 August 2021).

11 Katungulu Mwendwa. 'Everyday Superheroes', bit.ly/3z6XWeY (accessed 20 August 2021).

Reimagining Second-hand Markets in Africa

1 Esther Katende-Magezi, 'The Impact of Second Hand Clothes and Shoes in East Africa' (2017), cuts-geneva.org/pdf/PACT2-STUDY-The_Impact_of_Second_Hand_Clothes_and_Shoes_in_East_Africa.pdf (accessed 8 March 2021).

2 Nnaemeka Ugochukwu, 'Second-Hand Clothing May Be A Threat to Africa's Textile Industry, But It's Not All Bad', *Eco Warrior Princess* (29 February 2020), ecowarriorprincess.net/2020/02/second-hand-clothing-threat-africa-textile-industry-not-all-bad/ (accessed 13 February 2021).

3 Karen Tranberg Hansen, 'The Secondhand Clothing Market in Africa and Its Influence on Local Fashions' (2014), kci.or.jp/research/dresstudy/pdf/K_D64_HANSEN_The%20Secondhand%20Clothing_ENG.pdf (accessed 5 February 2021).

4 'Global Business of Secondhand Clothes Thrive in Africa' (26 April 2018), africanews.com/2018/04/26/global-business-of-secondhand-clothes-thrive-in-africa-business-africa/ (accessed 8 March 2021).

5 Andrew Brooks, 'The Hidden Trade in our Second-hand Clothes Given to Charity', *The Guardian* (13 February 2015), theguardian.com/sustainable-business/sustainable-fashion-blog/2015/feb/13/second-hand-clothes-charity-donations-africa (accessed 5 February 2021).

6 Kevin Moss and Manish Bapna, '4 Indicators that the Reuse and Resale Market Is on the Rise', *World Resources Institute* (21 December 2020), wri.org/insights/4-indicators-reuse-and-resale-market-rise (accessed 24 March 2021).

7 Dan Banik with Kaja Elise Gresko, 'Why is Used Clothing Popular Across Africa? We Found Out in Malawi', *The Conversation* (21 April 2020), theconversation.com/why-is-used-clothing-popular-across-africa-we-found-out-in-malawi-136438 (accessed 8 March 2021).

8 Julian Hattem, 'Can "Made in Africa" Mend a Textile Industry Dominated by Throwaways', *BRIGHT* Magazine (19 April 2018), brightthemag.com/textile-second-hand-clothes-fashion-uganda-cotton-made-in-africa-20f83de98138 (accessed 24 March 2021).

9 Rick Leblanc, 'The Basics of Textile Recycling' (9 December 2020), thebalancesmb.com/the-basics-of-recycling-clothing-and-other-textiles-2877780#sources-of-textiles-for-recycling (accessed 24 March 2021).

10 SgT Group, 'Sustainable Fashion Transformation: Recycling and Reuse' (21 August 2018), sgtgroup.net/textile-quality-management-blog/sustainable-fashion-transformation-recycling-and-reuse (accessed 26 March 2021).

BIBLIOGRAPHY

Peter Adler and Nicholas Barnard, *African Majesty* (London 1992)

Joan Anim-Addo and Suzanne Scafe (eds), *I am Black/White/Yellow: An Introduction to the Black Body in Europe* (London 2007)

Willem Ankersmit, 'The Wax Print: Its Origin and Its Introduction on the Gold Coast', Master's Thesis, University of Leiden, 2010

Gloria Anzaldúa, *Borderlands/La Frontera: The New Mestiza* (San Francisco, CA 1987)

James Baldwin, *Dark Days* (London 2018)

Jane Barbour, 'Nigerian "Adire" Cloths', *Baessler-Archiv,* N.F. (1970), vol.18, no.2, pp.363–426

Malcolm Barnard, *Fashion as Communication* (Oxford 1996)

Homi K. Bhabha, *The Location of Culture* (Abingdon 1994)

Edward Kamau Brathwaite, 'Caribbean Man in Space and Time', *Savacou* (September 1975), nos 11–12, pp.1–11

Edward Kamau Brathwaite, *History of the Voice* (London 1984)

Sarah C. Brett-Smith, *The Silence of the Women: Bamana Mud Cloths* (Milan 2014)

Michael A. Bucknor, 'Rooting and Routing Caribbean-Canadian Writing', *Journal of West Indian Literature* (November 2005), vol.14, nos 1 and 2, pp.i–xliii

Margaret Busby, *Daughters of Africa* (London 1992)

Muriel E. Chamberlain, *Decolonization* (1999) (Malden, MA, and Oxford 2004)

Christine Checinska, *Colonizin' in Reverse!,* unpublished PhD dissertation, Goldsmiths, University of London, 2009

Christine Checinska, 'Aesthetics of Blackness?', *Textile: Journal of Cloth and Culture* (June 2018), vol.16, issue 2, *Aesthetics of Blackness?: Cloth, Culture and the African Diasporas,* pp.118–25

Henri Clouzot, *Tissus nègres* (Paris 1931)

Boubacar Doumbia, *L'Evolution des Teintes naturelles: Basilan, Bogolan, Gala* (Mali 2006)

W.E.B. DuBois, *The Souls of Black Folk* (1903) (New York 1994)

Joanne B. Eicher, *Encyclopedia of World Dress and Fashion: Africa* (Oxford 2010)

Akwaeke Emezi, *The Death of Vivek Oji* (New York 2020)

Frantz Fanon, *Black Skin, White Masks* (1967) (London 1986)

Frantz Fanon, *The Wretched of the Earth* (1963) (London 1990)

Leora Farber, 'Hypersampling Black Masculinities, Jozi Style', *Image & Text: a Journal for Design* (9 January 2015), vol.26, no.1, pp.111–36

Leora Farber (ed.), *Critical Arts: (Re)Fashioning African and African Diasporic Masculinities* (June 2017), vol.31, no.3

Henry Louis Gates Jr, *The Signifying Monkey: A Theory of African-American Literary Criticism* (Oxford 1988)

Elke Gaugele and Monica Titton (eds), *Fashion and Postcolonial Critique* (Vienna 2019)

John Gillow, *African Textiles: Colour and Creativity across a Continent* (San Francisco, CA 2003)

Paul Gilroy, *Between Camps: Nations, Cultures and the Allure of Race* (London 2004)

Amanda Gilvin, 'Hot and Haute: Alphadi's Fashion for Peace', *African Arts* (Summer 2014), vol.47, no.2, pp.40–55, jstor.org/stable/43306220 (accessed 17 March 2020)

Suzanne Gott and Kristyne Loughran, *Contemporary African Fashion* (Bloomington, IN 2010)

Suzanne Gott et al. (eds), *African-Print Fashion Now!: A Story of Taste, Globalization, and Style,* exh. cat., Fowler Museum at UCLA, Los Angeles, CA 2017

Stuart Hall, 'What is this "Black" in Black Popular Culture? (Rethinking Race)', *Social Justice* (Spring/Summer 1993), vol.20, no.1–2, pp.104–14

Julie Halls and Allison Martino, 'Cloth, Copyright, and Cultural Exchange: Textile Designs for Export to Africa at the National Archives of the UK', *Journal of Design History* (September 2018), vol.31, issue 3, pp.236–54, doi.org/10.1093/jdh/epy007 (accessed 25 July 2021)

Jennifer Harris, *A Companion to Textile Culture* (Hoboken, NJ 2020)

Martin Heidegger, *Poetry, Language, Thought,* trans. Albert Hofstadter (New York 1971), faculty.arch.utah.edu/miller/4270heidegger.pdf (accessed 17 July 2021)

Jessica Hemmings, *Cultural Threads: Transnational Textiles Today* (London 2015)

Hildi Hendrickson, *Clothing and Difference: Embodied Identities in Colonial and Post-Colonial Africa* (Durham, NC and London 1996)

Patricia Hill Collins, *Black Feminist Thought: Knowledge, Consciousness, and the Politics of Empowerment* (New York and London 1991)

bell hooks, *Ain't I a Woman: Black Women and Feminism* (London 1982)

Shona Hunter and Christi van der Westhuizen, *Routledge Handbook of Critical Studies in Whiteness* (Abingdon and New York 2022)

John Hutnyk, *Beyond Borders* (London 2012)

Pascal James Imperato and Marli Shamir, 'Bokolanfini: Mud Cloth of the Bamana of Mali', *African Arts* (Summer 1970), vol.3, no.4, pp.32–41, 80

Maria Angela Jansen, *Moroccan Fashion: Design, Tradition and Modernity,* e-book, 2015, bloomsburyfashioncentral.com/products/berg-fashion-library/book/moroccan-fashion-design-tradition-and-modernity (accessed 19 May 2021)

Helen Jennings, *New African Fashion* (Munich, London and New York 2011)

Koyo Kouoh, *Hollandaise: Un Voyage à Travers un Tissu Emblématique/Hollandaise: A Journey into an Iconic Fabric* (Dakar 2013)

Alisa LaGamma, *Sahel: Art and Empires on the Shores of the Sahara,* exh. cat., Metropolitan Museum of Art, New York 2020

Alisa LaGamma and Christine Giuntini, *The Essential Art of African Textiles: Design Without End,* exh. cat., Metropolitan Museum of Art, New York 2008–9

Joan Livingstone and John Ploof, *The Object of Labor: Art, Cloth, and Cultural Production* (Chicago, IL, Cambridge, MA and London 2007)

Catherine E. McKinley, *The African Lookbook: A Visual History of 100 Years of African Women* (New York 2021)

BIBLIOGRAPHY

Patricia E. Mears, 'Jessie Franklin Turner: American Fashion and "Exotic" *Textile Inspiration', Textile Society of America Symposium Proceedings. Paper 191* (1998), http://digitalcommons.unl.edu/tsaconf/191 (accessed 25 July 2021)

Ietse Meij (ed.), *Fashion and Ghana,* exh. cat., Gemeentemuseum Den Haag, The Hague 2001

Kobena Mercer, *Welcome to the Jungle: New Positions in Black Cultural Studies* (New York and London 1994)

Monica L. Miller, *Slaves to Fashion: Black Dandyism and the Styling of Black Diasporic Identity* (Durham, NC and London 2009)

David Murphy, *The First World Festival of Negro Arts, Dakar 1966: Contexts and Legacies* (Liverpool 2021)

Molara Ogundipe-Leslie, *Re-Creating Ourselves: African Women and Critical Transformations* (Trenton, NJ 1994)

Chief (Mrs) Nike Okunadaye, *Adire: An Unspoken Language: The Patterns and Meanings of an Indigenous Yoruba Textile* (Lagos 2017)

Pat Oyelola, *Nigerian Artistry* (Ibadan 2010)

John Picton with Rayda Becker et al., *The Art of African Textiles: Technology, Tradition and Lurex,* exh. cat., Barbican Art Gallery, London 1995

John Picton and John Mack, *African Textiles* (London and New York 1989)

Claire Polakoff, *Into Indigo: African Textiles and Dyeing Techniques* (Garden City, NY 1980)

Christopher Richards, 'The Models for Africa. Accra's Independence-Era Fashion Cultures and the Creations of Chez Julie', *African Arts* (2016), vol.49, no.3, pp.8–21

Christopher Richards, *Cosmopolitanism and Women's Fashion in Ghana History: Artistry and Nationalist Inspirations* (Abingdon and New York, forthcoming 2022)

Doran H. Ross (ed.), *Wrapped in Pride: Ghanaian Kente and African American Identity,* exh. cat., Newark Museum, Newark, NJ; Fowler Museum at UCLA, Los Angeles, CA 1998

Victoria L. Rovine, *Bogolan: Shaping Culture through Cloth in Contemporary Mali* (Washington, DC 2001)

Victoria L. Rovine, *African Fashion, Global Style: Histories, Innovations, and Ideas You Can Wear* (Bloomington, IN 2015)

Jonathan Rutherford, *Identity: Community, Culture and Difference* (London 1990)

Antwaun Sargent, *The New Black Vanguard: Photography between Art and Fashion,* exh. cat., Aperture Gallery, New York, 2019–20

Felwine Sarr, *Afrotopia* (Minneapolis, MN 2019)

Roy Sieber, *African Textiles and Decorative Arts,* exh. cat., Museum of Modern Art, New York 1972–3; Los Angeles County Museum of Art, CA 1973; M.H. de Young Memorial Museum, San Francisco, CA 1973; Cleveland Museum of Art, OH 1973

Lucy Siegle, *To Die For: Is Fashion Wearing Out the World?* (London 2011)

Doig Simmonds, Pat Oyelola and Ṣẹgun Ọkẹ (eds), *Adire Cloth in Nigeria 1971–2016* (Ibadan 2016)

Anne Spencer, *In Praise of Heroes: Contemporary African Commemorative Cloth,* exh. cat., Newark Museum, Newark, NJ 1982–3

Lowery Stokes Sims and Leslie King-Hammond, *The Global Africa Project,* exh. cat., Museum of Arts and Design, New York, 2010–11

Margaret Trowell, *African Design* (1960) (2nd ed., New York 1966)

Carol Tulloch, *Black Style* (London 2004)

Grace Wales Bonner, 'Threads Across the Black Atlantic: Grace Wales Bonner', *Frieze* (June/July/August 2019), no.204, pp.25–6

Alice Walker, *The Color Purple* (San Diego, CA 1982)

Alice Walker, *In Search of Our Mothers' Gardens: Womanist Prose* (San Diego, CA 1984)

Frantz de Zeltner, 'Tissus africains à dessins réservés nu décolorés', *Bulletins et Mémoires de la Société de Anthropologie de Paris* (1910), ser.6, vol.1, pp.224–7

GLOSSARY

Àdìrẹ

An indigo-dyed cloth traditionally produced by Yorùbá women in south-western Nigeria. A range of resist-dye techniques can be used.

Agbádá

A men's long, loose-fitting robe with wide sleeves. The term can also refer to a set of garments consisting of the outer robe, an undershirt, drawstring trousers and a cap.

Akwardzan (*also* **Akwadzan**)

A Ga word referring to the dressing practice of draping and wrapping the upper torso with cloth.

Akwete

Handwoven cloth of cotton and sometimes raffia, hemp or silk, featuring decorative motifs created with supplementary weft threads. Produced by the Igbo population of Nigeria.

Ankara

Printed cotton cloth. Also referred to as 'African wax' prints and 'Dutch wax' prints.

Aṣọ-òkè

Handwoven cloth historically produced by Yorùbá people in south-western Nigeria.

Batik

A resist-dying technique of patterning cloth using wax, originating in Indonesia.

Bazin

A heavy and very finely woven cotton fabric that is highly polished and lightly starched to give it a distinctive sheen and stiffness. Often made of imported cotton with patterns woven in to it, which is then dyed and processed in Mali. The layering of the dye and the process of hammering the starched cloth is what gives it its shine.

Bògòlanfini

A patterned cloth, most associated with the Bamana people of West Africa. Cotton or wool cloth is dyed with leaves before decoration is hand-painted or stencilled on with mud. Sometimes woven in narrow strips that are stitched together to form a width. Also known as 'mud cloth'.

Boubou

A men's long-sleeved outer robe.

Bziouia

A very finely woven, semi-transparent cloth of wool and sometimes silk, usually used for men's garments such as *djellabas*, originating from Bzou, Morocco.

Caftan (also **Qef-tan**)

A loose-fitting long robe with wide sleeves, sometimes belted.

Dashiki

A loose-fitting, short-sleeved tunic top, usually featuring decoration around the neck opening.

Djellaba

A long, loose-fitting outer garment with full sleeves and usually a hood, worn by men and women in North Africa.

Gèlè

The Yorùbá word for a headdress, usually voluminous, created from cloth wrapped around and tied or otherwise fixed on the head.

Gendura (also **gandora**)

A short-sleeved, full-length tunic usually featuring embroidered decoration around the neck and arm openings, worn by men and woman in Morocco.

Inkehli

A traditional headdress worn by married Zulu women.

Ìró

Yorùbá word for a full-length skirt that is wrapped around the body and tied at the waist. Also known as a wrapper. Usually worn with a matching top known as a *bùbá*.

Kaba

Ghanaian women's tailormade garment consisting of a fitted bodice and full-length fitted skirt.

Kanga (also **khanga**)

A piece of cloth, usually of cotton and rectangular in shape, printed with a decorative border running around all four sides and a central pattern featuring a motto or other text. Often sold in pairs and worn by women as shawls or headwraps.

Kente cloth

Formed by stitching together narrow strips of handwoven (typically silk) cloth that feature colourful woven patterns. The term is particularly used to refer to the silk cloth traditionally produced by Asante and Ewe people in West Africa.

Kita

A narrow handwoven cloth comparable to *kente* produced by Baule people in Côte d'Ivoire, West Africa.

Kuba cloth

Cloth of handwoven raffia, often subsequently embroidered, dyed, appliqued or otherwise decorated. Produced by Kuba people in DRC (Democratic Republic of the Congo).

Òkènè

A handwoven cloth, traditionally of cotton and bast fibres, produced by the Ebira population of Central Nigeria.

Riga

A voluminous ceremonial robe, usually made up of many narrow, woven strips stitched together and subsequently embroidered with decorative motifs. Worn by Hausa men in northern Nigeria.

Sankofa

A word in the Akan Twi and Fante languages of Ghana that literally translates as 'retrieve' ('san' return; 'ko' go; 'fa' take) and is often interpreted as outlining the value of obtaining knowledge and inspiration from the past.

Tafe

A wrap-around skirt worn by woman in Mali.

Tagalmust

A turban and mouth-veil of Indigo-dyed cotton that wraps around the head and bottom half of the face, worn by Tuareg and Sanhaja people in North Africa.

Takchita

A Moroccan women's full-length layered garment consisting of a front-opening robe worn over a dress, often belted. Typically worn for celebrations, particularly weddings.

Tòbí

Underskirt or slip.

Umushanana

Ceremonial dress worn in Uganda, Burundi and Rwanda consisting of a wrapped skirt and sash draped on one shoulder, typically worn with a bustier or other top underneath.

Compiled by Connie Karol Burks with advice on Yorùbá from Kólá Túbòsún.

We have sought to use the correct accents and characters for words from other languages, but we are aware that common usage and standardization can vary.

AUTHOR BIOGRAPHIES

Omoyemi Akerele is founder of Lagos Fashion Week and the creative development agency Style House Files.

Amine Bendriouich is a fashion designer based in Casablanca. In 2018 US *Vogue* included him in their list of 100 most exciting Street Style creatives.

Gus Casely-Hayford is Director of V&A East and was previously Director of the Smithsonian, National Museum of African Art. A cultural historian, in 2014 he presented the BBC TV series *Lost Kingdoms of Africa* and was author of the accompanying book. He is author of *Timbuktu: The Secrets of the Fabled but Lost African City* (2018).

Christine Checinska is the inaugural Senior Curator Africa and Diaspora: Textiles and Fashion at the V&A. A creative designer in the fashion industry for over 30 years, including for iconic brands such as Margaret Howell, she is a Research Associate at VIAD, University of Johannesburg.

Sunny Dolat is an independent fashion curator, cultural producer and creative director. He is co-founder with Dr. Njoki Ngumi of The Nest Collective, Nairobi.

Bonnie Greer is a playwright, novelist and author. Her work includes the play *Douglass* (2021), the novel *Entropy* (2009) and the book *Langston Hughes: The Value of Contradiction* (2011). She was formerly Deputy Chair of The British Museum, the first woman of colour to hold that position.

Monica L. Miller is Professor of English and Africana Studies at Barnard College, Columbia University. Her book, *Slaves to Fashion: Black Dandyism and the Styling of Black Diasporic Identity*, was published in 2009.

Elisabeth Murray joined the Performance, Furniture, Textiles and Fashion department at the V&A in 2016, working across the twentieth-century and contemporary fashion collections. She is the Project Curator for *Africa Fashion*. She also contributed to the *Mary Quant* exhibition and accompanying publication.

Njoki Ngumi is an artist, writer, film-maker and healthcare professional. She is a co-founder with Sunny Dolat of The Nest Collective, Nairobi.

Hadeel Osman is an award-winning Sudanese creative director, designer, researcher and fashion sustainability consultant. She is the founder of multidisciplinary creative agency DAVU Studio and works with several global organisations for a decolonized, conscious and ethical fashion industry.

Roslyn A. Walker is Senior Curator of the Arts of Africa, the Americas, and the Pacific and The Margaret McDermott Curator of African Art at the Dallas Museum of Art. Her book *The Arts of Africa at the Dallas Museum of Art* (2009) was the first catalogue devoted solely to the DMA's collection of African art, and more recent titles include *The Power of Gold: Asante Royal Regalia from Ghana* (2018).

ACKNOWLEDGEMENTS

Africa Fashion has been years in the making. It would not have been possible without the foundational work done by my V&A predecessors, such as Machel Bogues, Janet Browne, Helen Mears, Nicola Stylianou and Carol Tulloch, who highlighted the need to better represent African and African diasporic fashions and textiles in our permanent collections and popular exhibitions. Carol Tulloch's pioneering work, central to the field of Black and African Fashion Studies – the field in which this publication sits – must be acknowledged.

Many colleagues at the V&A and elsewhere have contributed to the research, development and actualization of this project. I would first like to thank the core Africa Fashion curatorial team: my right-hand person Elisabeth Murray, our Consultant Researcher Sunny Dolat, and my colleagues Connie Karol Burks, Jessica Harpley and Stephanie Wood. Elisabeth Murray, as Project Curator, ceaselessly worked on the exhibition and book, writing her own article and interviewing the 'Agents of Change' creatives. I extend thanks to Christopher Wilk, an unofficial member of the core team and Keeper of the Performance, Furniture, Textiles and Fashion Department. I am grateful for the advice of fellow departmental colleagues Sonnet Stanfill and Oriole Cullen. Thanks are due to Gus Casely-Hayford, Director of V&A East, for his support; our Textiles and Fashion Conservation collaborators Lara Flecker, Gill MacGregor and Katy Smith; the Paper Conservation team Eoin Kelly and Jane Rutherston; Director of Exhibitions Daniel Slater and his team Sarah Scott, Rachel Murphy, Ana Belén-Martínez, Meg Hogg, Sophie Parry, Charlotte King and Rocío Mayol Sánchez; Head of Interpretation Bryony Shepherd and her team Lenny Cherry and Corinne Jones; also to our volunteers Tosin Adeosun, Henry Dowson and Samriddi Gurung who assisted with research.

Conversation and collaboration have helped to shape this project's uniquely African-centred character. I would therefore like to thank the following people who encouraged and challenged us along the way, enriching our process and end results: Heather Akou, Omoyemi Akerele, Lucilla Booyzen, Michael Burgess, Avis Charles, Sunny Dolat, D. Denenge Duyst-Akpem, Edward Enninful, Allana Finley, Paul Goodwin, Erica de Greef, Bonnie Greer, Xiomara Grosset, Neshane Harvey, Rachel Hemingway-Hurst, Afua Hirsch, Shona Hunter, Angela Jansen, Kimberly Jenkins, Helen Jennings, Nisha Kanabar, Barbara Kennedy-Brown, Lesiba Mabitsela, Helen Mears, Monica L. Miller, Diana N'diaye, Hadeel Osman, John Picton, Cher Potter, Christopher Richards, Victoria Rovine, Hanelli Rupert, Sarah Schleuning, Jacqueline Shaw, Nicola Stylianou, André Leon Talley, Nana A. Tamakloe, François Vergès, Roslyn A. Walker, Gloria Wavamunno, Elizabeth Way, Ajamu X, Dina Yassin, Johanna Zetterstrom-Sharp. In addition, we benefited from the insights of the Africa Fashion Youth Group and our Community Panel, alongside those of the V&A Global Narratives Network. Both the exhibition and book have benefited from the generosity of many foundations, private individuals and fashion houses, too numerous to list in this limited space, who have either loaned or donated garments, accessories and contextual matter. I am particularly grateful to Fọlashadé 'Shade' Thomas-Fahm and Fauzi Fahm, Lalage Bown, Emmanuelle Courrèges, Alphadi and Lalla Seidnaly, Awa Meité, Reine Okuliar and Lydie Ullmann, Ryan Ansah and Joey Ansah of the Kofi Ansah Foundation, and Makeba Boateng Utip and Jennifer Phoenix of MCPR Africa and Fashion Forum Africa.

The production of this book drew on the expertise of countless people. I would like to thank Coralie Hepburn and Tom Windross in Digital Media and Publishing for their guidance during the early stages of the process, our Editor Rebecca Fortey for her patience, and Fred Caws and Andrew Tullis for clearing the image copyright. I am also grateful to Sarah Duncan and Kieron Boyle in the V&A Photographic Studio, book designer Aaron Yeboah of 2dots Space, copyeditor Linda Schofield, and Production Manager Emma Woodiwiss. Finally, I thank my fellow authors Bonnie Greer, Gus Casely-Hayford, Monica L. Miller, Roslyn A. Walker, Elisabeth Murray, Akosua Afriyie-Kumi, Gouled Ahmed, Imane Ayissi, Maxwell Boko, Lafalaise Dion, Ami Doshi Shah, Lisa Folawiyo, Mariam Hazem, Nisha Kanabar, Sindiso Khumalo, Doreen Mashika, Lukhanyo Mdingi, Awa Meité, Laduma Ngxokolo, Bubu Ogisi, Adebayo Oke-Lawal, Nkwo Onwuka, Mmuso Potsane, Hend Riad, Neo Serati Mofammere, Baay Sooley, Laure Tarot, Adeju Thompson, Moses Turahirwa, Sunny Dolat, Njoki Ngumi, Hadeel Osman, Omoyemi Akerele and Amine Bendriouich.

– Christine Checinska

IMAGE CREDITS

INDEX

Illustrations and their captions are denoted by the use of *italic* page numbers.

INDEX

INDEX